DISSENTING VOICES AND TRANSFORMATIVE ACTIONS

Social Movements in a Globalizing World

Edited by

DEBAL K. SINGHAROY

MANOHAR
2010

First published 2010

ISBN 978-81-7304 869-2 (Hb)
ISBN 978-81-7304-875-3 (Pb)

Published by

Ajay Kumar Jain *for*
Manohar Publishers & Distributors
4753/23 Ansari Road, Daryaganj
New Delhi 110 002

Typeset at

Digigrafics
New Delhi 110 049

Printed at

Salasar Imaging Systems
Delhi 110 035

To
Prof. T.K. Oommen
for all his encouragement
and inspiration

Contents

V. GRASSROOT INITIATIVE IN A GLOBALIZED WORLD

Preface

Social movements have emerged to be a core area of social research in recent decades and has acquired substantive theoretical sophistication and empirical depth. This area has marched ahead leaving behind the age of intellectual apathy of the functionalist scholars in considering social movements to be part of the mainstream social science discourse. It has also left behind the Marxian approach of class deduction and economic determinism to be the sole discourse of social movement studies. Since last three decades, especially since early 1980s there have been the pre-dominance of 'identity driven new social movements' and 'political process oriented resource mobilization' perspectives in contemporary social movement studies. Scholars have also developed preceptive critically on these analytical orientations in view of enormous process of de-contextualization taking shape in the contemporary world in the wake of globalization, economic liberalization and fast expansion of information and communication technologies. These critical perspectives have generated new varieties of intellectual contestation to the pre-existing articulation that recognized a process of 'construction of social solidarity' in social movements with the articulation of the notion of 'fluidity in social collectivities' and in collective mobilizations. Similar contestations have been articulated to revisit the construction of 'contentious collectively' with 'conscientized subjectivity'; 'contextual social movements' with 'movements of social movement', and 'social movements' with 'social anti movements' and so on. Moreover local collective actions are examined to locate the new array of global linkages and connectivity and network of networks. Social movements have widely emerged as reaction to sustained process of marginalization and social exclusion. Which are no more solely locally circumscribed; by globally intenliked and conditioned. In a globalized world there have not only been social movements from below to resist the oppressive hegemony of the corporate world, state and ruling class, but also a process of guided mobilization from the above in the wake of co-option of the popular intiatives and civil society activisms by the state. While social movements are manifested to resist all forms of dominations, these are also directed to rejuvenate the process of social development.

There have been substantive intellectual efforts all over the world to examine all these processes and their local and gobal interlinkages with emerging theoretical perspectives and in-depth empiricism. This collection of essays has tried to capture a glimpse of the scholarly efforts on social movement studies in the globalized world by collecting relevant contributions from the prominent scholars working in this field.

This collection has taken concrete shape out of sustained desire of a group of scholars to develop an organized body of knowledge in comprehending the dynamics of social movements in perplexing globalized world with critical and analytical vigour. Here I am especially thankful to noted scholars like Partha Nath Mukherjee (India), Gail Omvedt (India), James Goodman (Australia), Tova Banski (Israel), Benjamin Tejerina (Spain), Hakan Thorn (Denmark), Lauren Langman (USA), Daniel Kunzler (Switzerland), Helen Schwenken (Germany), Marek Herkenrath, (Switzerland), Sharit Bhowmik (India), M.N. Panini (India), Elizbieta Budakowska (Poland), Sergio Tamayo (Mexico), Leo Zeiling (South Africa), Shashi Bhushan Upadhyay (India), Swaraj Basu (India), Dip Kapoor (Canada), Tejwant Chana (Canada) and Archana Prasad (India) for their contribution.

I am especially thankful to Professor T.K. Oommen (India), Peter Jay Mike (Canada), Tim Jordan (UK), Roger Spadling (UK) for their encouragement and constant support.

I am extremely thankful to Prof. V.N. Rajasekharan Pillai, Vice-Chancellor, Indira Gandhi National Open University, who kindly extended his support under his Chairpersonship to organize the International Conference on Social Development, Social Movements and the Marginalized in Indira Gandhi National Open University, New Delhi in February 2008 with the co-sponsorship of the Research Committee 48: 'Social Movements and Collective Action and Social Change' of International Sociological Association (ISA) Madrid, Indian Council of Social Sciences Research (ICSSR), New Delhi and United Nations Development Programme (UNDP), New Delhi. I am sincerely thankful to ISA, ICSSR and UNDP for their kind gesture. A large number of papers in this collection were initially presented in this conference and subsequently revised and modified. A good number of papers were also specially invited to suit the thematic requirement of this collection. I would like express my heartiest thanks and gratitude to all the scholars who agreed to contribute.

I am also thankful to Prof. Pravin Sinclair, Pro-Vice-Chancellor,

Prof. Uma Kanjilal, Director, School of Social Sciences of Indira Gandhi National Open University for their proper advice and guidance.

My sincere thanks are due to Prof. Omprakash Misra, Pro-Vice-Chancellor, Indira Gandhi National Open University and Prof. Maitrayee Chaudhuri, Professor of Sociology, Jawaharlal Nehru University, New Delhi for their valued contribution towards shaping this collection. Prof. Omprakash Mishra has always taken personal initiative and shown keen interest in bringing out this collection.

I am highly indebted to my colleagues in IGNOU, especially to Prof. S.C. Garg, Professor of Physics, Prof. Perdeep Sahni, Professor of Public Administration, Prof. Darvesh Gopal, Professor of Political Science, Prof. A.S. Narang, Prof. Kapil Kumar, Professor of History, Prof. E. Vayunandan for their encouragement and support.

I am thankful to my department colleagues Prof. Tribhuwan Kapur, Dr. B. Kiranmayi, Dr. Nita Mathur, Dr. R. Vashum, Dr. Archana Singh and Dr. Rabindra Kumar for their cooperation. Ms T. Jitha deserves special thanks for her initiative at the early stage of organizing this collection.

I am especially thankful to my wife Dr. Prava Debal for her observations, comments on my papers and timely support despite her own professional and other commitments. I am thankful to my daughter Purbali and son Anirudha, for their cooperation and for allowing me to remain engaged with my commitment; and for sacrificing their share of attention.

My office staff Sri Shailendra Kumar Singh and Ms Sonia Singh have always shown commitments and promptness towards the completion of this work. Indeed it would have been impossible for me to organize such voluminous work without their support and help.

Thanks are also due to Mr. Ramesh Jain, Manohar Publishers for bringing out this volume with utmost efficiency. I am also thankful to Siddharth Chowdhury, for this ever friendly approach in completing this work.

DEBAL K. SINGHAROY

Introduction

DEBAL K. SINGHAROY

The contemporary world has borne witness to the resurgence of new varieties of social movements on the one hand, and the decline of class-based social movement on the other. However, notwithstanding such shifts in its culture, social movement, as organized civil actor, remains at the core of social conscience and has acquired renewed significance in the contemporary world to reorient the pathways of social progression with assured justice and liberty. Touraine (2002) underlines the essence: 'If I maintain the central importance of the concept of social movements in strict sense, it is because of the future of democracy, of freedom, of justice . . .' (Touraine 2002).

Social movements occupy the core of the social dynamics by integrating social tension, crisis, conflict, change and transformation with the processes of rejuvination and progression of the society. They produce social space for their emergence, challenging the existing values, norms and societal arrangements and in the process pave the way for the emergence of new culture, ideas, knowledge and societal arrangements. In essence, 'social life is produced by cultural achievements and social conflicts and at the heart of the society burns the fire of social movements'; and 'social movements are the expressions of the collective will . . . (and they) are not exceptional or the dramatic events: they lie permanently at the heart of the social life . . .' (Touraine 1981: 29). However, 'social movements are not a marginal rejection of order. They are not merely an outcome of the crisis. Social movements generate new sources of power. 'They force this power out into the open and give it a shape and a face. . . . They speak a language that seems to be entirely of their own, but they say something that transcends their particularity and speak to us all. They signal a deep transformation in the logic and processes that guide complex societies' (Melucci 1996). Movements are the representatives of people's will and power; and power is embodied in social movement is derived from people's participation in the movement. Gradually 'power in movements grows when ordinary people join the forces in continuous confrontation' (Tarrow 1995). People live in society and participate in the social movements to bring change in several societal arrangements, norms, values and institutions of the society to which they adhered to for long. Thus the key to understand the emergence of social movements is to understanding social structures over a period of time. Human societies have progressed from pre-agrarian to agrarian, from agrarian to industrial and from industrial to post-industrial and knowledge society. However, many of the societies continue with the major traits of more than one society at a time. However, all the societies have produced their own societal arrangements, and patterns of domination and resistance.

Though the sociology of social movement is of very recent origin—barely half a century old, it has been very eventful in terms of the transition of society and proliferation of social movements of diverse forms during this period. The decades of late 1930s and early 1940s saw the expansion of Nazism and totalitarianism followed by proliferation and consolidation of anti-colonial movements in the 1940s and 1950s. Significantly 'working class movements—the characteristic features of the industrialist society were at their peak in the 1960s. Indeed the working class movement became the founding perspective of social movements and remained identified with the framework of state and nation for long' (Wieviorka 2005). The 1970s saw the proliferations of the students, women, black civil rights, environment and such new varieties of social movements based on the consolidation and shaping up of transnational humanitarian consciousness and identities. These emerging phenomena had called for a new explanation. The founding class perspective of social movement studies were unable to explain the emerging dimensions of 'new social movements' (Touraine 1981).

In the present juncture of transition of society, the existing social, economic and political arrangements have emerged to be complex and the facets of domination and resistance have emerged to be multi-faceted. Hence Touraine (1981) observes that 'we are living through a transition from industrial to the programmed society and hence experiencing the decline of a certain type of class relations and conflicts and emergence of a new generation of social movements'. To him the present moment of the society is 'marked by the appearance of new problems and new social movements which must be understood and which can no longer be explained by invoking another order of the phenomena—the laws of the capitalist development or the consequences of modernization . . .'. It is also a different intellectual moment 'causing inability to the traditional left to understand social and the political events' of this era: 'Our most urgent need is to learn how to name and analyse the new social practices and the new forms of collective action which are shaping the societies of today and tomorrow' (Touraine 1981: 25). To Melucci (1996) 'the social space for social movements has become a distinct area of the system and no longer coincides either with the traditional forms of organization of solidarity or with the conventional channels of political representation. Again the 'the notion of movement itself, which originally stood for an entity acting against the political and governmental system, has now been rendered inadequate as a description of the reality of reticular and defused forms of collective action.' New social movements is a relative concept and it had a temporary function to indicate the comparative difference between the historical forms of class conflict and today's emergent form of collective action.

In the wake of globalization and resurgence of world capitalism the crises in the class-based social movement culture have rather been very explicit. Contemporary world has been marked by the decline of conventional class-based social movements and the emergence of multiple varieties of social movements and collective actions. The dependency theorists are of the view that in the world system there have existed multiple movements that have protested and organized against the multiple injustices of the existing system and have offered alternatives which they believe would bring about a fundamental change in the society (S. Amin, G. Arrighi, A.G. Frank, Wallerstein, 1990). However these movements (environment, women's, human rights, gay rights, black civil rights, and so on) were primarily triggered by the sense that the old movements—the social democrat, the communist and the nationalists had failed in many of their objectives (Wallerstein 1990). Again despite popular mandates and official pretensions, states everywhere have failed to address or resolve problems of economic exploitation and deprivations, political oppression, peace threatening and disturbing insecurity, environmental degradation, ethnic, religious, gender, age, class discrimination, marginalization, injustice, regional, sectoral, and community (mal)-integration or segregation, individual and other crises of identity which are more or less rampant everywhere. Recently these state failures have received important political expression and official recognition (Andre Gunder Frank and Matra Fuentes, 1990).

Besides globalization and economic liberalization, the processes of emergence and transformation of social movements have been widely influenced by expansion of information and communication technology and shaping up of network society. Now 'with the technological revolution, transformation of capitalism, and the demise of the statism, we have been experiencing the widespread surge of powerful expression of collective identity that challenge globalization and cosmopolitanism on behalf of the singularity and people's control over their lives and environment'. It has created a paradox of its own. 'In the network society thus, on the one hand the dominant global elites inhabiting in the space of flows tend to consist of the identity less individuals (citizens of the worlds); while on the other hand, people insisting economic, cultural, and political disfranchisement trend to be attracted to communal identity.' Thus in the network society together with the state apparatuses, global networks, and self-centred individuals, there are also communes formed around resistance identity (Castells, M. 1997: 356).

In this emerging vicissitude there have been diverse processes relating to the emergence of social movements and the frameworks of their social analysis. The symbolic interactionist, Marxian, functionalist, new social movement/identity theorists and resource mobilization scholars have provided strong intellectual foundations in analysing the origin, source of power, process of sustenance of social movements with in-depth understanding. The functionalist theorists have observed social movements as potential threats to social stability and structural coherence; the Marxists' economic determinism has explained social movements as manifestations of class conflicts; the symbolic interactionists has found in social movements a source of new life, and the new social movement/indentity theorists have identified social movements as processes of rejuvenation of multiple collective identity and freedom of life and choice. To the identity theorists the dimensions of subjectivity, emotion, commitment and cognition have remained the core issues in the progression of social movements. The resource mobilization theorists on the other hand have emphasized on the 'end and means' relationships in social movement participation. To them availability of political opportunities, rationality of collective action, construction of contention and innovation have got a prominent role to play in the social movement analysis. It has also been asserted by these political process analysts that movements are created when political opportunities open up for social actors who usually lack them. To the resource mobilization scholars, at the base of all social movements lies the repertories of contentions which are nurtured and reconstruted by social movement entreprenuers. Indeed the contentious forms of collective action are framed to challenge opponents, bring out solidarities, and have meaning within particular population group, situation and political culture (Tarrow 1995: 3).

Framing of collective action thus is an important aspect of resource mobilization. It is accepted that each political system has degree of consensus around its legitimizing symbols and that citizens contribute towards the maintenance of the system by their knowledge of and support for these symbols. Out of a cultural toolkit of possible symbols, movement entrepreneurs choose those that they hope will mediate among the cultural underpinnings of the group they appeal to (ibid.: 123).

In the contemporary globalized world the nature of social movements has undergone a phenomenal change along with the fast transition taking place in the society. Hence 'the era of new social movements is behind us now. It corresponded to a transitional phase between the working class movement of yesterday and the global movements of today, between industrial society and the societies which we now refer to as network societies rather than industrial societies'. Student movements have mostly disappeared, most of the ecological movements have become institutionalized, feminism has become primarily a political pressure group with varieties of intellectual and philosophical reflection. Thus 'contrary to a sort of sociological optimism, the new social movements have not marked the entry into a new type of society directly and distinctly'. However in the contemporary juncture neither the working class movement of 1960s, nor new mobilizations of 1970s have entirely disappeared. Their reminiscent have become institutionalized and

> incapable of rising to the level of historicity to challenge the overall control of the major orientations of collective life, or else had been radicalized and was prepared, in particular, to take the form of violence or of ideologies of rupture. The most visible assertions of identity seemed more likely to lead to withdrawal into communities, or to be set in a context of sectarianism, nationalism—even terrorism—than to have any relation with social movements. (Wieviorka 2005)

Globalization has affected the pre-existing patterns of social solidarity and the ways and means of shaping this solidarity. It has generated new metaphor of network and varieties of fluid. In the wake of globalization now there have been 'global fluids', in the form of the 'heterogeneous, uneven and unpredictable mobilities of people, information and objects, money, images and risks that move chaotically across regions strikingly faster and unpredictable shapes. Such global fluids have no clear point of departure, or arrival, just de-territorialization of movement and mobility' (Urry 2000). The concept of society itself has undergone changes. In this context within the contemporary social movements there has been a shift from 'solidarity' to 'fluidarity' and from 'collective identity' to one of 'public experience of self' (McDonald 2002).

In these backdrops globalization has again generated new varieties of social, economic and political processes. It has provided the space for diverse varieties of collective actions. A section of the social movement scholars are of the view that there has evolved an 'empire' over a period of time (constituted with the United States IMF, UN, G8, NATO, WTO, and transnational and multinational corporations) that accepts no boundaries and limits to capitalist expansion. The expansion and dominance of transnational corporation and post-industrial forms of labour and production have converted the 'entire world now into an integrated workplace, a giant social factory', a single market through competition and technological innovations and competition. By the way of promoting new political order of globalization, cultural and economic transformation, new forms of network and communication, control and domination, articulation of identities and exclusion the empire has provided new contexts of protests and social movements. Within these empires varieties of rebellions and protests have taken shape in the form of traditional labour, feminist, ecological, civil rights, national liberation and so on over the decades. However in the process of increasing communication and informationalism, connections are developed to connect these instances of rebellions as nodes of common struggle against exploitation (Hardt and Nagri 2001). The emerging phenomenon has also produced the culture of movements of social movements. While transnational collective action has emerged to be a reality, local resistance against global are also taking shape simultaneously.

Contemporary world has seen the organization and proliferation of several varieties of social movements. Wieviorka (2005) however cautions that a social movement must not be confused with its inverted image—the social anti-movements which are reverse and negative expressions. A social anti-movement in essence is 'deformed, inverted and perverted aspects of a social movement. Social anti-movements are not the defensive dimensions of the social movements but on their contrary, are their enemy. Instead of promoting a social or a cultural identity, they are champions of some abstract entity, essence or symbol, and speak in the name of a purity or homogeneity. Instead of defining an adversary, they have one or several enemies, and search for or eliminate scapegoats, traitors or spies; they give the impression of a collective paranoia that has no bounds. Instead of building relationships with other actors, agreeing on the principles of debates and negotiations, they champion absolutes, and adopt do or die attitudes. And if they appear in an arena where social movements also exist, they try to destroy these movements, and fight against them' (Wieviorka 2005). Though these have been facilitated by globalization, in actual practice these are the darkest aspects of globalization. Globalization may explain the formation of anti-movements but the latter are not necessarily global themselves. Throughout the world today globalization is indeed a powerful factor in cultural fragmentation and in the reinforcement of social inequalities, and these phenomena may give rise to all sorts of anti-movements: sects, for example, communities which turn to violence, do not in themselves have the slightest connection with the global approaches of classical social movements which disintegrate and invert to such an extent that they resemble social movements (Della Porta and Tarrow 2005).

Across the globe the human sociaties now largely experience the phenomena of increasing fluidity in social relations, decline of old social values and norms, emergence of parochial social anti-movements, decline of old varieties of social protests and resistance, and surpassing of the stage of new varieties of collective actions. Notwithstanding these developments, social movements still occupy the core of social dynamism to construct an alternative world-view to ensure equality and justice for all members of the society in the globalized world. As against these backdrops several questions are raised as to, has there been a common pattern in the manifestation of social movements in the wake of globalization? What have been the emerging perspectives to analyse the social movements in a globalized world? If we have left behind the era of new social movements, what are the major varieties of social movements taking shape empirically in contemporary world? Despite the decline of class-based social movements, why and how are the 'old social movements' continuing in many parts of the globalized world? What have been the nature and form of local resistance against emerging form of global domination? What has been the nature of the present form social protests of the pre-defined social categories like caste, race, tribe, and ethnic groups? What has been the emerging nature of protest of women, farmers, students, migrants in a changing scenario? How are the social issues articulated in these movements? This volume has endeavoured to examine all these questions by critically examining the relevance of major theoretical perspectives on social movements and incorporating specific studies on social movements in parts of North and South America, Eastern and Western Europe, Africa, Asia and Australia.

The contributions of the social movement scholars on these emerging issues are presented in five interrelated sections in this collection and they deal with broad theoretical issues and their specific applications, transnational activisms, issues of labour and farmers, facets of caste, tribal, ethnic and women's movements.

In Section I of this collection there are six papers dealing with theoretical issues and their specific applications. Benjamín Tejerina in his paper on 'The Logic of the Alterglobal Movement' elucidates the emerging patterns of mobilizations taking shape in the globalized social movements in the contemporary world. To him, new forms of discontent and resistance are now fast spreading geographically, even though in an uneven way, acquiring public visibility and affecting consciousness of civil society and thus increasingly becoming internationalized. In this backdrop his paper aims to contribute to the understanding of the social meaning of what has been defined as the 'movement of movements' by Della Porta and Tarrow (2005). He points to the facts that social backgrounds of the participants are directly linked to the material foundations of the social movements and that there are also several cross-currents in these movements in terms of sectoral and global issues and diverse identities involved in these movements. With in-depth empiricism Tejerina has examined the characteristics of the activists who, proceeding from different sectors, come together in the movement in favour of global justice. He also analyses the details of the issues of compatibility or incompatibility between the different levels of identification, e.g. sectoral *vs* global, particular *vs* general and of the relationship among the participants. He explains how the ideal of global in the context of social movement undergoes different processes of construction and reconstruction and contributing towards the concretization of alterglobalization movements. To this end he delineates a possible conception of the world that supersedes the plurality of political cultures present amongst the activists of the Alterglobal Movement. He also examines with perceptive orientation the tension between the conditions of mobilization, and the activists' conditions of existence, which involve very different living experiences that are at times, distinct from the solidarity-based demands of globalization. In the emerging scenario, he indicates that the old variety of 'middle-class radicalism' is being complemented in the alterglobal movements by a growing presence of professionals of knowledge and information. To him a significant section of the alterglobalization activists also participate in the new social movements. This paper shows a conceptual and empirical interface of the alterglobal movement with new social movements of 1980s.

James Goodman in his paper Counter-Globalist Movements and 'Post-Globalisms of the Marginalized' discusses the emergence of post-Globalism as challenge to globalism and manifestations of counter-global movements with distinctive ideological orientations. He delineates that the imposition of globalism through 1980s and 1990s has radically undermined the stability of financial, social and ecological systems of the world and dramatically delimited the political authority and legitimacy of political elites, especially in peripheral zones and subordinated the society to the impulse of the market. In this backdrop the counter-globalist movements have emerged to assert both autonomy and solidarity, geared to deep democratization, and engaged to the agendas for decommodification, including the assertion of the commons. This movement thus 'instigates struggles for a world beyond exhaustion, fought-out between social forces that benefit from accumulation and those that bear its costs'. The central themes of the counter-globalist movement are to strengthen the processes of subordinating markets into society, enabling a collective delinking from market dependence, embedding markets for societies, rather than the reverse. These relate to the de-globalization dynamics that are built in the form of trans-local subsistence or sufficiency movements, through delinking moves at the national level, and through inter-state multilateral delinking, mostly from blocs of southern countries. Clearly to him, counter-globalism potentially encompasses a wide range of political forces, from the communal to the global, ranges against dominant globalist ideologies, is powerfully generative, offering pathways from opposition to aspiration, and poses alternatives to possibilities for post-globalism.

This movement moreover offers the possibility of generating new ideological formations capable of charting new models for post-globalism as it emerged in the ideological logic of the 'Global Justice Movement' of 1990s viewing post-globalism 'from below and articulating an alternative ideology of justice globalism against the dominant ideology of corporate globalism'. He also points out that the counter-globalism has challenged globalism across state borders, contesting agendas set in international contexts by the corporate power, embodied in transnational corporations, imperial power exercised by governmental and intergovernmental institutions, and normative globalism expressed in consumerist culture-ideology. Ideology, to him, acquires distinctive meaning in the context in which a movement has taken a shape. Goodman argues that 'globalism brings with it a normative dimension expressed as a culture-ideology of consumerism, carried by an increasingly visible transnational capitalist class. Globalism, as a dominant ideology, to him, is self-consciously developed and promulgated by legions of neo-liberal think-tanks, media conglomerates, management consultancies and semi-state agencies. In contesting this dominant ideology, counter-globalist ideology has to likewise constitute a bloc of social forces. That are necessarily embedded in social experiences, translating existent social antagonisms into public contestations and transforming counter-globalist social forces from passive existence 'in themselves' into active assertion 'for themselves'.

Lauren Langman in his paper on 'Global Justice as Identity: Mobilization for a Better World' discusses the emergence and proliferation of global justice movements and several of their contemporary dimensions. He points out that in the backdrop of triumph of neo-liberal global capitalism since the last decade, there has been a proliferation of resistance and contestation by various social mobilizations of this emerging global order. These resistance and contestations have acquired significance of global dimensions in the wake of fast penetrations of information and communication technologies. To him the Internet has made it possible to create 'virtual public spheres' that are also transnational, and in turn, there have been the emergence of 'internetworked social movements' articulating a global justice identity, working toward a more progressive vision than ever before. Collecting evidence from the World Social Forum, as well as various feminist and democratic movements in the Middle East the author suggests that if the pen is mightier than the sword, then the computer keyboard is potentially more powerful than the institutions that maintain domination.

In the paper on 'Globalization, Social Movements and Social Development: Emerging Discourses' Gail Omvedt, has examined the issues relating to transformation of social movements in India in the wake of globalization. Focusing on the Dalit movement she gives a critical analysis of globalization and the struggles against it. She points out that in India the process of globalization has been misunderstood and misinterpreted especially by the Marxists, as they predominantly saw reincarnation of old imperialism, and weakening the position of national capitalists by the multinational capitalists in the process of expansion of globalization and emergence of the new economic order. Taking the clue from the study by Michael Hardt and Antonio Negri (2003), she points out that in the global system of economy 'production is defused and decentralized; that the old borders and boundaries increasingly have little meaning'; that new forms of production take place increasingly based upon information and communication technologies; that they represent a post-industrialism and a post-modernism in cultural terms; and that that there is a major change in mass movements. With the change in the economic framework of the society the nature of working class itself has also changed, fragmented and differentiated. As against these backdrops several protest movements are arising on different issues and are searching for new ways of communication. Within this profound change the world capitalism and the society around it are reorganizing themselves at a global level. Omvedt finds capitalism to have become in a real sense a global mode of production. Herein she expresses the need for a new analysis of social movements to comprehend these changes. Taking into account the phenomena that exploitations are 'increasingly operative on a global scale, and yet their direct global communication is minimal' she found that people support and stand with social movements without necessarily understanding all the issues. However they identify themselves with the opposition to the exploitative globalization. In this wider context she examines the proliferation of the Dalit movements in India and shows that these movements today are connected with fragmentation and increasingly with the problematic of identity and dispersion over many fields of action and ideology. To her, though these social movements today are fragmented and this fragmentation also means that they increasingly overlap. And given the global possibilities of communication, sometimes the most 'localized' movements can make the leap in a way that the movements of the 'classic' era could not. Furthermore, she recognizes that there is a sense of solidarity among these diverse movements irrespective of multiplicity of struggles of resistance and a deep rooted recognition of a common enemy and way to a new future.

Social movements are parts of historicity and inseparable parts of historical analysis of social dynamics. Partha Nath Mukherjee, in his paper 'Social Movements, Conflicts and Change: Towards a Theoretical Orientation' proposes a theoretical framework that is not constrained by any historicity. His analytical framework promotes the analysis of the historical evolution of social movements in their social and cultural specificity. To him, though the culture of social movements owes its origin within the democratic framework of the West, it has got universalized over a period of time. South Asia in general and India in particular now provide extraordinarily rich experiences of numerous varieties of social mobilizations. He examines several dimensions of these movements and provides a broad analytical framework to social movements. Based on his researches on agrarian, 'revolutionary' and other movements he 'suggests a comprehensive theoretical orientation/ framework for a more efficient comprehension of the dynamics of social movement and change'. Towards this endeavour he uses a good deal of indigenous input for the universalization of the particular. He holds the position that indigeneity is an essential condition of universalizing social sciences and that the search for 'truth' in this kind of thinking cannot be circumscribed within any single theoretical school or paradigm (new social movements, resource mobilization, etc.), nor does it mean that we necessarily have to involve all existing paradigms. He uses the illustrations of the Maoist movement in India for the formulation of his proposed theoretical orientation/ framework.

Debal K. SinghaRoy in his paper entitled 'Changing Trajectory of Social Movements in India: Towards a Holistic Analytical Perspective' examines the relationships among social mobility, collective mobilization and social movements as constituents of social progression and proposes a resilient-holistic perspective in explaining the processes of social transition and social movements in India. He examines dominant theoretical perspectives on social mobility, conflicts, collective mobilization and social movements to explore their applicability in explaining emerging facets of social transition and social movements in contemporary India. He points out that in the context of globalization and increasing socio-cultural disembededness, societies in India have been introduced to new processes of social mobility and segregation, exclusion and domination, articulation of new interests and identities, conflicts and resistance and manifestation of new forms of collective mobilization and social movements at the grassroots which were hitherto unknown to these societies. He elaborates these processes with in-depth information and analyses inadequacies of the prevailing theoretical perspectives in explaining the emerging intertwining among them. After examining facets of contemporary social movement in the backdrop of emerging socio-economic transitions SinghaRoy proposes an alternative resilient-holistic perspective to explain the emerging intertwining among social mobility, conflicts, collective mobilization and social movements. This perspective, to him, adheres to the principle of flexibility and culture of accommodation of conflicts within the social structure which has been transitional in nature and diversely connected by the integrated logic of social mobility, conflict and collective mobilizations within its ambit.

There are five papers in Section II of this collection which deal with contemporary issues taking shape cutting across the borders and geographical boundaries transnationally. These scholars have dealt with these issues both conceptually and empirically with in-depth perceptive understanding. Hakan Thorn in his paper on 'The Anti-Apartheid Movement and Global Civil Society' focuses on the transnational anti-apartheid movement that connected thousands of groups, organizations including solidarity organizations, union, churches, women, youth, students, etc., in more than 100 countries. To the author the transnational anti-apartheid movements depict the emergence of global civil society with global political culture and collective actions. To him the new social movement perspective is inadequate to explain the phenomena of the anti-apartheid movement as so many old social movements have integrated within this movement and are becoming 'movements of movements' and that this new social movement theory projects some Euro-centric assumptions. He suggests to delink contemporary collective action from the euro-centric implications and proposes the 'post-colonial theory on social movement' that emphasizes on the significance of colonial legacy in the context of globalization and the influence of decolonialization process in present-day politics. He views anti-apartheid movement as a transnational movement which goes beyond nation state-oriented analysis of social movement and looks into the constraints and opportunities for social movements which operate at different levels of international politics. He points out that in the context of political globalization several political communities with distinctive identities and interests are shaped by the phenomena of post-coloniality and the Cold War. There have also been the formation of several transnational and international organizations which promote anti-apartheid struggle. In this backdrop the transnational anti-apartheid movement has become 'movement of movements'—a space of intersection for a wide range of collective actors. He points out that while there has been a construction of transnational political culture from the above; there was also processes of political globalization from below. Torn concludes that the anti-apartheid movement provides an important case of present-day global politics and that the supranational political institutions like WTO, IMF and the World Bank have historical links to post-war, transnational political culture that the anti-apartheid movement is a part of.

Hip Hop movements based on Rap music are spread all over the globe and has become increasingly subject to scientific analysis mainly focusing on the USA and Europe. Nevertheless, to Daniel Künzler Hip Hop in Africa, south of the Sahara is rather a scientific black box. In his paper 'Hip Hop Movements: The Local Adaptation of a Global Culture' elucidates the role of Hip Hop movements based on Rap music in constructing identities and in empowering a marginalized group and in local adaptation of a global culture. Based on the analysis of tapes and CDs, written documents, scientific literature and the Internet sources on African Hip Hop movements in Burkina Faso and Mali, he points out that these movements are essentially politico-cultural in nature and are integral part of civil society in Africa. By critically discussing the political, socio-economical and cultural aspects of this music led movement, the author delineates the 'corrective function' of the Hip Hop movement. To him, although Rap music was known in Africa before, the Hip Hop movements gained massive popularity especially during the social crisis in the 1990s, being led by charismatic Rappers. While at the beginning, the Hip Hop movements were dominated by the children of the urban petty bourgeois in the environment of universities and secondary schools, the social base has extended to the urban lower classes over the decade. There is a process of individuation among the young urban, allowing unknown levels of autonomy and the appropriation of new spheres of cultural expression. Hip Hop movements based on Rap music, as the 'CNN of the poor', are especially important in the context of illiteracy and low education, and in its connection with elements of the traditional African cultures. The author, however, points out that although Hip Hop movements stand for different values and norms, they don't present a counter-concept to the neo-patrimonial state and will most probably not be the basis of an alternative society.

Helen Schwenken in her paper 'Contesting Europe's Borders: The Self-organization of Undocumented Migrants in Borderlands' focuses on the conflicts in the borderlands that are increasingly taking place at the margins of the European Union. Based on intensive empirical research, she analyses political mobilizations by undocumented migrants in the borderland between France and the United Kingdom. The paper explains the following questions: why the refugee camp was first tolerated, but then became a domestically and internationally contested issue? How did the undocumented migrants in transit/ borderlands challenged the barriers to organize themselves? How did the migrants frame their demands? What were the dynamics of the alliances between undocumented migrants and civil society (anti-racist groups, churches, but also: the private transportation sector)? How did their framings and strategies differ? The author uses the perspective of 'framing' and 'political opportunity structures' as elaborated by the resource mobilization theorists to explain the political strategies employed by the undocumented migrants and refugees to gain access to other countries. She highlights that borderlands are highly contested geographic spaces and herein irregular migrants are among the relevant actors, although their mobilizations are extremely precarious. She also points out that in these borderland the issue of entry, exit, citizenship, identity, etc., remain contested and are subject to contestation and negotiation. Based on a case study of Sangatte she has discussed the criteria for a successful movement and a typology of political mobilizations in the field of irregular migration and has shown that some elements of the Sangatte-case study can be generalized.

In recent years though there have been phenomenal proliferations of transnational political and civil society activism and their transnational networking capability. Mark Harkenrath in his contribution 'Social Movements and the Challenges of Transnational Coalition-Building' makes an in-depth enquiry into the emerging patterns of networking of transnational social movements. Focusing on Hemispheric Social Alliance (HSC)—a network organization connecting grassroots movements, labour unions and other non-governmental organizations from many different parts of Americas, Harkenrath charts the struggle of this organization against the Free Trade Area of Americas. The HSC has emerged to be an excellent case study to depict the conditions and strategies that help social movement coalitions to manage internal tensions, build trust across borders, ways to cope with opportunities and threats, organize sustained mass mobilization with grassroots participation in transnational civil society organization. The author himself was a participant in this movement. He combines his experience of participant observer in the movement with the emerging theoretical perspectives on the transnational movement. Based on in-depth empiricism and a sound theoretical grounding the author analyses the growing significance of this transnational coalition and protest; challenges (like unequal access to resources, internal power disparities, complex and multiple layers of political environments, existence of contradictory local, national and international opportunities, diverse cultural contexts of the participants) encountered by this coalitions; and also strategies adopted by them in overcoming these challenges. Social cohesion is an important aspect of transnational coalition movement. He records that cohesion among the members are maintained largely through the diplomatic skills and intellectual competence of the coordination committee members who demonstrated a high level of conflict tolerance and respect for diversity of opinions. It is again pointed out that the regional collective identities which were formed based on shared historical experiences of resistance against external oppression of the colonial and imperialist forces have helped unite the participants of this coalition despite the interregional cultural differences and contradictions. According to Harkenrath these selected historical materials were significant for the reconstruction of a common collective identity downplaying contradictory diversities.

Tova Benski in her paper 'The Coalition of Women for Peace in Israeli Society' presents a portrait of the central, currently active, women's peace movement in Israel. The central argument presented in this paper is that the coalition challenges are one of the central structures of modernity in Israeli society and it forms an integral part of the new, alternative discourse that is emerging therein. She has conducted extensive field studies for this research in Israel since 1985 through participant observation at meetings, conferences and other activities organized by the Coalition and its members; group interviews, in-depth open-ended interviews with regular activists; analysis of e-mail messages distributed to the mailing list maintained by the Women's Coalition for a Just Peace, etc. Based on this primary source of information she has presented a portrait of the coalition and proceeds to elaborate on its values, activities, and local orientations and its integration into the global space. Besides analysing the model of 'Nation-in-Arms' that dominated Israeli modernity till the late 1970s she has also discussed the alternative visions and creations of civilian alternative spaces since the 1980s in the Israeli society. She has located the Coalition of Women for Peace and civilian alternative peace movements within the transition of this society.

The issues of land and labour are focused in Section III. Sharit Bhowmik in his paper on 'Trade Union Movement in India: A Critical View' analyses the growth of the labour movement in India and assesses its future trends. Within the broad conceptualization of labour movement, i.e. 'the ways and means through which labour organizes itself in order to improve its working and living conditions' he focuses on the emerging trends of trade union movements in India. He elucidates that the trade unions have remained to be the most important organizations to mobilize labour for improving their working and living conditions. He, however, points out that given the heterogeneity and the vast numerical size of these organizations they have been able to mobilize only a small section of the labour force in India. He simultaneously recognizes the roles played by the political parties, non-government organizations, and other types of grassroots organizations in mobilizing the labour in India. Besides presenting a historical background of the emergence of trade unions, and elaborating their early features, he also highlights the problems faced by the working class in the wake of structural adjustment and globalization, and the means adopted by the labour movements to counteract these problems. To him the changes taking place in the economy through the policies of liberalization poses the greatest challenge to the labour movement in India as these are leading to job losses in the organized sector while expanding the base of the unprotected sector. He also points out that fragmentation and divisions among the working class are crucial problems in counteracting the adverse effects of globalization and economic liberalization by the labour movement. Notwithstanding these issues he is strongly of the view that the role of the trade unions cannot be undermined or replaced as they are the only means for protecting the interests of the working class and no other institution, be it a benevolent bureaucracy, a political party or even an NGO, can substitute for trade unions.

In the paper on 'Dynamics of Early Labour Mobilization: Bombay City, 1890-1919' Shashi Bhushan Upadhyay explores the dynamics of labour mobilization in the early phase of globalization of late nineteenth and early twentieth century and explains the remarkable militancy of textile workers therein. For this purpose he focuses on three major events in a period of about thirty years which effected three biggest mobilizations among them—the communal riots in 1893, the famous protests against Tilak's conviction in 1908 and the industry-wide general strike in 1919, which witnessed the closure of all the mills and the mobilization of the workers on the streets. He elucidates the basic thesis that although the grim conditions of their existence and the consequent struggle for adjustment and survival shaped their consciousness, the workers, at any given moment, possessed not one but several identities. He points out that some of these identities might be their cultural inheritance from the villages, while others would be engendered and acquired in the city through a variety of political and social ideas and activities. According to the scholar these processes have constantly intermingled and determined the behaviour-pattern of the workers. Thus the militant mobilizations should not be viewed solely in class terms, although class identity was a crucial element in them.

M.N. Panini in his paper entitled 'Farmers Against Globalization?: The Role of Karnataka Rajya Raitha Sangha' assesses the role of Karnataka Rajya Raitha Sangha (KRRS) under Professor M.D. Nanjundaswamy in the anti-globalization movements in Karnataka in the wider context of globalization and proliferation of anti-globalization movement (AGM) in several parts of the country. With empirical investigation of this movement he examines Hardt and Negri's (2003) thesis of viewing AGM as an 'emerging' movement that uses 'networks of networks' to evolve antagonistic strategies that subvert the hegemony of the 'empire'. He examines KRRS as an instance of the AGMs at several levels—local, national and international. He points out that even though at the local level KRRS failed to convert the farmers from their economism, and at the national level it has failed to reverse the trend towards globalization due to diversities of approaches of different state level farmers/peasant associations and of several NGOs, at the global level of the AGM, the KRRS has played a crucial role in undermining the hegemony of multinational corporations, multilateral institutions of governance and their supportive state structure. He however points out that the KRRS movement has been unable to offer viable and practical alternatives to the institutions that prop up the current regime of globalization due to certain inherent weaknesses of this movement. These altogether lead him to examine whether this failure leads to the acceptance of globalization as a *fait accompli.*

The Section IV of this collection deals with the contemporary movements dealing with the issues of caste, ethnicity student and also the electoral movement. Sergio Tamayo in his paper on 'Dynamic of Contention: Post-electoral Movement in Mexico' discusses the mobilization against electoral fraud and for democracy in Mexico. Describing several dynamic and innovating tactics involved in this mobilization he elucidates the role of this movement in paving the way for a period of transition in Mexico by transgressing several institutions and creating ample space of protest and political change therein. In analysing the sequence of this movement against he has highlighted opportunities and risks involved in this mobilization and the possibilities of success thereafter. He has used the analytical perspective of 'framing and contention' as proposed by the political process and resource mobilization theorists in explaining his view on the proliferation and sustenance of this mobilization.

Elżbieta Budakowska in her paper 'Combating Historical Ethnic Stigmatization: BRASPOL in Brazil' examines the dynamic role of the New Social Movement, BRASPOL, in stimulating the Polish post-immigrant generations' actions to challenge negative historical stigmatization of their ancestors in a pluralist society of Brazil. Besides analysing the main elements of the historical development of Polish immigration to Brazil, it presents the process of manifestation of this movement within the 'new social movement' perspective. She explains that social mobilization that aims to redress the issues of historical stigmatization is closely linked to the individual and collective identity formation. However, as the identity-oriented mobilization is manifested in fragmented social and cultural contexts, this also leads to the fragmented identity formation. The processes of the individual and collective identity formation also simultaneously intertwine with the global and local context of multiculturalism.

Multiculturalism, based on the recognition and acceptance of difference, to her, allows new forms of difference to emerge and co-exist. Since the national culture is plural and not a single cultural vision of one group, coherent macro-culture is seen as something in a constant state of becoming. The interaction and intercultural exchange led to strngthen the bonds and citizenship, especially in an isolated Brazilian interior. Multicultural context served as a background of revalourization of the origin. She concludes that if the New Social Movement creates a positive collective identity based on cultural heritage of the active social actors, it can help in overcoming the stigmatization of marginalized community.

Leo Zeilig in his contribution 'Students' Protest and Activism in Sub-Sahara Africa' examines the historical evolution of student activism in sub-Saharan Africa. The paper argues that students have acquired a politically privileged status in much of the continent, which was linked to the role the student-intelligentsia played in the struggles for Independence in the Sub-Saharan Africa. He highlights the nature of student action using a range of literature that emerged during the student revolts of the 1960s and thereafter. To him, immediately after Independence student activism was an important political feature of the new states. In the specific circumstances student activists continued to occupy a politically privileged position in the 1960s and 1970s in sub-Saharan Africa. However, globalization and structural adjustment programme have posed several limitations to students' movement. Herein the student activisms since 1990s have had to negotiate with new form of political and economic forces and contested in waves of popular protest. This paper explains the implications of such negotiations.

Swaraj Basu in his paper on 'Kshatriyahood to Statehood: Voices of the Rajbansis of North Bengal' analyses the transformation of the Rajbansi movement, as it proliferated in the northern part of Bengal, from a quest for upper caste Kshatriya identity to a separate statehood. Making a historical analysis the scholar points out that socially and economically the Rajbansis along with other lower castes are in the margins compared to the upper castes of the region. Making a historical analysis he points out that during the colonial rule in Bengal, the Rajbansi caste movement for upward social mobility and under the banner of the Kshatriya Samiti they asserted their demand for social equity and justice and they took part in the electoral politics in pre-Partition India. In post-independent India, the Rajbansi Kshatriya movement lost its momentum, but over a period of time from a perceived sense of marginalization the Rajbansis raised their voices for a separate state—either in the name of 'Uttarakhand' or 'Kamtapur' or 'Greater Coochbehar'. The reasons for the manifestation of this movement, the process of transformation of this movement, response of different political parties towards the demands of the Rajbansis are analysed in this paper. It has been concluded that the creation of the state would not lead to the end of the existing problems of the Rajbansis or other indigenous groups unless the state machinery gears up to undertake corrective measures to remove socio-economic disparities and backwardness of this region.

There are two papers in Section V of this collection dealing with the issues of grassroots mobilizations. Dip Kapoor and Tejwant Channa in their paper 'Adivasi Social Movements in Orissa: Development, Marginalization and Dispossession' provide an overview of the processes of extraction of valuable resources from the Adivasi (tribal) areas of Orissa, by the trans/national corporate bodies and the response of the Adivasis towards such development. Based on the case study undertaken by the Centre for Research and Development Solidarity (CRDS) on the Kondh and Saora Adivasi movement these scholars develop subaltern insights of the articulations of assertions of these people. Herein using the theoretical and praxiological utility of Gramscian-strains of subaltern studies they underline the contradictions between the emerging developmental dynamics and the tribal peoples' response towards such perspectives of development. They posit the issue of the tribal articulation and collective assertion in the context of the UN Declaration on the Rights of Indigenous Peoples the one hand and expansion of the philosophy of economic liberalization on the other. They delineate the contradiction in the prospects with resource extraction and capitalist accumulation that predictably collides with indigenous peoples' lands, livelihood and culture and their way of development. Such developments they suggest are only likely to exacerbate relations with Adivasis and agri-based communities (e.g. Kashipur struggle) in a state whose people predominantly rely on agricultural livelihoods/ways. They conclude that as indigenous international agendas and transnational and local movements take on counter-hegemonic proportions with or without the use of boomerang strategies, the increasingly corporatized Indian state will be compelled to pay heed to the various assertions of its rural, forest and land-based citizenry, especially the tribals, the subaltern constituencies.

Archana Prasad, in her paper on 'Mahila Panchayat: An Alternative Mode of Collective Action' develops a comprehensive understanding of alternative modes of collective action by women at the grassroots. He highlights that the 'Mahila Panchayat', as a redressal forum for disputes in the community, serves as a vigil group on violence against women and children especially girl children. Functioning in the similar ways to that of Village Panchayat in rural areas this group of women as leaders of the community constitute the Mahila Panchayat to act as a fact-finding team, a pressure group and offers solutions to the problems, which are honoured by the community. The Mahila Panchayat is also a powerful women's forum putting pressure on the family and community to resolve marital and other disputes. Against the backdrop of increasing violence against women in Indian society, persistent state failure to tackle this problem, inadequate legislative measures, delay and denial of justice this paper examines the position of women in the Panchayat as a collective forum for addressing problems, contradiction between the philosophy of women's reservation and the prevalence of patriarchal environment in the Panchayat, effectiveness of state initiatives to protect women against violence, increasing roles of civil society in organizing Mahila Panchayat for marginalized women from poor communities and the need to legalize the women forum so as to give them the legal status.

This collection of esseys have raised several issues related to the dynamics of deprivation, marginalization and inequality and also social and human under development. These issues are addressed in another two collections dealing with the social, cultural, political and historical dynamics of marginalization and social development in the contemporary world.

REFERENCES

Amin, S., G. Arrighi, A.G. Frank, and I. Wallerstein (eds) (1990), *Transforming Revolution: Social Movements and the World System*, New York: Monthly Review Press.

Castells, M. (1997), *The Information Age: Economy, Society and Culture,* vol. II, *The Power of Identity*, Oxford: Blackwell Publishers.

della Porta, Donatella and Tarrow Sidney (2005), *Transnational Protest and Global Activism*, Lanham: Rowman & Littlefield Publishers.

Frank, A.G. and M. Fuentes (1990), Civil Democracy: Social Movements in Recent World History', in S. Amin, G. Arrighi et al. (eds), *Transforming the Revolution: Social Movements and the World System.*

Hardt, M. and A. Negi (2000), *Empire*, Harvard: Harvard University Press.

McDonald, K. (2002), 'From Solidarity to Fluidarity: Social Movements Beyond Collective Identity: The Case of Globalization of Conflict', *Social Movement Studies*, vol. 1, no. 2, 109-278.

Melucci, A. (1996), *Challenging Codes: Collective Action in the Information Age*, Cambridge: Cambridge University Press.

Olson, Mancur, Jr. (1965), *The Logic of Collective Action: Public Goods and the Theory of Groups*, Cambridge: Harvard University Press.

Tarrow, Sidney (1995), *Power in Movements Social Movements: Collective Action and Politics*, Cambridge: Cambridge University Press.

Tourine, A. (2002), 'The Importance of Social Movements', *Social Movement Studies*, vol.1, no. 1. pp. 89-95.

——— (1981), *The Voice and the Eye: An Analysis of Social Movements*, Cambridge: Cambridge University Press.

Urry, John (2000), 'Mobile Sociology', *British Journal of Sociology*, vol. 51, no. 1, 185-203.

Wieviorka, M. (2005), 'After New Social Movements', *Social Movements Studies*, vol. 4, Issue I: 1–19.

Wallerstein, I. (1990), 'Antisystemic Movements: History and Dilemmas', in S. Amin, G. Arrighi et al. (eds), *Transforming the Revolution: Social Movements and the World System*.

I. SOCIAL MOVEMENTS AND SOCIAL TRANSFORMATION: REFLECTIONS ON CONCEPTUAL ISSUES

CHAPTER 1

The Logic of the Alterglobal Movement*

BENJAMÍN TEJERINA

INTRODUCTION

For a little over a decade we have been witnessing the growth of a type of mobilization that had previously only expressed itself on a few occasions and around events of great social relevance. Seattle, November 1999, was the moment when this form of protest acquired planetary visibility, thanks to the social impact of the images of the demonstrators outside the World Trade Organization Summit broadcast by the mass media. This was neither the first mobilization against one of the bodies that best represents the tendencies of economic globalization, nor was it the most important in terms of its mobilizing capacity or social effect; however, it was the moment when a form of discontent and resistance, geographically spread in an uneven way, acquired public visibility and affected the consciousness of a civil society that was becoming internationalized.

It is not its relative novelty that interests us, but the rapid spread of this form of protest and its meaning (Della Porta and Tarrow, 2005). In order to contribute to the understanding of the social meaning of what has been defined as the 'movement of movements', we propose to answer four questions that we believe to be of key importance.

In the first place, I will briefly analyse the possible material foundations of the mobilization. One of the debates that has been the object of reflection by the social movements in recent years is related to the supposed structural foundations of collective action.

*I would like to thank the following for their active participation in this research: Iñaki Martínez de Albeniz, Andrés Gómez Seguel, Beatriz Cavia and Amaia Izaola.

While the roots of the workers' movement were to be found in unequal property structures, and social class became a supposition of its objective definition and an opportunity structure for subjective belonging, the social movements that are characteristic of the 1980s and 1990s reveal themselves to be interclass realities. In the majority of cases, they reflect a middle-class radicalism that aspires to oppose the degradation of the conditions and quality of everyday life, as well the colonization of the space of privacy, pushing the social sectors most affected by these characteristic processes of late capitalism towards mobilization. We propose to answer the question: who are, and what are the characteristics held by the activists who, proceeding from different sectors, come together in this movement in favour of global justice?

In the second place, I would like to know if there is compatibility or incompatibility between the different levels of identification—sectoral-global, particular-general—or if, on the contrary, these are watertight compartments without relationship between them. It is worth recalling that while the workers' movement, and the social and historical movements, drew their main issues from aspects of social existence such as exploitation at work, the relations of domination between persons of different gender, sex, ethnic condition, place of residence or threatened culture, as well as from more general aspects such as the defence of the environment or peace, the movement against neoliberal globalization shows an internal diversity so wide that it is presenting problems for the management of its kaleidoscopic reality of demands.

In the third place, we will consider what could be called the process of construction of the global and alterglobalization: how is the global to be defined and how does alterglobalization acquire concrete form? To this end, we will attempt to delineate a possible conception of the world that supersedes the plurality of political cultures present amongst the activists of the Alterglobal Movement.

In the fourth place, I want to delve deeper into the tension between the conditions of mobilization, which pass through periods of maximum visibility around counter-summits and global protest actions, and the activists' conditions of existence, which involve very different living experiences that are, on occasion, distant from the more solidarity-based demands of globalization.

I will use the four sections of this communication to try and answer these four questions. The information presented here proceeds from a questionnaire that was answered by 166 activists, and the corresponding fieldwork was carried out during the spring months of 2005. The same questionnaire has been used in other European countries and will enable us in the future to compare answers and analyse similarities and differences. In addition, between the months of January and February 2006, 25 interviews were carried out with activists from different organizations, associations and groups that consider themselves part of the Alterglobal Movement, with the aim of analysing other aspects relating to identity, political culture and the movement's alternative proposal.

THE ACTIVISTS OF THE ALTERGLOBALIZATION MOVEMENT

In some social movements the fundamental source of recruitment coincides with a social category: job, ethnic group, gender, age, place of residence. Precisely those social categories that the social scientists use in their questionnaires as independent variables have become significant elements and the object of demands. In spite of the fact that many social movements recruit many of their activists from specific categories, we find in all of them individuals who do not proceed from those categories, while, on the other hand, not all the individuals who belong to certain categories become activists.

According to Claus Offe the characteristics

> of the nucleus of activists and sympathisers of the new social movements proceeding from the new middle class consist of a high level of education, relative economic security and employment in the sector of personal services. [. . .] Besides, they include elements from other groups and strata with which they tend to form a more or less stable alliance. Amongst these other groups, the most important are: a) the 'peripheral' or 'de-commercialised' groups and b) elements of the old middle class. (Offe 1988: 195-6)

Ronald Inglehart has suggested the thesis that the emergence of new social movements is largely due to what he calls cognitive mobilizations, that is, 'the gradual increase in the level of political skill amongst the masses of the population, which in its turn is due to the further spread of education and the intensification of political information' (Inglehart 1991: 421).

I am interested in determining both the socio-demographic characteristics and the characteristics of belonging of the alterglobalization activists interviewed. Amongst the former, it has been pointed out that the new social movements respond to a new 'radicalism of the middle classes'. The origin of this radicalism would lie in the fact that the processes of structural change have contributed in different ways to weakening the foundation of the traditional social conflicts (Eder 1993). Together with these transformations, we are witnessing the emergence of social groups that are notable due to their level of education and to their occupying a social position different from that of the traditional middle class (Della Porta and Diani 1997: 65). These new middle classes would be the link between structural change and new social conflicts. Amongst some of the socio-demographic characteristics of the alterglobalization activists interviewed, we could point to their pronounced youth, 72.3 per cent are younger than 34 years; their high level of education, 70.5 per cent are educated, above the average level of the population, 70.5 per cent; more than 70 per cent have university qualifications; and a high level of use of new information and communication technologies, 60.8 per cent use a computer everyday, 47 per cent use the Internet, and 51.8 per cent use e-mail.

The activists interviewed have different occupations, with a considerable number (30.1 per cent) still studying, and 18.7 per cent carrying out work of an intellectual type or related to the scientific sphere. Those with jobs show a lower level of job insecurity (22.9 per cent) than the level of the employed population as a whole (33 per cent in 2006).

The most outstanding characteristic is the high level of mobilization, since 90.4 per cent take part in some social or political organization (Table 1.1).

Militancy in more than one organization seems to be another outstanding characteristic amongst those interviewed, with participation in 1.65 organizations per activist (Table 1.2).

TABLE 1.1: PARTICIPATION IN SOCIO-POLITICAL ORGANIZATIONS

Participation in socio-political orgs.	Absolute frequency	Percentage
Yes	150	90.4
No	16	9.6
Total	166	100.0

TABLE 1.2: TYPE OF ORGANIZATION TO WHICH THOSE INTERVIEWED BELONGED

Type of organization	Absolute frequency	Percentage
Political parties	26	17.3
Trade unions	18	12.0
Social movements	79	52.7
Associations	26	17.3
Voluntary orgs.	46	30.7
Others	15	10.0
No answer	38	25.3
Total	248*	100.0

Note: *The total does not add up to 166 because the answer is multiple

In relation to their political identity and their feeling of belonging to a global movement, the majority of those interviewed stated that their political identity lay in the social movements (pacifism, ecologism, feminism, autonomous or solidarity).

In the second place, were those who stated that their political identity lay in the workers' movement and, after that, we find those who felt they belonged to a global movement (Table 1.3).

Those who belonged to historical (neighbourhood, students), nationalist or religious movements had less weight amongst those interviewed, some 10 per cent of the cases. Paradoxically, the political identity situated in different social movements seems compatible with a more general and abstract identification, as 81.3 per cent of

TABLE 1.3: POLITICAL IDENTITY OF THE ACTIVISTS INTERVIEWED

Political identity	Absolute frequency	Percentage
Workers' movement	58	34.9
Social movement	127	76.5
Historical movement	21	12.7
Religious movement	11	6.6
Nationalist movement	18	10.8
Global movement	50	30.1
No answer	3	1.8
Total	288*	100.0

Note: *The total does not add up to 166 because the answer is multiple.

those interviewed stated that they felt part of a global movement (Table 1.4).

TABLE 1.4: FEELING OF BELONGING TO A GLOBAL MOVEMENT

P. 10 Do you feel part of a global movement?		
	Absolute frequency	Percentage
Yes	135	81.3
No	19	114
No Answer	12	7.2
Total	166	100.0

THE IDENTITY OF THE ALTERGLOBALIZATION MOVEMENT

The new social movements approach emphasizes those aspects of the social movements that are related to the process of construction of new collective identities, but it has not considered the personal sphere of identity in sufficient depth. The general tendency has been to study processes and social factors that determine the evolution and impact of the social movements. In this approach, the micro-social processes pass into the background.

Omi and Winant (1983), in an evaluation of the civil rights movement in the USA, have pointed out that beyond the legislative achievements or the spread of mass mobilization, the great success of this movement must be sought in its ability to create a new 'subject' and to redefine racial identity and race itself in North American society.

There is an unequal treatment of identity amongst the different social movements. The social centrality of the issues with which the social movements concern themselves is not always accompanied by the same degree of centrality for activists or sympathizers. While certain movements with a religious or nationalist character can involve a high degree of personal commitment for some of their activists, for others they can represent an identification that is transient or instrumental. Other social movements deal with aspects of social life that are directly situated in personal life experience, such as the case of the feminist movement or the movement of gays, lesbians, bisexuals and transsexuals. With respect to personal strategies, the activists of any movement can commit themselves to a greater or lesser degree to the practices of their organization. But the idea we wish to stress is that, from the viewpoint of the construction of personal identity, practices involving an intervention of gender or sexual relations appear to have, in general, greater social meaning than those that affect aspects such as relations with the environment or solidarity with the underprivileged. By this we do not wish to say that for any feminist, gay or lesbian activist his/her commitment involves the same identity. In cases like these, there are important differences in how commitment is lived and how homosexuality is experienced; there are even different ways of defining and becoming homosexual (Plummer 1981; Bell and Weinberg 1978).

Together with personal identity, groups also provide a collective identity. According to Melucci, collective identity is a process that contains three interrelated dimensions that can be separated analytically: (a) it formulates systems of interpretation concerning ends, means and the sphere of action; (b) it activates relations amongst the actors, who interact, communicate, influence each other, negotiate and take decisions; (c) they make emotional investments that permit individuals to recognize themselves (Melucci 1988: 343; 1989: 35; 1995 and 1996).

A similar definition has been made by Polletta and Jasper, according to whom collective identity is (2001: 284):

> an individual's cognitive, moral, and emotional connections with a broader community, category, practice, or institution. It is a perception of a shared status or relation, which may be imagined rather than experienced directly, and it is distinct from personal identities, although it may form part of a personal identity. A collective identity may have been first constructed by outsiders (for example, as in the case of 'Hispanics' in this country), who may still enforce it, but it depends on some acceptance by those to whom it is applied. Collective identities are expressed in cultural materials—names, narratives, symbols, verbal styles, rituals, clothing, and so on—but not all cultural materials express collective identities. Collective identities do not imply the rational calculus for evaluating choices that 'interest' does. And unlike ideology, collective identity carries with it positive feeling for other members of the group.

Although we basically agree with both Melucci's and Polletta and Jasper's definition of collective identity,[1] we would emphasize some distinctive aspects. 'Collective identity' is a concept by which we refer to a feeling of belonging shared by the members of a group or several groups, through which reality is interpreted and defined, directing the actions of those who participate in that feeling. Collective identity can crystallize and objectify itself, but it is constantly subjected to the possibility of change and re-elaboration. Collective identity is not something purely symbolic—belonging to the world of signs and interpretations; it also belongs to the world of social practices (Tejerina 1999).

Taylor and Whittier (1992) have noted down three analytical tools for understanding the construction of collective identity: frontiers, consciousness and negotiation. Now, from the point of view of ideological contents, the constitution of a sense of a differentiated 'we' (frontiers), the formulation of an alterglobalizing sentiment (consciousness), and the establishment of a shared (negotiated) collective action, the statements of the activists interviewed show a clear collective identity.

We asked the activists about motivations, the aspects most valued by the movement, the objective and interest in maintaining relations with other groups. Their answers are shown in Table 1.5.

With respect to the reasons why activists take part in the alterglobal movement, we asked them to answer a question concerning their motivations: 'I take part in collective actions against globalization in order to (...)'. The sentiment on which there was most agreement was opposition to economic domination (4.5 points and the least standard deviation). It was followed in importance by the transformation of political structures and democracy (4.45 points) and affirming moral principles of equality and justice (4.44 points).

With respect to the degree of solidarity amongst activists, those interviewed shared a broad space of solidarity that was expressed in a strong agreement with respect to the transformation of a social reality that they didn't like (4.66 points), building a feeling of solidarity against what they considered to be an imposition (4.45), sharing the same demands (4.24) and reaching understanding about common interests (4.16).

We also formulated a question on the aspects of the movement that were most highly valued, with the reply that the plural composition obtains the most positive assessment (4.18 points) amongst all of the proposed alternatives for assessment, followed by the horizontal and democratic character of the movement (4.10) and its reference to transcultural questions (4.04).

With respect to the aim of the movement, the ideas of extending consciousness of the risks of globalization (4.35 points) and of changing the perspective on globalization (4.25 points) were the affirmations that obtained the highest level of agreement amongst those interviewed, in the double sense of perception of the effectiveness

TABLE 1.5: MOTIVATIONS, OBJECTIVE, INTEREST

P. 12. 'I take part in collective actions against globalization in order to . . .' (rank from 1 'total disagreement' to 5 'total agreement')

		N	Average	Standard deviation	Coefficient of variation (%)
P1201	Affirm moral principles of equality and justice	163	4.44	0.79	17.70
P1202	Oppose economic domination	163	4.50	0.74	16.44
P1205	Transform political structures and democracy	160	4.45	0.93	20.90
P1301	Share my demands	166	4.24	0.90	21.13
P1303	Generate solidarity in face of those who impose globalization	165	4.45	0.86	19.30
P1304	Change a social reality that I don't like	161	4.66	0.70	15.00
P1801	Plurality of components	161	4.18	0.90	21.56
P1803	Horizontal-democratic character of the movement	152	4.10	0.81	19.80
P1804	The fact they deal with events that cross-cultural frontiers	162	4.04	0.96	23.64
P1902	Change the perspective on globalization	160	4.25	0.90	21.27
P1903	Raise awareness of the risks of globalization	161	4.35	0.83	18.97
P3001	Build the widest possible movement	162	4.12	0.98	23.86

of mobilization and the progressive expansion of one's own awareness. Finally, the desire to construct a broad social movement obtained a high level of agreement (4.12 points).

THE POLITICAL CARTOGRAPHY OF ALTERGLOBALIZATION

According to the classical formulation of Almond and Verba, 'the term *political culture* thus refers to the specifically political orientations—attitudes toward the political system and its various parts, and attitudes toward the role of the self in the system. We speak of a political culture just as we can speak of an economic culture or a religious culture. It is a set of orientations toward a special set of social objects and processes' (Almond and Verba 1965: 12). This definition refers to a cultural corpus that is specifically political; a differentiated and separable set of beliefs, values, behaviours, symbols, discourses, memories, expectations, roles and manners that revolve around the political. Resounding within this is a type of universalist vision of the political that results, firstly, from a dissociation of politics and culture and, secondly, from the articulation of a specifically political cultural system that is characterized by a strong universal (transcultural) identification between the political and the sphere of activity characteristic of the institutions (Martínez de Albeniz 2003).

The theoretical problem that is raised by considering political culture as a special case of Culture is that the terrain of the relationships and links between the two spheres is left unexplored, which affects a more exact understanding of their process of production and transmission. On the other hand, an important empirical problem arises, since anti-institutional or extra-institutional sectors, anti-system forces, groups of the disenchanted or incivility are not always found behind the new political cultures.

Political culture can be considered from another perspective. It can be understood as a set of attitudes, opinions and behaviours with respect to the norms that regulate processes of social conflict existing in society, as well as the cognitive, affective and practical elements involving the agents who intervene in decision-making processes. It also implies moral evaluations on the attribution of responsibility both to collective actors and to the institutions that intervene in managing and planning the future of a society. These include all those that compete for responsibility in decision making in the sphere of the state and supra-state regulations.

With this definition we are attempting to widen the narrow margins into which political culture—understood as institutionally orientated political culture, political culture of the national sphere, and the majority or dominant political culture—has been fit. In any case, it would be preferable, and sociologically more appropriate, to talk of political cultures in the plural. However, on differentiating amongst the different components of political culture(s), we observe that this concept reveals itself to be unsuitable for rendering what has been taking place in the alterglobalization movement. Rather than seeking for a differentiated political culture, the question we must answer is whether the orientations and practices should be considered as part of the political cultures of the citizenry or whether, on the contrary, when studying political culture we should refer exclusively to opinions and attitudes facing institutionalized actors and political spheres.

In our opinion, the first option contributes elements that are basic to the analysis and understanding of political processes in advanced societies, and if they are not taken into consideration the latter remain opaque. Above all, they shed light on the social processes of production of new cultural dynamics that emerge on the limits of institutionalized politics, with which they compete for new definitions, contributing to their transformation.

Besides, the global and alterglobalization constitute a terrain in dispute in the process of redefinition, some of whose formulations are to be found in the alterglobalization movement, which is why any one-dimensional attempt at reification is highly unsatisfactory. At the same time, the concept of political culture is still too homogeneous, too compact, smooth and lacking in edges to be able to render the plurality of tensions enclosed by: (a) the instituted and the instituting; (b) the political and the cultural; (c) the visible and the hidden; (d) having and living. To speak of a political cartography of alterglobalization, instead of a political culture, has the advantages that: (a) it represents a guide to different and differentiated times, places and practices; (b) it permits a better understanding that similar practices can give rise to diverse trajectories and interpretations; (c) it is better adapted to understanding a reality resembling an open world, one full of possibilities, but—at the same time—with well-trodden paths, which contains the new and the old, and is yet identifiable and discernible.

That is how we understand it and the construction of the questionnaire has been directed towards capturing this fluid and changing reality, with the interviewees questioned about those aspects that form a relevant part of the characteristic *weltanschauung* of technologically orientated societies undergoing a process of increasing globalization. The five spheres on which we have concentrated are: (1) the context of work; (2) the interests existing behind knowledge, research and training; (3) the models of consumption; (4) the relations of domination in the sphere of culture; and (5) the regulating role of the political institutions. We will briefly consider the views on these five spheres of society expressed by the activists of the alterglobalization movement.

It hardly seems unnecessary to recall that work has been, and continues to be, a fundamental institution of society. The majority of the evolutionary typologies of society refer to the dominant character of labour for defining each of its types and constitutive stages. In the questions we put to the interviewees we combined characteristic elements of the current employment situation, its expressive character, its conditions, consequences and agents (Table 1.6). What seemed to most concern the activists is the power of the multinationals and financial groups (4.75 points) and the labour conditions of globalization (4.64 points). The unequal distribution of power and its consequences for one of the sides—the workers—who intervene in global production thus appears as an outstanding element in the evaluation. This emphasis on, or sensitivity towards, inequality, the scarcity of justice and the opposition to economic domination had already appeared previously as an element giving cohesion to the movement. Lack of employment (4.43 points) and uncertainties surrounding professional life (flexibility, mobility, insecurity, precariousness)—4.11 points—appear next as features of the present-day world of work that cause the greatest concern. The

TABLE 1.6: EVALUATIONS ON THE CONTEXT OF WORK

P.43 'Evaluate the following features of the today's world' (rank from 1 'it doesn't cause me any concern at all' to 5 'it causes me a lot of concern')

		N	Average	Standard deviation	C.V. (%)
P4301	Lack of employment	161	4.43	0.80	17.99
P4302	Uncertainty of professional life	160	4.11	0.91	22.17
P4303	Difficulty for expressing one's own creativity at work	157	3.83	1.00	25.98
P4304	Having to work as an employee or for the labour market	157	3.75	1.06	28.16
P4305	The power of multinationals and financial groups	161	4.75	0.53	11.1
P4306	Labour consequences of globalization	160	4.64	0.63	13.53

possible lack of expressiveness, or difficulty in expressing one's own creativity at work (3.83 points) and lack of independence (3.75 points), on having to work as an employee, cause less concern although it is still significant.

We frequently refer to present-day society as a knowledge society. Although knowledge is not an aspect exclusive to this age, the central role of science and the generation of reflexive processes associated with its technological advances, has made it possible to generalize labels such as society of science (Lamo de Espinosa), information

TABLE 1.7: EVALUATIONS ON EDUCATION AND KNOWLEDGE

P.43 'Evaluate the following features of the today's world' (rank from 1 'it doesn't cause me any concern at all' to 5 'it causes me a lot of concern')

		N	Average	Standard deviation	C.V. (%)
P4307	Lack of relation between the knowledge acquired in the educational system and personal needs	160	4.11	0.95	23.16
P4308	Disconnection between the knowledge taught in the educational system and insertion into the labour market	156	3.78	1.16	30.74
P4309	Transmission of knowledge linked exclusively to the system of dominant values	156	4.43	0.80	17.97
P4310	Educational system too closely linked to the needs of the market	159	4.28	0.93	21.82
P4311	Policies of privatization of teaching and research	158	4.63	0.63	13.67
P4312	Educational system excessively determined by a neo-liberal perspective	158	4.41	0.82	18.64
P4313	Difficulty of access to knowledge	157	4.24	0.80	18.77
P4314	The fact that science and technology are not dedicated to resolving basic social problems	156	4.51	0.76	16.81

society (Castells) or knowledge society (Stehr). The capacity for social intervention in our own nature has reached levels that were unthinkable a short time ago (Melucci), which has spread the idea that science, knowledge and the educational system—responsible for the former two's transmission—occupy a central place in today's society. We asked the activists about the use and orientation that education, research, science, technology and knowledge in general should have. The element that caused the greatest concern was the policy of privatizing education and research (4.63 points), as well as the fact that science and technology are not dedicated to resolving basic social problems (4.51 points). The privatization of certain uses of research and dedication to basic social problems seem to be situated in the same evaluative continuum, almost a composition in terms of axiological antagonism.

A short distance behind, we find the answers on the transmission of knowledge linked exclusively to the dominant system of values (with a level of rejection of 4.43 points), and the existence of an educational system that is excessively determined by a neo-liberal perspective (4.41 points). Dominant values and a neo-liberal perspective appear to refer to the same sphere of evaluation. The fact that the educational system is too closely linked to the needs of the market produces a high level of rejection (4.28 points), as do the difficulties in access to knowledge (4.24 points), and the lack of relation between knowledge acquired in the educational system and personal needs (4.11 points). The idea that causes the least objection, although it continues to be significant, is the disconnection between knowledge taught in the educational system and insertion in the labour market (3.78 points). From the above, we can conclude that there is rejection of the privatization of research; of the fact that basic social problems are not its priority; that education and knowledge are directed by the market, by dominant values or by a neo-liberal perspective; as well as the lack of democracy in the access to knowledge and its dissociation from personal needs.

The drastic changes that have occurred in industrial societies have brought about a transformation in the structure of plausibility of that form of collective identity that was articulated around the world of work. The decline in the rate of trade union affiliation, the fall in the number of workers employed in certain branches of production, the dispersion of social enclaves that were culturally homogeneous in terms of class density are some of the factors that have resulted in class mobilization losing its political relevance, and class identity its social meaning.

The social conditions of work in post-Fordist society restrict the recourse to this source of identity. In the words of L.E. Alonso: 'the dictates of the new spirit of capitalism dissolve both the profession—vocation—and the collective consciousness of the organizations, which become dissolved on the surface of the network society' (Alonso 2000: 217). The point is being reached where this process could put an end to work as a source of collective identity, since in post-modern society '[this approach] announces the loss of social references by subjects in the place of production (...) and considers consumption as a form of adventure making possible plasticity and expressiveness; it always forgets that social subjects in this situation can disintegrate into pure individuals enclosed in an autistic and egotistic world filled with lack of commitment and disinterest for the group' (Alonso 2000: 217).

The question we wish to pose in this respect is whether indeed the consumerist society transforms us into such malleable persons, into such autistic and egotistic subjects lacking in interest for the group, or whether amongst the activists of alterglobalization we can find traces of that culture of work that are not wholly individualistic. Solidarity is also present amongst those interviewed, although it has adopted other meanings. The search for a model of consumption that does not ignore ecological balance (4.68 points), abandoning consumption oriented towards economic speculation (4.62 points) and rejection of products elaborated under exploitative conditions in developing countries (4.58 points), are the evaluations that reach a higher degree of concern (Table 1.8). Other aspects appear that are related to unequal access to consumption, both between developed and non-developed areas (4.43 points) and within the developed areas between different social sectors (4.18 points), the instrumental use of consumption as a status symbol (4.35 points), and the relative lack of control over important aspects of one's own life (4.37 points). Justice, equality, solidarity, the non-exploitation of people, ecological balance and social control over life would be the constituent evaluative components of this political cartography of questions relating to the consumer society.

What is political about culture, or what political culture is to be found in the cultural and institutional models? This issue is raised by the questions in Tables 1.9 and 1.10. What most concerns the

TABLE 1.8: EVALUATIONS OF THE MODELS OF CONSUMPTION

P.43 'Evaluate the following features of the today's world' (rank from 1 'it doesn't cause me any concern at all' to 5 'it causes me a lot of concern')

		N	Average	Standard deviation	C.V. (%)
P4315	Consumption of products produced under exploitative conditions in developing countries	158	4.58	0.79	17.29
P4316	Unequal access to consumption in developed areas	156	4.18	0.85	20.24
P4317	Unequal access to consumption between developed and non-developed areas	156	4.43	0.79	17.79
P4318	Consumption of goods as a status symbol	156	4.35	0.82	18.80
P4319	Consumption oriented towards economic speculation	157	4.62	0.60	13.07
P4320	Consumption that ignores ecological balance	157	4.68	0.59	12.59
P4321	Lack of control over important aspects of one's own life	151	4.37	0.71	16.20

interviewees with respect to the cultural models is the excessive concentration of power by capital (4.71 points); they also share a pronounced sense of justice between women and men, strongly rejecting the absence of equity between the genders (4.69 points). The domination exercised by those who control information at the world level also generates a strong sense of concern.

Once again, a special feeling is expressed against those who have accumulated a great measure of power. In the second place, a series of items appear relating to the repression of alternative lifestyles (4.47 points), the lack of social control by individuals over the model of society (4.35 points), cultural reproduction planned by cultural industry (4.34 points), imposition and lack of individual freedom (4.27 points), and recognition of cultural diversity (4.36 points).

TABLE 1.9: EVALUATIONS OF THE CULTURAL MODELS

P.43 'Evaluate the following features of the today's world' (rank from 1 'it doesn't cause me any concern at all' to 5 'it causes me a lot of concern')

		N	Average	Standard deviation	C.V. (%)
P4322	Lack of control by individuals of the model of society	154	4.35	0.75	17.33
P4323	Repression of alternative lifestyles	158	4.47	0.69	15.50
P4324	Cultural production planned by the culture industry	152	4.34	0.71	16.34
P4325	Domination exercised by those who control the production of information at the world level	154	4.65	0.62	13.35
P4326	Excessive concentration of power by capital	155	4.71	0.53	11.34
P4327	Imposition of models of individual freedom	155	4.27	0.87	20.37
P4328	Lack of recognition of cultural differences	157	4.36	0.73	16.63
P4329	Absence of equity between the genders	156	4.69	0.49	10.45

These indicate the existence of a culture of resistance and a search for cultural patterns as an alternative to those that, in the opinion of the interviewees, are being imposed by authorities with more power. Numerous examples appear in the interviews with activists, of experiences that attempt to construct, occupy and inhabit alternative spaces on the margin of the controls of economic, political and cultural power.

It is not clear whether the critique of the institutions that appears in this specific political cartography involves more or less politics. We are inclined to think that it is more a critique of failings than of excess, that is to say, what is desired is more politics and more intervention by the political institutions and not less, as would be demanded, for example, by a critique from neo-liberal positions, or from positions

you, that is, the friendships I personally made there, friendships with people you know for 3 or 4 days. Although you've only seen them again a couple of times, the truth is it's like you've known them all your life, because of everything you've shared in that short space of time', 'they serve to form networks, share experiences, and for returning home with new capacities for analysing international reality', 'you come back with renewed energy, because you see people who are working better than you, doing really important things'.

From the statements of the interviewed activists it is possible to establish a triple conception of the global: (a) as an isolated, odd, strange, and extraordinary moment that displays a peculiar kind of time and space with specific social relationships, that is to say, in which experiences that have their own social logic take place; (b) as a festive, relaxed moment, in which entertainment pleasure and expression of demand go hand in hand; and (c) as an event with a meaning that transcends the limits of the exact moment in which it takes place.

The local appears to present a greater degree of coherence and unanimity, inasmuch as it is the place where interactions take place and where the structures that make it possible to build and maintain the movement are found: 'the most important thing is getting close to your milieu, the [activity] that's done on a small scale', 'it's getting involved in small projects, in small campaigns that you can see actually working, reaching people', 'it's not in the big summits where most of the work of the alterglobalization movement is found, but in what's local', 'always starting out from the local, because of the closeness of people of your milieu, the people who live in your community', 'as the construction of alternative spaces of another sociality, of another type of relationships', 'your relationship with social change is not only standing behind a banner, or mobilizing. It's in your everyday relationships, starting with your friends, your partner, relationships of every type', 'the alterglobalization movement is nothing unless it has a basis of struggle and resistance at the local level'.

The local ambit appears as the original place where demands are made, the space of authenticity. It is an immediate, accessible, nearby, completely visible, and therefore apprehensible, kind of time and space. It also appears as the place of the concept of 'we', of the people, the space in which we meet everyday, the space of the real and the space of personalization (face-to-face personal relationships).

A third space is delineated between the local and the global; insofar as it is a space in the process of being created it is symbolic, a virtual architecture between both spheres of activity. It is a 'place' traversed by contradiction, tension and imbalances, but also by additions and superimpositions, although the transition between the two is not easy. Three meanings appear clearly prefigured. In the first place, as a way to define the movement: 'the feeling that the rebels from different issues, organizations, spheres of intervention seek each other out is, in my opinion, a fundamental key that differentiates today's processes from those of before', 'the fact of having shared many processes of struggle with many different people, in different countries, in different situations', 'meeting so many people from different continents who think the same way, has given me immense hope, an immense faith in humanity: we are capable of doing anything, and besides I believe it'.

In the second place, tension defines some of the testimonies gathered: 'there are two levels in the alterglobalization movement: (a) there are some people who are paid workers, teachers or people who want to participate in this movement and this coordination at the international level that takes people by plane from here to there, and (b) there is local coordination', and 'I wouldn't say it's plural, rather I'd say it's contradictory, it's clearly contradictory'.

In the third place, another interpretation appears around the idea of a necessary evil: 'one shouldn't make a legend out of summits. They are necessary experiences, but the work is at home, the work lies in making proposals in your milieu, and in the end we live in a world full of micro-realities, which require micro-political actions', and 'integrating that solidarity and that spirit of cooperation in your everyday life, that is something that always gets through to people, because the very essence of action is that it's done with people'.

The statements about the glocal are structured around three meanings: (a) that which defines the movement and gives it a specific value and importance compared to previous mobilization processes, as a space of struggle and search, of meeting between rebellious and disobedient activists, resistance fighters, and as a space of re-signification; (b) as a space of coordination in permanent tension between the fixed (here and now) and the mobile (there and before–after); (c) as a necessary evil that connects the non-genuine, dispensable and non-essential macro-space (idealized/legendary) with the space of the micro, of the real, of the genuine and the truly essential.

CONCLUSION

The social characterization of the alterglobalization activists interviewed indicates some differences compared with those features traditionally attributed both to the members of the workers' movement and to those of the new social movements. In comparison with the latter, their profile places more accent on their youth, their higher level of educational training, greater contact with the new information technologies, a more pronounced presence of women and less exposure to job insecurity.

Everything seems to indicate that the old category of 'middle-class radicalism' is being complemented by a growing presence of professionals of knowledge and people accustomed to managing information of both a general and a professional kind. However, it would be complex to elaborate further than we have here in presenting this conclusion, since a significant part of the alterglobalization activists also participate in what have been called the new social movements.

Militancy in more than one organization seems to be a frequent feature amongst the activists interviewed, with a small presence of affiliates of political parties and trade union organizations, and a massive presence of other social movements, voluntary associations and non-governmental organizations. Activism is subjected to frequent renewal and collaboration is limited in time, with a scarce presence of activists having more than five years involvement, although the majority participate regularly and only a small percentage get involved at specific times. Ideologically they are situated on the extreme left, the great majority declare themselves to be non-believers and to be non-practising in religious terms.

A minority situate their political identity in their belonging to a global movement (17 per cent) against a majority who prefer to situate themselves in other types of movement (83 per cent). Does this mean that the majority do not consider themselves to be part of a global movement? Is it possible to make both feelings of belonging compatible, or for them to be considered the same thing? Only 11.4 per cent rule out belonging to a global movement, 30.1 per cent affirm that their political identity is linked to their belonging to the global movement, and as many as 81.3 per cent feel themselves to be a constituent part of that movement. In terms of belonging, there is a terrain that makes it possible to make political identification with a sectoral movement and belonging to a wider movement compatible.

If Melucci is right when he says that collective identity is a shared definition, produced by interaction amongst individuals, which makes reference to the orientations of their action as well as to the opportunities and limits within which this action takes place, then we would be facing a collective identity with a very clear, precise profile that is widespread amongst the interviewees. The activists appear to be conscious that: (a) through their action they want to build the widest possible movement; (b) that they personally mobilize to oppose economic domination, to affirm moral principles of equality and justice, and to transform the political structures and democracy; (c) that their interest in uniting with others rests on the possibility of altering an unwanted social reality, generating solidarity, constructing common interests and sharing demands; (d) that the alterglobalization movement is effective because it is contributing to raise awareness of the risks of globalization and to change the perceptions held of it; and (e) that the most problematical aspects of organizing a movement (pluralism, diversity) are what appear to make it most attractive to the activists: the plurality of its components, the horizontal and democratic character of the movement and the fact that it deals with questions that transcend cultural frontiers. But is this possible? Can such dissimilar components and political perspectives coexist without resulting in disintegration? Can they inhabit the same terrain?

The cartography sketched by the answers of the alterglobalization activists delineates a three-dimensional space resulting from the intersection of two planes: one horizontal (the plane of what should be), which indicates the desire for egalitarian comparison, from which the second (the plane of what is) is judged. The latter indicates and denounces the structures of social and economic inequality (power of the multinationals, absence of scientific and technological knowledge for the resolution of social problems, absence of ecological balance, economic exploitation and speculation, concentration of power and absence of equity).

The evaluations of the alterglobalization activists structure a social space, a space which is at the same time symbolic, a cosmovision making it possible to define globalization and its malcontents around three axes: the first refers to the spatial, the second to the relational, and the third to the practices carried out by the different participating agents.

(a) Inside–outside, inclusion–exclusion as can be seen in the items: 'Lack of employment', 'Labour consequences of globalization', 'Difficulty of access to knowledge', 'Conditions of exploitation',

'Unequal access to consumption', 'Domination exercised by those who control the production of information', or 'Absence of equity between the genders'.

(b) Up–down, imposition–repression corresponds to the items: 'Uncertainty of professional life', 'Policies of privatization of teaching and research', 'Educational system too closely linked to the needs of the market and determined by a neo-liberal perspective', 'Consumption of goods as a status symbol', 'Lack of control over important aspects of one's own life', 'Lack of control by individuals of the model of society', 'Repression of alternative lifestyles', 'Excessive concentration of power', 'Imposition of models of individual freedom' or 'Lack of recognition of cultural differences'.

(c) The practices, agents and institutions that shape the space of conflict: 'the unemployed', 'multinationals and financial groups', 'scientists and technologists', 'developing countries', 'developed countries', 'alternative lifestyles', 'models of society', 'cultural industry', 'capital', 'national institutions', 'states'.

All of this gives shape to a cosmovision, and also to living spaces, spaces that are habitable, or that are at least intended to be habitable, on the basis of another way of understanding globalization and antiglobalization practices.

Such agreement around the diagnosis of globalization that we have found amongst the alterglobalization activists is truly striking if we recall the great constituent diversity of its structural support; above all because the first identification in the majority of cases does not occur as members of a global movement but as actors of other movements and organizational forms. Both elements, globalization and alterglobalization, with their multiplicity of living spaces, on the one hand, and the structural plurality as the material support of an excessively coherent diagnosis, on the other, pose a paradox that we cannot elucidate here, but that we cannot resist stating: How is it possible, out of the fragmentation, plurality and diversity of a 'movement of movements', to affirm a common belonging to a global movement? Is the global movement formed by a series of homeomorphic expressions (definitions provided with proximity and continuity) or is the 'global' an empty signifier in which all demands are possible, a signifier that makes it possible to articulate very different demands, a type of ecumenism of demands?

From the standpoint of the movement: (1) the global is viewed as an unreal space for simulation, visibility, entertainment, sharing, talking, and meeting with everybody; (2) the local is defined as a real space of the genuine, for invisibility, seriousness, and the place of the making, building, and the space of the 'we'.

From the point of view of the social logics: (1) the global is defined with the following concepts: the isolated, the momentary, the discontinuous, the space for desire, the space for building networks, telling and sharing experiences, mutual recognition, and space for sharing with strangers; (2) the local is identified with: small, near, communal, sociability, everyday life, concrete, continuous, returning home, carrying out experiences, face-to-face relationships with your friends, your colleagues, little by little building, your milieu.

NOTE

1. We do not fully agree with Polletta and Jasper's assertion that collective identity is the perception of sharing the same status or relation (cognitive, moral and emotional connections with a broader community) which is or can be imagined rather than directly experienced. There are numerous testimonies by activists that narrate how they have directly experienced those connections with other activists at times of mobilization or of carrying out massive actions of resistance or opposition, and how their effect has stayed alive in their consciousness for a long time.

REFERENCES

Almond, Gabriel A. and Sidney Verba (1965), *The Civic Culture*, Boston: Little Brown.

Alonso, Luis Enrique (2000), *Trabajo y postmodernidad: El empleo débil*, Madrid: Fundamentos.

Barth, Frederic (1976), *Los grupos étnicos y sus fronteras*, México: F.C.E.

Bell, Allan and Martin Weinberg (1978), *Homosexualities: A Study of Diversity Among Men and Women*, New York: Simon and Schuster.

Berger, Peter and Thomas Luckmann (1967), *The Social Construction of Reality: A Treatise in the Sociology of Knowledge*, Harmondsworth: Penguin Books.

Bourdieu, Pierre (1997), *Razones prácticas. Sobre la teoría de la acción*, Barcelona: Anagrama.

Castells, Manuel (1998), *La era de la información: Economía, Sociedad y Cultura. El fin del milenio*, vol. III, Madrid: Alianza.

Cohen, Anthony P. (1985), *The Symbolic Construction of Community*, London: Routledge.

Codol, Jean-Paul (1981), 'Une approche cognitive du sentiment d'identité', *Information sur les sciences sociales*, 20, 1.

Dahrendorf, Ralf (1990), *El conflicto social moderno*, Madrid: Mondadori.

Della Porta, Donatella and Mario Diani (1999), *Social Movements*, Oxford: Blackwell.

Della Porta, Donatella and Sidney Tarrow (2005), *Transnational Protest & Global Activism*, Lanham: Rowman & Littlefield Publishers.

Durkheim, Emile (1982), *Las formas elementales de la vida religiosa. El sistema totémico en Australia*, Madrid: Akal.

Eder, Klaus (1993), *The New Politics of Class: Social Movements and Cultural Dynamics in Advanced Societies*, London: Sage.

Eisenstadt, Samuel N. (1969), 'El Estado, la Sociedad y la formación de Centros. Algunos problemas en la evolución de la Sociología Política', *Revista Española de la Opinión Pública*, no. 18 (Oct.-Dic.).

Erikson, Erik H. (1966), 'The Concept of Identity in Race Relations: Notes and Queries', *Daedalus*, 95.

Guiot, Jean M. (1977), 'Attribution and Identity Construction: Some Comments', *American Sociological Review*, 42, October.

Habermas, Jürgen (1975), *Problemas de legitimación en el capitalismo tardío*, Buenos Aires: Amorrortu.

Inglehart, Ronald (1991), *El cambio cultural en las sociedades industriales avanzadas*, Madrid: CIS-Siglo XXI.

Kastersztein, Joseph (1981), 'Aspects psychosociaux de l'identité', *Information sur les sciences sociales*, 20, 1.

Martínez De Albeniz, Iñaki (2003), *La poética de la política. Los usos de la política en el País Vasco*, Bilbao: Servicio de Publicaciones de la Universidad del País Vasco.

Melucci, Alberto (1988), 'Getting Involved: Identity and Mobilization in Social Movements', in *International Social Movement Research*, 1, pp. 329–48.

———, (1989), *Nomads of the Present: Social Movements and Individual Needs in Contemporary Society*, London: Hutchinson Radius.

———, (1995), 'The Process of Collective Identity' in Hank Johnston and Bert Klandermans (eds.), *Social Movements and Culture*, London: UCL Press, pp. 41–63.

———, (1996), *Challenging Codes: Collective Action in the Information Age*, Cambridge: Cambridge University Press.

McAdam, Doug (1982), *Political Process and the Development of Black Insurgency, 1930-1970*, Chicago: The University of Chicago Press.

Offe, Claus (1988), *Partidos políticos y nuevos movimientos sociales*, Madrid: Sistema.

Omi, Michael and Howard Winant (1983), 'By the Rivers of Babylon: Race in the United States', part II, in *Socialist Review*, 72 (November/December), pp. 35–52.

Plummer, Ken (1981), *The Making of the Modern Homosexual*, Maryland: Rowman & Littlefield Publishers.

Polletta, Francesca and James M. Jasper (2001), 'Collective Identity and Social Movements', *Annual Review of Sociology*, 27, pp. 283–305.

Shils, Edward A. (1961), 'Center and Periphery', in *The Logic of Personal Knowledge: Essays Presented to Michael Polanyi*, London: Routledge & Kegan Paul.

Smith, Anthony D. (1991), *National Identity*, London: Penguin.

Taboada-Leonetti, Isabelle (1981), 'Identité individuelle, identité collective', *Information sur les science sociales*, 20, 1.

Tajfel, Henri (1974), 'Social Identity and Intergroup Behaviour', *Social Science Information*, 13, 2.

Tarrow, Sidney (1994), *Power in Movement: Social Movements, Collective Action and Politics*, Cambridge: Cambridge University Press.

Taylor, Verta and Nancy E. Whittier (1992), 'Collective Identity in Social Movements Communities: Lesbian Feminist Mobilization', in A.D. Morris and C.M. Mueller (eds.), *Frontiers in Social Movement Theory*, New Haven: Yale University Press, pp. 104–29.

Tejerina, B., Sobrado Fernandez, J.M. and X. Aierdi (1995), *Sociedad Civil, Protesta y Movimientos Sociales en el País Vasco*, Vitoria-Gasteiz: Servicio Central de Publicaciones del Gobierno Vasco.

Tejerina, Benjamín (1999), 'El poder de los símbolos. Identidad colectiva y movimiento etnolingüístico en el País Vasco', *Revista Española de Investigaciones Sociológicas*, no. 88, Octubre-Diciembre 1999, pp. 75–105.

Tejerina, Benjamín and Iñaki Martínez De Albéniz (1999), 'Movimientos sociales y globalización en Euskal Herria' in J. Beriain and R. Fernández Ubieta (coords.). *La cuestión vasca. Claves de un conflicto cultural y político*, Barcelona: Proyecto A, pp. 244–56.

Weber, Max (1984), *La acción social: Ensayos metodológicos*, Barcelona: Península.

Weiner, Richard (1982), 'Collective Identity Formation and Social Movements', *Psychology and Social Theory*, 3, spring-summer.

Zald, Mayer N. and John D. McCarthy (1987), *Social Movements in an Organizational Society: Collected Essays*, New Jersey: Transaction Publishers.

CHAPTER 2

Counter-Globalist Movements and Post-Globalisms of the Marginalized

JAMES GOODMAN

Over the last ten years social movements of the marginalized have acquired remarkable public visibility and political traction. Movements based on sectors that were previously assumed to have been superseded, left behind by the march of history, have come to claim central significance in the unfolding drama of corporate-led globalization. Subsistence peasants, urban poor, indigenous peoples, domestic workers, migrants, and others, have gained a consciousness and capacity to act in the face of commodifying pressures imposed through market globalism. In the process they have forged new strategic alignments, mounting counter-globalist challenges that have seriously disrupted globalist prescriptions. This paper addresses some of these themes, discussing how counter-globalist agency may now be generating new post-globalist ideological orientations.

Globalization is best understood as an outcome rather than a cause of social change. It signifies a spatial reorientation that itself is a symptom of a large-scale reorganization of societies driven by changing social relations (Rosenberg 2000). The most recent wave of globalization contrasts with mercantilist and colonialist antecedents in being driven primarily by corporate interests. The key social agents of corporate globalization are transnational capitalist classes that coalesce executives of transnational corporations, state and inter-state elites, and consumerist cultural elites (Sklair 2000). These social forces have deep roots in the earliest manifestations of capitalist expansion, but with the latter third of the twentieth century they have become increasingly autonomous and self-conscious political players, evidenced in a panoply of globalist institution-building efforts and related ideological expressions. Transnational capitalist classes have thereby globalized material, institutional and info-cultural power sources, and have promulgated powerful globalist ideologies of neo-liberalism and marketization.

Counter-globalists assert both autonomy and solidarity, geared to deep democratization, and to agendas for decommodification, including the assertion of the commons. The primary effect of globalism has been the commodification and consequent exhaustion of existence: unavoidably it is the realms of reproduction—uncommodified or de-commodified realms on the frontiers of accumulation—that are the chief targets and sites of conflict. It thus instigates struggles for a world beyond exhaustion, fought-out between social forces that benefit from accumulation and those that bear its costs. A central theme is to embed markets in society, rather than embedding society in markets (McMicheal 2003). At the international level such an agenda expands the concept of the right to development into a 'right to wealth', and into the idea of 'ecological debt', such as the North's climate debt, posing a real challenge to the current model of distribution.

These themes directly address structures of global inequality, and are geared towards enabling people to determine their own futures, as self-determining, self-governing entities. As globalist agendas have destabilized societies, counter-strategies have swiftly developed into post-globalist agendas, offering the possibility of new ideologies and programmes grounded in the exercise of popular sovereignty. A key starting point is the practice of multipolar delinking, where the political institutions of globalism are rendered irrelevant as multiple social forces collectively construct their own autonomous mechanisms. These de-globalization dynamics are built in the form of trans-local subsistence or sufficiency movements, through delinking moves at the national level, and through inter-state multilateral delinking, mostly from blocs of southern countries.

Clearly counter-globalism potentially encompasses a wide spectrum of political forces, from the communal to the global, ranged against dominant globalist ideologies (Goodman 2007a). The primary lines of antagonism centre on realms of social, cultural and ecological reproduction (Bakker and Gill 2003). Rather than simply resisting globalism, these counter-forces pose alternatives to it and pre-figure the possibilities for post-globalism. In this respect they are powerfully generative, offering pathways from opposition to aspiration. This paper addresses these post-globalist agendas through discussion of structures, values and alternatives. Section one sketches an overview of shifting structures of globalism, including a recent spiraling into increasingly coercive modes of command politics. Section two offers a provisional framework for interpreting counter-globalist politics, identifying structural fissures, channels for mobilization, and associated value orientations. Section three suggests how counter-globalism may develop its characteristic modes of post-globalist ideology.

GLOBALISM IN CRISIS

As a global hegemonic force globalism has faltered. Since at least the late 1990s we have been living through what Wallerstein has characterized as the 'Age of Transition'—an interregnum characterized by both disruption and possibility. The crisis has its roots in deep contradictions, which generate sources of transformative agency and ideological potential.

CONTRADICTIONS

Corporate-driven globalization is geared primarily to securing heightened commodification of social relations, and in the process creates new imperatives and social disciplines. The 'new-constitutionalism' is expressed in strengthened structural disciplines, enforced through the threat of capital flight, as well as through formal interstate structures (Gill 2002). Such 'global governance' enforces globalist precepts, generating powerful contradictions. These emanate from three underlying contradictions, now writ large across the globe. First is the social contradiction between capital and labour, manifest in the exponential widening and deepening of global social divides. Second is the contradiction between capital and nature, manifest in an intensifying logic of ecological exhaustion at the global level. Third is the contradiction between fractions of capital that engage in self-destructive dynamics of marketization and volatility, and inter-imperial competition and conflict.

Under global governance these contradictions are systemically (and deliberately) displaced from core to periphery (indeed, globalization is in large part characterized by this process of social, ecological and financial dumping). Increasingly, though, the resulting crises are revisiting the heartlands, generating a social, environmental and financial backwash that cannot be ignored. Global social inequality produces southern social implosions, global insurgencies, and growing south-to-north refugee and migrant flows. Global ecological crisis produces resource exhaustion and climate instability in the north as well as in the south. Global marketization produces financial contagion that overwhelms northern as well as southern contexts. We may say then, that globalism is producing truly global crises.

At the same time, globalism undermines institutional capacity, generating vulnerability as well as exposure. Concentration of ownership at the transnational level leads to a hollowing-out of state capacity at both the national and international level (Goodman 2007b). In a context of deepening state implosion on the periphery, growing resource insecurity and inter-state resource rivalry, and increased global insurgency, there is an increased resort to coercion. Northern heartlands increasingly behave like enclaves, under siege from the rest of the world. There has been increased resort to the coercive imposition of globalist strictures, orchestrated by the core enclave and in response, contender blocs and social forces have emerged, especially in South America and the Middle East, with more assertive imperial challenges, notably from Chinese and Russian state elites. Pre-emptive intervention and coercive militarism, striking out and striking back at the symptoms of the crises, is now at the core of globalism.

In sum, the imposition of globalism through 1980s and 1990s radically undermined the stability of financial, social and ecological systems and dramatically delimited the political authority and legitimacy of political elites, especially in peripheral zones. Heartlands are increasingly under siege from the resulting contagion and backwash.

Agency

If we accept that what is distinctive about globalism is the insistent drive for commodification, what some characterize as the 'commodification of everything', then the search for post-globalist social forces should begin here. Globalism's chief target are peoples engaged in or dependent upon relatively uncommodified reproductive activities (Bakker and Gill 2003). Reproduction in all its facets has become the target of current globalist modes of accumulation, and has become the new territory of social conflict and mobilization.

We all, in one way or another, depend upon uncommodified reproductive capacities, but some are more immediately vulnerable and actively resist the unravelling of reproductive frameworks. These groupings set the conditions for the existence of productivism, and exist as a 'meta-industrial class', a class of peoples who engage in 'metabolic' rather than the 'instrumental' labour. As Salleh, and other eco-feminists like Shiva and Mies argue, in the current crisis, these peoples move to centre-stage (Salleh 2004). From this perspective a multiplicity of social forces, such as subsistence farmers, unpaid domestic workers, slum-dwellers, indigenous peoples, and other de-formalized social sectors, that were previously assumed to be secondary to capitalist social relations, acquire both the capacity and the consciousness to engage in transformative action.

A key site is ecological exhaustion, where nature is reduced to a measure of value flow and societies are confronted by the materiality of ecological insecurity. Ecological degradation and resultant social exhaustion generates reciprocal mobilization for the commons against exchange value. In northern contexts, efforts to reclaim leisure time, to secure the liberation of time from exploitation, are reflected in a pervasive so-called 'work-life collision'. In southern contexts a parallel de-formalization of work reduces security and threatens livelihoods, producing broad-based movements for survival. Subsistence peasants, indigenous peoples, landless labourers, and urban poor, social groupings often assumed to have passed into history, acquire new agency. The Slum-dwellers International for instance has made considerable headway in mobilizing urban poor communities. Likewise, Via Campesina has emerged effectively as the new peasant International, forcing a new politics of refusal into international arenas.

Despite these possibilities there are also difficulties: meta-classes are internally divided and diverse. Their leverage, moreover, may be less than apparent, as they are, by definition, excluded from power. Such exclusion, though, may itself be a strength, in fostering autonomy for a 'meta-social' claim to legitimacy. The challenge of meta-classes indeed may be especially powerful in centring on livelihood and survival, and manifested as a value orientation grounded in widely-shared normative spheres. In an age of exhaustion, of multiple and profound crises of belief in commodified productivism, there is a craving for embedded and embodied modes of existence. In that context Salleh's meta-industrial class perhaps may be acquiring greater leverage.

One key site is the commodification of knowledge and the assertion of new commons in the appeals of health care workers against intellectual property regimes, or the campaigns of consumers and farmers against genetically-modified organisms. Another is the defence of resources, as played out in anti-mining or anti-dam campaigns, or in the campaigns of peasant farmers for food sovereignty against 'free' trade. Another is the multiplicity of campaigns for the civil commons, against privatization, such as through the 'Our World is Not For Sale Network'.

Ideology

The destabilization of dominant ideologies and their associated modes of regulation produces intense reflection, reorientation and renewal. Under the weight of its own contradictions, globalism is radically destabilized: we live with the legacies of globalist projects, but sit on the cusp of a potentially post-globalist world ideological order. As in earlier periods of ideological transformation, we are witnessing an opening-up of the political space, with social movements reflecting on dominant contradictions, generating new visions and possibilities.

In the past, counter-ideologies have undergone periods of generation and renewal as contradictions overwhelm dominant operating systems. The early twentieth-century interregnum between Pax Britannica and Pax Americana saw an intense process of reflection leading to the transition from an imperial model of regulation to a model of embedded liberalism. A further redefinition of dominant ideology occurred from the 1970s with the crisis of Fordist welfarism and the transition to neo-liberal globalism (Pijl 1998). In each period of ideological fluidity social movements gain remarkable traction. Accordingly, today we see social movements directly confronting the contradictions of globalism, actively generating alternative visions.

For political elites, the end of globalism as an ideology capable of garnering sufficient consent requires the emergence of new dominant ideological formations capable of managing current and emergent world-scale contradictions. For counter-globalists, it offers the possibility of generating new ideological formations capable of charting new models for post-globalism. The implosion of globalism poses the question of whose post-globalist future will prevail: post-globalism 'from above' or post-globalism 'from below'? As Wallerstein notes, 'the struggle is not about whether or not we are in favour of capitalism as a world-system. The struggle is about what should replace it, given the implosion of the present world-system' (Wallerstein 2005: 1275).

Amongst counter-blocs the emergence of coercive globalism generated initial disarray. The ideological logic of the 'Global Justice Movement' as it emerged in the 1990s posed an alternative ideology of justice globalism against the dominant ideology of corporate globalism. With the US-led 'War on Terror', a resort to unilateralist military action against would-be contenders, advocates for global justice was put onto the defensive. Former critics of multilateral institutions found themselves outflanked by a growing unilateralism. The tables were turned on the counter-ideology that had sustained the global justice movement, and a reorientation was required to refocus on state power. Rupert argues this was achieved by late 2002, culminating in the global protest against the intervention in Iraq, the largest mobilization the world has seen (Rupert 2003).

The shift reflected a need to balance between contesting a globalized power nexus expressed in globalist ideology and the imperial power nexus expressed in revived ideologies of imperialism. Imperial structures had clearly remained in place under globalism, but had become dramatically more salient as dominant powers sought to maintain control of the process. As Saul argues, 'The fact is that 'Empire' (the world of capitalist globalization) and 'empire' (the world of Western imperialism) coexist'; Bush and the Bank, he argues, have to be taken together (Saul 2003: 227). Out of this context new agendas of de-globalization, post-globalism and delinked sufficiency and sovereignty have flourished.

RESISTANCE STRATEGY AND DIALOGUE FOR ALTERNATIVES

As globalism has imploded under the pressure of its own contradictions, and its public legitimacy has faltered in the face of persistent counter-globalist forces, we enter a world of possibilities. In this period, political spaces that were previously non-existent, and ideological leverage that was once unavailable, begin to open up.

Challengers to globalism have mobilized across state borders, contesting agendas set in international contexts. Three specific targets are evident—corporate power, embodied in transnational corporations, imperial power exercised by governmental and intergovernmental institutions, and normative globalism expressed in consumerist culture-ideology. The process of contestation creates post-globalist infrastructures and alternatives: corporate power is confronted with de-commodification, imperial power with demands for deep democracy, global norms with dialogic solidarity.

First, movements target commodification and its chief agent—the transnational corporation. Production, finance and the media shed national legitimacy, and are revealed as powerful political agents. Workers, environmentalists, indigenous peoples, and human rights advocates work together to demand that corporations conform to popular priorities. Movements share an anti-corporate agenda and enter into multiple forms of dialogue geared to asserting and extending realms of uncommodified provision, often through the rhetoric of 'the commons' and in the name of eco-sufficiency (Johnston, Gismondi and Goodman 2006). Specific corporates or sectors are targeted by international networks of locally-based movements, constructing and leveraging cross-national linkages. Two relatively new pressure points are manifested—mass consumer activism, emerging from the success of cross-national corporate branding, and investor activism, emerging from the volatility and sensitivity of highly inter-connected finance markets. At the same time the broader role of corporate lobby-groups, such as the World Economic Forum, is contested through local convergences designed to challenge and politicize corporate legitimacy. In both contexts protestors articulate alternative visions, exploiting public disquiet at the corporate takeover of public life.

Second, movements challenge globalist governance, arguing for democratic regulation of transnational relations. Nationally-based coalitions become increasingly correlated in international contexts, creating networks that directly link 'grassroots' groups with expert-status NGOs. These counter-globalist networks operate as fluid entities, grounded in a politics of horizontalization. They disrupt international hierarchies, establishing relatively routinized protest practices and channels for influence, plaguing the would-be legislators for corporate globalism. These networks of deep democracy may be understood as a form of trans-localism where multiple locally-engaged perspectives are brought into play, reconfiguring locality for counter-globalism. In Southern contexts such projects can offer alternative frames for a national developmentalism geared to local commons rather than to global commodification. In northern contexts efforts at extending neo-liberal governance have been met with forceful challenges, that re-assert popular sovereignty, one example being the 2005 referendum in France against the European constitution. The outcome is a form of politics that builds shared north-south frameworks for deep democracy and sovereignty, against corporate imperialism.

Third, movements subvert dominant global norms. Globalism brings with it a normative dimension expressed as a culture-ideology of consumerism, carried by an increasingly visible transnational capitalist class (Sklair 2000). Where norms of corporate globalism seek to naturalize globalized marketization as an inevitability, social movement challengers actively assert the existence and legitimacy of 'multipolar' interactions and alternatives (Amin 1997). The assertion of plurality, of a 'world of many worlds', poses a powerful challenge to the absolutism of one-world corporate globalism. Challenges are embedded in local or national contexts and differences, brought into relationship with one another through forms of mutual dialogue. These frameworks translate local actions, transferring their meaning and symbolic significance into a broader interpretative context. The logic of mutual engagement validates differences as the basis for solidarity but at the same time constructs shared perspectives: in doing so counter-globalist movements create connections that build conceptual themes and linkages across identifications, rather than simply between them.

Dialogues for Alternatives

Across these three channels, the political infrastructures of globalism are confronted by connected actions, constituting powerfully reflexive counter-globalisms. While there is no collapse into an unvariegated global movement; neither is there a break-up into fragmented autonomies. Instead, what emerges is an intense imperative for dialogue and reflexive strategizing, invigorating locality within globality. A new inter-cultural ethic of solidarity comes into play, constituting political community around situated universalisms—feminist unity is re-embedded in gender difference, human rights in cultural rights, eco-globality in living environments, worker solidarity in differing development priorities. The assertion of a single model for social change is displaced by autonomy and mutual recognition. The process of addressing—not settling—differences becomes the key issue.

Universal commitments can no longer be assumed, and dilemmas of constructing counter-hegemony across ideological, national and socio-cultural contexts rise to the top of the agenda. The imperative to act in concert may be highly contingent, dependent on a particular arrangement of political forces. For tactical manoeuvring to develop into forms of strategic engagement connectivity must emerge as a necessity. Shared visions for change emerge from the creative interaction across differing perspectives, forcing new ideological and political programmes into view.

Internationally, this dialogic methodology of solidarity-building has its most impressive manifestation in the World Social Forum (WSF) that was established as a counter to the corporate-led World Economic Forum (WEF), and met for the first time in 2001 at Porto Alegre, Brazil. For its organizers, the WSF is a generative engagement, a pre-condition for a future possibility of co-related visions and programmes, for a future ideological offensive against globalism (Leite 2005). In the interim the Forum rests on the assertion 'another world is possible', expressing a democratic plurality of 'many worlds' against the authoritarian singularity of 'one world' globalism. It signals a self-conscious move from oppositionalism to the production of alternatives: here the politics of the 'programme' and the 'mass' gives way to the politics of interacting programmes and interacting masses, forcing mutual reorientation and transformation, building shared agendas for the new sources of power. The models, programmes and strategies appear permanently provisional and transitional, yet they mark new frontiers of contestation and transformation, in a fluid and creative praxis.

COUNTER-IDEOLOGY AND POST-GLOBALISM

An ideologue is often seen as someone who is necessarily authoritarian or dogmatic. In colloquial use ideology has strong pejorative connotations, denoting a separation from social engagement and authentic expression. An ideological statement is one deemed to have no merit; it is driven by conviction or faith rather than a genuinely-felt expression of experience and aspiration. In contrast, practical or common sense knowledge and its prescriptions are said to be ideology-free, naturalized as pragmatic and necessary. Here, ideology is revealed in its denial: the effort invested in asserting 'there is no alternative', the insistence on the necessity of such strictures, reveals their hegemonic purposes.

The denial of ideology extends well beyond popular culture. It is deeply rooted in much academic theorizing about social movements and social change. Ideology is rejected as necessarily hierarchic and programme-orientated, a meta-narrative that contrasts with the networked, practice-centred logic of contemporary social movements. With the post-structural turn, the production of visions and programmes is understood as an exercise of power, exceeding the intellectual's legitimacy and capacity. Faith is vested in the process of contestation, in the struggle. Theorists analyse 'frames' of practice, they explore movement of resources and opportunities, they foreground identity and cultural embeddedness, they rarely analyse the process of generating ideas and visions and how these are manifest in practice as ideologies. Ideology, Buechler argues, is the 'orphan' of social movement theory (Buechler 2000: 200).

Anti-ideological themes are also evident amongst movements themselves, where the rejection of ideology forms part of a broader embracing of difference over collectivity. Ideology necessarily involves the exercise of power—it requires the power to prioritize and privilege a particular world-view while subordinating and excluding others. Dialogic politics can disassemble power hierarchies, and can be highly productive in terms of creating connectivity and solidarity. But it may also signal a politics of avoidance, where situatedness becomes an end in itself. Counter-globalist movements have underlying unifying values—decommodification, deep democracy and autonomy amongst them—but with dialogic politics these remain subterranean, underlying themes rather than elements of an encompassing counter-ideology. Indeed, the counter-globalist mantra, 'one no, many yesses' is permanently in danger of collapsing into its plurality, constituted by what it stands against, rather than what it stands for. Movement intellectuals can be left grasping the thinnest of mantles—a faith in the process of mutual engagement and dialogue around shared problems.

The political problem of generating transformative ideology is expressed in the WSF process, which remains in large part prefigurative of alternative political agendas rather than constitutive of them. Frustrations with the Forum centre on its limits as a reflective and dialogic process, a talking shop for alternatives, rather than as a forum for deliberation. The desired end point of a counter-hegemonic 'movement of movements', adequate to the task of superseding as well as destabilizing globalism, has been elusive. The task is not simply a matter of synthesizing ideas: there have been attempts along these lines, but with little in the way of an overarching model of interpretation and vision for transformation (see for instance Polet et al. 2004). One example, said to have been one of the most significant recent attempts of its kind, was the 'Porto Alegre Manifesto', issued by nineteen prominent activist-intellectuals at the 2005 WSF which summarized some of the key issues in counter-globalism (Reitan 2007: 145). The Manifesto integrated its twelve points into three overarching themes—respect for life, a just and peaceful life for all, and humanity and democracy for all—but beyond this did not offer a broader integrated challenge.

From Dialogue to Ideology?

Post-globalist ideology clearly cannot be seen as somehow emanating in the abstract from deliberation. Ideology is a normative claim on society, pursued in the public sphere and articulated through civil society. Ideologies are constituted as action-oriented ideas, but only exist insofar as they garner political leverage: they are, as Buechler argues, 'meaning in the service of power' (Buechler 2000: 201). In this respect, ideologies are inseparable from social power: conflicts between ideologies are not simply conflicts between ideas, they are conflicts between social forces.

Globalism, as a dominant ideology, is self-consciously developed and promulgated by legions of neo-liberal think-tanks, media conglomerates, management consultancies and semi-state agencies. These organizations house the organic intellectuals of the transnational capitalist class, and their ideological work plays a central role in both constituting the ruling bloc and its authority: without them there would be no capacity to define a shared framework for action, nor to make a claim on the public sphere, or to act for the public interest, to garner public consent for the globalist agenda. In contesting this dominant ideology, counter-globalist ideology has to likewise constitute a bloc of social forces. These social forces are necessarily embedded in social experiences, translating existent social antagonisms into public contestations and transforming counter-globalist social forces from passive existence 'in themselves' into active assertion 'for themselves'.

Movement ideologies bring values to bear on immediate experiences, interests and aspirations, creating an interpretative frame, a shared way-of-seeing. On this foundation, movements can develop transformative agendas, and strategize means of getting there, in the form of a political programme. Experiences of globalism are diverse, and aspirations can diverge, especially across deepening global divides. Reflecting the disparate and diffuse challenges to globalism, the interpretative frame of counter-globalism is especially fluid. In the volatile flux of globalization the management of ideological uncertainty and disharmony becomes a central issue; particularly in transnational contexts, movements have to navigate across ideological divisions and be able to recombine and regenerate agendas; at the same time, a pervasive sense of disempowerment under globalism paradoxically intensifies emotional engagement, while creating strong tendencies to demobilization and disengagement (Freeden 2001: 7).

Against pressures for disaggregation, social forces displaced by globalism find unity in their shared experiences. As noted, marginalized 'meta-industrial' classes provide powerful structural underpinnings to counter-globalism. The capacity of these groupings to disrupt globalism is already evident. In Thompson's schema, dominant ideology works by legitimizing power sources, obscuring and dissimulating interests, by asserting unity behind the dominant bloc, while seeking to divide contenders (Thompson 1990). In response, movements develop counter-ideological strategies—they delegitimize and reveal power relations, they highlight lines of social division and extend solidarity to subordinates, and most important, they relativise the exercise of power, showing it to be assailable (Buechler 2000: 202). In many respects, counter-globalist social forces currently engage in all these elements, and increasingly take-on more proactive roles: in Castells' terms they already move beyond resistance to develop transformative project identities.

Certainly, as argued here, there is an emerging configuration of meta-class social forces, bound into a broad agenda for de-commodification and sufficiency, deep democracy and de-linking, and for recognition and autonomy. The key is how these and other themes may be correlated to constitute an emergent global social bloc. Movements themselves embody alternatives, and engage with one another to develop broader-scale visions and programmes, clearly though, this process of ideological creativity is permanently in danger of collapse, and needs to be constantly regenerated. Carroll argues that 'prospects for global social justice hinge significantly on discovering political methodologies that activate democratic social learning as to how we might live differently' (Carroll 2007: 54). Social infrastructures are needed to channel the creative force of movements into a process of collective ideological reflection, enabling a self-conscious process of ideological creativity, a permanent exercise in the ideological imaginary.

These observations require a much more self-conscious process of working with counter-globalist configurations and social forces, to build beyond foundational value orientations as they have become manifest to date. We may even speculate that such an initiative requires and presages a more thorough-going World Political Forum. An ideological offensive of this sort could present normative prescriptions, express aspirations and set new horizons for transformative vision and hope for post-globalism. It could offer both interpretative and instrumental leverage: providing a public narrative and explanation of the current malaise, a means of transcending the present, and a programme for the future.

The dominant form of market globalism is best understood as an ideological strategy of transnational capitalist classes. Its principal effect is to deepen the commodification of social relations, and in the process flexibilize and informalize structures of social and ecological reproduction, generating widespread crises of exhaustion. Through the 2000s market globalism has become increasingly coercive, but also increasingly unstable. Social, ecological and financial crises, exacerbated by marketization, have deepened this instability.

In response, counter-movements of the marginalized have proliferated, generating shared post-globalist agendas. In many contexts, antagonisms centre on reproductive spheres, and involve struggles for decommodification, for the commons and deep democracy, enacting trans-local autonomy and solidarity. These post-globalisms 'from below' have created new political spaces for deliberation, and for democracy. As argued here, these dialogues for alternatives point the way to more explicitly political movements, and to counter-ideologies capable of taking us beyond prevailing crises of exhaustion.

REFERENCES

Amin, S. (1997), *Capitalism in the Age of Globalization*, London: Zed Books.

Bakker, I. and S. Gill (2003), *Power, Production and Social Reproduction*, London: Palgrave Macmillan.

Buechler, S. (2000), *Social Movements in Advanced Capitalism: The Political*

Economy and Social Construction of Social Activism, New York: Oxford University Press.

Carroll, W. (2007), 'Hegemony and the Global Field', *Studies in Social Justice*, vol. 1, no. 1, Winter 2007, pp. 36–66.

Freeden, M. (2001), 'Political Ideologies in Substance and Method: Reappraising a Transformation', in M. Freeden (ed.), *Reassessing Political Ideologies: The Durability of Dissent*, New York: Routledge.

Gill, S. (2002), *Power and Resistance in the New World Order*, London: Palgrave Macmillan.

Goodman, J. (2007a), 'Reflexive Solidarities: Between Nationalism and Globalism', in J. Goodman and P. James (eds.), *Nationalism and Global Solidarities*, London: Routledge.

——— (2007b), 'Non-state Actors: Multinational Corporations and Non-government Organizations', in R. Devetak, A. Burke and J. George (eds.), *Introduction to International Relations*, Melbourne: Cambridge University Press.

Heywood, A. (2007), *Political Ideologies: An Introduction*, Basingstoke: Palgrave Macmillan.

Johnston, J., M. Gismondi, and J. Goodman (eds.) (2006), *Nature's Revenge: Sustainability in an Age of Corporate Globalism*, Toronto: Broadview.

Leite, J. (2005), *The World Social Forum: Strategies of Resistance*, Toronto: Haymarket Books.

McMicheal, P. (2003), *Globalization*, Cambridge: Cambridge University Press.

Pijl, K. Van (1998), *Transnational Classes and International Relations*, New York: Routledge.

Polet, F. et al. (2004), *Globalizing Resistance: The State of Struggle*, London: Pluto.

Reitan, R. (2007), *Global Activism*, New York: Routledge.

Rosenberg, J. (2000), *Follies of Globalization Theory*, London: Verso.

Rupert, M. (2003), 'Globalising Common Sense: A Marxian-Gramscian Revision of the Politics of Governance/Resistance', *Review of International Studies*, no. 29, pp. 181–98.

Salleh, A. (2004), 'Theorizing the Meta-industrial Class', in R. Albritton, et al. (eds.), *New Socialisms: Futures Beyond Globalization*, New York: Routledge.

Saul, J. (2003), 'Globalization, Imperialism, Development: False Binaries and Radical Resolutions', in *Socialist Register 2002,* London: Merlin Press.

Sklair, L. (2000), *The Transnational Capitalist Class*, Cambridge: Polity.

Thompson, J. (1990), *Ideology and Modern Culture*, Stanford: Stanford University Press.

Wallerstein, I. (2005), 'After Developmentalism and Globalization, What?', *Social Forces*, 83, 3, 1263–78.

CHAPTER 3

Global Justice as Identity: Mobilization for a Better World*

LAUREN LANGMAN

INTRODUCTION: THE DIALECT OF GLOBALIZATION

At the end of Second World War, a number of strategic decisions were made regarding the shape of the post-war world. Following the 1944 Bretton Woods Conference, the dollar replaced the pound sterling, the convertibility rates of the currencies were set, a banking system (International Bank for Reconstruction and Development [IBRD], later the World Bank [WB], as well as the International Monetary Fund [IMF]) was created to encourage economic growth, and a new set of rules were established to relate trade and tariffs (General Agreement on Trade and Tariff [GATT], later the World Trade Oraganization [WTO]). In the early post-war years, the primary concerns were the rebuilding and retooling of Europe and fostering economic growth in the 'underdeveloped' colonies, lest adverse economic conditions foster mass sympathy for communists or Third World nationalists. Perish the thought! These then relatively obscure organizations, making seemingly arcane financial decisions, laid the foundations for an unprecedented expansion of capitalist markets and their integration.

The next 45 years, roughly 1945–90 were shaped by the 'cold war' between the Soviet Union and the 'peace loving democracies of Europe and the US'. The attempts to preserve European imperialism proved futile as various nationalist movements in India, Algeria and Vietnam gained independence for their respective countries, often

*This paper is rooted in an earlier work on the role of the Internet (Langman 2005), and linking micro and macro levels of analysis.

through long, arduous and bloody conflicts. For various reasons, many of these conflicts, rebellions, national liberation movements, and peasant wars were seen through an East/West, communist–capitalist prism and various 'rebels' were labelled as communist dupes.[1] Notwithstanding, international trade showed 'healthy growth'. By the 1970s, this trade, often the sale of cheap resources from poor countries to the West, and the sale of expensive manufactured goods to the East, was understood through the 'dependency theory'. While enriching some local elites, the benefits of such trade did not trickle down very far. But meanwhile, just as many African and Asian colonies sought self-determination, so too did many of the Soviet states seek economic and political self-determination. Going back to the Bretton Woods agreements, not only were raw materials quite cheap for the US and even a resurgent Europe, but so too were the costs of labour. Lo and behold, as foreign industrial capacities were rebuilt, and their economies grew, high quality products of skilled labour became competitive with those of the advanced countries. Indeed, it was often less costly to import steel from Japan than produce it.[2] Enter de-industrialization.

Meanwhile back at the bank, the hegemony of Keynesian economics was challenged by the free market ideals of people like Hayek and Friedman who claimed that when the economy was unfettered by government regulations or social concerns (entitlements), it would not only produce greater wealth, but that the wealth would be more equitably distributed; as they argued, 'the rising tide would raise all ships'. The resurrection of Smith's vision of a 'liberal market' became known as 'neo-liberalism'.

As neo-liberalism slowly but surely transformed the nature of international markets, as its intellectuals promised, it would promote rapid economic growth, and as they say, the rest is history. Transnational capitalist corporations now dominate the world economy; transnational regulatory agencies, beholden to capital regulate and control trade and investment. Thus we might talk of the current moment of globalization as a seamlessly integrated, deterritorialized neo-liberal market that has, as its prophets predicted, produced great profits. But most of these profits have gone to small numbers of transnational capitalist elites. These mantras of unfettered Foreign Direct Investment (FDI), ending trade barriers, privatization, anti-unionism and structural readjustment have become the 'received wisdom' of the contemporary world, celebrated by writers like Tom Friedman.

But globalization as a force of 'creative destruction' (Schumpeter) has not only created vast profits and transformed the nature of contemporary life, but has created major social disruptions, stresses, strains and hardships starting with declining wages for industrial workers and many service workers in the advanced countries. The forces of globalization have led to massive social dislocations and migrations as destitute and often landless peasants have flocked from rural hinterlands to big cities—only to find unemployment, underemployment, and the impersonality and anonymity of the city.

Consider Mexico City, Cairo, Jakarta or Sao Paulo. Many people from poorer countries have migrated, often illegally to the richer countries, and find the conditions of the poor slums, barrios, favelas, banlieues and ghettoes filled with hardship, crime, violence and despair. Meanwhile, in the name of profits, environmental despoliation has not just become rampant, but the proliferation of wastes, global warming, species depletion and desertification threaten the very viability of human life. 'The problems generated by globalization transcend national boundaries and cannot be addressed by national actors; therefore, new kinds of global social movements are necessary to meet the new kinds of challenges' (cf. Bennett, 2003).

I. GLOBAL JUSTICE MOBILIZATIONS

Crisis Tendencies of Global Capital

The dialectical understanding of society, rooted in the Hegelian-Marxist framework, rests on the concept of negation, understood as the inherent nature of contradiction that would seek to resolve itself. The 'power of negativity' would seek the 'negation of negation' to overcome contradictions. As such, negativity fosters change. In terms of political economy, the contradiction of class domination fosters crises and in turn disposes changes/challenges that would transform class relations to overcome crises tendencies based on those inherent contradictions. (And systems of domination seek to neutralize, control or deflect efforts at change.) Sociologically, social mobilizations become one means of mediating between structural and/or ideological domination/contradictions and overcoming these contradictions experienced as crises with various collective stresses and strains experienced individually and collectively that may involve anxiety, anger, shame, humiliation, and so on. But how do crises and contradictions foster social mobilization? Habermas (1975) formulated a comprehensive theory of legitimacy crises fostering social mobilizations. His analysis can yet be useful for understanding Global Justice Movements (GJM).[3]

As has been suggested, the globalized production of goods, services and entertainment that provides vast corporate profits has had onerous social consequences for many people, beginning with the vast disparities of wealth, power and lifestyles of the elites of the transnational capitalist class and the vast multitudes. Notwithstanding the 'joys of shopping' gleaned through goods that provide the 'good life' for the few, the clothes, toys, gadgets and electronics of consumerism are often produced in inhumane 'satanic mills'—the Third World sweatshops run using exploited and oppressed women workers, often in toxic environments. While to be sure large numbers of people have moved from poverty to a better life, for the majority, the conditions have worsened. Meanwhile, power stations, factories, and transportation systems billow forth vast amounts of CO_2 and SO_4. Global warming continues unabated. For analytic purposes five such contradictions of neo-liberal globalization foster various kinds of system and subsystem contradictions and crises, though in practice these often overlap (cf. Buechler 2000). For example, young women may be sexually exploited to gain/keep a job in a polluting enterprise without rights or political recourse. Following Habermas (1975) crisis tendencies occur when a society fails to provide for economic/material needs, the government fails to secure legitimacy, the integration of the society becomes problematic, and finally identity and motivation withdraw from the dominant order. This suggests multiple crises.

Economic/Material

Globalization in its current neo-liberal form has generated massive amounts of wealth as well as massive redistributions of wealth from the poor to the rich as 'corporations now rule the world' (Perucci and Wysong 2002; Korten 2001; Stieglitz 2002). Privatization has raised water and electricity costs while the race to the bottom the attempt to find lowest possible wages has contracted incomes. Between desertification and appropriation, many have lost their lands. Moreover, the mass production of goods has created various externalities, not the least of which is massive pollution of air, land and sea (think food chain, think mercury) and in turn, global warming that is causing rising sea levels (think Bangladesh/South Florida underwater).

Political

Globalization has led to an erosion of the autonomy of individual state policy and attenuation of self-determination that has defined the modern state. Transnational firms and agencies dedicated to the WTO, IMF and World Bank increasingly dictate trade policies, tariff rates, investment laws, copyrights and labour conditions. With the invisibility of many global policies, there is little citizen awareness and in turn, citizens have little voice in the policies that impact them.

Cultural

There has been a growing concentration of the means of communication, a universalization of homogenized popular culture and transformation of news into entertainment (Bagdikian 1997; McChesney 2000). Media-fostered consumerism increasingly serves the political and economic interests of globalization by providing media spectacles and forms of subjectivity and cultural identification apart from political economy (Langman 1992).

Environmental

There has been vast environmental despoliation, destruction of ecosystems, deforestation, the loss of many species, and the definition of genetically modified organisms as a social problem (Kovel 2002; Foster 2002).

Human/Labour Rights

Many types of human rights/worker rights based global social justice movements have arisen since the 1960s with greater awareness of oppression, torture, and even murder as a state-sponsored or state-tolerated practice in non-democratic societies.[4] In many places, governments repress if not murder union organizers or civil libertarians. Race, gender and gender preference-based oppressions ranging from genocide in Sudan to Female Genital Mutilation (FGM) or rape as punishment endure. Meanwhile a mass sex trade has flourished, often involving children. Some of the pornography of the Internet is dependent on coercive practices of the global sex trade. These issues of social justice have complex interactions with class, state polities, national cultures and religion. Insofar as these problems now cross-national boundaries, so too must various NGOs and associated social movements take a transnational course.

Culture, Identity and Motivation

The dysfunctions, contradictions and crises at the structural levels as well as the ideological level, where the promises of freedom and prosperity become issues of domination and poverty, *foster crises of legitimacy* at both the collective and experiential levels. In face of the structural crises, contradictions and dislocations due to globalization, there is often a migration from the political/economic to cultural/collective identity and emotional realms. Customary identities regarding work, gender, gender orientation and religion face economic and/or cultural challenges and crises that in turn impact identities and cause emotional distress to actors. Thus we have a long history showing how financial crises lead to anxiety and depression. I shall return to this important, but often ignored point.

Identity, Stability and Change: Hegemony and its Contestation

For Foucault, power and domination work through the inscription and control of identity through various disciplinary/discursive practices (cf. Buechler 2000). Gramsci's notion of cultural hegemony depends on mediation though identity to naturalize the historical (Langman 2000). Thus a crucial aspect for certain contemporary social movements is rejection or refashioning of identities/values to influence the future direction of a society.[5] From what has been said, collective identity can be seen as a contested terrain in struggles for hegemony. The historic blocs in power defend their clout and privilege by fostering identities in which subjugation is cloaked and most people accept their domination (ruling bloc interests) as 'normal', 'common sense' and 'in their best interests'. In other words, the production of identities is a part of hegemonic processes that sustain structures of domination at the level of the person. And the acceptance and performances of those identities is not without certain emotional gratifications for most people most of the time. The extent to which such identities are embraced without question, and reproduced in performance over time, sustains the continuity of the society. This has been the essential nature of the structuration process for Giddens and the nature of the *habitus* for Bourdieu. Most notions of identity locate the person/group within certain structures of hierarchy and domination. This may be racial or ethnic. Colonizers impose subaltern identities upon the colonized, the acceptance of which empowers the colonizer, even if the colonized turns violence on his/her self (Fanon 1986). Women have been socialized to be subordinate to men, but Simone de Beauvior noted the suffering of women as Other, and Freidan called it the illness without a name. Gays have long suppressed their identities.

Nevertheless, at certain times, to paraphrase Marx, the maintenance of 'typical' and earlier identities becomes a problem for both the society and the people and must be discarded. At times of social change, often due to material factors arising from technological innovation, people must attenuate certain identities and embrace new ones.[6] But this is a long-term process. Crises are often very sudden and there come times in a society where for various reasons, the typical identities become problematic in the face of crisis. Further, and until there are emotional consequences to macro structural crises and/or official policies, most people do not interrogate their identities or values. Various social movements, often the vanguard of would-be blocs, would seek new cultural understanding and identities that would result in political and economic transformations shaping the values and directions of a society. Collective identities can be thought of as locus where a number of material and ideological influences converge to control the culture in ways to sustain the power of a particular historic bloc despite various challenges and contestations.[7]

Following Castells (1997), network society fosters four types of collective identities:

1. *Legitimizing identities* sustaining the social order—typically these include patriotic, religious or consumerist orientations. Such identities, the most typical in any society, maintain the *status quo*.
2. *Resistance identities*—attempt to retain or restore waning identities that oppose globalization and its impacts. For example, the fragmentation of community, often tied to economic decline, leads some people to turn away from the global and embrace reactionary movements from nationalisms to fundamentalisms that would restore a [mythical] lost world or 'Golden Age' of strong communities of the past and defend

a particular cultural framework that would secure heretofore privileged, traditional identities. In some cases, there may be progressive forms of resistance albeit romantic, anarchic, and individualistic, but they are unlikely to foster mobilizations.

3. *Ludic identities*—they locate subjectivity in the liminal anti-structures of late modern mass culture that privilege privatized hedonistic indulgence and mass-mediated forms of escapism and/or simulated contestations that allow subcultural withdrawal of self and identity from the larger society; what has been called 'retreatism'.[8] But while most such identities withdraw from the political, some of the contemporary GJMs include numbers of more marginal youth whose playful antics, bizarre appearances and strange attire can be understood as cultural protest. Alternative subcultures of style and 'transgressive' identities such Goths, punks, and metalheads allow a 'withdrawal' from the dominant order through the embrace of an 'oppositional' culture.
4. For our purposes, the most important, if often least frequent pattern, are the *project identities* that challenge the hegemony of the dominant class at several levels, not the least of which are proposing alternative identities that typically resist rationalization and/or commodification and consumerism. These project identities pose fundamental challenges to late capitalist modernity in which rational technologies, as forms of domination, colonize the world as well as collective identity, child rearing, family life, work, organizational spheres and even the pursuit of pleasure (Giddens 1991; Habermas 1975; Hochschild 1997). The attempts to re-negotiate and/or fashion new forms of tolerant democratic identities that embrace alternative futures in turn act to impel progressive social transformations.[9] Such people seek to transform people and society in terms of greater equality, freedom and democracy. But these project identities are emergent in the interaction of struggle; they are neither a priori nor clearly envisioned goals.

The articulation of identities/social goals by one group necessarily conflicts with those of other groups. Those who seek social transformation must confront the entrenched powers that have not only secured cultural and psycho-social hegemony but also provides various rewards to those who willingly assent to their power and authority.

Similarly those who embrace of fundamentalism as a critique of modern values and the limited economic opportunities stand in conflict with secularids who are often the very ones who are best trained to deal with the complexities of the global economy. Feminists must challenge both patriarchy and the many women whose identities and values sustain patriarchy and subjugation. Thus as will be seen, an intrinsic aspect of mobilization is the articulation of new identities that challenge the *status quo* and offer new forms of identity.

From Crisis to Action: Mediated Through Identity

How do structural crises and contradictions impel social mobilization? The global market has now colonized the life worlds of most human actors. Crises, contradictions, stresses and strains at the structural level thus contextualize and impact the everyday life, worlds and experiences of actors.[10] Jobs are lost, new ones found, communities change, immigration/emigration become salient. I would suggest that the emotional reactions to crisis are the initial moment of social mobilization. This is not to revert to the 'irrational mob' theories of LeBon/Freud, but rather is an appeal to 'bring emotions back in' (Goodwin and Jasper 2000; Goodwin et al. 2001).[11]

Human beings have a number of fundamental needs/desires tied to their emotional life and affect system.[12] People are fundamentally social. They need attachments and ties to others, not only for their very survival, but for the pleasantries of social interaction and inter-subjective relations, for their own sake. The pleasure of friendship and company is sought in every society, just as isolation, abandonment and loss of attachments are unpleasant and avoided. People seek recognition of who they are, they seek a degree of self-esteem and dignity and would avoid shame and/or degradation. They would seek to assert agency, have some impact on others and on the world, and would avoid powerlessness.[13] Finally, most people need to find their life meaningful, lest they suffer anxiety, despair and worthlessness. When macro structural crises adversely impinge on people's lives—directly as victims, or indirectly through value-based empathy, people respond with strong emotional reactions such as fear, anger or shame. Others may be angered and outraged by famines, human rights/labour rights/animal rights abuses, pollution, genocide, torture, rape, illness or the sex trade—much of which is often based on social policies amenable to change. Similarly, as Scheff (1994) argued, repressed shame can foster rage, and violent nationalisms. I would suggest that emotional reactions to crises, tragedies and contradictions, directly or indirectly experienced, refracted [understood] through a person's identity, impel actions that would hopefully alleviate the adversity. Consider the case of

> Hamas leader Dr. Abdel Aziz al-Rantissi, who was assassinated by Israel in April of 2004. Rantissi took over Hamas after its founder, Sheik Ahmed Yassin was assassinated by the Israelis in March of that year. Rantissi was born in what is now Israel and driven from his home in 1948 during the war that established the Jewish state. He, along with more than 700,000 other Palestinian refugees, grew up in squalid camps. As a small boy he watched the Israeli army enter and occupy the camp of Khan Younis in 1956 when Israel invaded Gaza. The Israeli soldiers lined up dozens of men and boys, including some of Rantissi's relatives, and executed them. The memory of the executions marked his life. It fed his lifelong refusal to trust Israel and stoked the rage and collective humiliation that drove him into the arms of the Muslim Brotherhood and later Hamas. He was not alone. Several of those who founded the most militant Palestinian organizations witnessed the executions in Gaza carried out by Israel in 1956 that left hundreds dead.[14]

For various reasons, people who are either directly and adversely impacted by dysfunctions and hardships, or have awareness and empathy with 'distant' others who face adversities are likely to seek out means of amelioration. In still other cases, people in certain structural locations are more likely to be exposed to certain information and/or experiences. What is being suggested is that a fundamental factor for many mobilizations, at least the GJMs, is the alienation of actor(s). Otherwise said, a degree of alienation is a pre-condition for seeing and understanding things in a slightly different way. Much as Simmel described the [alienated] 'stranger' as both 'within' and 'without' and thus a more acute observer, the 'alienated' can see and/or be open to seeing what most might ignore. Alienation may come from his/her structural location, or conflicting locations, especially if s/he is both emotionally impacted; s/he feels powerless and seeks to foster change.[15] I am not necessarily talking about the powerlessness of class position, indeed many educated, affluent people feel a need to assert agency and foster ameliorative transformation.[16] How do we now move from feelings to action?

II. EXPLAINING SOCIAL MOBILIZATION

Perhaps the most vile and despicable social movement in history was the rise of Fascism. That said, there were important lessons learned about social movements that have been slowly forgotten. The fascist mobilizations were much more than mesmerized crowds at midnight rallies or berserk brown shirts running amok on *Krystallnacht* (crystal knight, when fascist mobs went about madly breaking windows of Jewish-owned shops throughout Germany and Austria). While surely the crises of world capital in the 1930s made people fearful, anxious, angry and desperate, the 'mass psychology of fascism' was not simply about jobs and benefits. It was concerned with creating a valourized identity tied to a *volk*, a disinct people, that appealed to needs to submit to authority, restoring national pride, and seeking 'revenge' against enemies from without, and even from within—'impure' Jews and treasonous leftists.

The GJMs of today are different than the more traditional interest-based, instrumental movements of workers struggling over wages, working conditions or organizing unions. Similarly, anti-slavery, Prohibition, suffrage or civil rights movements were concerned interests in preserving or gaining status and/or privileges. The changing nature of societies and its contentious mobilizations, dealing with more individual/personal factors such as the colonization of the world and the private sphere and the colonization of consciousness marked a move toward issues of culture, hegemony, legitimacy and even identity.[17] Thus, identity, emotions, experiences, including at times sexuality, became central concerns. As Giddens (1991) noted, for the emerging lifestyle politics, new forms of valourized identity and recognition are central for feminist women, racial ethnic minorities, gays, and so on. Such movements are more concerned with creating and/or gaining 'recognition' of newly empowered 'collective identities' than material benefits.[18] These mobilizations do not really fit the classical models of strain and irrational response, nor are they the rational pursuits of knowing actors who rationally pursue self-interests that may be mobilized by 'social movement entrepreneurs'. Rather, I would suggest that for [some] GJM movements, the concerns with culture and identity are more salient, and indeed, such pursuits may be detrimental to material gain. As such, GJMs are a particular kind of new social movements (NSM). For Melucci (1989), structural theories may explain why a movement begins, but fail to specify how structural factors impel actual actors, while resource mobilization (RM) may explain the processes of how movements may emerge, but not why.

Social crises, stresses and strains at economic, political, cultural or motivation-identity levels can and do migrate from one realm to another. Contradictions and crises produce victims who find their plight disconcerting and feel anger, rage and shame. Some distant others may identify with concrete victims or more abstract notions of justice and/or experience emotions as a result of information mediated through locally situated interpersonal networks. When people saw bulldogs attacking civil rights advocates or Buddhist monks immolating themselves, many were upset. While the directions of chains of influence are variable, in most cases, crises in political or economic spheres have differential impact on people at given social locations and within that location. Variations in identity that are associated with gender, in some cases race/ethnicity, and individual psychological differences impact the consequences of events and their understandings.

Identity-motivation has a crucial role in social mobilization; for example, an economic or political change, or anticipated change, may bring some people advantages and other people losses that might impel them to organize and act. Those potentially advantaged would tend to support the *status quo*, while those burdened might (i) passively accept the new status, especially if understood through a hegemonic ideology; (ii) they might seek to retreat or withdraw from the adverse circumstances; or finally, (iii) they might come together, discuss their plight, attempt to understand their circumstances, and attempt transformation.[19]

At this point the fundamental theoretical question is how crises at multiple levels in the global capitalist structure and its neo-liberal ideology can foster social mobilizations that recruit, socialize, organize and mobilize actors?[20] If we understand society as consisting of groups in conflict over material or symbolic resources (recognition/honour), we can understand how social movements consist of communities of actors engaged in the contested terrains of the public sphere who seek to influence the political to refashion the larger society in terms of their identities, goals/visions (Melucci 1989). The mediations between structural contradictions, injustices and adversities, which are often far removed from personal experience, nevertheless lead to actual participation in concrete social movements. This depends on a number of factors, as noted above, the antecedent factors including emotions, a personal disposition and structural location or circumstances that allow one to take a critical stance against the *status quo*.[21] That said, mobilization then depends on: (i) access to information and the way an issue or crisis is framed; (ii) a personal identity/emotional constitution that is receptive to this information which may be discrepant from the 'received' wisdom; (iii) a structural location or position conducive to activism; and (iv) establishing linkages or ties with 'embedded networks' of social actors with similar concerns and goals that join together.[22] This is not sequential; it can often work in many directions, e.g. activists with more flexible work schedules and who are typically better educated are more likely to be exposed to certain information not often part of local circles or mainstream media. Conversely, activists are likely to get information most people either don't get or have any interest. How then are actors recruited, and how do actors foster social change?

New Social Movements

We have argued that hegemony includes the production of identities— and therefore, counter-hegemonic struggles must target the nature of identity (cf. Langman 2005; LaClau and Mouffe 1985). Moreover, emotions play a central role in prompting the actor to action, and membership in communities provides various joys and emotional gratifications, not the least of which are attachments to a group and recognition by others and finding meaning as part of a 'movement'.[23] Further, contemporary GJMs tend to be more open, fluid and democratic; 'leaders' are more like cheerleaders than directors or movement entrepreneurs. Finally, the tendency for transnational advocacy networks, social movement organisations (SMOs) and International non-government organisations (INGOs), often located in different continents, to exchange information, work out alternative frameworks and strategies, and even forge alliances is unprecedented and must be theorized.

The NSM perspective emphasizes the cultural nature of the new movements and views them as struggles by active agents seeking control over the production of meanings/values and the constitution of new collective identities. It stresses the expressive aspects of SMs and places them exclusively in the terrain of civil society as opposed to the state. This approach also emphasizes discontinuity by highlighting the differences between the new movements and traditional collective actors.[24] New social movement theories specifically address the conditions for the construction and emergence of collective identity formation and collective action of the GJMs in the contemporary world. These theories have emerged in response to changes in the goals, strategies and constituencies of social movements that have emerged as a result of the neo-liberal globalization. Although social movements may still pursue political and social gains, for the NSMs there is greater stress on the construction and legitimation of collective identities for solidarity, meaning and to articulate resistance.

NSMs often carry out organization and resistance on symbolic or cultural grounds rather than through traditional political channels. Further, in modern societies in which power is dispersed and expressed in various signs and symbols, NSMs often challenge those signs and symbols. The organizing base of NSMs has been theorized as more dispersed, diverse, fluid and complex in structure than the more defined and fixed structures of previous movement organizations (e.g. labour movements). Further, NSMs generally value autonomous, reflexive individuals who engage in participatory democratic relations with decentralized forms of organization (Castells 1997; Melucci 1989, 1996); these factors combine to create more informal, submerged networks than those of past movements or 'vanguard' parties.

Following Touraine (1985) we can suggest that NSMs be seen as groups that struggles over historicity—the ability of society to 'act upon itself' and develop new values, goals and lifestyle to shape social life. Social movements seek to change the future directions of post-industrial society. Touraine suggests there are three main components of social movements, they seek to:

(i) *Assert a collective identity 'I'* (self-definition and self-understanding) in the face of social fragmentation in general. These struggles take place in the public sphere.
(ii) They *challenge opposition and adversaries 'O'* (e.g. the crises and contradictions of neo-liberal globalization).
(iii) *The struggles seek control the future and outcome of the social totality 'T'.*

Some movements are defensive attempts to assert a reactionary agenda based on a mythical return to a utopian past—what Castells called 'resistance identities' for example with the recent upsurge of nationalisms and/or fundamentalisms as attempts to 'restore' a 'Golden age' of a community now fragmented by globalization and cast a drift in 'liquid modernity' (Langman 2008; Beck 2006). Thus it is not surprising that the lower middle classes, the lumpen proletariat, and waning segments of the elites are most likely to embrace reactionary movements that restore a previously valued self by restoring an earlier age which has now been lost. Conversely, others seek a more progressive, utopian alternative collective identity (project identities). Let others seek alternative futures for those adversely affected by its neo-liberal policies. Progressives more likely come from proletarian or upper middle/professional classes. But in either case, one central aspect of mobilization is the crafting of a collective identity within a struggle. As Bartholomew and Mayer (1992) note in their review of Melucci:

> In attempting to grasp how individuals get involved in collective action Melucci stresses the concept fo collective identity as the crucial mediating variable missing in much exciting work on social movements. 'Collective identity' is not equivalent to 'mobilizing interests' (as in Resource Mobilization's market conception of interests and benefits), but is precisely a constructivist concept, which can appear only outside the assumptions and framework of (pluralist or elite) liberal theory. It requires an intermediate level of analysis which brings into relief how individuals come to decide that they share certain orientations and decide to act collectively. Many approaches to social movements have been bedeviled by the problem of bridging the gap between the structural foundations for action and the collective action itself.

As Melucci (1995) pointed out: 'Collective identity is an interactive, shared definition produced by several individuals (or groups at a more complex level) . . . that must be conceived as a process because it is constructed and negotiated by repeated activation of the relationships that link individuals (or groups) [to the movement].' While activists may realize their identities and values in their political/cultural activities, they are at the same time, involved in the submerged networks of everyday life and networks of meanings they produce and reproduce (Melucci 1989: 71). The everyday life and network and communities are identities that are fashioned and negotiated. It is important to note that for the GJMs, and many other movements as well, identity is not so much given as the product of interaction and negotiation that are part of the struggle. To Simmel, and whose work in turn influenced Coser, in situations of conflict, identities are created, negotiated and consolidated. That said, emergent identities depend on the kinds of concrete performances that secure recognition and confirmations of identity that come though participation in a social movement. To be sure, as any activist knows, much [most?] of the activity consists of long, boring meetings. As Weber (1918) pointed out, 'politics is a strong and slow boring of hard boards. It takes both passion and perspective'. While activism includes demonstrations, actions and protests, lobbying, handing out literature, collecting signatures, canvassing and so on, it is important to note that such activities, and we might even note repressions, arrests, and often violence, take place among groups more or less defined by a commitment to social transformation. Again, as Bartholomew and Mayer (1992) point out:

> In order to pursue the level of analysis necessary to analyze contemporary movements as composite action systems, Melucci attends to the networks which constitute the submerged reality of the movements before, during and after [visible] events' (1988: 338). Networks are the small groups, submerged in everyday life, which require a personal involvement and produce 'alternative frameworks of meaning' (1989: 70). They *are* 'networks of meaning' or signs (1989: 58) which put into practice the alternative meanings which they produce and reproduce (1989: 71). The form of the movement is thus *itself* a message (1989: 60).

That meaning may well come from the shared ideology that would foster struggles, challenges and political action/change to so transform the self-production of society to make the world 'better'—however 'better' be defined, from the embrace of Jesus, stopping abortions or restoration of the Caliphate, to ending patriarchy, neo-liberalism or abolishing of capital. For Melucci, a key element in the ideology of a movement is the 'negation of the gap between expectations and reality'. The birth of a movement is marked by 'moment of madness' when all things seem possible. . . . Ideology thus overcomes the inadequacy of action (1992: 133).

Global Justice as a NSM

Today the life worlds of everyone have been radically changed by neo-liberal capital. If the mediations between the crises and contradictions of globalization are (i), framed though ideology, (ii) mediated through an emergent collective identity as locus of action and meaning, (iii) impact actors emotionally, and (iv), counter-hegemonic struggles are often over culture, identity and lifestyles, it should now be obvious that the NSM theory, while rooted in the new social movements of the 1970s and 1980s, help us understand the various GJMs of today. The emergent 'internetworked social movements' share many of these characteristics; however, the influence of new technology on mediation has created a new type of movement that requires new theoretical examination. Today the major differences are the global context of crises, contradictions and adversities and a part of that context, it should be noted, is that many of the activists in these movements were first 'called' to activism in those earlier movements. And I use the term 'called' in much the way that Weber (1918) saw politics as a 'calling, an expression of an inner determination'. 'Only he has the calling for politics who is sure that he shall not crumble when the world from his point of view is too stupid or too base for what he wants to offer. Only he who in the face of all this can say "In spite of all!" has the calling for politics.'

To understand contemporary AGMs, it is necessary to have a social movement model that connects identity, ideology, and network formation to understand how collective action may be mobilized. The NSMs were grounded in the resistance of the middle class to the rationalizing forces of modernity, social fragmentation, injustices, identity and the importance of recognition. The NSM theory speaks to the cultural critiques of Critical Theory (Habermas/Offe) and in turn post-structuralism (Foucault/LeClau and Mouffe), and then moving to NSM theories of Touraine and Melucci. We can see that social movements provide communities with intersubjectively meaningful ties, relationships and realms of sociality. Such communities provide the individual with a number of personal gratifications as well as a sense of meaning through the attempt to shape the future. Thus, the GJM social movements can be thought of as identity granting/recognizing, interacting/socializing communities of meaning devoted to fostering political and/or cultural changes. Thus, for example, the environmentalist movements are not simply concerned with installing scrubbers on smokestacks, detoxifying industrial wastes or saving polar bears. They are seeking to promote lifestyles and values that reject consumerism in general, and more specifically dangerous forms such as fossil fuel based energy, transportation or products as well as say fast food which require vast factory and farms—read massive deforestation. More specifically, the contemporary AGM movements follow much the same patterns and dynamics as the earlier movements studied by NSM students. The major differences are the global nature of the problems and the role of the computer-mediated communication (CMC).

As Sassen (1998) pointed out, most of the activity of the global economy is financial and most of that takes place in the 27,000 or so private networks. Further, the various command, coordination and control of transnational corporations, whether financial, manufacturing or services, as well as the many transnational regulatory agencies are all dependent on the Internet. But the rise and proliferation of the Internet has introduced fundamental changes in the way that information is freely available, and the way people/ groups can communicate across great distances. The consequences of neo-liberal globalization—growing global inequality, labour injustices (from child labour to the sex trade), exploitation and the oppression of women, global warming, human rights abuses—are ever more visible thanks to the Internet, cell phone cameras, and of uploading pictures onto the Internet.

Sociologists like Castells, Sassen, and Wellman began to chart the emergence of new forms of networks and organizations in the 1990s. It was found that not only has the Internet changed the nature of communication, but has enabled new forms of [virtual] community and political formations. These networks enable 'virtual public spheres' where people can have access to information, and can also communicate wide and far. We can suggest that for theorizing AGMs, given crises, contradiction and adversities and suffering of globalization, (1) some people, informed by media, get recruited by self or others to form or join networks and organizations. They are often engaged via a computer terminal, where people have access to 'virtual public spheres' and where people can freely attempt to create and negotiate understandings, glean 'consensual truths', debate and articulate critiques, propose alternative imaginaries and explore various strategies to realize these goals. As a result, (2) 'Internetworked Social Movements' (ISMs) of various kinds have emerged, with often contentious relations to states. Some provide alternative information, others initiate various kinds of actions that might contest, resist and even transform adversities and injustices through pressures on states and/or economic actors to change policies or, in some cases, change governments. These might include lobbying, consumer boycotts, demonstrations, and even direct forms of 'netwar' such as 'hactivism'. As has been noted (Langman 2005):

> The 'virtual public spheres' of a global civil society not only provide information and communication but act as identity-granting subcultures that foster collective identities. The 'virtual public spheres' of the Internet enable what Kahn and Kellner (2003), call 'post-subcultures', interpersonal networks of discussion, debate and clarification that, however virtual, nevertheless

foster or create spaces for the democratic construction, negotiation and articulation of new constellations of project identities that are decoupled from national, ethnic or religious moorings. These 'post-subcultures' allow people the freedom to re-define and construct themselves on the basis of the alternative cultural and/or political forms and experiences.

Moreover, the global nature of the Internet has fostered a greater awareness of often far-removed injustices and adversities that in turn mobilize ameliorative strategies rooted in political or economic practices. Internet 'post-subcultures' have taken up the questions of local and global politics and are attempting to construct globally oriented identities and strategies to act both locally and globally, which are now possible because of nature of the Internet. Social justice movements are organized around articulating collective identities that seek to attain some public good(s).[25] Those who acquire a global justice identity through the Internet are more likely to join GJMs. Such identity-based networks impel resistance, contestation and new forms of net-based progressive cyberactivism.[26] These include globally based peace movements, feminisms, gay rights and environmentalism as well as AIDS activism. Other AGMs embrace more traditional causes amplified by globalization such as trade unionism, job creation, poverty, inadequate medical services, civil/human rights, genocide, the sex trade, and regional trade agreements (taxes tariffs, migration), landless/homelessness or family violence.

It is now generally accepted that many 'local' problems cannot be solved locally, like acid rain destroying vegetation thousands of miles away. The rapid creation of industrial and service jobs in developing countries has impacted Europe and the US. Much of the tuna in the world now has dangerous levels of mercury—a by-product of burning fossil fuels. The pollution of the Pearl River basin impacts every man, woman and child on the planet. As has been noted, the contradictions of globalization generate negativity that in turn might have transformative powers. But that requires the dedication and devotion of millions of activists devoted to global justice.

CONCLUSION

While social scientists may quietly debate the nature of social movements, the contemporary world is now dominated by a regime of neo-liberal capital that as such faces unprecedented contradictions and adversities. Never before has so much wealth been generated in a short time—albeit the wealth being highly concentrated within the transnational capitalist elites (Sklair, 2002). Millions of people have moved from abject poverty to moderate levels of comfort, but far more people now face a life of greater poverty, deprivation and violence. In response to the contradictions of global capital, we have seen the emergence of a vast number of global justice movements, NGOs, INGOS, and SMOs. Aided and abetted by the same Internet technologies that make the current moment of globalization possible, there has been a vast and growing proliferation of Alternative Global Movements (AGM). But just as these movements argue that humanity must develop new paradigms of identity and meaning, so too must social scientists rethink the understanding of these new social movements. One of the common themes of the GJMs, most clearly seen as the motto of the WSF is that a better world is possible. Between the growing proliferation of nuclear weapons technology, the growing shortages of resources from oil to land to water, and growing environmental dangers, we might suggest that these movements may not just make the world better, but enable the very survival of humanity.

NOTES

1. Eisenstadt (1993) has shown how the collectivist orientations of socialism were more compatible with the more familial and tribal orientations of many underdeveloped countries.
2. The story of how Deming's pleas for quality controls were ignored by US industries, while embraced by the Japanese is now standard business school curriculum. Toyota will soon displace General Motors, most US televisions come from foreign companies, especially Japanese and Korea.
3. While economic crises may well foster social movements, this does not mean embracing either classical economic reductionism, or ignoring a plurality of identities other then the proletarian—often a conservative element. Thus issues like gay rights or environmentalism are not working class struggles.
4. It was only when digital photos of the abuses of Abu Ghraib went out over the Internet that these practices became well known outside of human rights organizations.
5. See below. While the present analysis is sympathetic to the notions of the discursive production of hegemonic identities as LaClau and Mouffe (1985) argue, they completely lose sight of the larger political economy, which in terms of the present analysis is neo-liberal globalization.
6. As will be noted, many fundamentalist or nationalist movements today can be seen as attempts to maintain values and identities under siege by global forces. Progressive activists would say, 'you can't go back, we must fashion a new kind of society'.

7. For Althusser, the subject is 'interpellated' (constructed/hailed) by Ideological State Apparatus, and his/her sense of agency is an illusion. While he is half right in that schools, media, churches and families socialize identities that sustain a social order, the NSM perspective argues that indeed it is the agency of the actor that enables social transformation, and that is the constriction upon agency that can impel action.
8. Castells did not use this term.
9. Such identities might also include contemporary instantiations of progressive trade unionists, anti-war activists, and human rights activists.
10. This is not to assume that most people understand how global finances work or see how their lifestyles impact the environment. But when the dollar falls, losing almost half its value since 2000, people feel how imported goods are more expensive.
11. Reactionaries, fascists and fundamentalists have long understood the relations of emotion, identity and social mobilization. They have no problem manipulating fear, revenge and outrage. Progressives and liberals who appeal to either reason or logic and/or the 'good will of people', always lose in struggles.
12. While essentialism may be disdained by post-modernists, and the nature of what is human and human desire are socially constructed, given the universality of the human body, and its innate affect system which is a product of evolution, there are some general tendencies of all people. There are of course many variations, for example, psychopathology. See Tompkins (1995) Ekman (1973).
13. The need for community/attachment, recognition/esteem, agency/empowerment can be found in Marx's critique of alienated labour that rendered people powerless to outside forces, fragmented community and truncated his/her humanity, leaving her/him little different from a pack animal.
14. Chris Hedges, http://www.truthdig.com/report/item/20080121_the_lessons_of_violence/
15. Fromm (1941) argued over 60 years ago that the feelings of powerlessness that came from social change disposed an anxiety and in turn a submission to authority via a new collective identity—in the sixteenth century, it was Protestantism, in the twentieth, Nazism.
16. A central premise of NSM theory argues that these movements are not class based as in classical Marxist theory. But at the same time, in many movements, workers/peasants may well be the most powerful factions. for example, consider the power of the Workers Party (PT) Brazil or the Korean Federation of Trade Unions.
17. The works of Habermas, Offe, LeClau and Mouffe, and Marcuse can now be seen as important precursors to the New Social Movement perspective.

18. In many ways, various reactionary/fundamentalist movements follow the same model. This was anticipated in Lipset's analyses of 'status anxiety' in the conservatism of the 1950s, especially McCarthyism.
19. In some ways, this typology is somewhat like Merton's classical model of conformity, retreatism, innovation, rebellion or retreatism.
20. Neo-liberalism becomes a material force when resources or government services are privatized, structural adjustment is implemented, when land is confiscated for WB projects, etc.
21. Thus someone who was adversely affected by political policies, say a relative of someone who died in combat, denied an insurance claim or whatever, often sees first hand how the 'system' operates which is often quite discrepant from its public presentations.
22. With all due respect to Tilly and Tarrow, the political opportunity structure also plays a role in social mobilization, but the present concern focuses on identity/emotion following a NSM perspective.
23. For the sake of full disclosure, the author has been a member of many activist organizations. Members of such organizations see each other as 'movement' people, sort of a valourized 'we' *versus* a 'them' that includes the nefarious evil elites as well as the bulk of people indifferent to the political/cultural struggles beyond voicing opinions.
24. The RM theory, in contrast, stresses the political nature of the new movements and interprets them as conflicts over the allocation of goods in the political market. Hence, it focuses on the strategic-instrumental aspects of action and places social movements, simultaneously, at the levels of civil society and the state. It also places emphasis on continuity between the new and the old collective actors.
25. In many cases, membership and participation in a social movement organization serves more to sustain and confirm collective and personal identity than to actually impact policy over what sometimes seem to be intractable adversities. Consider the Israeli-Palestinian conflict. Some of the peace activist groups have spent decades trying to foster reconciliation—so far to no avail.
26. There have been earlier notions of global justice organization, for example, the World Federalists. But these tend to be more formal and less likely to engage in protest mobilizations.

REFERENCES

Bagdikian, B. (1997), *The Media Monopoly*, Boston: Beacon.

Bartholomew, A. and Margit Mayer (1992), 'Nomads of the Present': 'Melucci's Contribution to New Social Movement Theory', *Theory, Culture and Society,* (9), 141–59.

Beck, U. (2006), 'Living in the World Risk Society', *Economy and Society,* 35, pp. 329–45.

Bennett, W. (2003), 'Communicating Global Activism', *Information, Communication & Society*, 6, pp. 143–68.

Buechler, S. (2000), *Social Movements,* New York: Oxford University Press.

Castells, M. (1997), *The Power of Identity*, Malden, MA: Blackwell Publishers.

Eisenstadt, S. (1993), *The Political Systems of Empires*, Piscataway, NJ: Transaction Publishers.

Ekman, P. (1973), *Darwin and Facial Expression, A Century of Research in Review*, New York: Academic Press.

Ekman, P. (2003), *Emotions Revealed*, New York: Times Books.

Fanon, F. (1986), *Black Skin, White Masks*, tr. C.L. Marhham, London: Pluto Press.

Foster, J. B. (2002), *Ecology against Capitalism*, New York: Monthly Review Press.

Giddens, A. (1991), *Modernity and Self-Identity: Self and Society in the Late Modern Age*, Stanford: Stanford University Press.

Goodwin J. and J. Jasper (2000), 'The Return of the Repressed: The Fall and Rise of Emotions in Social Movement Theory', *Mobilization*, 5(1), pp. 65–84.

Goodwin, J., J. Jasper and F. Polleta (eds.) (2001), *Passionate Politics: Emotions and Social Movements*, Chicago: University of Chicago Press.

Habermas, J. (1975), *Legitimation Crisis*, Boston: Beacon Press.

Hochschild, A. (1997), *The Time Bind: When Work Becomes Home and Home Becomes Work*, New York: Metropolitan Books.

Korten, D. (2001), *When Corporations Rule the World*, San Francisco: Berrett-Koehler.

Kovel, (2002), *The Enemy of Nature: The End of Capitalism or the End of the World?* New York: Zed Books.

LaClau, E. and C. Mouffe (1985), *Hegemony and Socialist Strategy: Towards a Radical Democratic Politics*, New York: Verso.

Langman, L. (2000), 'Identity, Hegemony and the Reproduction of Domination' in Altschuler, R. (ed.) *Marx, Weber and Durkheim*, New York: Gordian Knot Press, pp. 238–90.

Langman, L. (2002), 'Globalization, Cyberspace and Identity', *Information Technology Education and Society*, 3, p. 2.

Langman, L. (2005), 'Virtual Public Spheres and Globalized Social Movements', *Social Theory*, 3(1), pp. 42–74.

Langman, L. (2008), 'The News of the Death of Nationalism May be Premature' Plenary Address, Annual Meeting, *Global Studies Association*, Pace University, New York.

McChesney, R. (2000), *Rich Media, Poor Democracy: Communication Politics in Dubious Times*, New York: The New Press.

Melucci, A. (1989), *Nomads of the Present*, Philadelphia: Temple University Press.

Melucci, A. (1992), 'Frontier Land: Collective Action Between Actor and Systems', in Maria Diani and Ron Eyerman (eds.), *Studying Collective Action*, London: Sage.

Melucci, A. (1995), 'The Process of Collective Identity', in H. Johnston and B. Klandermans (eds.), *Social Movements and Culture*, Minneapolis, M.N: University of Minnesota press.

Moghadam, V. (2000), 'Transnational Feminist Networks: Collective Action in an Era of Globalization', *International Sociology*, 15 (1), pp. 57–85.

Perucci, R. and E. Wysong (2002), *The New Class Society*, Langham, Md.: Rowman & Littlefield Pub Inc.

Sassen, S. (1998), *Globalization and its Discontent: Essays on the New Mobility of People and Money*, New York: New Press.

Scheff, T. (1994), *Bloody Revenge: Emotions, Nationalism, and War*, Boulder: Westview Press.

Stieglitz, J. (2002), *Globalization and its Discontents*, New York: Allen Lane/ The Penguin Press.

Tompkins. S. (1995), 'Exploring Affect', in Virginia E. Demos (ed.), *The Selected Writings of Silvan S. Tompkins*, New York: Press Syndicate of the University of Cambridge.

Touraine, A. (1985), *Social Movements and Social Change*, London: Sage.

Weber, M. (1946), 'Politics as a Vocation' in *From Max Weber: Essays in Sociology*, tr. and ed. H. Gerth and C. Mills, New York: Oxford University Press.

CHAPTER 4

Globalization, Social Movements and Social Development: Emerging Discourses

GAIL OMVEDT

Globalization is today a highly contested concept (and phenomenon). At the same time it is taken for granted that 'social movements', in India at least, have been transformed, and in most cases have declined since the 1990s, that is, since the advent of globalization. So, among its other characteristics, it is said that globalization stifles social movements. But not through simple repression. The present paper will examine this problem, with a special focus on the Dalit movement. First, it will give a critical analysis of globalization and the struggles against it, then look at the new shape of social movements, and finally examine the Dalit example.

GLOBALIZATION: CAPITALISM AS A WORLD MODE OF PRODUCTION

The discourse on globalization has been a strange one: too often it has simply been taken as a slogan. Rather than analysing what is really new about the current phase of world capitalism, leftists have seen it as the 'reincarnation' of the old imperialism. They have talked about multinationals as a 'new East India Company', and in the early 1990s most of the left in India were predicting that Indian capitalists would be 'eaten up' by multinational capital. Wrong analyses lead to wrong predictions: globalization indeed has involved new inequalities and new forms of exploitation, but the Indian capitalist class, far from being endangered, has surged forward with it.

The result has been for all to see: not knowing really how to analyse globalization, leftists have swung from incoherent opposition to implicit acceptance in their own realms. The result we see in Nandigram. No real policy for the current stage of imperialism has been formulated. No real alternative is given in most of today's discourse on globalization. Instead, there is a tendency to look back with nostalgia on the past, when villages and nations were relatively independent. The 'local' is posed against the global, the nation-state against 'imperialism'. As a recent study has pointed out:

> In the long decades of the current crisis of the communist, socialist, and liberal Left that has followed the 1960s, a good portion of critical thought . . . has sought to recompose sites of resistance that are founded on the identities of social subjects or national and regional groups, often grounding political analysis on the localization of struggles. Such arguments are sometimes constructed in terms of 'place-based' movements or politics, in which the boundaries of place (conceived of as identity or as territory) are posed against the undifferentiated and homogeneous space of global networks. At other times such political arguments draw on the long tradition of Leftist nationalism in which (in the best cases) the nation is conceived as the primary mechanism of defense against the domination of foreign and/or global capital. Today the operative syllogism at the heart of the various forms of 'local' Leftist strategy seems to be entirely reactive: If capitalist domination is becoming ever more global, then our resistance to it must defend the local and construct barriers to capital's accelerating flows'. (Hardt and Negri 2000: 35)

In India, this means that opposition to 'globalization' (or 'LPG—liberalization/privativization/globalization') implied an effort to defend the old state-capitalist society with its protectionism and its public sector and presumed welfare policies, along with a simple proclamation of the evils of the current day, a proclamation that has confronted the hopes that people keep putting into these.

Thus we need a new analysis. Much groundwork for this has, I feel, been laid by the recent study by Michael Hardt and Antonio Negri cited earlier, the latter a 'workers' autonomist' from Italy who has done most of his writing from jail. They contrast what they call 'Empire', the new era of globalization, from the old imperialism in two ways.

First, where the old imperialism involved competition among nation states, each with its group of dependent colonies, the new 'Empire' is more genuinely a global system. Production is defused and decentralized; the old borders and boundaries increasingly have little meaning. Multinationals—now genuinely transnational—may produce anywhere, and use a mélange of territorial places and a variety of ethnic personnel. While the US is the most powerful 'nation' remaining, it does not dominate in the way that the old nations dominated; it is not a Britain of the new era. The US itself is increasingly becoming multicultural and multiracial, its government forced to confront a citizenry that is diverse and representative of nearly the whole globe. (For example, the largest mass movement of recent years in the US has been that of immigrants, fighting efforts to declare them illegal and send them out of the country.) The recent presidential election, where there was hardly a 'WASP' (White Anglo–Saxon Protestant—a slang-term for ethnic elite in the US) male among the leading candidates, is symptomatic of this. Whereas the British, an ethnically identified group, clearly ruled their empire, the hegemony of the white European male is now under serious challenge. In many ways, there is no ethnically identifiable group that quite so clearly rules; somewhat like the situation that developed in the old Roman empire. This does not mean 'racism' does not exist, but it takes new forms; Hardt and Negri argue that it is distinguished and ideologized in cultural terms.

Similarly, economically the old division of labour in which colonies produced raw materials while the dominant manufacturing was carried on in the imperial centres has now nearly vanished. The rising new economic powers are former colonies and dependencies such as India and China. Even culturally, they are making a clear impact. The new 'Empire' is a system that is qualitatively different.

The second major feature is the new forms of production that take place. Increasingly these are based upon information and communication technologies; they represent a post-industrialism and a post-modernism in cultural terms. Negri and Hardt call what this involves as 'bio-political' production and new forms of control. They talk about regulation through 'control' as opposed to the old forms of 'discipline'. Whereas the old society, the imperialism of the nation states, was based on more clear use of force and discipline, now control is much more internalized. It produces an emotional 'affect' with all the power of symbolism. There is an insidious attractiveness about the existing system that hypnotizes the subordinated groups within it, makes them desirous, distracts them from the possibilities of realizing a future, more self-directed society.

Hardt and Negri also argue that there is a major change in mass movements. The working class itself is changed—fragmented and differentiated. The two writers refer to the 'multitude' rather than the working class. They argue that while so many protest movements are arising on different issues, they can no longer easily communicate; in fact they are becoming 'incommunicable' in their terms. In the past, we may note, movements had internationals—international union organizations, lines of control and communication and leadership running through the nation to the international level. This is no longer true. While there are efforts at global alliances today, they certainly cannot work as in the past, and movements in fact are searching for new ways of communication.

We can put this all in more classical Marxist terminology: capitalism is becoming in a real way a global mode of production. Whereas it arose at the local (often urban, only later spreading to the countryside) and national level, emerging as many capitalist modes of production dominating social formations that were in effect nation states with colonies (the classical 'imperialism'), now the nation state form is gradually becoming secondary. Capitalism is organizing itself and the society around it at a global level. This is a profound change. Hardt and Negri are right in rejecting the possibility of going backwards; reading Marx and Engels, especially in the *Communist Manifesto*, we may also do so.

SOCIAL MOVEMENTS OF THE MARGINALIZED

The old 'Left' paradigm of social movements was fairly simple: these were movements of the masses against exploitation; but exploitation was assumed to be within the context of the nation state, with the situation varying according to whether the nation was independent or a colonial dependent. Not only was the working class movement privileged as the vanguard, but the national movement, in colonized countries, was also privileged as the decisive social movement to which other issues should be subordinated. Thus, for example, after 1936 when the Comintern theses made this clear, the Communist Party of India brought its front groups and all the activists it could influence into the Congress Socialist Party, effectively seeking to operate as a pressure group within the Congress. This orientation to nationalism remained even during periods such as the Second World War and the agreement between Hitler and Stalin, when the CPI took an apparently anti-national stance. Up to today, this nationalist orientation has remained.

During the 1970s and 1980s, what were then referred to as the 'new social movements' burst forth in various countries throughout the world. These could not be contained, either under the old Left/ nationalist leadership, or theoretically within the traditional analysis. In India such movements were extremely strong. They involved sections which did not fit easily into the working class/nationalist paradigm, people organizing in terms of the racial, caste, gender and even religious issues which remained unresolved. They also included sections oppressed in different ways, dam evictees fighting for rehabilitation, farmers demanding better prices.

Since the new movements did not fit easily into the traditional Left paradigm, the concept began to develop that they represented 'identity politics', a politics fairly empty of economic issues and focused more on cultural and with it political assertion of the groups in question. However, this fit some of the movements but by no means all of them. Nearly all the movements had economic aspects; some were simply survival fights of groups which were affected by misguided development policies. Movements such as the farmers movement in India defined themselves as 'economic', stressing the price demand, but also stressing that their battle was against the state.

The 'new social movements' never could unite, and remained diverse but sometimes allied. However, after 1990 all movements seem to have gone into crisis. Core issues remain unresolved; struggles go on, the movements obviously survive, in some form, but are fragmented and diversified, and increasingly people within them question whether there really is a movement. No longer are there such huge mass rallies or campaigns—lakhs of people travelling without tickets on the train, for example, to demonstrate in Delhi or Mumbai.

Today, we need a new analysis of social movements to comprehend these changes. Among the phenomenon that must be taken into account is the fact that they are increasingly operative on a global scale, yet their direct global communication is minimal. People act in support of, or along with, social movements in far-off places, without necessarily understanding all the issues yet somehow identifying with the cause of opposition to an exploitative globalization.

Let us take the Dalit movement in India as an example of these changes.

DALIT MOVEMENT TODAY

The 'classic' era of the Dalit movement was of course the pre-Independence period. In spite of many local diversities, and in spite of leadership factions, it emerged as a fairly solitary movement under the leadership of Dr. Ambedkar. All the regional Dalit leaders paled before him; they either became his lieutenants, or remained simply local leaders, or worked directly in alliance with the Congress (such as Jagjivan Ram) as more or less a counter. This movement retained its autonomy from the Congress and from the Left, fought (in its own way) both imperialism and the nationalist leadership, and won some real gains. It was in that sense a classic social movement, though it was not nationalist and not under Left leadership.

Today many raise the question of whether there is a Dalit movement at all. It is extremely factionalized, organizationally and politically. On one hand, Uttar Pradesh Chief Minister Mayawati has emerged as a powerful national political leader and an unquestioned Dalit icon; yet it is clear that neither she nor her mentor, the founder of the Bahujan Samaj Party (BSP), the late Kanshi Ram, is a movement leader in the sense that Ambedkar was. Nor, we may say, do they aspire to be: Mayawati today seems to be aspiring to do something rather different, mainstreaming the party, speaking in the name of *sarvajan*—clearly aiming to become an alternative to Congress as a political party at the national level. This is to make Dalits a 'ruling community' in the old aim of Ambedkar, but it is not quite a Dalit movement either.

On the other hand, local Dalit politics remain as factionalized as ever; three Republican factions in Maharashtra, two Dalit parties in Tamil Nadu, small groups here and there. A number of local activist leaders, disgusted with Mayawati's apparent compromise with Brahmins, are speaking of starting 'real Dalit parties'. These represent the sectional interests of Dalits, yet can achieve very little.

In other ways, there is a new globalization of the Dalit movement, one that can be dated to perhaps 2001 when the United Nations conference against racism took place in Durban, South Africa. This was after ten years of economic reforms, which had given some impetus to growth in India and which a section of Dalits, due to benefiting from the history of reservations, could take advantage of. They were beginning to organize in new ways: taking to the internet and discussing on chat groups, sending out messages, forming their own NGOs. A small section that was abroad, in the US, Dubai, UK, Europe, was becoming newly conscious and communicating very often through the internet. They got involved in organizing and attending international conferences and meetings, raising money for scholarships, various types of aid. Here there are alliances with African-Americans, or occasionally (without much communication) with Burakumin in Japan, communication with Dalit groups in Nepal and Pakistan. In these ways, the Dalit movement has begun to go significantly beyond old national boundaries.

At the same time, we see another kind of fragmentation: tensions within Dalits, between different *jatis* especially. Specifically, those castes that were more educationally and economically backward for long periods of time—Madigas in Andhra, Matangas in Maharashtra, the Bhangi groups in northern India—are beginning to mobilize, and occasionally their mobilization is directed against the formerly dominant communities (Mahars, Malas, Chamars, and so on). They have often met with a stark lack of sympathy and defensive attitude from the more 'leading' Dalit castes. In addition there are new movements among Dalit Christians, Dalit Muslims, and so on. to demand the status of 'Scheduled Caste'; these are also met with varying responses from the Dalits, who often object to seeing new groups crowding out their reservation opportunities. But they pose problems.

There is also a new tension between Dalits and the Other Backward Castes (OBC). During the colonial period too there were differences, but these could often be papered over against the common enemy of 'Brahmanism'. Today, OBCs have also become assertive, and many have attained a clear political strength. Yet their economic and cultural (intellectual) status does not match this. Their sense of neglect and oppression (often intensified since many are in the crisis-ridden rural sector) very often gets turned against the Dalits. This results in notorious cases such as Khairlanji in Maharashtra, where a family of Dalit farmer was massacred. On the whole, it is clear that in vast parts of the country some of the most prejudiced attitudes and practices against the Dalits remain. Yet the OBCs, who also suffer from discrimination and being viewed with scorn by the elite, do not seem to aim for unity.

Finally, it is important to note the fragmentation of themes pushed by various sections of the Dalit movement. The BSP takes up purely political issues. In contrast to the era of Ambedkar's fairly detailed economic programmes and policies, it never has bothered to have an economic programme. The other sections of Dalit parties (the Republican Party of India factions and so on) mostly borrow their political rhetoric from the Left. The Dalit NGOs concentrate mostly on atrocities and exposure of these.

At the same time, it is important to note that assertion is going on at all levels: political, cultural (new writers, new interest in writing, concern about symbols and symbolization), economic (there are a number of efforts, both at the individual and collective level, to begin small businesses), educational, and so on.

Some of these changes can be related to the shifting and more heterogeneous position of Dalits (and other castes) within the global capitalist mode of production. The years of reservation have produced a small intellectual and political elite; these are now making their presence felt. There has also been migration, even by the poor, to new areas of the world. During the Durban conference period, for example, many educated Dalits who had found themselves overseas in comfortable positions, for one reason or another, found themselves identifying with their old community. While casteism and discrimination remain strong, this new 'middle class' now produces a certain leadership; it is at the same time increasingly fragmented in terms of ideology and political stance. There are socialists and democratic capitalists among Dalit intellectuals; there are supporters of BJP as well as of the Congress and Left parties. The 'masses' of Dalits themselves are fragmented and hierarchized.

In fact, the question we have to conclude with is, why a 'Dalit' movement? Although the identification is fairly strong and specific, still the terminology began to be widespread only after the 1970s, and still was perhaps never fully known among the masses. There have always been sections that have dissented from the term, taking 'Dalit' to mean only one section of the broad caste category of former untouchables. There have also been those who have rejected it, preferring to identify themselves as 'Buddhists' or some such. And, finally, the strongest 'Dalit' political party, the BSP, has never identified itself as a Dalit party, and has been quite specific in claiming to represent a broader category of oppressed caste that includes the OBCs and minorities (and now, under Mayawati, it is moving towards a 'sarvajan samaj' position literally forming "all peoples society" but referring but specifically to the inclusion of Brahmins).

Thus, if we were to summarize the condition of the 'Dalit movement' today, we would have to stress its expansion connected with fragmentation, its increasingly problematic identity, and its dispersion over many fields of action and ideology.

CONCLUSION

Hardt and Negri refer not to the traditional proletariat as the 'working class', but to the 'multitude'—stressing the diversity of those exploited by capital in the new era of 'Empire'. Their movements are also fragmented, a point that they make. Negri and Hardt argue that in contrast to the 'classic' struggles of the old imperial era—when the general strike and the nation-based insurrection were the preferred forms—in the 'concrete alternatives' emerging in the new era, 'What appears here is not a new rationality but a new scenario of different rational acts—a horizon of activities, resistences, wills and desires that refuse the hegemonic order, propose lines of flight, and forge alternative constitutive itineraries'. In other words, various struggles of resistance emerge, locally based but each pointing in their own way to a new future.

But unity remains a problem. Previously since all movements had common features, there was a fairly simple understanding and events in one area could set-off, like a chain, insurrections, movements and events elsewhere. In the new conditions of 'Empire', being locally based and constituted, the movements often use a discourse not easily 'translatable' or understood by those struggling elsewhere. There is a global sense of solidarity, yet often a difficulty in expressing these. Hardt and Negri see the movements as 'incommunicable' in a new sense, yet argue that this means their only choice is to make a leap for the global and attempt direct communication.

'We can recognize powerful events on the world scene that reveal the trace of the multitude's refusal of exploitation and that signify a new kind of proletarian solidarity and militancy', write Hardt and Negri. They mention Tienanmen Square in China, Infitada in Israel, and the Chiapas uprising in Mexico and other events. To these we might add the increasing Dalit assertion and resistance. All of these, they note, are very specific in the exploitation they focus against, and have difficulty in communicating their aims. They have sparked powerful though scattered sympathy throughout the world, but real understanding is often missing.

Though social movements today are fragmented, this fragmentation also means that they increasingly overlap. And given the global possibilities of communication, sometimes the most 'localized' movements can make the leap that Hardt and Negri want, can put their specific needs on the global agenda—in a way that the movements of the 'classic' era could not. Furthermore, there is a sense of solidarity:

even when the specifities of movements are not really comprehended, this solidarity gets expressed; underlying this is a recognition of a common enemy.

Social movements today, argue Hardt and Negri, are 'constituent struggles, creating new public spaces and new forms of community'. They are not easily understood, but the obstacles that block communication can be overcome. They call for analysis of the current situation, a 'new language' that will facilitate communication between struggles that involve very different forms of exploitation. All of this is achievable.

REFERENCES

Arrighi, Giovanni, 'Globalization, State Sovereignty and the "Endless" Accumulation of Capital', revised version of paper presented at Conference on States and Sovereignty in the World Economy, University of California, Irvine, 21–23 February 1997.

Balakrishnan, Gopal (2000), 'Review of Michael Hardt and Antonio Negri, *Empire*', in *New Left Review,* 5, September-October.

Becker, Gary (2007), 'Globalization and Inequality', October 14, http://www.becker-posner-blog.com/archives/2007/10/globalization a 1.html

Bhagwati, Jagdish (2004), *In Defense of Globalization,* Oxford University Press.

Birdsall, Nancy (2007), 'Inequality Matters', *Boston Review*, March–April, http://bostonreview.net/BR32.2/birdsall.php

Desai, Meghnad, 'Globalisation and its Contents', *The Little Magazine*, vol. V, issue 4-5.

Firebaugh, Glenn and Goesling (2004), 'Accounting for the Recent Decline in Global Income Inequality', *American Journal of Sociology*, September.

Firebaugh, Glenn (2008), 'Debate about Income Inequality', http://ucatlas.ucsc.edu/blog/?p=55

Giddens, Anthony (1999), 'The Runaway World' (Rath Lectures No. 1), 10 November.

Hardt, Michael and Antonio Negri, *Empire*, Cambridge, Mass: Harvard University Press 2000.

Held, Devid (2004), 'Inescapably Side by Side: A Interview with Devid Held' by Mikkel Thorup and Mads P. Sorensen, *Polity*, February.

Hensman, Rohini (2007), 'Globalisation or Militarist Imperialism? India Must Choose', www.countercurrents.org, 19 November.

Human Development Report (2007–8), Tables, United Nations.

International Monetary Fund (2007), 'Recent Trends in Globalization and Inequality', Chapter 4 of 2007 report.

Jaffer, Abbas (2008), 'A Third Way: Globalization from the Bottom', *Foreign Policy in Focus*, 6 August.

Omvedt, Gail (1994), *New Social Movements and the Socialist Tradition in India*, New York: M.E. Sharpe.

Petras, James (2001), 'Empire with Imperialism: Review Essay on Michael Hardt and Antonio Negri, 29 October, www.globaljusticecenter.org/papers/saenz_noters.htm -16k

Progressive Policy Institute (2005), 'Shares of World GDP' http://www.globalpolicy.org/socecon/inequal/income/tables/history.htm

Salai-i-Martin, Xavier (2002), 'The Disturbing "Rise" of Global Income Inequality', NBER Working Paper no. 8904, April, http://www.nber.org/papers/w8904

Sen, Amartya (2004), 'Sharing the World', *This essay is based on the author's address to the General Assembly of the United Nations on 29 October.*

Stiglitz, Joseph E. (2002), *Globalization and Its Discontents,* W.W. Norton and Company.

UNCTAD (2004), *Development and Globalization: Some Facts and Figures*, New York and Geneva: United Nations.

Vadaele, John (2008), 'Globalisation 'Localises' Inequality', Inter Press Service, 11 March Glf@Globalpolicy.Org

——— (2007), *The Silent Death of Neoliberalism.*

Wade, Robert, Reply to Firebaugh and Goesling (2004), http://ucatlas.ucsc.edu/income/debate.html

Wallerstein, Immanuel (2008), 'The Demise of Neoliberal Globalization', *Commentary*, no. 226, 1 February, www.binghamton.edu/fbc/226en/htm

CHAPTER 5

Social Movement, Conflict and Change: Towards a Theoretical Orientation*

PARTHA NATH MUKHERJI

INTRODUCTION

'As they evolved in Western countries,' contends Charles Tilly,

> social movements combined three major elements: (1) sustained campaigns of *claim-making*; (2) an array of *public performances* including marches, rallies, processions, demonstrations, occupations, picket lines, blockades, public meetings, delegations, statements to and in public media, petition drives, letter-writing, pamphleteering, lobbying, and creation of specialized associations, coalitions, or fronts—in short, the social movement repertoire; and (3) repeated *public displays* of worthiness, unity, numbers and commitment (WUNC) by such means as wearing colors, marching in disciplined ranks, sporting badges that advertise the cause, displaying signs, chanting slogans, singing militant songs, and picketing public buildings. (Tilly 2006: 183–4; emphasis added)

Two other points Tilly makes merit noting: (1) social movements have only now become ubiquitous, 'at least in relatively democratic countries', but come to think of it, they 'had never existed anywhere in the world three centuries ago'. 'Western Europeans and North Americans' were the ones to have put 'the elements of a new political form' in the late eighteenth century, which became available to the 'ordinary people' in these countries in the first half of the nineteenth

*Paper presented at the international conference 'Social Development, Social Movements and the Marginalised: Perspectives and Concerns', organized by the Indira Gandhi National Open University, New Delhi, 17–18 February 2008.

century even 'as it began spreading to the other parts of the world' (Tilly 2006: 182), (2) Social movements had to be distinguished from collective violence, which refers to phenomena such as civil war and terrorism, including revolts, rebellions and state sponsored terrorism[1] (ibid.: 118–50).

In this formulation, social movements perform a functional role within a largely democratic framework. The means and mode of protest lie within the permissible limits of regulation of social order. Implicitly, there was a pre-social movement era, much the same as the pre-modern era. It is indigenous to the West, but getting universalized.

Wallerstein distinguishes between 'social' and 'national' movements, which nonetheless reveal 'a series of shared features' within the period 1850 and 1970. The former 'were conceived primarily as socialist parties and trade unions; they sought to further the class struggle within each state against the bourgeoisie or the employers'. The latter, 'were those which fought for the creation of a national state, either by combining separate political units that were considered to be part of one nation—as, for example, in Italy—or by seceding from states considered imperial and oppressive by the nationality in question—colonies in Asia or Africa, for instance' (2002: 29). He locates the emergence of these movements in the second half of the nineteenth century. The role of violence or its absence is left open in this framework.

In recent times the distinction is made between 'old' and 'new' social movements (NSM), the former referring to labour and working class movements, whilst the latter to movements in the 'post-industrial' society in which 'other social cleavages become more salient and generate new identities, and the exercise of power is less in the realm of work and more in "the setting of a way of life, forms of behavior, and needs"' (Touraine, cited in Edelman 2001: 288). Touraine 'excludes from this category, however, forms of "collective behavior" that "defend" the social order or "social struggles" directed at the state' (Edelman 2001: 288). In general, 'the NSMs emerge out of the crisis of modernity and focus on struggles over symbolic, informational, and cultural resources and rights to specificity and difference' (ibid.: 289). Melucci identifies three important dimensions of social movement: (a) commonalities, shared identities, objectives and understandings among the actors; (b) 'adversarial relations with opposition who claim the same goods or values'; and (c) 'actions that exceed the tolerance limits of a social system, thereby pushing it to change' (ibid.: 289).

In the largely European discourse the theoretical premises of both the old and new social movements have their structural bases in social conflict having consequences for social change. Mainly developed in North America, the 'rational-actor postulate' (Olsen) and the 'strategy oriented' paradigm (Cohen) underlie the resource mobilization (RM) theorization. Couched in terminologies of 'social movement industries', 'social movement organizations', 'movement entrepreneurs', who 'had the task of mobilizing resources and channeling discontent into organizational forms', the RM theories considered 'collective action mainly as interest group politics played out by socially connected groups rather than by the most disaffected' (ibid.: 289). To this was added the proposition of political opportunity structure (POS) which introduced the element of perceived opportunities or threats posed by the 'challengers', and equally, the element of facilitation or repression likely to be exercised by the authorities.

Historical and contextual factors such as a strong Marxist tradition leading to a social democratic consensus in Europe; its absence in North America, and the strong civil rights movement that has characterized it provide the two models that are consistent with their respective historicities. Each of these experiences has an element of indigenousness with respect to its evolution. It follows that if these experiences of collective action could differ across the Atlantic, then they need not qualify to be universal for other regions of the world like Asia or Latin America or Africa, although, surely, their experiences cannot be discounted in reaching out for more universalistic formulations.

I propose to attempt a theoretical orientation/framework that is not constrained by any historicity, while permitting analysis of the historical evolution of social movements in their social and cultural specificity. The South Asian experience in general, and the Indian, in particular, provide extraordinary rich experience of numerous varieties of social mobilizations over time. The claim that social movement is of Western origin linked with an earlier stage of the plight of the working class during the industrial revolution and development of capitalism; and subsequently, with social and cultural alienations that the post-industrial era produced, will have to be re-examined in the light of the experiences of the post-colonial and developing world.

Drawing from my personal researches on agrarian, 'revolutionary' and other movements, I have been attempting a comprehensive theoretical orientation/framework[2] (as distinguished from theory *per se*) for a more efficient comprehension of the dynamics of social movement and change. It has therefore a good bit of inductive indigenous input, consistent with the position I hold that indigeneity is an essential condition of universalizing social sciences, as long as we are searching for the universals in the particulars in different knowledge and cultural contexts. Such an exercise, I believe, benefits from an approach which Merton long ago described as 'disciplined eclecticism'. The search for 'truth' in this kind of thinking cannot be circumscribed within any single theoretical school or paradigm, nor does it mean that we have necessarily to involve all existing paradigms. It does mean that in the course of 'truth seeking' no holds are barred in following the logic of selection from the available repertoire of theories and paradigms. In this paper I propose to extend and build on the theoretical exercise I began in 1977. I shall confine my illustrations to the Maoist movement in India.

THEORETICAL ORIENTATION[3]

Three essentials without which social movements cannot be conceptualized are social conflict, social or collective mobilization and social change, *in their interrelation*. None of these singly constitute social movement. Collective mobilization in the face of sudden natural disaster, or for the Pulse Polio campaign, or for combating AIDS, by itself does not qualify as a social movement. If it leads to collective mobilizations against perpetrators of environmental degradation, or against those who in the medical profession/general public practice unwarranted discrimination against AIDS victims, then such mobilizations link up with conflict and change.

The central concern in the study of movements, as Gusfield long back observed, is 'its relation to the analysis of change and social conflict' (1970: 8). This leads us to question: do revolts, rebellions and revolutions fall outside the pale of social movements, as Tilly, based on his Western historical experience seems to contend explicitly?[4]

I argue that this can be answered if we regard social movement as the *generic*, and the other forms of socially mobilized social conflicts as the *species* type. This would unfold a complex variety of social movements and conflicts that would tend to dilute analytical precision.

To counter this it is important to interrelate social movement, conflict and change within a single dynamic framework that can capture structure, change process and change. In our framework, social movement, when it has to do with social change, includes resistance to change.

The first step is to classify the variety of social changes. Since social movements are inevitably related to social conflict and to social change (either change promoting or resisting), classification of social change is primary to an understanding of social movements. Only then will we be able to relate social movements with the changes they *intend* to address and the nature of conflicts involved.

This requires some notion of a social system that is structured in terms of *interrelated*[5] and *interpenetrating* 'parts' (structures), such that changes in any one or more of these will have likely consequences for one or more or all of the others. Both Marxist and non-Marxist theoretical approaches that sport a preference for a structural understanding of society, either in the functional or dialectical frame, entertain some notion of 'social system'. What distinguishes various approaches to this conceptualization lies in how the structures are conceived and in what manner of relationships they are constitutive of the system. In the broadest sense, a social system is a system of social interaction of its 'parts' (or structures). Lastly, any social system is an abstraction relative to a *system referent* (family, caste, bureaucracy, party, society, country, international, global, and so on).

Social conflicts, as they are understood here, are overt manifestations of collective behaviour, rather than as potentials for action and to subjective states. They refer to conflicts 'in which the parties are an aggregate of individuals, such as groups, organizations, communities and crowds, rather than single individuals, as in role conflict.... [S]ocial conflict encompasses a broad range of phenomena: class, racial, religious, and communal conflicts; riots, rebellions, revolutions, strikes and civil disorders; marches, demonstrations, protest gatherings, and the like' (Oberschall 1973: 291). While there can be no social conflict in the absence of any relations of antagonism, it is equally true that the mere presence of social antagonism does not trigger a social conflict. Manifestation of social conflict is 'contingent upon to what extent and in what manner a given society is structured, permitting or inhibiting the articulation or expression of dissent or antagonisms and their resolution or neutralization through institutional means' (Mukherji 1986: 26). Many studies of social conflict start with a typology 'based on the forms it takes and the ultimate outcome, e.g. revolution, rebellion, riot, *coup d'etat*, or guerilla war, or classification based on the social categories of the participants and social institutions primarily affected, e.g. peasant rebellion, political conflict or economic conflict' (Oberschall 1973: 32; emphasis added). The general applicability of such typological efforts being less than satisfactory, their analytical utility is diminished.

Like social conflict, social change too admits of a wide array of phenomena from attitude changes to pattern variables to notions of development, progress, evolution, revolution, and the like. The inadequacy of classifications of conflict and change, unrelated to each other, is of limited salience. Precisely for this reason, I am arguing for classifying social change in relation to social movement and conflict.

Paradoxically, it is from the classical, conservative, functional perspective that Talcott Parsons makes the crucial classificatory distinction 'between kinds of change . . . in his analysis of change *within* and change *of* the system . . .' (Strasser and Randall 1981: 12). Two clarifications are crucial before I propose the classificatory scheme. First, social conflicts are not a necessary condition for social change. Social changes can and do occur independent of social conflicts, for example, through changes in technology, demography, environment and such other factors, or even as a consequence of natural disasters. Second, social changes occurring independent of social movements, in fact, may provide the objective conditions for the maturation of social conflicts and movements.

Social changes can now be classified in terms of:

- Changes occurring *within* a given social system;
- Changes occurring on account of the *emergence* of additional structures;
- Changes occurring due to the *elimination* or *loss* of structure/s;
- Changes occurring as a result of *replacement* of existing structure/s by alternative structure/s (Mukherji 1977 and 1986).

Social movements, in this framework, cover the entire gamut of social mobilizations that characterize Tilly's conceptualization of social movements; or movements that fall within the categories 'old' and 'new'; even revolutionary movements that do or do not employ violence. *Only when social/collective mobilizations emanate from sources of perceived, real or imagined, antagonistic relationships embedded in the contradictions within the social system would they qualify as social movements.* Contradiction and conflict are the key concepts in this scheme of analysis. Classification of social movements provides an analytical tool by which we can distinguish between the generic and the species types. Table 5.1 provides a classificatory schema in which classification of social movement follows the logic of types of social change.

Quasi-structural social movements operate *within* the social system. The changes sought to be brought about are accumulative and incremental, seeking to improve the capacity and efficient functioning

TABLE 5.1: CLASSIFICATION OF SOCIAL CHANGE, CONFLICT AND MOVEMENT

Description of change	Type of change	Type of conflict	Type of movement
Changes occurring within a given system	Quasi-structural/ Accumulative/ Intra-systemic	Intra-systemic	Quasi-structural social movement (e.g., role of pressure and interest groups, grievance redressal, etc.)
Changes occurring from emergence of additional structure/s			Structural-alternative social movement (e.g., introduction of wage labour in a feudal area with only attached labour; abolition of sharecropping).
Changes occurring due to elimination or loss of structure/s	Structural/ Alterative/ Systematic		
Changes occurring as a result of replacement of existing structure/s by alternative structure/s	Structural/ Transformative/ Systemic	Systemic	Structural-transformatory/ revolutionary social movement (e.g., replacement of state ownership of property by private ownership; the Maoist movement.)

Source: Adapted and revised from Mukherji (1987: 1608).

of the social system through pressure group demands and grievance redressal. Social movements in this category help in the gradual evolution of the social system. Tilly's conceptualization of social movements does not go very much beyond this threshold. Over a long stretch of time such accumulative changes may lead to structural changes.

Social movements that seek to or are instrumental in bringing about *alterative* changes in the social system, by *creation* of additional structure/s or *elimination* of structure/s are *structural-alterative* social movements. The addition or elimination of structure/s in some way alters the social system. For example, a feudal agrarian system based almost entirely on a landlord-tenant-attached labour undergoes *alterative* changes as wage labour becomes another structural component of the system. Or when sharecropping tenancy gets eliminated and a basically landowner-wage labour agrarian system emerges.

Structural-transformative social movements occur when replacement of one or more or all structures takes place bringing about transformative changes in the system. Consider replacement of private ownership by state ownership. It is a far-reaching transformatory change. Carried to its logical end, when all or most of the major institutions of society are replaced by *alternative*[6] structures, we are witnessing a *revolutionary social movement.*

While classification provides for much-needed conceptual clarification, it is not a substitute for a theoretical orientation, which should enable a better comprehension of the dynamic of social movements, and possibly generate meaningful hypotheses. With this in view, I have tried to factor in the *means employed to achieve movement ends*, namely, the notion of praxis, to introduce an element of the 'dynamic' in the model. Thus, *institutionalized* or *non-institutionalized* means or a combination of both can be employed as *short-term tactics* or *long-term strategies* by movements (see Table 5.2).

A few conceptual clarifications are important. Institutional means refer to the repertoire of forms of collective actions legitimated by the state for voicing dissent, seeking redressal of grievances, bargaining for better deals in the competition for power and scarce resources, and the like. Social mobilizations in antagonistic relations with others, *per se*, do not pose a threat to the social system. The rules of the game prevail in the means adopted for the pursuit of legitimate goals. This is the most predominant and pervasive form of social movement.

TABLE 5.2: SOCIAL MOVEMENT, CHANGE AND PRAXIS

Means/praxis	Change promoting/resisting movement	
	Intra-systemic	Systemic
Institutional	Quasi-structural movement, e.g. strikes, lockouts, protest marches for legitimate demands and redressal of grievances. *Stable state* [A]	Quasi-structural tending towards structural-alterative, e.g. Union claims for decision-making powers. *Unstable state* [B']
Non-institutional	Quasi-structural tending towards structural, e.g. peasant revolt for two-third crop share from existing half *Unstable state* [B'']	Tending towards revolutionary movements, e.g. Naxalite movement, Charu Mazumdar underground phase. *Unstable state: Flux.* [C']
Institutional-non-institutional	Quasi-social movement tending towards structural social movement. *Unstable state*, e.g. riots, rebellions, peasant revolts against oppression, exploitation. *Unstable state* [B''']	Situation of flux. Social transformatory and revolutionary movements, e.g. structural changes associated with rebellion, revolution, terrorism, civil disobedience, satyagraha, etc. *Unstable state: Flux.* [C'']

Source: Adapted and revised from Mukherji (1987: 1608).

Non-institutional means are of the opposite kind. Violent or non-violent, they attract the coercive power of the state and of those constituting the ruling elite, particularly when the threat perception to the system crosses permissive limits of tolerance. They pose a threat to the system and consequently to those entrenched in the system. Social movements don't necessarily have to be directed against the state.

It is essential to remember that all social movements *intend* to bring about certain changes in or of the social system, but there is no guarantee of their total or partial fulfilment. On the contrary, they often result in *unintended* consequences as well. Social movements may remain resilient if the contradictions that gave rise to them persist. If these contradictions lose their primacy, either on account of movements having partially or fully achieved their goals or because of some other external factors, the movements either routinize into a party or some organization, or shift goals more relevant to other emerging contradictions, or just fade away. Movement outcomes are a function of the dialectic of social conflict between contending groups.

This dynamic model envisages six types of situations:

- Social movements seeking quasi-structural, accumulative changes through legitimate institutional means. Trade union mobilizations for better emoluments, service conditions, and against perceived victimization would fall in this category [A].
- Social movements seeking systemic changes but through institutionalized means. Trade unions are now demanding a share in the power of decision making, e.g. membership in the board of directors. This is not permitted in the existing system. The demand is potentially destabilizing. If the social movement persists and the authorities are intractable in their stand, the collective mobilization may take recourse to non-institutionalized means. Hence the situation is at a low unstable state [B′]. Trade unions may decide not to pursue the demand beyond a certain point.
- Social movements seeking quasi-structural changes through non-institutionalized means reflect an unstable situation. The threat is not to the system as such and yet the disaffection and alienation of the collective mobilization is sufficiently strong to push it towards adopting non-legitimate means. The agrarian struggle in Bengal in the 1940s with the tenants demanding two-thirds of the crop share, already recommended by the British, led to violent class struggle. The radical slogan of 'land to the tiller' found expression during the course of the movement. Subsequently, this would acquire a revolutionary form under Maoist inspiration in Andhra Pradesh, West Bengal, Bihar and present Chhattisgarh [B″].
- Social movements seeking systemic changes through non-institutionalized means provide a situation of flux that can escalate into transformative or revolutionary movements. The militant underground phase of the Naxalite (Maoist) movement under Charu Mazumdar that spread from West Bengal to Andhra Pradesh and to some other states with lesser intensity is a classic example of such a transition [C′].
- Social movements seeking quasi-structural changes through a combination of institutional and non-institutional means reflects an uncertain situation inasmuch as there is greater persistence

and insistence on change outcomes against resistance. Social movements that employ mass movements along with covert instruments of violence would qualify as an illustration. Again, this would include Maoist parties that have not abjured violence in their ideology, keeping it handy for exceptional circumstances, but actually furthering their cause through mass movements and participation in so-called bourgeois parliamentary democracies [B‴].

- Social movements seeking transformatory and revolutionary social changes clearly target institutions that they aim to replace with alternative institutions by a combination of non-institutional and institutional means. Such movements make use of all variety of available or possible social mobilizations directed towards quasi-structural, structural-alterative demands that cumulate under a more overarching, transformative and revolutionary ideology and mobilization. The Gandhian *sarvodaya–gramdan* movement of the 1960s and the Maoist movement post-1970s are classic illustrations. Nationalist and secessionist nationalist movements too can fall in this category [C″].

The model integrating social movement, conflict and change can now be situated within a broader theoretical perspective. I have already clarified that the notion of social system is analytically more useful if it is shifted out of its functionalist description as *interdependency* of 'parts', to that of a system of asymmetrical *interrelationship* of its 'parts'.

A social system at the macro-societal level can be conceived as constituted of *domains* of social relations of asymmetries. The number of domains a social system can be divided into is the researcher's prerogative, although the major ones drawn from the substantive field of the discipline will carry consensus. I have suggested that we conceive of society being composed of five major domains of asymmetries—discrimination (ethnic), exploitation (class), oppression (power), gender discrimination, and the eco-environmental asymmetry. These are counter-concepts describing a social system. No society (except in utopia) in contemporary times is likely to be free from these domainal asymmetries. These domains are interrelated, interpenetrating and hence, *interfaced*.

Discrimination essentially conveys the context of normatively legitimated relations of asymmetry that are internalized generally from birth through family and childhood socialization. This is the domain of primordial, ascriptive loyalties that provide major cultural anchorages on the basis of language, caste, race, religion, creed, and so on. This is the *ethnic* domain.

Exploitation is best applied in the context of unequal economic exchanges in the normatively defined role of the market, and in the relations of production. This is the *class* domain.

Oppression has to do with the control and exercise of power. It defines the relationship between the dominant and the dominated. It also implies deliberate impediments created to obstruct access to power of the less privileged. This is the *power* domain.

Gender discrimination refers to the iniquitous relationship between male and female in a system of gender relations.

Eco-environmental asymmetry is basically the asymmetry between humankind in its relation of exploitation of nature.

Embedded in each of these asymmetries are contradictions, 'defined as actual or potential oppositions arising out of differences that are socially perceived, sooner or later, and/or ideologically/theoretically constructed, having change/transformation (or resistance to change/transformation) consequences for the social system under reference' (Mukherji 1999: 61). Contradictions can be antagonistic but not always. The presence of antagonistic contradictions does not *ipso facto* give rise to social conflicts nor to social movements. However, a strong social movement is the surest indication of the existence of antagonistic contradiction/s that triggered the movement.

The type of a social movement can be identified in terms of the locus of its *primary contradiction.* Competing/conflicting interests associated with the conflict facilitates the location and identification of the primary contradiction/s. Caste conflicts and movements, for instance, would mean that the primary contradictions lie in the asymmetrical domain of social discrimination. An agrarian conflict will signify the location of primary contradiction in the domain of exploitation. A movement against *sati* is surely centred on the primary contradiction of gender inequity.

In this framework, the primary contradiction is not deterministically fixed in any domain. A social movement arising out of primary contradiction in any one domain may be overtaken, at a subsequent stage, by another in the same or different domain. This is because the domains are interfaced. A strong caste-ethnic movement, with the primary contradiction located in the domain of discrimination, for example, is likely to have interfaces with secondary contradictions within the same domain (say in religious ethnicity) or in the domain of class exploitation, cutting across caste.

I have classified social movements at two different levels of abstraction: (a) with respect to classification of social change and conflict; and (b) at the domainal level of asymmetries of social relationships. By and large, the social space within which social movements have been taking place have had boundaries circumscribed within 'national', 'country', or 'societal' territories. With the advent of technology-driven, time-and-space-compressing-globalization, the space for social movements has also expanded to global proportions. This has given birth to a new species of transnational social movements in response to transnational institutions that operate over and above the nation states. The market liberalizing economic regime that dominates the world has consequences for nation states across the globe. The World Trade Organization (WTO) and the expanded role of the International Monetary Fund (IMF) are global structures that have come about in response to the liberalization of world trade. Summit meetings of the world's largest market players are necessitated to decide on future economic strategies that have consequences for people at the 'local' level in different countries. This has led to structural responses at the global level, namely, transnational activism; International Non-Governmental Organizations (INGO); World Social Forums (WSF) held at intervals; anti-corporatist social movements; and the like.

While this is not the place to go into this vast social terrain that is still unfolding, two points have to be kept in mind. First, globalization as it is impacting on the local has become a new source exacerbating existing contradictions and giving rise to new ones. For example, acquisition of agricultural lands for corporate private industrialization (special economic zones) has generated a contradiction that has led to strong social movements opposing such capitalist penetration. Even with globalization, the operational space for such movements remains largely unaltered—bounded by the 'national', 'societal' or 'country'. The abstraction of domainal asymmetries remains valid. Second, large amorphous transnational social movements that operate at the global scale within a transnational global space, responding to contradictions that have global import, creating, as some suggest, the ground for global civil society, are too complex to fathom at this initial stage of its evolution. Whether the interests opposing economic globalization are truly global concerns (climate change) or still country-specific (subsidy for agriculture) has not yet been firmly established (see Edelman 2001, Nash 2005).

I shall now make a brief attempt to understand Naxalism as a pervasive structural–transformative–revolutionary movement.

NAXALISM: INDIAN MAOISM

Consistent with the theoretical orientation, I have argued that similar goals in different societal contexts may have different implications of their being achieved. A structurally evolved, socially and politically differentiated democratic societal context is more likely to generate and accommodate quasi-structural movements associated with intra-systemic conflicts. The capacity of adaptive changes is higher in such societies with institutionally legitimated groups, representing competing and conflicting interests than ones in which structural elaboration is less developed. In the latter context, the intensity of conflict even for intra-systemic changes can run very high and the scope for structural–alterative–transformative–revolutionary changes is relatively greater.

I will argue that Naxalism or the Mao-inspired social movements for structural–transformative–revolutionary changes that have taken place almost exclusively in remote, backward, mostly tribal, less-communicable areas of the country are the very regions where the responsible role of the democratic state has least penetrated, leaving feudal enclaves to persist and prosper outside the ambit of governance of the state. The demolition of these feudal vestiges may be transformatory with respect to the backward region, but not so for the environment external to it, where feudal structures are getting dismantled through market and other social forces such as farmers movements. By stating this, I will not like to undermine the complexity of the phenomenon nor cling exclusively and narrowly to my theoretical position.

It is impossible to do justice to the immensely complex phenomena of Naxalite politics within the scope of this paper. One cannot be certain how many parties and groups are involved and active in this overarching politics,[7] save and except those that have expanded in their operations of violent class struggles to the point where the national government feels threatened and is compelled to act.[8]

It is the Naxalite formation following the merger of the CPI-ML People's War Group (PWG) with the Maoist Communist Centre

(MCC) in September 2004 that has posed a real threat to the state. Balagopal, one of the most authentic voices of the poor, whose appreciation for the Naxalite achievements is well known, traces the passage of the PWG movement (later known as, CPI-Maoist) through several phases. In the late 1970s and early 1980s, it was through mass organizations of agricultural labourers, students and youth fronts that the spread of Maoism as ideology and political practice was initiated. In the *second* phase, the achievement of a heightened awareness of 'attainability of justice was [itself] a fundamental change' in the psyche of the exploited and oppressed tribal population, but it was accompanied by a gradual, barely perceptible, dependence of the people on armed squads. Consequently, 'oppressors of local society, whether upper caste landlords or insensitive public officials, started dreading the wrath, initially of the awakened masses, and later of well-armed squads composed of cadre born and brought up in poor families of the very same villages'. In the *third* phase, old landlords were gone, but new local elites had emerged, instilling the fear among the poor that without the Naxalites they would face a survival threat (Balagopal 2006: 3183). Apparently, the dependence on the Naxalite armed squads was now established. The gradual shift from institutionalized to non-institutionalized means for the accomplishment of structural changes in the prevailing feudalistic agrarian system had taken place during this period. The social system was moving from a stable to a less stable state.

The Naxals were 'remarkably successful', observes Balagopal, in eliminating the institution of *begar* or the system of unpaid labour, and were able to enforce 'close to minimum wages for rural labour'. Two 'constitutional tasks' were achieved (ibid.: 3184). On the issue of land, the fight was 'not so successful', as the lands belonging to 'runaway landlords' remained fallow under police protection. However, they were more successful in getting forests cleared over a period of fifteen years in four lakh acres of land making it fit for cultivation. Thereafter, they stopped felling trees in the very interest of the tribals (ibid.: 3184). The elimination of *begar* certainly altered the structural arrangement of the prevailing feudal agrarian system.

The use of violence by Naxals that 'lived by its own norms, which [were] enforceable only by itself', attracted heavy State suppression. Maoists decided to take on the state and began hitting back from onwards of June 1985, killing police personnel. Frequency of encounters with police went on increasing and with it the decapitation of limbs of police informers by Naxals. Special police forces that 'were allowed to operate totally incognito', were formed for the express purpose of eliminating Naxalites (ibid.: 3185). These encounters led the State to craft a new instrument of repression—the 'Greyhounds', 'a well-trained anti-guerrilla force that live[d] and operate[d] as the Naxalite armed squads [did] and [was] bound by no known law, including the Constitution of India' (ibid.: 3185).

By 2000, the PWG 'declared the entire tribal forest region that include[d] Bastar and extend[ed] into Maharashtra and Madhya Pradesh as guerilla zone, i.e. a region where People's War would attempt to prevent state officials and forces from maintaining their rule and create alternative institutions of what it termed 'people's rule' (Fact Finding Report 2006: 11). By creating a guerrilla zone involving three adjacent states, the movement prompted the formulation of 'inter-state joint task force' by the state as a matching counter measure. By the unilateral declaration of the replacement of the authority of the states by that of the authority of the social movement, the Maoist movement got into a structural-revolutionary mode.

The game of establishing military supremacy over the States became an obsession with the text of the ideology, deflecting attention from the context of decreasing involvement of the masses in the decisions that affected their lives and livelihood. The suspicions that breed in secret underground guerrilla operations and the benefit of doubt that is invoked in favour of maintaining secrecy, often result in the ruthless killings of innocent people suspected of being police informers. Party and ideology take precedence over the people for whom the revolution is meant. Balagopal postulates an invariant law of sociology of armed insurgency, '[w]ithout exception, all militant movements have killed more people of their own social base than their purported enemy classes. . . . The very fact that this is true of the Naxalites, the most politically sensitive of all insurgents, is proof enough' (ibid.: 3185). The movement in the course of revolutionizing its praxis, at the same time, set in motion a reversal of the process of its activation of quasi-structural movements, thus weakening its mass base.

Spiraling violence led to peace talks initiated in Andhra Pradesh by the Congress government between July–October 2004. Two fundamental issues led to its failure: (a) the Naxalites maintained that 'the question of carrying arms and conducting armed struggle were non-negotiable', and (b) the state government expressed its inability 'to undertake land reforms on the scale and manner suggested by the Naxalites' (Nayak 2006). Even as the talks were on, Naxalites continued their armed struggle in other states, e.g. landmine blasts in eastern Uttar Pradesh killed 15 policemen (ibid.). Violence escalated exponentially on both sides after the failure of the talks.

With the Greyhounds gaining the upper hand in Andhra Pradesh in the game of spiraling violence and counter-violence, the Maoists concentrated in the neighbouring Dantewada district of Chhattisgarh. The story that unfolds in this adjacent district is very similar to that of northern Telengana and other areas in Andhra Pradesh. A number of ML groups initiated peasant struggles in the 1970s. In the 1980s the Dandakaranya Adivasi Kisan Mazdoor Sangh (DAKMS) was formed. It took up: (a) issues relating to oppression and exploitation by 'outsiders', primarily by personnel of the forest and revenue departments, the police and moneylenders; and (b) the *patta* issue of vesting ownership rights on forest lands brought under cultivation. The DAKMS 'deployed methods of chasing away forest and revenue officials from villages and attacking forest posts' (Fact Finding Report 2006: 11). Later, in the 1980s, 'internal contradictions in the adivasi society started being addressed. Portions of land under control of a few families of large landholdings, mostly village headmen and *sarpanches*, were expropriated and distributed among the landless. Grains also were distributed likewise (ibid.: 11). Forcible seizure of cultivable land from landowners and their distribution amongst the landless clearly indicates the use of non-institutionalized violence for 'illegal' appropriation and distribution of land, made possible by an alternative structure of authority in defiance of the existing legitimate authority.

This was followed by the creation of *sanghams*, with the ultimate objective of replacing the existing traditional structures of authority at the village level. They articulated village issues and settled disputes (ibid.). Later still, they fixed the prices of forest produce, notably, that of *tendu* leaves; prevented *sarpanches*/headmen from misusing government funds; mobilized labour for creating irrigation facilities; created seed banks; maintained land records of all cultivated lands; encouraged afforestation (ibid.). By the time the new State of Chhattisgarh was created, 'the CPI(ML) had created substantial bases in the forest areas of Bastar, Kanker and Dantewada' (ibid.). It was in 2000 that the area was declared a guerrilla zone. The *sangham* was an additional structure introduced within the social system to replace the traditional structure and authority of the headmen/ *sarpanches.* It helped activate a number of quasi-movements to bring about intra-systemic changes with mass participation.

Soon after the *sanghams* were established, in July–August 1990, the headman of village Badre near Kutru was killed. The retaliatory attacks against Maoist sympathizers sowed the seeds of the Jan Jagran Abhiyan, which later got transformed into Salwa Judum (May–June 2005), a counter mobilization of the local people, with armed support of the State, against the Maoists and the *sanghams.* The leadership was taken up by a tribal, Mahendra Karma, earlier of the CPI, later of the Congress party. With political support from parties like the Bharatiya Janata Party (BJP) in Madhya Pradesh, the Abhiyan and the Maoists had alternating successes. The landownership issue, unlike in Andhra Pradesh, became a highly 'contentious issue in enormously differentiated villages' (ibid.: 13). The escalating retaliatory violence after the formation of Salwa Judum, from both the ends of the pole resulted in huge loss of lives and in mass dislocation of population, with nearly 50,000 people driven into makeshift camps after forced or fearful desertion from their villages. The declaration of a sovereign guerrilla zone followed by increased violence for the elimination of headmen and sarpanches was a direct assault on the sovereignty of the state and its legal and constitutional obligations. The ensuing contestation between usurped authority of the movement and established authority of the state has resulted in a full-scale war-like condition in which democratic space of the affected people has shrunk to zero; who now find themselves disenfranchised having been displaced from their homes and properties and reduced to the status of refugees.

The declaration of the forest strongholds as guerrilla zones by the Maoist movement, the creation of a sovereign space within which a new people's democracy was sought to be established and governed, under the revolutionary authority of a few hard core doctrinaire leaders, sounds ominously problematic. Balagopal perceptively observes, 'the real challenge for the Maoists is not whether they can militarily get the better of the greyhounds, who have a clear upper hand at present, but whether they can retain active support from one generation to the next while retaining the Maoist strategy . . .' (2006: 3186).

The Maoist ideology recognizes the contradictions of gender, caste, religion and so on, but only as subsidiary and subject to the deterministic dialectic in which the primary contradiction is fixed in the domain of exploitation. While in theory the whole array of quasi-structural, structural-alterative, structural-transformative mobilizations of the proponents of the movement are regarded as important for building a mass base, in practice, this has at best been limited to the initial stages of the movement. The propensity for militarization of the conflict carries within its womb the seed of its own denouement, as the mass base erodes; the people become fearful and suspicious of gun-toting squads who tend to turn extortionist. The romantic notion of a people's democracy, a construction of the party elite, is thrust upon an unsuspecting people who find their culture and customs denigrated for their alleged obscurantism.

In the end, I will raise some questions. What do we make of the growing spread of the Maoist movement? Given its ideological anchorage in anti-feudal contradictions, a dedicated, ideologically committed party or group will find objective conditions ripe for its role in the most backward, isolated, feudal enclaves, where not only the states have failed to extend their governance, even Left parties in electoral politics are conspicuous by their absence. Given their romanticized vision of capturing national state power through the barrel of AK 47s, rocket launchers, landmines combining guerrilla warfare tactics, it is anybody's guess what progress they can achieve beyond forest covers and simple, illiterate, uneducated tribal masses. Besides, no matter how much good a militant movement does to people, violence begets state violence. As long as State violence is able to establish its superiority over movement violence, its success is doubtful. In this respect the conditions in India and Nepal are oceans apart. This has been demonstrated since the Naxalbari peasant mobilization and the phase of annihilation of class enemies during the Charu Mazumdar regime.

Are there any unintended consequences of such militarized Maoist movements? Yes. First, it dismantles the feudal structures. Then by overstretching their claims for guerrilla zones, they attract disproportionate involvement of the state in establishing their superiority in quelling the rebellion. This is followed by high inputs of 'development' from the government for creation of employment, improvement in productivity, building roads and bridges, developing markets, and so on. With the feudal structures dismantled, the development process may become more effective.

The second unintended consequence is that the state is able to gain in experience in controlling such situations more effectively in the future. For example, in Andhra Pradesh, the state was able to create an anti-guerrilla greyhound force that is already being prescribed for places other than Andhra Pradesh. The experience in Chhattisgarh has contributed to the formulation of the Salwa Judum. Although this has attracted widespread condemnation, the repertoire of counter-guerrilla actions is increasing.

Are such movements vulnerable to internal contradictions? Generally yes. Firstly, there is the fallacy that the primary contradiction is fixed in the domain of economic exploitation or class. This tends to assign secondary importance to the domains of discrimination, oppression and gender bias. The top leadership is reluctant to loosen its grip over the movement organization. Secondly, the logic of instruments of violence is itself alienating for the common people.

There are so many other questions, but there has to be an end.

NOTES

1. Rajendra Singh in his book on social movements is in close agreement with Tilly on this point. He observes, '[u]nlike movements, however, riot and rebellion necessarily involve violence. Revolution is necessarily violent and unlike movement, riot and rebellion, it involves all sections of society living in its territory' (2001: 36). Non-violent revolution in his scheme is axiomatically out, and so is it from Tilly's framework. Besides, while revolution involves mobilization of *all* sections of population, social movements involve only *a* section. The scope of social movements, therefore, is limited to seeking 'redressal of a grievance or to struggle for specific goals and objectives' (ibid.: 36).
2. A theoretical orientation as distinguished from theory is 'the set of ideas, assumptions and methodological approaches that serve to guide or orientate the researcher in his examination of substantive issues . . . it does not in itself form a consistent system of interrelated propositions which are capable of being tested empirically, although it may facilitate the formulation of such hypotheses or theories' (Long 1977: 4).
3. I have drawn liberally from my following articles: (1) 'Social Movement and Social Change: Towards a Conceptual Clarification and Theoretical Framework' (1977); (2) 'Social Conflict and Social Change: Towards a Theoretical Orientation' (1986); (3) 'Study of Social Conflicts: Case of Naxalbari Peasant Movement' (1987); (4) 'Nation-State Reformulated: Interrogating Received Wisdom' (1999). This paper has gone beyond the earlier ones in stating my present position.

4. Rajendra Singh tows the same line. Disagreeing with Smelser he emphatically states: 'Social movements may lead to or transform itself into revolution. When it does transform itself into revolution, it ceases to be a movement.' The reason he gives sounds arbitrary rather than convincing. He assigns to social movements the limited role of struggle for grievance redressal and pursuit of 'specific goals and objectives'. Violent methods are not for social movements (2001: 36).
5. My preference for 'interrelatedness' (rather than 'interdependence') between the 'parts' in a social system is prompted by the fact that a social system may be constituted of dominant, dependent and independent structures. Such a system can accommodate antagonistic and non-antagonistic relations of competition, conflict and cooperation. It permits the presence of structural asymmetries that embed antagonistic or non-antagonistic contradictions. In contrast, 'interdependence' implies mutuality of dependence.
6. It has been my singular misfortune that in some of my earlier publications the term 'alterative' has been printed as 'alternative' creating confusion most confounded. This has been one instance of the printer's devil that has wrought great damage to the author.
7. Manoranjan Mohanty identifies three streams of Naxalites since 1977: (1) CPI-ML Liberation which is the first breakaway faction from the original CPI-ML founded by Charu Mazumdar. It was led by Satya Narayan Sinha, a member of the first Polit Bureau when the party was formed in 1969. After his death the leadership was with Vinod Mishra, who in turn, was succeeded by Dipankar Bhattacharya. The party focuses on mass movements and organizations, and participates in electoral politics. (2) The Communist Organization of India-ML (COI-ML), led by the legendary Kanu Sanyal, who was the architect of the peasant revolt in Naxalbari, under the leadership of Charu Mazumdar. The party is engaged in consolidating the Naxal parties and groups that believe in creating mass organizations, and participates in electoral politics. (3) CPI-ML People's War Group (PWG) founded by Kondapalli Sitharamayya, followed the Charu Mazumdar line of rejecting parliamentary politics and eventual seizure of state power through a people's liberation guerrilla army. Based in the backward tribal region of north Telengana in Andhra Pradesh, it merged with CPI-ML Party Unity of Bihar in 1996 to extend its territorial reach. In September 2004, it merged with the Maoist Communist Centre (MCC), which had emerged as a parallel organization to the CPI-ML led by Charu Mazumdar and was strong in Bihar and Jharkhand. In 2004, the armed wing of the PWG merged with that of the MCC, forming the People's Liberation Guerilla Army (PLGA), having as many as 3,500 trained fighters who can handle sophisticated arms like AK-47, rocket launchers, grenades, and landmines. Ganapathy ousted Sitharamayya from power. It will be obvious that it is this last combine, rechristened, the

CPI-Maoist, that has instilled the fear of the devil in the state, with its operations strongly felt in Andhra Pradesh, Chhattisgarh, Bihar and Jharkhand (Mohanty 2006: 3165–7).

8. On 19 September 2005 the Union Home Ministry in a meeting in New Delhi, attended by chief ministers, home secretaries, director-generals of police and other senior officials from 12 Naxalite affected states, decided to set up inter-state joint task forces to 'facilitate coordinated and synergized anti-naxalite operations across State boundaries' and 'strengthen intelligence networks' for this mission. This was described as a historic decision without precedence in countering Naxalite threat (Ramakrishnan 2005).

   On 13 April 2006 Prime Minister Manmohan Singh addressed the chief ministers of six states outlining the factors contributing to the growth of Naxalism: 'exploitation, artificially depressed wages, iniquitous socio-political circumstances, inadequate employment opportunities, lack of access to resources, underdeveloped agriculture, geographical isolation and lack of land reforms' (Gupta 2008).

REFERENCES

Balagopal, K. (2006), 'Maoist Movement in Andhra Pradesh', *Economic and Political Weekly*, 41(29), 22 July, pp. 3183–7.

Edelman, Marc (2001), 'Social Movements: Changing Paradigms and Forms of Politics', *Annual Review of Anthropology*, available at arjournals.annualreviews.org. Site accessed on 21 January 2008, pp. 285–317.

Gupta, Tilak D. (2006), 'Maoism in India: Ideology, Programme and Armed Struggle', *Economic and Political Weekly*, 41(29), 22 July, pp. 3172–6.

Gusfield, J.R (1970), *Protest, Reform and Revolt*, New York: John Wiley and Sons Inc.

Long, Norman (1977), *An Introduction to the Sociology of Rural Development*, London: Tavistock Publications.

Mohanty, Manoranjan (2006), 'Challenges of Revolutionary Violence: The Naxalite Movement in Perspective', *Economic and Political Weekly*, 41(29), 22 July, pp. 3163–8

Mukherji, Partha N. (1977), 'Social Movement and Social Change: Towards a Conceptual Clarification and Theoretical Framework', *Sociological Bulletin*, 26(1), March, pp. 38–59.

——— (1986), 'Social Conflict and Social Change: Towards a Theoretical Orientation', in Urmila Phadnis, S.D. Muni and Kalim Bahadur (eds.), *Domestic Conflicts in South Asia*, Vol. 1: *Political Dimensions*, New Delhi: South Asian Publishers, pp. 24–53.

——— (1987), 'Study of Social Conflicts: Case of Naxalbari Peasant

Movement', *Economic and Political Weekly*, 22(38), 19 September, pp. 1607–17.

——— (1999), 'Nation-State Reformulated: Interrogating Received Wisdom', *Man and Development*, 21(4), December, pp. 51–68.

Nash, June (2005), 'Introduction: Social Movements and Global Processes', in June Nash (ed.), *Social Movements: An Anthropological Reader*, Malden: Blackwell Publishing, pp. 1–26.

Nayak, Nihar (2006), 'Naxalite Movement in Bihar: A Domino Effect of Nepal'?, Society for the Study of Peace and Conflict, Article No. 94, 24 November. Available at http://www.sspconline.org/article_details.asp?artid=art104 [site accessed on 11 January 2008]

Oberschall, A. (1973), *Social Conflict and Social Movement*, Englewood Cliffs N.J.: Prentice Hall Inc.

People's Union for Civil Liberties (PUCL) (2006), *Fact Finding Report: Where the State Makes War on its Own People: A Report on the Violation of People's Rights during the Salva Judum Campaign in Dantewada*, Chhattisgarh, April (no mention of place of publication).

Ramakrishnan, Venkitaesh (2005), 'The Naxalite Challenge', *Frontline*, 22(21), 8–21 October, http://www.flonnet.com/fl2221/stories/20051021006700400.htm [site visited 1 May 2008]

Strasser, H. and Susan C. Randall (1981), *An Introduction to Theories of Social Change*, London: Routledge and Kegan Paul.

Singh, Rajendra (2001), *Social Movements Old and New: A Post-modernist Critique*, New Delhi: Sage.

Tilly, Charles (2006), *Regimes and Repertoires*, Chicago: University of Chicago Press.

Wallerstein, Immanuel (2002), 'New Revolts Against the System', *New Left Review*, 18, November–December, pp. 29–39.

CHAPTER 6

Changing Trajectory of Social Movements in India: Towards a Holistic Analytical Perspective

DEBAL K. SINGHAROY

The processes of social mobility, collective mobilization and social movements are important constituents of social progression with important continuities and connectedness. At times, one of these processes becomes the extension of another or paves the way for the emergence of another as the reflective continuum of social progression. In the context of globalization and increasing socio-cultural dis-embeddedness, rural societies in India have been introduced to new processes of social mobility and segregation, exclusion and domination, articulations of new interests and identities, conflicts and resistance and manifestation of new forms of collective mobilization and social movements at the grassroots which were hitherto unknown to these societies. As against this backdrop the present paper aims to examine the emerging facets of these processes; their implications for social mobility, collective mobilization and social movements in rural India; and the adequacies and inadequacies of the prevailing theoretical perspectives in explaining the emerging intertwining among them. This paper is presented in four sections. In the first section of the paper dominant theoretical perspectives relating to social mobility, conflicts, collective mobilization and social movement are discussed. Section two discusses the major facets of socio-economic transformation in contemporary India and in section three implications of these transformations for the emerging intertwining among social mobility, conflicts, collective mobilization and social movement are delineated. In section four the scope and limitations of applicability of prevalent theories in examining the contemporary Indian scenario are analysed and a resilient-holistic perspective is evolved to explain the emerging intertwining among social mobility, conflicts, collective mobilization and social movements.

SOCIAL MOBILITY, CONFLICTS, COLLECTIVE MOBILIZATION AND SOCIAL MOVEMENT: THEORETICAL INTERTWINING

In social science, a vast body of literature has emerged in theorizing social mobility, social conflicts, collective mobilization and social movements. Significantly many of these literatures have delineated the underlying linkages among these processes.

Social mobility as an inevitable process of social progression has always attracted the attention of sociologists. It is intrinsically related to social inequality, stratification and to the culture of resistance in a society. Indeed, there has scarcely been a society whose strata were absolutely closed, or in which vertical economic, political and occupational mobility was not present and that 'there has never existed a society in which vertical social mobility has been absolutely free and the transition from one social stratum to another has had no resistance' (Sorokin 1959).

Karl Marx visualized social mobility in terms of class mobility and class struggles through historical epoch whereby 'the history of hitherto existing society has been the history of class struggles' and that 'each time the struggles ended either in a revolutionary re-constitution of society at large, or in the common ruin of the contending classes'. To him the historical epoch of the modern capitalist era, has been characterized by absolute concentration of the means of production and upward mobility of the class of bourgeoisie (i.e. capitalists, owners of the social means of production and employers of the wage labour) through the modern developmental processes (extension of market, navigation, rail and road communication, industry) and exploitation of the proletariat (i.e. modern wage earners, who having no means of production of their own, are reduced to sell their labour power in order to live). In this era the proletariats are sharply downwardly mobilized and sell themselves piecemeal as a commodity, like every other article of commerce, and are

> consequently exposed to all vicissitudes of competition, to all fluctuations of market. . . . With the development of industry the proletariat increases in greater number by recruiting members from lower middle class, small

manufacturers, shopkeepers, artisans, peasants and lowest layers of the society. The modern labourers instead of rising with the progress of industry sink deeper and deeper below the condition of existence of his own class. He becomes a pauper and pauperism develops more rapidly than population and wealth.

The increasing quantum of downward mobility and pauperization contributes to intensify class struggle. For Marx, the proletariats bring a halt to their pauperization through a violent struggle and revolutionary change in the society (Marx 1847, rpt. 1972: 118–27).

Mobility however can be smooth, according to some experts, if it is institutionalized.

It is observed that in societies in which upward social mobility is institutionalized, in which achieved rather than ascribed status dominates; hostility between various strata is mingled with a strong positive attraction to those higher in the social hierarchy, who provide some models of behaviour. . . . It is (however) also true that the structure of the system is maintained partly by these reciprocal antagonisms which preserve gradations of status. Nevertheless, members of the lower strata often emulate the higher, and aspire to membership in higher strata. (Coser 1956: 36)

With the expansion of education and occupational diversification in contemporary world there have been phenomenal changes in the pattern and quantum of social mobility. Today in the post-industrial society, no social stratum, group, or class can remain completely stable for more than one generation. By developing a critique of Marxian analysis of social mobility, Dahrendorf (1959) points out that institutionalization of social mobility through both the educational and the occupational systems contradicts quite clearly the prediction of a continuous increase in the intensity of class conflict. To him,

social mobility has become one of the crucial elements in the structure of industrial societies; and one would be tempted to predict its 'breakdown' if the process of mobility were ever seriously impeded. . . . Social mobility, which, for Marx, was the exception that confirmed the rule of class closure, is built into the structure of post-capitalists society and has therefore become a factor to be reckoned with in all analyses of conflict and change. In post-capitalist societies there is a great deal of movement, upward and downwards as well as on social level, between generations as well as within them, so that the individual who stays at his place of birth and in the occupation of his father throughout life has become a rare exception. (Dahrendorf 1959: 56–9).

With the changes in society, from ascription to achievement orientation, the structure of stratification system is undergoing changes. In the process of such transition 'if ascriptive values are institutionalized, mobility tends to be collective; if achievement values are institutionalized, mobility tends to be individual'. Though the rate of upward mobility is closely related to the type of economic system and dependent in large part on continued economic expansion and the occupational shifts that accompany it, it would be hazardous to posit a simple continuation of the recent trends given the uncertain prospects of the nation's and the world's continued economic growth (Smelser 1962: 91).

Social conflict, very often than not, is closely embedded with occupational mobility and economic growth. Conflict theorists, while analysing social stratification, delineate that social groups are unequally posited in the society in terms of their uneven access to or control over economic, social or political resources; that social groups indulge in conflict for the optimization of their access or control over resources. It is generalized that 'men have an instinct for herding together and fighting with other herds. This instinct underlines the formation of all the divisions and subdivisions that arise within a given society and occasion for moral and physical conflicts' (Mosca 1939). Hence to many social scientists conflict has positive contribution in social life and it is considered to be one of the most vivid social interactions and 'a part of sociation—a particular pattern of interaction through which human beings relate to each other. Thus conflict is expected to resolve divergent dualisms; and it is perceived to be a potential way of achieving some kind of unity and resolving the tension between contrasts' (Simmel 1946, cf. Wolff 1950).

Conflict is also a potential resource to human beings who are 'sociable but conflict prone animals. There is conflict because violent coercion is always a potential resource in pursuing one's own interests. These are very explicit in situations where power is involved and interests are inherently antagonistic' (Collins 1974) and groups are hierarchically arranged. It is also illuminated through historical evidences that 'in every type of social structure there are occasions for conflict, since individuals and subgroups are likely to make from time to time rival claims to scarce resources, prestige or power positions'. However the safeguard against conflict disrupting the consensual basis of relationship is contained in the social structure itself:

It is provided by institutionalization and tolerance of social conflict . . . conflict tends to be dysfunctional for a social structure in which there is no or insufficient toleration and institutionalization of conflict. What threatens the equilibrium of such a structure is not the conflict as such, but the rigidity itself, which permits hostilities to accumulate and to be channeled along one major line of cleavage, once they break out in conflict. (Coser 1956: 151–7)

In his materialistic interpretation of history Karl Marx (1976 rpt.) underlines social inequality in terms of class inequality based on unequal control of the means of production. To Marx consciousness is the mediating factor for social conflict and is a part of development in human society. 'But it is not the consciousness of men that determines their existence but on the contrary their material condition of existence that determines this consciousness' (Marx 1976: 504). Marx indeed has privileged economy over other forces as the determining factor to social division and social conflict.

Social bases of conflict however have acquired different dimensions in post-industrial societies. The processes of democratic decision-making, institutionalization of social mobility, relative deprivation and comparative gratification and dissociation between industry and the state have intensified conflicts in the post-industrial societies based on unequal distribution of authority. Social classes and class conflicts are present in these societies based on the issues of unequal distributions of authorities over social positions. Moreover,

Class division based on unequal distribution of authority in the post-industrial society is qualitatively sharper than the material based class division in the capitalist society since the unequal distribution of authority is absolute, while the unequal distribution of material resources is relative. The process of decomposition of capital and labour by the separation of ownership and control has produced new forms of social differentiation in the advanced industrial society and new forms of conflict and mobilization. (Dahrendorf 1959: 241–8)

Collective mobilization is an induced process of social progression. It involves a process of shaking, organizing, rejuvenating, and activating collective resources to attain a collectively defined goal. It is essentially attitudinal—a commitment to action, and a means of translating commitment into action or observed behaviour (Nettl 1967: 32). It calls for the 'induction of new structure into the system to meet the new challenges. That is mobilization necessitates the creation of new institutions and their institutionalization'. Thus mobilization is a continuous process with a varying scale and intensity over a period of time. Oommen (1984) points out that the processes of mobilization and institutionalization do co-exist and that 'institutionalization provides new possibilities of mobilization' (Oommen 1984: 238). It alters the power relations in the society by way of challenging the pre-existing power structure and generating new societal identities. It is thus considered an important component of social movements.

Social movements are broader processes than those of social mobility, conflict and mobilization. They depict holistic aspects of society. 'Social movements lie permanently at the heart of the social life. They are not a marginal rejection of order; they are the central forces fighting one against the other to control the production of society by itself and the action of classes for the shaping of historicity' (Touraine 1981: 29). Social movements are 'a sign. They are prophets of the present. They announce the commencement of change; not, however, a change in the distant future but one that is already a presence'. However, 'the notion of movement itself, which originally stood for an autonomy from the political system, has now been rendered inadequate as a description as there have emerged diverse, and at time defused, forms of collective action' (Melucci 1996: 9). Large varieties of collective initiatives, actions and interventions are described as social movements.

> Each movement shares some features in common with other movements, without any features being sufficiently inclusive and sufficiently exclusive to demarcate and identify the set. What all movements share in common they tend to share with things other than movements and yet those characteristics which are unique to some are not shared by all. Even within the same movement we find diversity, and all movement change. Furthermore we cannot define the term of our definition, other than arbitrarily, because collective, protest and other such terms like social movement itself belong to our everyday language and derive meaning from their diverse uses in specific contexts. (Crossley 2002: 2)

In social science a vast body of literature has emerged in the area of social movements with distinctive intellectual perspectives and theoretical traditions. One is to bear in mind that social movements are conceptualized in a given context of space and time. For decades the area of social movements' studies was relegated to the margin by the dominant Functionalist and Marxist schools of thoughts. The

Marxist social scientists have reduced all varieties of collective mobilizations and social movements to class conflicts as to them social classes are the sole agents of social transformation. The functionalist on the other hand considered social movements as the potential agency of disruptions to the social order. For example, in America, Haberle (1951) conceptualized social movements as the potentially dangerous forms of non-institutionalized collective political behaviour that threaten the stability of the established social order. Similarly the scholars of collective behaviour perspective, especially Turner and Killian (1957), Parsons (1969), Smelser (1962), and others viewed social movement as non-institutionalized collective actions, which are not guided by existing social norms, formed to meet undefined or unstructured situations and are understood in terms of a breakdown either in the organs of social control or normative integration, due to structural changes (Cohen 1985: 71–2, cf. Jamison and Eyreman 1991: 14). However, in symbolic interactionists like Blumer have identified the desire for new life in social movements (Blumer 1951: 99).

Social movement studies have entered into a new trajectory of theorization with the resource mobilization theorists using the dimensions of entrepreneurship, cost and benefit in the analysis of social movements since the early 1970s. They study social movements as a political process of institutionalized protest or collective actions to get the share of political power by using various resources. Charles Tilly (1985) explained the occurrences of the popular protest in terms of the emerging the 'political opportunities' caused by the involvement of the state with the welfare activities and the increasing importance of parliamentary politics that accommodated collective mobilization and gave legitimacy to petitions, demonstrations, strikes, mass meetings, and so on as democratic process. He has explained the occurrences of collective action in terms of the pursuit of common interest and the rationality of human action, whereby the participants in the social movement calculate the costs and benefits of their participatory action in collective mobilization. Similar view has also been furthered to show that social movements are manifested when the required resources are pumped into it by the rich for their benefits (Jenkins and Perrow 1977), and that social movements generate a 'demand' similar to an economic demand, to which 'political entrepreneurs' respond by forming a counter-movement as business (McCarthy and Zald 1977). Hence the social movements compete for resources within a broader movement industry and struggle for resources against the demands of the public, private and third sectors.

In recent years a shift is marked in resource mobilization theory to describe the emergence of social movements in terms of expanding political opportunities through indigenous organizational strength on the one hand and cognitive liberation on the other. It states that these cognitions 'are overwhelmingly not based upon observation or empirical evidence available to participants, but rather upon cuings among groups of people who jointly create the meanings' (McAdam 1982). In this context the dimensions of 'framing and contentious politics' have emerged to be important issues in social movement analysis. According to Tarrow (1995) 'movement organizations draw people into collective action through known repertoires of contention and by creating innovations around their margins. The organizers exploit political opportunities, create new collective identities, bring people together in organizations and mobilize them against more powerful opponents . . .' (Tarrow 1995: 3). Thus social movements construct meaning through interpretative schemata that signifies and condenses the 'world out there' by 'selectively punctuating and encoding objects, situations, events, experiences, and sequences of actions within one's present and past environment' (David Snow and Robert Benford 1992). The movement entrepreneurs are also 'effectively engaged in "naming" grievances, connecting them to other grievances and constructing larger frames of meaning that will resonate with population's cultural predispositions and communicate a uniform message to power holders and others' (A. Marris and C. McClurg Mueller 1992: 136–7).

However, the resource mobilization theory has emerged to be very limited in its scope and analysis. Many scholars find it is simplistic, rigid and static (Goodwin and Jasper 1999; McAdam 1999; McAdam, Tarrow and Tilly 2001). To these scholars the resource mobilization interpretation observes social structure as fixed entities through which political opportunities are drawn. Indeed 'there may be no such things as objective political opportunities before or beneath interpretation or at least none that matter; they are all interpreted through cultural filters' (Goodin and Jasper 1999: 33). Hence to overcome the structural bias or structural determinism, McAdam (1999) suggests to combine the structuralist, culturalist and rationalist tenets with the forms of contention to develop a complete understanding of the origins of movements (McAdam 1999: xxxvii). Thus many scholars highlight the need of developing models of analysis that recognize identity as relational, contingent and socially constructed, as opposed to non-problematic resources to be mobilized and affirm that identities are not durable or encompassing attributes of persons or collective actors as such (McAdam, Tarrow and Tilly 2001: 133; Bevington and Dison 2005: 287–9).

It is now imperative for us to look into the nuances of the identity perspective that has been widely used in west European countries to study social movements since the early twentieth century. This intellectual tradition has emerged against the backdrop of proliferation of preponderant labour movements, development of industrial democracies, Fabian socialism and welfare state in the UK and other countries on the one hand, and mobilizations of nationalist feelings in countries like Germany on the other. Indeed institutionalization of reformist and social democratic labour movement in western Europe affected the way social movements were conceived by social scientists in these countries (Eyerman and Jamison 1991: 17–18).

However, since the 1960s, going away from the economic determinism and recognition of newness were the major thrusts to study social movements. Touraine (2002) makes it very explicit:

> After the World War II and even very recently—especially in the 1960s—many people, including myself tried to discover new forms of collective actions in a so called, at that time, post-industrial, society and what we call now an information society. . . . I was convinced at the end of the twentieth century and beginning of the twenty-first century, the social and the political scene would be dominated by the growing role of these new and the cultural movements. . . . Many people were convinced that priority should be given to the formation of what I had myself called 'new social movements'.
>
> (pp. 89–92)

It was widely realized that not merely the empirical and the economic class position, but rather the issue of values, culture, subjectivity, morality, and empowerment have also played crucial roles towards the formation of new collective identities in these movements. Touraine (1981, 1983) observed 'new social movement as potential bearers of new social interests' and that social movements are characterized by the realization of historicity, by self-conscious awareness and collective identity. Bertaux (1990) has added the view that 'subjectivity' and 'idealism' are essential elements of social movement and that 'subjectivity refers to the subject in its totality . . .

it concerns with the drastic change in the fabric of social life that takes place when a new movement is born' (1990: 53). Social movements help generate a sense of collective identity and new ideas that recognize the reality from a new perspective. Collective identities are formed as an achieved definition of a situation, constructed and negotiated through the constitution of social networks which then connect the members of a group or movement through collective action to provide distinctive meaning to collective action. Thus social movements grow around relationship of new social identity that are voluntarily conceived 'to empower' members in defence of this identity (Melucci 1992, 1996). To Melucci

> newness of the new social movements is a relative concept and it had a temporary function to indicate the comparative difference between the historical forms of class conflict and today's emergent form of collective action. The reality in which we live has in entirety become a cultural construct and our representations of it serve as filters for our relationship with the whole world. . . . Social movements too seem to shift their focus from class, race, and other more traditional issues towards the cultural ground. . . . (Melucci 1996: 8–9)

In the world of cultural interactivity and co-construction social movement provides public spaces for generating new thoughts, activating new actors, and generating new ideas

> Thus by producing new knowledge, by reflecting on their own cognitive identity, by saying what they stand for, by challenging the dominant assumptions of the social order, social movements develop new ideas that are fundamental to the process of human creativity. Thus social movements develop world-views that restructure cognition, that recognize reality itself. The cognitive praxis of social movements is an important source of new social images and transformation of societal identities (Eyerman and Jamison 1991: 161–6)

Thus social movements involve actions for 'doing'. 'The involvement in an action is a matter of conscience and emotion, of responsibility and intention, of reflection and compassion, it is basically moral, global and individual' (Hegedus 1990: 266).

Social movements are however linked not only to the understanding of common social identity but also of common interest (Scott 1991: 6). With the growing space for globalism and informationalism while the notion of identity has emerged to be idealistic and hegemonic at one end, it is also tending to be diluted, fragmented and self-oriented on the other. In view of the changes in the contemporary society, critiquing the domination of the identity theory has also been a possibility and necessity. It is widely delineated that with the technological revolution, transformation of capitalism, and the demise of statism, informationalism is disintegrating the existing mechanism of social control and political representation. With the exception of a small elite of global politics (***half beings, half flows***), people all over the world have experienced loss of control over their lives. In the network society, 'thus on the one hand the dominant global elites inhabiting in the space of flows tend to consist of the identity less individuals (citizens of the worlds); while on the other hand, people insisting economic, cultural, and political disfranchisement tend to be attracted to communal identity' (Castells 1997).

Hence the concept of collective identity has also become an obstacle to explore the forms of mobilizations increasingly taking place in the networks and flows. The fluid-like characteristics of the emerging society with increasingly unequal flows of people, information, money, images, risks, practices and emotions, with no clear beginning or end points have become the dominant phenomena. Within these emerging complexities, social systems increasingly manifest fluid-like characteristics and become increasingly subject to shockwaves of fluidarity rather than solidarity. Herein the public experiences of self rather than collective solidarity are the emerging paradigm of contemporary social movements (Urry 2000 cf. McDonald 2002).

These emerging phenomena have induced a good deal of complexities in comprehending social movement theoretically, and in understanding the nature of collectivities on which the very foundation of social movement is laid. A social movement group is understood as a variant of social collectivities and is usually understood within the conceptual formulation of 'community'. Now it has also been understood as a collectivity of informal networks which mobilizes on conflictual issues through the frequent use of various forms of protest' (della Porta and Diani 1999: 16). Moreover, there are diverse types of adherents in social movements, i.e. activists, participants, sympathizers (Neidhardt and Rucht 1991). Social movement collectivities are loosely formed, many a times independent of geographical boundary. Their collective identity is formed based on temporarily perceived and articulated ideals and common interests, and that many participants tend to be members of more than one collectivities simultaneously. Significantly many of these collectivities

In the wake of globalization and the emerging interplay of several new forces a large part the society is undergoing a profound process of socio-cultural de-contextualization. This has generated new varieties of social change and mobility and has led to the articulation of diverse interests and identities; and expression of diverse varieties of protests, conflict, collective mobilization and social movements. Significantly many of the processes are intertwined with each other. Societies in India are experiencing fast processes of transformation caused by the unprecedented expansion of the service sector of the economy, penetration of information and communication technology, increasing flow of migration, introduction of new development initiatives, increasing literacy rates and fast economic growth rate on the one hand and sharp decline in the land-man ratio and decline of work participation in agriculture, stagnation of vast section on abject poverty, livelihood insecurity, unemployment and underemployment on the other. These phenomena have generated composite processes of vertical and horizontal social mobility; new forms of social conflicts locally and globally, and concurrent radicalized and institutionalized social mobilizations and collective actions, and rejuvenations of several old forces of collective action in the new context. The relationships between the state and social movements have acquired several new dimensions.

In the emerging scenario while on the one hand, there have been processes of cooption of collective mobilization by the state, and a decline of culture of collective protests, there have also been resurgence of people's protest at the grassroots, which are looking for new mediums of expressions and societal recognition. In the changing context several new contradictions have emerged in shaping the essence of social movements and in comprehending them in totality. These contradictions can't be explained simply by contra-positing and privileging one organizing principle of collective mobilization over the other, for example, interests *vs.* identities, subjectivity *vs.* objectivity, morality *vs.* rationality, solidarity *vs.* fluidarity, structure *vs.* process, framing *vs.* cognition, singularity *vs.* plurality, anti-social *vs.* social. Rather in view of historicity and contemporarility, resilience and resurgence of these social conflicts and collective mobilizations and their interface with emerging patterns of social mobility, these are required to be explained by understanding the broad processes of socio-economic transitions of the society and by juxtapositioning and combining many of the organizing principles of social movements together with in-depth reflexivity and resilience. As a pre-condition to this understanding let us have glimpses of socio-economic transition in contemporary India.

GLIMPSES OF SOCIO–ECONOMIC TRANSITION

Shift in the economic order: Though India is still predominantly an agricultural country, she stands on the threshold of a new economic order which is characterized by occupational diversification, fast expansion of the service sector, and decline in work participation in the agricultural sector. In India work participation in the service sector has increased from 15 per cent in 1960 to 39 per cent in 2007, while it has declined in agriculture from 74 per cent to less than 52 per cent. Work participation in the industrial sector has remained constant at around 11 per cent during the same period. As a corollary, the service sector of economy which minimally contributed to India's GDP in the 1960s now occupies the prime position by contributing 56 per cent of the GDP, whereas agriculture and industry contributed to the extent of 21 per cent and 24 per cent of the GDP respectively (UNDP 2006; World Bank 2007).

Erosion of the bases of traditional economy and increasing downward mobility and migration: Rural societies in India in general now characterized by decline in the traditional bases of natural resources and in the land-man ratio, and sharpening the process of vertical and horizontal social mobility for the largest segment of the households. It is substantiated by the fact that per household landholding has declined from 1.78 hectares in 1961–2 to 0.73 hectares in 2003. In rural India though there has been a significant decrease in the number of landless households, there has also been a phenomenal decline in the category of medium and large category of landowning households. However, the steep process of downward mobility is evidenced at the lower strata and are reflected in patterns of landholding and work participation. In rural India 10.5 per cent of the households are landless. The landless and semi-landless households (having less than 0.04 hectares of land which is mostly for residential purposes) altogether form 40.2 per cent of the rural households. The semi-marginal and the marginal cultivators, who altogether formed 62 per cent of the rural landowning households in 1981, constituted 80 per cent of households in 2003. The landless, semi-landless and the marginal cultivators (owning less than 1 hectare) who altogether form over 90 per cent of the rural households have emerged to be highly economically vulnerable (NSSO 2003).

Over the years, as already pointed out work participation in agriculture has declined from 74 per cent in 1961 to 52 per cent in 2001. The proportion of cultivators as main workers has declined from 51 per cent to 32 per cent and the proportion of agricultural labourers has increased from 19 per cent to 27 per cent during the period 1961 to 2001. The decline in the category of cultivators and increase in the category of agricultural labourers is related to the issue of increasing unemployment and under-employment in rural areas and increase in the quantum of rural–urban migration. It has been visibly marked in the increase in the category of 'marginal workers' (getting less than 180 days of employment) from 4 per cent in 1981 to 11 per cent in 2001. These have generated instability in the rural economy, causing spatial mobility and migration. According to the NSSO 2000 report, about 27 per cent of the Indian population was migrant and the proportion of migrant in the urban areas and rural areas were to the extent of 33 per cent and 24 per cent respectively. Among the urban migrants 59 per cent of the males and 58 per cent of the females were from rural areas (NSS 2000). About 67 per cent of the household migrated from rural to rural areas and 60.2 per cent migrated from rural to urban areas for the purpose of employment (NSS 1999).

Increasing vulnerability of the marginalized: Within the emerging processes of spatial and occupational mobility the socio-economic position of the marginalized sections of the society has emerged to be highly vulnerable. Among the Scheduled Castes (SC) there have been more cultivators than agricultural labourers with 23.47 per cent and 52 per cent respectively. While among the Scheduled Tribes (ST) the proportion of the cultivators are more with 47 per cent against 38 per cent for agricultural labourers. However, the STs, have the highest extent of work participation as agricultural labourers among all social categories because of the predominance of sub-marginal and marginal landholdings among them. The incidence of poverty is also highest among them with more than 47.3 per cent living below the poverty line. Among the SCs around 37 per cent live below the poverty line; and for the general 28.3 per cent live below the poverty line.

While there has been a predominance of sub-marginal and marginal holdings in the agrarian society, the extent of such holdings has been very preponderant among the SCs and STs (see Table 6.1). Due to these emerging patterns of landholding and downward mobility the extent of work participation as agricultural labourers among the SCs, STs has risen in recent years. It is culturally important here that while the marginal sizes of landholding pushes the other categories of social groups to look for self-employment outside agriculture, the SCs and STs look for employment as labourers either in agriculture or elsewhere. Higher caste women usually don't work in the field as manual agricultural work is considered demeaning and is socially stigmatized. There is also a tendency among the SCs and the Other Backward Classes (OBC) to withdraw from manual agricultural activities once their economic condition improves. Hence the higher is the extent of economic downward mobility higher the extent of work participation in agriculture or elsewhere as labourers.

Though the extent of poverty and unemployment is high among the SCs and STs, not all of them prefer to migrate to the urban areas. Due to low levels of education, skill and knowledge and lack of information about spatial mobility, they mostly slog in the rural areas. It reflects in the social composition of the slum areas which accommodate most of the migrant labourers. In India 19 per cent and 2 per cent of the population belong to the category of SCs and STs.

TABLE 6.1: LANDHOLDING AMONG SCHEDULED CASTES, SCHEDULED TRIBES, OTHER BACKWARD CASTES AND OTHERS IN INDIA (2003)

Social Categories	% of Household	% of area owned	Average size of holding	Landless households	Households with .01–.04 (ha)	Households with .041–1.00 (ha)	Households with 1.01–2.00 (ha)	Households with 2.01–4.00 (ha)	Household with 4.01+ (ha)
ST	10.5	11.5	0.77	9.01	25.5	41.3	14.2	7.3	3.5
SC	21.6	9.4	0.30	5.7	51.2	34.4	5.8	2.2	0.6
OBC	41.6	43.5	0.75	6.3	31.9	41.5	11.4	6.2	3.6
Other	26.3	36.3	1.00	6.8	24.3	40.9	12.7	8.3	6.2

Source: National Sample Survey, 2003.

Occupational diversification: India stands at the threshold of economic diversification and fast occupational shift. According to the 2001 census 48 per cent of the rural workers are engaged in non-agricultural activities. This indicates interpenetration not only of new economic forces in the rural areas but also of the emergence of new patterns of social mobility and social interaction. Increase in literacy and rural communication networks have largely helped sustain such occupational diversifications. The occupational diversification has takan shape based on the localized resources available in the given area, and types of communication networks expanded in the concerned areas. The emerging patterns of occupational diversification has mostly contributed to the economic and social horizontal mobility for the vast section of rural population. For example, a marginal cultivator is now becoming a milkman or an agricultural labourer becoming a construction labourer.

Expansion of literacy and education: In 1951, 18.33 per cent of Indian population was literate while the rural literacy rate was only 12.1 per cent. In 2001 all-India literacy rate increased to 65.4 per cent and in the rural areas to around 60 per cent. In 2002–3 an estimated 82 per cent of the children aged 6–14 years attended primary school. Retention of students at various levels of learning has increased substantially and the extent of drop-out has declined at all levels. According to the Ministry of Human Resource Development, Government of India Annual Report, students' drop-out rate has declined at the primary level from 58.7 per cent in 1981 to 40.7 per cent in 2001 and at the middle and secondary levels from 73 per cent to 54 per cent and 83 per cent to 69 per cent respectively during the same period.

Spread of mass communication networks: Mass communication networks are spreading very fast in contemporary India. According to Asian Mass communication Research Centre there are more than 23,000 registered newspapers in India, 106 radio stations, around 200 transmitters. According to the 2001 census, 86 people and in the urban metros 22 per cent population in rural areas own TV sets. In the rural areas, 42 per cent of the population watches TV programmes.

Fast expansion of ICTs: Over the decades the usage of internet has significantly increased from less than 0.01 per cent in 1990 to 5.5 per cent in 2005, mobile phones from 0.02 per cent to 8.2 per cent and telephones from 0.6 per cent to 4.5 per cent during the same period (www.internetworldstats.com 2007). This sector is now expanding very fast. India produces 28 per cent of the knowledge workers servicing the global IT industry. As much as 82 per cent of the US companies choose India as their first choice for software outsourcing. India's share in the total global IT offshoring is $17 billion, which is 53 per cent of this total market share. Ever more people are now employed in the information and communication sector. IT is expanding its horizon to the small towns and villages. 'C' class cities now account for more than 50 per cent of the PC sales in India (*Hindustan Times*, 6 July 2005). These have together created the space for increasing social, political and economic communication in the rural areas and a process of redefining and reconstructing social lives by offering several options.

Changing facets of development initiatives and civil society intervention: In India development perspectives have got reoriented several times. Immediately after Independence India followed the growth with stability model. Against the backdrop of imbalanced economic development and sharp downward mobility of a vast section of the population, this development policy was reoriented in the early 1970s to incorporate the philosophy of 'social justice' in the development discourse. The development model was reoriented once again in the mid-1980s to associate the notion of empowerment with 'development' to 'ensure full participation of the people in the development process in accordance with the constitutions, laws and procedures consistent with international law and obligation' (UN 1995). The emerging development has also envisaged state 'partnership with free and representative organizations of civil society, and strengthening of the abilities and opportunities of civil society and local communities to develop their own organizations, resources and activities' (ibid.). In the wake of globalization and the introduction of the structural adjustment programme, the emphasis has been on the increasing role of the civil societies 'to take the burden off the state, by involving citizens and communities in the delivery of the collective goods' (World Bank 1997: 3). In recent years there has been a phenomenal proliferation of civil society activism in India. Social scientists have attributed this phenomenon to the crises and legitimization deficit in the states on the one hand and the market triumph on the other.

In contemporary India, civil societies like non-governmental organizations (NGOs) play a crucial role for the social development of the marginalized people, especially in the sectors of health, education, employment generation, livelihood security, protection of human rights, animal rights, participatory sustainable development, disaster management, relief distribution, dissemination of information, political participation, and so on. In many parts of the country the civil society activism has provided alternative modes of organizing collective initiatives.

Practice of democracy at the grass roots: The 73rd Amendment to the Constitution of India has made revolutionary changes in rural society. It has made the traditional Panchayati Raj Institutions (PRIs—three-tier bodies for local self-governance) statutory bodies, made election for a term of five years compulsory and introduced 30 per cent reservation for women in these elected bodies. It has also empowered these bodies to formulate and implement development initiatives at the grassroots. As an institution of democracy it holds the key to elect 3 million peoples representatives every five years, of which one million are women and 0.8 million are SCs and STs.

Rural development programmes: Rural India has seen the proliferation of several rural development programmes initiated by governmental agencies. Besides the pre-exiting Integrated Rural Development Programme (IRDP) and the National Rural Employment Programme (NREP), several other programmes have been initiated to rejuvenate the process of rural development. Some of the employment generation programmes like the Pradhan Mantri Gram Sadak Yojana, Swarnjayanti Gram Swarozgar Yojana, Sampoorna Grameen Rozgar Yojana (SGRY), National Rural Employment Guarantee Programme and National Social Assistance Programme have generated strong waves of social and political activisms at the grassroots in most parts of the country as these have provided the scope of alternative livelihood security for the rural poor.

Millennium development goals and collective mobilizations: The state and civil society actors in India are under tremendous pressure to achieve the Millennium Development Goals of the UN which specifically aim to eradicate extreme poverty and hunger, achieve universal primary education, promote gender equality and empower women, reduce child mortality, improve maternal health, combat HIV/AIDS, malaria and other diseases, ensure environmental sustainability, and develop a global partnership for development (UNDP 2000). As these goals are to be achieved by 2015 several developmental schemes relating to the above-mentioned goals are formulated time to time with the participation of international experts in collaboration with grassroots workers at the village level. Several multinational and bilateral agencies have also made their presence felt in the rural areas.

Notwithstanding all the developmental initiatives and increase in the local-global connectivity, rural India has remained the breeding ground for several social ills with the concentration of the problems of unemployment, poverty, illiteracy, high infant mortality, low longevity, inadequate safe drinking water, lack of proper road, drainage, health care facilities, domination of traditional authority, caste hierarchy, conservatism, fractional politics, and so on. All these provided the basis for regular mobilization of rural population on several issues including land reform, self-employment, micro-credit, and poverty elevation. The emerging patterns of transition of society have profound implications on the processes of social mobility, social conflicts, and collective mobilization and largely on the culture of social movements of these societies.

POSITING SOCIAL MOBILITY, SOCIAL CONFLICTS AND SOCIAL MOBILIZATIONS IN TRANSITION

The conventional and pre-existing patterns of vertical social mobility in rural India have been diluted in the wake of decline in the land–man ratio, increase in occupational diversification and rural–urban migration. With the expansion of new avenues of employment and communication networks a section of rural poor are now horizontally mobilized socially and economically. A section of them have also migrated to the urban areas and got absorbed in the unorganized sector.

Occupational diversification has widened the scope of horizontal and upward social mobility of the upper strata as well. Business relating to transport, modern amenities, electronic and electrical goods, cable television network, telecommunication hubs, internet kiosks, etc., have not only provided the upper strata new avenues of earning but also the scope to provide employment to others. Since they have already got access to modern education, communication and social network they easily take advantage of the new economic opportunities and emerging avenues of employment.

These have caused the emergence of multiple employer–employee relationships even in rural areas. The predominant and stable forms of agrarian employer–employee relationships (landlord–tent or landlord–agricultural labourer) are now being replaced by unstable, infrequent relationships with multiple employers or service users. The multiplicity of work relationships is reflected in the functions of an agricultural labour simultaneously as a milkman, a construction labour, a *bidi* maker, and simultaneously as migrant labour in the local town. Similarly, landowners are also simultaneously village businessmen, ICT or IPO hub owners, transporters, teachers or government servants. Significantly, such relations go beyond the boundaries pre-defined notion of domination and hierarchy.

The traditional structure of authority and the primordial form of domination have been widely questioned with the emergence of NGOs and the functioning of PRIs at the grassroots. In the emerging contexts gender, religious minority, SC, ST and OBC issues and identities are widely articulated with the activities of the NGOs and PRIs to frame collective mobilizations against the hostile forces of patriarchy, feudalism and caste and ethnic hegemony. The emerging scenario of mobility has destabilized the pre-existing practices of social inequality; patterns of primordial power hierarchy and domination; and the caste-based employer–employee relations. Thus for many the emerging forms of social mobilities are liberating ventures from the pre-existing structures of domination.

In spite of such occupational mobility, the economic vulnerability of the marginalized segment of the population has not been altered. The association of caste and other primordial identity with the phenomena of economic vulnerability still show a historical continuity. Social mobility through the cultural path of sanskritization is also gradually losing its hold among many communities in the wake of emergence of several alternative role models. As the caste order has remained historically oppressive, resistance against this order is articulated by taking advantage of modern education, occupational diversifications, and professionalizing traditional occupations and most importantly collective mobilization. Sustained economic vulnerability and social exclusion have got new political meaning for assertive and transformative collective actions. Herein causes of social conflicts have been cumulative; and collective mobilizations are extended to new areas of these conflicts. The struggles of the Dalits and the tribes for economic emancipation have been extended to the areas of struggles for political empowerment and to the struggles for their caste and ethnic identities.

The practice of democracy at the grassroots and their increasing connectivity with the regional and national politics have generated a space for self-assertion among the marginalized groups on diverse issues and have contributed to the continuity of the culture of collective mobilizations and re-articulation of regional, ethnic and gender identities. These have redefined the paradigm of legitimacy of conflict, protest and collective mobilization and processes of articulation of new interests and identities. For example, the Telangana region of Andhra Pradesh, which has seen a proliferation of peasant movements (viz., the Telangana movement between 1948 and 1952, the Naxalite movements 1972 onwards) has now seen the growth of numerous collective mobilizations at the grassroots. For example, the resurgent separate Telangana statehood movement based on the ethnic identity of the Telangana people, mobilization of the agrarian poor and sustained agrarian conflict spearheaded by the CPI(ML) (Peoples' War Group, now known as Maoist) and various other Naxalite outfits; mobilization for the protection of civil rights of citizens by the Andhra Pradesh Civil Liberties Committee (APCLC), Organization for the Protection of Democratic Rights and Citizens Forum; mobilization of STs by Thudum Debba (a militant organization of the STs); mobilization of Maadigga (a group of SC) by Maadigaa Reservation Porata Samithi (MRPS) for re-categorization of the SCs into four groups based on their contemporary educational and economic status for the purpose of reservations in jobs, education, etc.); moblization of cultivators by Roytu Seva Samithi, Jala Sandhana Samithi (demanding irrigation facilities for the peasants); anti-arrack movement to mobilize women against production and consumption of liquor and also for women's liberty, political participation and social development and so on, are the contemporary realities of collective mobilization in rural Andhra Pradesh.

Similarly, in West Bengal there have been the Tebhaga (1946–7), Naxalite (1967–71) and Operation Banga movements (1977–till late 1990s), Gurkhaland movements (1980s and onward), Kamtapur movement (1980s and onward), resurgence of Naxalite extremism in the southern part of West Bengal since early 2000, movements against acquisition of agricultural lands by the Krishi Jami Suraksha Committee (Committee to Protect Agricultural lands) in Singur and Krishi Bhumi Ucched Pratirodh Committee (Committee Against Eviction from Agricultural Land) in Nandigram, tribal villager's, resistance to police oppression through the People's Committee Against Police Austrocities in the Midnapore district and several other grassroots mobilizations.

The state now has provided the liberal democratic space to articulate issues, interests,, and identities for collective mobilizations. Within this available space many of the radical mobilizations have got transformed to be institutionalized, co-opted, and have become partially reformative. Hence the processes of institutionalization of conflicts have been privileged by the state and society over radicalization of the same. Against this backdrop there have been paradigmatic transitions in the nature of organization, ideology, mobilization and interests involved in these movements and also in the span of mobilization, state's response, direction and immediate fall-out of these movements. Tables 6.2 and 6.3 depict these transitions.

Evidences from West Bengal and Andhra Pradesh show that sustained mobilizations have opened up the possibility of articulation of new issues, identities and mobilizations of the marginalized sections of the population. In India, a vast section of the population has remained economically insecure in agriculture. However, they prefer to retain agriculture as their prime source of livelihood security as they are unable to get fully integrated with the emerging new avenues of employment due their low state of education, training and capacity building. According to an NSSO report, more than 40 per cent of the agricultural people in India prefer farming as their occupation. Significantly the sub-marginal, marginal and the small cultivators give more preference to farming than the medium and large cultivators. They look for avenues for self-fulfilment in the rural society itself through diverse means and encounter the daily hardship and domination of cumulative marginality that adversely affects their aspirations. Hence they resort to or take part in the collective mobilization as an effective and alternative tool for livelihood security, collective self-assertion and resistance against domination. As the state has emerged to be the primary provider, intrinsically dominant collective mobilizations are frequently directed against the state.

In recent years, however, the patterns of collective mobilization have been different from those of the previous ones. Even the major revolutionary and extremist political parties that once propagated seizure of state power through armed struggle have joined parliamentary politics. In the process of continuous political mobilization the difference between the state and the political party has been minimized in many parts of the country; and many of the civil society initiatives have got co-opted by the state. The society now sees the cropping up of several new issues, new patterns of conflict, mobility and mobilization, while many of the old ones has taken a new shape in the present context. In the emerging scenario the relationship between social mobility, conflict, mobilization and social movements have been extensive and implicit. The fast social and economic transitions of the society have generated a big momentum for social mobility. The quantum of upward social mobility has been faster for those segments of the population in rural societies who have better access to economic, political and other social resources, while spatial and horizontal social mobility has been substantive for the marginalized sections. Though the increasing quantum of horizontal mobility has not altered many of the pre-existing arrangements of domination and underlying coercion these have helped question the bases of legitimacy of such domination and coercion.

These assorted forms of social mobility have reformulated boundaries of several social identities. This reformulation has helped to articulate distinctive strategy to protect the pre-existing forms of gender, caste and ethnic identity. This reformulation has also sharpened their views on social, economic and political interests and identities; and has encapsulated many of these identities as projects to attain specific political goals. Hence they not only question the bases of legitimacy of pre-existing arrangements but also assert for a share in the social, economic and political spheres in the established order. The imbalanced and assorted forms of mobility have induced social conflict and extensive collective mobilizations at the grassroots. These mobilizations however are not isolated, but are linked to the wider social processes of collective identity formation and political assertion which are reflected in the people's struggle to protect their dignity, livelihood, land, for greater political participation, and equal status in society. The democratic polity in India has provided the opportunity for the articulation, sustenance and accommodation of these conflicts and collective mobilizations. These identities and conflicts however are not fixed. They get articulated, re-articulated and rejuvenated both synchronically and diachronically on diverse issues in diverse

TABLE 6.2: ANDHRA PRADESH

Name of Movement	Nature of Organization, Ideology & Mobilization	Types of Demands	Span of Mobilization	Nature of State's Response	Direction of Movement	Social Collectivities Involved in Mobilization
1948–52: Telangana movements	Radical and Uninstitutional-ized	Explicitly economic, implicitly political	Episodic and intensive at particular points of time	Strong opposition	Suspended/ collapsed	Class based, predominantly represented by SC, ST, BC and women
1970–1: Srikakulam Uprise	Radical and Uninstitutional-ized	Explicitly economic, implicitly political	Episodic and intensive at particular points of time	Strong opposition	Collapsed, remained partly active in small groups	Class based, predominantly represented by SC, ST, BC and women
1980 onward: Peoples' War	Radical and partly disguised	Explicitly economic, cultural, gender & implicitly political	Continuing over a period of time	Opposition and negotiation	Sporadic but sustained and networking with related civil societies	Class based, predominantly represented by SC, ST, BC and women
1960s onward: Telengana statehood movement	Partly institutionalized and partly radical	Explicitly political and cultural	Sustained and continuous	Opposition, cooption and negotiation	Sporadic but sustained and networking with related civil societies	Regional and linguistic predominantly represented by SC, ST, BC and women

Civil liberty movement	[illegible] institutionalized and partly radical	Explicitly political and cultural	Sustained and continuous	Integration and negotiation	Networked, sustained and expanding	Political and secular identity predominantly represented by SC, ST, BC and women
1985 onward: Anti-arrack	Mostly institutionalized	Explicitly cultural, implicitly political and economic	Episodic	Encourage-ment and integration	Networked, sustained in diverse forms	Resurgence of gender identity
1995 onward: Maadigaa Reservation Porata Samithi	Mostly institutionalized	Explicitly cultural, economic, implicitly political	Sustained and continuous	Integration, cooption	Expanding	Caste based, predominantly represented by SC
1995 onward: Malla Reservation movement	Mostly institutionalized	Explicitly cultural, economic, implicitly political	Sustained and continuous	Integration, cooption	Integration, cooption	Caste based, predominantly represented by SC
1990s onward: Thudum Debba movement	Mostly institutionalized	Explicitly cultural, eco-nomic, impli-citly political	Sporadic and continuous	Integration, cooption	Integration, cooption	Caste based, predominantly represented by ST
1990 onward: Farmers', Roytu Seva Samithi, etc., movements	Mostly institutionalized	Explicitly economic, implicitly political	Sustained and continuous	Integration, cooption	Integration, cooption	Rejuvenation multiple identities and new political forces

TABLE 6.3: WEST BENGAL

Name of Movement	Nature of Organization, Ideology & Mobilization	Types of Demands	Span of Mobilization	Nature of State's Response	Direction of Movement	Social Collectivities Involved in Mobilization
1946–7: Tebhaga movements	Radical and uninstitutional-ized	Explicitly economic, implicitly political	Episodic and intensive at particular points of time	Strong opposition	Collapsed	Class based, predominantly represented by SC, ST, and women
1967–71: Naxalite	Radical and uninstitutional-ized	Explicitly economic, implicitly political	Episodic and intensive at particular points of time	Strong opposition	Collapsed remained, partly active in small group	Class based, predominantly represented by SC, ST, women
1977–till date: Operation Banga and land distribution	Institutionalized	Implicitly economic and political	Sustained and continuous	Integration and negotiation	Networked, sustained and cooption	Class and political identity caste based pre-dominantly represented by SC, ST, minorities and women
1981–till date: Gorkhaland	Partly institutionalized and partly radical	Explicitly cultural implicitly political and economic	Sustained and continuous	Opposition, negotiation, accommodation	Sustained	Ethnic identity; Predominantly represented by ST

1979–till date: Kamtapuri	Partly institutionalized and partly radical	Explicitly economic and cultural	Sustained and continuous	Opposition	Partly active in small groups	Caste identity predominantly represented by SC
1995–till date: Janjuddha/ Maoist	Partly institutionalized and partly radical	Explicitly economic and cultural	Segregated, sporadic	Opposition	Active in small groups	Class identity predominantly represented by SC, ST & BCs
2007–till date: Krishi Bhumi Ucched Birodhi Andolan	Partly institutionalized and partly radical	Explicitly economic and cultural	Sustained	Opposition	Active in small groups	Agriculturalist identity predominantly represented by SC, ST, minorities and women
2008-till date Movement Against Police Atrocities on the Tribes	Initially institutional now radical in 2009	Explicitly economic and cultural	Sustained for more than year	Opposition	Active in some area	Tribal and backward caste, women forest dowellers identity

contexts. They move like a pendulum in these mobilizations getting fixed at one end and flexible and liberated at the other.

In general, the shift is widely delineated from radicalization to institutionalization and further rejuvenation of social conflicts and collective mobilization. The increasing quantum of social mobility, both horizontal and vertical, shows a positive correlation with the process of institutionalization and rejuvenation of collective mobilization. Hence there is a need to develop a holistic resilient and reflexive perspective on social movement in view of the changing nature of social mobility, social conflict and collective mobilization in the present society.

INTERFACE AND ALTERNATIVES

In India a vast body of sociological literature has emerged in the area of social mobility. In the functional perspective the social and cultural dimensions of change and mobility have been privileged over the economic dimensions. The process of sanskritization has widely been depicted to explain such mobility whereby a 'low' caste Hindu, or tribal or other group, changes its customs, ritual, ideology and way of life in the direction of a high, and frequently, 'twice born' caste (Srinivas 1956). The Marxian analysis, however, has emphasized on the economic dimension. The process of proletarianization has also been widely used to explain the process of downward mobility of the lowest section of rural agrarian population (for details, see Mukherjee 1957; Desai 1971; Byres 1981). In the wake of adoption of new technology in agriculture scholars have highlighted the process of accentuation of transformation of the 'rich peasant class-in-itself' into a powerful dominant class with the characteristics of capitalist farmers and a process of proletarianization of a large number of completely landless labourers, disposed tenants, poor peasants, and an unknown number of ruined village artisans and craftsmen (Byres 1981: 425–37).

A good body of studies on social conflicts, collective mobilizations and social movements in India has used well-knit theoretical perspectives of Marxian, functionalist, nationalist, subaltern and transformative social analysis. The Marxian scholars have examined conflicts, social mobilizations and social movements within the framework of class formation and class conflict and provided an economic explanation of these phenomena (Dhanagare 1983; Desai 1981; Sen 1982;

Dasgupta 1974; Gupta 1998; and many others). The functionalist scholars on the other hand have emphasized on the issues of structural maladjustment or instability in the society and have highlighted the socio-cultural issues involved in conflicts, social mobilizations and social movements (Rao 1985; Oommen 1985). The Gandhian perspective of mass mobilization, which lays its foundation on the principle of nonviolence, passive resistance, civil-disobedience, transformation of consciousness, social upliftment programme, and establishment of a moral order has been widely accepted by the nationalist scholars to explain the process of mass mobilization during the independence struggle (Chandra 1996; Mukherjee 2004).

The subaltern studies in India have brought forth the issue of autonomy of social conflicts, social mobilizations and movements, their localized specificity and very micro dynamics. It is argued by them that subaltern politics which included a wide variety of generally autonomous modes of thought and action expressed through local conflicts, rebellions, riots and popular movements constituted an autonomous domain which neither originated from elite politics nor depended upon the latter for its existence. To rebel was to destroy many of the familiar signs which were a spontanous, motivated and a conscious undertaking on the part of the rural masses. Therefore to them, rebellion was not merely some automatic reflex action to external economic or political stimulus; it was 'peasant praxis', the expression through peasant action of the collective consciousness of the peasantry (Guha 1983b). In fact, autonomy has been emphasized, and to them 'to deny autonomy to the subalterns would be to petrify this aspect of historical process . . .' (Chatterjee 1998: 166).

A large number of scholars have also examined the transformative dynamics of social conflicts, social mobilizations and social movements (Mukherjee 1979; Oommen 1984 and 1985; SinghaRoy 1992 and 2004). These studies have made significant contributions in delineating the process of transformation in social mobilizations and social movements from radicalization to institutionalization, from interest to identity orientations, and also profound reformulations towards the orientations of new social movement. It is shown that sustained mobilizations have helped generate multiple and alternative collective identities that look for liberation from the coercive bases of dependency and domination (see SinghaRoy 2004).

In rural India most social movements have retained their continuity for a considerable period of time in one form or the other. Many have retained their legacy through diverse modes of collective mobilizations. As the root causes of the conflict—poverty, unemployment, and livelihood insecurity, social and cultural indignation and the like—have remained to be eradicated, collective mobilizations and social movements against such ills have remained an inseparable part of social progression therein. Collective mobilizations of the marginalized people are also politically constructed surrounding those issues of deprivation, inequality, domination and social isolation. At times local issues have got politically interlinked with wider ideology and organizations. Herein in terms of historicity, while many of the ideologies, organizations, and collective mobilizations of radical movements have got transformed to be institutionalized, social movements emerging out of daily resistance are also routinizing social conflicts and collective mobilizations. Resurgence of violent protests has been part of this ongoing dynamics. The normative and the institutional arrangements of the society have now provided the required space with the democratic framework to accommodate cultures of protest, resistance and collective mobilizations at the grassroots. Herein, the resurgence of the Naxalite uprise in various parts of the country has not been seen with a perspective of democratic inclusion. Political parties and civil society organizations now play significant roles to integrate these mobilizations and protests with the democratic processes of the country. Hence not only the issues of law and order, but also social and economic deprivation of the protesters have got vital attention. It is aptly expressed in the utterance of Prime Minister Manmohan Singh that 'Naxalite movement not a law and order problem, but deep rooted social and economic problem in country' (*Times of India*, 12 October 2009).

In a composite scenario there has been fast expansion of the forces of globalization, ICTs, cultural disembeddedness, change in the economic structure of the society, expansion of knowledge economy, erosion of the bases of traditional economic resources, increasing occupational diversifications, dilution in the conventional modes of social mobility, emergence of multiple employer–employee relationships, emergence of civil societies and practice of democracy at the grassroots. These have profoundly diffused many of the pre-existing modes of social mobility, social conflicts and collective mobilization. Increasing connectivity and communicability with the wider world, regular political interventions at the grassroots and inculcation of new identities have opened up the possibilities of multiple collective mobilizations of same sets of people on diverse issues and interests—economic, social, cultural and political. Social collectivities are formed and mostly politically mediated based on economic class or professional, ethnic, regional, caste, gender, environment, human rights and related interests and identities. These collectives are in essence interconnected and are formed crosscutting pre-existing boundaries. With the sustained intervention of state and civil societies these collectivities have now emerged to be highly mobilized and flexible and have taken the form of social movement society—an interconnected collectivity regularly mobilized on the principle of fragmentation at one end and unification at the other, and in a process of continuous renewal and rejuvenation.

These phenomena can't be analysed solely in terms of economic, ideational, localized, or any particularistic determinism. Marxists analysis of class transformation is effective in examining the economic dimensions of social conflict and collective mobilizations. However, it is unable to accommodate the dynamics of several societal identities and the new form of ethnic, regional, caste and Dalit protests, which have been rejuvenated and reconstructed in the contemporary society even though maximum participants in these protests are from the categories of agricultural labourers, tenants, poor artisans, marginal cultivators, construction labourers, and so on. The functional analysis is unable accommodate in its scheme of analysis the emerging forms of social conflicts as taking shape in contemporary rural India. Explanation of continued social conflicts and collective mobilizations of these groups and the newly form collectivities in terms of structural inadequacy, disfunctioning of normative orders and institutional failure appears to be highly inadequate. Moreover functional analysis is unable to explain the process of sustenance and rejuvenation of collective mobilization and conflicts that question stability of the established social order. The scholars on the subaltern studies, on the other hand, are mostly concerned with the issue of autonomy of the localized formation of the protests whereby the issues of connectivity and communicability of these groups with the wide world is conspicuously missing. The process of formation of social collectivities, articulation of collective issues, initiation and sustenance of collective actions are no more isolated phenomena. The scholars on subaltern studies ignore the emerging dimensions of local–global interconnectivity, potential political and ideological and organizational interventions through which collective actions are largely framed at the grassroots. The collective assertions of women, ethnic minorities, Dalits, tribals, agricultural labourers, tenants, and poor artisans are indeed no more autonomous of the socio-economic formations of other domains of the society.

The cost benefit analysis of resource mobilization theorists has excluded the aspects of cognition and morality from the ambit of social movement analysis. The emotional zeal and subjectivity, which form a crucial part of a social movement, hardly find any recognition in their overwhelming emphasis on economic rationality. It has not only privileged structure over process, it has been over-deterministic so far as the rationality of human thoughts are concerned in their response to social exigencies. The overwhelming participation of women in the collective actions related to land and environment, or the participation of the ethnic minorities, Dalits, tribals, agricultural labourers, peasants and others in the collective action related to education, human rights, cultural autonomy, etc., issues can't be adequately explained in terms of economic rationality alone. The new social movement scholars though have largely been involved in redefining the process of cognition, new identity formation, empowerment, collective subjectivity; they have analysed movements only as discrete, episodic manifestations. They have also tacitly developed an ideological containment against economic analysis of social movements. They describe new social movements as essentially non-violent, pragmatic, non-integrated, non-hierarchical, non-coercive, cross-class, cross-ideology and cross-age in their constituencies (Hegedus 1990: 263) and autonomous in character (Scott 1990: 18–20). It has privileged subjectivity in collective identity formation over rationality of thought and actions; consequently identity has been privileged over interest. Many a time however, subjectively articulated identity is also used in the pursuit of material interests. For example, the Maadigaa Reservation Porata Samithi and the Malla Reservation Movements of the SCs in Andhra Pradesh used caste identity for economic benefits, while the Rajbansi and the Gorkhaland movements in the northern part of West Bengal have been using the caste and ethnic identity to highlight the economic plight of their people. The overwhelming participation of the SCs and the tribal population in the peasant movement only shows deep-rooted intertwining between identity and interest.

The Gandhian perspective takes into cognizance morality of the community as a whole whereby conflict will be resolved with the surrender of the opponents to the moral demands of the society.

Though it takes into consideration the issue of ideological transformation and a relentless process of mobilization, it tends to eliminate conflicts from its paradigm, and emphasizes on self-reliance based on khadi and other conventional technologies.

In India the contemporary phase of social transformation has been marked by the composition of multiple social realities of agrarian, industrial, and post-industrial societies together; wherein the processes of social mobility, social conflicts and collective mobilizations have not only been interlinked but also diversely constructed with the interplay of apparently contradictory but interrelated principles of organizing collective sentiments and actions. These composite processes help generate and reshape new collective identities and rejuvenate old identities in a new context. As given in Tables 6.1 and 6.2, collective mobilizations and identities are formed based on multiple issues which are interlinked. Collective identities are indeed articulated based on the common collective experiences of economic class exploitation, power hierarchy, ethnic and caste segregation and gender inequality. These experiences indeed are not autonomous of each other; rather they are interlinked. Many of the historical experiences of social conflicts and collective mobilizations have remained associated with the process of articulation of new collective identity and their transformation. Thus the processes of solidification and fluidarity of collective identity go hand in hand and the dynamics of 'identity' and 'interest', 'morality' and 'rationality', 'primordiality' and 'modernity', 'autonomy' and 'dependence' function as combinations of these composite social processes by becoming dichotomous forces in one context and complementary in another. Hence social movements are required to be understood with a flexible resilient-holistic perspective going beyond a particularistic strand of analysis.

This perspective aims to anchor all the possible emerging dynamics of contradictions and complementarities within the ambit of its analysis by locating the flow of social mobility, social conflict and interactivity among social groups as integrated social processes affected by multiple social forces and processes. This perspective visualizes social movements as recurrently organized and sustained as mobilizations of interactive civil actors to have access to and control over the cultural, social, and economic and the political resources to enable them for upward social mobility, to demolish the structure of domination and reorient their collective identities for self-expression and fulfilment. These interconnected civil actors are highly flexible as social collectivities that are regularly mobilized on the principle of fragmentation at one end and unification, on the other, and are in a process of continuous renewal and rejuvenation in the process of crystallization of the culture of social movement society. As the structure of domination has remained institutionalized, social conflicts and collective mobilizations rejuvenate themselves to articulate a space to transform the structure by contesting the structure of domination.

This resilient-reflexive perspective lays its foundation on the following premises: that social mobility, social conflict and collective mobilizations are integral part of the social movement society; that social imbalances are produced, sustained, and furthered through unequal access over social, economic and political resources which condition social mobility; that unequal quantum of mobility create underlying tension and competition for potential collective mobilization; that persistent social imbalances cause social conflict and cause of social conflicts are inherently multidimensional—material and non-material, emotional, moral; that conflicts and collective mobilizations are parts of democratic practices and development initiatives at the grassroots; that greater the capacity of the structure to co-opt/accommodate social conflict and collective mobilization, greater is the potential for the sustenance of the structure; that social movements get transformed with the changes in the cause of conflict, space of mobility, response of the structure to mobilization; and that social progression reproduces and rejuvenates social conflicts and collective mobilization although the process of institutionalization of social movements generates and accommodates new ideas and actions.

This perspective adheres to the principle of flexibility and culture of accommodation of conflicts within the social structure, which is widely transitional in nature. As the causes of social conflicts and process of collective mobilizations are getting widely diffused and simultaneously diversely connected, this perspective accommodates several new social, political and economic processes within it to integrate multiplicity and diverse formations within the ambit of social movement society. It is presented as a simple diagram in Figure 6.1.

However, the holistic perspective does not accommodate social anti-movements within the ambit of its analysis. Since social anti-movements are basically non flexible, non-compromising, undemocratic and remain as a threat to social movement society and propagate the absolute (Wieviorka 2005). It also breeds a variant of resistant identity with the expressions being exclusion of the excluded by the excluders (Castells 1997).

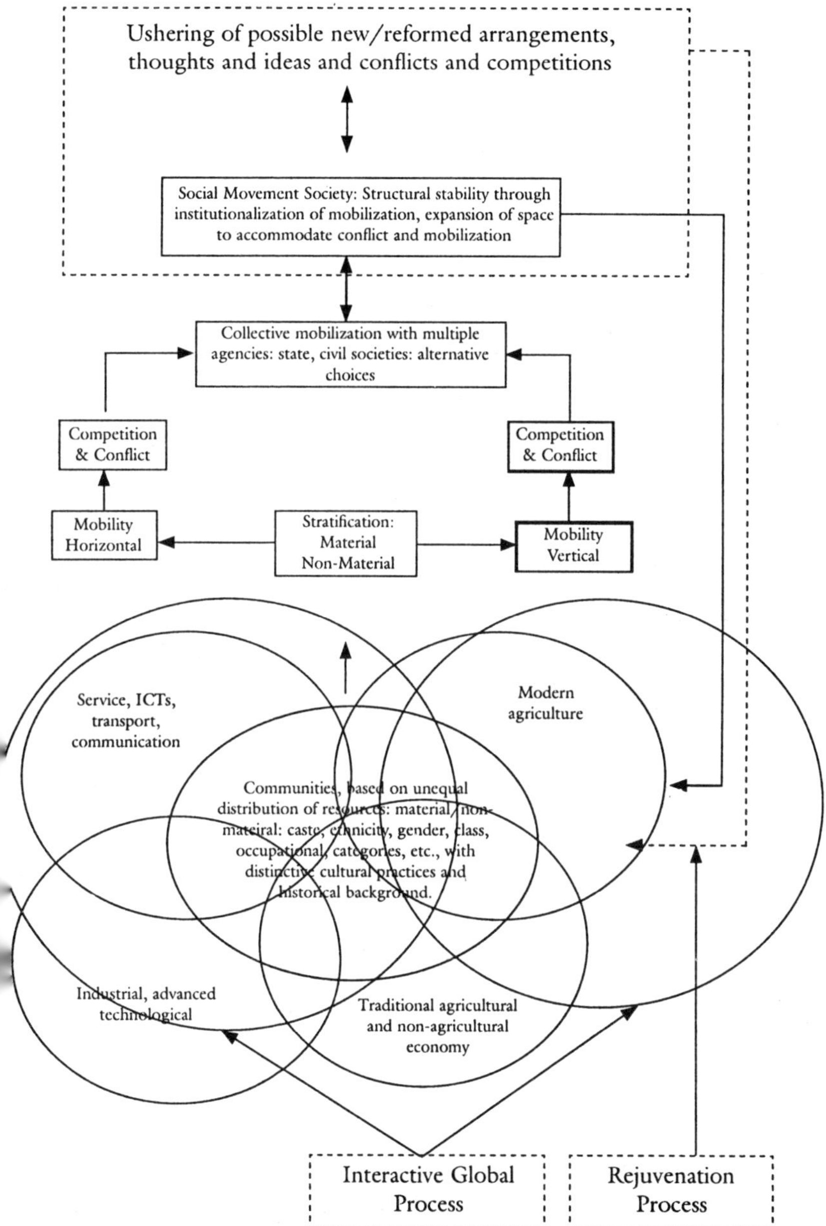

FIG. 6.1: FRAMEWORK OF RESILIENT HOLISTIC UNDERSTANDING OF SOCIAL CONFLICT, SOCIAL MOBILITY AND SOCIAL MOVEMENTS

Rural societies in India stands at the threshold of a social order widely characterized by intensive interactivity with, apparatus of the state, local social groups, ethnicity and new identities. Sharp depletion of the sources of livelihood security, increasing quantum of livelihood insecurity, migration, occupational mobilization, spread of education, urbanization, physical transport and information and communication networks have accentuated the processes of social mobility, conflicts and collective mobilizations. Sustained social conflicts have rejuvenated the process of multiple social identity formation, which constantly question the structure of their domination in society through everyday forms of collective mobilization and increasing quantum of social conflict. The struggles of poor peasants, SCs, STs, women, ethnic minority groups are as much related to the issues of livelihood security as to the issue of their identity that questions the several dimensions of their domination in society. These issues and collective mobilizations are related to the wider social system.

Social change and mobility have emerged to be integral parts of contemporary political conflicts, which are linked to the issues of cultural identity and wider social processes. These social conflicts, social mobility and social change have helped generate a new network of relationship between state, social movements and society across the space and have challenged many of the cultural values, social and political institutional arrangements and added new meaning to them. In the emerging contexts the seeming disjunctions between social mobility, collective mobilizations, social conflict and social change now tend to decline; for social conflict and collective mobilizations are no longer emergent responses to the exigencies of the society; rather they remain integrated as the valid arrangements of the social movement society. Hence there is the need to integrate the analyses of social structure with the processes of social mobility, conflicts, mobilizations and change.

In a social structure there are institutionalized forms of domination and also potential forms of challenges 'coming from new actors in history and society' as 'society is structured around conflicting positions which define alternative values and interests'. Such relationships between people and society are well depicted in every-day and in every context of social conflicts and collective mobilizations whereby 'people acting individually or collectively, produce or reproduce the rules of their society, and translate them into their spatial expression and their institutional management'. Here social movements as collective actions consciously aims at the transformation of the social interests and values embedded in the forms and functions of a historically given society and 'a movement develops not only in relationship to its own society, but also in relationship to a world-wide social system' (Castells 1983: i-xvi). In this context of technological revolution, there has been a widespread surge of powerful and multiple expressions of collective identity that challenge globalization and cosmopolitanism (Castells 1997), locally and globally.

REFERENCES

Amin, S., G. Arrighi, A.G. Frank and I. Wallerstein (eds) (1990), *Transforming Revolution: Social Movements and the World System*, New York: Monthly Review Press.

Banaji, Jarus (1994), 'The Farmers' Movements: A Critique of Conservative Rural Coalitions', *Journal of Peasant Studies*, 21(2), January.

Banerjee, A. et al. (2002), 'Strategy for Economic Reform in West Bengal', *Economic and Political Weekly*, vol. XXXVII, no. 41, pp. 4203–18.

Bartelson, J. (2000), 'Three Concepts of Globalization', *International Sociology*, vol. 15, no. 2: 180–96

Bell, D. (1976), *Coming of Post-Industrial Society: A Venture in Social Forecasting*, Harmondsworth: Penguin.

Bertaux, S. (1990), 'Oral History Approaches to an International Social Movement', in E. Oyen (ed.), *Comparative Methodology: Theory and Practices in International Social Research*, London: Sage.

Bevington, D. and C. Dixon (2005), 'Movement-relevant Theory: Rethinking Social Movement Scholarship and Activism', *Social Movement Studies*, vol 4, no. 3: 185–208(24).

Blumer, H. (1951), 'Social Movements', in A.N. Lee (ed.), *New Outline of Principles of Society*, New York: Baines D. Noldi.

Bourdieu, P. and L. Wacquant (1999), 'On the Cunning of Imperialist Reason', *Theory, Culture and Society*, vol. 16, no. 1, pp. 41–50.

Byres, T.J. (1981), 'New Technology, Class Formation and Class Action in the Indian Countryside', *The Journal of Peasant Studies*, vol. 8, no. 4, pp. 405–54.

Castells, M. (1983), *City and the Grassroots: A Cross Cultural Theory of Urban Social Movements*, California: University of California Press.

——— (1997), *The Rise of the Network of Society*, Oxford: Blackwell.

——— (1997), *The Information Age: Economy, Society and Culture: The Power of Identity*, vol. II, Malden: Blackwell Publishers.

Chandhoke, N. (1995), *State and Civil Society: Exploration in Political Theory*, Delhi: Sage.

Chandra, B. (1996), *Indian National Movement: The Long-term Dynamics*, New Delhi: Vikas.

Cohan, J.L. and A. Arato (1994), *Civil Society and Political Theory*, London: MIT Press.

Cohen, J. (1985), 'Strategy or Identity: New Theoretical Paradigms and Contemporary Social Movements', *Social Research*, 52(4), pp. 663–716.

Collins, Randall (1974), *Conflict Sociology*, New York: Academic Press.

Coser, Lewis (1956), *The Functions of Social Conflict*, Toronto, Ontario: Collier-Macmillan Canada.

Crossley, N. (2002), *Making Sense of Social Movements*, Buckingham: Open University Press.

Dahrendorf, Ralf (1959), *Class and Class Conflict in Industrial Society*, Stanford, CA: Stanford University Press.

Dasgupta, Biplab (1974), *The Naxalite Movement*, Mumbai: Allied Publishers.

Desai, A.R. (ed.) (1979), *Peasant Struggle in India*, Bombay: Oxford University Press.

della Porta, D. and S. Tarrow (2005), *Transnational Protest and Global Activism*, Lanham: Rowman & Litterfiled Publishers.

Dhanagare, D.N. (1983), *Peasant Movements in India, 1920-50*, Delhi: Oxford University Press.

Drucker, P.F. (1994), 'Knowledge Worker and Knowledge Society', http://www.kgs.harvard.edu

Edwards, M. (2000), *NGO Rights and Responsibilities*, London: The Foreign Policy Centre.

Elster, J. (1989), *Nuts and Bolts for the Social Sciences*, Cambridge: Cambridge University Press.

Eyerman, R. and A. Jamison (1991), *Social Movements: A Cognitive Approach*, Cambridge: Polity Press.

Ferree, M.M. (1992), 'The Political Contest of Rationality: Rational Choice Theory and Resource Mobilization', in A. Morros and C. Mueller, *Frontiers in Social Movement Theory*, New Haven: Yale University Press, pp. 29–52.

Ferguson, M. (1992), 'The Mythology About Globalization', *European Journal of Communication*, vol. 7, no. 1: 69–93.

Firth, R. (1946), *Malaya Fishermen: Their Peasant Economy*, London: Kegan Paul, Trench, Trubner & Co.

Giddens, A. (1991), *Modernity and Self-identity*, Cambridge: Polity Press.

Goodwin, J. and J.M. Jasper (1999), 'Caught in a Winding, Snarling Vine: The Structural Bias of Political Process Theory', *Sociological Forum*, vol. 14, no. 1, pp. 27–54.

Government of India, 1961, 1971, 1981, 1991, 2001, *Census of India*, New Delhi: Ministry of Information and Broadcasting.

Gramsci, A. (1998), *Selections from the Prison Notebooks* (rpt.), Chennai: Orient Longman.

Guesfield, J.R. (ed.) (1971), *Protest, Reform and Revolt: A Reader in Social Movements*, New York: John Wiley & Sons.

Guha, R. (1998), *Dominance Without Hegemony: History and Power in Colonial India*, Delhi: Oxford University Press.

Gupta, D. (2005), 'Wither the Indian Village: Culture and Agriculture in Rural India', *Economic and Political Weekly*, vol. XL, no. 8.

Gupta, Dipankar (1998), 'Country-Town Nexus and Agrarian Mobilization: The Bhartiya Kisan Union as an Instance', *Economic and Political Weekly*, 16 (37).

Haberle, R. (1951), *Social Movements*, New York: Appleton Century-Croft

——— (1972), 'Types and Functions of Social Movement', in *International Encyclopedia of Social Sciences*, New York: Macmillan Company Free Press.

Hagedus, Z. (1990), 'Social Movements and Social Change in Self-creative Society: New Initiatives in the International Arena', in M. Albrow and E. King (eds.), *Globalization, Knowledge and Society*, London: Sage.

Hardt, M. and A. Negri (2000), *Empire*, Harvard: Harvard University Press.

Jenkins, C. (1983), 'Resource Mobilization Theory and the Study of Social Movements', *Annual Review of Sociology*, 9, pp. 527–53.

Jenkins, C. and C. Perrow (1977), 'Insurgency of the Powerless Farm Workers Movements (1946-1972)', *American Sociological Review*, 42(2), pp. 249–68.

Jessop, B. (2003), 'The Future of State in an Era of Globalization', *International Politics and Society*, 3/2003.

Larana, E., H. Johnston and R. Guesfield (1984), 'Identities, Grievances and New Social Movements', in E. Larana, H. Johnston, and R. Guesfield (eds.), *New Social Movements: From Ideology to Identity*, Philadelphia: Temple University Press.

Marris, A. and C. McClurg Mueller (1992), 'Master Frames and Cycles of Protests', in A. Marris and C. McClurg Mueller (eds.), *Frontiers of Social Movement Theory*, New Haven and London: Yale University Press.

Marx, K. (1852, rpt. 1974), Excerpts from 'The Class Struggle in France 1848–1850', and 'The Eighteenth Brumaire of Louis Bonaparte', in K. Marx and F. Engels, *Selected Works*, vol. 1, London: Lawrence & Wishart.

——— (1976, rpt.), *Selected Writings*, Moscow: Progress Publishers.

Marx, K. and F. Engels (1748, rpt. 1972), 'Manifesto of the Communist Party', *Karl Marx and Frederick Engels Selected Works*, vol. 1, Moscow: Progress Publishers.

McAdam, D. (1982), *Political Process and the Development of Black Insurgency*, Chicago: University of Chicago Press.

——— (1999), *Political Process and the Development of Black Insurgency, 1930-1970*, Chicago: University of Chicago Press.

McAdam, D., S. Tarrow and C. Tilly (2001), *Dynamics of Contention*, Cambridge: Cambridge University Press.

McCarthy, J. and M. Zald (1977), 'Resource Mobilization and Social Movements', *American Journal of Sociology*, 82(6), pp. 1212–41.

McDonald, K. (2002), 'From Solidarity to Fluidarity: Social Movements Beyond Collective Identity: The Case of Globalization of Conflict', *Social Movements Studies,* vol. 1, no. 2, 109–278.

Melucci, A. (1996a), *Challenging Codes: Collective Action in the Information Age*, Cambridge: Cambridge University Press.

——— (1996), 'The Symbolic Challenge of Contemporary Movements', in S.M. Buechler and F.K. Cylke Jr. (eds.), *Social Movements: Perspectives and Issues*, California: Mayfield Publishing Company.

Mosca, Gaetano (1939), *The Ruling Class*, New York: McGraw Hill.

Mukherjee, R.K. (1957), *Dynamics of a Rural Society*, Berlin: Academic Verlag.

Mukherjee, M. (2004), *Peasants in India's Non Violent Revolution: Practice and Theory,* New Delhi : Sage.

Mukherji, Partha (1979), 'Naxalite Movement and the Peasant Revolt in North', in M.S.A. Rao (ed.), *Social Movements in India*, New Delhi: Manohar.

Naisbitt, J. (1986), *Reinventing the Corporation: Transforming Your Job and Your Company for the New Information Society*, London: Nicholas.

Nettl, J.P. (1967), *Political Mobilization: A Sociological Analysis of Methods and Concepts*, New York: Basic Books.

NSSO (1971), (1992), (2003), *Reports of the National Sample Survey*, New Delhi: Ministry of Statistics and Programme Implementation.

Oommen, T.K. (1984), *Social Transformation in Rural India: Mobilisation and State Intervention*, New Delhi: Vikas Publishing House.

——— (1985), *From Mobilization to Institutionalisation: The Dynamics of Agrarian Movement in 20th Century Kerala*, Bombay: Popular Prakashan.

Parsons, T. (1969), *Politics and Social Structure*, New York: Free Press.

Planning Commission (2001), *Tenth Five Year Plan 2002-2007*, New Delhi: GOI.

Powel, B.H. (1957) (rpt.), *The Indian Village Community*, New Haven: HRAF Press.

Pradhan, T. (2002), 'Kantapuri Andolan Kon Pahe' (Bengali), *Ajkal*, 19 August.

Prasad, P. (1973), 'Production Relations: Achilles Heal of Indian Planning', *Economic and Political Weekly*, vol. VIII, no. 19, pp. 869–72.

Rao, M.S.A. (1985), *Social Movements and Social Transformation: A Study of Two Backward Class Movements in India*, New Delhi: Manohar.

Rucht, D. and F. Neidhardt (2002), 'Towards a Movement Society? On the Possibilities of Institutionalizing Social Movements', *Social Movement Studies*, vol. 1, no. 1, pp. 1–30.

Scott, A. (1991), *Ideology and New Social Movements*, London: Unwin Hyman.

Sen, S. (1982), *Peasant Movements in India: Mid-Nineteenth to Twentieth Centuries*, Calcutta: K.P. Bagchi & Co.

SinghaRoy, D.K. (2001), 'Critical Issues in Grassroots Mobilizations and Collective Action', in D.K. SinghaRoy (ed.), *Social Development and Empowerment of the Marginalized Groups: Perspectives and Strategies*, New Delhi: Sage.

——— (2004), *Peasant Movements in Post Colonial India: Dynamics of Mobilization and Identity*, New Delhi: Sage.

——— (2005), 'Peasant Movements in Contemporary India', *Economic and Political Weekly*, 24 December.

Smelser, N. (1962), *Theory of Collective Behaviour*, New York: Free Press.

——— (1976), *The Sociology of Economic Life*, Englewood Cliffs, New Jersey: Prentice-Hall Inc.

Smith, P.J. and E. Symthe (1999), 'Globalization, Citizenship and Technology: The MAI Meets the Internet', *Canadian Foreign Policy*, 7(2): pp. 83–105.

Sorokin, Pitirim (1959), *Social and Cultural Mobility*, New York: The Free Press.

Snow, D.A. and Robert D. Benford (1992), 'Master Frames and Cycles of Protests', in A. Marris and C. McClurg Mueller (eds.), *Frontiers of Social Movement Theory*, New Haven and London: Yale University Press, pp. 133–55.

Srinivas, M.N. (1956), *Religion and Society Among the Coorgs of South India*, Mumbai: Asia Publishing House.

Streten, P. (1998), 'The Contribution of Non-Governmental Organizations to Development', *Political Economy Journal of India*, vol. 6, no. 2, pp. 111–21.

Tarrow, S. (1995), *Power in Movements Social Movements, Collective Action and Politics*, Cambridge: Cambridge University Press.

Therborn, G. (2000), 'Globalizations: Dimensions, Historical Waves, Regional Effects, Normative Governance', *International Sociology*, vol. 15, no. 2, pp. 151–79.

Thompson, E.P. (1963), *The Making of the English Working Class*, London: Victor Gollancz.

Tilly, C. (1985), 'Models and Realities of Popular Collective Action', *Social Research*, vol. 52 (Winter).

Toffler, A. (1980), *The Third Wave*, London: Pan Books.

Tonnies, F. (1957), *Community and Society*, East Lansingh: Michigan State University Press.

Touraine, A. (1981), *The Voice and the Eye: An Analysis of Social Movements*, Cambridge: Cambridge University Press.

——— (1983), *Anti-Colonial Protest*, Cambridge: Cambridge University Press.

——— (2002), 'The Importance of Social Movements', *Social Movement Studies*, vol. 1, issue 1, pp. 89–95.

Turek, J. (2003), Review of Maurell Castell's Publication, *The Information Age*, www.capimu.de/fgz/reviews/30.php

Turner, R. and L. Killian (1957), *Collective Behaviour*, Englewood Cliffs: Prentice Hall.

UN (1995), 'Declaration of the Social Development Summit, Copenhagen', New York: UN.

UNDP (1993), 'UNDP and Civil Society', New York: UNDP.

——— (1995), 'Declaration of the Social Development Summit, Copenhagen', New York: UN.

——— (1997), *Human Development Report*, New Delhi: Oxford University Press.

——— (2001), *Human Development Report 2001*, New Delhi: Oxford University Press.

——— (2005), *Human Development Report*, New Delhi: Oxford University Press.

——— (2007), *Human Development Report*, New Delhi: Oxford University Press.

Urry, John (2000), 'Mobile Sociology', *British Journal of Sociology*, vol. 51, no. 1, 185–203.

Wallerstain, I. (1990), 'Antisystemic Movements: History and Dilemmas', in S. Amin, et al. (eds.), *Transforming the Revolution: Social Movements and the World System*, New York: Monthly Review Press.

Wieviorka, M. (2005), 'After New Social Movements', *Social Movements Studies*, vol. 4, Issue 1 : 1–19.

Wilson, J. (1973), *Introduction to Social Movements*, New York: Basic Books.

Wolff, Kurt H. (tr.) (1950), *The Sociology of Georg Simmel*, Glencoe, IL: The Free Press.

World Bank (1997), *World Development Report*, New Delhi: Oxford University Press.

Zald, M. and J. McCarthy (1987), *Social Movements in an Organizational Society: Collected Essays*, New Brunswick: Transaction.

II. SOCIAL MOVEMENTS, GLOBALIZATION AND TRANSNATIONAL ACTIVISMS

CHAPTER 7

Solidarity Across Borders: The Anti-Apartheid Movement and Global Civil Society

HÅKAN THÖRN

INTRODUCTION

Given the number of people that participated in the transnational anti-apartheid movement, as well as its geographical dispersion and its achievements, there is no doubt that it was one of the most influential social movements during the post-war era. In addition to the South African movement organizations, the transnational anti-apartheid network connected thousands of groups and organizations, including solidarity organizations, unions, churches, women's, youth and student organizations in more than 100 countries. For example, only in Britain more than 184 local groups were affiliated to the British Anti-Apartheid Movement (AAM) in 1990; and its list of international contacts included anti-apartheid solidarity organizations in 37 countries (MSS AAM 13 & M). Existing as a transnational movement for more than four decades, its impact was not limited to the South African context, as it created transnational networks, organizations and collective action forms that made—and still make—an impact on national as well as transnational political cultures.

Although the significance of this movement has often been recognized (Della Porta and Kriesi 1999; Keck and Sikkink 1998; Cohen and Rai 2000), little research has been done on anti-apartheid, especially from the perspective of social movement theory. Further, while one of the most crucial aspects of this movement was its construction of *transnational* networks and forms of action, most research has focused on its national aspects, looking at the Australian,

British, American or South African AAMs (Fieldhouse 2005; Massie 1997; Jennett 1989; Voorhes 1999; Seekings 2000).

In this article I analyse some of the crucial aspects of the action forms and identification processes of the anti-apartheid movement, relating it to relevant political and historical contexts. I argue that the transnational anti-apartheid struggle proves a relevant case for contemporary theorizing and research on transnational social movements and the emergence of a global civil society.

ANTI-APARTHEID AND SOCIAL MOVEMENT THEORY: BEYOND EUROCENTRISM

In the cases where the anti-apartheid struggle has been analysed in terms of a social movement, it has often been related to the discourse on 'new social movements' (NSM). In an article on the British AAM, Stuart Hall argues that it could be seen as one of the new social movements, since it 'cut across issues of class and party, and organizational allegiance' (Hall 2000: 52). In a similar mode Christine Jennett has analysed the Australian AAM as a new social movement, emphasizing its cultural orientation (Jennett 1989). I agree that the AAM displayed many of the central features of NSM as these have been defined in the context of NSM theory (Della Porta and Diani 1999; Melucci 1996; Kriesi et al. 1995; Cohen and Rai 2000). The struggle against apartheid was part of the emergence of a new transnational political culture during the post-war era, that also included other solidarity movements, as well as student's, green, peace and women's movements, often conceptualized as 'the NSMs'. It was able to unite an extremely broad 'rainbow coalition' of organizations and groups, with extremely diverse social basis and ideological orientation. Further, the AAM had a strong cultural orientation, it was highly media oriented and the production and dissemination of information was one of its central activities. Finally, although its actions often had the purpose of putting pressure on governments and political parties, it engaged in extra-parliamentary political action, such as civil disobedience and boycotts, the latter its most important form of collective action.

It is however not possible to use NSM theory to analyse the transnational AAM without making a few modifications. *First*, 'old social movements', predominantly labour movements and church networks, and their increased internationalization during the post-war era were an integral part of the AAM, which could be defined as a 'movement of movements'. *Second*, and more important, the case of anti-apartheid as a transnational social movement reveals some highly problematic Eurocentric assumptions made in the context of NSM theory.

Although the global dimensions of contemporary collective action has often been pointed out, especially by Alberto Melucci (1989; 1996), Western nation states and their transformation to 'post-industrial', 'complex' or 'informational' societies have been the point of departure for theorizing on NSMs. In general, NSM theorists have pointed to new social conditions of 'advanced Western societies' as a precondition for emergence of NSMs. Consequently, where no such new conditions are clearly present, no new movements can possibly emerge. In spite of this, the concept of 'NSMs' has in a few cases been applied in analyses of collective action in the South (Slater 1985; Wignaraja 1992), however often without theoretical debate. One important exception is Ernesto Laclau (1985), who has argued that:

> . . . is it not the case that this plurality of the social and this proliferation of political spaces which lie behind the new social movements, are basically typical of advanced industrial societies, whilst the social reality of the Third World, given its lower level of differentiation, can still be apprehended in terms of the more classical categories of sociological and class analysis? The reply is that, besides the fact that this 'lower level of differentiation' is a myth, Third World societies have never been comprehensible in terms of a strict class analysis. We hardly need to refer to the Eurocentrism in which the 'universalization' of that analysis was based. (Laclau 1985: 30)

Thus, as Peyman Vahabzadeh has argued: 'the presence of new social movements in non-western societies (i.e., gay, women's or ecological movements) problematizes the explanatory linkage between the postindustrial society and the new social movements' (Vahabzadeh 2001: 24).

The implicit Eurocentric and evolutionist thinking often expressed in NSM theory is clearly formulated by Christine Jennett as she applies Alain Touraine's theory of social movements in her analysis of the Australian AAM. The movement organization Australian AAM, consisting of predominantly white middle-class Australian solidarity activists, is by Jennett defined as a 'NSM', characterized by its orientation toward participatory grassroots democracy. The exile liberation movements, including the African National Congress

(ANC), Pan Africanist Congress (PAC) and Azanian People's Organisation (SZAPO), are by the same author defined as 'historical movements', characterized by hierarchical forms of organization and nationalist ideology (Jennett and Stewart 1989: 21; Jennett 1989: 136, 147).

In a sense the NSM theory has often implicitly been reproducing the Eurocentric evolutionist thinking of classical modernization theory, in which each country in its development has to pass through similar stages, and where the 'underdeveloped' countries of the south are always lagging behind the developed countries of the north. This mode of thinking is also based on what has been called 'methodological nationalism' in the sense that the nation state is always the basic unity of the analysis, and development/under-development thus always is related to 'internal factors' (Beck 2000). This paradigm ignores the existence of global power relations and economic and political interdependence. In the case of theories of post-industrial society, it is often 'forgotten' that the transformation to post-industrial economies in the north presupposed moving industrial production to so-called 'low-wage' countries in the south. Although few advocates of classical modernization theory are to be heard today, many of its assumptions are still implicitly present in current social theory. This is the case even in recent globalization discourse, as social conditions and trends specific to countries in the north are often being universalized (Castells 1996; Paolini 1997).

As I see it, the NSM theory has contributed with many valuable insights on contemporary collective action, but it must be delinked from its eurocentric implications. Social movement studies could thus benefit from integrating perspectives from post-colonial theory (Hall 1996; Bhabha 1994). Post-colonial studies have not only emphasized the importance of the presence of a colonial legacy in the context of the latest phase of the globalization process, but also the presence and influence of the de-colonization process and the politics of anti-colonialism on present-day politics (Young, 2001; and 2004).

Applying this perspective to the transnational AAM, and relating it to the debate on NSMs, it is evident that this movement, displaying all the characteristics associated with so-called 'NSMs', emerged out of *transnational* interactions located in the context of de-colonization. It was initiated under strong influence of not just ANC, PAC and the political community of South African exiles, but also of the broader anti-colonial struggle.

The first international AAM organization was the International Defence and Aid Fund (IDAF), formed with the purpose of providing legal support to individuals prosecuted for violating the apartheid laws and to support the families of 'apartheid prisoners' (Herbstein 2004; Shepherd 1977). It was initiated in 1956 (but formally founded as an international organization only in 1965) as an outgrowth of Christian Action, a group inspired by the anti-colonial movements, engaging in solidarity action and civil disobedience. However, the broader international campaign against apartheid took off in the late 1950s and early 1960s. In June 1959, the anti-colonial Committee of African Organizations (CAO) held a meeting in in London, in response to the call of the South African Congress Alliance to boycott South African goods. One of the speakers at the meeting was Julius Nyerere, president of the Tanganyika Africa National Union. The Boycott Committee was formed, and soon it evolved into the independent Boycott Movement, which in 1960 changed its name to the AAM, run by South African exiles and a few of their British supporters (MSS AAM 1; Guerney 2000). In 1964 the AAM decided to pay special attention to the coordination of the transnational anti-apartheid network (MSS AAM 13 & M).

The de-colonization process clearly marked established politics as well as the emerging alternative political culture in Britain at this time. Both IDAF and AAM were formed as part of what in Britain in the late 1950s and early 1960s was called 'new politics', as I see it an early conceptualization of certain forms of collective action, foreshadowing the latter 'new social movements'. At the same time in the 1950s that IDAF was initiated, the British peace movement initiated a mobilization process influenced by the Indian anti-colonial movement. It was called 'Operation Gandhi', and organized 'sit-ins' outside of the British Ministry of Defence. The founder of IDAF, Canon John Collins, was also the chairman of the Campaign for Nuclear Disarmament (CND), the dominant peace movement organization in Britain at the time. A public personality involved in the more militant civil disobedience actions that the peace movement at this time continued to stage (and which amongst other things led to the trial against Bertrand Russell, that gained media attention around the world) was Reverend Michael Scott. Scott was a priest who had been participating in militant Indian civil disobedience actions as well as black political activism in South Africa. Banned in South Africa in 1950, Scott initiated the anti-colonial Africa Bureau in London, supporting African de-colonization. Just like the Movement for Colonial Freedom, the Africa Bureau was an important part of an emerging anti-colonial political culture in Britain in the late 1950s. As the AAM started to reach outside of the exile circles, it attracted individuals who were part of this political culture.[1]

To conclude the discussion on the implications of the case of the AAM in relation to the debate on NSMs: I argue that if we use this concept, it must be recognized that NSMs in the West partly emerged out of the *global context* of de-colonization, and that the collective experiences and action forms of the anti-colonial struggles in the south were extremely important sources of influence. I think that the reason for this influence being largely neglected in the context of NSM theory is partly due to the methodological nationalism which for a long time has dominated not just social movement studies but the social sciences in general (Beck 2000).

However, recently a new inter-disciplinary field of research has emerged, dealing with transnational collective action and the changing role of the nation state in the context of the increasing importance of processes of globalization (Della Porta and Tarrow 2005; Della Porta and Kriesi 1999; Tarrow 1998a; Keck and Sikkink 1998; Smith, Chatfield and Pagnucco 1997). As Keck and Sikkink (1998) showed, this approach is not only valid in relation to the recent wave of transnational collective action, but also to historical cases.

Emphasizing their theoretical model of 'political opportunity structures', social movement theorists like Della Porta, Kriesi and Sidney Tarrow argue that changes in international contexts and the emergence of international institutions have created new opportunities for social movements to act transnationally. However, in relation to what Tarrow (1998a) calls 'the strong transnational thesis', according to which national opportunity structures are giving away to transnational structures, these social movement theorists have generally taken a more cautious or sceptical approach (Tarrow 1998a; 1998b). Tarrow, as well as Della Porta and Kriesi emphasize that the nation state still is, and for some time will continue to be the most important context for social movement mobilization.

According to some proponents of the 'strong thesis', transnational collective action has resulted in the emergence of a global civil society (Anheier, Glasius and Kaldor 2001 and 2004/5; Kaldor 2003). However, sceptics like Tarrow have argued that 'it is hard to find, combined in the same movement, the conditions necessary to produce a social movement that is, at once, integrated with several societies, unified in its goals, and capable of sustained interaction with a variety of political authorities' (Tarrow 1998a: 240). In a similar vein, Keck and Sikkink argue that 'there is a lack of convincing studies of the sustained and specific processes through which individuals and organizations create . . . something resembling a global civil society' (Keck and Sikkink 1998: 33).

However, I would like to argue that the transnational AAM fulfils the criteria that Tarrow mentions. In this sense the interactions of the AAM was part of the construction of a global civil society during the Cold War, if we understand this concept as a transnational space where different political cultures intersect (Thörn 2002 and 2006, forthcoming).

There is no doubt that national policies, national organizations as well as national political cultures played a significant role in shaping the anti-apartheid struggle in different parts of the world. Globalization does not necessarily mean that the nation state, understood as a political space, is fading away. *Rather, the nation state gains new meanings in the context of globalization, just as globalization has different meanings in different national contexts.* However, I also think that in social movement studies focusing on political opportunity structures, the relevance of a global perspective on social movement interactions, networks and contexts has been underestimated. It is not just the issues and the networks of the new movements that have become increasingly global during the post-war era. The structural processes that create the preconditions for the emergence of new forms of collective action are transnational, rather than bound to any *specific* nation states. Further, looking at the case of anti-apartheid, the different opportunities and constraints facing anti-apartheid organizations in the context of specific nation states, were to a large extent determined by the belongings of those states to different international communities and their interests, as well as by wider global and historical contexts. Hence, the nation state cannot be used as the basic unit of the analysis of anti-apartheid collective action.

Turning to theories on the emergence of a global civil society, these have recently been fuelled by the appearance of the 'global justice movement' (sometimes called the 'anti-globalization movement') in the streets of Western cities, as well as in a globalized media space (Della Porta and Tarrow 2005; Sen et al. 2003; Anheier, Glasius and Kaldor 2001; Bond 2001). In these discussions, the internet is often highlighted as important in the making of a global civil society (Naughton 2001). However, I would like to argue that more importantly, the present global civil society has historical links to the post-war, transnational political culture in which the AAM played a significant role.

In the following section, I will look at the context in which anti-apartheid emerged as a transnational social movement. In an attempt to go beyond the nation state-oriented analysis of social movements, Della Porta and Kriesi (1999) suggest that we should look at how international *constraints and opportunities* operate at different levels of international politics. However, as my focus is on transnational *political culture,* I prefer to use the concept of *context* rather than opportunity structure. This is in order to emphasize how transnational collective action at any given time is structure not just by the presence of formal political international institutions, but through historically instituted discursive formations and processes of identity construction at a global level.

DEFINING THE CONTEXT OF ANTI-APARTHEID: POLITICAL GLOBALIZATION, POST-COLONIALITY AND THE COLD WAR

In the widest sense the appropriate structural context for the transnational AAM is the process of intensified political globalization during the post-war era (Held et al. 1999; Thörn 2002). Here, it is also relevant to make an analytical distinction between *globalization from above*, and *globalization from below* (Falk 1999). Political globalization from above is constituted by the increasing number and importance of inter-governmental organizations (IGOs) and international treaties, a process taking off during the post-war era (Held et al. 1999: 53). It is important to emphasize that this increasingly complex international system is not just composed of formal institutional arrangements. It should be conceived of as a conglomeration of overlapping *international communities*, understood as 'sites of identity and interest' (Klotz 1995: 27). When looking at the political context of the global anti-apartheid struggle, a number of international communities were important. For the European AAM, the EEC was of course important. For example, the British AAM built relationships with members of the European Parliament and met the European Parliament Socialist Group. In April 1985 the

EEC agreed to partial sanctions, which were extended in 1986 (Fieldhouse 2005). Globally, even more important were however particularly the OAU, the Commonwealth, and the UN, being the largest and most complex of the international communities during the post-war era (Klotz 1995). The foundation of these communities, as well as the articulation of their political identities and interests, were in turn shaped by two wider and overlapping global and historical contexts: *post-coloniality* and *the Cold War*.

Situated in the context of *post-coloniality*, the issue of apartheid was articulated as an issue of de-colonization, particularly by newly independent states and anti-colonial movements, and the patterns of conflicts and positions taken in the context of international communities were conditioned by the political history of colonialism. Situated in the context of the Cold War, the anti-apartheid struggle, like any significant political field during the post-war era, national as well as transnational, was divided along the conflict lines that constituted the Cold War. The Cold War was a crucial factor in the circumstances that made it possible for the South African apartheid government to sustain its position internationally. It was also the Cold War that made it possible to define ANC as part of a bloc that threatened world peace and security, because the organization did not only receive support from Western states, but also from the Eastern bloc.

POLITICAL GLOBALIZATION FROM ABOVE: THE OAU, THE COMMONWEALTH AND THE UN

Divided on many issues, especially in relation to Cold War conflicts, the African states declared unity on advocating racial equality and de-colonization when the Organization of African Unity (OAU) was formed in 1963. The OAU was thus founded on the construction of a post-colonial Pan-African identity and became an important inter-state actor in the anti-apartheid struggle, which it articulated in terms of de-colonization and national self-determination. When the UN General Assembly in 1973 declared that it was the South African liberation movements (ANC and PAC) that were the authentic representatives of the (national) people of South Africa, it referred to an earlier declaration made by the OAU (UN 1994: 30). In 1964, the OAU called for an oil embargo on South Africa. It also encouraged its member states to give active support to the liberation movements and gave strong support for the call for sanctions made by the transnational AAM (Klotz 1995). This support was partly a result of persistent pressure from the AAM, particularly the exiled liberation organizations ANC and PAC.

During the period of the anti-apartheid struggle, the Commonwealth, an informal organization based on the historical legacy and political identity of the British Empire, was transformed into a post-colonial community. This was felt by South Africa, which in 1961 was more or less forced to withdraw its request for readmission into the Commonwealth after it had become a republic. It was also felt by Britain itself, becoming more and more constrained as the numbers of newly independent states grew, as did the commitment to issues of decolonization and anti-racism. The issue of apartheid caused a large battle in the Commonwealth, in which Britain resisted the overwhelming majority of nations advocating sanctions. In doing this Britain confirmed that if it was losing its grip over its old colonies, it still had status as a world power, being one of the leading members of the political community of the Western powers and its military alliance NATO, formed in the context of the Cold War. (It was only as a result of strong pressure from other European countries that Britain, under protest, in 1985 accepted the EEC policy of partial sanctions.)

The transnational anti-apartheid movement was allowed a space for lobbying during the Commonwealth meetings.[2] Under the leadership of Shridath Ramphal, the Commonwealth Secretariat gave the ANC accreditation to attend the meetings together with journalists, something which upset the British, as the ANC at this time was labelled a terrorist organization by Prime Minister Margaret Thatcher.

The international community that became most important for the transnational AAM, in terms of providing a space for mobilization, was the UN. In 1963, the UN Special Committee against Apartheid was formed (Korey 1998; Shepherd 1976). At this time, NGOs did not have the kind of official recognition in the UN that they have at present. In this sense, the Special Committee against Apartheid was unique when it became a crucial node in the network of transnational anti-apartheid activism. The committee supplied anti-apartheid organizations with well-researched information material and, from the late 1970s, in a few cases some financial support. The committee also sent delegations to various countries to consult with national and international NGOs.[3]

However, the most important aspect of the activities of the

committee was the organization of conferences, where representatives from anti-apartheid organizations could come and make important contacts. According to activists, what really mattered was not so much what happened during the formal sessions, but what took place in the context of informal meetings in between them. Here, information was exchanged, overall strategies were discussed, cooperation on campaigns, national as well as transnational, were coordinated, and friendships were made. These conferences might actually be seen as the predecessors of the alternative NGO-conferences that since the 1970s are regularly held 'outside' the large official UN meetings.

However, as any issue in the UN at the time, the apartheid issue was clearly defined by the tensions and conflicts of post-coloniality as well as of the Cold War. Activists, particularly those in the United States, also felt this. According to Jennifer Davis, a South African exile and a leading activist in the New York-based solidarity organization American Committee of Africa (ACOA), the UN was regarded with suspicion in the US during the Cold War. 'It was regarded as the creature of somebody else—either the Third World or the Soviet Union.'[4] In the context of the UN, the activities of the Special Committee were thus also regarded with suspicion in certain camps. Defining the issue in Cold War terms, the major Western powers opposed sanctions against South Africa in the Security Council and boycotted the Special Committee (none of the Western countries ever joined the committee). The committee consisted of representatives mainly from Asian, African and Latin American countries, as well as a few from Eastern Europe.

The apartheid issue points to the 'Janus face' of the UN as a political community and a central institution of global politics. On the one hand, as an inter-state organization, the UN is subjected to the power hierarchy of the inter-state system. The dominant state powers in the Security Council can block or manipulate decisions in accordance with their national interests, as was the case with the issue of effective sanctions against South Africa. On the other hand, the UN might also be seen as part of a global civil society, as relatively independent UN organizations like the Special Committee interact with NGOs from various countries, bypassing the state level, and giving space for transnational social movements opposing the interests of dominant state powers. To conclude, the case of anti-apartheid shows that the UN can be perceived as political space where the processes of globalization from above and below sometimes intersect.[5]

POLITICAL GLOBALIZATION FROM BELOW: LIBERATION MOVEMENTS AND SOLIDARITY NETWORKS

The emergency of a global civil society during the twentieth century was constituted by the increasing number of NGOs, transnational networks and social movements organizing across borders (Held et al. 1999, McGrew 1997). During the post-war era, a transnational political culture emerged through the increasing internationalization of old movements, such as churches and the labour movement, as well as the emergence of new social movements, which addressed global issues in new ways, e.g. colonialism/imperialism, solidarity, ecology, peace and gender inequality. The transnational anti-apartheid movement was part of this process and became, as a 'movement of movements', a space of intersection for a wide range of collective actors.

Social movement studies have emphasized the importance of previously organized networks for the mobilization of a social movement (Della Porta and Diani 2000; Tarrow 1998b). Since networks are carriers of values, previously organized networks bring a historical legacy into the formation of a new movement. In the context of the AAM, the churches, the labour movement and the anti-colonial movements provided such networks.

The tensions and ambiguities of post-coloniality were particularly evident in the church networks. On the one hand the presence of the European and North American churches in southern Africa was part of cultural colonialism. On the other hand, many key activists and prominent figures of the AAM were based in the churches, for example, Albert Luthuli of ANC, Trevor Huddleston of AAM, Canon John Collins of IDAF and George Houser of American Community of Africa (ACOA). Another relevant case is that of Gunnar Helander, who in the 1930s went to South Africa to spread the word of Swedish Protestantism. In the late 1950s he came back to Europe on a completely different mission, becoming a leading anti-apartheid journalist and author in Sweden, initiating the Swedish chapter of IDAF, and later becoming its vice-chairman in London. Still, old colonial links in some cases influenced positions that were taken by Helander and his church, as for example, in relation to the debate on sanctions *versus* 'constructive engagement'. The latter signified a standpoint that opposed sanctions against South Africa, and instead proposed that apartheid should be resisted through successive reforms, which should be forced through by multinational companies with subsidiaries in South Africa (a standpoint that the core of the AAM regarded as a cover for doing 'business as usual' in South Africa). Although many intense debates on the issue of isolation *versus* involvement were held within the networks of the Swedish churches, and ambivalence as well as internal opposition was frequently expressed, it was only in 1986 that the Swedish Church finally sold off its shares in Swedish South African companies. In this matter, it is relevant to mention the close contacts that the Swedish Church Mission had with chief Mangosuthu Buthelezi of KwaZulu Natal, a leader of the Inkatha organization, which opposed ANCs call for sanctions. This was a link going back to the late nineteenth century when the mission started its South African adventure in Zululand (Sellström, 1999 and 2002).

Tensions of post-coloniality also defined the relations between South African exile movements and Western solidarity movements. In her Australian study, Christine Jennett emphasized that the solidarity organizations were dependent on good relations with the exile movements for their legitimacy in relation to their supporters and the general public. However, just as important, it was the other way round as well. For example, it was very difficult for the ANC or the PAC to stage its own public meetings in Britain in the 1960s as 'black' and 'foreign' organizations.[6] However, with AAM providing the platform by organizing the meeting, the ANC and PAC leaders could give public voice to their issue. I think that this interdependence between exile and solidarity organizations highlights some of the paradoxes characterizing the condition of post-coloniality, in which colonial dependencies can be reproduced, rearticulated and sometimes transgressed.

Understood in its broadest sense, the international labour movement played an extremely important role in the transnational anti-apartheid struggle. However, it also brought into the movement its historical legacy of factional divisions, which had gained a new meaning and a new significance in the context of the Cold War. Particularly the reluctance among many Western labour unions to support the ANC and its call for sanctions against South Africa must be related to Cold War divisions between Soviet Communism and Western Socialist Reformism. Especially during the 1970s, the strong anti-Communism within the Western the International Confederation of Trade Unions (ICFTU) caused suspicion against ANC, since its main union ally at this time was South African Confederation of Trade Unions (SACTU), that was affiliated to the Communist-dominated World Federation of Trade Unions (WFTU).

Thus, it was not just through its impact on inter-state relations that post-colonial and Cold War tension, ambivalence and conflict conditioned the anti-apartheid struggle; they were also structuring the movement's internal organization, its debates and action strategies.

In retrospect, transnational support to the struggle against apartheid in South Africa might appear to have been something uncontroversial in most parts of the world. And sometimes it was. But to *sustain* support to the struggle in South Africa against apartheid through the decades from the 1950s until the 1990s, and especially to support the call for sanctions made by the ANC, was not always an easy affair. I would argue that, at certain moments, anti-apartheid action in this context constructed what Homi Bhabha has called a *third space*, understood as 'an intervention into a situation that has become extremely polarised'.[7] As a position, 'third space' does not signify neutrality, rather it is a condition in which the conflicts, contradictions and ambivalences of a political order is felt most strongly. This condition was undoubtedly experienced by the anti-apartheid activists who were not just occasionally participating in a boycott or a demonstration, but spent years and decades in order to sustain support to the struggle against apartheid.

In the following section, I will analyse how this space was constituted through collective action, defining transnational anti-apartheid collective action as a social movement.

DEFINING ANTI-APARTHEID AS A TRANSNATIONAL SOCIAL MOVEMENT

Departing from the so-called 'identity paradigm' (Melucci 1996; Eyerman and Jamison 1991; Cohen and Arato 1985) I *analytically* define a social movement as a form of collective action that articulates a social conflict and ultimately aims at transforming a social order; it is a process of action and interaction involving as a fundamental element the construction of a collective identity, or a sense of community, of 'us', sharing a set of values and norms, and 'others', i.e. antagonistic actors, or 'enemies' (Thörn 1997). This is a process that not only involves consensus building but also tensions and conflicts. Although social movements may appear as homogeneous phenomena in public space, they must be conceived as action spaces constituted by heterogeneous and sometimes contradictory constellations of actions (Melucci 1996). I would even argue that tension and conflict are constitutive of dynamic social movement processes. This is particularly the case with the transnational AAM, which was a 'movement of movements', consisting of an extremely broad alliance between liberation movements and solidarity movements, the latter composed of different 'blocs'—churches, unions, youth wings of political parties (predominantly liberals and social democrats), women's, student and solidarity movements.

What then, united the different actors struggling against apartheid, in spite of their many internal differences and debates? They were of course united in the common goal of ending the apartheid system in South Africa. However, a common goal is not enough for a constellation of actors to compose a social movement. What is required is a shared collective identity, and I would like to argue that in the context of the *transnational* AAM, 'solidarity' was the central identity concept. According to the activists that I have interviewed, 'solidarity' was a concept that was recognized across the variety of actors in the movement. Church activists, Communists, Union activists, exiled South Africans, Liberals and, of course, solidarity activists, shared an identification with the concept of solidarity. Whatever one was doing, whatever one was participating in, an organization, a demonstration, a boycott, it was defined as an act of solidarity. Solidarity was thus constructed as a fundamental value that defined the collective identity of the transnational AAM, its ideas as well as its practices.

In terms of collective identity, sustained transnational anti-apartheid action across borders was thus made possible through the construction of *an imagined community of solidarity activists*. I think it is particularly useful to use Benedict Anderson's influential concept here (Anderson 1991), since it emphasizes the possibility of a shared sense of community among people dispersed over large geographical distances, not the least with the help of the communication media. To borrow an expression from John B. Thompson (1995), the transnational AAM was constituted by 'action at a distance'. According to Thompson, this is a form of action that, through the use of various forms of communication media, 'enables individuals to act for others who are dispersed in space and time, as well as enabling individuals to act in response to actions and events taking place in distant locales'

(Thompson 1995: 82). However, as we shall see in the next section, not just media, but also mobility—or travel—played a crucial role in the organization, mobilization and articulation of anti-apartheid across borders.

FORMS OF TRANSNATIONAL ACTION: MOBILIZATION, ORGANIZATION, MEDIA AND MOBILITY

I would like to argue that the central aspects of the construction of a movement space for transnational anti-apartheid action, as part of a much wider process of political globalization from below, can be analysed through the following interrelated themes: organization, mobilization, media and mobility (travel).

1. *Transnational organization and mobilization:* As in the case of most social movements, mobilization in the AAM was done through social movement organizations (SMOs) (McCarthy and Zald 2004). Some of them were national, like the British AAM, some of them were international, like the IDAF, and some of them consisted of networks of local groups, like the South Africa Committees and the Africa Groups (before they were formed into a national organization) in Sweden. These organizations were all part of a transnational solidarity network, which had at least two important nodes on the northern hemisphere; London as a 'post-colonial capital', where exiled African political activists played a crucial role in initiating the Boycott Movement, and New York, where the UN Special Committee against Apartheid became an important forum for interaction. The anti-apartheid struggle also involved alliances between states and actors in global civil society, as states such as India, Tanzania, Nigeria, Holland and the Scandinavian countries in a few cases funded, and exchanged information with, movement organizations across national borders. For example, the Swedish government supported the British Defence and Aid Fund, which was in strong opposition to the policy of the British government.

The British AAM was initiated in 1959 under the name of the Boycott Movement, and *I would argue that boycott was the most important form of mobilization* in the context of the AAM. The ultimate aim of the economic, cultural and sports boycotts was of course to put pressure on the South African government by isolating the country culturally and hurting it economically. However, as several activists that I have interviewed have pointed out, the anti-apartheid organizations also viewed the boycott as an important tool for mobilization and 'consciousness raising' of large numbers of people. Through the launching of boycott campaigns, the organizations offered people an opportunity for 'everyday' participation in solidarity action. It was argued that in the long run such active participation would generally raise public consciousness about the issue, and eventually increase the pressure on national governments and international organizations, like UN or EU, to impose sanctions. From this point of view, to participate in a boycott could also be seen as 'voting' for sanctions (the British AAM called boycott action 'people's sanctions'). It could also be argued that participating in a boycott could be seen as a form of expressive action that was a fundamental aspect of the construction of the collective identity of the movement. It was an act through which the individual subject could feel that s/he became a part of an imagined global community of solidarity activists. In this sense, the boycott was a form of 'identification at a distance' through local action. From this point of view the boycott also *emotionally* connected grassroots activists in different parts of the world.

2. *Transnational media space*: Media and information work was a crucial part of anti-apartheid activism. The rise of the international AAM parallels with *the growth of a transnational media space*, which can be see as a part of the process of globalization (Thompson 1995). This is not only a space for the immediate transmission of news across the globe, but also a site of political struggle, where different political actors, through symbolic actions, are trying to influence public opinions.

Since the 1960s new social movement groups and organizations are increasingly staging media-oriented public manifestations addressing a global audience (Gitlin 1980; Peterson and Thörn 1994 and 1999, Jong, Shaw and Stammers 2005, Opel and Pompper 2003). At the same time movement mobilizations are sometimes shaped in *response* to events that are globally reported by the media; movement intellectuals and groups take part in the struggle over the interpretation of the political implications of these events. Sometimes political mobilizations have taken place simultaneously around the world in an immediate response to events reported globally by the media. This was for example the case with the reports on the shots in Sharpeville in 1960, which lead to an intensified mobilization against apartheid in different parts of the world.

exchange of information and experiences between individuals representing groups, communities and organizations from different locations in the world; and making identification with 'distant others' something concrete for grassroots activists in the solidarity movement.

THE LEGACY OF ANTI-APARTHEID

To conclude, I would like to argue that the history of the anti-apartheid struggle provides an important historical case for the analysis of present-day global politics. During the process of my research it became evident that the present mobilization of a global civil society, addressing economic globalization and supra-national political institutions like the WTO, IMF and the World Bank, has historical links to the post-war, transnational political culture that the AAM was part of. Movement organizations, networks and individuals that took part in the anti-apartheid struggle are present in this context. For, example, as I was doing my first interviews for this project in Stockholm in October 1999, two veteran anti-apartheid activists told me that they were busy interacting with NGOs in various parts of the world, preparing a protest against the WTO meeting in Seattle in December. 'It is going to be big', they told me.[8] Their organization Diakonia, earlier member of the Swedish anti-apartheid coalition ISAK, was one of the 1,448 organizations that signed the 'Appeal from the International Civil Society' that was published on the internet during the protests in Seattle.

An example of the fact that different individuals can carry the learning processes of the AAM into very different contexts, is showed in Ben Cashdan's documentary *The Two Trevors Go to Washington*. It follows two South Africans, Trevor Manuel and Trevor Ngwane, both of them former anti-apartheid activists, on their journey to the IMF/World Bank meeting in Washington in 2000. Trevor Manuel visits the meeting as South Africa's Minister of Finance and as the chairman of the boards of governors of the IMF and the World Bank. Trevor Ngwane is a grassroots activist from Soweto that goes to Washington to protest against the global policies of the IMF and the World Bank. The example thus displays not only the importance of previously existing transnational networks for the formation of new transnational movements, but also that transnational movements sometimes even provide global politics with new elites.

NOTES

1. Interview with Dorothy Robinson, who was active in the Africa Bureau in the late 1950s and AAM in the early 1960s.
2. Interview with Patsy Robertson, Commonwealth Secretariat; Ethel de Keyser; and Mike Terry, both at different times Executive Secretaries of AAM.
3. For example, expenses for NGOs to participate in committee-sponsored conferences, seminars and sessions were provided. However, the budget of the committee was limited and it could only provide expenses for a few anti-apartheid groups that did not have expenses for travel. Interview with E.S. Reddy, former Principal Secretary of the UN Committee Against Apartheid. See also Korey (1998), p. 96.
4. Interview with Jennifer Davis.
5. For a theoretical discussion on the interaction between social movements and the UN, see also Passy (1999).
6. Interview with Reg September, former ANC Chief Representative in London.
7. On the notion of 'third space', Bhabha (1994). The particular definition of the concept used above is quoted from a lecture by Homi Bhabha, Göteborg, 19 September 2002.
8. Interview with Bo Forsberg and Magnus Walan.

REFERENCES

Anderson, B. (1991), *Imagined Communities: Reflections on the Origin and Spread of Nationalism*, London: Verso.

Anheier, H., M. Glasius and M. Kaldor (2001), *Global Civil Society Yearbook*, London: Sage.

——— (2004/5), *Global Civil Society Yearbook*, London: Sage.

Beck, U. (2000), *What is Globalization?*, Cambridge: Polity Press.

Bhabha, H.K. (1994), *The Location of Culture*, London and New York: Routledge.

Bond, P. (2001), *Against Global Apartheid: South Africa Meets the World Bank, IMF and International Finance*, Cape Town: UCD Press.

Castells, M. (1996), 'The Net and the Self: Working Notes for a Critical Theory of the Informational Society', *Critique of Anthropology*, 1(16).

Cohen, J.L. and A. Arato (1985), 'Strategy or Identity?: New Theoretical Paradigms and Contemporary Social Movements', *Social Research*, no. 52.

Cohen, R. and S. Rai (eds.) (2000), *Global Social Movements*, London: Athlone Press.

Crawford, N.C. and A. Klotz (eds.) (1999), *How Sanctions Work: Lessons From South Africa*, London: Macmillan.

Della Porta, D. and M. Diani (1999), *Social Movements: An Introduction*, Oxford: Blackwell.

Della Porta, D. and H. Kriesi (1999), *Social Movements in a Globalizing World: An Introduction*, in D. Della Porta, H. Kriesi and Rucht (eds.), *Social Movements in a Globalizing World*, London: Macmillan.

Della Porta, D. and S. Tarrow (2005), *Transnational Protest and Global Activism: People, Passions and Power*, Oxford: Rowman and Littlefield.

Eyerman, R. and A. Jamison (1991), *Social Movements: A Cognitive Approach*, Pennsylvania: Penn State University Press.

Falk, R. (1999), *Predatory Globalization: A Critique*, Cambridge: Polity Press.

Fieldhouse, R. (2005), *Anti-Apartheid: A History of the Movement in Britain: A Study in Pressure Group Politics*, London: Merlin Press.

Gitlin, T. (1980), *The Whole World is Watching: Mass Media and the Making and Unmaking of the New Left*, Berkeley: UCLA Press.

Guerney, C. (2000), ' "A Great Cause": The Origins of the Anti-Apartheid Movement, June 1959–March 1960', *Journal of Southern African Studies*, vol. 26, no. 1.

Hall, S. (1996), 'When was the "Post-Colonial": Thinking at the Limit', in I. Chambers and L. Curti (eds.), *Common Skies, Divided Horizons*, London: Routledge.

——— (2000), 'The AAM and the Race-ing of Britain', in *The Anti-Apartheid Movement: A 40-Year Perspective. Symposium Report*, London: Anti-Apartheid Movement Archives Committee.

Held, D., A. McGrew, D. Goldblatt and J. Perraton (1999), *Global Transformations: Politics, Economics and Culture*. Cambridge: Polity Press.

Jennett C. and R.G. Stewart (eds.) (1989), *Politics of the Future: The Role of Social Movements*, Melbourne: Macmillan.

Herbstein, D. (2004), *White Lies: Canon Collins and the Secret War against Apartheid*, Cape Town: HSRC Press.

Jennett, C. (1989), 'Signals to South Africa: The Australian Anti-Apartheid Movement', in C. Jennett and R.G. Stewart (eds.), *Politics of the Future: The Role of Social Movements*, Melbourne: Macmillan, pp. 98–155.

Jong, de W.D., M. Shaw and N. Stammers (eds.) (2005), *Global Activism, Global Media*, London and Ann Arbor: Pluto Press.

Kaldor, M. (2003), *Global Civil Society: An Answer to War*, Oxford: Blackwell.

Keck, M.E. and K. Sikkink (1998), *Activists Beyond Borders: Advocacy Networks in International Politics*, Ithaca and London: Cornell University Press.

Korey, W. (1998), *NGOs and the Universal Declaration of Human Rights*, New York: St Martin's Press.

Klotz, A. (1995), *Norms in International Relations: The Struggle Against Apartheid*, Ithaca and London: Cornell University Press.

Kriesi, H., R. Koopmans, J.W. Duyvendak and M.G. Giugni (1995), *The Politics of New Social Movements in Western Europe: A Comparative Analysis*, Minneapolis: University of Minnesota Press.

Laclau, E. (1985), 'New Social Movements and the Plurality of the Social', in D. Slater (ed.), *New Social Movements and the State in Latin America*, Amsterdam: CEDLA, pp. 27–42.

McGrew (eds.) (1997), *The Transformation of Democracy? Globalization and Territorial Democracy*, Cambridge: Polity Press.

Massie, R.K. (1997), *Loosing the Bonds: The United States and South Africa in the Apartheid Years*, New York: Doubleday.

McCarthy, J.D. and M.N. Zald (eds.) (2004), *Comparative Perspectives on Social Movements: Political Opportunities, Mobilizing Structures and Cultural Framings*, Cambridge: Cambridge University Press.

Melucci, A. (1989), *Nomads of the Present: Social Movements and Individual Needs in Contemporary Society*, London: Hutchinson.

——— (1996), *Challenging Codes: Collective Action in the Information Age*, Cambridge: Cambridge University Press.

Naughton, J. (2001), 'Contested Space: The Internet and Global Civil Society', in H. Anheier, M. Glasius and M. Kaldor (eds.), *Global Civil Society 2001*, Oxford: Oxford University Press, pp. 147–68.

Opel, A. and D. Pompper (eds.) (2003), *Representing Resistance: Media Civil Disobedience and the Global Justice Movement*, London: Praeger.

Paolini, A. (1997), 'Globalization', in P. Darby (ed.), *At the Edge of International Relations: Post-Colonialism, Gender and Dependency*, London/New York: Pinter.

Passy, F. (1999), 'Supranational Political Opportunities as a Channel of Globalization of Political Conflicts: The Case of the Rights of the Indigenous Peoples', in D. Della Porta, H. Kriesi and Rucht (eds.), *Social Movements in a Globalizing World*, London: Macmillan, pp. 148–69.

Peterson, A. and H. Thörn (1994), 'Social Movements as Communicative Praxis: A Case Study of the Plowshares Movement', in *YOUNG: Nordic Journal for Youth Research*, 2.

——— (1999), 'Movimientos sociales y modernidad de los medios de communicación. Industria de los medios de communicación: amigos o enemigos?', in *Comunicación y Sociedad*, 35, pp. 11–43.

Seekings, J. (2000), *The UDF: A History of the United Democratic Front in South Africa 1983-1991*, Claremont: David Philip.

Sellström, T. (1999), *Sweden and National Liberation in Southern Africa*, vol. 1: *Formation of a Popular Opinion 1950-1970*, Uppsala: Nordiska Afrikainstitutet.

——— (2002), *Sweden and National Liberation in Southern Africa,* vol 2: *Solidarity and Assistance 1970-1994*, Uppsala: Nordiska Afrikainstitutet.

Sen, J. et al. (2003), *Challenging Empires: Reading the World Social Forum*, Delhi: Viveka Foundation.

Shepherd, G.W. (1977), *Anti-Apartheid: Transnational Conflict and Western Policy in the Liberation of South Africa*, London: Greenwood Press.

Slater, D. (eds.) (1985), *New Social Movements and the State in Latin America*, Amsterdam: CEDLA, s. 27–42.

Smith, J. and C. Chatfield and R. Pagnucco (1997), *Transnational Social Movements and Global Politics: Solidarity Beyond the State*, Syracuse: Syracuse University Press.

Tarrow, S. (1998a), 'Fishnets, Internets and Catnets: Globalization and Transnational Collective Action', in M. Hanagan, L.P. Moch and W. Brake (eds.), *Challenging Authority: The Historical Study of Contentious Politics*, Minneapolis: University of Minnesota Press.

——— (1998b), *Power in Movement: Social Movements and Contentious Politics*, Cambridge: Cambridge University Press.

Thompson, John B. (1995), *The Media and Modernity: A Social Theory of the Media*, Cambridge: Polity Press.

Thörn, H. (1997), *Modernitet, sociologi och sociala rörelser*, Göteborg: Sociologiska institutionen, Göteborgs universitet.

——— (2002), *Globaliseringens dimensioner: nationalstat, världssamhälle, demokrati och sociala rörelser*, Stockholm: Atlas.

——— (2006), *Anti-Apartheid and the Emergence of a Global Civil Society*. New York and Basingstoke: Palgrave Macmillan.

UN (1994), *The United Nations and Apartheid 1948-1994*, New York: UN.

United Nations and Apartheid 1948-1994, New York, 1994.

Vahabzadeh, P. (2001), 'A Critique of Ultimate Referentiality in the New Social Movement Theory of Alberto Melucci', *Canadian Journal of Sociology* 26, pp. 611–33.

Wignaraja, P. (eds.) (1992), *New Social Movements in the South*, London: Zed.

Voorhes, M. (1999), 'The US Divestment Movement', in N.C. Crawford and A. Klotz (eds.), *How Sanctions Work: Lessons From South Africa*, London: Macmillan, s. 103–26.

Young, R.J.C. (2001), *Postcolonialism: A History*, Oxford: Blackwell.

——— (2004), *White Mythologies: Writing History and the Present*, London and New York: Routledge.

ARCHIVES

ANC Historical Documents Archive, www.anc.org.za
Bodleian Library, Oxford-
Archive of the Anti-Apartheid Movement 1959–95: (for a list of contents, see www.bodley.ox.ac.uk/dept/rhodes/aam/aam.html.)
MSS AAM 1: Committee of African Organizations' papers concerning establishment of Boycott Movement, 1959–60.
MSS AAM 13: AAM annual reports, 1962–90, and political reports, 1992–3.
M: Overseas anti-apartheid organizations 1963–95.

THE LABOUR MOVEMENT ARCHIVE, STOCKHOLM

AGIS Annual Reports
ISAK Annual Reports

MAYIBUYE CENTRE, UNIVERSITY OF WESTERN CAPE, CAPE TOWN

ANC London papers

INTERVIEWS

Fifty-two interviews had been carried out for the research project on which this article is based. The following are referred to in the text:

Jennifer Davis, New York, 20 June 2000
Bo Forsberg, Stockholm, 30 June 1990
Ethel de Keyser, London, 30 March 2000
Enuga S. Reddy, New York, 21 June 2000
Patsy Robertson, London, 27 October 2000
Dorothy Robinson, London, 2 March 2000
Reg September, Cape Town, 21 February 2001
Mike Terry, London, 07 March 2000
Magnus Walan, Stockholm, 30 September 1999

CHAPTER 8

Hip Hop Movements: The Local Adaptation of a Global Culture

DANIEL KÜNZLER

INTRODUCTION

Globalization is manifesting itself in culture in general and music in particular. Hip hop and rap music are popularly seen as examples of an American culture diffused worldwide. Indeed, the signs of hip hop culture can be found in Rwanda's capital Kigali, in Timbuktu at the fringe of the Sahara desert in Mali, in public transports in Tanzania, at the court of a traditional Baariba king in northern Benin, in short all across sub-Saharan Africa. A closer analysis of hip hop in sub-Saharan Africa based on written documents and music tapes reveals a nuanced perception: hip hop is not just an adoption of the American model, but this global culture is locally adapted and used to respond to global challenges. As part of the civil society, African hip hop artists represent the local scene of a comprehensive politico-cultural movement. Within the network of hip hop artists, rap music is a powerful means of mass communication. It is used to raise awareness and shape a collective identity of a 'lost generation'. Marginalized from the access to power and resources, young (male) urban Africans analyse the situation of African societies and voice their protest publicly through rap music. This helps to cope with problems of modernization and social change. Rap music is therefore a mode of social action and rappers can contribute actively to social change, as the examples of Senegal and Kenya show.

SOCIAL MOVEMENTS IN THE ERA OF GLOBALIZATION

The Ambiguous Concept of Civil Society

There is no authoritative definition of civil society. Barely defined, the concept is widely used and of Western origin (Bliss, 2003; Künzler

2006). Civil society is here seen as the sphere between the state and the market, or in other words as the part of the society that is non-governmental and not for profit without necessarily being in the public interest. The state is founded on coercion, the market on competition and civil society on voluntary cooperation. Civil society is characterized by the public character of its activities addressed mainly, but not solely, to the state and thus by a contribution to a public opinion. By creating a public sphere and a counter-power to the state, civil society is limiting and controlling the power of the state. The question whether a certain collective actor like an non-governmental organization (NGO), association or self-help group is part of civil society should be the subject of empirical analysis, as their respective labels say nothing about their real nature.

There has been a certain tendency to see civil society uncritically as the great white hope in the wake of the debate about the failure of the African state. This entailes a discussion on whether the concept of civil society is applicable to Africa at all (Künzler 2004). As African societies are characterized by the straddling or the interpenetration of the state and other parts of society, there is often limited autonomy for the organization and aggregation of interests and the participation of interest groups in society. Forms of vertical cooperation are gaining importance, but still, African societies are often vertically segmented along ethnic, local and family loyalties. The state classes are prone to co-opt protagonists of civil society and create new clientelist relations in order to widen their base of power, thus blocking the impulse for change by the emerging civil society. In rent economies, the potential of refusal of performance is very limited for civil society and the likelihood for toppling state classes is rather minor. Collective actors in the African civil society have nevertheless a certain potential of pressure through the creation of a public sphere.

Actors on the Borders of Civil Society: Social Movements

NGOs and other formal organizations are seen as important actors of civil society without consistent definition. Rather than blindly assume, their belonging to civil society should be the subject of empirical analysis. Already during colonial times, associations with religious or wildlife conservation aims had been founded. Others have existed since the nationalist period, but most have appeared with the democratic changes in the early 1990s. In the wake of the denationalization of development aid and its channelling through NGOs, they gained more importance. Several types of NGOs can be distinguished in the African context (Bliss 2003):

- The national subsidiaries of international NGOs having not necessarily African members or a mandate to represent Africans,
- Advocacy NGOs having a certain number of African members and a high legitimation to represent a certain segment of society,
- Development NGOs being by far the most common in Africa. Surely, some try to aid development with commitment, but most of them exist more or less just on paper. These *de facto* self-employment projects of jobless academics or side-projects of civil servants and even politicians are not that independent from the state as they are supposed to be (Künzler 2004, 2005). As successful adaptations to changed conditions for the access to foreign resources, they are not necessarily a sign of a transformation in the civil society and sometimes even reinforce the power of the state class and local elites.

It is thus social romanticism to see NGOs as the panacea: they are not a priori democratic or noble. Neglecting organization and legitimation problems, their potential has been overrated. But nowadays, there is ample scientific work on NGOs. It is thus more promising to enquire on the margin of society among the informal actors.

Informal social movements are another form of collective action in civil society. A network of organizations and individuals sharing a collective identity and mobilizing in order to trigger, oppose or rescind social change can be defined as a social movement. Without tight organization, they are often centred on a core and use different tactics including non-institutionalized ones. They don't take part directly in the political decision-making process in contrast to political parties and associations. Social movements seek influence via the public sphere and the help of mass media, using protest as an important means for the construction of social problems. They develop where there is discontent and relative deprivation and where resources are mobilized and there is some kind of organizational effort to tackle this deprivation. Social movements can pave the way to social change and thus be early signposts for social change (Bornschier 1998 [1996]). They are often preceded or accompanied by cultural innovations like popular music among others. Artists as emblematic leaders help to mobilize for social change and popular music is helpful in articulating protest and counter-concepts. Popular music therefore is a means for political transformation and chooses not the exit option, but the voice option as a form of social action. As Cohen (1993) shows, some social movements crystallize around a particular form of popular music or around a cultural movement. Of course, there are many forms of modern popular music in Africa originating in regional centres: Zouglou and Coupé Décalé from Côte d'Ivoire, Soukouss from Congo, Kwaito from South Africa, Highlife from Ghana, Afro-Beat from Nigeria or Makossa from Cameroon. Furthermore, there is Reggae and Ragga in several African countries. Rap music as a part of the hip hop culture is very popular all across Africa. This paper thus focuses on hip hop and especially on rap music in Africa south of the Sahara.

Hip Hop as a Politico-Cultural Movement

The demarcation of the terms rap and hip hop is confusing. Often, hip hop is seen as the generic term of a cultural expression including musical elements based on 'rap' (spoken rhymes creating a flow) and deejaying, graphical elements (graffiti, tag), fashion elements (baggy style) and elements based on motions (breakdancing) and body-languages (posing). Not always all elements are present and their respective importance varies from local scene to scene. The musical element is often called rap music and rapping is surely the most important element of hip hop. This form of expression developed out of Afro-American cultural forms at the end of the 1970s in New York's neighbourhood of Bronx, according to the generally accepted historiography (Toop 2000). First, it was a form of expression for low class Afro–Americans and Caribbeans and thrived in high schools, community centres, public places, record shops and other places. It spread from New York to other cities in the USA and other countries, but also to white and middle-class people. Nowadays, hip hop movements crystallizing around rap music are spread across the globe. hip hop is not only a public phenomenon and a subject of scientific analysis, but also a political phenomenon as rappers are criticizing the elites in power in countries all around the globe.

Hip hop involves ideologies, attitudes and manners shaping a culture with its own codes and languages. Rapping is often said to be of African origin, from where it supposedly spread to the West Indies and the USA (Toop 2000: 31). To justify this allegedly African origin, reference is made especially to the—often paid—songs of praise and allusion widespread in western Africa and to other forms of oral traditions in Africa that value the spoken word, satirical poems, the art of verbal improvization and the fast verbal reaction to events. But this hardly-contested idea of African roots is superficial, as traditional cultural forms that are somehow predecessors of rap exist all around the globe and (competitive) rhyming is probably just part of the nature of languages (Arnaud 1999; Maraszto 2002; Klein and Friedrich 2003; Verlan 2003; Englert 2004). The smooth worldwide acceptance of rap music cannot be explained by reducing rap to a *black* cultural expression (Verlan 2003: 139). Rap isn't either *just* a form of cultural expression, even if some rappers merely perform personality commercials. Since the early times of rap, there has been 'message rap' or what sometimes is called 'conscious hip hop' with lyrics reflecting political and social problems. Some rappers started to report about the life in American ghettos, but the enlightened character was soon lost and rapping reduced to boasting about drugs, violence and sex. This dual character still marks hip hop. But conscious hip hop is without doubt transmitting political topics into cultural practices and thus a politico-cultural movement as defined by Abner Cohen (1993: 148). A cultural form is used to develop independent identities and resist the dominant social order. Hip hop thus can be seen as a political counter-power and a form of politics.

The Local Adaptation of a Global Culture

Even if hip hop is globally spread, it is not a mere adoption of the American model, as it is locally adapted in very different contexts within a specific infrastructure involving production, distribution and promotion. Rap music is thus paradigmatic for the local adaptation of global cultures (Androutsopoulos 2003). Of course, the local adaptation of global culture is not a new phenomenon or restricted to hip hop. Interestingly, some other forms of popular music are hardly taken up in Africa, as especially the examples of rock music, heavy metal or punk show. What makes hip hop one of the most widespread forms of popular music is its easily accessible oral form of expression. This allows an active coping with local conditions. Of course, the integration of global cultural symbols into local cultures forms hybrid identities, but it is in the nature of culture itself to produce hybridities out of mutual influences (Klein and Friedrich 2003). One important side effect is the revaluation of local languages, music and traditions by a young generation previously rather sceptical about those issues. In what is considered to be a global movement, nodal local scenes around a town are represented (Mikos 2003). While sometimes, these local scenes are centred on central protagonists, studios or clubs, they are in other countries split up in various groups without much exchange or even in opposition. This opposition might be based on a 'generational' gap between early and later rappers as in Senegal or Nigeria and or on a social gap between upper class and lower class rappers as in Côte d'Ivoire or Tanzania. African hip hop mostly follows the general pattern of a spread from the metropolis to the hinterland (Künzler 2006).

Hip hop movements led by charismatic rappers gained momentum in Africa with the social crisis in the 1990s, even if rap music was known before. Among the countries where hip hop arrived early, there is Côte d'Ivoire (around 1980), Senegal (1982), Tanzania, South Africa and Guinea (1980s), Gabon (around 1985) and Nigeria (around 1987). A little later, it was brought to Ghana (early 1990s), Benin (1992) and Kenya (around 1993) and rather late to Uganda, Burkina Faso and Mali (mid-1990s). Now there are hip hop movements based on rap music all over the African continent. Without doubt, the epicenter is Senegal and especially Dakar with 1,500 to 5,000 hip hop crews according to different estimates.[1] Even in regions devastated by civil war, hip hop is present and former child soldiers from Sudan, Sierra Leone and Liberia cope with their trauma by making hip hop.

The liberalization of the media has been an important effect of the 'wind of change' that allegedly blew across Africa in the beginning of the 1990s. The private radio and TV stations were extremely important for the boom of hip hop in Africa, as they offered a platform for the civil society in general and rap music in particular. This allowed for the multiplication of the audience for African rap music and its messages as well as the interactive discussions on rap lyrics. While this is surely true for many countries, the room to manoeuvre varies considerably and is far less extensive in countries as such Guinea,

Togo or Cameroon, not to mention Zimbabwe and other authoritarian countries.

Rap music is obviously something to be afraid of, as is shown by its ban during the 2000 elections in Zanzibar, during a while at the end of 2001 in Nigeria or in the Democratic Republic of Congo in 2004. Of course, even proforma freedom of the press means not automatically access to the media for rap music. Airtime frequently has its price and the examples of profiteering journalists and other media professionals are legion. Concerning rap music, there seems to be some kind of symbiotic relation between rappers and media professionals. At least, all across Africa, many hip hop artists thank the press for the support on their record covers.

There is quite a similar pattern of the local adaptation of hip hop all around the globe. There is an initial phase of pure consumption of foreign—mainly but not solely American—hip hop. Then, the first protagonists start to imitate their models in Western languages or to freestyle, often in the environment of secondary and/or high schools. This borrowing and identification with foreign hip hop allows as some kind of learning process for the later adaptation of hip hop to local conditions including especially local languages and substandards as well as sometimes musical traditions (Scholz 2003). At times, the former colonial languages are used, as are other European languages. The use of English by rappers from Francophone countries is an important symbol of emancipation. Quite often, there is also code switching between European and African languages, whether regional languages as Haussa or Kiswahili or local languages, especially those more common in the big cities. In countries like Tanzania, local languages prevail. An impressive range of semantic techniques is used, as the linguistic research on rap lyrics has shown. Several topics are covered by rap lyrics (Scholz 2003): personality commercials, scene discourses, social critiques, reflections, love/sex, party/fun, drugs, religion, and family. One could add diseases, culture/traditions, history and political critique for the African context. The frequencies of these broad categories vary of course considerably.

While in the beginning performances were the main contact with the public, soon the first tapes were produced, be it in the initial phase of borrowing and imitation or in the later phase of adaptation to local conditions. The first tapes were produced in Côte d'Ivoire and South Africa around 1990, in Guinea around 1996, in Benin and Burkina Faso from 1997 onwards, in Cameroon and Uganda around 1998 and in Kenya as well as in Mali at the end of the 1990s. Different countries adapted this global culture differently depending on the local conditions. Often, the lyrics were increasingly critical and denouncing, as the degree of 'message rap' in proportion to 'gangsta rap' varied, but in general was quite high. This paper views the hip hop movements as parts of the African civil societies, fully aware that there is no such thing as a stable identity of the disperse and inconsistent protagonists. Nevertheless, even they use the concepts of movement, identity and community, even though with a critical understanding (Menrath 2003 [2001]).

HIP HOP AS THE VOICE OF MARGINALIZED GROUPS

YOUNG (MALE) URBAN: THE SOCIAL BASE OF AFRICAN HIP HOP

Rap music was brought to Africa mainly by young people living or studying abroad and sending it to their friends and relatives in Africa. This was mostly in relatively well-off families that could afford to buy rap music, stereo systems and TVs. The early African rappers were thus mostly the children of the urban petty bourgeoisie in the environment of universities and secondary schools. Still nowadays many rappers are well educated in comparison to the average of the population (Maraszto 2002). This is a sign that most rappers don't come from the lowest classes of society, as education is socially biased (Künzler 2005). The information analysed confirm this presumption for Mali and predominantly also for Burkina Faso (Künzler 2006). In other African countries as Côte d'Ivoire, Senegal, South Africa, Tanzania or Gabon, hip hop has diversified its social base more markedly to the urban 'lower classes'. This spread from 'middle class' to 'lower class' is exactly contrary to what happened in the USA, where it started in the 'lower class' and ended in 'middle class'. As hip hop artists tend to live mostly in urban areas and access to music and TV is easier, there is clearly an urban bias in the production of hip hop. But increasingly, people from rural areas are listening to rap music. It is diffusing also across ethnic groups, generations and even sexes, although the production of hip hop is still dominated by male artists. Rap lyrics thus represent often a male perspective on social and political problems and therefore, it is more difficult for girls and women to identify with (Maraszto 2002).

As members of society who were born at approximately the same time and exposed to similar social problems, African rappers share a view of the world different from generations at other points of time or in other places. They see themselves as being part of a 'sacrificed' or 'lost generation' (*Yeleen* 2001): 'Génération sacrifiée'; *SNK featuring Dodou Soul* (2003): 'Je vois'; *Sofaa* (n.d.): 'Le Beatraad'; *Wed Hyack* (n.d.): 'Humanités troubles').[2] They are 'sending out an SOS' (*Koumankan* (n.d.): 'Sombre futur'). African rappers declare themselves as marginalized in society. As they have no access to power and other resources and as young people have a rather low status in African societies, they are effectively marginalized. As in most African countries, more than half of the population is younger than 25 years and yet this biggest part of society is excluded from power and resources. However, the youth are nevertheless not at the periphery of society. Hip hop artists represent the different social groups (family, ethnic group, neighbourhood, social networks). They are rooted in family, ethnic group, neighbourhood, social networks as spokespersons; they express experiences and define identities (Auzanneau 2003 [2001]; Wittmann 2004a). Having a voice is what makes hip hop special in Africa, as young people normally are not supposed to express their opinion in public.

Hip hop appeals thus to a huge potential of ostracized young Africans and is a catalyst of social change. The process of individuation among young urban releases unknown levels of autonomy and makes the appropriation of new spheres of cultural expressions possible. One possible form of cultural expression, rap music, is often but not always progressive and radical as it criticizes the neopatrimonial state from the fringe of society. It can be also quite conservative and rap music as a means of coping with postcolonial modernities should not be seen with social romanticism and naïve wishful thinking (Wittmann 2004a). The level of criticism varies from country to country. In some countries, rappers still fight to get a voice at all, while they can use this voice widely in other countries. The use of language and the directness of expression according to different strategies allows for a differentiation from the older generations. Rap music is the speaking tube for young male urban Africans, but speaks also for larger segments of society. It addresses the general population and the politicians and helps to raise awareness and denounce injustices. In the context of illiteracy and low education, it has a special importance due to the use of local languages and its connection with elements of the traditional African cultures. As a politico-cultural protest movement, rap music is tackling economic, social and political realities. African rappers see themselves increasingly as part of an international

Diouf himself was ambivalent towards hip hop. He qualified rappers in public as 'insane young people'. This made hip hop a symbol of resistance against Diouf (after Diouf complained in public Diouf rappers). On the other hand, he tried to buy critical statements by rappers against Wade. The money offered was plainly refused despite the poor economic resources. As already mentioned, most rappers were supporting the voting out of Diouf and less Wade as a personality or any specific political party. In 'Kunu Abal Ay Beut' by *Omzo* (Various Artists 2001) a Senegalese comedian is ironically repeating a speech by Wade where he is stating that the youth is his force. Wade is under critical observation by the 'Bul Faale' movement. Rappers of the 'Bul Faale' movement state quite forthright that Wade is now under critical observation (Denis 2004). *Sen Kumpe* for example states in 'Lou deux bi blath'[8] (Various Artists 2001): 'If he is not keeping his promises, he will have to leave also.' The same kind of warning is stated by *BMG 44* (Various Artists 2002b): 'Hey, President, don't forget March 19, 2000. We celebrated together your victory, but don't forget your promises!' *Las-MC* (2002) wants in 'Batanaal' for Wade to share the sufferance and problems of the people. *Alif* (2003),[9] one of the few female hip hop crews, deplores in 'Joolaa' the victims killed on the ferry with the same name that sunk in front of Gambia's coastline toward the end of 2002; a tragedy Wade is blamed for. One can be sure that Wade will be the topic of quite another bunch of rap lyrics. The example of Senegal thus illustrates clearly the socio-political dimension of hip hop.

The Anthem of Kenya's Change of Power

The political life in Kenya from 1960 to 1964 was dominated by two rival parties.[10] The first president Jomo Kenyatta was leading the rather conservative and pro-Western 'Kenya African National Union' (KANU), with its support mainly among the Kikuyu[11] and their close relatives Embu and Meru as well as among the Luo and Kamba. The different Kalenjin-groups, Luhya-groups and Masai were mainly supporting the rather radical 'Kenya African Democratic Union' (KADU) that was dissolved in 1964. Most members were integrated into the KANU as a countermove to some ministerial posts. There was a small, but radical opposition in favour of squatters. His sympathy for this movement cost Oginga Odinga his post as the vice-president. This Luo politician founded together with some other former KADU-

Sofaa' and by *Yeleen* (2001) in 'Génération sacrifiée'. On the eve of independence, African soldiers participated in Second World War and on their return contributed to the independence movements (Künzler 2005). In French-speaking West Africa, the 'Senegalese privates' (tirailleurs sénégalais) were not paid right wages and a protest movement in Dakar's suburb Thiaroye ended in a massacre by French troops in 1944. This topic is widely discussed in West Africa as the last surviving privates still fight for their compensation and are mentioned by several rappers (*Faso Kombat featuring Yeleen* (n.d.): 'Pourqoui c'est comme ça'; *Les Escrocs* (2001): 'Tounga'; *Smockey* (n.d.): 'Ma dignité'; *Sofaa* (n.d.): 'Tchéfari'). After independence, statesmen such as Thomas Sankara in Burkina Faso rose and fell, but are still reverenced by several rappers (*Smockey* (n.d.): 'On est tous innocent'; *Sofaa* (n.d.): 'Tchéfari'). However, African leaders are more often linked with the probably most widespread topic in African hip hop: Corruption (*Faso Kombat* (n.d.): Konscientization; *Rage* (2000[1998]): 'Interlude'; *Tata Pound* (2002): 'Cikan–le message'; *Tata Pound feat. Tiken Jah Fakoly* (2002): 'Deliverance'; *Wed Hyack* (n.d.): 'Honte à Babylon'). *Sofaa* (n.d.) criticizes in 'Tchéfari' African presidents transferring stolen money to their famous Swiss bank accounts; *Lassy King Massassy* (n.d.) mentions in 'Jamana Jo' corrupt police officers and the arbitrariness of the repression apparatus, the latter being a long-running issue in hip hop all around the globe.

The relation with the former colonial master France is topic of discussion too. While for *Smockey* ('Le Cycle', n.d.) the Gallic cock has lost its cock-a-doodle-doo, independence is a myth for *Rage* ('Acide constat', 2000), *Yeleen* ('Génération sacrifiée', 2001) and *Sofaa* ('Tchéfari', n.d.). *Sofaa* (n.d.) in 'Tchéfari' says it is quite clear in which hands the steering wheel is, referring to what is commonly called 'Françafrique'. The criticism is also addressed to French domestic politics, as by *Faso Kombat* (n.d.) in '2 poids, 2 mesures'. *Yeleen's* (n.d.) focus in 'Outro' is on the 'world policeman' USA and on some contemporary problems of the American society. Rap lyrics from French-speaking countries is dominated by topics of African unity and Pan-Africanism (Künzler 2006). The reality on the continent is different and civil wars shatter the dream of unity. Civil wars and the fate of child soldiers attract the attention of *La Censure* ('Pourqoui', n.d.), *Lassy King Massassy* ('Fabara', n.d.), *TA-K-MI* ('Enfants soldats' 2003) and *Yeleen featuring Faso Kombat* ('Même combat', n.d.). Civil wars are often caused by the scramble for natural resources and too is in danger when voices get too critical. *Tata Pound* received death threats in the run-up to the publication of their album 'Yelema-La Révolution' (2006). State radio and TV censured their popular songs 'Yelema' and 'Monsieur le maire'. While 'Yelema' deals, critically with privatization and the pseudo-changes in Mali, 'Monsieur le maire' incriminated some mayors elected in 2004, but who quickly forgot their electoral promises and even illegally sold estates.

Poverty, the Lack of Public Welfare and Education: Hip Hop as a Voice for Socio-Economic Questions

Evidently, economic problems are prominent themes in African rap lyrics. Some rappers mention specific topics such as *Lassy King Massassy* (n.d.), pointing in 'Jamana Jo' to the issue of imports threatening domestic production and transforming Mali's farmers into simple consumers. *Smockey* (n.d.) deplores in 'Ma dignité': 'Imported religion, imported policy, imported economy, conditioned by the WTO. I hope we'll not have to import our sperms in order to continue to live.' *Tata Pound featuring Tiken Jah Fakoly* (2002) in 'Deliverance' criticize privatization as only a few billionaires profit from this policy implemented with the advent of democracy in Mali. At the same time, there would be a huge potential, as *Yeleen featuring Faso Kombat* (n.d.) underline in 'Même combat': 'We are rich, but the continent is poorly exploited'. Sometimes, general analyses are made about unemployment (*Rage* (2000): 'Acide constat'; *Wed Hyack* (n.d.): 'Humantié troublés') or the lack of economic progress (*Yeleen* (2001): 'Génération sacrifiée'). As *SNK featuring Dodou Soul* (2003) state in 'Je vois':

> I see guys taking drugs, guys drinking alcohol, I see guys being fed up, abandoning school. (. . .) I see guys not respecting neither their fathers nor their mothers. I see guys that would kill their brothers for money. I see guys drudging. (. . .) I see despaired guys never becoming what their fathers hoped. (. . .) It is not a secret, since 1991 there was no progress [in Mali].

Even when assessing the lack of progress, rappers do not ask for more development aid. On the contrary in 'Ma dignité', *Smockey* (n.d.) sees pity coming in the name of development cooperation. And in his song 'ONG' he describes the bitter logic of humanitarian NGO-staff driving around in big four-wheel drive vehicles:

> You are hungry? We are here. You have health problems? We are here. You want what? You want everything??? Ehm, we're not here anymore. If we

give you everything, you don't need anything anymore, so you don't need us anymore. This is the social business.

Poverty and misery are of course abundant as subjects of rap lyrics and seen as the source of violence and crime (*La Censure* (n.d.): 'Pourqoui'; *Fanga Fing* (2000): 'Wari'; *Yeli Fuzzo* (2003): 'Mankene', *SNK featuring Dodou Soul* (2003): 'Je vois'). As *Rage* (2002) state in 'Interlude':

It is true that there is no township, no ghetto as in the United States. You don't get shot. There is no tribal war as in Rwanda, inch'Allah, not yet. But corruption, fiddling, laxity, poverty are very well reality, you see! There is no social welfare system. (. . .) The termites empty the treasures of the state.

While rappers from countries with big cities are describe life in the shanty towns of Lagos, Dakar, 'Nairobbery' (Nairobi) or Johannesburg (Künzler 2006), there are no such big cities and ghettos in Mali. Rapping about ghetto life would be seen as a cheap imitation of American gangster rap. But Mali's capital Bamako also attracts villagers with the promise of economic success and a better lifestyle. *Yeli Fuzzo* (2003) tells in 'Ladji Kabako' the story about a failing migrant to Bamako:

Ladji Kabako (. . .) was the most respected man in the village for his kindness and his courage. What was the destiny of Ladji Kabako? To go to the big city, the capital Bamako! He was going for the good of his community. He didn't know his destiny. Ladji loves to party, Ladji loves the big city, Ladji loves the vice of the city. Ladji, everything is fun for you! Ladji loves to party, Ladji loves to have fun, Ladji loves the money, Ladji, everything is fun for you! Ladji Kabako has arrived in the big city. The man in the city doesn't live in the reality. He lives for the women, the power and the money. He doesn't care about his origin, he just wants to go to Paris. Ladji understood it all, the businesses and the money. Yes, he went to the big city for his community, but he chose the women and they choose his destiny. (. . .) Ladji became the king of the big city; Ladji lost the sense of reality. He was the most respected man in the village. He forgot and repudiates his inheritance. The women took all his money. Ladji Kabako doesn't have any friends anymore. We are all Ladji Kabako. We are all blind and lost in Bamako. He went to the big city for his community. He came back to the village with nothing to give.

African rappers also frequently bring up the prevention of AIDS, trying to combat the spreading of the disease and fighting the exclusion of those already infected (Künzler 2006; *Les Ecrocs* (2001): 'Le SIDA'). Rap lyrics also often talk about the lack of social services reality. What I know is that a lot of women are in fact suffering. Don't touch my sister, don't touch, my mother. I'm scared. It is time to open the eyes and to consider the happiness of my sister. No to the laws of an ageing practice. This lonely women died alone in her room. Victim of suicide I still see her under the pall. (. . .) Educate . . . the parents! Educate . . . the awareness! Educate. . . . It is a question of mentalities. Everybody is talking about this, everybody is singing about. But what is done to change it?

Another question that is often presented as 'tradition' is forced marriages, tackled by *Faso Kombat* (n.d.) in 'Pananki Pananzoï'. Women don't accept any longer to be seen as objects under male domination and therefore, *Ta-K-Mi* (2003) sees in 'Mah kana kasi' some signs of change. Young women only interested in material gains and working their way along lovers or even having several loves at the same time is also widely criticized, although this kind of behaviour is not considered prostitution. But 'the quality of their feelings depends on the wallets', as *Sofaa* (n.d.) remark in 'Profile-bas'. *Smockey* (n.d.) denounces in 'Le truc qui rend digne' not only men exploiting young girls, but also criticize female genital mutilation and the prohibition of abortions:

Money is not everything, money is the only thing. Dare to ask the little girls in the age of 13-14 years, consumed by paedophiles who behave like dignitaries. To complete the education of their daughters our mothers exert themselves to cut the clitoris they lost yesterday themselves the same way. And our sons accept this sacrifice. E-E-Enough of this general hypocrisy. Those forbidden abortions that bring nothing as those young mothers try it nevertheless in totally miserable conditions. Husbands and wives that don't love each other but live together and tolerate it for the good functioning of society. Those lies about fidelity leading to seropositivity. Cousin, you have only one choice: The condom! Later . . . you don't have a choice anymore.

Identities, Traditions and the Dream of Migration: Hip Hop as a Voice for Cultural Questions

Rap music assists young people in contemporary Africa with the creation and formulation of identities. As *Yeli Fuzzo* (2003) puts it: 'I rap, therefore I am.' The behaviours as cheap copies of American rappers or the imitation of imported lifestyles are dismissed by many artists. The latter is seen by *Yeleen* (2001) in 'Génération sacrifiée' as 'mental slavery' replacing the taste of the African identity. Towards African traditions, there is a differentiated approach. African rappers want traditions like respect towards parents and elders in general to be maintained (*Les Escrocs* (2001): 'Demissenw'; *Yeleen* (2001): 'Génération sacrifiée'; *Yeli Fuzzo* (2003): 'Mali Djaka'). But there is no uncritical glorification of cultural traditions and their contemporary manifestation. The critical texts about the role of women have been already mentioned above. Another example is *Sofaa* (n.d.) and their warning of the instrumentalization and abuse of witchcraft by politicians in '25ème heure'. For *SNK featuring Ta-K-Mi & Mizé* in 'Fiers d'être malien' (2003) the approach is to respect traditions and build on them, but also to change them where seems necessary:

> Malian, I'm proud to be. (. . .) You have to be linked, to keep the bonds, not to forget like the guards of passed times. Remember our empires to construct our future, to recover this feeling of glory, this feeling of power, freedom, pride. Towards yourself, towards him, towards your country, Mali. (. . .) Always on the quest, for improvement, for a better regime. But we are proud, of our culture, proud of our origins.

While about 80 per cent of Mali's population is Muslim, the figure is around 30 per cent for Burkina Faso. Hip hop artists in both countries rarely deal with Islam and the identity of young Muslims in Africa, in contrast to their Senegalese counterparts (Wittmann, 2004a; Künzler 2006). However, Malian artist *Lassy King Massassy* (n.d.) in 'Religion' blames the mixture of religion with politics for many of the country's ills. He also mentions that there are political killings in Algeria, a 'supposed' Islamic country, and that slavery still exists in Mauritania and Sudan.

The lifestyle of Europe and the USA is tempting for many young Africans who dream of migrating. But this dream may turn into a nightmare, as many migrants experience racism and hardship, according to *Les Escrocs* in 'Tounga' (2001). *Yeli Fuzzo* (2003) tells us in 'A mon retour' about the frosty social relations in the host country and the depressed migrants. The disillusioning story of a migrant is also central in 'Le chemin de l'exil' by *Yeleen* (2001):

> Shackled by the chains of exile you have to leave. It is dry here; you have to go to enrich yourself. Better not that people say 'look, this is the son without future'! The morning will come when you pack your bags. (. . .) On the sill you will see the disapproving glance of your worried father, red of hate and thinking he's the reason for this pain. You will go with an almost empty bag (. . .) and the hope of returning one day. (. . .) Over there, it will be cold and there will be nobody anymore. Nobody, because over there it is everybody on its own (. . .). You are going to forget your parents and only keep your

these companies are looking for music fitting into the pigeonhole of 'World Music'. What emerged in the early or mid-1980s as a category used for the marketing of music and not for its production is more and more structuring the production and reception of music (Mallet 2002). Yearly 10,000 *novelties* (new releases) join this important market, making 12 per cent of the total music sales in Europe with 25,000 titles available (Mallet 2002: 832). But labels as well as consumers have some expectations for access to that market: World music is supposed to be exotic and linked to supposed musical traditions. Acceptance by the European public is not following rapping skills, but more folklore connotations linked to the African origins of rappers (Various Artists 2001). Far too independent for this kind of cultural ghetto, African hip hop does not easily fit in that pattern, even if some artists try to adapt to those conditions. There is a redefinition of African hip hop into world music. This limitation on its cultural character while denying the political components is what happens very often to politico-cultural movements (Cohen 1993; Menrath 2003 [2001]). Of course, hip hop *has* cultural characteristics, as its self-perception is far from being homogeneous. It contains cultural as well as political notions and very often a combination of them.

Considering the quickly emerging market for rap music and its commercial viability, hip hop in the USA has not surprisingly 'been co-opted by the multinational music industry' but with an 'apparently low level of intervention in a potentially controversial form of music' (Toop 2000: 206). Especially in its commodified version, hip hop has become an opportunity for upward mobility for the mostly Afro–American lower classes. Rap also has been very quickly harnessed by politics, an early example being Jesse Jackson's campaign for the 1984 Democratic nomination for president. As with other forms of politico-cultural movements, the idea of buy-out and commercialization via the cultural industry as a threat to the resistance of the politico-cultural movement is abundant in hip hop (Klein and Friedrich 2003). Youth cultures very often have contradictory relations to commodification and capitalism and hip hop is no exception. It can be a form of modern praise song, where the diffusion of messages is paid as some examples show (Künzler 2006). In Mali, as in Senegal, some politicians tried fruitlessly to buy rappers during the electoral campaign in 2002, knowing well that two-third of Mali's population is younger than 25 years and young voters are thus an important electorate. Some rappers are directly involved in commercials. Many use the French Cultural Centres or similar institutions for performances in Africa. These centres representing the dominant cultural forms of Europe are also used for hip hop festivals and award ceremonies, as examples across Africa show. The impact is difficult to assess, but the artists seem to enjoy a certain degree of liberty. Also national and international NGOs and development projects try to profit from the popularity of hip hop (Künzler 2006). USAID and local NGOs supported the original production of 'Votemania' by *Rage* (2000) in 1997 as they wanted to mobilize young people to register to vote. *Yeleen* from Burkina Faso as well as *Didier Awadi* from Senegal, among other artists, are still supporting the fair trade campaign 'Big Noise' by Oxfam. These are just two examples among many across Africa. Hip hop movements are surely less instrumentalized by the neopatrimonial state or international organizations than many NGOs. But the musicians are still threatened, as one can hardly survive on music in Africa and rappers need economic resources.

CONCLUSION: AN IMPORTANT CRITICAL VOICE, BUT NO COUNTER-CONCEPTS

What is the impact of hip hop as a politico-cultural movement and as a part of African civil society? It is obvious that rappers criticize commodification and capitalism from within without being able to change the system (Androutsopoulos 2003; Menrath 2003 [2001]). Even if they stand for different values and norms, they don't present a concrete counter-concept to the neopatrimonial state. Hip hop movements are thus critical voices without going far beyond this corrective function. But this criticism is not to be underrated. It is opening a new channel for criticism as it is creating a public sphere for a once excluded social group, the young (male) urban. This is more than other forms of protest music reached.[20] Several examples show that this criticism is noticed by the state. Hip hop can give a voice to other social movements and help mobilize people for them, but it will most probably not enter into closer collaboration with other movements and thus not widen its social base. Civil society is threatened by economic and political dependency from the state (satellization) as *Tata Pound* (2002) states in 'Politicien'. Without being the bases of an alternative society or a signpost for the future, hip hop movements can wake agency among young urban Africans.

Cohen, Abner (1993), *Masquerade Politics: Explorations in the Structure of Urban Cultural Movements*, Berkeley/Los Angeles: University of California Press.

Denis, Jean-Michel (2004), 'Rythme Dakar: La rap-City', in *AM*, 227/228, pp. 84–8.

Englert, Birgit (2004), 'Africa Raps Back: Reflections on Hip Hop from Tanzania and South Africa', in Anne Schröder (ed.), *Crossing Borders: Interdisciplinary Approaches to Africa*, Berlin: Lit Verlag, pp. 77–97.

Greenpeace Magazine (2002), 'Als laute Stimme ihrer Generation klagen Dakars Rapper bessere Chancen für die Jugend ein', in *Greenpeace Magazin*, 4. Download from http://www.greenpeace-magazin.de/magazin/reportage.php?repid=540 on 23 April 2005.

Grignon, François (1998), 'La démocratisation au risque du débat? Territoires de la critique et imaginaires politiques au Kenya (1990–1995), in Denis-Constant Martin (dir.), *Nouveaux langages du politique en Afrique orientale*, Paris: Éditions Karthala and Nairobi: IFRA, pp. 29–112.

Havard, Jean-François (2001), 'Ethos "Bul Faale" et nouvelles Figures de la Réussite au Sénégal', in *Politique Africaine*, 82, pp. 63–77.

Hauck, Gerhard (2001), *Gesellschaft und Staat in Afrika*, Frankfurt am Main: Brandes & Apsel.

Human Rights Watch (2004), 'Unfinished Democracy: Media and Political Freedom in Angola', A Human Rights Watch Report, 14 July 2004. Download from www.hrw.org/backgrounder/africa/angola/2004/ on 5 March 2006.

Klein, Gabriele and Malte Friedrich (2003), 'Populäre Stadtansichten. Bildinszenierungen des Urbanen im HipHop', in Jannis Androutsopoulos (ed.), *Hip Hop. Globale Kultur—lokale Praktiken*, Bielefeld: Transcript, pp. 85–101.

Künzler, Daniel (2004), *Wo die Elefanten tanzen, leidet das Gras. Staat und Entwicklung in Afrika*, Münster: Lit Verlag.

——— (2005), 'L'éducation pour quelques-uns? Enseignement et mobilité sociale en Afrique aux temps de la privatisation: le cas du Bénin', unpublished manuscript.

——— (2006), 'The "Lost Generation": African Hip Hop Movements and the Protest of the Young (Male) Urban', World Society Focus Paper Series. Zurich: World Society Foundation, Paper to be published on www.wsf.unizh.ch

Mallet, Julien (2002), ' "World Music". Une question d'ethnomusicologie?', in *Cahiers d'Études Africaines*, 42, 4, 168, pp. 831–52.

Maraszto, Caroline (2002), 'Sozialpolitische Wende? Zur Entwicklung des Rap im Senegal', in Stichproben, *Wiener Zeitschrift für kritische Afrikastudien*, 2, 4, pp. 81–104.

Maupeu, Hervé (2003), 'Kenya: Les élections de la transition' in *Politique Africaine*, 89, pp. 149–66.

Medico International (2005), *Der Stoff aus dem Kriege sind. Rohstoffe und Konflikte in Afrika*. Medico International e.V., Frankfurt am Main und DGB Bildungswerk/Nord-Süd-Netz, Düsseldorf.

Menrath, Stefanie (2003): '"I am not what I am": Die Politik der Repräsentation im Hip Hop', in Jannis Androutsopoulos (ed.), *Hip Hop. Globale Kultur—lokale Praktiken*. Bielefeld: Transcript, pp. 218–45 [Reworked version of the chapter of the same name in: Stefanie Menrath (2001): Represent what . . . Performativität von Identität im HipHop. Argument Verlag, Hamburg]

Mensah, Ayoko (1999): L'âge de raison des Positive Black Soul. Entretien avec Didier Awadi (PBS), in *Culture Hip-Hop. Africultures*, 21, pp. 17–18.

Mikos, Lothar (2003): 'Interpolation and sampling: Kulturelles Gedächtnis und Intertextualität im HipHop', in Jannis Androutsopoulos (ed.), *Hip Hop. Globale Kultur—lokale Praktiken*, Bielefeld: Transcript, pp. 64–84.

Nyairo, Joyce and James Ogude (2005), 'Popular Music, Popular Politics: Unbwogable and the Idioms of Freedom in Kenyan Popular Music', in *African Affairs*, 104, 415, pp. 225–49.

Scholz, Arno (2003), Rap in der Romania. Glocal Approach am Beispiel von Musikmarkt, Identität, Sprache, in Jannis Androutsopoulos (ed.), *Hip Hop. Globale Kultur—lokale Praktiken*, Bielefeld: Transcript, pp. 147–67.

Servant, Jean-Christophe (2000), Neue Musikrichtungen in Afrika, in *Le Monde Diplomatique*, 6323, 15 December, p. 17

Toop, David (2000), '*Rap Attack 3: African Rap to Global Hip Hop*', expanded 3rd edn., London: Serpent's Tail.

Verlan, Sascha (2003): HipHop als schöne Kunst betrachtet—oder: die kulturellen Wurzeln des Rap. In: Jannis Androutsopoulos (ed.), *Hip Hop. Globale Kultur—lokale Praktiken*, Bielefeld: Transcript, pp. 138–46.

Wafula Wekesa, Peter (2002), 'The Politics of Marginal Forms: Popular Music, Cultural Identity and Political Opposition in Kenya', paper to be presented during the CODESRIA General Assembly on the theme 'Africa in the New Millenium'. Kampala, 8–12 December 2002. Download from www.codesria.org on 13 March 2005.

Wittmann, Frank (2004a), Sexismus, Islamismus und Ghettoromantik. Die Dakarer HipHop-Bewegung *Bul faale* im Kontext der globalen Postmoderne, in Eva Kimminich (ed.), *Rap: More Than Words*, Frankfurt am Main: Peter Lang Verlag, pp. 181–204.

——— (2004b): Die Klippen des Black Atlantic. Engagierter Pop und politische Gewalt in Westafrika, in *Neue Zürcher Zeitung*, International Edition, 15 April, p. 36.

Zona de Obras (2002), *Diccionario de Hip-Hop y Rap Afro Latinos (España,*

CHAPTER 9

Contesting Europe's Borders: The Self-organization of Undocumented Migrants in Borderlands

HELEN SCHWENKEN

INTRODUCTION

Conflicts in borderlands are increasingly taking place on the margins of the European Union. In the autumn of 2005 TV pictures of hundreds of irregular migrants with faces full of desperation trying to enter the Spanish enclaves of Ceuta and Melilla have moved the general public. All of those migrants had been deported by both Spain and Morocco; many were abandoned in the desert, even in areas pitted with land mines. After a short public outcry, the EU agreed on an action plan with a well-equipped budget to intensify European border surveillance. The TV pictures did not only show images of poor and desperate migrants; they also revealed that they were organized. They developed collective action on the one hand in the sense of attacking the border fence collectively and on the other hand in a more social movement sense of collective action as they were in contact with humanitarian NGOs and reported about their destiny via mobile phone while being deported.

Some time ago a comparable, but even longer-lasting incident—which I will analyse in the following sections—took place. In the course of three years, from autumn 1999 to autumn 2002, about 80,000 undocumented migrants and refugees crossed the maritime border between France and the United Kingdom in an unauthorized way. First their migratory movements were *de-facto* tolerated, but after a while, the British government started to highlight it. So it

As in other border regions, it is a common sight to see thousands of migrants constantly strolling around Sangatte. They try to cross the channel again and again, some succeed, some get discouraged, many get deported and quite a few migrants die (for figures: see UNITED 2004). In order to deal with the challenges of the large and permanantly changing transit population, the Red Cross France established in September 1999 a camp for irregular migrants in Sangatte. They provided food and shelter, some local non-governmental organizations took care of the children and provided medical and legal assistance.

The socio-demographical background of the inhabitants in Sangatte was clear: the average age of the inhabitants was 25 years, 95 per cent of them were male and of Muslim origin (Laacher 2002: 27), 55 per cent were Afghan nationals and 33.5 per cent were Kurds from Iraq (ibid.: 28f.). The average level of education was relatively high and did not differ significantly between Iraqi Kurds and Afghans. About 40 per cent had finished high school and most had further years of education, 40 per cent had left school after 'Secundaria', 13 per cent after 'Primaria' and only 6 per cent have no formal education (ibid.: 31). Most of the migrants belonged to the middle class or upper middle class in their countries of origin (ibid.: 34). They were employed as salesmen, craftspeople, workers or in liberal professions, or were students or professionals (ibid.: 32f.). For many of the migrants/refugees, not being able to find a job adequate to their education was a reason to leave the country, besides the general precarious conditions created by prolonged (civil) wars.

This situation, the large amount of irregular border crossings and the existence of the Red Cross shelter, led to diplomatic dissonances between France and Britain. The British government blamed the French government of tolerating and actively promoting the migrants' passage, thus getting rid of the unwanted migrants. During the pre-election and the election for the French presidency the problems was one of the most important campaigning issues in France. The Center-Conservative Party put the fight against the Red Cross Center on their banners. After they won the elections in 2002, everything changed quickly. It was a top-priority issue for the newly elected Center-Conservative French minister of the interior, Nicolas Sarkozy. Britain and France agreed on the closure of the Center. It was closed down at the beginning of December 2002, despite protests by the migrants and anti-racist organizations. On 31 December 2002, the centre was destroyed. This did not stop migrants from crossing the border without authorization and since then hundreds of migrants keep strolling around trying to cross the Channel.

The conflict around the Red Cross Center in Sangatte has rarely been analysed by academic scholars. One discourse analysis of the British policies was carried out (Thomson 2003) and one empirical study on the social structure of the migrants in the Red Cross shelter was conducted (Laacher 2002). The media and political actors were mostly interested in the political struggles between France and Britain. But what was and is often overlooked is that the migrants organized themselves and tried to articulate and fight for their demands. They were an important factor in the actual political struggles. In the media they appeared only as an anonymous mass moving in the dark. The following section, will shed some light on these political mobilizations. The conflict will appear in a different light as the range of actors and their capabilities is much wider than is usually assumed.

METHODOLOGICAL FRAMEWORK: EVENT ANALYSIS AND FRAME ANALYSIS

The analysis was carried out with the help of two methods—event analysis and frame analysis.

As the conflict around the Red Cross Center in Sangatte has not been researched on, no chronicle existed on which I could base my analysis. Thus I reconstructed the events from different primary sources: local and national media articles in France and Britain, leaflets, speeches, e-mails and other sources. The central unit of the sources taken into consideration was 'political mobilization'. Overall I analysed 336 articles from one local paper (*La Voix du Nord*) and one national paper (*Le Monde*); all articles during the course of the conflict were analysed. Articles from a number of other papers, including British newspapers, were included when important events took place. The reconstruction of events based only on media coverage has certain characteristics: media tend to report on spectacular or violent events; they focus on prominent persons and speakers; movement; complex issues are simplified and events are isolated. Thus, newspaper reports often lack background information and complexity (c.f. Barranco/Wisler 1999; Koopmans/Rucht 2002). For a thorough analysis, these characteristics of media coverage would have led to deficient results. So I included other kinds of sources: 89 grey materials and publications

Analysing the empirical material, two main frames applied by the undocumented migrants in Sangatte can be identified: I call the first one 'autonomy of migration' and the second one 'refugee protection frame'.

Frame I: 'Autonomy of Migration'

The name of this frame is borrowed from a discussion which mainly developed among French intellectuals and anti-racist activists since the 1990s. A starting point of the concept is the existing reality of undocumented migration all over the world and the acknowledgement of the failure of migration control and management. Political demands which are connected with this perspective promote the regularization of undocumented migrants and the extension of their rights. The definite right to stay somewhere is given a higher priority than the right of free movement which is based on the assumption that migrants bestow themselves with the right of free movement anyway.

We can identify the frame of 'autonomy of migration' mainly in the actions performed by the undocumented migrants in Sangatte. The frame is seldom articulated discursively or discussed in a strategic way. On various occasions a few hundred migrants penetrated the fenced territory of the Eurotunnel and entered the tunnel itself.[1] These mass invasions can be regarded as political actions for two reasons. The migrants are not as naïve as to hope to reach the other side of the tunnel without being caught. The second indicator for the political intentions are the chosen dates. For the invasions, the migrants went on days like Christmas day 2001, when public attention was high for the situation of despaired refugees (*La Voix du Nord*, 27 December 2001; *Le Monde*, 27 December 2001). On another occasion they did it in Spring 2002 when the French border control police was reorganized due to the change of government (BBC 17 May 2002). Each time such large number of people entered the tunnel and the media coverage was quite impressive.

On a demonstration in October 2001, the undocumented migrants demanded that the borders be opened within and into the European Union (Réfugiés Afghans du camp 2001; Réfugiés Afghans/Herin 2001). This was one of the few occasions the frame 'autonomy of migration' was verbally expressed. Another example happened during the phase of the closure of Sangatte. After 5 November 2002 no further migrants were accepted to Sangatte (*Le Monde*, 7 November

2002; *La Voix du Nord*, 5 and 7 November 2002). As a result, the migrants and French supporters occupied a gym and a church (e.g. *Le Monde*, 10 November 2002). The migrants, most of them Iraqi Kurds, demanded a transit permit with one month validity (*Le Monde*, 12 November 2002) in order to have enough time and the possibility to reach Great Britain without getting into trouble with the border police.

These examples show that the frame 'autonomy of migration' has a certain relevance for the political activities of undocumented migrants in Sangatte.

Frame II: 'Refugee Protection'

The refugee protection frame refers to the responsibility of nation-states and societies to provide safe havens for persecuted persons. It includes the right of asylum and other protective measures with regard to the Geneva Refugee Convention of 1951. This basis is shared by broader parts of the political and civil society, e.g. church-based groups and human rights organizations as well as countries which signed the respective conventions.

The 'refugee protection' frame is articulated in Sangatte by the undocumented migrants mainly discursively in petitions, declarations and on banners and slogans at demonstrations. On 2 August 2001 the migrants demanded the mediation of the United Nations in their case (*Libération*, 3 August 2001; *La Voix du Nord*, 3 August 2001). Two weeks later they wrote a letter to the UNHCR in which they expressed their causes to flee, among them war, persecution and poverty (*Le Monde*, 23 August 2001) and demanded just asylum procedures. After the 11 September 2001 events the Afghan refugees publicy condemned the terrorist attacks and explained their experiences in Afghanistan during the Taliban regime as their main reason to leave the country (*Immigrés Afghans*, 2001; *Le Monde*, 20 September 2001, *La Voix du Nord*, 19 September 2001). They also mentioned the situation of Afghan women at a planned demonstration and intended to show a documentary about the situation of women (Réfugiés Afghans du camp 2001; Réfugiés Afghans/Herin 2001).

These examples could be extended to every demonstration or to every petition delegations of undocumented migrants from Sangatte passed on to politicians or official representatives.

(b) The second type of mobilization can be called 're-regulation' as the most important aim is to regulate migration and to shape it in a more just way. The main protagonists are pro-migrant-organizations, a number of migrants' organizations and some actors in EU institutions, as well as International Organizations (IOs). Migration should be regulated for the benefit of all: the migrants as well as the sending and receiving societies. Migrants are regarded as human beings who suffer from economic and racial injustice. The perspective is more state-centered than the first one as the state is considered to be the regulatory institution. The 'refugee protection' frame in the case of Sangatte can be subsumed under this type.

(c) There is a third type of mobilization, which I have labelled 'repressive migration management'. It differs from the first two types in that the aim is to combat irregular migration and migrants. The problems is externalized, e.g. by deportations and increased border security. The stakeholders are mostly governments and the European Union, parts of IOs and counter-movements. In the case of Sangatte it included the governements of the UK and France, especially the French minister of the interior and the British home affairs minister. Thus this is not a 'typical' social movement type of mobilization. However, the reason it is important to take it into consideration when dealing with migrant and pro-migrant-organizations will be explaned in the following paragraph. The migrants in this frame are conceived either as victims (as in the case of trafficking in women) or as criminals (in the case where they cross borders and work illegally, as was the case in Sangatte).

The policies and strategies of the undocumented migrants and refugees in Sangatte fit mostly to the first type and to some degree, as they demanded protection for refugees or collaborated with others, to the second type. The policies and strategies of the support and advocacy-organizations in Sangatte are best described by the second type. However, due to the conflation of irregular migration, trafficking and security issues, there may be a danger in some collaborations with state actors and International Organizations like the International Organisation of the Migrants (IOM). Therefore it is crucial to consider the third type also as a type of mobilization. In line with the thinking of Antonio Gramsci, the state is not only consisting of institutions

TABLE 9.2: TYPOLOGY OF MOBILIZATION

Type of mobilization	Stakeholders	Approach to migration policy	Status of the migrants	Case 'Sangatte'
'Migrants' interests' or: 'right for rights'	Migrants, (part of) pro-migrant-organizations	Migration cannot be controlled; migration as a human right	Normalization	Realization of individual migratory projects; tactical and temporary collective actions; Frame: 'autonomy of migration'
'Re-regulation'	Pro-migrant-organizations, part of migrants, EU institutions, International Organizations	Migration can be regulated and just; balancing of interests	Regularization	Refugee protection; international norm compliance Frame: 'refugee protection'
'Repressive migration management'	Governments, EU, part of IOs, counter-movements	Combating irregular migration is pre-condition for legal migration	Scandalization	Discursive nexus of 'illegal migration' and crime; combating of trafficking in women; human smuggling and undeclared work Frame: 'Combating of trafficking in women'.

Source: Helen Schwenken, own compilation.

such as governments and ministries, but also of the so-called 'extended state'. This has to be taken into consideration as important processes of the formulation of consensus and other forms of mobilization take consensus is *not* positively sanctioned, instead actors who behave in a confrontational way. For other cases like lobbying policies, it is the other way round, only actors who follow the written and unwritten rules of lobbying are able to use the spatial and discursive opportunity structure. It can be concluded that the undocumented migrants in Sangatte were only able to organize themselves because the space 'borderland' was a terrain of resistance and as the mobilizations became a conflict over the space itself and its migratory significance. Thus, following the classical work of Henri Lefebvre, 'it is only *in* space that such conflicts come effectively into play, and in doing so they become contradictions *of* space' (Lefebvre 1991 [1974]: 365).

NOTE

1. Empirical evidence can be found in Home Office, 2001; *Le Monde*, 4 September 2001; *Le Monde*, November 2001; *Le Voix du Nord*, 27 December 2001; *Le Monde*, 27 December 2001; *Le Monde*, 22 January 2002; BBC, 27 May 2002.

REFERENCES

Abdallah, Mognis H. (2000), 'Die Bewegung der Sans Papiers—ein Höhepunkt in Frankreichs Einwanderungsgeschichte', in Autor Innenkollektiv (Hg.), *Ohne Papiere in Europa. Illegalisierung der Migration–Selbstorganisation und Unterstützungsprojekte in Europa*, Berlin/Hamburg: Schwarze Risse, Rote Straße, VLA, 17-67.

Alvarez, Robert R. (1995), 'The Mexican-US Border: The Making of an Anthropology of Borderlands', *Annual Review of Anthropology*, 24, pp. 447–70.

Anderson, Bridget (2000), *Doing the Dirty Work: The Global Politics of Domestic Labour*, London, New York: Zed Books.

AutorInnenkollektiv (Hg.) (2000), *Ohne Papiere in Europa. Illegalisierung der Migration–Selbstorganisation und Unterstützungsprojekte in Europa*, Berlin/Hamburg: Verlag Schwarze Risse/Rote Strasse, VLA.

Barranco, José and Dominique Wisler (1999), 'Validity and Systematicity of N wspaper Data in Event Analysis', *European Sociological Review*, 15, 3, pp. 310–22.

Benford, Robert D., David A. Snow (2000), 'Framing Processes and Social Movements: An Overview and Assessment', in *Annual Review of Sociology*, 26, pp. 611–39.

Cissé, Madjiguène (2002), *Papiere für alle. Die Bewegung der Sans Papiers in Frankreich*, Berlin/Hamburg/Göttingen: Assoziation.

Cornelius, Wayne A. (2000), 'Death at the Border: The Efficacy and "Unintended" Consequences of U.S. Immigration Control Policy', 1993-2000', Working Paper No. 27, November 2000, The Center for Comparative Immigration Studies, University of California-San Diego. http://www.ccis–uesd/LICATIONS/wrking27n (16 October 2009).

Cornelius, Wayne A., Takeyuki Tsuda, Philip L. Martin, James F. Hollifield, (eds.) (2004), *Controlling Immigration: A Global Perspective*, 2nd edn., Stanford, California: Stanford University Press.

Figueroa, Hector (1998), 'Back to the Forefront: Union Organizing of Immigrant Workers in the Nineties', in Jo-Ann Mort (ed.), *Not Your Father's Union Movement: Inside the AFL-CIO*, London: Verso, pp. 87–98.

Geddes, Andrew (1998), 'The Representation of "Migrants' Interests" in the European Union', in *Journal of Ethnic and Migration Studies*, 24, 4, pp. 695–713.

——— (2000), *Immigration and European Integration: Towards Fortress Europe?*, Manchester/New York: Manchester University Press.

Guiraudon, Virginie (2001), 'Weak Weapons of the Weak? Transnational Mobilization around Migration in the European Union', in Doug Imig, Sidney Tarrow (eds.), *Contentious Europeans: Protest and Politics in an Emerging Polity*, Lanham/Boulder/New York/Oxford: Rowman & Littlefield Publishers, pp. 163–83.

Heyman, Josiah (1994), 'The Mexico–United States Border in Anthropology: A Critique and Reformulation', in *Journal of Political Ecology*, 1, pp. 43–65.

Heyman, Josiah McC. (1999), 'Why Interdiction? Immigration Control at the United States-Mexico Border', in *Regional Studies*, vol. 33.7, pp. 619–30.

Home Office, UK (2001), 'Measures Announced to Improve Immigration Control', 19 September 2001, Immigration & Nationality Directorate, 214/01, www.ind.homeoffice.gov.uk/news asp? News Id=86 & Section Id = 1 (27 May 2002).

Imig, Doug and Sidney Tarrow (eds.) (2001), *Contentious Europeans: Protest and Politics in an Emerging Polity*, Lanham/Boulder/New York/Oxford: Rowman & Littlefield Publishers.

Immigrés Afghans, Sangatte (2001), 'Les Afghans de Sangatte contre les terroristes et l'anéantissement de leur pays. Déclaration écrite parvenue à l'AFP', 26 September 2001, http://hns.samizdat.net/article.php3?id_article=369 (16 October 2009).

Jackson, Richard T., Shirlena Huang, and Brenda Yeoh (1999), 'Domestic

Workers and Transnational Migration: Perspectives from Singapore and Philippines', in *Revue Europeenne des Migrations Internationales*, 15, 2, pp. 37–67.

Jurado Guerrero, Teresa (ed.) (2000), 'Easy Scapegoats: Sans Papiers Immigrants in Europe. State Strategies and Intervention Strategies for the Civil Society', Weinheim: Freudenberg Stiftung.

Koopmans, Ruud, Dieter Rucht, (2002), 'Protest Event Analysis', in Bert Klandermans and Suzanne Staggenborg (ed.), *Methods of Social Movement Research*, Minneapolis, London: University of Minnesota Press, pp. 231–59.

Kyle, David and Rey Koslowski (eds.) (2001), *Global Human Smuggling: Comparative Perspectives*, Baltimore/London: John Hopkins University Press.

Laacher, Smaïn (2002), *Après Sangatte. nouvelles immigrations, nouveaux enjeux*, Paris: La Dispute.

Laubenthal, Barbara (2006), ' "Papiere für alle". Proteste illegaler Einwanderer in Murcia' (Spanien) in *IMIS-Beiträge*, Institut für Migrationsforschung und Interkulturelle Studien der Universität Osnabrück, 27, pp. 109–29.

Lavenex, Sandra (2001), 'Migration and the EU's New Eastern Border: Between Realism and Liberalism', in *Journal of European Public Policy*, 8, 1, pp. 24–42.

Le Voy, Michele, Nele Verbruggen and Johan Wets (eds.) (2004), *Undocumented Migrant Workers in Europe*, Brussels/Leuven: Picum, Katholieke Universiteit Leuven.

Lefebvre, Henri (1991 [1974]), *The Production of Space*, Oxford/Cambridge: Blackwell.

Lindemann, Ute (2001), 'Sans-Papiers-Proteste und Einwanderungspolitik', in *Frankreich*, Opladen: Leske+Budrich.

Lindio-McGovern, Ligaya (2004), 'Alienation and Labor Export in the Context of Globalization. Filipino Migrant Domestic Workers in Taiwan and Hong Kong', in *Critical Asian Studies*, 36, 2, pp. 217–38.

Lüthje, Boy and Christoph Scherrer (2001), 'Race, Multiculturalism, and Labour Organizing in the United States: Lessons for Europe', in *Capital & Class*, 73, pp. 141–71.

Martínez, Oscar J. (1998), *Border People: Life and Society in the U.S.–Mexico Borderlands*, Arizona: Arizona Press.

Milkman, Ruth (eds.) (2000), *Organizing Immigrants: The Challenge for Unions in Contemporary California*, Ithaca, London: ILR Press, Cornell University Press.

Mujica Petit, Javier (2004), El desafío de la solidaridad. Condiciones de vida y de trabajo de los migrantes peruanos en Chile. Oficina International del Trabajo, OIT. 178. (ACTRAV). Proyecto 'Los sindicatos y el trabajo decente en la era de la globalización en Améria Latina', Lima: OIT.

Ness, Immanuel (1998), 'Organizing Immigrant Communities: UNITE's Workers Center Strategy', in Kate Bronfenbrenner, Sheldon Friedman, Richard W. Hurd, Rudolph A. Oswald and Ronald L. Seeber (eds.), *Organizing to Win: New Research on Union Strategies*, Ithaka, London: ILR Press, Cornell University Press, pp. 87–101.

O'Dowd, Liam (1998), 'Negotiating State Borders: A New Sociology for a New Europe?', Inaugural Lecture, 10 March 1998 at Queen's University, Belfast, www.qub.ac.uk/ss/ssp/cibr/odowd.html (13 August 2001).

Ramasami, P. (2003), 'International Migration and Conflict: The Case of Foreign Migrant Labour in Malaysia', Centre for History, Political Science and Strategy, University of Kebangsaan, Malaysia (unpublished).

Reflex; IM'média, L'agence (ed.) (1997), *Sans Papiers—Chroniques d'un Mouvement*, Paris.

Réfugiés Afghans du camp, Sangatte (2001), Manifestation, 31 October 2001, Calais, www.gisti.org/dossiers/sangatte/actions.html (Abruf: 26 November 2001).

Réfugiés Afghans, Sangatte; Herin, Christophe (2001), Calais: manifestation de 'réfugiés' afghans du camp de Sangatte le mercredi, 31 octobre 2001. http://maison-des-sans.org/palabre.php3?id_article=17 (12 January 2003).

Routledge, Paul (1993), *Terrains of Resistance. Nonviolent Social Movements and the Contestation of Place in India*, Westport, Conneticut/London: Praeger.

——— (1996), 'Critical Geopolitics and Terrains of Resistance', in *Political Geography*, 15, 6/7, pp. 509–31.

Schwenken, Helen (2005), 'The Challenges of Framing Women Migrants' Rights in the European Union', in *REMI—La Revue Européenne des Migrations Internationales*, 21, 2, pp. 177–94.

Sherman, Rachel and Kim Voss (2000), ' "Organize or Die": Labor's New Tactics and Immigrant Workers', in Ruth Milkman (ed.), *Organizing Immigrants: The Challenge for Unions in Comtemporary California*, Ithaca, London: ILR Press, Cornell University Press, pp. 81–108.

Soysal, Yasemin Nuhoglu (1994), *Limits of Citizenship: Migrants and Postnational Membership in Europe*, Chicago/London: The University of Chicago Press.

Spener, David (2001), 'Smuggling Migrants through South Texas: Challenges Posed by Operation Rio Grande', in David Kyle and Rey Koslowski (eds.), *Global Human Smuggling: Comparative Perspectives*, Baltimore/London: John Hopkins University Press, pp. 129–65.

Thomson, Mark (2003), 'Images of Sangatte: Political Representations of Asylum Seeking in France and the UK', Sussex Migration Working Papers No. 18. University of Sussex. www.sussex.ac.uk/migration/publications/working_papers/mwp18.pdf (10 April 2004).

UNITED, UNITED for Intercultural Action (2004), 'The Deadly Consequences of "Fortress Europe"—More than 4,500 Deaths', information leaflet no. 24, www.united.non-profit.nl/pages/info24.htm (20 August 2004).

Waldinger, Roger, Chris Erickson and Ruth Milkman et al. (1998), 'Helots No More: A Case Study of the Justice for Janitors Campaign in Los Angeles', in Kate Bronfenbrenner, Sheldon Friedman, Richard W. Hurd, Rudolph A. Oswald and Ronald L. Seeber (eds.), *Organizing to Win: New Research on Union Strategies*, Ithaca, London: ILR Press, Cornell University Press, pp. 102–19.

CHAPTER 10

Social Movements and the Challenges of Transnational Coalition-Building*

MARK HERKENRATH

INTRODUCTION

As cases of transnational political activism have become more numerous over the past few years, so have sociological studies analysing these cases. Excellent analyses of transnational movement coalitions can be found, for instance, in the recent volumes edited by Bandy and Smith (2005a), and Khagram, Riker and Sikkink (2002). Yet, as research on transnational social movement cooperations is still in its infancy, many important questions have remained unresolved. Little is known, for example, about how transnational social movement networks manage internal conflicts, and how their participants forge unity amidst diversity. In his various publications on transnational activism, Sidney Tarrow (e.g. 2003, 2004) emphasizes that the

*This research has been made possible by a grant from the Swiss National Science Foundation (PBZH1-104372). A very preliminary version of this paper was presented at the International Studies Association Annual Convention, 2006, San Diego, California (USA), 22–5 March, Session SD38 on 'Transnational Social Movements' (organizer: April Linton). The current version was presented at the 16th ISA World Congress of Sociology in Durban (South Africa), 23–9 July 2006, in the RC44 Session 8 on Transnational Organising (coordinator: Peter Evans), and in the RC48 Session 4 on Social Praxis of Counter-Globalization (coordinator: James Goodman). I would like to thank Marisa von Bülow, Christopher Chase-Dunn, Ellen Reese, Ruth Reitan, Amory Starr, and Thomas Volken for their comments and valuable insights.

challenges for movement leaders engaged in cross-border coalition building are legion. Not only is transnational activism plagued by the manifold difficulties inherent to intercultural and inter-organizational communication, but social movement coalitions are also embedded in a complex, multi-level political environment, which calls for equally complex contentious strategies and collective action frames. Transnational movement coalitions, Tarrow (2004: 16) argues, 'must overcome cultural differences, correct imbalances in resources, and bridge the differences in opportunities and constraints that their different states and societies impose on activists once they return home'. Grasping these dilemmas of coalition formation, he then states, 'is a major task of students of transnational activism today' (Tarrow 2004: 15).

I address this task in the present study by looking into the Hemispheric Social Alliance (HSA) and its participants' struggle against the Free Trade Area of the Americas (FTAA) and other regional free trade agreements. The HSA is a network organization connecting grassroots movements, labour unions and other non-governmental organizations from many different parts of the Americas, and can be seen as a paradigmatic case of effective transnational coalition building and durable coalition maintenance. Although its participants represent various types of organizations from different cultural and socio-economic contexts, the HSA (colloquially: the Alliance) has now existed for more than ten years. Also, it has been able to increase the number of associated organizations, as well as win the support of several governments. Among others, it has strong ties to the Chávez administration in Venezuela; and Bolivia's head of state, Evo Morales, has been a participant of the HSA for many years. The HSA is an excellent case, then, to identify the conditions and strategies that help social movement coalitions to manage internal tensions, build trust across cultural and organizational borders, and find ways to cope with changing opportunities and threats. On a more critical note, however, it is important to emphasize that grassroots activists are concerned about the HSA's inability, or unwillingness, to enable sustained mass participation outside the metropolises. Therefore, the Alliance also constitutes an interesting case to investigate into the limits of grassroots participation in transnational civil society organizations—a problem that challenges movement leaders and scholars alike.

This study draws on data collected by means of participant observation techniques, semi-structured interviews and qualitative content analysis of the HSA's publications. To understand how the HSA has forged unity amid diversity, I participated in one of the organization's international coordination meetings, the 1ro *Encuentro hacia la Cumbre de los Pueblos* (June 2005), and its 3rd Peoples' Summit of the Americas in Mar del Plata (November 2005). During these events, I conducted a series of semi-structured interviews with movement leaders who serve as international delegates in the HSA's international boards, the Coordinating Committee and the Hemispheric Council. I also carried out a field study on the HSA's local network partners in Argentina, the *Autoconvocatoria No al ALCA*, to investigate questions of mass participation and within-movement accountability. During this field study, which lasted for a total of almost four months, I regularly participated in the *Autoconvocatoria's* weekly meetings, and interviewed over a dozen grassroots activists from both Buenos Aires and Argentina's heartland.

THEORETICAL AND EMPIRICAL PERSPECTIVES ON TRANSNATIONAL MOVEMENT COALITIONS

Of the many theoretical perspectives social movement research has developed since the 1960s, Resource Mobilization, Political Opportunity Structures and New Social Movements have been the most influential. As della Porta and Diani (1999: 3) cogently argue, these theoretical perspectives do not contradict and mutually exclude each other, but simply 'approach the issue from different directions'. It is only by combining these theories that researchers can develop a comprehensive understanding of social movement dynamics.

When applied to the analysis of transnational movement coalitions, the existing theoretical perspectives show that transnational activists face the same challenges as activists operating at the national and local levels. Transnational movements, too, must mobilize resources, find ways to take advantage of given political opportunities, create powerful collective action frames, and support the development of a sustained collective identity. In this respect, then, the currently dominant theoretical perspectives, although developed to analyse national and local activism, reveal important insights into the challenges and dynamics of transnational movements.

It should be clear, however, that in the case of transnational activism the same challenges are more complex than in the case of activism at the national and local levels. *Firstly*, as the participants of transnational movement coalitions tend to have unequal access to resources, externally imposed inequalities may translate into internal power disparities. Thus, transnational movements, particularly those involving participants from the global north and the global south, not only need to mobilize resources, but they also have to redistribute these resources in such ways that this internal redistribution may not create clientelism and dependency.

Secondly, transnational movements operate in a complex multi-layered political environment, which offers them various yet often contradictory local, national, and international opportunities. Activists thus need to develop strategies that not only match the diverse political situations in various countries, but also take advantage of the opportunities presented by the relevant international organizations. *Thirdly*, transnational movements have to find collective action frames universal enough to resonate with the various cultural contexts of the activists' home countries (or flexible enough to be adapted locally).

How, and under what conditions, may transnational social movement coalitions succeed in overcoming these challenges? How do they manage the strategic conflicts these challenges may produce among participants? Unfortunately, the currently dominant approaches in social movement theory do not seem to have convincing answers to these questions. Existing theoretical approaches help shed light on the various strategic difficulties transnational activists must cope with, yet the same approaches have not provided convincing solutions to these difficulties. In particular, it remains open as to how transnational movement coalitions may bridge internal divisions and foster cohesion among culturally and politically heterogeneous participants. It thus comes as no surprise that contemporary analyses of transnational social movement activism often do without recourse to the existing theoretical approaches. The case studies in Bandy and Smith's *Coalitions Across Borders* (2005a), for instance, 'waste little time trying to reconstruct existing theories' (Tilly, 2005: xiii); they rather follow the inductive approach of thinking through concrete cases in order to reach new theoretical insights.

Looking beyond the area of social movement research, useful theoretical insights into how transnational movement coalitions may create unity amid diversity can be found in research on group cohesion. In experimental studies, this research strand has found group cohesion to be strongly influenced by the frequency of successful interaction and productive exchange among group members. As group members interact with one another and jointly solve certain practical problems, their sense of belonging to the group grows and they increasingly perceive their being part of the group as a gratifying experience (Lawler and Yoon 1998). Also, it has been shown that repeated successful interaction is causally linked to group cohesion not primarily through uncertainty reduction and the emergence of mutual trust, but through an affective process creating positive emotions (Lawler, Thye und Yoon 2000). These findings thus support the theory of relational cohesion (Lawler and Yoon 1998; Lawler, Thye, and Yoon 2000; cf. also Thye, Yoon, and Lawler 2002), according to which successful social interaction and joint accomplishments create mild, everyday feelings that the actors then attribute not only to the participants involved but the group as a whole:

> [A]ctors are motivated to understand the sources of these feelings . . . [T]hey want to reproduce good feelings and avoid bad feelings in the future. Yet, the source of these feelings is unclear, given that exchange entails a joint accomplishment. This presents actors with an attribution problem. . . . The result is 'cognitive work' by individuals, in which social units—exchange relations or groups—are part of their explanation for the emotions felt. In productive exchange, then, groups become objects of attachment to the degree that they are perceived as a source of positive individual feelings. Cohesion and commitment behavior are consequences of this. (Lawler, Thye, and Yoon 2000: 626)

Transferring these findings to the study of social movement activism, a first factor potentially contributing to cohesion in transnational movement coalitions becomes apparent: the capacity of social movement leaders to convincingly portray important political events as the outcomes of coalition efforts. To the degree that movement leaders and coalition coordinators succeed in presenting such events—e.g. the collapse of free trade talks or the breakdown of other international negotiations—as the merit of transnational contention, activists develop positive feelings cognitively attributed to the movement coalition. As Bandy and Smith (2005b: 245) put it, 'coalitions are sustainable when they can convince members that there is reasonable progress toward common goals. . . . With every success, however minor or fleeting, coalitions achieve greater legitimacy for participants.'

Joint protests and other large gatherings—especially those that include not only movement leaders but also rank and file activists—

constitute another factor that, according to the theory of relational cohesion, may contribute positively to the survival of transnational social movement coalitions. While facilitating the exchange of information and the planning of future events, protests and meetings also have a positive effect on coalition maintenance by generating what Kohler (2006) calls 'networking moments', i.e. personal and sometimes very emotional intercultural encounters among participants. In these gatherings, activists learn to respect each other's experiences and visions, and to the extent that some of the participants use the event as a platform to publicly express themselves through artistic means such as photographs, music and other performances, their encounters also manage to overcome language barriers. However, as Wood (2005) and several others have pointed out, transnational movement meetings tend to suffer from an over-representation of participants from the global north, as these have more access to travel funds and rarely face restrictive visa regulations. There is a risk, then, that transnational meetings become dominated by cliques of northern activists and other frequent participants.

The existence of hierarchical relations constitutes a factor, which, according to research on relational cohesion, can endanger the development of person-to-group attachment in transnational social movement coalitions. As Lawler and his colleagues (Lawler und Yoon 1998; Lawler, Thye and Yoon 2000) demonstrate in group experiments, repeated successful cooperation increases person-to-group attachment only in such settings in which group members have been endowed with the same degree of centrality and power. In groups showing an unequal distribution of power, social cohesion remains virtually unchanged as the frequency and success rate of interactions increase. Total cohesion is presumably greatest in such transnational social movement coalitions that show a relatively equitable distribution of power and a homogeneous distribution of interaction frequencies among participants. According to Bandy and Smith (2005b), sustained transnational cooperation is most likely to happen in movement coalitions whose organizational culture is flexible and democratic.

Yet another factor fostering the cohesion and survival of transnational movement coalitions is the leadership of skilled movement brokers (Bandy and Smith 2005b)—that is, the capability of movement leaders and coalition coordinators to accommodate different movement cultures. In their role as 'bridging persons' (Brown and Fox 1998), movement leaders need to have certain qualities to undertake the process of coalition building and maintenance work. The case studies reviewed by Bandy and Smith (2005b: 241f.), for instance, show that for coalitions to be successful and enduring, brokers need to have abundant charisma and enjoy a high level of legitimate authority. Also, leaders and coordinators of successful movement coalitions tend to be skillful communicators, culturally sensitive interpreters, and patient listeners. 'They may translate languages, but they also translate between different discourses of grievance and forms of action used by members. They promote dialogue among members, and thus mutual learning, trust, and the sharing of resources' (Bandy and Smith 2005b: 241). To the degree that movement leaders and coalition coordinators can draw upon these capabilities, they may not only transform potential and actual conflicts into productive learning experiences, but also help activists engaged in transnational movement coalitions develop a sense of belonging and collective identity.

In summary, the above considerations make it clear that for transnational social movement coalitions to survive and succeed, leaders and activists need to overcome several challenges. These challenges are similar to those usually faced by movements operating at the local or national level, but they typically show a greater degree of complexity. As Bandy and Smith (2005b: 231) emphasize, transnational movement coalitions have to deal with many differences among participants which, when not addressed properly, not only creates social strain, but can lead to ruptures. 'It is very difficult even for nationally based movements to survive as they challenge power holders, but transnational networks must traverse even larger gaps in power, wealth, ideology, culture, strategic interests, and organizational forms.' As Lesley Wood (2005: 97) puts it, 'In transnational coalitions, participants often speak different languages, operate within different national and local contexts, have distinct organizational cultures and histories, and come from movements as diverse as rural fisherfolk in Bangladesh and Canadian trade unionists.' However, given several cases of coalitions that have overcome these challenges, it should be clear that building and maintaining long-lasting transnational movement coalitions is by no means impossible. In a comparative analysis of several case studies, Bandy and Smith point out that all cases of successful long-term coalition maintenance show four commonalities: (i) they are able to convince members that there has been reasonable progress toward stated goals; (ii) they create coalition forums such as the World Social Forum in Porto

Alegre or PGA's Hemispheric Encounters, in which activists can build intercultural ties; (iii) they show a relatively flat hierarchy and flexible organizational culture; and (iv) they can count on the intercultural competence of their coalition delegates and movement leaders. Interestingly, these findings corroborate the theory of relational cohesion outlined above. In the following sections, I will analyse as to whether the same success factors have been at work in the case of the Hemispheric Social Alliance, as well as what other factors need to be taken into account.

THE HEMISPHERIC SOCIAL ALLIANCE AND THE STRUGGLE AGAINST THE FTAA

To analyse how transnational collaboration has been sustained in the case of the HSA, this study will first give a descriptive account of the organization's history, organizational structure, and repertoire of contention. Although politically influential through its protests and other activities, the HSA is relatively unknown to the general public, especially outside Latin America. The mass media tend to address the HSA in terms of the organization's activities, referring to their members as 'the organizers of the Peoples' Summit of the Americas', or 'the coordinators of the mass rally against the latest ministerial meeting of the Organization of American States'. And while there is a vast scholarly literature on civil society protests against the North American Free Trade Agreement (NAFTA) treaty, there are relatively few studies on the struggle against the FTAA and other regional free trade agreements. Some important exceptions notwithstanding (Massicotte 2003 and 2004; Foster 2005; von Bülow 2006; and Saguier 2005), the present analysis of the HSA appears to be breaking new scholarly ground.

Historical Roots

As one of the participants in the 3rd Peoples' Summit of the Americas put it, the history of the HSA and its campaign against the FTAA goes further back than the history of the FTAA itself. The organizational roots of the Alliance can be traced to the collective struggles against the bilateral free trade agreement between the United States and Canada (CUSFTA), and against NAFTA agreement. As Foster (2005) reports in his study on civil society struggles against NAFTA, negotiations around free trade in North America originally gave rise to a broad variety of relatively unconnected local protest movements, but eventually several of these movements came to coordinate their struggles in four national and regional network organizations: the Alliance for Responsible Trade (ART) in the United States; the Red Mexicana de Acción Frente al Libre Comercio (RMALC) in Mexico; Common Frontiers in the English-speaking regions of Canada; and the Réseau Québéquois sur l'Intégration Continentale (RQUIC) in Québéc. These were the organizations, which, at a later stage, initiated the creation of the HSA.

When the US administration under Bill Clinton announced its plans to launch the FTAA initiative, it was clear to the members of the trilateral coalition against NAFTA that they had to build a pan-American resistance movement. In South America and parts of Central America, many social movement activists and progressive non-governmental organizations knew only little about the implications of neoliberal free trade agreements, and they knew even less about how to effectively fight such agreements. The networks that had formed the trilateral alliance against NAFTA thus decided they would have to reach out, educate civil society organizations in other countries about these topics, and mobilize potential network partners across the continent (source: interview with a founding member from Brazil). Conversely, there was a widespread belief among North American politicians, as well as in the North American population in general, that people in Central and South America generally favoured free trade because it would produce economic and political development. Therefore, it seemed very important to North American activists to become more connected with Latin American activists, as only direct testimonies from their southern partner organizations would make a plausible case that people in the global South were indeed *opposed to* free trade (source: interview with a US American participant).

After a while, the 'NAFTA veterans' (Foster 2005) were able to mobilize the support of several civil society organizations in Chile, and of various organizations in Brazil. The latter eventually created a network organization called REBRIP (*Rede Brasileira pela Integração dos Povos*: 'Brazilian Network for the People's Integration'), and together with the initial North American networks, the future REBRIP members organized a transcontinental civil society meeting in 1997 in Belo Horizonte, Brazil. It was in this meeting, described by Foster (2005: 220) as a 'diverse gathering of trade union, antipoverty, environmental, and other NGOs', in which the participants not only decided to found the Hemispheric Social Alliance but also began to organize the First Peoples' Summits of the Americas, which then took place in 1998 in Santiago de Chile, as a counter event to the official Summit of the Americas held by the Organization of American States. The HSA's actual founding act, in which the participants signed a founding charter, took place during a meeting in 1999 in Costa Rica. By this time, the initiators had been joined by two other participants: Vía Campesina, a global association of small-scale peasants, and ORIT (Organización Regional Interamericana de Trabajadores), the inter-American association of labour unions.

Since its informal creation in 1997, and even more so since the formal founding act in 1999, the HSA has experienced a quite unexpected growth, as several additional organizations, big and small, have joined in. Currently, the HSA has national chapters and affiliated partners in at least twenty American countries, including Argentina, Bolivia, Chile, Colombia, Cuba, the Dominican Republic, Ecuador, and Guatemala, to name just a few (www.asc-hsa.org). The third HSA-organized Peoples' Summit of the Americas in Mar del Plata (November 2005) attracted movement leaders and grassroots activists representing over 500 organizations. The final mass rally mobilized about 50,000 people (according to official sources; according to the organizers, there were 60,000 people). Press coverage of the event, although overshadowed by reports on violent clashes between the police and autonomous radicals later in the evening, was vast and surprisingly sympathetic.

Aims and Organizational Structure

While opposition to the FTAA was the HSA's *raison d'être*, several other objectives have been relevant to the organization as well. The founding charter (HSA 1999), for instance, emphasizes the need to struggle against the World Trade Organization (WTO) negotiations and the Organisation of Economic Cooperation and Development (OECD's) Multilateral Investment Agreement. And over the last years, the HSA has also become engaged in protests against bilateral free trade negotiations between the United States and individual countries in Central America, as well as against negotiations between Common Market of the South (Mercosur) countries (Argentina, Brazil, Paraguay and Uruguay) and the European Union. More recently, the campaign against U.S. military bases in Latin America, and support for Jubilee South's struggle for the cancellation of foreign debts, to have become almost as crucial to the HSA as the initial campaign against the FTAA. The anti-FTAA campaign, in turn, gradually developed a kind of life of its own, as it was increasingly supported and co-sponsored by organizations which do not consider themselves participants of the HSA. An organizational 'emancipation' of this campaign took place, which is expressed symbolically by the fact that its participants created their own website (http://movimientos.org/noalca/). The website states that the participants 'give priority to the campaign—not just consider it as just one more activity'. Coordination meetings, however, were organized by the HSA (especially its Cuban chapter), and the HSA staff in Brazil was in charge of the campaign's Operations Secretariat.

The Hemispheric Social Alliance is organized as a 'coalition of coalitions' or 'mega coalition'. Although the Alliance recognizes individuals and individual organizations as possible participants, all members of the HSA's international coordination boards, the Organizing Committee and the Hemispheric Council are themselves coalitions of groups from various segments of civil society. More specifically, the Hemispheric Council consists of so-called Thematic Networks and National Chapters, which represent two different organizational principles. The Thematic Networks combine organizations from various countries working on the same topics, whereas the National Chapters usually combine organizations from the same country working on different topics. The *Organización Continental Latinoamericana y Caribeña de Estudiantes* (OCLAE), for instance, is a typical Thematic Network as it combines students associations from several places in Central America and the Caribbean. The Argentinean *Autoconvocatoria No al ALCA* (recently renamed Movimiento por La Soberanía e Integración de Los Pueblos [MOSIP]), in turn, is a typical National Chapter as it represents human rights organizations, nation-wide trade union associations, neighbourhood councils in Buenos Aires, unemployed workers, and many other segments of Argentina's civil society.

Interestingly, in its founding charter and its website the HSA never characterizes itself as an 'organization'; it rather uses the terms 'forum', 'process under construction', 'space', and 'platform' to describe its organizational form. The intention of its founding members and participants has always been to avoid strict hierarchies, keep the organizational structure as decentralized as possible, and give its participants maximum autonomy. By evading the term 'organization' the participants want to make it clear that the Alliance is never to develop a strictly hierarchical structure with 'NGO-like' professional staff and institutionalized mechanisms to sanction non-compliance with group decisions. It is important to note, however, that the Alliance does have an institutionalized division of labour in that it has formed an administrative secretariat, which is in charge of organizing meetings, maintaining communications, and dealing with other day-to-day business. Political guidelines are developed by the HSA's Hemispheric Council, whereas actual policy decisions are made by the international Coordinating Committee. The Hemispheric Council, which meets once or twice a year to discuss the broad policy lines, consists of delegates of about 30 organizations, whereas the Coordinating Committee consists of delegates of only 8 organizations. The latter meet several times a year and share information through a steady exchange of e-mails, fax letters and international phone calls.

In sum, while, there are elements of formal organizational structures in the HSA, the participants try to keep these as minimal as possible. In fact, the minimization of hierarchies and centralization are addressed explicitly in the founding charter, which states that 'although the HSA does not conceive itself as an organization with structures and hierarchies', participants cannot avoid 'the creation of coordinating spaces and instances', as only these can 'ensure that the HSA be not confined to a concept, but become an instrument for action and contestation'. Yet, coordinating instances are to be kept 'minimal and flexible' (HSA 1999).

Repertoire of Action

On the website of one of its founding members, Common Frontiers, the principal objectives of the HSA are identified as follows: (i) to impact, and eventually stop, the FTAA by lobbying, influencing public opinion, and developing corresponding media strategies; and (ii) to mobilize broad-based support for this struggle in collaboration with the trade union movement, environmentalists, women's organizations, 'and all other social movements, especially those most marginalized by the present economic model' (www.commonfrontiers.ca). In other words, the HSA aims at building support among like-minded civil society organizations, while also raising public awareness and influencing the opinions of people outside the social movement sector. To reach these goals, HSA participants have developed a broad repertoire of contentious activities. Or, as the website of Common Frontiers states emphatically, 'The HSA is not short of ideas!' (ibid.) Among other things, the HSA issues press statements, maintains a newslist to disseminate updates on the ongoing free trade negotiations, and initiates coordinated mass rallies and so-called 'Hemispheric Days of Action' across the Americas.

As a core element of its campaign against the regional free trade agreements, the HSA has been conducting sporadic *consultas populares*—unofficial plebiscites—in several countries. These plebiscites serve the threefold purpose of raising public awareness of the ongoing free trade negotiations, informing critically about the agreements possible effects, and surveying people's opinions. The methodology of how the *consultas* are conducted can vary in accordance with the available resources and political opportunities in each country. In Chile, for instance, the *consulta* process has been restricted so far to a survey-based consultation among left-wing civil society organizations, whereas in Peru the consultation has been carried out in gatherings of grassroots movements (Berrón and Freire 2004). But the intended procedure (as implemented in Brazil and Argentina, for example) is that of a broad-based plebiscite 'from below'. In these plebiscites, activists put up stands with ballot boxes in as many major (and sometimes minor) localities as possible, and during approximately a week they talk to passers-by about the planned free trade agreement. The passers-by are then asked to vote anonymously on whether or not they agree to their government continuing the negotiations.

A first wave of *consultas* concerned with the FTAA took place over the years 2002 and 2003 in Argentina, Brazil, Paraguay, Mexico, and several other countries. The response this first wave managed to produce varied significantly from country to country. In Paraguay, for instance, the HSA's national chapter collected only 1,63,000 votes (with an overwhelming majority, obviously, opposing the FTAA), while in Uruguay the campaign was never really able to take off, and the *consulta* was cancelled before it had even begun. But in other cases, the *consulta* turned out to be a considerable success. In Argentina, the HSA was able to collect 22,50,000 votes, while in Brazil, with the help of several thousand grassroots activists, it collected an overwhelming 10 million votes (95 per cent of which opposed the free trade agreement; Berrón and Freire 2004). To date, then, the *consulta* process has enabled the face-to-face dissemination of critical information about the regional free trade initiatives to several million people, especially in the most powerful economies of the Southern Cone, Brazil and Argentina.

While the first wave of the *consulta* campaign was focused almost exclusively on the negotiations around the Free Trade Area of the Americas (though in some cases combining this with the issue of bilateral free trade agreements and the Central American Free Trade Area (CAFTA)), the HSA-organized Peoples' Summits of the Americas have been broader thematically. They run counter to the official Summits of the Americas held by the Organization of American States, the platform for the American heads of state to negotiate the multilateral free trade agreements and advance several other mechanisms of regional integration. There have been four Peoples' Summits so far, the first in Santiago de Chile (1998), the second in Québéc (2001), and the third in the Argentinean beach resort Mar del Plata (2005) and the fourth on the Island of Trinidad and Tobago 2009. The organizational format of these Peoples' Summits is that of a semi-structured forum. Alongside plenary events and discussion rounds organized by the HSA, the Peoples' Summits also provide open space for a broad variety of self-organized events by other civil society groups. Hence, the Peoples' Summits constitute ideal opportunities for the HSA to strengthen their ties with other civil society organizations in the Americas. The 2005 version of the Peoples' Summit, for instance, hosted a well-attended meeting of indigenous resistance movements, a workshop on the economic effects of genetically engineered soy production on small-scale farmers, and a workshop on non-violent protest tactics, to name just a few of over hundred self-organized events. But the main objective of this most recent Peoples' Summit was to promote a broad-based discussion on socially and environmentally sustainable alternatives to the FTAA. As one of the organizers put it, the first two Peoples' Summits had intended to raise public awareness of the FTAA initiative and build a broad-based resistance movement. These aims being reached, the time seemed ripe to begin discussing more seriously the issue of possible counter-proposals to the FTAA.

The HSA has provided an inspiring basis for the discussion of counter-proposals to the regional free trade in the form of its

'Alternatives for the Americas', a 'living document' under continual revision. Formulated by several HSA participants from Canada, Mexico and the United States, a first version of this policy paper was presented and discussed at the occasion of the First Peoples' Summit of the Americas in 1998. Since then, several international working groups have been in charge of revising and updating each chapter by collecting and coordinating input from various conferences and working meetings. The participants in these international working groups have continually circulated draft versions of the document by email and met in various countries to discuss and advance their respective chapters. As each revision has taken into account suggestions raised during plenary discussions in the Peoples' Summits (and several other broad-based civil society meetings), the policy paper is reflective of the HSA's particular mélange of 'top-down' and 'bottom up' approaches. While the original draft had been elaborated 'top down' by movement leaders and professional NGO staff, it has gradually turned into a construction 'from below', increasingly integrative and conducive to the strengthening of the HSA's collective identity. According to one interviewee, the HSA's policy paper has served as an important source of inspiration for the ALBA (*Alternativa Bolivariana para la América*), the counter-proposal to the FTAA put forward by the Hugo Chavez administration in Venezuela.

What has been Accomplished?

In assessing what the HSA has accomplished to date, it is worthwhile to note that no kind of pan-American free trade agreement has not come into effect yet. While the original FTAA initiative envisaged the implementation of the agreement by January 2005, the negotiations did not even produce a consensual working draft yet. In fact, the regional free trade talks are effectively blocked, as the Venezuelan government under the leadership of Hugo Chávez refuses to proceed with the negotiations altogether. Also, the Argentinean and Brazilian governments have stated that their future participation in regional free trade talks is conditional upon the elimination of agriculture subsidies on the part of the United States, and the provision of effective market access in all those sectors, in which the United States itself has been trying to protect its businesses from Southern American competitors. In other words, Argentina and Brazil are not opposed to pan-American free trade altogether, but demand it to be really free. And yet, as their demands seem currently unrealizable in the US, this position amounts to a temporary veto against any pan-American free trade initiative.

It should be clear, of course, that the current deadlock in pan-American free trade negotiations initiative must not be credited to the efforts of the HSA alone. As Tarrow (2003: 20) puts it, 'the most impressive roadblock to the successful completion of the FTAA is not the notable transnational educational and lobbying activities of the Hemispheric Social Alliance, but formidable and growing objections of Brazil to US domestic trade policies.' And these, it should be added, have been reflective of, or a pretext for, Brazil's geostrategically motivated interest to remain South America's uncontested economic leader. Brazil's inclusion in the FTAA would have turned the most powerful economy in the South America into a 'junior partner' of the United States, whereas the strengthening of the Mercosur, the Southern counterweight to the NAFTA, would improve the geostrategic position of both Brazil and Argentina. Hence, geostrategic interests seem to have been at least equally decisive for the stagnation of the FTAA process as the popular resistance against the agreement.

However, while the role of the HSA should not be overrated, nor must it be underrated. As discussed above, the HSA was able to inform several million people about the FTAA's potentially devastating social and environmental consequences—and it has also heightened pre-existing resentment toward the United States by framing the proposed agreement as an imperialistic attempt on the part of this country to oppress the rest of the continent. On the website of the Argentinean *Autoconvocatoria No al ALCA*, for instance, textual and pictorial representations of this (anti-)imperialistic frame were legion. 'The United States need the FTAA to solve their economic problems, and to satisfy their ambition to dominate', the site states; and: 'This is not regional integration; this is an ongoing attempt to finalize our imperialist annexation.' In the *consulta popular*, several of the organizers recount, such (anti)imperialistic slogans had massive resonance. If the Argentinean government were to sign the any kind of pan-American free trade treaty, many activists speculated during interviews, this would probably cause mass protests similar to the ones that overthrew several presidents in 2001 and 2002.

ANALYSIS

The historical account above has made it clear that the HSA can be seen as a successful case of transnational coalition building and maintenance. But what has made this success possible? And to what extent will it be possible for movement coalitions in other regions to replicate the HSA's experiences?

Regional Factors

Although the interviews for this study tended to take unexpected thematic turns, the issue of diversity and potential divisions come up in all of them. What has enabled the participants of the HSA to overcome the challenges imposed on them by their cultural and organizational diversity? Interestingly, almost all respondents explain the HSA's success by emphasizing, first and foremost, the crucial role of historical and regional factors lying beyond their sphere of influence. In fact, one activist states (in an unrecorded and informal conversation) that in the case of the HSA the issue of diversity must not be overrated, as the American continent in general is far more homogeneous, culturally and linguistically, than other continents. The American peoples have all been shaped by the same European influences, this respondent argues, and while in Africa and Asia, for instance, there exist hundreds of different languages, American peoples are able to communicate in just four languages: Spanish, Portuguese, English, and French.

Other respondents, of course, contradict this notion of homogeneity. Instead, they emphasize that the notable heterogeneity of the American peoples has filtered down into the HSA and other transnational movement coalitions. In the words of one of the Argentinean interviewees (my translation), 'the movement is politically diverse, . . . it shows diversity in terms of politics, culture and religious beliefs, to name only three important aspects of this diversity, . . . and this has to do also with different national identities and many others things.' However, nearly all interviewees emphasize the notion that the American peoples have gone through the same historical experience—namely, the suffering of colonialism and neocolonial imperialism—and that this shared experience has unified the Americans beyond any cultural differences. The common past of the American countries, the respondents seem to suggest, has lead the inhabitants to develop a kind of multiple collective identity: they have come to define themselves as both, a collective of culturally diverse American peoples in the plural, and as one American people in the singular.

As an Argentinean labour unionist explains, a collective American identity, based on the common desire for independence from oppression, had existed long before the HSA set out to bring together activists from across the entire continent: 'America, especially Latin America, is the outcome of an invasion; therefore, its identity is one of continual struggle for liberation. This is an identity that runs through the whole hemisphere' (my translation). The same respondent then recapitulates the history of the Americas over the last six centuries as a history of continual domination and resistance. In a remarkably elaborate narration, he manages to rhetorically connect the (ambivalent) role of the Guaraníes in Artiga's liberation movement with the Bolivarian revolution and to link the latter with the HSA's ongoing resistance against the FTAA and other free trade initiatives in the Americas.

While most of the other respondents are less eloquent than the labour unionist just quoted, the same basic idea reappears throughout nearly all interviews: while foreign domination, in various forms, has left a mark in the collective memory of all American people(s), resistance against this foreign domination has become part and parcel of a distinctive (Latin) American identity. This collective identity has been present in all participants of the Hemispheric Social Alliance since the coalition's very beginning. Therefore, the respondents suggest, the HSA has always been more likely to turn out an enduring endeavour than have similar coalitions in other regions.

In a similar vein, most interviewees point to the importance of popular resentment towards US foreign policy over the last century. They depict this resentment as both, a particularly significant element of the (Latin) American collective identity, and a favourable condition for the HSA's success in mobilizing enduring support for its campaign against the mutual free trade in the Americas. As an Argentinean human rights activist put it, the continent-wide struggle against the FTAA clearly profited from the fact that people were tired of US American economic and political interventions:

> It should be clear that this was a continent in uproar, fed up with U.S. American domination, with years of misery caused by this domination, and with the local social elites that had made way for all of this. (. . .) There was this special social climate—this seems very important—and in this social climate (. . .), (. . .) our collective intelligence—because I don't think this

has been the work of one or two people in particular—succeeded in detecting the connection between the FTAA and the old imperialistic strategy of domination. Because, this is nothing new. There is a history that is very much soaked with pain—and pain leaves scorch marks—. . . with pain and with struggle. Not with passive pain, but with the struggle of various sectors of the continent (my translation).

In short, what the activists suggest in their (highly analytic) narrations is that the HSA has profited from the effects of structural and historical circumstances over which the movement coalition had no control whatsoever. Possible explanations that connect the HSA's longevity with the agency of the participants themselves are usually brought up at a very late point in the interviews, and given little, if any, importance. Instead, the respondents emphasize as success factors the comparatively high degree of linguistic homogeneity and the important role of what could be called 'historical opportunity structures' specific to the Americas.

This emphasis on contextual success factors means bad news, of course, for coalitions outside the Americas. If unity among the participants of the HSA has been rooted primarily in structural and historical characteristics of the American continent, other movements may be unable to copy the HSA's successful experience with coalition building. As these regional characteristics are unique to the Americas, and external to the movement, movements struggling in other regions and for other issues cannot replicate them.

It is debatable, however, whether or not these factors have really been as decisive as most of the interviewees seem to argue. Firstly, even though the activists themselves have not attributed much importance to factors related to agency and organizational form, these internal factors (see below) may have been just as important as contextual ones. Secondly, the external 'factors' emphasized so far are not as factual as the activists have depicted them. References to a common American culture, history, and collective memory, are by no means references to undisputed realities 'out there'. Rather, they must be seen as the outcomes of a framing process, which has taken place within the (Latin) American Left, and the HSA in particular, over the last decade or two. The historical material that these frames have been constructed from is probably unique to the American continent; but material for similar frames can be found in other places as well.

The notion of cultural and linguistic homogeneity among the American peoples is a good case in point. While the American continent is relatively homogeneous when compared to others, in absolute terms its inhabitants are too diverse for a well-working and broad-based pan-American movement coalition to be taken for granted. In fact, the idea proposed by one activist, that diversity 'must not be overrated', as 'there are only four languages on this continent', neglects the presence of several hundred First Nations and their native languages. Similarly the notion of a common American history represents a perspective that is far from consensual. For the Italian immigrants in Buenos Aires, for instance, the allegedly 'shared' history of oppression and resistance has been another than for the First Nations in Peru, or for the African slaves in Brazil.

What this suggests, then, is that the respondents' narratives are reflective of a movement frame, rather than a factual, or consensual 'reality'. They constitute selective, and strategic, (re)constructions of reality that suppress notions of difference, while simultaneously reinforcing unifying perceptions of possible commonalities. As such, they do not necessarily represent frames that have been proffered by the HSA to convince external audiences of their political claims; they are elements of what could be termed subcultural or 'in-house' framing.

Organizational Decentralization and Flexibility

Transnational movement coalitions tend to experience deep internal conflicts over divergent organizational demands (Bandy and Smith 2005a). While some participants usually champion decentralized mass participation and 'horizontal' coordination processes, others favour hierarchies and the centralization of decision making. Comparative research has demonstrated that a central commonality of durable transnational coalitions has been their ability to find a balance between these two opposite principles. As Bandy and Smith (2005b: 244) put it, 'both demands—efficient coordination and decentralized participation—are vital to coalition survival'. Coalition maintenance requires that participants develop 'a flexible organizational culture that accommodates members' autonomy and diversity, while nonetheless uniting them around common goals—a strategy of reconciling difference with unity, the universal and the particular' (ibid.: 244).

The sustained survival of the HSA corroborates this finding, as the HSA's internal politics have been reflective of what could be termed 'subsidiary federalism' (to borrow a term used by the European

Union and Switzerland). The Alliance provides its participants with institutionalized means to coordinate their struggles, and with the possibility to be perceived as a powerful unitary actor by the media and politicians, but decisions are made at the lowest organizational level possible. Likewise, decisions that need to be made at the 'hemispheric' level—by the Hemispheric Council and the Coordinating Committee—usually leave a broad margin for flexible adaptation at the local and national levels. Not only does the HSA lack formal means to sanction non-compliance, but also decisions made at the uppermost organizational level usually have the form of general guidelines rather than binding rules. The idea of 'thinking globally, acting locally', though developed by business advisors for transnational corporations, seems to apply here as well.

A good case to illustrate that the HSA operates on the principles of organizational flexibility and decentralization is its 'living' policy paper, the 'Alternatives for the Americas', discussed in the previous section. Another case in point is the *consulta popular*. As described above, this informal plebiscite has taken on different forms in different countries, although the initiators originally wanted the process to have the same format throughout the whole continent. While the intended format has been implemented in just a few countries (e.g. Argentina and Brazil), in others the process has needed to be adapted to the capabilities of the local organizers and to specific political opportunity structures. And yet, despite these cross-national variations, the *consulta popular* has not only been made possible, but local organizers have also managed to give it a unitary appearance by using the same slogans and logos.

The notable diversity in how the *consulta popular* has been carried out can be interpreted as an ambivalent outcome of both, organizational 'strength' and 'weakness'. On the hand, as suggested by Massicotte (2004: 35; my translation), the flexible implementation of the plebiscite is a sign of weakness in that it is reflective of divisions among the HSA's leaders:

> (It) reveals the presence of divergent opinions as to the most efficient way of organizing the campaign and reaching out to the citizens. There seems to have been dissension on available resources and strategic options. In the end, the delegates came to an understanding which was based on the need to stay flexible in order to realize their common objectives. They kept adhering to the principle of consensual decision-making, but the consensus reached indicated notable discrepancies among the various movements on the continent.

On the other hand, the *consulta's* flexible implementation must also be seen as a pragmatic and strategically adequate response to cross-national differences in political and cultural opportunities. In view of these differences, a 'one-size-fits-all' model would have been unreasonable. Decentralization and flexibility 'have permitted each organization and coalition to adapt the campaign to the particularities and needs of the popular forces in their respective region' (ibid.; my translation). In this sense, then, the flexible implementation of the campaign is not so much a sign of weakness, but has allowed the campaign to become embedded within the local context. Moreover, it has permitted the local organizers to develop a strong sense of ownership for the campaign.

Participatory Deliberations and Consensus-Oriented Decision Making

While organizational flexibility has been critical for the HSA's survival, consensus decision making has been crucial to build cohesion among its participants. International meetings (such as the Hemispheric Encounters for the Struggle Against the FTAA) and the meetings of national chapters (such as the Argentinean *Autoconvocatoria*) operate on the principles of consensus: participants are expected to deliberate and are encouraged to express dissent, and decisions are only made if all participants agree. In large meetings, deliberations usually take place in parallel discussion groups consisting of twenty to thirty people, and the results of these decentralized discussions are gathered, and deliberated once more, in a plenary round. If the group reaches no consensus, but there is a majority championing the same option, matters are adjourned until the next day, or the next meeting.

While none of the activists interviewed for this study has criticized the principle of consensus decision-making, several have emphasized its merits. Firstly, they argue, the consensus method helps to strengthen group cohesion and build up a collective identity, as it leaves no room for participants with minority positions to be continually overruled. No group can ever feel like its views are not welcome. Secondly, consensus decision-making increases compliance with the outcomes. As the decisions are 'owned' and supported by all participants, effective implementation is ensured. Thirdly, the search for consensus involves an intense exchange of ideas and information. To substantiate their respective positions, participants in consensus-oriented debates often refer to the history and political situation in the countries, or provinces, they come from, and to the current situation of the group they represent. Hence, consensus decision making sparks mutual learning, which in turn brings participants closer together. Fourthly, as one respondent argues, consensus decision making is slow, but remarkably effective. In meetings operating on the principles of majority voting, discussions are usually cut-off as soon as there is a selection of two or three options to vote on. Yet, the proffered options are not necessarily the most useful. Consensus decision making being a slower, yet more creative process, it often produces solutions that are not only consensual but also more adequate and clever. As Polletta (2002: 2) puts it, 'The sheer diversity of input into tactical choice that participatory democracy makes possible, (. . .) enable(s) activists to outpace their opponents in generating novel tactics.'

This is not to say, however, that consensus decision-making will invariably have positive effects on any kind of group. Rather, the effectiveness of this method depends on specific group characteristics and social context. Polletta's (2002) case studies suggest that for consensus-oriented forms of participatory decision making to work, participants must share the same basic goals and have a similar understanding of their situation. As each participant can use the right of veto to continually block the decision making process and immobilize the group, the consensus method can hardly create cohesion in groups with fundamentally different interests. In fact, problems also arise when a participant who repeatedly expresses dissent is just *suspected* of trying to immobilize the process. Hence, mutual trust and respect, too, are important preconditions for the consensus method to produce satisfactory outcomes.

Basic Similarities of Participating Groups and Frequent Interaction Among Leaders

In the case of the HSA, it can be argued, the preconditions for successful consensus finding—a common understanding of the situation, shared goals, and mutual trust—have been fulfilled since the organizations' onset. The Alliance was created by a core group of initiators through the mobilization of like-minded groups with which there had been previous ties. In other words, the Alliance has grown in what could be described as a concentric process of self-selection. When the core group of coalitions that had fought against the NAFTA agreement began searching for potential partners to build a hemispheric network, they reached out to groups they already knew to be trustworthy and share the same interests. Once these groups joined in, they in turn began mobilizing others, which they happened to know from previous struggles.

Moreover, as one of the founding members recounts, in many Southern American countries the progressive left knew very little about the FTAA and its possible consequences. The members of the trinational coalition against NAFTA were thus expected by potential partner organizations to educate them about this matter. Drawing on the expertise they had achieved in the struggle against the NAFTA agreement, the North American networks informed southern civil society organizations on their experiences and insights, and thereby contributed to the diffusion of a shared understanding of what was at stake. Hence, the HSA has never been in a situation where it needed to bridge fundamentally divergent perspectives on the same cause.

This is not to say, however, that there have not been any conflicts. On the contrary, despite manifold initial commonalities among its members, the Alliance has gone through all of the conflicts that Bandy and Smith (2005b: 238) see as typical for transnational movement coalitions, 'including those over representation, decision-making, divisions of labor, leadership styles, hierarchy, and centralization'. Not surprisingly, there have also been 'debates over strategies that vary between radical and reformist, legal and illegal, nonviolent and violent' (ibid.: 240), as well as between cooperative and disruptive. Several of the initial participants reported in the interviews for this study that in the first years there was a deep conflict on whether the Alliance should struggle for a socially tolerable reform of the FTAA, or reject the treaty altogether. As one respondent put it, the way towards the now uncontested strategy, to stop the FTAA altogether, was 'tough, very tough' (my translation).

That strategic and tactical differences have not produced major frictions has been, to a great extent, the merit of the movement leaders who represent the National Chapters and Thematic Networks in the HSA's international boards. The delegates in the Coordinating Committee and the Hemispheric Council have repeatedly acted as skilled and committed interlocutors, or bridging individuals, and managed to negotiate viable compromises despite manifold centrifugal forces (cf. Brown and Fox 1998). Moreover, as there has been relatively low fluctuation in the composition of these boards, the delegates have been able to build up emotional bonds. As Massicotte (2003: 110) notes, the HSA 'reaches out to grassroots movements, but only a few social leaders coordinate its regular activities'. In fact, several founding members have been delegates in the Coordinating Committee and the Hemispheric Council since the HSA's very beginning. Hence, just like in the cases of durable coalitions discussed by Brown and Fox (1998: 455), 'direct, repeated, sustained contact among bridging individuals appears to have been an important factor in the development of solidarity, trust, and shared values among participants'.

THE UNRESOLVED PROBLEM OF GRASSROOTS PARTICIPATION

The previous sections have depicted the HSA as a case of effective coalition maintenance. There are, however, unresolved difficulties, especially with regard to grassroots participation at the local level. Whether or not the HSA's experiences should be evaluated as a 'success', thus depends on the evaluation criteria. Taking into account that many transnational movement coalitions are short-lived and centered around a single-issue campaign, the HSA can indeed be seen as a success story. It has survived manifold internal crises, and grown increasingly more inclusive in terms of both, participating organizations and issues covered. And yet, measured against one of the HSA's main objectives, to strengthen local civil society organizations and encourage their political empowerment, the balance seems more ambivalent. According to its founding charter, the Alliance aims at creating 'participatory democracy at the hemispheric level' (my translation), but critics point out that in reality it has allowed less mass participation than would have been possible, and been unable to avoid the reproduction of internal asymmetries.

Massicotte (2003), for instance, points out the notable over-representation of professional NGO staff, researchers, and union leaders in the HSA's Coordinating Committee and the Hemispheric Council. She notes that,

> While it has gained the support of mass organizations, only a few *leaders*, maybe a hundred, from key national and regional coalitions, regularly participate in the HSA's activities. Its limited resources and the 'hemispheric'

scale at which it primarily functions make it extremely difficult for grassroots participation. (Ibid.: 111)

Moreover, Massicotte emphasizes the notorious underrepresentation of delegates from areas outside the major metropolises:

> The Alliance is not as hemispheric as its name suggests. Regular participants live in major cities, and come from about ten countries. Being in large cities provides leaders with easier access to information and governments for their lobbying strategies, especially national offices dealing with interstate trade. (2003: 121f)

The consequences of this overrepresentation of professionals with similar social backgrounds are, of course, ambivalent. On the one hand, the relatively pronounced homogeneity and stable composition of the HSA's hemispheric boards appear to have been crucial for the organizations' survival. On the other hand, the regular participants in these boards can be argued to have become an elite, increasingly detached, perhaps, from the ideas, needs, and interests of grassroots activists. Based on interviews conducted in the United States, Canada and Mexico (ibid.: endnote 19), Massicotte observes that local activists indeed perceive a gap between their own work and that of their regular delegates in the HSA's hemispheric boards:

> Many grassroots activists (. . .) are disappointed about not being able to participate. They often see coalition politics as the preserve of a few social leaders who can travel to meetings and participate in conference calls to deepen their analysis and plan joint activities. Many are therefore sceptical about the idea that coalition-building strengthens their struggles for deeper democracy and justice. The HSA promotes the latter goals, but there are continual dilemmas and debates about how to ensure representativity and democratic participation, especially at 'transnational' levels. (Ibid.: 121)

Interestingly, however, Massicotte's findings do not quite correspond to the perceptions of Argentinean grassroots activists. The Argentinean activists interviewed for the present study seem to have a more pragmatic perspective on the issue of transnational representation and participation than the North American respondents in Massicotte's study. While they find hemispheric coalition-building very important, many Argentinean rank and file activists see it as 'normal' and 'logical' that only a few leaders can afford travelling to international coordination meetings. As they cannot think of any viable alternative, they do not seem to be disappointed, or angry, about not being able to participate.

Moreover, most of the Argentinean respondents seem quite confident that the participants in the Coordinating Committee and the Hemispheric Council have maintained strong connections to the movement's popular base. And they trust the hemispheric delegates to represent this base to the best of their knowledge. As one of the respondents put it, increased grassroots participation in the HSA's hemispheric international boards would probably not change their policies, as the boards are already aware, and sufficiently reflective of grassroots interests. Another respondent, however, emphasizes the autonomy of local activists to implement the HSA's policies as they wish. If the decisions made by the HSA's coordination boards appear useless, she says, the local participants 'just do it differently' (my translation).

In sum, then, a certain lack of mass participation in the HSA's coalition politics does not seem to be a major concern for Argentinean grassroots activists. However, grassroots activists from outside Buenos Aires emphasize, and criticize, that there is a notable lack of grassroots participation at the *national* level. This is interesting, for the HSA's Argentinean chapter, the *Autoconovocatoria No al ALCA*, not only operates on the principles of participatory democracy, but also constitutes what participants call an 'open space'. That is, deliberations and decision-making take place in weekly plenary meetings, and these are open to anybody who agrees to the *Autoconvocatoria*'s basic objective—to stop the FTAA. The problem is that these meetings take place on weekdays in the capital, invariably and exclusively, and activists living in remote (and not-so-remote) areas cannot attend. Most grassroots activists in the hinterland cannot afford to travel to Buenos Aires, and those who can, usually have no time to do so except on weekends. Hence, grassroots activists operating outside the metropolitan centre are almost entirely excluded from the *Autoconvocatoria's* participatory decision making.

Activists in the hinterland have thought of several creative solutions to resolve this problem, but their suggestions seem to have fallen on deaf ears. Therefore, the *Autoconvocatoria's* inability to stimulate mass participation outside Buenos Aires has come to be seen as the result of arrogance and indifference. As an activist in the province of Santa Fe puts it,

> They always talk about Buenos Aires and the situation in the Latin American subcontinent, but the Argentinean heartland, *el interior*, never comes up. Really, it's like we're reproducing the very logic of the model we've been

fighting against. We have so many difficulties in democratizing all levels and spaces. (. . .) (. . .) But it's as if in Buenos Aires they don't see the problems of small organizations: that we don't have money, that we only get by because we put in a lot of volunteer work, that we don't have all this infrastructure that big organizations have—the ones that participate in the Hemispheric Council, and in the World Social Forum, in which we are unable to participate. (my translation)

Quite surprisingly, however, most of the other local activists in the Argentinean heartland do not conceive the lack of mass participation in the *Autoconvocatoria* in terms of a lack of representativity and internal democratic accountability. Most respondents agree that the ideas and interests of the *Autoconvocatoria's* participants in Buenos Aires are more or less identical with those of grassroots activists in the hinterland. As another respondent from Santa Fe emphasizes, the actual differences are small:

Suppose you conduct a poll about this. . . . You would find that there are no differences between what the comrades in Buenos Aires have in mind and what the [people from the other] provinces would ask for if they were included. (my translation)

What the grassroots activists outside Buenos Aires *do* emphasize are motivational problems. As their comrades in Buenos Aires seem to pay very little attention to what goes on at the local level, several respondents in the heartland report that they often lack the energy to continue with their struggle. It is difficult for them to keep in mind, they argue, that they are part of a 'hemispheric' movement if the regular participants of the national chapter keep excluding them.

CONCLUSION

Coalitions of social movement organizations and activists from different countries can take advantage of a great variety of strategic inputs. As Khagram (2002: 288f.) has shown in his analysis of social movement struggles against the World Bank's Narmada Dam project in India, transnational civil society coalitions pursue their goals using an innovative combination of various protest forms and other actions—'combining and coordinating the full range of strategies, from grassroots protest to elite lobbying, in the widest possible range of institutional contexts, from the local to the international level'. Also, transnational coalition building helps civil society organizations gain symbolic weight and political capital. The Hemispheric Social Alliance, for instance, claims to be a joint project of all the people from Alaska to *Tierra del Fuego*. In many respects, then, transnational coalitions are more than just the sum of their parts. To the casual bystander, the transnational form of these coalitions suggests that the problem the activists struggle against is not only crucial, but also universal: why else would participants take on the significant effort of cross-border organizing? How could a problem of only minor significance create such outrage?

Having said this, building and maintaining transnational coalitions is by no means an easy task. The challenges that transnational activism must cope with are legion. 'Coalitions are difficult wherever they occur, but the diversity of languages, political experiences, and national cultures within transnational coalitions as well as the uncertainties and complexities of intergovernmental negotiating arenas create some unique challenges for organizers' (Smith and Bandy 2005: 7). For skeptical observers such as Sidney Tarrow (2003, 2004), successful cases of transnational coalition maintenance therefore constitute the proverbial exceptions confirming the rule. Normally, skeptics suggest, transnational activism consists of short-lived and monothematic campaigns, which tend to fall apart easily.

The present study demonstrates this skeptical perspective to be overly narrow, as the empirical object of this study, the HSA, has been in existence for more than a decade now. Initiated in the mid-1990s by a group of social movement organizations in Canada, the United States, and Mexico, the HSA now has participants in over twenty countries across the Americas and the Caribbean. Member organizations include politically influential actors such as CUT, the Brazilian trade union association, but also hundreds of lesser known human rights organizations and rural grassroots projects. Hence, the example of the HSA demonstrates that sustained transnational coalition maintenance is possible even in the presence of high levels of heterogeneity and ideological diversity.

To understand how the HSA has forged unity amid diversity, it is important to take into account its organizational culture. *Firstly*, decision making operates, at all organizational levels, on the principles of participatory deliberation and consensus-orientation. This participatory consensus method encourages a respectful exchange of views and thus fosters the development of mutual trust and understanding. *Secondly*, the HSA works according to the principles of subsidiarity and greatest possible local autonomy. While the HSA provides its participants with structured means to coordinate their activities, exchange ideas, and have a joint public appearance, its campaigns and other activities show a significant margin of flexibility in local implementation. Local participants typically have the right (as well as the responsibility) to adapt the coalition's activities to their individual context. *Thirdly*, cohesion among the HSA's member organizations and participants can also be attributed to the diplomatic skills and intercultural competence of the national and regional delegates to the coalitions' steering boards, the Coordinating Committee and the Hemispheric Council. In many cases, the personal biographies of these delegates contain multicultural elements such as multilingualism, personal migration experience, and transcultural marriage. Also, interviews with these delegates suggest a high level of conflict tolerance and respect for diversity of opinions.

In general, the findings presented here lend further support to the results of studies on other transnational movement coalitions (Bandy and Smith 2005a; Fox und Brown 1998; Khagram et al. 2002). Those studies too emphasize the importance of a flexible and decentralized organizational culture (Bandy and Smith 2005b) and of coalition coordinators being skilled leaders and intercultural interlocutors (Fox and Brown 1998). However, in addition to these well-established factors, the present study reveals the importance of yet another element of social cohesion in transnational movement coalitions—the presence of a (regional) collective identity. In the activists' own accounts, this seems to be the single most important explanation for the HSA's longevity: their belonging to a regional collective is mentioned by some respondents as the first, by others as the only success factor. In fact, almost all respondents attribute social cohesion among HSA activists to their common historical experience of resisting external oppression. The century-old struggle against foreign colonial and imperialist forces, they suggest, has united the American peoples despite any cultural differences—and made it relatively easy for the HSA to create sustained group attachment.

It should be clear, of course, that the activists' historical narratives represent an understanding of American history that is unconventional and rather selective. Nevertheless, this selective reconstruction of American history seems to have enabled the HSA's participants to create a sense of belonging and mutual respect. It can be seen as a collective identity frame, the purpose of which is to put emphasis on participants' commonalities whilst downplaying potentially conflictive differences. Though the historical material, from which this identity frame has been constructed, is unique to the Americas, movement coalitions in other regions will surely find similar material from which they can build functionally equivalent constructs.

In summary, this study contends that sustaining long-term cooperation in transnational movement coalitions is difficult, but by no means impossible. Exaggerated skepticism as to the possibilities and limits of transnational activism seems unjustified. However, caution is warranted when overly enthusiastic observers portray contemporary progressive movement coalitions as the unmistakable precursors of an emergent 'planetary democracy' (Ziegler 2003; own translation) and see these coalitions as having the potential to not only bring about selective reforms but also radically transform global politics altogether (Monbiot 2004). Typically, such assessments are not based on rigorous empirical research, but result, to a significant degree, from wishful thinking. In fact, empirical research demonstrates that transnational movement coalitions tend to suffer from internal democratic deficits and power imbalances, which not only reduce their potential to produce transformative innovations, but also help opponents undermine the coalitions' legitimacy (Bandy and Smith 2005a; Khagram et al. 2002). In the case of the HSA, portrayed as a 'success story' of sustained transnational activism in this study, movement leaders and coalition coordinators have so far failed to produce the participation and empowerment of local grassroots activists that the organization's founding charter (HSA 1999) deems so critical (cf. Massicotte 2003 and 2004). In Argentina, for instance, grassroots organizations working outside the capital city have virtually no influence on the decisions made by the HSA's national chapter, the *Autoconvocatoria No al ALCA*. The *Autoconvocatoria* operates on the principles of participatory and consensus-oriented deliberation, but local grassroots activists simply cannot afford frequent trips to Buenos Aires.

REFERENCES

Bandy, Joe and Jackie Smith (eds.) (2005a), *Coalitions Across Borders: Transnational Protest and the Neoliberal Order*, Lanham, MY: Rowman and Littlefield.

Bandy, Joe and Jackie Smith (2005b), 'Factors Affecting Conflict and Cooperation in Transnational Movement Networks', in ibid. (eds.): *Coalitions Across Borders: Transnational Protest and the Neoliberal Order*, Lanham, MY: Rowman and Littlefield, pp. 231–52.

Berrón, Gonzalo and Rafael Freire (2004), 'Los movimientos sociales del Cono Sur contra el mal llamado "libre comercio".' *Revista del Observatoria Social de América Latina*, 13, pp. 297–306.

Brown, Jonathan A. and L. David Fox (1998), 'Accountability within Transnational Coalitions', in L. David Fox, and Jonathan A. Brown (eds.), *The Struggle for Accountability: The World Bank, NGOs, and Grassroots Movements*, Cambridge, MA; and London: MIT Press, pp. 439–83.

della Porta, Donatella and Mario Diani (1999), *Social Movements: An Introduction*, MA, Malden and Oxford: Blackwell.

Foster, John W (2005), 'The Trinational Alliance against NAFTA: Sinews of Solidarity', in Joe Bandy and Jackie Smith (eds.), *Coalitions Across Borders: Transnational Protest and the Neoliberal Order*, Lanham, MY: Rowman and Littlefield, pp. 209–30.

Hemispheric Social Alliance (HSA) (1999), 'Coordinación Hemisférica de la Alianza Social Continental. Actas de la reunión de los días 12, 13 y 14 de marzo de 1999', La Catalina, San José, Costa Rica. (Unpublished founding charter of the Hemispheric Social Alliance; electronic copy sent to the author by Graciela Rodriguez, REBRIP, a founding member of the HSA.)

——— (2002), 'Alternatives for the Americas', http:://www.commonfrontiers.ca/Current_Activities/AFTA.html.

Khagram, Sanjeev, James V. Riker and Kathryn Sikkink (eds.) (2002a), *Restructuring World Politics: Transnational Social Movements, Networks, and Norms*, Minneapolis, MN, and London: University of Minnesota Press.

Khagram, Sanjeev, James V. Riker and Kathryn Sikkink (2002b), 'From Santiago to Seattle: Transnational Advocacy Groups Restructuring World Politics', in ibid. (eds.), *Restructuring World Politics: Transnational Social Movements, Networks, and Norms*, Minneapolis, MN, and London: University of Minnesota Press, pp. 3–23.

Kohler, Kristopher (2006), 'The World Social Forum and a Counter-Hegemonic Vision: Towards a Theory of Transnational Identity Formation', paper presented at the International Studies Association Annual Convention, San Diego, CA, 22–5 March.

Lawler, Edward G., Shane R. Thye and Jeongkoo Yoon (2000), 'Emotion and Group Cohesion in Productive Exchange', *American Journal of Sociology*, 106 (3) 616–57.

Lawler, Edward J. and Jeongkoo Yoon (1998), 'Network Structure and Emotion in Exchange Relations', *American Sociological Review*, 63 (6), pp. 871–94.

Massicotte, Marie-Josée (2003), '"Local" Organizing and "Global" Struggles: Coalition-Building for Social Justice in the Americas', in Gordon Laxer and Sandra Halperin (eds.), *Global Civil Society and Its Limits*, New York, NY: Macmillan, pp. 105–25.

——— (2004), 'Forces d'émancipation et démocratie participative dans les Amériques : un regard sur l'Alliance sociale continentale', *Politiques et Sociétés* 23 (2–3).

Monbiot, George (2004), 'The Age of Consent.' On-line article: http://www.monbiot.com/archives/2004/06/01/the-age-of-consent/

Moody, James, and Douglas R. White (2003), 'Structural Cohesion and Embeddedness: A Hierarchical Concept of Social Groups', *American Sociological Review*, 68 (1), pp. 103–27.

Paxton, Pamela, and James Moody (2003), 'Structure and Sentiment: Explaining Emotional Attachment to Group', *Social Psychology Quarterly*, 66 (1), pp. 34–47.

Polletta, Francesca (2002), *Freedom is an Endless Meeting: Democracy in American Social Movements*, Chicago, and London: University of Chicago Press.

Saguier, Marcelo (2005), 'Convergence in the Making: Transnational Civil Society and the Free Trade Area of the Americas', Centre for the Study of Globalisation and Regionalisation: CSGR Working Paper No. 137/04.

Tarrow, Sidney (2003), '"Global" Movements, Complex Internationalism, and North-South Inequality', Workshop on Transnational Contention at Cornell University: Working Paper, 2nd draft (Oct 10). http://falcon.arts.cornell.edu/sgt2/contention/default.htm. (Accessed: 15 January 2006).

——— (2004), 'The Dualities of Transnational Contention: "Two Activist Solitudes" or a New World Altogether?' Workshop on Transnational Contention at Cornell University: Working Paper (7 September 2004). http://falcon.arts.cornell.edu/sgt2/contention/default.htm. (Accessed: 15 January 2006).

Thye, Shane R., Jeongkoo Yoon, and Edward D. Lawler (2002), 'The Theory of Relational Cohesion: Review of a Research Program', *Advances in Group Processes*, 19, pp. 139–66.

Tilly, Charles (2005), 'Foreword' in Joe Bandy and Jackie Smith (eds.), *Coalitions Across Borders: Transnational Protest and the Neoliberal Order*, Lanham, MY: Rowman and Littlefield, pp. ix-xiii.

Von Bülow, Marisa (2006), 'When North and South Meet: Civil Society and Trade Agreements in the Americas', paper presented at the International Studies Association Annual Convention in San Diego, CA, 22–5 March.

Wood, Lesley J. (2005), 'Bridging the Chasm: The Case of People's Global Action', in Joe Bandy and Jackie Smith (eds.), *Coalitions Across Borders: Transnational Protest and the Neoliberal Order*, Lanham, MY: Rowman and Littlefield, pp. 95–117.

Ziegler, Jean (2003), *Die neuen Herrscher der Welt und ihre globalen Widersacher*, München: Bertelsmann.

CHAPTER 11

The Coalition of Women for Peace in Israeli Society*

TOVA BENSKI

There is general agreement among scholars that the movements that have emerged in Western society during the 1960s–80s were related to basic and deep transformations of social structures of modernity (Kriesi, Kuupmans, Duyvendack and Giungi 1995; Pakulski 1991). Some of these changes seem to have reversed or were at the process of reversing 'many of the normal patters of modernity' (Pakulski 1991: 1), giving rise to new visions, perceptions and forms of political, social, and cultural organizations (Eisenstadt 2000). The chief carriers of these new visions were: the feminist, the ecological and the peace movements. Women's peace movements that have appeared in Israel since the early 1980s, can be viewed as part of this general trend, both reflecting wider social processes of the decline of structures of modernity in the Western world and in Israel, as well as the architects of new visions.

This chapter presents a portrait of the central, currently active, women's peace movement, 'The Coalition of Women for Peace' (CWP) in Israel. The chief argument of this paper is that the coalition challenges one of the central structures of modernity in Israeli society, the 'Nation-in-Arms' model and that the coalition forms an integral part of the new, alternative discourse that is emerging in Israeli society, of the embryonic emergence of trends at civilianizing Israeli society.

The analysis is based on field studies conducted in Israel since 1985, but most of the data that will be discussed is taken from an

*Parts of this paper appeared in the Hebrew language (Benski 2006). This chapter is narrower in focus; it is updated and includes additional sources and different analyses.

ongoing research project, entitled: Documenting Women's Peace Activision in Israel, that began in February 2002, in which various qualitative methods (triangulation) were employed to collect data.[1]

The paper is divided into three parts. In the first part the 'Nation-in-Arms' model that dominated Israeli modernity till the late 1970s and the alternative visions that emerged since the 1980s are outlined. More specifically the focus is on the civilian alternative and its characteristic features. In the second part a portrait of the coalition is presented, along with its values, activities, local orientations and its integration into the global space. These characteristics locate the coalition within the civilian alternative space of the Israeli left. In the third part, the analysis presented shows how the CWP identified the 'Nation-in-Arms' model through its diagnostic framing activity, using the concept of 'militaristic culture', the challenges that it poses to this model and the prognostic frames and activities directed at demilitarizing Israeli society and contributing to its civilianization.

THE 'NATION-IN-ARMS' MODEL, ITS EFFECT ON THE STATUS OF WOMEN AND ITS POST-MODERN/LATE MODERN ALTERNATIVES

The 'Nation in Arms'[2] model is central to Israeli modernity. It is a collectivistic model that evolved during the formative stages of the state in response to the Israeli–Palestinian conflict and the continued state of belligerence that often erupted into armed confrontations and wars. It was shaped through processes of both state building and constant preparations for war and combat readiness. These processes were central in the shaping of societal institutions and political culture, and as a result, the military became a central institution in Israeli society, and the lines dividing between the military and civilian society were fluid and penetrable (Lissak 1999).

Within this model, that dominated Israeli society up to the late 1970s, the Israeli–Palestinian conflict was constructed as a routine (Ben Eliezer 1994), unchangeable reality, a kind of 'destiny' in the Greek tragedy style. The most basic assumption underlying this model was that of a constant existential threat posed by the Arab nations to Israel. This led to the framing of the issue of national security in Israeli society in military terms within the doctrine that the continued existence of the state of Israel depended on its military might and could be guaranteed only by the use of arms. National security came to be equated with the military and compulsory army service for Jewish Israeli citizens, both male and female. This was built into the new society as a patriotic duty and up to the 1980s was taken for granted and to a large extent served as an 'entry ticket' to Israeli society (Kimmerling 1993; Lissak 1999).

The centrality of the military and security considerations, typical of this model, find expression in the collective identity, which is one of the central symbols of the collective and the embodiment of patriotism. Within this model, military considerations and issues defined as pertaining to 'national security' take the highest priority on the national agenda. These considerations became part of the organizing principles of the collective. All other issues were subjected to secondary position. These characteristics are at the heart of various definitions of militarism (Kimmerling 1993; Ben Eliezer 2003).

This model affected the position of both men and women in Israeli society. The construction of masculinity and femininity in societies mobilizing for war is intertwined with the gendered duties of fighting *versus* nursing/nurture (Helman 1999). According to Bercovitch (1999), within this same political culture, a series of criteria evolved that measured good citizenship according to the individual's contribution to national security. Hence, military service, especially in combat units, defined good male citizenship, whereas motherhood defined good female citizenship.[3] War-making and nation-building have been associated with the reproduction and sharpening of gender and other divisions (Melman 1998; Reardon 2005). Israel's political culture thus contributed to the genderization of the public/private division, a process that culminated in gender inequality, the exclusion of women from the political-security discourse and the marginalization of issues that were important for women (Herzog 2003).

History has shown that as early as the beginning of the twentieth century, women in Israel resisted their exclusion and marginalization and demanded integration within the community's political and economic institutions (Bernstein 1987; Fogiel-Bijaoui 1992; Safran 2001; Izraeli 1984). At the same time, many women accepted the centrality of the security threat and the developing hierarchy, according to which social issues (including those that affected the status of women) were viewed as subordinate to security issues at the national level.

Concurrent with processes of decomposition of central components of Western modernity during the late years of the twentieth century

(Kriesi, Kuupmans, Dyvendack and Giungi 1995), the 'Nation-in-Arms' model has been on the decline. Since the 1980s Israeli society is described as being in a post-revolutionary state (Eisenstadt 1989), or on the verge of a new era, a post-hegemonic/post-modern stage (Ben-Eliezer 2003; Ram 2003; Reznik 2003).

The debate over alternative models has been viewed as evidence of the tension existing between diametrically opposed visions driving the conflict over Israel's image and future (Eisenstadt 1989). These alternatives are phrased in polarized terms, as trends toward a civilian society that is post-modern/post-Zionist/post-militaristic as opposed to trends toward increased nationalism that are neo-Zionist/militaristic/neo-militaristic (Ben-Eliezer 2003; Ram 2003; Reznick 2003). The trends promoting civilian society are perceived as post-modern and post-Zionist challenges to the entire complex of values on which the state based its control, i.e. the 'Nation-in-Arms' model, whereas the military/neo-nationalist alternative is viewed as 'defensive nationalism', a reaction to the threats posed by ('classic') ethnic or ethnic-religious nationalism (Ram 2003: 493).[4] According to Ben-Eliezer (2003), these two trends represent the foundations of two societies: civilian society and neo-militarist society. Since this paper focuses on the Coalition of Women for Peace as part of the civilian alternative, we will now focus on this alternative.

It is important to note two important points related to the position of the Israeli variant of the civilian alternative in addition to the position of women's peace movements within this process of civilianization. First, in the Hebrew language the same word is used to refer to both 'civil' and 'civilian'. I prefer to use the concept 'civilian society' in a way that resonates with that of Norbert Elias' use of the 'civilizing process' (1988, 1994). That is, as contesting the legitimacy ascribed to political problem-solving by means of force (1988, 1994). Ben-Eliezer (2003) presents this trend of the emergent civilian society that has been observed in Israel as challenging the basic principles of the 'Nation-in-Arms' model (Ben-Eliezer 2003). This trend consists of a wish to resolve the conflict through diplomatic means based on negotiations, compromise and concessions. The political and social attitudes of the emerging civilian society are linked to global developments, to liberal and individualistic attitudes and way of life, and with a civic stand that accepts pluralism and conceives politics as an arena of compromise and consensus. Its attitude towards the army is suspicious, to say the least, and it is opposed to the central position of the army and security considerations in the socio-political life in Israel. This description is consistent with Ram's (2003) analysis of post-Zionist/post-modern trends.[5]

Second point to note is that Ben-Eliezer recognizes the central role played by women's peace movements in the 'birth'[6] and formation of Israel's fledgling civilian society. He accurately outlines the main theme espoused by these movements—objection to war. Ben-Eliezer nevertheless ignores the tight linkage forged between anti-militarism and feminism within these movements. In this paper I claim that the mix of peace politics with feminist politics, together with their incorporation into the global arena, has transformed women's peace movements into a unique phenomenon within Left wing Israeli Politics.

COALITION OF WOMEN FOR PEACE: A PORTRAIT

This part of the paper focuses on the involvement of the coalition in the development of the civilian alternative in Israeli society. It will therefore focus on the Coalition of Women for Peace's (CWP) value and action orientation and on its integration in the global space.

Women's peace movements in Israel began with a small number of organizations immediately following the break out of the first Lebanon War in June 1982 (Azmon 1997; Gilath 1987; Zukerman-Bareli and Benski 1989). By the turn of the third millennium, two distinct cycles of women's peace activism could be identified. The first cycle began after the outbreak of the first Palestinian *Intifada*, in January 1988, and receded in 1993 or 1994 with the signing of the Oslo Agreement.[7] The second cycle began with the onset of the *Intifada al-Aqsa* (October 2000), and is still active, though it has passed its peak.[8]

The CWP was founded in November 2000. It mobilizes women in support of human rights and a just peace between Israel and its Arab neighbours, and emphasizes women's contribution to democracy within Israel. Like many other new movements that have emerged in the West, the coalition consists of interaction networks between individuals, groups or organizations exhibiting different levels of organizational consolidation (Della Porta and Diani 1999),[9] and allows for multiple and overlapping membership in various organizations

(Melucci 1985). The coalition brings together individual women and nine women's peace organizations. The descriptive account of these nine movements and groups is attached in Appendix A.

Analysis of the activists' socio-demographic profile indicates that despite differences between the groups, the majority of women respond to the definition of the new middle-class or of 'socio-cultural experts' (Kriesi et al. 1995).[10] Representing a broad spectrum of the Israeli left, they were motivated to join women's peace movements by their wish to put an end to the Israeli occupation started in 1967 and to achieve a just solution to the Israeli–Palestinian conflict by peaceful means and to make place for women's voices in the security discourse.

The CWP represents a new model of political action within Israel's glocal environment in that it links feminist concerns and the conflict. This is their focal point at the local level. At the same time, they are linked with globalization in myriad ways. The local emphases are anchored in the issues, principles and activities upheld by the coalition and its constituent groups whereas the global characteristics are anchored primarily in the wide-reaching international linkages, coalitions and activities in which the coalition and its members are involved.

The Local Scene: Value Orientations and Activities

The value orientations of the coalition resonate with the general value orientations of the new social movements that appeared in Western society in the 1980s and with the values that are associated, according to Ben-Eliezer (2003), with the civilian alternative in Israeli society. These value orientations can be inferred from the nine basic principles of the coalition and from the activities of the coalition and its constituent groups.

The principles of the coalition as they appear on the website are:

1. An end to the occupation;
2. The full involvement of women in negotiations for peace;
3. Establishment of the state of Palestine side-by-side with the state of Israel based on the 1967 borders;
4. Recognition of Jerusalem as the shared capital of the two states;
5. Israel must recognize its share of responsibility for the results

of the 1948 war, and cooperate in finding a just solution for the Palestinian refugees;
6. Opposition to the militarism that permeates Israeli society;
7. Equality, inclusion and justice for Palestinian citizens of Israel;
8. Equal rights for women and all residents of Israel;
9. Social and economic justice for Israel's citizens, and integration in the region. (http://www.coalitionofwomen4peace.org)

Three of these nine principles have not been articulated by former women's peace movements in Israel. These are: the demand for the full involvement of women in the peace process; the demand that Israel recognizes its responsibility for the results of the 1948 war and the opposition to the militarism that permeates Israeli society. The elevation of these three demands to the status of pivotal principles that condition membership in the coalition represents both the widening of issues of the women's peace camp and their radicalization compared with the first cycle of women's peace activism.[11]

Analysis of the nine principles indicates that the coalition's agenda can be grouped into three categories of issues: (1) those related to the Israeli–Palestinian conflict and its conclusion; (2) issues internal to Israeli society, its image and its citizens; and (3) a feminist agenda involving equal rights for women and their participation in the peace process. One of the central slogans of the CWP demonstrates this very clearly: 'There is no democracy without peace, and there is no peace without women' (Noga 2002: 1). Thus, the demands for ending the conflict and for gender equality are inseparably intertwined within a rather comprehensive vision of a just and egalitarian society, while at the same time they decompose the world taken for granted in the 'Nation-in-Arms' model.

Analysis of the coalition's annual reports for the years 2000 to 2007 reveals plurality of both forms of action and issues in which these groups are involved and supports the above conclusion. Four most persistent types of activity that were found were:

Expression of protest: The coalition has organized demonstrations and protest marches around its three major areas of activity. At the focus of its protest actions are the occupation, the human rights violations as well as the military operations conducted in the occupied territories and the impact of these on the lives of the Palestinians. Recent activity has focused on the wall (constructed by the Israeli government inside the west bank to prevent potential suicide bombers to enter Israel) and recent events in the Gaza strip.

Pragmatic, empathic activities: These are focused mostly on humanitarian assistance to the Palestinian population. For example, the coalition organizes convoys carrying tons of food and other equipment for children, school and kindergartens and personal hygiene supplies in response to requests made by Palestinian women in the territories.

Education and information: Events such as discussion groups, seminars, conferences and fact-finding trips, primarily for Israelis, with the intent of increasing awareness of the difficulties of the life of Palestinians under the occupation, and to the scope and extent of militarism in Israeli society.

Struggles for social justice and equality: The coalition has engaged in a large variety of struggles to promote equality and social justice in Israeli society. The coalition is an active member of the 'World Social Forum', an umbrella organization for dozens of peace and social justice organizations targeting socio-economic issues.

The value orientations of the CWP—as can be inferred from the descriptive account of the movements presented in Appendix A, as well as from their principles and various activities—are universal, post-materialist values such as: human rights, peace, cooperation, justice, equality, integration, citizenship and opposition to militarism. Interviews conducted show that the women joining these movements come from a background that can be classified into three interrelated value systems: universal humanistic values, political left wing values and feminism. Their participation in the coalition brought these three sources together and merged them. This has led to the strengthening of each element and together led the coalition to anchor its claims and statements more and more on human rights which is the meeting point of these three ideological frames. These three ideological frames find their direct expression in the principles of the CWP, as shown above.

Pluralism, rejection of one sole organizing principle, and uniform voice are major characteristics defining the coalition and post-modernity itself. Pluralism is expressed in the coalition's principles, activities and the range of its constituent groups. For example, one interviewee stated: 'The coalition is a type of mosaic. Each organization in the coalition has a role, and they [the groups] complement each another' (interview with Orit Livnin-Dgani [A.-L. D.] 23 March 2004). The majority of groups in the coalition are indeed single-issue organizations, with actions focused on one distinct aspect or area of action. Together these nine organizations form a pluralistic, multi-issue movement and the result is an open, flexible, decentralized, polysepalous structure that is considered typical of the new social movements (Pakulski 1991).

The coalition's *modus operandi* flows from a feminist world-view that upholds decision making following discussion and of a consensus rather than top-down imposition of decisions. According to one interviewee: 'The pattern that we are attempting to apply is also feminist. Work is initiated on a consensual basis in an attempt to find the common denominator of all the groups of the coalition. We leave room for expression of the individual group's unique identity' (interview with D.L. (initial of the women interviewed. Due to sensitivity only initials of the respondent is provided), see Isachar 2003: 73). Similar statements were made regarding other coalition member groups.

Integration into the Global Space

Globalization is another characteristic of both post-modernity and the civilian alternative to the 'Nation in Arms' model. Although the coalition focuses on local issues, it operates in a global space. Usually, discussions of globalization focus on the effects of the global on the local. In the case of the coalition, globalization works both ways. The coalition is influenced by global trends, at the same time it contributes to the continued globalization of the Israeli–Palestinian conflict and its issues.

One area in which we can identify the reciprocal effects of globalization is that of modes of activity. The CWP includes groups inspired by earlier movements of women who protested and created a public space for women to be heard. Some women from Women in Black (WIB), for example, stated that Black Sash in South Africa, and the Madres de la Plaza de Mayo in Argentina were their models (www.womeninblack.org/history.html). 'Machsom Watch' was modelled after a group that had been active in Guatemala (Isachar

2003, interview with I.K., p. 44). Others became local branches of international movements, for instance, WILPF and TANDI. At the same time, the opposite process of the export of ideas about women's peace activism also occurred. The most prominent of these groups is WIB, which has become a model for emulation throughout the world, and given rise to the international movement of WIB. It has also inspired the emergence of an international group linked in an Internet list, 'Wibcomm', that originated at the International WIB conference held in Marina Di Masa, Italy, in the summer of 2003 (Cockburn 2005, 2007).

The second area of reciprocal international influence is that of integration into the global information and communication network. The coalition maintains an Internet site in Hebrew and English that functions as an information platform in which data on its member groups, activities, articles, opinions and so forth are made readily available (www.coalitionofwomen4peace.org). It also includes links to websites of its constituent groups. This simplifies direct access to international organizations as well as the bidirectional flow of information and solidarity. In addition, the CWP and some of its constituent groups maintain e-mail lists which they use extensively to disseminate information, petitions, organize various activities, coordinate their actions, and engage in various discussions and debates with international and local participants.

International cooperation in the organization of international events represents the third area of reciprocal global flows. The coalition organizes and participates in international actions together with more than 100 women's organizations and peace activists worldwide (Greenblatt 2002). Such participation contributes to the continuing globalization of activities related to the Israeli–Palestinian conflict. The coalition also contributed to the publication of a trilingual (Arabic, Hebrew and Dutch) journal in cooperation with Holland's Pax Christi and the Palestinian organization Panorama of Palestine within the context of a major campaign involving numerous participants, organized by the coalition in May–June 2003 in commemoration of the 36th anniversary of the occupation (see internal documents, and the coalition's Internet site). In addition, the coalition participates in common projects with Dutch and Norwegian peace organizations as well as other international human rights movements such as International Solidarity Movement (ISM), some of whose members were injured in the course of demonstrations held in Israel. Furthermore, WIB is organizing a series of biannual international conferences of International WIB. The last was held in Spain in the summer of 2007.

Significant international exposure and recognition is the fourth area of global influences. The coalition members are frequently invited to international conferences in order to present the organization and its positions. During the years 2002–4 the coalition representatives participated in conferences in more than 15 countries and assisted in the preparation of 11 internationally produced films on the efforts of the Israeli women's peace movement.[12] A particularly important event mentioned in the coalition's Activities Report was the speech given by a Bat Shalom representative at the UN Security Council on 7 May 2002.[13]

This exposure has paved the way for international recognition and respect, demonstrated by the prestigious international awards and prizes the coalition has received. For instance, WIB has been awarded four international peace prizes and, together with Serbian WIB, the movement was nominated for the Nobel Peace Prize in 2001 and 2002. In March 2004, New Profile was honoured with the 'Courage of Conscience' award by the Peace Abbey, located in Sherborne, Massachusetts. Other recognition of coalition activists includes the Bremen (Germany) Solidarity Prize, the PEN Prize and the Aachen Peace Prize, the last awarded in 2004 to an Israeli–Palestinian woman active in WIB, TANDI, and the Coalition as well as other peace and human rights organizations.

Last, and possibly most important, is the contribution of globalization to the formation of individual identity. As demonstrated, the value orientations of the coalition are typical post-materialist humanistic values, a combination of leftist and feminist values. In this the coalition has joined the global trends exhibited by new post-modern social movements active in the West. There is no doubt that some of these values are indigenous to Israeli society and that others penetrated as a result of globalization and were adjusted to the Israeli reality (Emmett 1996; Safran 2001).

At the personal level, many of the women that were interviewed were exposed to feminist and post-national ideas either through reading the classical feminist works or through studying in the US. Some of the women were from Anglo–Saxon origin, raised abroad and immigrated to Israel at a relatively mature age. While abroad, these women were exposed to other modes of life, perspectives and ways to construct reality. One of these women commented: 'I am glad that I have lived a few years in a different place because there, my whole perspective changed. Suddenly I was exposed to a different way of thinking, critical thinking on Israeli society, and I could choose' (Hellman 2003). Or as Mazali and Gor, among the founders of the New Profile report said, a reading of the feminist works of Virginia Woolf, Sara Ruddick, Bell Hooks and others gradually taught them to take a critical view of Israeli society. These experiences led them to understand their education and how they had been channelled to accept Israel's militaristic culture as taken for granted; they also perceived the place and roles that such a culture designates to women (Gor and Mazali 2001). It therefore appears that their comprehension of the Israeli hegemonic culture and socio-political reality was facilitated by the act of travelling—physically or metaphorically—beyond the socio-political-cultural boundaries of Israel. From there, they could observe their society from the outside, from a different perspective, from a world in which the 'taken for granted' was very different.

CHALLENGING THE 'NATION-IN-ARMS' MODEL AND THE CONTRIBUTION TOWARDS CIVILIANIZING SOCIETY

The civilian discourse and activity within the coalition consists of three major groups of practices: (a) identification of the 'Nation-in-Arms' model, (b) challenges posed to the basic tenets of the 'Nation-in-Arms' model, and (c) action taken to oppose the model and to offer alternative civilian practices in all walks of life. In terms of framing theory (Benford and Snow 2000; Snow and Benford 1988; Snow and Byrd 2007; Snow et al. 1986), the first two practices definitely fall under the category of 'diagnostic frames', while the last category can be viewed as a mix of 'prognostic', 'motivating' frames and agency.

Within the coalition and its constituent groups there evolved a rhetoric that includes phrases such as 'soldiers' state', 'army state', 'cultural militarism', and 'a deep process of militarization'. Through these concepts, the CWP identifies the model and frames it in terms of the 'Militarism that permeates Israeli society' (the sixth principle of the coalition as listed on page 317 in this chapter) while linking it directly with the position of women in Israeli society. The roots of this discourse are grounded in the first cycle of women's peace activism. At the Ninth Feminist Convention held in Givat Haviva in May 1993, during a workshop entitled *The Feminist Movement and the Struggle for Peace*, the representative of women's peace activism on the panel identified what she called the prevailing 'male militarisic culture', which she claimed was responsible for women's marginal position in society, the occupation and war as well as the emergence and institutionalization of a definition of citizenship that was contingent on the individual's contribution to the nation. In her own words:

There exists (in Israeli society) a system of values, a normative system that gave rise to, and nurtures the occupation and at the same time it oppresses women and uses the occupation to legitimate the continued oppression of women in Israel. This cultural system is a *militaristic male* value system. The soldier is a culture-hero. This cultural system sanctifies the state and state security and its perpetual state of war. . . . The concepts of universal 'civil rights' and 'individual rights', per se, not related to one's contribution to the state do not exist in Israeli culture. The concept of citizen's rights is subjugated, to a large extent, to the conditions of state security and the continued existence of the state. . . . Any struggle for women's liberation that is not directed at the roots of the occupation, at the roots, or expression of Israeli patriarchy, MILITARISM, will only have partial achievements.

[T.P. (Respondent) 1993].

In terms of framing theories, this is a diagnostic frame that answers the questions 'what is wrong' and 'who is to blame' (Snow et al. 1986; Snow and Benford 1988; Snow and Byrd 2007). The frame presented in the statement describes the essence of Kimmerling's 'civilian militarism' (1993) from a feminist stance. It can further be interpreted as a hybrid feminism that is partially constituted by its anti-militarism, conflating Ruddick's (1998) argument regarding feminism's links to anti-militarism. Women are thus committed to struggle against this model in the name of feminist values, as Ruddick describes it: 'Militarism an extended expression of the domination of women that feminists are committed to eradicating' (Ruddick 1998: 215).

Within the CWP, New Profile is the movement that has elaborated this line more thoroughly. The movement views 'cultural militarism' as the major factor shaping Israeli society. It claims that militarism penetrates all walks of life, constructing a 'world taken for granted' at the cultural, cognitive and emotional levels which makes it very difficult to expose the dynamics and mechanisms that create, shape, and perpetuate it, and very difficult to oppose it. They touch on many elements of the 'Nation-in-Arms' model. They relate to the 'dehumanization' of the enemy, to 'the expectation that war will occur sooner or later' and to the fact that 'War itself is accepted as a reasonable, inevitable solution to state problems' (Gor and Mazali 2001).

The educational system is held responsible for instilling the young with militaristic values:

> The educational system . . . acts to solidify a definition of reality in which war is a reasonable political policy, and is harnessed to preserve the central position of the army, that is presented as an important and worthy value. The educational system links the transition from childhood to maturity, to manhood in particular, with army service. (Gor and Mazali 2001)

Furthermore, they also claim that the militaristic culture is closely linked with gender issues and a dichotomous view of reality.

A more recent diagnostic frame promoted by the CWP focuses on the concept of 'security'. On the coalition website, in a short article entitled 'Reframing Security', the following claim appears:

> . . . the concept of 'security' is a powerful one. For years, politicians have used it to justify human rights violations and the occupation itself as carried out in the name of 'security'. Yet few Israelis stop to think whether these military and policing measures have in fact provided us with the long-sought security. ('Reframing Security', 22 July 2008)

Having identified the basic elements of the 'Nation-in-Arms' model, they set out to challenge them. They refuse to accept the assumption of a real 'existential threat' posed to Israel by the Arab nations. They refuse to accept the 'no choice' assumption basic to the 'Nation-in-Arms' model (Gor and Mazali 2001). They also refuse to accept the basic premise that security is necessarily linked with military might (Gor and Mazali 2001; 'Reframing Security', 2008). Thus they directly challenge basic premises of the hegemonic model and decompose the equation: security = military might.

They expose the gender roles constructed and allocated to women in Israel claiming that enacting these roles represent collaboration with the militaristic culture. They claim that their lives are 'mobilized' to prepare their children to accept army service as natural, and that in a 'soldiers' state' women are supposed to support the soldiers in their families and supply 'the warm embracing home. This home is a refuge, and at the same time it needs protection and justifies war'

(Mazali 2002). These considerations have led them to 'refuse to enact the roles that the culture of war' expects from them (Mazali 2002). 'We refuse to continue to mobilize, to raise children for the draft, to support partners, brothers, and fathers who perform army service, when the heads of state continue to use the army instead of looking for other solutions' (AMANA, June 1999).

Having challenged and decomposed the basic tenets of the 'Nation-in-Arms' model, the CWP offers some answers to the question 'what is to be done?' which is at the core of prognostic framing. As noted by Benford and Snow (2000), while the proposed solutions and strategies may not necessarily flow from the prognostic frames, there is usually a great deal of correspondence between the two. Indeed within the CWP a number of prognostic frames have evolved, all connected with and flowing from the diagnostic frames.

Given the centrality of the conflict to the emergence and consolidation of 'militarism' or the 'Nation-in-Arms' model, the first prognostic frame focuses on the peaceful resolution of the Israeli–Palestinian conflict. This is highly visible in the CWP's slogan: 'The era of generals has ended. It is time for women to talk peace.' All groups included in the coalition call for ending the historic conflict through talks and compromise, based on mutual respect and principles of justice, equality and peace. This line of thought replaces guns with words, as women in the first cycle of activism repeatedly said: 'War is the masculine way of resolving conflicts, through occupation and oppression. . . . The feminine approach is different. It is based on communication and mutual consent. It aims at the conservation of human relationships, not at ruination' (Carmela Shalev, quoted by Harpaz Yoram 10 March 1989). This line is further developed in the second cycle by all groups of the CWP. One particular example is found in the movement 'The Fifth Mother'. They call for a conclusion of the conflict by means of fair negotiations, mutual respect and consideration for the needs of both sides. Their ambition is to make place for a new language in the security discourse, a language of conflict resolution, by introducing professional arbitration [interview with A.L. (Respondent), 23 March 2004]. Hence, their motto is 'War is not my language'.

The CWP also demands the participation of women in peace negotiations as is evident from the CWP's principles. This is clearly articulated in the words of Terry Greenblat, in her address to the UN Security Council on May 2002:

You need us, because if the goal is not simply to cease fire but also to establish viable peace based on cooperation and security, then we, the women, are a very important factor. . . . We have the courage to cross the lines of the differences between us. And we have developed the wisdom to do it without guns and bombs . . . we will talk. We will not use guns. . . . We are prepared to sit together at the same side of the table, to examine together our complex common history and to commit not to stop till we reach a mutual understanding. We will start a new historic move and will fulfill our common destiny. (Greenblatt 2002: 17)

This is consistent with the characteristics of the emerging civilian alternative to the 'Nation-in-Uniform' model (Ben-Eliezer 2003).

The second most prominent prognostic frame of the CWP is focused on changing 'the profile' of Israeli society from a 'militarized' to a peaceful, equalitarian, civilian society (www.newprofile.org). New Profile, the movement that is focused on this goal within the CWP suggests 'canceling compulsory conscription and legally recognizing the right to conscientious objection' (Gor and Mazali 2001) as a central strategy in uprooting 'militarism'. Indeed, compulsory conscription is one of the pivotal features of the 'Nation-in-Uniform' model and the citizenship discourse. This is the first women's peace movement in Israel to suggest such a measure. The movement quotes on its website facts and figures concerning the extent of draft dodging, claiming that, in effect, the most securely guarded military secret in the state of Israel is that compulsory army service does not really exist any more. The women of New Profile support the right of all men and women to resist the draft, to conscientious objection and refusal to serve in the occupied territories (www.newprofile,org). They do so through dissemination of information on their website, through lectures, the media, conferences and other events. One of the sections on the website contains information, practical tips and guidance to the 'would be conscientious objector' and to 'ambivalent youths and parents'. The movement further operates an escort service to objectors, escorting them through the whole process of objection, providing legal, social and moral aid. This is also easily accessed through the movement's website.

Third, New Profile targets the educational system and youth as central arenas for activity. The women oppose the accepted practice of para-military education in schools. They are opposed to visits to schools by army personnel and generals for lectures and draft attempts to combat units. The women object to this phenomenon, framing it within a category of 'military brain-washing at school'. They suggest stopping educating and preparing the youth to the army service and instead, preparing them to contribute towards the community and civil society organizations. They suggest reformulating the goals of the educational system in the direction of 'an educational system that engages in democratic civilian education, practical education for peace and conflict resolution instead of education for soldiering and the acceptance of belligerence' (AMANA June 1999). They also act directly towards these goals in schools where they have cooperative PTAs and boards. They organize seminars, lectures, excursions and special events in these schools in an attempt to insert into the syllabi civilian and antimilitaristic content. They also organize activities among the youth in Israel and form special youth groups to discuss their uncertainties, questions and ambivalent feelings towards the army service (Activity Report for January–May 2008, www.newprofile.org).

Fourth is the suggestion to act towards reframing the concept of security in a much broader, civilian frame. Having decomposed the equation 'security = military might' they suggest to broaden the scope of the concept of security to include personal and social concerns such as economic security, security from violence (personal safety) and environmental security. They have organized campaigns that suggest the concept of 'human security' as asserted by the 2003 report of the UN Commission on Human Security. They quote the following 2003 assertion on their website: 'Human security means protecting vital freedoms. It means protecting people from critical and pervasive threats and situations, building on their strengths and aspirations. It also means creating systems that give people the building blocks of survival, dignity and livelihood' ('Reframing Security', 2007). They suggest that 'initiating public discourse about human security will provide first, critical stage in attitude change in Israeli society, opening the door to more far-reaching changes in public policy and priorities' ('Reframing Security', 2007). By this they insert a new civilian direction to the concept of 'security', reclaiming it from its hegemonic usage, relocating it at both the private and the public realms of the envisaged civilian society.

EPILOGUE

The analysis presented in this chapter has demonstrated that the CWP has established a unique civilian discourse within the public sphere of Israeli society. The special combination of feminist, humanistic and peace-oriented political views and their integration in the global space of peace and human rights activism has created a unique feminist peace project. This project has deconstructed the basic assumptions and manifestations of the taken-for-granted world of the 'Nation-in-Arms' model that has characterized Israeli modernity. At the same time, the project opens new avenues for feminist work in promoting non-violent civilian social relationships, new insights, visions and perhaps even hopes for Israeli society.

The CWP is innovative in its activities, constructing a new praxis that is simultaneously a medium and a message. By doing so it is directly linked to innovative international trends such as those described by Melucci (1985: 810–12). The following excerpts from Melucci's work seem to summarize the spirit of the work of the CWP: 'Movements present to the rationalizing apparatuses questions which are not allowed . . . they ask where we are going and why. . . . Their voice is difficult to hear. . . . Nevertheless, they speak to the whole society' (p. 810). Having discussed the problems that the youth movement, the women's and the ecological movements of the 1970s–1980s have presented to society, Melucci continues:

> All these forms of collective action challenge the dominant logic on a symbolic ground. They question definitions of codes. *Nominations* [italics in the original text] of reality. . . . They act as new media: they enlighten what every system doesn't say of itself, the amount of silence, violence, irrationality which is always hidden in dominant codes. At the same time, through what they do, or rather through how they do it, movements announce to society that something 'else' is possible. (Melucci 1985: 812)

NOTES

1. These methods include participant observation at meetings, conferences and other activities organized by the coalition and its members; group interviews, in-depth open-ended interviews with regular activists; analysis of e-mail messages distributed to the mailing list maintained by the Women's Coalition for a Just Peace, New Profile and Machsom Watch; as well as articles, publications and other materials appearing in the movement's websites. In addition I referred to interviews conducted with peace activists as published in newspapers and Hedva Isachar's book (2003). I should also note that this article reflects only a small portion of the data collected during the period of the research.

2. There is disagreement among Israeli sociologists over the nature of the links between the military and society in Israel. However, there is general agreement to the effect that there are extensive links. The concepts used in various formulations are 'Militarism' (Ben-Eliezer 2003; Helman 1997; Kimmerling 1993); 'Partially militarized society' (Horwitz 1982); the 'Nation-in Arms' model; 'the security ethos' (Lissak 1999); 'a powerful military ethos' (Eisenstadt 2006). I do not wish to enter this debate as that is not the aim of this paper. Therefore, I chose to use the term 'Nation-in-Arms' since it is less controversial and is sufficient for the purposes of this paper.
3. Lissak partially accepted Bercovitch's position and the argument that Zionism equated the good citizen with the male soldier, as a result of which women were shifted to the margins of the public sphere (Lissak and Knei-Paz 1996).
4. Parallel to these two options, other trends—e.g., the classic 'Nation-in-Arms' model—continue to exist, accompanied by the persistent special status of the military in Israel (Ben-Eliezer 2003; Ram 2003). Hence, the boundaries between any two new alternatives are not always precise. These boundaries may vary from clear to blurred, based on events and conditions (Ben-Eliezer 2003).
5. We should also note that the social infrastructure of the civilian alternative in Israeli society, as delineated by Ben-Eliezer, is quite narrow and based on peace movements, considered as one specific category of social change organizations within Israeli civil society (Gidron et al. 2002). Yishai refers to a specific segment of the organization of civil society—that which challenges the political system (Yishai 1998). It appears that despite the broad support for the peace process found in contemporary society, the anti-militarism that is at the core of this position is characteristic of a very small minority of the Israeli public. For instance, Smooha (2003) cites data from research conducted in 1993 that found that only 4.9 per cent of the young, secular, university-educated Ashkenazi youth maintained post-Zionist views. Survey data from 2001 indicated a similar proportion.
6. Ben-Eliezer employs the concept 'birth' of Israel's civilian society to describe the arguments of Shoshana Shmueli, a founder of the movement 'Parents Against Silence'. We may assume that his use of this concept is utilitarian and meant to indicate the (at least) partial feminization of Israel's emergent civilian society.
7. For research on the first cycle of protest and for the mothers' protest movement that preceded it, see: Atzmon 1997; Bareli and Benski 1992; Chazan 1991; Emmett 1996; Gilath 1987, 1991; Hellman 2003; Hellman and Rappoport 1997; Kaminer 1996; Mayer 1994; Sassoon-Levi and Rappoport 2002; Shadmi 2000; Sharoni 1995; Zukerman-Bareli and Benski 1989.

8. I would like to clarify that by identifying 'cycles' I am not implying that all activism came to a halt between the first and second cycles. Quite a number of movements continued their activities but their intensity was much lower.
9. Since this phenomenon is neither homogeneous nor uniform, when referring to the coalition's constituent social movements I use the terms organizations, movements and groups interchangeably.
10. During the first wave of women's peace movement activity, I distributed questionnaires to three samples of activists in a range of organizations. The findings indicated quite consistently that these women were of Ashkenazi origin, in their mid-life, predominantly secular, university-educated, primarily in the social sciences and the humanities, more than 80 per cent were active in the labour market and the majority practised professions typical to the new middle class—engineering, medicine, law, psychology, social work, consultancy, university lecturing and teaching. The majority also came from a Western sociocultural background. As to the present wave of activism, I have not distributed questionnaires but I based my analysis on an examination of the details of the participants in two conferences held by the coalition—one in October 2002, the other in December 2002. It appears that this profile has remained intact. The main difference lies in the fact that about 25 per cent of the participants in the 2002 conferences were Israeli–Arab women and most of them were members of TANDI, a part of the coalition. In addition, an analysis of the participants in activities conducted by the Haifa and Tel Aviv vigils of WIB indicated that the women's age structure has changed, that is, about half the women were in the 20–35 years age groups. This means that feminist peace activism continues and that several generations of feminists are now represented by the coalition.
11. For more data on the issues and value orientation of the first cycle of women's peace activisim in Israel, see references cited in note 7.
12. See the coalition's *Activities Report* (2002–3) and internal documents. See also the coalition's Internet site.
13. The full text of the speech given by Terry Greenblatt is reprinted in *Noga*, 41, Summer 2002, pp. 16–17.

REFERENCES

AMANA, June 1999, Retrieved 28 January 2002 from http://www.newprofile.org/

Azmon, Y. (1997), 'War, Mothers and a Girl with Braids: Involvement of Mothers Peace Movements in the National Discourse in Israel', *Israel Social Science Research*, 12(1), pp. 109–28.

Bareli, C. and T. Benski (1992), ' "Women and Peace" and "The Women's Peace Net": A Comparative Analysis of Two Peace Movements in Israel', paper presented at the First Conference of European Social Movements, Wissenchaft Center, Berlin, 29 October–1 November.

Ben-Eliezer, U. (1994), 'The Nation in Arms and War: Israel and its First Year', *Zmanim*, 49, pp. 51–65 (in Hebrew).

——— (2003), 'Civil Society and Military Society in Israel: Neo-Militarism and Anti-Militarism in the Post-Hegemonic Era', in M. Al-Haj and U. Ben-Eliezer (eds.), *In The Name of Security: The Sociology of Peace and War in Israel in Changing Times*, Haifa: Haifa University press, pp. 29–76 (in Hebrew).

Benford, D.R. and D.A. Snow (2000), 'Framing Processes and Social Movements: An Overview and Assessment', *Annual Review of Sociology*, 26, pp. 611–39.

Benski, T. (2005), 'Enreaching Events and the Emotional Reactions of the Public: Women in Black in Israel', in F. Helena and D. King, *Emotions and Social Movements*, London: Routledge, pp. 57–78.

——— (2006), 'The Coalition of Women for a Just Peace: The Feminist Peace Project as One of the Trends to Naturalize Israeli Society', in U. Cohen , E. Ben-Rafael, A. Bareli and E. Ya'ar (eds.), *Israel and Modernity: In Honor of Moshe Lissak*, Sde Boker: The Ben-Gurion Research Institute, Ben-Gurion University of the Negev and Jerusalem: Yad Izhak Ben-Zvi, pp. 523–48 (in Hebrew).

Bernstein, D. (1987), *The Struggle for Equality: Women Workers in the Palestine 'Yishuv'*, Tel Aviv: Hakibbutz Hameuchad (in Hebrew).

Berkovitch, N. (1999), 'Women of Valor: Women and Citizenship in Israel', *Israeli Sociology*, 2 (1), pp. 277–317 (in Hebrew).

Chazan, N. (1991), 'Israeli Women and Peace Activism', in B. Swirski and M.P. Safhir (eds.), *Calling the Equality Bluff: Women in Israel*, New York: Pergamon Press, pp. 152–61.

Cockburn, C. (2005), 'Feminist Antimilitarism: Scope, Problematic and Difficulties in a Global Social Movement', Lecture for the Colloquium Intended and Unintended Suffering: The Legacy of Meg Stacey's Ideas and Work, 29 June 2005.

——— (2007), *From Where We Stand: War, Women's Activism and Feminist Analysis*, London: Zed Books.

Della Porta, D. and M. Diani (1999), *Social Movements: An Introduction*, Malden, MA: Blackwell.

Eisenstadt, S.N. (1989), *The Transformation of Israel Society*, Jerusalem: The Magness Press (in Hebrew).

——— (2000), 'Multiple Modernities', *Daedalus*, 129 (1), pp. 1–29.

——— (2006), 'Israeli Society's Wrestling with Modernity in the Age of Globalization', in U. Cohen, E. Ben-Rafael, A. Bareli and E. Ya'ar (eds.), *Israel and Modernity: In Honor of Moshe Lissak*, Sde Boker: The Ben-Gurion Research Institute, Ben-Gurion University of the Negev and Jerusalem: Yad Izhak Ben-Zvi, pp. 13–29 (in Hebrew).

Elias, N. (1988), 'Violence and Civilization: The State Monopoly of Physical Violence and its Infringement', in J. Keane (ed.), *Civil Society and the State,* London: Verso, pp. 177–98.

——— (1994), *The Civilizing Process*, Cambridge: Blackwell.

Emmett, A. (1996), *Our Sisters' Promised Land: Women, Politics and Israeli-Palestinian Coexistence*, Ann Arbor: The University of Michigan Press.

Fogiel-Bijaoui, S. (1992), 'On the Way to Equality? The Struggle for Women's Suffrage in Israel: 1917–1926', *Megamot*, XXXIV (2), pp. 262–84 (in Hebrew).

Gidron, B., M. Bar, and H. Katz (2002), 'Characteristics of the Organized Civil Society in Israel', *Israeli Sociology,* 4(2), pp. 369–400 (in Hebrew).

Gelbloom, A. (2000), 'We Refuse to be Enemies' (translation of the Hebrew title), *Noga*, 41, pp. 18–24.

Gilat, N. (1987), 'Thundering Silence—Parents against Silence', M.A Dissertation, School of Political Science, Haifa University, Haifa.

Greenblatt, T. (2002), 'No Guns, No Shells' (translation of the Hebrew title), *Noga*, 41, pp. 16–17.

Gor, H., and R. Mazali (2001), 'Militarization of Education: A Feminist Point of View (translation of the Hebrew title)', retrieved 1 April 2001, from http://www.newprofile.org/showdata.asp?pid=279

Harpaz, Y. (1989), 'Lo Yorot, Lo Bochot' ('They (Women) are Not Shooting, They are Not Crying'), *Kol Hair* (daily newspaper), 10 March 1989.

Hellman, S. (1997), 'Militarism and the Construction of Community', *Journal of Political and Military Sociology*, 25, pp. 305–32.

——— (1999), 'From Soldiering and Motherhood to Citizenship: A Study of Four Israeli Peace Protest Movements', *Social Politics*, 6 (3), pp. 292–313.

——— (2003), 'Citizenship, Peace Protest and the Construction of Ethnic Boundaries', in M. Al-Haj and U. Ben-Eliezer (eds.), *In The Name of Security: The Sociology of Peace and War in Israel in Changing Times*, Haifa: Haifa University press, pp. 557–74 (in Hebrew).

Hellman, S., and T. Rappoport (1997), ' "Women in Black" and the Challenge to the Social Order', *Theory and Criticism,* 10, pp. 175–92 (in Hebrew).

Herzog, H. (2003), 'The Fighting Family: The Impact of the Arab-Israeli Conflict on the Status of Women in Israel', in M. Al-Haj and U. Ben-Eliezer (eds.), *In The Name of Security: The Sociology of Peace and War in Israel in Changing Times*, Haifa: Haifa University Press, pp. 401–20 (in Hebrew).

Horowitz, D. (1982), 'The Israeli Defense Forces: A Civilianized Military in a Partial Militarized Society', in R. Kolkowitz and A. Korbonski (eds.), *Soldier, Peasants, and Bureaucrats*, London: George Allen and Unwin, pp. 77–106.

Hyman Alonso, H. (1993), *Peace as a Women's Issue: A History of the US Movement for World Peace and Women's Rights*, Syracuse: Syracuse University Press.

Isachar, H. (2003), *Sisters in Peace: Feminist Voices of the Left*, Tel-Aviv: Resling (in Hebrew).

Izraeli, D.N. (1984), 'The Socialist Zionist Women's Movement in Eretz Israel', *Cathedra*, 32, pp. 109–41 (in Hebrew).

Kaminer, R. (1996), *The Politics of Protest: The Israeli Peace Movement and the Palestinian Intifada*, Sussex: Sussex Academic Press.

Kimmerling, B. (1993), 'Militarism in Israeli Society', *Theory and Criticism*, 4, pp. 123–40 (in Hebrew).

Kriesi, H., R. Koopmans, J.W. Dyvendak, and M.G. Giungi (1995), *New Social Movements in Western Europe: A Comparative Analysis*, London: UCL.

Leshem, R. and E. Brindet (2000), 'The Same Mother, Only the War has Changed' (translation of the Hebrew title), *Yediot Aharonot, Seven Days* weekly supplement, 15 March, pp. 16–19.

Lissak, M. (1999), 'Uniqueness and Normalization in the Military-Government Relations in Israel' (translation of the Hebrew title) in R. Cohen-Almagor (ed.), *Basic Issues in Israeli Democracy*, Tel Aviv: Hakibutz Haa'rtzi, pp. 225–45 (in Hebrew).

Lissak, M., and B. Knei-Paz (1996), 'Epilogue: Israel in the Peace Era' (translation of the Hebrew title), in M. Lissak and B. Knei-Paz (eds.), *Israel Towards the Year 2000: Society, Politics and Culture*, Jerusalem: The Magness Press, pp. 429–38 (in Hebrew).

Machsom Watch (2004), *A Counterview: Checkpoints 2004*, Jerusalem: Machsom Watch.

Mansbach, D. (2007), 'The Power of the Duality: The Protest of the "Checkpoint Watch" Movement', in *Theory and Cricism*, 31, pp. 77–99.

Mayer, T. (ed.), (1994), *Women and the Israeli Occupation: The Politics of Change*, London: Routlege.

Mazali, R. (2002), 'Women Refuse' (translation of the Hebrew title), Retrieved 13 April from http://www.newprofile.org/showdata.asp?pid=252

Melman, B. (1998), 'Introduction', in B. Melman (ed.), *Borderlines: Genders and Identities in War and Peace 1870-1930*, London: Routledge, pp. 1–25.

Melucci, A. (1985), 'The Symbolic Change of Contemporary Movements', *Social Research* , 52 (4), pp. 789–817.

Pakulski, J. (1991), *Social Movements: The Politics of Moral Protest*, Melbourne: Longman Cheshire.

Ram, U. (2003), 'Pre-, Pro-, Post-, Neo-: A Socio-political Map of Israel at the Beginning of the 21st Century', in M. Al-Haj and U. Ben-Eliezer (eds.), *In The Name of Security: The Sociology of Peace and War in Israel in Changing Times*, Haifa: Haifa University Press, pp. 489–508 (in Hebrew).

Reardon, B. (2005), 'Sexism and the War Mechanism', in H. Gor (ed.), *The Militarization of Education*, Tel Aviv: Babel, pp. 59–85 (in Hebrew).

'Reframing Security' retrieved 22 July 2008 (http://www.coalitionofwomen.org/home/english/activities/security/)

Reznik, S. (2003), 'Law-Breaking Movements on the Right and on the Left: The Jewish Underground and the Conscientious Objection Movement 1979–1984', in M. Al-Haj and U. Ben-Eliezer (eds.), *In The Name of Security: The Sociology of Peace and War in Israel in Changing Times*, Haifa: Haifa University Press, pp. 509–34 (in Hebrew).

Ruddick, S. (1998), ' "Women in Peace": A Feminist Construction', in L.A. Lorenzan and J. Turpin (eds.), *The Women and War Reader*, New York: New York University Press, pp. 213–27.

Safran, H. (2001), 'The American Connection: The Influence of the American Feminism on the struggle foe women's Suffrage in the Yishuv (1919-1926) and Women's Equality in Israel (1971-1982)', doctoral dissertation, Department of General History, Haifa University, Haifa.

Sasson-Levy, O. and T. Rapoport (2002), 'Body, Ideology and Gender in Social Protest', *Megamot*, XLI (4), pp. 489–513 (in Hebrew).

Shadmi, E. (2000), 'Between Resistance and Compliance, Feminism and Nationalism: Women in Black in Israel', *Women's Studies International Forum*, 23(1), pp. 23–34.

Sharoni, S. (1995), *Gender and the Israeli-Palestinian Conflict: The Politics of Women's Resistance*, Syracuse: Syracuse University Press.

Smooha, S. (2003), 'Implications of the Transition to Peace for Israeli Society', in M. Al-Haj and U. Ben-Eliezer (eds.), *In The Name of Security: The Sociology of Peace and War in Israel in Changing Times*, Haifa: Haifa University Press, pp. 455–88 (in Hebrew).

Snow, D.A. and S.C. Byrd (2007), 'Ideology, Framing Processes, and Islamic Terrorist Movements', *Mobilization* 12, pp. 119–36.

Snow, D.A. and R.D. Benford (1988), 'Ideology, Frame Resonance, and Participant Mobilization', *International Social Movement Research* 1, 197–217.

Snow, D.A., E.B. Rochford, S.K. Worden and R.D. Benford (1986), 'Frame Alignment Processes, Micro-Mobilization, and Movement Participation', *American Sociological Review*, 51, pp. 564–81.

Yassour-Borochovitz and Helena Syna Desivilya (2007), 'Locking and Unlocking Gender: The Case of "Machsomwatch"—A Human Rights Women Organization', *Social Issues in Israel*, 1 (3), pp. 136–65.

Yishai, Y. (1998), 'Civil Society in Transition: Interest Politics in Israel', *ANNALS, AAPSS*, 555, pp. 147–62.

Zuckerman-Bareli, C. and T. Benski (1989), 'Micromobilization Processes and Precondition for the Emergence of Protest Movements: The Case of Parents Against Silence', *Megamot*, XXXII (1), pp. 27–42 (in Hebrew).

APPENDIX: THE MOVEMENTS CONSTITUTING THE COALITION OF WOMEN FOR PEACE

Women in Black (WIB) is an international feminist peace movement organized in the form of a network of vigils. It has won four international prizes for peace activism and was nominated twice for the Nobel Prize, in 2001 (the Israeli and Serbian WIB), and in 2002. WIB started in Jerusalem in January 1988, a month after the outbreak of the first Palestinian uprising but soon spread to locations all over the country and all over the world. WIB consists of a weekly silent vigil in central places in Jerusalem, Haifa, Tel-Aviv, and other busy road junctions in different locations. The vigil is conducted on a regular basis, every Friday afternoon between 13:00–14:00, regardless of weather conditions and political situation. The women wear black and hold signs in the form of a hand that is copied from the traffic sign 'stop'. The hand is black and on it, in white ink, is written the slogan 'Stop the Occupation' in three languages: Hebrew, English and Arabic. This has become the identifying slogan of the movement. (For additional information on WIB see Benski 2005.)

Machsom Watch—Women for Human Rights, was founded in February 2001. Its main activity consists of observation at the checkpoints between Israel and the Palestinian territories that are operated by the Israeli Defense Forces (IDF) and the Border Police. The women observe and document the soldiers' behaviour at these checkpoints. In cases of 'gross violations of human rights, severe intimidation and restrictions' (Machsom Watch 2004), the women try to intervene and where possible to prevent them. They are working to change the policy that limits the freedom of movement of Palestinians within the territories and to dismantle the checkpoints. On 25 March 2004, the movement was awarded the Emil Greenzweig Human Rights Award by the Association for Civil Rights in Israel. (For analyses of this movement see Mansbach 2007; Yassour-Borochowitz and Desiviliya 2007).

New Profile describes itself as 'The Movement for Civilization of Israeli Society' (www.newprofile.org). The movement was founded in October 1998. It is a feminist movement aiming at changing 'the profile of Israeli society from a militarized society of war and might, to an actively peacemaking community in which the rights of all its citizens are protected and promoted equally, and the human rights of all people residing inside and outside Israeli borders are respected' (www.newprofile.org). Its focus on raising public awareness of the level of militarization of Israeli society and deepening critical discussion of this issue distinguishes New Profile from the other social movements in the coalition. It supports conscientious objectors and acts mainly within the educational system and youth.

WILPF, or the Women's International League for Peace and Freedom is an international organization founded during First World War—1915—in The Hague by European women for the purpose of expressing their opposition to the war as well as to search for means to achieve peace and women's equality (Hyman Alons 1993). Its main theme is the unity of freedom and peace (Gelbloom 2000). WILPF maintains about 45 branches throughout the world; its headquartered in Geneva, Switzerland, and maintains ties with the United Nations. The Israeli branch of the WILPF was established in 1980 with the aim of promoting a dialogue between Jews and Arabs as well as furthering equality between the two peoples within Israel in addition to achieving a just conclusion to the Israeli-Palestinian conflict.

The Fifth Mother was established in March 2002; its name refers to Hagar, Ishmael's mother. Its founders were originally members of former peace movements, 'Four Mothers' and 'Women in Black' in particular. These women felt the need to create 'a mass movement . . . and to attach themselves to the public at those points where the public was ready to listen, ready to assimilate' their message (Leshem and Brindet, p. 16, 15 March 2000). Members of the movement attempt to project 'the other voice', the motherly female voice that knows how to 'the absorb pain, feel compassion, confront fear and uncertainty and solve conflicts through dialogue and mutual respect' (*The Fifth Mother: Another Language—The Feminine Voice*, 2003, internal document). Members of the movement call for a conclusion of the conflict by means of fair negotiations, mutual respect and consideration for the needs of both sides. Their ambition is to make place for a new language in the security discourse, a language of conflict resolution by introducing professional arbitration (interview with A.L., 23 March 2004). Hence, their motto is: 'War is not my language'.

Noga is a feminist journal. The magazine's first issue was published in 1980. Its name was derived from the Hebrew word for Venus, the female planet, which is identified with feminine symbols as well as the Canaanite goddess Ashtar. Coalition members use the journal as a major means of communication, dissemination of news, announcements and articles that deal with the coalition actions as well as the activities of other women's peace movements.

NELED—Women for Coexistence, was created in 1988 by several women who chose to work for coexistence between Israelis and Palestinians, Jews and Arabs. Its original members were Jews and Arab citizens of Israel. According to I.G., one of its founders (interview with I.G., 23 March 2004), during the first cycle of women's peace activism, the movement's approach was more radical and its activities more widespread than they are today. At present, a small number of women are active in the organization and they focus primarily on social and cultural activities conducted within their homes.

One of its purposes is to recruit women from the moderate left. In W's words: 'Women who don't think like me, women who aren't radicals' (interview with W, 11 May 2004).

TANDI (The Movement of Democratic Israeli Women) is among the oldest movements and exhibits the broadest range of objectives; it is also the most diverse in terms of its member profile. Established in 1948 by women from leftist, primarily communist circles, and inspired by the World Federation of Democratic Women that was founded at the end of Second World War, TANDI is considered to be one of the Federation's branches. TANDI has focused its actions on the following issues: women's and children's rights, the promotion of Jewish–Arab congeniality within Israel's borders, conclusion of the occupation, achievement of a peace agreement and the struggle against the deployment of atomic weapons (taken from a movement pamphlet entitled *Women Who Care*, undated). The movement maintains several dozen branches throughout Israel, with Jewish and Arab Israeli participation. In the public mind, the movement is identified as a female extension of Hadash (Israel's communist party) even though some of its members disagree with that attribution.

Bat Shalom—The Women's Network for Peace, was founded in 1994. Bat Shalom is active in promoting a just peace between Palestinians and Israelis, equality between men and women and equality between Jews and Arabs within the State of Israel. This movement's uniqueness lies in its projects, such as participation, together with the Jerusalem Center for Women (JCW), in the 'Jerusalem Link' project. The JCW, located in East Jerusalem, represents an umbrella organization for several Palestinian women's organizations. Other unique Bat Shalom activities include the Peace Tent, which the movement erects at the Megiddo Junction during the Succoth holiday. Under the tent, diverse activities are conducted, such as lectures, seminars, workshops and so forth.

III. GLOBALIZATION, LABOUR AND FARMERS' MOVEMENTS

CHAPTER 12

Trade Union Movement in India: A Critical View

SHARIT K. BHOWMIK

INTRODUCTION

Trade unions are unique organizations in many ways. They are formed mainly for protecting the interests of workers or employees against those who would harm them. These could be the employers, the state or any agency identified as such. In this sense trade unions can be viewed as opposition organizations. Most trade unions broadly centre around this basic objective. Secondly, trade unions are a product of industrialization. They were born out of the industrial revolution and as such had no connections with any pre-industrial form of social organization. Thirdly, the most important feature of trade unions is that theory did not play much part in their initial formation. In other words, there are no theoretical roots to the origin of trade unions. Their convergence was a spontaneous, healthy process which grew out of the needs of common people (Flanders 1970: 1). The result is not a neat and tidy pattern but something which is complex and overlapping. Hence in order to understand the nature of trade unions one has to go back to their origins. In this chapter we will deal with the features of trade unions in India and in doing so we will start with the origin and growth of trade unions and then discuss the problems of trade unionism in the country.

Trade unions had their origins in England and they were a result of the industrial revolution. In the early stages they were formed to regulate competition among workers. The industrial revolution had impoverished the village artisans as the goods they produced were replaced by goods mass produced in factories. These people were forced to flock to the industrial townships in different parts of the country. They were desperate for work and they provided cheap labour for factory owners. The factories were damp, unhealthy places with little light or ventilation. The hours of work were long. Men, women and children worked for over 16 hours everyday in order to get a wage that would cover their minimum requirements. The wages were low and the entire family had to work in order to eke out an existence. Child labour was prevalent and children were used to clean machines or carry goods from under the machines. They were small and could easily crawl under the machines.

Low wages and appalling conditions of work were mainly because the number of unemployed was large. There was constant competition between the low paid workers and unemployed job-seekers. If a worker was unwilling to work for a particular wage, the employer could find several others who would be willing to work for even less. This competition for jobs depressed the wage rates and provided total power to the employers. Friedrich Engels (1973: 115) wrote in 1848 that this was the 'worst side of the present state of things in its effects upon the workers, the sharpest weapon against the proletariat in the hands of the bourgeoisie'. Workers tried to overcome this competition by forming associations, through in the face of stiff opposition from the employers. In fact, trade unions were a result of these spontaneous attempts of workers to end competition.

Engels explains that at first these associations carried out their activities underground as they were not given legal status. They were able to organize a few strikes. Which were ruthlessly crushed by the state. The trade unions expressed their grievances through acts of sabotage or by beating up managers. These conditions meant that these associations had to function in secrecy, and, as Engels notes, it was this secrecy that prevented these associations from spreading among all sections of the working class. Thus these efforts remained isolated instances that depended more on violence than on mass action of the working class.

It was only in 1824 when the British parliament granted the right to free association through the Freedom of Association Act that trade unions could finally take-off. As a result, 'These combinations were soon spread all over England and attained great power' (ibid.: 252). The unity achieved through trade unions gave workers a feeling of confidence resulting from collective action. It also gave them better awareness. Trade unions strove to remove competition among the workers and changed the conflict between individuals within the class to conflict between classes. The working class gradually realized that the only way of improving their conditions of existence was through confrontation with their employers rather than fight among themselves for jobs. The workers also realized that the supremacy of their employers lay in their being disunited. This is one of the most important contributions of trade unions.

ORIGINS OF INDUSTRIALIZATION IN INDIA

Factory production started in India in the early part of the 1850s. The objective then was to export manufactured goods to markets in Britain. Factories were thus established in the port towns of Calcutta and Bombay (now Kolkata and Mumbai) to facilitate export. Cotton textile mills were established in Mumbai and jute mills in Kolkata. Later, factories were established in Madras (now Chennai), another port town. One of the reasons for setting up industries was that costs of production were much lower in India as labour was available at very cheap rates. A couple of decades earlier, in 1839, tea plantations came up in the north-eastern province of Assam. The tea produced was again for consumption in Britain.

The existence of cheap labour was mainly due to two reasons. First, the indigenous economy had been devastated with the introduction of colonial rule of the East India Company a hundred years earlier. During this period the local crafts were replaced by cheaper imports of factory produced goods from Britain. This led to the gradual rout of rural artisans in the country. The peasants were no better off as in many parts of the country they were forced to cultivate cash crops in the place of food crops, which were needed as raw materials for factories in Britain. Besides, the cultivators paid higher taxes due to the new types of land settlements and land revenue imposed by the colonial rulers. As a result, there was a general impoverishment of the rural population. These people served as pools of cheap labour when the factories came up.

The other reason for labour being cheap was that in the initial stages of industrialization the colonial government did not regulate work or wages. The workers were unorganized and the industrialists were able to make them work for long hours at low wages. Women and children were most affected in this system, as their wages were even lower.

The miserable plight of the textile workers, especially the children, caused concern among social workers. One of them, Shapoorjee S.

Bengalee, a Parsee philanthropist and social reformer, tried to convince the government to enforce some legislation to protect children working in factories. He even drafted a bill on this subject and sought the help of his friends in England to help convince the British government to pass regulations.

Meanwhile, the textile mill owners in Lancanshire in England were unhappy over the state of affairs. The lack of any regulations on the textile mills in Bombay had helped the mill owners to sell their goods at cheap rates. The cost of production of the cloth produced in the textile mills of Bombay were cheaper than that of Lancashire mainly because labour costs were lower. The average textile worker in Bombay earned six times less that the worker in Lancashire. There was no regulation on working conditions or time. Workers in Bombay, males, females and children, worked in the factories for 16 hours a day or more. It was not possible to increase wages as there were no such regulations at that time. Hence if there were regulations on work and the timings, it would be possible to increase prices. The Lancashire textile mill owners pressed for government regulations on working conditions. This move was not out of concern for the conditions of the Indian factory workers but more because such regulations would lead to increase in costs of production of the textiles produced in India.

Pressures from both sides led the government to pass the First Factories Act in 1881. This was the first legislation that regulated working conditions in the factories. However it had hardly any effect on the working conditions. The main impact of the Act was that it reduced the working hours of children to nine hours a day.

However, it provided no mechanisms for enforcing such a measure and it was left to the good offices of the owners to implement the provisions. Ten years later, in 1891, the Second Factories Act was passed that reduced the working time of children to seven hours and of women to eleven hours a day. A half hour recess was allowed for workers to take their meals. At the same time there was no move to regulate the working hours of males and also wages.

M.D. Morris notes that most textile mills did not follow the regulations. The few that did, resorted to paying the women and children less for the reduced time. This in fact increased the burden on male workers as they had to work longer hours to make up for the reduction in family income. Working hours of male workers were regulated only after the passing of the Third Factories Act in 1911 which laid down that men could not work for more than 12 hours in a day.

The industrial base in India remained narrow during the initial years mainly because industries were set up for export and not for the local market. Industries were thus largely concentrated in the three port cities, namely, Bombay, Calcutta and Madras, and they manufactured mainly cotton textiles and jute. The census of 1911 showed that there were around 8,00,000 engaged in the secondary and tertiary sectors. Of these 5,24,000 were employed in factories and plantations. In fact, the jute industry and tea plantations employed 4,00,000 workers, namely, half the total labour force. The situation improved with the onset of the First World War in 1914. The war created a need for industrial goods and the colonial government sought to meet this by expanding the engineering goods sector in India. During this period the first steel mill was set up in Bihar, a region with an abundance of mineral wealth. The railways, introduced in the 1860s primarily to carry raw materials to the cotton textile mills in Bombay and the jute mills in Calcutta, increased its network (Gadgil 1982).

FEATURES OF THE LABOUR FORCE

The organized sector and the unorganized sector of the labour force in India can be distinguished from each other on the basis of the labour market and legal rights of the workers. The labour market in the unorganized sector is largely unstructured and unregulated. In legal terms too the unorganized sector hardly offers any protection to its workers. Given the number of unskilled job seekers in this sector, the wages are low and the workers lack bargaining power. The labour market in the organized sector, in comparison to the unorganized sector, is more structured and regulated. In addition, workers in this sector have better skills and are more protected due to the operation of laws regulating their work and employment conditions. These basic differences between the organized and the unorganized sectors also underline the wide gap between the working and living conditions of labour in the two sectors.

The bulk of the labour force is engaged in the unorganized sector. The 1991 census noted that the total working population in the country was 317 million, of which 290.2 million (92 per cent) was in the unorganized sector while only 26.8 million (8 per cent) was in the organized sector. The earnings of the workers in the two sectors differed considerably. Though the organized sector employed only 8 per cent of the total labour force, the workers collectively earned around 33 per cent of the country's total wages and incomes (Davala 1995).

The organized sector comprises mainly workers who get regular wages or salaries and have greater security of employment. Their services cannot be terminated at the whim of their employers, their working time is regulated and they get benefits of social security. It is significant that the major group of employers in this sector are in the public sector and the government. Around 70 per cent of the workforce in the organized sector is employed in these agencies (Papola 1994: 68).

The unorganized sector comprises two types of workers, namely, self-employed and casual wage earners. The self-employed are those who earn paltry incomes through their own assets. In the urban sector these would include petty vendors, rag-pickers, artisans, domestic servants, and so on. In the rural sector small and marginal farmers would be included. The entire employment in agriculture, 75 per cent of the employment in the manufacturing sector, 36 per cent of the employment in the construction sector and 50 per cent of the employment in the transport sector are in the unorganized sector (Papola 1994).

THE TRADE UNION MOVEMENT AFTER INDEPENDENCE: SPLITS IN WORKING CLASS UNITY

The most striking trend in the trade union movement of India before and after Independence is that in the earlier period there was a tendency towards unity while in the latter period splits became the order of the day. The All India Trade Union Congress (AITUC), formed on 31 October 1920, was the first national federation of trade unions. Till the eve of Independence it remained as the representative of the working class with all shades of political forces, ranging from the communists to the liberals, under its umbrella. The federation underwent two major splits over ideological issues during this period. The first split occurred in 1929 when liberals such as V.V. Giri, N.M. Joshi and others broke away to form a separate federation. The issue was over representation in the Royal Commission on Labour in India. The communists and the supporters of the Indian National Congress in the AITUC wanted to boycott the Commission but the liberals (known as the Rightists) wanted to support it. When the majority in the Executive Committee of the AITUC decided to support the move to boycott the Commission the Rightists broke away and formed the Indian Federation of Trade Unions (IFTU). In the following year the communists broke away to form the Red Flag Trade Union Congress. However, they rejoined the AITUC within two years and the IFTU decided to merge with the parent body in 1939 (see Sen 1979, and Revri 1958, for details).

The communists managed to gain control over the AITUC during the last few years of colonial rule. Soon after Home Rule was declared, the leaders of the Congress decided that since the working class would have to play a crucial role in the new pattern of planned development, it could not allow the trade union movement to be led by those who would not fully support its policies. The Congress decided to start another trade union centre which would rival the communist-controlled AITUC's hold over the working class. Thus the Indian National Trade Union Congress (INTUC) was formed in May 1947, three months before Independence. The remarks of Kandubhai Desai, one of the founders, make the purpose clear: While inaugurating the new federation he said. 'It is high time that those interested in building up strong trade unionism dissociate themselves from the communists if not for anything else to demonstrate to the world that whatever prestige and status the movement had was because of non-communist trade union workers' (Johri 1967: 10). Apart from anti-communism, a more important reason was of dovetailing trade unions with the government's policies. Desai admitted, 'It is also felt by many active trade union men that with the advent of the country's Independence, the trade union movement would have to play its destined and legitimate role of influencing the trends toward the elimination of political, economic and social exploitation.' The underlying meaning of this statement is that the existing federation, with its pro-communist slant could not be a dependable ally of the Congress and its policies.

The formation of the INTUC marked the first step of the state in controlling the labour movement. Some industrial relations experts, like C.K. Johri (1967: 11–12) tried to justify this by arguing that industrial peace was necessary during the period of national re-construction, especially when there was a consensus that 'economic development must take place under the aegis of the government'.

This in fact means that the government will have to play the role of employer in this system. Hence, trade unions would have to considerably soften their role as an opposition group. Johri (1967) asserted that in such a situation the government of a newly independent country could achieve its policy objectives easier if the trade union movement, or a major part of it, was ideologically aligned and politically close to the party in power.

It is, however, necessary to consider the long-term effects of the policy of state intervention. Usually it was found that though the state influenced the labour movement with all good intentions in the initial stages, its continued involvement did not help the working class movement. The movement became too dependent on the state for protective legislation, their implementation and even in solving industrial disputes. Moreover, in the case of India, there is enough evidence to show that in case of major industrial disputes the state rarely sided with the workers.

The split in the AITUC in 1947 paved the way for further splits based on narrow party lines with the result it almost became mandatory for every political party to have its trade union front. When a political party splits its trade union front also splits, thereby fragmenting the working class movement further. Similarly, a new political party invariably floats its own trade union.

At the time of the formation of the INTUC the pro-socialist group within the Congress did not support the federation and their trade unions remained with the AITUC. A year later, in 1948, this group broke away to form a new political party called the Praja Socialist Party (PSP) and decided to have its own trade union front which would attract the non-Communist and non-Congress trade unions together. Thus the Hind Mazdur Panchayat (HMP) was formed in that year. The party's objective was partly realized as the Indian Federation of Labour which was inspired by M.N. Roy, a former communist who later became severely anti-communist, merged with the HMP to form a new federation called Hind Mazdur Sabha (HMS). In 1949 the unions supported by the Revolutionary Socialist Party (RSP), a Marxist group having influence mainly in West Bengal and Kerala, which had earlier joined the HMS, decided to form their own federation, the United Trade Union Congress (UTUC).

In 1952, the Bharatiya Jan Sangh, a political party having a Hindu fundamentalist background, was formed and in 1955 initiated another trade union centre known as Bharatiya Mazdur Sangh. Meanwhile the socialists kept splitting and rejoining to form new parties. In 1965, a new party comprising breakaway groups from the PSP and Socialist Party was formed known as the Samyukta Socialist Party. Its most important trade union leader, George Fernandes, broke away from the HMS to form a new Hind Mazdur Panchayat. However, till the early 1970s, the most important trade union bodies in the country were the INTUC, AITUC and HMS.

The split in the communist movement, in the wake of the Chinese aggression in 1962, led to the formation of another communist party—the Communist Party of India (Marxist)—in 1964. Though initially the unions loyal to both communist parties remained with the AITUC, in 1970 the CPI(M) decided to set up another trade union centre known as Centre for Indian Trade Unions (CITU) which took away a large section of unions from the AITUC, especially the ones in West Bengal and Kerala. The other pro-communist federation of trade unions, the UTUC, was also split when a splinter group within the RSP (which later became a separate political party, the Socialist Unity Centre), formed its own UTUC. The two federations are distinguished from each other by the locations of their headquarters in Calcutta (Bow Bazaar and Lenin Sarani).

Apart from the working class being divided on lines of political parties at the national level, regional parties too started forming their own trade union centres since the late 1960s. This process was started by the Dravida Munetra Kazhagham (DMK) when it formed the state government in 1967 in Tamil Nadu (then known as Madras state). Later when the All India Anna Dravida Munetra Kazhagham (AIADMK) was formed in 1977, it too set up its rival centre.

The year 1967 saw the birth of the Shiv Sena in Mumbai. In its early phase the Shiv Sena claimed to represent the interests of Maharashtrians, more particularly the Marathi-speaking people in Mumbai. It was avowedly anti-south Indian and anti-communist. It formed its own labour wing, the Bharatiya Kamgar Sena. It was widely believed that the Shiv Sena and its labour wing had the backing of the industrial houses (most of which were non-Maharashtrian) in the Mumbai–Pune industrial belt to combat the communist unions which were very strong then.[1] It managed to divide the working class in Mumbai on regional lines and gain in strength. By the mid-1970s, its trade union had become fairly strong.

The birth of the Shiv Sena was linked, to a large extent, with the deteriorating economic situation in the country. In 1966–7, the country reeled under a recession which led to a decline in production and subsequently to job losses. Mumbai, being the financial and industrial capital of India, suffered the most. The existing trade unions, including the communists, were unable to cope with this phenomenon as their traditional means of seeking redressal, namely, work stoppage, mass rallies, and so on, were ineffective. The legislations granting protection to workers in the organized sector provided little solace to retrenched workers. The Shiv Sena was formed at this time. It aggressively asserted that job losses were due to the influx of south Indians into the city as these people were taking away available jobs from the local population. The Shiv Sena's influence over the organized working class based on this reasoning could not be stemmed by the traditional trade unions. It was only in the mid-1970s that Datta Samant, a medical practitioner turned trade unionist, could put an effective check on the Shiv Sena. The methods used by Dr. Samant were similar to those used by the Shiv Sena unions to oust the opposition, namely, intimidation and violence.

Thus the underlying feature of the trade union scenario is: proliferation of political parties results in proliferation of trade unions. Alongside there is a growing tendency towards unions based on regional, communal and caste lines. There are also a number of unions which are created by individuals in order to get political mileage or other person-centred benefits. A number of large enterprises, especially of the multinational companies (MNCs), have their internal unions which are run by their own members. These unions are independent in the sense that they are not affiliated to any of the federations. These are called enterprise unions and they have their own strengths and weaknesses (see Davala 1996). While commenting on the chaotic trade union scenario in india, an International Labour Organization (ILO) report (1992: 64) notes: 'The early (post-Independence) splits in Indian trade unionism tended to be on ideological grounds each lined to a particular political party. Much of the recent fragmentation, however, has centred on personalities and occasionally on caste or regional considerations.'

Hence we can see that the trade union movement, which was fairly united during the colonial rule, stands badly divided. This has considerably weakened the working class movement and has deprived it of whatever little power it has in challenging capital and the state. Quite often, inter-union rivalries are stronger than the conflicts between management and labour. Moreover, the mushrooming of unions make it difficult for labour to get proper representation in the national policy making bodies such as the Indian Labour Conference (ILC) and the Planning Commission. The government, in consultation with the ILC, has laid down three conditions for recognition of national trade union centres. First, the centre must have a total membership of 5,00,000. Second, its membership must be spread over at least four states, and third, the membership must be in at least four industries. There are seven such centres which are recognized as national federations. These are the INTUC, BMS, CITU, HMS, AITUC, UTUC (Bow Bazar, in Kolkata), and UTUC (Lenin Sarani, Kolkata). These unions collectively represent the overwhelming majority of the unionized labour force, but given the level of unionization of the total labour force the total membership is a mere drop in the ocean. In the following sections I discuss the problems of unionization in the various sections of the working class.

TRADE UNION MEMBERSHIP

Apart from the problem of fragmentation of unions, the number of unionized workers is also very low. It is difficult to state the actual number of members of trade unions as there is no authentic data on this. The Registrar of Trade Unions is expected to maintain records of union membership based on the returns submitted by the registered unions. However, these figures are not totally reliable as there are cases of underestimation, when unions do not send their returns regularly, and overestimation of membership. The membership of unions is restricted mainly to the 8 per cent in the organized sector. The rate of unionization in the public sector, which employs 70 per cent of the organized sector, is estimated to be around 80 per cent. Unionization in the private sector is much lower. Taking into account these facts the total percentage of unionized workers in the organized sector should be around 50 per cent. Membership in unions in the unorganized sector is small. With the Self-Employed Women's Association (SEWA), the largest union, having a membership of around 2,00,000, the total percentage of unionized workers should be around 5 per cent of the total labour force. The number of employees covered by collective wage agreements works out to a mere 1 per cent of the labour force (Venkat Ratnam 1994: 6). At the same time the unionized section of workers in the organized sector is more vocal and able to wrest more benefits from its employers as well as the government.

THE STATE'S ROLE IN FRAGMENTING THE LABOUR MOVEMENT

The colonial government had a covert pro-employer bias. After Independence, the government tried to rectify the balance by passing a series of protective legislations. Thus, in 1947, the Industrial Disputes Act (ID Act) was passed which attempted to protect workers by curbing some of the rights of the employers such as the right to terminate employment, shut down establishments arbitrarily, and so on. It also recognized trade unions as an essential feature of industrial relations. In addition, a number of legislations covering minimum wages, bonus, disciplinary procedures, recruitment policies, and so on, which grant security to the workers, were passed in order to ensure that the workers, whose strength was weaker compared to the collective strength of the employers, could get security and justice.

At the same time government intervention, especially through the labour department, increased considerably. For example, the ID Act of 1947 provided for conciliation by the government in disputes between labour and management. If this failed, the parties were compelled to submit their differences to arbitration. This provision was aimed at preventing workers from striking work and had been taken from the Defence of India Rules passed by the colonial government during the Second World War (Ramaswamy 1986: 25).

It can be argued with equal emphasis that the state's policies were, in fact, aimed at blunting the workers' initiatives in organizing themselves against the might of capital as well as the state through its bureaucracy, projecting itself as the protector of the workers. This, in fact, has made workers and their trade unions increasingly dependent on the government rather than on their own abilities for sorting out problems with their employers. In order to perpetuate this dependence the state has selectively passed laws which, while granting protection to the workers, has undermined the trade unions. For example, the Trade Unions' Act of 1926 (TU Act), which has remained unchanged since its inception, allows for registration of a trade union. However, there is no legislation which provides for recognition of a trade union as an agent for collective bargaining.

The issue of recognition is left to the management's discretion. Even when states pass legislation on recognition, the method of recognizing a union leaves much to be desired.[2] Another interesting aspect of the TU Act is that it does not distinguish between trade unions and associations of other sectors. Hence, even an association of employers can be registered as a trade union. In fact, the Employers Federation of India (EFI), the most powerful body of employers, is registered under this Act.

The ID Act allows any trade union or an individual worker to raise a dispute before a conciliating officer with the result that any minority union, with little or no following, can intervene in a labour dispute. This practice and the recognition issue encourage multi-unionism in industries. The managements too can maniplate unions and create inter-union rivalries through these methods. They can recognize unions of their choice or even if there is a recognized union they can encourage other unions to raise disputes. Another aspect of this Act, which adversely affects labour, is that of dealing with strikes and lock-outs. If a lock-out by the employer is declared illegal by the labour department the employers have to pay a fine of only Rs. 50 per day whereas in the case of an illegal strike the workers are deprived of their wages. It is no wonder that more human days are lost through lock-outs than through strikes.

It can thus be found that, in general, the state's intervention in regulating industrial relations has created several problems for the workers and their trade unions. Besides the problems discussed above, the elaborate legal structure and the emphasis on the bureaucracy have placed workers in a vulnerable position. It has increased their dependence on outside leaders as workers find the complicated legal process difficult to tackle on their own. Moreover, ordinary workers are unable to deal with the bureaucracy of the labour department independently and, hence, they have to find leaders with the correct political contacts to.do so.

The legal process for redressal of grievances is lengthy, complicated and expensive and instead of providing a framework for justice it has, in fact, encouraged militancy among the workers. Workers often resort to violent outbursts or wildcat strikes to get quick redressal. The rise of militant leaders like Dr. Datta Samant can be attributed to this. E.A. Ramaswamy's study of Mumbai's working class shows the growing impatience of the workers with the legal process. Samant (cf. Ramaswamy 1987: 20) has said, 'When the workers get something good from the lower courts the employer goes to the Supreme Court and straight away 10–15 years are lost. The workers cannot wait that long to get things changed.'

An examination of the industrial relations scene will clearly indicate that despite the projected pro-labour attitude of the state, whenever there has been any major confrontation between labour and management, it has invariably intervened on behalf of the management. Ramaswamy's (1986) study of two industrial disputes in Tamil Nadu in the 1970s, one in the textile industry and the other in the automobile industry, provides a graphic account of the state's manipulation in favouring the employers.

Another significant example is the strike of textile workers in Mumbai in 1982–3. This strike was led by Datta Samant and lasted for eighteen months. For the first fifteen months the entire textile industry in the city was at a standstill and this is regarded as the longest industry-wide strike in the country. The workers put forth demands which included regularization of casual workers, increase in wages and so on. But the most important demand was that of de-recognition of the RMMS.[2] However, despite the display of unity by the workers and their determination to fight, the strike petered off to a failure. The government extended total support to the employers and the RMMS did all it could to break the strike (see Bakshi 1987; Wersch 1992). In fact, during this period, the then chief minister of the state, Babasaheb Bhosale was replaced by Vasantdada Patil who was once the president of RMMS. This was obviously done with the intention that the new chief minister would be more competent in breaking the strike as he had once been a leader of textile workers.

Such instances reveal that the state has rarely taken a pro-working class stand in cases of major labour-management conflicts. In most cases the state has sided with the employers and has used its authority to break the workers' movement. Hence, the legal provisions regarding recognition and their subsequent effects in fragmenting trade unions may not necessarily be an act of omission. The state fears that if the trade union movement is truly autonomous it may emerge not only as the opponent of capital but of the state (more specifically, the party in power) as well. The formation of the INTUC by the Congress as an opposition to the AITUC was a clear indication of this fear.

MAIN ISSUES BEFORE THE WORKING CLASS MOVEMENT

The discussion has so far focused mainly on labour in the organized sector. However, a large section of the working population in India is employed in the unorganized sector. This sector with a heterogeneous composition of workers and it has been expanding. The problems of workers in this sector are manifold and are further compounded due to the near absence of trade unions. This has reduced the 'visibility' of workers in this sector as they are unable to articulate their problems as a collective.

Most of the larger trade unions do not appear to be interested in unionizing workers in the unorganized sector. Davala's study (1995: 7–8) showed that workers in the unorganized sector constituted less than 1 per cent of the total membership of most of the national trade union centres. As a result, representatives of labour in the unorganized sector are rarely called to the national policy-making bodies such as the Planning Commission, ILC and so on and their interests are not taken into account. In order to overcome this problem, some of the larger unions in the unorganized sector such as SEWA, Indian Federation of Construction Labour, National Forum of Fishworkers, Sarva Shramik Sangha and some of the unions of forest and agricultural workers got together to form another national centre. Thus the National Centre for Labour was formed on 1 May 1995. However, though the centre's collective membership is higher than some of the recognized national federations, it is yet to be invited to participate in the ILC.

At the same time employment in the unorganized sector has been growing while that in the organized sector has been on the decline as a result of some of the strategies adopted by the large firms. First, labour is being replaced by new technology. Second, most of these firms use the 'putting out' system to save costs.[3] Perhaps the most important reason for the growth of this system is that it gives the large-scale sector greater control over the labour process. Instead of manufacturing the entire product in their own factories, these firms prefer to farm out the manufacture of their products to smaller production units in the unorganized sector. Heather and Joshi (1976) had dealt with this aspect in their study on migrant labour in Mumbai. Holmstrom (1985) later did a more detailed analysis of the link between the two sectors. He saw this as a complimentary division of labour between the large-scale and small-scale sector where the later can find its market in the large-scale, organized sector (Holmstrom 1985: 13–25). Since costs of production are lower in the small-scale sector, the larger firms are able to procure the products cheaply. Labour productivity in the small enterprises is low, but costs are reduced due to the low level of wages.

The main attraction of the larger manufacturers towards the unorganized sector, besides low costs, is the flexibility of labour in this sector. There are hardly any regulations relating to working time, security of employment and social security. Hence workers work for long hours at unstructured timings and at very low wages. Besides they can be removed from employment at the will of the employer and the production unit too can close down at will. In the organized sector this is not possible because legal restraints and trade unions prevent the employers from acting arbitrarily. Hence by putting out to the unorganized sector the employers do not have to face these constraints. In other words, they face fewer controls from the government, the workers and their trade unions. In this way they, in fact, exert greater control over the labour process as they can get their products manufactured on their own terms and conditions through the unorganized sector.

The flexibility involved in home-based work, which is another major activity in the unorganized sector, is even greater. This sector comprises workers working at piece rates through labour contractors. A large section of this workforce comprises women. The remuneration is usually very low and often children are included in the workforce in order to increase the remuneration. There are practically no laws regulating work or wages and, in fact, the actual number of people working in this sector is not known as, in most cases, they are not even recognized as workers.

Liberalization in the economy due to globalization has boosted the putting out system because the emphasis is now on producing cheaply for the world market. The common refrain of the larger industries and the business press in the country is that over-protection of the organized sector workers is the biggest hurdle to increasing productivity. Soon after the new industrial policy was announced in July 1991, all the associations of the employers started pressing for an exit policy through which it would be easier to shut down industries. The government has so far not introduced this policy due to opposition from trade unions, but it has made conditions for laying off workers much easier. At the same time it should be noted that the liberalization policy introduced in 1991 did not create a flexible and unprotected labour force. It was already in existence and liberalization has boosted the process.

Though these changes are taking place at a fairly rapid pace, the trade unions in the organized sector have so far not been able to respond to these effectively. The response to the government's Industrial Policy Statement of 1991 of the trade unions has been very traditional. They have reacted through conventional means like organizing a national strike and holding a few demonstrations and meetings where the leaders gave fiery speeches full of rhetoric. These have hardly had any effect on changing the policies. In fact, the pace of liberalization has accelerated despite these protests.

One of the major problems of the trade unions is that they are unable or unwilling to expand their membership to sectors outside the organized sector. For example, within the organized sector there is an unorganized sector comprising casual and contract labour which is not protected by the legal framework. Davala's (1992) study of casualization of labour in eight industries showed that, in many large industrial units, the casual and contract labour outnumbered the permanent workers. Yet, in most cases, these workers were not unionized. In fact, in some of the units, the unions viewed these workers with suspicion and as potential threats, as the management could manipulate them easily and counteract work stoppages through them. Had these workers been brought into the trade union fold the managements would not have been able to manipulate them in their favour. Their wages and working conditions would have improved and the unions would have emerged stronger in counteracting managements' strategies for reducing the labour force.

The situation in the small-scale industries is similar. Had these workers been unionized by the unions in the industry, the bargaining power of both sections of workers would have improved. There would have been a common cause among all workers and workers in the small-scale sector could have improved their working conditions.

Unfortunately, instead of unionizing workers outside the organized sector, trade unions have become more inward looking. Their main concern lies in getting as much possible for their own members without any concern for other sections of workers. One can argue that trade unions are primarily responsible to their own members and it would be wrong to expect them to take up issues which do not affect their members. However, under the present circumstances, ignoring workers in the unorganized sector can further erode the gains of workers in the organized sector. The two sectors, as explained earlier, are linked with each other and the employers manipulate these sectors to their own benefit, thus increasing their control over the labour process. Hence, protecting the rights of workers in the unorganized sector through unionization will benefit both sectors.

The central trade unions do not seem to see things this way. They have rarely focused on issues of labour in the unorganized sector. For example, in the ILC held on 24–5 October 1996, the main issue raised by the national centres was that of raising the ceiling on bonus. This issue was discussed for a full day in the two-day conference. Though the issue was valid it concerned less than 5 per cent of the total workers. An issue which could have been discussed in the conference was the ILO convention on home-based workers. After a great deal of lobbying among the governments and the trade unions, the ILO's general body ratified a convention on home-based workers in August 1996 in which there are provisions for maintaining registers of home-based workers, granting them the right to unionize, provision of social security, minimum wages, and so on. These provisions of the convention need to be incorporated in the legal systems of different countries and the trade unions could have raised this in the ILC. The present attitudes of the trade unions are, in fact, aiding the process of liberalization as they result in dividing the working class.

PROBLEMS OF MARGINALIZED SECTIONS

Though trade unions are the most effective organizations of the working class, they also need to be sensitive to the problems of the socially marginalized sections. The two main issues which trade unions in the organized sector have overlooked are the problems of women workers and of workers belonging to the socially oppressed groups such as the Scheduled Castes (SC) and marginalized groups such as the Scheduled Tribes (ST).

From the 1940s till the 1970s the number of women employed in the organized sector declined drastically. This happened in industries which had high levels of unionization, such as cotton textiles in Mumbai, jute in Kolkata and mines in central India. In 1948, women constituted 12 per cent of the workforce in the cotton textile mills in Mumbai, 8 per cent in the jute mills in Kolkata and 15 per cent in the mines. By 1975 the proportion of women workers fell to

2.5 per cent in cotton textiles, 2 per cent in jute and 5 per cent in mines (Gothoskar n.d.). This happened when these industries were expanding and their labour force had increased in number. It was believed that the statutory protection given to women workers such as maternity leave, provision of crèches at the workplace, restriction from working in the night shifts and, in the case of mines, working underground made the working hours of women workers less flexible and also increased costs for the management. However, all these provisions are enforced in the plantation industry as well but this has not resulted in the reduction of women in the workforce, who still continue to constitute 50 per cent of it. Apart from the attitudes of the employers, who seemed only too eager to lay off women workers, the trade unions too did not take up this issue as they were not gender sensitive while framing union policies. Thus trade unions, riddled with their male bias, have not been effective in safeguarding women's employment rights when the employers sought to retrench them.

A similar situation prevails in the employment of SCs and STs in the organized sector. Trade unions have often overlooked their specific problems of social deprivation and prejudice or have sidelined them in union activities. For example, the report of the Commissioner of Scheduled Castes and Scheduled Tribes reviews the implementation of the job reservation policy in a sample of public sector enterprises. It is invariably found that the employment quotas for Class Four employees and factory workers are never filled up. Is it really so difficult to find candidates for these categories or is it merely due to the caste bias of the senior officers in these undertakings? Similarly the promotion policy for these sections, based on the roster system, is hardly ever implemented. The fact is that both the job reservation policy and the system of promotion are statutory requirements which are backed by law. However, none of the national trade unions deem it necessary to take up these legal issues.

There are other problems of social discrimination which have been ignored by the trade unions. One of the more shocking incidents is that of SC workers in the textile mills in Mumbai. They have been prevented from working in some sections in the mills because of the belief of the so-called upper caste workers that they would pollute the thread and hence no other worker would be willing to touch the cloth later. This happened in an industry which had a high level of unionization and militancy in trade union action. None of these unions thought it necessary to educate the workers on the evils of this issue. It is because of this indifference of trade unions to issues relating to caste and tribal affinities that often led these sections form their separate associations and distance themselves from the trade unions. For example, a study of coal mine workers in the Jharia–Ranigunj belt noted that the tribal workers (Santhals) did not join the existing trade unions and instead formed 'kalyan mandals' through which they pressed forth their demands. The working class is thus divided on caste lines due to these associations. But the point is that they are formed because the existing trade unions are not interested in taking up issues affecting these sections and hence they are forced to form their own fronts to protect their interests.

Caste and gender differences have existed among the workers but the significant aspect is that none of the national trade union centres think it necessary to give due importance to these problems or even educate the tradition ridden workers on these issues. The present situation is even more complex. The divide between the organized and unorganized sector workers is not only based on the degree of protection or the wage levels, but also on caste and gender basis. Women workers are largely engaged in the unorganized sector. The 1991 census showed that only 4.2 per cent of the total female workers are in the organized sector while 10.2 per cent of the male workers are in this sector. The proportion of male and female workers in the two sectors are: one female worker for every six male workers in the organized sector; and one female worker for every two and odd male worker in the unorganized sector. Similarly, upper castes have dominated the jobs in the organized sector while the SCs and STs are engaged in the unorganized sector. Hence there is every possibility of the present divide being exploited by caste-based organizations to create caste animosity. If this happens the tendency will then be to blame these organizations for creating casteism whereas the seeds have been sown by the present caste bias which has marginalized the so-called lower castes into a vulnerable position.

CONCLUSION

The changes taking place in the economy through the policies of liberalization pose the greatest challenge to the labour movement in India as these are leading to job losses in the organized sector while expanding the base of the unprotected sector. The main problem before the working class in the present situation is of fragmentation.

The divisions among the working class has resulted in its helplessness in counteracting the adverse effects of globalization and the consequent liberalization of the economy. The trade union movement could have counteracted the anti-labour policies but it has not been able to do so because it is divided. A united trade union movement is perhaps the most pressing need in the present situation. Every major trade union in the country has stressed this; yet, there seems to be no signs of its emergence. For example, the AITUC and the HMS decided to merge into one union in their respective conferences in 1992 but till date the merger has not been finalized.

Several reasons are put forth while analysing the phenomenon of fragmentation of trade unions, the most important being the links between trade unions and politics. It is felt that the political role of the trade unions has overshadowed its commitment to the workers' interests. This is, to a large extent, true. At the same time the political role of the trade union movement cannot be undermined. Trade unions are organizations of workers which are formed to protect their interests. Though trade unions are expected to counteract the power of the employers at the grassroots level, they cannot do so effectively without challenging the power of the state.

Besides trying to wrest a better deal for workers from the employers, the trade union movement has to influence the state so that the gains it has made out of its struggles are converted into legal rights. This can be done through its role in the political system which would include supporting of political parties. We can see most trade unions in the world are linked with political parties. The Trade Union Congress in the United Kingdom is closely linked with the Labour Party. In France, the largest trade union federation, the CGT, is linked with the Communist Party of France. Similarly a number of trade unions in the European countries are associated with the social democratic parties in their respective countries or with other political parties. In Canada, the Canadian Labour Congress has close associations with the New Democratic Party. Internationally too, trade unions are divided on the basis of ideology. The two major international trade union centres are the World Federation of Trade Unions to which most of the pro-communist trade unions are affiliated and the International Confederation of Free Trade Unions which comprises the socialist trade unions.

The major difference between the above scenario and the situation in India is that trade unions here are divided not on the basis of ideology but on the basis of political parties. Moreover, the political parties influence trade union policies rather than the other way around, with the result that the political parties set the agenda for their trade unions. This is often based on their political gains rather than the workers' interests. In the countries discussed above, it is the trade unions which affect the policies of political parties and even oppose them if they feel that they do not serve the interests of labour. The Trade Union Congress has been critical of some of the policies of the Labour Party and has, at times, threatened to withdraw its support if the party does not change its stand. Similarly the Canadian Labour Congress has often been critical of the policies of the New Democratic Party. Hence trade union unity becomes more difficult in india because this would presume that the political parties supporting the trade unions too have to unite.

It would not be totally correct to hold political parties solely responsible for the fragmentation of trade unions. In fact, the state has played a more important role in this process. We have seen that the legal framework for industrial relations on the one hand provides grounds for multiple unions and on the other hand makes the unions more dependent on government agencies for settlement of disputes. Moreover, the state itself has inevitably come out in support of the employers whenever there has been a major confrontation between labour and management. The state has thus provided the grounds for disunity within the working class which is capitalized by those with narrow political interests or other elements who want to use trade unions for personal gains.

One of the positive signs in the current situation is the near total consensus on opposing the liberalization process. However, this unity has arisen out of opposition and as such the trade unions have not developed alternative plans to replace the present policies. The opposition to policies comes mainly from the organized sector. One would have expected the unions to cover the unorganized sector as well, but unfortunately this has not happened. On the contrary, trade unions have become more conscious of protecting their own interests without a care for the vast section of the unorganized sector. One can argue that unions are primarily responsible to their own members, hence they cannot organize workers who are non-members. However, under the present circumstances ignoring workers in the unorganized sector will erode the gains of workers in the organized sector. The two sectors, as we have explained earlier, are linked with each other and the employers manipulate these sectors by pitting them against each other so that they can get the maximum benefits at the cost of labour. Hence, along with trade union unity, there is a need for closer links between labour in the two sectors. This will not only unite various sections of the working class but will, in addition, bring to the fore the problems of women workers and workers belonging to the socially oppressed groups.

Finally, while discussing the problems of the labour movement, the role of the trade unions cannot be undermined or replaced as they are the only means for protecting the interests of the working class. No other institution, be it a benevolent bureaucracy, a political party or even an NGO, can substitute for trade unions. Therefore, strengthening the labour movement can only be done through strengthening the trade union movement.

NOTES

1. For example, in the parliamentary elections in 1967, the Shiv Sena supported Harish Mahendra, an industrialist and candidate of the Congress, against S.A. Dange, a veteran communist trade union leader. Dange was elected to the parliament.
2. States such as Maharashtra, Gujarat and Madhya Pradesh have legislation providing for recognition of trade unions in some industries. These are based on the lines of the Bombay Industrial Relations Act (BIR) passed by the colonial government. The basic principle is of 'one industry one union'. The recognition of a representative union is on the basis of membership verification and not through election. There is a demand from all the central trade union centres, with the exception of the INTUC, that the representative union should be recognized through secret ballot but this has so far not been conceded. Soon after the BJP–Shiv Sena government came into power in Maharashtra it promised to amend the Maharashtra Recognition of Trade Unions and Prevention of Unfair Labour Practices Act to include this clause but it did not do so. The major problem with the membership verification method is that it is time consuming and once a union is recognized it is virtually impossible to replace it. This is the case with the Rashtriya Mill Mazdur Sangh (RMMS) in Mumbai. It was recognized as the representative union for the textile industry under the BIR Act and though other unions have proved to be more popular, such as the Mumbai Girni Kamgar Union led by the communists in the 1970s and Dr. Datta Samant's Maharashtra Girni Kamgar Union in the 1980s, they were unable to replace the RMMS as the sole bargaining agent as these unions had to prove that their

membership was higher by producing membership receipts which had to be verified case by case by the labour department. Similarly, if a union is derecognized by the management the same process of membership verification follows. For example, the Hindustan Levers Employees' Union was derecognized by the management in the mid-1980s and its membership verification process has yet to be completed by the labour department even though the factory was closed since early 2007.

3. In this system the larger industries get their components, and at times the entire product, manufactured in small-scale industries. As a result, the larger industries can lay-off their workers while procuring goods or components at lower prices as the costs of production in the small-scale sector are much lower due to low-paid workers and low capital investment. Though this system is very profitable for the larger industries it helps neither the workers in the small-scale sector as they are paid very low wages nor their employers as the selling prices of the goods are determined by the larger industries who purchase them. The consumer too does not benefit as the prices of the finished products marketed by the large industries is not lowered. This system is also known as outsourcing or vending.

REFERENCES

Bakshi, R. (1987), *The Long Haul*, Bombay: Build Documentation.

Dange, S.A. (1973), *Outlines of the Indian Trade Union Movement*, New Delhi: People's Publishing House.

Davala, S. (ed.) (1992), *Employment and Unionisation in Indian Industry*, New Delhi: Friedrich Ebert Stiftung.

——— (1995), *Unprotected Labour in India*, New Delhi: Friedrich Ebert Stiftung.

Davala, S. (1996), 'Independent Trade Unionism in West Bengal', *Economic and Political Weekly*, 31(52), L 44–9.

Engels, F. (1973), *Conditions of the Working Class in England in 1948*, Moscow: Progress Publishers.

Flanders, Alan (1970), *Trade Unions*, London: Faber and Faber.

Gothoskar, S. (1990), 'Declining Employment of Women in the Organized Sector' (Mimeograph).

Holmstrom, M. (1985), *Industry and Inequality: The Social Anthropology of Indian Labour*, Hyderabad: Orient Longman.

International Labour Organization (1992), *World Labour Report*, Geneva.

Johri, C.K. (1967), *Unionism in a Developing Economy*, New Delhi: Asia Publishing House.

Joshi, H. and V. Joshi (1976), *Surplus Labour and the City: A Study of Bombay*, New Delhi: Oxford University Press.

Mukherji, Radha Kamal (1955), *The Indian Working Class*, Bombay: Popular Prakashan.

Nehru, Jawaharlal (1955), *Autobiography*, New Delhi: National Book Trust.

Papola, T.S. (1994), 'Employment, Growth and Social Protection of Labour in India' in P. Sinha, C.S. Venkat Ratnam and G. Botterweek (eds.), *Labour and Unions in a Period of Transition*, New Delhi: Friedrich Ebert Stiftung.

Ramaswamy, E.A. (1986), *Power and Justice*, New Delhi: Oxford University Press.

——— (1987), *Worker Consciousness and Trade Union Response*, New Delhi: Oxford University Press.

Revri, C. (1958), *The Trade Union Movement in India*, Hyderabad: Orient Longman.

Sen, S. (1979), *The Working Class Movement in India*, Kolkata: K.P. Bagchi and Company.

Venkat Ratnam, C.S. (1994), 'Changing Role of Trade Unions in a Period of Transition', in P. Sinha, C.S. Venkat Ratnam and G. Botterweck (eds.), *Labour and Unions in a Period of Transition*, New Delhi: Friedrich Ebert Stiftung.

Wersch, H.V. (1992), *The Bombay Textile Strike 1982-83*, New Delhi: Oxford University Press.

CHAPTER 13

Dynamics of Early Labour Mobilization: Bombay City, 1890–1919

SHASHI BHUSHAN UPADHYAY

INTRODUCTION

Since the late eighteenth century the Indian subcontinent was subjected to the twin processes of colonialism and globalization. Establishment of colonial rule in significant pockets of the region was accompanied by its incorporation in the global network of trade, particularly in commodities and capital. This process of what has been termed as the 'first globalization' got intensified in the next century, reaching its peak in the late nineteenth century. Revolutionary breakthroughs in the technologies of communication and transportation, such as telegraph, telephone and railways, significantly supported this development. India's imports consisted of manufactured goods and capital. Thus, India's integration into a globalized market bore the stamp of its status as a colony.

Bombay (Mumbai) was among the most important cities in the country which became the focal point in this process of globalization. It served as a hub in the international network of trade through whose shores millions of tons of goods of all kinds passed. The successful launch of the initial wave of the modern cotton textile mills in the city was a part of this process. Capital was provided by the persons involved in the foreign trade, procurement of raw material was made easy by the already thriving trade in raw cotton and the machinery and technical personnel were imported from Europe, particularly Britain. Within a span of half century, Bombay became one of the major industrial centres in the world producing significant amount of textiles and exporting a major part of it.

The history of the labour movement in Bombay has also been particularly eventful. Several milestones in the history of the Indian labour movement have been associated with Bombay. The massive strike and demonstrations in 1908 against Tilak's imprisonment, the six-month long strike in 1928 and, the longest of all, the great strike of 1982 which lasted for about eighteen months, are some of the major instances of massive labour mobilizations which occurred in this city. It is true that there was a radicalization of labour movement all over India, especially under communist influence, but the labour militancy in Bombay has been remarkable. The cotton textile workers were particularly militant during the 1920s. There were six general strikes in the industry—in 1919, 1920, 1924, 1925, 1928 and 1929. Besides, there were innumerable small and large strikes on various issues. In fact, 'hardly a month went by without a strike in at least one department of one of the mills' (Newman 1981: 58). The working-class areas were in a constant state of fermentation during this period, the working-class organizations were extremely strong, and the communist presence was quite prominent.

The pre-1919 period was relatively quiet by these standards. However, it was not entirely eventless and, in fact, the foundations of the later militant mobilizations were laid during this period. Here we are mainly concerned with the pre-trade union period between the early 1890s, when the cotton textile industry in Bombay faced its first serious crisis after a long span of prosperity since its inception in 1856, and 1919, a few years before another long era of crisis began to trouble this premier manufacturing enterprise in early 1920s. This period also coincides with the first serious occurrences of workers' protests expressed in the form of small-scale but frequent strikes which continued with varying intensity over the years witnessing several ups and downs and ending with the first general industrial strike in 1919. This strike was around economic issues and was brought about by the workers' accumulated experiences and the generalized miseries of the war years.

Such industrial militancy typecast the workers in the framework of class, largely ignoring other forms of identities. When other identities, such as those of religious community, caste and region, became hard to ignore, they were sought to be explained as aberrations, as impediments which temporarily disturbed the onward march of class consciousness and disrupted the formation of class identity.

The Indian labour history until quite late had been chiefly concerned with the workers as economic beings for whom strikes constituted the only form of mobilization and the class was the only available identity. Even the formation of the workers as a class was assumed rather than elaborated. The presence of many other complimentary or competing identities was ignored. No attention was paid to the fact that the formation of class was closely allied with the growth of other corporate identities. Although these studies were significant in the sense of creating the tradition of labour history in India, they presented a rather one-sided picture of the workers and ignored the plurality of their existence (for example, Karnik 1967 and Sen 1977).

It is difficult to believe that the centuries' old tribal and peasant societies had no bearings on the minds and attitudes of the workers, whereas a few years of patchy, tardy capitalist industrialization could change the mentality and behaviour of the workers in the space of a few months or years. This is to imbue capital with magical qualities that could subdue with effortless ease the traditional societies with age-old values and norms.

In the recent historiography, it has been widely noticed that in the modern period people's identity assumes various shapes and forms, sometimes in apparent contradiction with each other. In the urban areas, particularly in the big cities, the volatile socio-economic and political situation creates many more avenues for such cross-currents. This fact is now increasingly coming to focus in labour studies and scholars are consciously exploring such cross-connections.

This paper explores the dynamics of labour mobilization in the pre-trade union period in Bombay. It also explains the remarkable militancy of textile workers in Bombay. For this purpose it focuses on three major events in a period of about thirty years which effected three biggest mobilizations among them. The communal riots in 1893, the famous protests against Tilak's conviction in 1908 and the industry-wide general strike in 1919 were the conjunctures which witnessed the closure of all the mills and the mobilization of workers on the streets.

Our basic thesis here is that although the grim conditions of their existence and the consequent struggle for adjustment and survival shaped their consciousness, the workers, at any given moment, possessed not one but several identities. Some of these might be their cultural inheritance from the villages, while others would be engendered and acquired in the city through a variety of political and social ideas and activities. The earlier identities were nurtured and widened in the city both due to the workers' attempts to survive in the new atmosphere and because of the general political activism induced by the colonial policies. The completely new identities relating to class, religious community and nation were often based on and around the previously existing consciousness of religion, caste and region, which were also in the process of change. They constantly intermingled and determined the behaviour-pattern of the workers. Thus the militant mobilizations should not be viewed solely in class terms, although class identity was a crucial element in them.

STRUCTURE OF THE INDUSTRY AND NATURE OF THE WORKFORCE

The cotton textile industry started in the 1850s and by the end of the century it had become prominent in the economy of the city. Depending on cheap labour and easy access to raw materials, the industry remained a profitable venture until the 1890s, despite the indifferent colonial government and a wary British textile industry which perceived it as a serious competitor. But the policies of the government, which were often influenced by its colonial imperatives, and its pro-Manchester attitude were inimical to the growth of the indigenous industry. As a result it remained unstable particularly because of its dependence on the export market in China. In the 1890s, a series of crises beginning with the colonial government's disturbing currency policy seriously undercut its competitive edge in the Chinese market for yarn. The availability of the foreign market remained uncertain while the home market was largely occupied by goods from the British industry. The indifferent attitude and the 'free-trade' policies of the colonial government left this newly emerging industry to fend for itself. Although it recovered by the turn of the century, the ups and downs continued till the beginning of the First World War which, by cutting down the imports, provided the opportunity for it to expand in the domestic market. It performed well until 1922 after which a long-term crisis began.

These uncertainties induced the industrialists to rely on the managing agents for the mobilization of capital and organization of production, and on the jobbers for procurement of labour and its management on the shop floor. No long-term solutions were devised.

The reliance on managing agents caused unnecessary overproduction as the agents were paid commission on the volume of production and the dependence on the jobbers resulted in the creation of an unstable and disorganized workforce.

There was no security of jobs and the workers worked for extremely long hours at relatively low payments, the working time stretching up to 12 to 15 hours a day during this period. The rapid development of mill-districts in the northern areas of the city where most of the mills were located and where the workers had moved *en masse* during the 1880s and the 1890s created a lot of sanitary problems. The polluted atmosphere in the neighbourhood, along with long hours in the equally polluted and hot mills weakened their bodies making them hosts of a variety of diseases. Sometimes the situation became so bad that Bombay resembled a city of death (Upadhyay 2004: 21–108).

The specific nature of industrial development in Bombay gave rise to two features which are of special significance here. Firstly, due to the insecurity of jobs and high rates of sickness and mortality, the workers had to depend on extra-industrial networks both in the villages and the city. The chain which joined the mill workers with their caste and kin people and with other workers stretched from the countryside to Bombay and moved back and forth. These links made them open to various influences which would otherwise not have been possible. The observance of strict caste rules even in matters of dining in Bombay was one such instance.

It was also quite decisive in shaping the nature of the workforce in the industry. There was a tendency for some groups to congregate in particular departments of the mills. A Bombay Mill Owners' Association (BMOA) survey, conducted in 1940, showed that 53.8 per cent of Hindu migrant workers from UP were in the 'mixing to speed frame' and formed about 46.8 per cent of the total workers in that department; 72.5 per cent of the Dalit castes were employed in the ring-spinning department and made up 39.5 per cent of all male workers; 52.2 per cent of all Muslim workers were employed in the weaving department where they formed 6.9 per cent of all the weavers (Morris 1965: 75). It may be expected that such community-centric concentration would have been more marked in earlier years. Contemporary observers attest to this trend of particularistic concentration [Burnett-Hurst 1925: 13]. In 1921, out of all the weavers, 61.7 per cent were Marathas, 21.9 per cent from the backward castes and 11.4 per cent from the Muslims (Newman 1981:

42). We find that the Marathas and Muslims were over-represented in this department in comparison with their industrial averages, which were 52 per cent for the former and 5.15 per cent for the latter. There was further concentration according to particular mills.

There was a bias against employment of low-caste people in certain departments, particularly the weaving sheds where the yarn had to be sucked by the workers into their mouths to put it on the shuttle, thereby constituting a danger of ritual defilement for the upper castes. It was due to this discrimination against them that the proportion of the lower castes in the weaving departments was just 0.6 per cent (Morris 1965: 76). In the earlier period, this practice seemed to prevail in the industry as a whole. J. Helm, the manager of the Bombay United Mill, said before the Factory Commission of 1875 that 'the operatives in my mill are almost all Hindus. There are a few Mahomedans and about half a dozen Parsees. No low-caste operatives are allowed to be employed in my mill' (*FC 1875:* 23). In 1908, Saklatvala, the manager of Petit Mill, stated: 'There were no low-caste men in the weaving shed. . . . When a man applied for work his caste was enquired into. *Caste, in fact, was a great consideration*' (*IFLC 1908:* 82, emphasis added). These problems persisted and in 1928 one employer commented: 'In our mills we have got people who go into various departments according to castes' (*BSEC* 1928–29: 674). The holidays given to the workers also followed the same pattern. The mills were closed mostly on Hindu holidays. One mill manager said that 'on Parsee and Mahomedan holidays we never stop the work. It is only on Hindu holidays that we do so' (*FC 1875:* 21). Another manager confirmed that they stopped the mill on 12 holidays in a year and 'they are all Hindu holidays' (ibid.: 28).

These caste- and community-based practices were quite common among the workers. Maya, a low-caste girl, told the Factory Commission of 1885: 'I belong to Mochee caste, consequently I cannot mix with the higher castes in the reeling room.' She wanted to work in the reeling department but could not do so. The statement given by Sakoo, the Maratha female overseer of the reeling department, confirmed this:

> There are different castes and the food would be defiled by the different castes and it would be practically impossible to do it. There are Mochees, Mahomedans and other castes and if any of them touched us or our food we should be defiled. . . . What is caste made for if it is not to be maintained?
>
> (*FC 1885*)

In 1922, one of the first grievances raised by the workers before the Tata Committee was 'the lack of separate water taps for untouchables' (Newman 1981: 279). Even where the Muslims and the Hindus worked in the same department there were separate arrangements for them for drinking water. In the mills with facilities for providing tea for the workers, there were generally two separate rooms for the Hindus and the Muslims. In cases of a single room and a single fireplace, two cooks belonging to each of the religions were employed to make tea (Kelman 1923: 134–6). The Chief Inspector of Factories, T.W. Johnstone, testifying before the *RCL*, said that the construction of a common dining shed might create 'caste difficulty in the mills'. He supported his statement by his experience of one mill in Ahmedabad :

> Some years ago . . . I happened to visit a mill and I found about 70 or 80 people fighting with rods they use in the blow room; half a dozen of them were laid out. They were all low caste people, wagris and dheds. The trouble arose through a wagri touching a dhed's food. (*RCL* 1931: 241)

The observation of caste rules among the workers as among other groups was a very strong sentiment and had its bearing on the composition and nature of the workforce and its distribution in various departments.

Despite such divisive tendencies, however, the development of the mill areas led to the concentration of a large number of workers in a relatively small space which provided the opportunity for easy mobilization. Moreover, it brought a large number of workers in one place and created more or less common grievances, particularly at the economic level. Thus, the same process of industrial development created conditions for unity as well as division among the working people.

THE THREE BIGGEST MOBILIZATIONS

The working-class crowds formed on innumerable occasions for various, sometimes contrasting purposes. Except for the nightly gathering for singing *bhajans* and other songs, the formation of crowds happened mostly, though not always, during the working time because it, particularly during the early period, encapsulated almost the entire waking time. The workers, therefore, had to absent themselves, often without permission, to participate in public events.

A significant portion of the crowd might, however, be composed of workers without jobs, the casually employed, the stragglers and destitute living in the mill areas and, of course, the children. These crowds could be mobilized with considerable ease. In fact, the mill areas witnessed a constant happening of crowds. They formed for strikes and impromptu demonstrations against working conditions, for cow-protection rallies, for Ganapati and Shivaji festivals, on Holi, Diwali and Dussehra (*ITJ* November 1901 and March 1904], for participation in nationalist rallies and demonstrations, and for temperance meetings. In fact, the working masses seemed to be available for any number of things one could think of. The crowds formed in so many ways, on so many occasions and for so many purposes that it is difficult to discern any clear pattern or to impute any fixed identities to the entire mass of workers. They were mobilized for the nationalist cause, but sometimes in opposition to it; against the millowners, but sometimes in their favour; against the government, but sometimes for them. The frequency of these mobilizations was so high that it is difficult to pinpoint the identities around which many of these took place.

But the three biggest mobilizations during this period with clear political purposes took place around the identities of religious community, nation and class. The communal riots in 1893 witnessed the first major collective mobilization of workers, though on a sectarian issue. All the mills were forced to close and almost the entire mass of workers was mobilized along sectarian lines. The next occasion for such a massive mobilization of the workers was in 1908 on a nationalist issue when Tilak was arrested and convicted. There occurred a largely pre-mediated general strike in the mills for seven days and the workers' protest-demonstrations happened almost continuously in the mill areas. The third such mobilization took place in 1919 in the form of a general strike on economic issues which was the biggest, more integrative and the longest ever strike. The class identity of the workers made it successful and this identity was strengthened during the course of the strike and its aftermath. In the following three sub-sections we will discuss each of these happenings chronologically.

I

Ironically, the first big mobilization of workers took place on a communal issue. The Hindu–Muslim riots which occurred in Bombay in August 1893 witnessed the first collective mobilization of workers on a grand scale. The mill workers were prominently involved in the happenings. Their involvement was viewed with much concern and was termed as a 'most serious aspect' and 'absolutely unprecedented'. The intensity and the spread of the riots were in large parts attributed to the 'capacity for cooperation which the Bombay mill-hands are beginning to display' [HD (Public) Proceedings 169–89, 1893: 72].

The riots were the result of a period of sectarian identity-formation which had been going on for quite some time in the city. The British policies and actions had also directly contributed to it. The colonial censuses played a great role in this process by accepting religious demarcation as their foundation. There were expected responses from the sides of their subjects. Many of the enumerated people began thinking and projecting themselves in terms defined by the censuses. The Census of 1901 duly noted the process of crystallization of religious communities, particularly in the wake of census operations. Various socio-religious groups which had hitherto been engaged in heterodox practices had started moving towards orthodoxy. It was reported that the Lingayats, who had earlier refused to recognize caste distinctions and the authority of the Brahmans, had submitted 'numerous representations' in 1891 to the census authorities 'claiming the right to be described as Virshaiv Brahmans'. Some of them had also submitted 'a complete scheme' showing the fourfold *varna* divisions among the Lingayat community (*Census 1901*). By 1901, these attempts by the Lingayats 'to revert to Brahministic Hinduism' had become even more pronounced (ibid.: 58). Similarly, it was reported that the Sikhs had been registering themselves in the censuses as 'Nanakshahi Hindus' for two decades (ibid.: 61). Therefore, while their actual number in 1901 in Bombay was 1,50,000, in the census figures the number of the Sikhs had been put down at 1,502, the rest being counted as Hindus (ibid.: 57). Along the same lines, the Animists whom the census of 1891 in Bombay had enumerated at 2,92,000 had declined to 95,000 in 1901, and one of the main reasons for this decline was said to the 'the tendency of such tribes to become converts to Hinduism with a view to raising themselves in the social scale' (ibid.: 65). In the view of R.E. Enthoven, the Chief Census Officer for Bombay, this trend could be attributed to the fact of 'the extraordinary attraction exercised on rival religions by the doctrines and social orders of orthodox Brahminism' (ibid.: 183).

Some of the truly heterodox sects like the Kabirpanthis who believed neither in the Vedas nor in the Koran and respected neither the Brahmans nor the *ulema*, faced a vertical division and dissolved themselves into Hinduism and Islam. Thus, the census of 1901 in Bombay returned from among the erstwhile Kabirpanthis 8,000 Hindus and 1,300 Muslims (ibid.: 61). It appears, therefore, that most of the heterodox sects such as the Lingayats, Satnamis, Margis, and Swami Narayanis increasingly subsumed under the overarching fold of Hinduism. The colonial impact, especially the censuses, had set in motion the process whereby most of the population started defining itself in terms of a few so-called 'great religious traditions'.

There was yet another level at which the intervention by the colonial officials tended to solidify the community identities. At the time of the census of 1881 in Bombay city, there were apprehensions that the entire exercise was viewed 'with much suspicion by the masses'. It was reported that there was general fear of 'social disasters' and 'material losses' and stories were circulating about 'conscription of labour, to extend even to women, to recruit forces from beyond the Indian frontier' (*Census 1881*: 4.) To overcome these obstacles and to ensure the 'sympathy and good will' of the people, the officials decided to rely so-called community leaders whom they called 'the elements of popular influence' (ibid.). For this purpose the supposed leaders of various religious communities were invited to the municipal office and meetings were held. For the Muslims, a meeting of the religious heads as well as some other prominent Muslims was called. Mohammad Ali Roghay and Badruddin Tyabji were some of those present. It was resolved that the leaders from each community should call meetings with people of their own religion, that the Anjuman-i-Islam and the Majlis-Akhwan-i-Sufa should play prominent roles in holding meetings with all classes of Muslims and familiarize them with the 'objects of the Census', advise them to 'cooperate with the census officers', and provide help in distributing posters and pamphlets brought out by the municipal authorities, that the names of the community leaders be included in the posters and pamphlets, and lastly, but equally importantly, *Muslim enumerators should be employed for the enumeration of the Muslim population*.

Meetings with Hindu leaders were held along the same lines and it was resolved that 'a general Committee of influential Hindoos should be formed to explain publicly the objects of the Census, and to disarm suspicion'. Following this, a meeting of the 'Hindoo inhabitants' was held at Madhav Bag and speeches were delivered by Varjivandas Madhavdas, Gopalrao Hari Deshmukh, Javerilal Yajnik, Raghunath Narayan Khote and others. Likewise, a meeting with the Parsi leaders was held in which Nowrozjee Furdoonjee suggested that the Parsi 'priests should be employed to explain to the lower classes the objects of the Census' (ibid.: 4-6).

Thus, even prior to the census operations, the people of Bombay were neatly divided into religious communities and some men were assumed as community leaders with influence on all classes of people supposedly following a particular religious faith. These communities were further assumed to be impervious to the influences from any other except the leaders from their own communities. All these assumptions derived warm and positive responses from these supposed community leaders who were equally anxious to assume and defend their leadership roles.

However, the responsibility for generating communal discord cannot be laid entirely at the doors of the colonial rulers. There were intense community-oriented social and cultural activities in Bombay in the latter half of the nineteenth century. Certain reform movements, like that of the Arya Samaj, tended, sometimes unintentionally, to encourage the closing of the community boundaries in basically two ways. Firstly, the reforming attempts were centred on religious or caste groups and tried to redefine, reform and purify the religious and caste practices, often resulting in weaning away people from the shared traditions. Secondly, these reform activities antagonized, revived and energized the conservative and reactionary sections within the community or caste and prompted them to close ranks and display aggressive behaviour not only towards the reformers but also towards the government and other religious groups.

The reform activities sometimes combined the religious and cultural with the social and economic. The improvement of the community's position in education and jobs was at times an important objective of the community/caste associations. Thus, B.M. Malabari, one of the most ardent and famous nineteenth-century reformers, feared the decline of Parsi position in the economic, social and educational spheres. 'We are afraid,' he wrote in 1883, that 'the future of the Parsi community in Bombay is a very unpromising one. With the loss of money they are losing their social prestige. In fact, they are being pressed out by the Hindus and the Mahomedans, till there is scarcely room for them in Bombay' (*Indian Spectator* 26 August 1883; quoted in Christine Dobbin 1972: 218).

Among the Muslims too both caste- and community-based associations were the order of the day, particularly among the elite. Both the traditional and modern elite were active in organizing and participating in associations which would boost their social position and competitive abilities in trade and jobs. The Khojas, Bohras, Memons and Konkanis were becoming increasingly self-conscious not only in terms of caste but also sect identities like Sunnis and Shias. Even the unifying bodies like the Anjuman-i-Islam were more successful when they took up communal issues like mourning the death of the Turkish sultan in 1876, collecting funds for the Turkish armies in 1877 or working for the promotion of Urdu as the language for all the Muslims than while trying to improve the educational standards of the Muslims or introducing secular reforms. Many of these groups also tried to eliminate the earlier shared customs and practices and impose a puritanical version of Islam on their members (ibid.: 229–46). These identities and activities seemed to have led to the Muslim-Parsi riots in 1851 and 1874.

Although all these activities tended to generate an atmosphere of communal antagonism, the cow-protection movement proved to be the most potent factor in mobilizing the Hindu masses and antagonizing the Muslims. The cow, as an essential symbol of Hinduism, could provide the platform where the broad community identity could be forged, where the high and low, the orthodox and heterodox, the *shetias* and the Western-educated, the Kunbis and Brahmans, the south Indian Kamathis and north Indian Hindus, the Gujarati and Marathi speakers, all could unite.

These sectarian mobilizations resulted in major riots which started on 11 August 1893 and continued, with varying intensity, till 20 August. The main events took place only on three days, but their intensity was such that, according to official estimates, 81 persons were killed, 700 injured and 1,550 were arrested; property worth lakhs of rupees was looted and destroyed. It also led to mass migration of people out of and within the city during and immediately after the riots. The textile workers were the single most dominant presence in these riots.

The relationship between the cow-protection movements, along with related riots, and the differential involvement of various groups has received a lot of scholarly attention [see, for example, John R. McLane 1977; S. Freitag 1990; Peter Robb 1986, and Gyan Pandey 1983]. With respect to the urban workers, this debate on communal conflict has been particularly intense in the context of the jute millworkers in Calcutta. Dipesh Chakrabarty finds a significant growth of sectarian tendencies which he describes as 'community consciousness', 'communal culture', and 'communal divisions' among the workers in the 1890s (Chakrabarty 1976) This he further defines as 'a consciousness to which religion was of crucial importance' (Chakrabarty and Das Gupta 1981: 7). Even though this consciousness developed in the 1890s, he charts it as something inherited, 'as an ensemble of relationship one is born into, as opposed to "class" which is based on an associational principle' (ibid.: 22). Thus the notions of community or/and communal consciousness, as emerges from his arguments, were phenomena which were not related to the particular historical and contextual developments. He reconfirms this position when he says that 'The jute workers . . . acted out of an understanding that was prebourgeois in its elements' (Chakrabarty 1989: 212).

Many historians have criticized the inadequacy and ahistoricity of this analysis and emphasized the colonial context as crucial to the development of such identity. They have stressed the centrality of economic and political factors as decisive in shaping the consciousness and actions of the workers (Das Gupta 1979; 1981; Bagchi 1990; Ghosh 1990).

What was the nature of the riots in Bombay in 1893? It is true that the workers were imbued with religious consciousness which was reinforced in the alienating atmosphere of the city. It did not, however, mean that it automatically led to communalism. The ideology of communalism must have a conception of the 'other' and this emerged and was shaped by the colonial ideology, policies and practices and was reinforced and strengthened by the political mobilization which took place in response to the colonial reality. The communal atmosphere and the consequent riots have to be placed in the particular historical context. The British policies and historiography turned the sectarian strife into communal riots and constructed distinct communities with disconnected culture and customs out of the varieties of castes and sects with shared traditions. What were until then feuds between different groups transformed into persistent battles between all-India communities defined by their religions.

But the responsibility for this was not entirely that of the colonial rulers. Several times actors from within the Indian social and political milieu mobilized opinions and people and their actions did not always conform to the rulers' ideology and interests. They also stood against the state. Therefore, the notion of communities based on religions was not inherited but was acquired during the late nineteenth century.

But the growth of communal identity cannot be explained in purely political and economic terms. Although political mobilization in the form of caste and community associations was taking place and the cow-protection movement pushed it to a much larger scale, the process of identity formation was social and cultural also. Why would a person or a group assume a certain identity and not another was also decided by her/his/their socio-cultural backgrounds and had its roots in the inherited consciousness of the people. In such situation, the socio-cultural inheritance interacts with political movements to shape a particular identity for a person or group.

The official and unofficial assessments about the role of the masses pointed towards relatively autonomous actions by people who, in most cases, did not belong to the criminal underworld and whose motivations varied widely. The leadership was localized and located in the caste groups or in smaller migratory communities based on linguistic or regional identities. However, there was an identification of the localized groups with the larger community. The speed with which the warring groups appeared on the streets and in the alleys pointed towards the process that had been going on for quite some time and that had helped to crystallize associational and conflicting identities making such massive mobilizations possible in the course of these riots. So, although a variety of motives went into the making of the riots, the lines between 'we' and 'they' were drawn along communal lines. All other motives and identities tended to dissolve into communal identity at that point of time. Caste, class, region and occupation were subordinated to the communal identity.

However, this was only for the time being. There were no congealed communal identities, at least for quite some time to come. The relative population of the Hindus in the Muslim-dominated areas or the Muslims in the Hindu-dominated areas did not show a major decline over the years, despite a few migrations. The Hindus, despite endeavours from various quarters to dissuade them, kept participating in the Muharram processions (Masselos 1982: 57). There were no communal riots again till 1929 and soon other loyalties manifested in different kinds of sectarian strifes. The Sunnis attacked the Bohras in 1904 and the Julahas in 1908 at the time of Muharram. In 1911, on Muharram day, Muslims and Hindus fought together against the police and in the ensuing police firing many Hindus were killed and injured along with many Muslims (Masselos 1976: 83–7).

II

The other occasion for a massive mobilization was the famous protest by the workers and others against Tilak's arrest and conviction in June–July 1908. Viewed against the background of ambiguous and indifferent relationship between the nationalists and millworkers, the events of 1908 stood as a towering instance of protest by the workers for the nationalist cause. Tilak was arrested on 24 June 1908. His first hearing was fixed on 29 June. From then until 29 July, that is, for a period of one month, there were almost regular protests in the city by workers, traders, petty shop-keepers and students. A six-year sentence was passed on him on 22 July and it was reported that an oath was taken in the mill areas to observe one-day strike for each year of the sentence. From 23rd to 28th all mills remained closed. The workers came out on the streets, held demonstrations, attacked the Whites and fought the police and military while the latter lathi-charged them or fired on them. At the end of it, many people had died, and many more were injured and arrested.

What propelled the workers to resort to such unprecedented level of defiance to register their protests against official action? The most favourite contemporary official explanation, supported by a large section of the press, was an organized conspiracy by Tilak and his followers. The pro-Tilak section of the press, however, completely discounted this interpretation of the 'disturbances' by stating that 'all this talk of secret emissaries is unmitigated moonshine' (*Rashtra-mat* 1 August 1908; in *RNP* 1 August 1908). Some mocked the government for failing to discover the supposed roots of the conspiracy. The Bombay police authorities themselves were confused about the agency behind the 'disorder'. In a revealing sentence the commissioner of police wrote that the mill workers had 'no organization, no leader, no common object and no weapons other than stones' (*JD* 1908, vol. 99, p. 141). The 'extremist' nationalist press also queried: 'why (would) ill-fed, ill-clad and half-starved people (should) by one common impulse strike work and . . . do deeds, which expose them to the fire of trained military men?' (*Rashtramat* 29 July 1908; in *RNP* 1 August 1908). Their explanation was that the workers and others were agitated because of the injustice done to Tilak by the government (ibid. Also, *Bombay Samachar* 31 July; *Indian Spectator* 1 August; *Mahratta* 2 August; *Rashtramat* 1 August; *Kal* 31 July; in *RNP* 1 August 1908. *Sanj Vartman* 5 August; *Gujarati* 2 August; *Bombay Samachar* 4 August; *Kesari* 4 August; *Chikitsak* 5 August; in *RNP* 8 August 1908).

But Tilak was not the only nationalist leader to be at the receiving end of the prosecution by the Bombay government. Many others were tried and convicted before him. Moreover, when Tilak was convicted in 1897, there were no protests by the workers then. So what had changed by 1908?

The nationalists did not have much practical interest in the workers. And whenever they took a stand it was not in favour of the mill workers even on crucial issues like long hours of work. The workers were left to the non-Brahman activists and philanthropists like Bengali, Lokhanday, Bole and Keluskar who did some welfare and rudimentary organizational work among them. These people were not sympathetic to Tilak's way of thinking. It is true that they did not have much influence on the activities of the workers but they were the only ones in touch with them.

A more immediate and potent form of influence on the workers was exercised by the jobbers. There is some evidence that Tilak and his followers had approached the jobbers in order to reach to the workers (JD, F.No. 5059, point 14). But these people, along with some others, were warned by the authorities not to create any problems. In any case, it would have been too much for any recognizable person to antagonize the authorities as well as the mill owners by inciting strikes and riots. Similarly, the 'Brahmin clerks' in the mills, whom the authorities, trying to find scapegoats, belatedly blamed for 'engineering' the riots (ibid., points 71 and 72), had much to lose by any such activity. In fact, what rendered the task of law-enforcing agencies even more difficult was the absence of any recognizable bodies or persons whom they could approach or command to control the workers.

It is true that Tilak and his followers became somewhat active among the mill workers during 1907–8, but their involvement was too brief and impermanent; their activities and organization among the workers were never strong enough to mobilize support at this level when people would go for total defiance of authorities both at the workplace and outside it and dare to challenge the might of the state. The fearless resistance offered by the workers and others to the police and troops revealed the very strong motivation behind their protests. This motivation and zeal derived from a source different from what the organization and activities by a few half-interested individuals could manage.

Right since the 1890s, Tilak had become somewhat involved in Bombay's political events. He was much upset by the riots of 1893 in Bombay and other parts of India. He also praised the mill workers for taking retaliatory action during the riots (*Mahratta* 20 August 1893, in Cashman 1975: 68–9). In order to dissuade the Hindus from participating in the Muharram rituals and to send a message to the British officials, he initiated the public celebration of Ganapati festivals by introducing several changes in the format of this traditionally popular festival (ibid.: 75–97). These innovations, though initially introduced in Pune, soon became popular throughout Maharashtra. The government officials feared that the festivals were a vehicle for spreading seditious messages (*SMHFM* II: 204–6). But it seems to be an overexcited reaction of an apprehensive officialdom and the festivals in the early years were mostly used as channels to unite the Hindus and berate the Muslims, if the songs sung during the celebrations were any indication. For example, one of the songs exhorted the Hindus to remember that:

The Arya religion is superior, other religions will not help you. The Ghodepir [Muslim *tabut*] is not worthy of your salutations (*JD* 1894, vol. 287, pp. 252–3. Quoted in Cashman 1975: 66, fn. 81).

Another song went along the same lines:

> Oh! Why have you abandoned today the Hindu religion? . . .
> Do not at all venerate the *tabuts*,
> The cow is our mother, do not forget her.
> (*JD* 1894, vol. 287, pp. 263–4; in ibid.: 78)

There were a profusion of similar songs and sentiments in the early phase of the movement. But Tilak also had other aims in mind. He wanted this and other festivals to become channels for the politicization of the masses. Once he commented in the *Kesari* (on 6 September 1896): 'Why shouldn't we convert the large religious festivals into mass political rallies? Will it not be possible for political activities to enter the humblest cottages of the villages through such means?' (in ibid.: 79).

In Bombay city also these festivals were celebrated with much enthusiasm in various quarters. The approximate number of festivals celebrated in Bombay city were 35 in 1895, 68 in 1896, 40–4 in

1900, 45 in 1906 and 46 in 1908 (ibid.: 226). The Bombay workers had also established their own Ganapati festivals modelled on the new lines.

The nature and character of these festivals began to change around 1900. They now acquired an anti-government tone. Songs exhorting people to abandon liquor, to adopt Swadeshi, to oppose the policies of the government, to regenerate Indian industries began to be sung in many of the Ganapati *melas.* Although the negative references to the Muslim rulers still remained and the fights of the Marathas against them were highlighted, it was through these channels that Tilak and others endeavoured to take an anti-imperialist stance. Thus, in 1901, in the course of the Shivaji festival in Pune, declared that 'Shivaji was greater than all European heroes' because he did not believe in appropriation of other's property but in the 'redemption of his religion and co-religionists and the deliverance of Brahmins and cattle from molestation at the hands of the Muhammedans' (*SMHFM* II: 210). Again, in 1902, he praised the Boers in South Africa who fought against the British by adopting a 'system of warfare . . . which Shivaji had adopted against the Muhammadans' (ibid.: 211).

Therefore, part of the political education of the workers in the nationalist ideology took place through the medium of these religious festivals and through religious, even communal, vocabulary. Beyond doubt, the workers had their own economic grievances and they were struggling to get them resolved. They also had anti-imperialist feelings through their experiences at the time of the famines and the plague. When Tilak came to attend their puja and spoke to them on other occasions on temperance and *swadeshi*, exhorting them to remember their ancestry, they must have felt elated and gratified. Even before that, through Ganapati and Shivaji festivals, a process of deifying Tilak had started by putting his photographs beside those of Ganesh and Shivaji. The workers who also initiated and participated in such festivals, must have known Tilak long before he came to speak to them. Thus, in the minds of the workers and the poor in general as well as the lower middle classes, the image of Tilak was that of a demi-God who was fighting against the British and suffering at the latter's hands for their benefit. So, when asked what Tilak had done for them, the workers 'unhesitatingly declared that he was fighting their battle with the government and that he was prosecuted because he attempted to rescue the people from the demon of drink. And when they were told that it was not due to this that he was convicted, 'they flew into a rage' (*Oriental Review* 29 July 1908; in *RNP* 1 August 1908). For many workers he was 'an incarnation of Vishnu' (Cashman 1975: 180). More often than not religious channels were used to disseminate the views of Tilak. It was reported that Tilak's 'doings and sayings were further spread by the many religious Hindu preachers, who are daily in the habit of reading Puranas to the millhands in their *chals*' (JD F.No. 5059, para 69). Some posters put in the mills and other places to mobilize people stated that 'the man who would continue to work would be thought guilty of killing kine' (*The Times* 19 August 1908; quoted in Chicherov 1966: 593).

The process of myth-making reached such an extent that superhuman stories had started to circulate. One, for example, was that 'the ship on which Tilak was being taken away had been turned back by Divine Providence' (ibid.). In fact, Tilak was transferred from Bombay in a train. In this situation it was no wonder that the 'multitude of people believed that Tilak was an incarnation of God and that a diabolical Government had put him behind bars' (ibid.). This sentiment was reflected even in the slogans shouted by the workers like 'Tilak Maharaj ki Jai' and in their demand put before S.M. Edwardes, when he went to the mill areas to pacify the workers: 'Let us have a look at Tilak Maharaj' (*Indian Spectator* 1 August 1908; in *RNP* 1 August 1908).

These were the sentiments which propelled the workers towards valiant and desperate acts to articulate their feelings of resentment. At the same time, however, this religious appeal alienated those sections of workers who came from different religious backgrounds. The Muslim workers, who formed a sizeable section of the total workforce not only kept away from the movement but also resented it. The police authorities congratulated themselves for the fact that

> throughout the trouble the Mahomedans kept aloof, though strenuous attempts were made by the Hindus to induce them to join forces. . . . It is believed that had the disturbances continued much longer this feeling might have eventually brought the Mahomedan operatives into actual collision with their Hindu co-workers. (JD F.No. 5061: 6)

Therefore, despite the lukewarm response of the nationalists, including Tilak, towards workers' grievances and the equivocal relationship between them, Tilak's personal appeal among Bombay workers remained quite high till the end.

The sentiments of the workers towards Tilak, therefore, operated in the arena where the religious and the political intermingled. The workers' protests against Tilak's imprisonment and their continued attachment to him cannot be explained by the fact of what he had done for them (which was pretty little) or even in terms of workers' nationalist feelings. Their strong motivation seemed to derive from a domain beyond these. At the same time, however, their actions cannot be taken out of the historical context which turned Tilak from a provincial (Maharashtrian) and city (Pune)-based politician into the most prominent Indian nationalist leader fighting against the might of the British government in support of the Indian, particularly Hindu, customs and practices and for the liberation of the Indian people from foreign domination. Therefore, what did not happen in 1897, at the time of his previous incarceration, became possible in 1908, particularly with the working classes of Bombay.

III

The general strike of 1919 in the Bombay textile industry was a watershed. It was a link between the earlier forms of individual, departmental, mill-level and multi-mill-level strikes of the earlier period and the general industrial strikes of the later period. It is not that the earlier forms disappeared later on. But even they acquired a new poignancy and militancy and inspired a new cohesiveness among the participants. The scale and success of the 1919 strike heralded a new era in the history of industrial relations in Bombay which culminated in the great strike of 1928 which was unprecedented in scale and in the formation of workers' consciousness. The leaders and organizations operating in the mill areas until 1918 became more or less redundant after 1919 and a new phase of leadership and organizational initiatives became relevant after that. The workers in Bombay successfully resisted the employers' attempts to cut wages in the mid-1920s even while the employers in some other industrial centres like Ahmedabad managed to do so. The collective strength and consciousness of the workers in the 1920s were on a higher level and it was different from those of either the preceding or succeeding decades. The strike in 1919 lasted for about 20 days, from 9 to 28 January, and, barring a few violent incidents, remained peaceful. The workers exhibited firm resolve and solidarity.

The contemporary observers, particularly in the initial phase of general strikes and militant action by the workers immediately following the War, were vexed to find 'the capacity of the operatives to remain on strikes for considerable periods despite the lack of any visible organization' (*IDC* 1922: 2). The Government of Bombay, after the 1919 strike, though surprised at the apparent lack of leadership despite such a level of industrial protest, talked about the 'probability of some controlling organization' (Chandavarkar 1981: 603). Similarly, the *Bombay Chronicle* commented in February 1924 that 'it is absurd to suppose that the men are lacking in leadership . . . it is clear that there is good sound leadership among them *somewhere*' (quoted in ibid.: 604, emphasis added).

How did this mobilization occur? Attempts have been made to explain this phenomenon. Newman has underlined the role of the jobbers as the leaders of the workers, while Chandavarkar emphasizes the role of the mill districts in sustaining the movement.

The jobbers did perform a certain level of leadership role at many junctures. They organized meetings, sent petitions, presented demands and represented the workers at various commissions of enquiries. Similarly, the neighbourhood provided the arena, particularly in the later period, where workers exchanged information, confabulated with each other, heard their well-wishers and potential leaders both from within their own ranks as well as from among the outsiders. It also served as the base for sustaining the strikes as it was here that credits in kind and cash were arranged and moral and material support of various sorts were given and received not only in times of conflicts and strikes but otherwise as well.

There is, however, one problem in attributing such a pivotal role to either the jobbers or the neighbourhood. The jobbers had been in existence almost since the beginning of the industry and the mill districts had also emerged since the 1890s. So why was it that the coordination of industry-wide strikes could be effected only after the War and not before that? This point leads us to an exploration of the workers' consciousness gradually forming itself around the demands related to their works in the mills and the growing realization of their common grievances and strength.

The behaviour-pattern of the workers had been sometimes explained in terms of their supposedly pre-industrial mentality. Newman talks about 'pre-industrial attitudes and relationships'. Moreover, there is the notion that the 'factory routine' obliterates such consciousness (Newman 1981: 1). He rightly points out that the earlier consciousness entered the new environment. But he very narrowly identifies it with caste and, even more narrowly, with the institution of jobber. Caste was a variable and evolving phenomenon while the institution of jobber was completely a modern creation, put in place for assisting the peculiar industrial system in colonial setting.

Ravinder Kumar is even more emphatic on pre-industrial nature of workers' mobilization. Analysing the general strike of 1919, he characterizes it 'as a species of a working class *Jacquerie*' which 'exhibited all the features of a peasant uprising: complete spontaneity; an absence of class consciousness, class organization and formal leadership; and finally, the expression of long standing grievances and pent up frustrations through a popular explosion' (1971: 3).

Although this evaluation succinctly comprehends the apparent formlessness of the strike of 1919 in the beginning, it misses a few vital points. Even though their activities in the initial stage took unorganized forms, the workers were fully cognizant of their grievances. Secondly, the strike was not particularly violent. The occasional violence which occurred was purposive and selective, not mindless and indiscriminate. Its purpose was to get the mills closed and achieve a full mobilization. Finally, there is no contradiction between spontaneity and consciousness. There can hardly be a movement without spontaneity and, in any case, the spontaneity of today is the accumulated consciousness of yesterdays. The cumulative experience of resistance and protests, combined with the generalized sufferings of the War-years, produced the first general strike. The strikes of the pre-War period could cover only a few mills at most, whereas the strikes of the post-War years could spread to all the mills. Spontaneity of the pre-War years was limited in scope; the spontaneity of the post-War period was realized at a much higher level. Spontaneity was not a static thing. It kept developing with the growth of consciousness among the workers.

This will take us into an exploration of the various forms of resistance and protests offered by the workers over the previous decades. Absenteeism, go-slow, leaving the work for short periods, and strikes were the forms of resistance offered by the workers against the difficult conditions of work. The emphasis on the nature of their protests changed over the years. For example, strikes became the more important form in later years. It should be clear, however, that no Chinese Wall can be erected between the supposedly distinct phases and different forms of protests, because, after all, it is the activities of the former phase which leads to the later one. Moreover, there is no linear progressive path; reverses occur quite frequently. But, as the industry matured and more and more workers constantly experienced the city life, the collective learning and its dissemination both in the urban and rural areas (from where the workers came) became wider in scope. The new migrants did not need to know the details of the industrial experience firsthand. The learning might occur from the old hands who had returned to the villages either permanently owing to failing health or joblessness or from those who moved to-and-fro between the city and the country for various purposes and under different circumstances. This previously acquired knowledge would have helped the newcomers in coping with the industrial situation more efficiently than would have been the case for a complete novice. The later newcomers, therefore, were not total greenhorns as they were the inheritors of the collective wisdom drawn and forged from the previous experiences. The collectivities were emerging and getting wider and more organized not only within the framework of the industry but the city as a whole. The numerous caste, regional and community associations which were springing in the city at regular intervals and which were operating in the working-class neighbourhood also helped the workers to fight their industrial battles and sustain them more securely outside the mills. It was on the point of getting more wages to offset the cost of living that their demands were getting concentrated now. The prices of the basic necessities of life had increased so much that all the workers were affected by this. This common demand combined with some success in frequent strikes during the War-years created a feeling of solidarity among them and a sense of strength *vis-à-vis* their employers. The experiences of protests and strikes tended to create a basis for relatively swifter mobilization at the industrial level. Thus began the new phase in the history of industrial relations in Bombay bringing general strikes in its wake. It was not the formal trade unions but the general strikes which separated the post-War years from the pre-War ones. And it was not the educated, mass-oriented middle-class individuals who, by forming trade unions, changed the course of workers' struggles, but the workers themselves, by entering the arena of general strikes, created the conditions for a wider solidarity thereby facilitating the growth of trade unions.

However, this solidarity and the sense of class identity were limited in nature. Two very important groups—the women and the Dalits—were not fully integrated. The existence of separate enclaves of women's work and the discrimination against the Dalits were responsible for this situation. The women did strike work in many instances and they also supported the collective actions by other workers. But they were not actively engaged in larger actions of the period. On many occasions, even their demands were not taken into consideration.

DYNAMICS OF IDENTITY-FORMATION AND MOBILIZATION

The process of identity-formation among the workers was shaped by various socio-cultural and political factors encompassing their inherited as well as acquired consciousness. The identities of caste, religion, language and region were carried by the rural folk seeking jobs over to the city. These were parts of their inherited baggage which had been handed over to them through generations and had defined their existence, outlook, attitude and behaviour until then. This does not mean, however, that these were static phenomena admitting no change. In the context of Maharashtra, these identities were constantly reshaped and redefined throughout the seventeenth and eighteenth centuries by the Bhakti movement and the battles and wars which the peasant armies and guerrillas had fought against the regional and central authorities. The whole array of Bhakti saints had sought to shape the religious and social outlook of the people at various levels.

Yet there was certain stability in a peasant society which was reflected in the relative fixity of status, position and attitudes following a generally predictable pattern. The impact of the British rule proved to be destabilizing for the Indian society, particularly in the urban situation. Here the social, political and economic changes were novel and rapid, various socio-political identities jostled with each other, sometimes in a symbiotic relationship and, at other times, conflicting and vying for supremacy. Bombay was a particularly pertinent example of this. During the nineteenth century, it underwent a reasonably fast economic and demographic growth. People from various economic, social and linguistic background thronged the city in pursuit of business and jobs. The sheer variety of people living in Bombay with their distinct languages, dresses, colours and occupations was quite noticeable by the end of the nineteenth century.

The marginal and uprooted peasants who flocked to Bombay in search of jobs brought their old-world socio-cultural identities with them. These were rooted in their consciousness of caste, religion, region and language. In the city they stayed with their relations and the people from their own regions. In many cases, the old workers who visited their homes prompted their relations and neighbours to come to the city for jobs. These old workers also helped them in finding the jobs and accommodated and supported them until they managed to find some work. The process of finding the jobs was difficult and retaining them was even more so. For this purpose, many formal and informal networks were established, used, activated and nurtured. Caste, kinship, region and language provided the most important social channels through which the job-seekers were brought, sustained and put on to the jobs in the city. These inherited identities proved to be extremely potent sustaining factors in the urban lives of the working masses. The workers from a particular caste, region and language tended to congregate in particular localities. These small collectivities gave them a sense of security and ease. They also helped to sustain them in times of adversities. These identities were maintained and strengthened through the endogamous marriages and continuing rural links.

In this way, the city environment, instead of eroding the old-world ties, reinforced and strengthened them further. But the process of reinforcement was not simple and unidirectional. The inherited identities were actively reshaped and remoulded. In the city, the terms of reference of these identities became wider. Therefore, the term 'Maratha' referred to a group of endogamous sub-castes from various regions of Maharashtra; the 'Bhaiyas' signified the Hindu migrants from north India, particularly the United Provinces; the 'depressed classes' denoted a wide group of untouchable castes. The Indian society was well aware of caste. However, what was happening, particularly in the urban areas was the construction of communities. Groups of endogamous castes were being transformed into putatively uniform communities, the members of which even now might not have nuptial relationships. The cohesive caste identity which earlier belonged to the group of adjoining villages could now extend to the entire region or the state or even the whole country. The proliferation of caste-based associations[1] in the mill areas and naming of various institutions including hospitals along the caste and community lines attested to the fact that the urban environment had expanded the reach of the community and turned a cultural phenomenon into a political one.

The city-life brought the workers in contact not only with people from their own caste and region but a variety of others as well. They interacted with middle-class educated persons professing various ideologies. These contacts with advocates of cow-protection, nationalists like Tilak and his followers, and later the trade unionists and the communists had their impacts on the workers. These incipient communal, nationalist and leftist ideas were to be picked by the workers in the course of time.

Although these mobilizations occurred around distinctly different identities, there were certain similar patterns discernible among them. One characteristic of these mobilizations was the lack of visible leadership. On all the three occasions the government authorities and commentators vaguely talked awhile about 'wire-pullers', 'ring-leaders' and 'mischief-makers' but failed to lay fingers on any individuals who played leadership roles and whom they could punish or with whom they could negotiate. In fact, the absence of any leadership in the modern sense was quite remarkable. The workers seemed to operate not only in a relatively autonomous domain but also in an arena where the self-conscious leaders did not have much role to play.

The most important characteristic, however, was that all these mobilizations, though of completely different nature and character, seemed to be based on the core consisting of the Maratha workers, who had wide links inside the city and some security of their rural links to fall back upon. A cohesiveness was also induced due to the newly emerging Maratha mass identity which was crucial both in the city and in the Presidency (O'Hanlon 1985: 41–9). Various castes among the Hindus such as Prabhus, Sonars, Sutars and the Marathas were organizing their caste associations for improvement of their social and economic position. In 1885 a group of Konkani Marathas numbering about 25,000 and consisting of 'millhands, office peons and private messengers' founded organizations called Kshatra Dharma Pratipadak and Dharma Fundolejaka Sabha. The caste activities among what is termed as the 'Maratha-Kunbi caste cluster' was particularly noticeable. There was a rapid emergence of Maratha identity during the 1860s and 1870s and several endogamous Maharashtrian peasant castes began to claim the Maratha identity, along with Kshatriya status. There was a constant movement among the Kunbi peasantry in the whole of Maharashtra to register themselves as Marathas in the censuses. Many of them had also started wearing the sacred threads (*janeyu*) associated with the twice-born among the Hindus. In Bombay city, this movement for upward social mobility was particularly noticeable with all the Kunbi migrants registering themselves as Marathas while nobody registered himself/herself as Kunbi in the census of 1901. This social consolidation was also reflected in political assertion and as this group formed about half of the total city's population and more than half of the textile workforce, no big mobilization was possible without taking them into account. Numerous caste-based associations mushroomed in the mill areas. Thus we find Maratha Aikyechhoo Sabha, Maratha Temperance Association, Maratha Educational Conference, Maratha Advisory Board and a host of other bodies based on this particular identity.

This core was big enough among the workers to effect a bigger mobilization. Thus, although the riots of 1893 were also against the minority Muslim workers, all the mills were forced to close and the masses of the workers were ranged on the Hindu side. Similarly, in 1908, although the Muslim workers were said to have resented the strikes and the consequent loss of their incomes, this never had any affect on the course of events. All the mills were forced to close and massive demonstrations occurred in mill areas and many of them led to violent confrontations with the police and military resulting in loss of many lives. The Marathas from the Konkan region, who were preponderant among the mill workers, were said to be mainly responsible for this mobilization. During the strike of 1919 also, although the Muslim weavers were among the most militant strikers, they were not significant enough to cause a general mobilization. The other groups like the 'Pardeshis', that is, Hindu workers from U.P. and the Dalit workers, although significant in number, could not bring about such mobilization. This mobilization was again based on the powerful group belonging to the 'Maratha-Kunbi caste cluster' with great mobilizational potential. Throughout they formed more than half of the total workforce. Over the years, as the weaving sections were added and expanded, many of them moved over to this better-paying department where they accounted for about 62 per cent of all the weavers. The weavers' capacity for mobilization and propensity for militancy were based on this regionally powerful group which was upwardly mobile in social and political contexts and had their rural connections largely intact to fall back upon in times of adversity. Without taking this group into account, no big mobilization was possible in the working-class areas. When this group was won over to the communists in the late 1920s, the latter became a big force to reckon with. S.H. Jhabvala, an important labour leader in Bombay, commented on this phenomenon:

> Labour activity in Bombay is largely Mahratta in its nature. The leaders must be conversant firstly with the Mahratta language, secondly with Mahratta habits of life and with a good deal of social outlook upon life that is Mahratta partly in its character. (Chandavarkar 1981: 646)

However, even though the workers operated in a relatively autonomous domain, with respect to some of the mobilizations and the moving force behind the bigger mobilizations was provided by the Maratha workers, the ideas were derived from many sources. Autonomy of action was guided by inter-connecting discourse. The ideologies behind the bigger mobilizations transcended the parochial boundaries and sometimes assumed a pan-Indian character. The overarching identities woven around religious community, nation and class were based on the narrower identities, but they also tended to subsume them in the course of time integrating increasingly more numbers around them.

The communal riots, as witnessed in 1893, disappeared from the map of Bombay for more than thirty-five years, only to reappear in 1929. Nationalist sentiments were more constantly present, but its manifestations were only occasionally witnessed. Class experiences and struggles were repeated everyday either at the workplace or in the neighbourhood. It does not mean, however, that class identity was more of a presence in workers' lives than religious or caste identity. The fact that the class identity was antagonistic made its presence more marked in the records. Religious or caste identity was more broadly accepted and, therefore, more generally and subtly present. Almost since a child was conceived until s/he died, it was operative in various ways. We have seen how it was working during the nationalist mobilization. It was definitely present at home and in the neighbourhood; but it was also present at the shop floor, when a new machine was particularly worshipped and exorcized of demons, when religious holidays were demanded and granted, and where caste discriminations were observed in the name of religion.

Thus the community/caste identity was not eroded at the time of class mobilization, nor was the class identity erased during communal mobilization. We have to make a distinction between identity and mobilization. Identity is historical and ontological, whereas mobilization is contingent. Identity is historically constructed over a period of time. It is also ontological in the sense that lived experiences are sought to be structured in terms of available knowledge-categories. Mobilization, on the other hand, is caused by a specific constellation of circumstances. In fact, quite often the putatively conflicting identities help strengthen the solidarity at the time of mobilization.

REFERENCES

Government Records and Reports

BSEC	*Bombay Strike Enquiry Committee*, 1928–9, Proceedings.
Census 1881	*Census of the City and Island of Bombay taken on 17 February, 1881, by T.S. Weir* (Bombay, 1883).
Census 1901	*Census of India, 1901*, vols. X & XI (Bombay, 1901).
FC 1875	*Bombay Factory Commission, 1875* (Bombay, 1875).
FC 1885	*Bombay Factory Commission, 1885* (Bombay, 1885).
HD	Home Department
IDC	*Report of the Industrial Disputes Committee* (Bombay, 1922).
IFLC	*Indian Factory Labour Commission, 1908, Report and Evidences*, 2 vols. (Simla, 1908).
JD	Judicial Department
RCL	*Report of the Royal Commission on Labour in India, 1929* (HMSO, London, 1931).
SMHFM	*Source Material for a History of the Freedom Movement in India*, Government of Bombay, vol. II, 1885–1920 (Bombay, 1958).

Newspapers and Periodicals

BC	*Bombay Chronicle*
ITJ	*Indian Textile Journal*
RNP	*Report on Native Newspapers*
TOI	*Times of India*

Books and Articles

Bagchi, A.K. (1990), 'Working Class Consciousness', *Economic and Political Weekly*, vol. XXV, no. 30, PE-54–PE-60.

Burnett-Hurst, A.R. (1925), *Labour and Housing in Bombay: A Study in the Economic Condition of the Wage-Earning Classes of Bombay*, London: P.S. King.

Cashman, R.I. (1975), *The Myth of the Lokamanya: Tilak and Mass Politics in Maharashtra*, Berkeley and Los Angeles: University of California Press.

Chakrabarty, Dipesh (1989), *Rethinking Working-Class History: Bengal, 1890–1940,* New Delhi: Oxford University Press.

——— (1976), 'Communal Riots and Labour: Bengal Jute Mill Hands in the 1890s', *Occasional Paper No. 11*, Kolkata: Centre for Studies in Social Sciences.

Chakrabarty, Dipesh and Ranajit Das Gupta (1981), 'Some Aspects of Labour History of Bengal in the Nineteenth Century: Two Views', *Occasional Paper No. 40*, Kolkata: CSSS.

Chandavarkar, R. (1981), 'Workers' Politics and Mill Districts in Bombay between the Wars', *MAS*, XV, 3.

Chicherov, A.I. (1966), 'Tilak's Trial and the Bombay Political Strike of 1908', in N.M. Goldberg and I.M. Reisner (ed.), *Tilak and Struggle for Indian Freedom*, New Delhi: PPH.

Das Gupta, R. (1979), 'Material Conditions and Behavioural Aspects of Calcutta Working Class, 1875-1899', *Occasional Paper No. 22*, Kolkata: CSSS.

Dobbin, Christine (1972), *Urban Leadership in Western India: Politics and Communities in Bombay City, 1840-85*, London: Oxford University Press.

Freitag, Sandria (1990), *Collective Action and Community: Public Arenas and the Emergence of Communalism in North India*, New Delhi: Oxford University Press.

Ghosh, Parimal (1990), 'Communalism and Colonial Labour: Experience of Calcutta Jute Mill Workers, 1880–1930', *EPW*, vol. XXV, no. 30.

Karnik, V.B. (1967), *Strikes in India*, Mumbai: Manaktalas.

Kelman, J.H. (1923), *Labour in India: A Study of Conditions of Indian Women in Modern Industry*, London: George Allen and Unwin.

Kumar, Ravinder (1971), 'The Bombay Textile Strike, 1919', *IESHR*, VIII, 1.

McLane, John R. (1977), *Indian Nationalism and the Early Congress*, Princeton: Princeton University Press.

Masselos, J.C. (1976), 'Power in Bombay "Moholla", 1904–1915: An Initial Exploration into the World of the Indian Urban Muslim', *South Asia*, VI.

——— (1982), 'Change and Custom in the Format of the Bombay Mohurrum during the Nineteenth and Twentieth Centuries', *South Asia*, n.s., 5, no. 2.

Morris, M.D. (1965), *The Emergence of an Industrial Labour Force in India: A Study of the Bombay Cotton Mills, 1854-1947*, Berkeley: University of California Press.

Newman, Richard (1981), *Workers and Unions in Bombay, 1918-29: A Study of Organization in the Cotton Mills*, Canberra: Australian National University Monographs.

O'Hanlon, Rosalind (1985), *Caste, Conflict, and Ideology: Mahatma Jotirao Phule and Low Caste Protest in Nineteenth-Century Western India*, Cambridge: Cambridge University Press.

Pandey, Gyanendra (1983), 'Rallying Round the Cow: Sectarian Strife in the Bhojpuri Region, *c.* 1888-1917', in R. Guha (ed.), *Subaltern Studies*, vol. II, New Delhi: Oxford University Press.

Robb, Peter (1986), 'The Challenge of Gau Mata: British Policy and Religious Change in India, 1880–1916', *MAS*, 20, 2.

Sen, Sukomal (1977), *The Working Class of India: History of Emergence and Movement*, Kolkata: K.P. Bagchi & Company.

Upadhyay, S.B. (2004), *Existence, Identity and Mobilization: The Cotton Millworkers of Bombay, 1890-1919*, New Delhi: Manohar.

CHAPTER 14

Farmers Against Globalization?: The Role of Karnataka Rajya Raitha Sangha

M.N. PANINI*

INTRODUCTION

Karnataka's distinct contribution to peasant movements in India has been the formation in 1980 of the Karnataka Rajya Raitha Sangha (KRRS), a Kannada name that translates into English as the Karnataka State Farmers' Organization. The KRRS is distinct because it recognized that the 'local' problems of the peasants could be traced to global trends controlled by multinational agribusiness corporations operating in concert with pliable governments. The KRRS adopted the 'direct action' method of mobilization and protest that dramatically debunked authorities and reduced them into passive spectators in public displays of defiance. Professor M.D. Nanjundaswamy (MDN), a socialist in the mould of Ram Manohar Lohia was for long the undisputed leader of the movement. He carefully crafted the 'direct action' strategy and emerged as a prominent leader in the global network against globalization. He was such a militant, knowledgeable and eloquent opponent of globalization that even ministers and government officials hesitated to challenge his assertions in public. MDN's impact was so powerful that he even undermined the legitimacy of scientists who supported the application of modern biotechnology in agriculture. A leading biotechnologist and a member of the Genetic Engineering Approval Committee of the Government of India felt so exasperated with what he called 'half truths'[1]

*I dedicate this paper to my colleague and friend Professor T.K. Oommen who has been a pioneer in the study of social movements and protests.

propagated by MDN that he even referred to him as a CIA agent determined to prevent India from emerging as an independent global power! Such wild statements made by the responsible scientist reveal the powerlessness he experienced in dealing with unrelenting propaganda against the application of biotechnology in agriculture. This contrasts with the authority and respect that an earlier generation of Indian scientists commanded in ushering the 'green revolution' in India. In other words, MDN became a principal global actor in the drama that undermined the legitimacy of the discourse of development based on the application of modern science and technology.

In this paper I attempt to assess the role of KRRS under MDN's leadership to study the dialectic between the anti-globalization movement (AGM) on the one hand and the processes generated by globalization of agriculture on the other. There is a view that follows Hardt and Negri's thesis of regarding AGM as an 'emerging' movement that uses 'networks of networks' based on 'weak' relations to evolve antagonistic strategies that subvert the hegemony of the 'empire'[2]. I propose to study the role of KRRS as an instance of AGM to assess this point of view. My study points to the need to assess KRRS as an instance of AGM at several levels. At the local level the KRRS failed to convert the farmers from their economism despite its astounding success. At the national level as well, the KRRS failed to reverse the trend towards globalization due to diversities of approaches of different, state-level, farmer/peasant associations and of several NGOs. Despite these failures, it is possible to note that at the global level of the AGM the KRRS played a crucial role in undermining the hegemony of multinational corporations, multilateral institutions of governance and their supportive state structures. This study of the KRRS movement also points to the weakness of the AGM in offering viable and practical alternatives to the institutions that prop up the current regime of globalization. In the end I propose to examine whether this failure leads to the acceptance of globalization as a *fait accompli*.

THE SETTING

In judging the KRRS, I rely mainly on my fieldwork conducted intermittently during the years 1998–2003 on agribusiness in the state of Karnataka in India. The Government of Karnataka was the first in the country to spell out a coherent agricultural policy that formally allowed the entry of private corporations in the field of agriculture.[3] The intention was to generate a growth dynamic in the rural economy that was for long suffering from the dominance of government and governmental controls imposed ostensibly to meet the requirements of food security. The new policy recommended market-oriented agriculture with emphasis on the cultivation of commercial crops such as cotton and oil seeds, seed production, horticulture and floriculture besides the development of poultry, livestock farming and dairy development. The policy encouraged the participation of agribusiness corporations through contract farming and the application of modern biotechnology in agriculture. My fieldwork sought to assess the social implications of the new agricultural policy. Even as I was engaged in my fieldwork I heard echoes of MDN's green discourse in the villages and small towns and in the government offices that I visited. I could note that MDN's discourse had sensitized even the technicians working in some of the private floriculture 'poly houses' that dotted the rural landscape north of Bengaluru. Private floriculture firms were engaged in exercises that sought to reduce the use of chemical fertilizers and pesticides by increasing the use of poultry litter and farmyard manure. Even officials of the department of agriculture had become sensitive to ecological issues and they proudly took me on a tour of a rundown fertilizer processing unit that they had converted into a granulated poultry litter plant to demonstrate their green orientation. They pointed out that the consumption of chemical fertilizers was showing a decline in Karnataka suggesting that it confirms the environmental awareness of the farmers of the state.

There was a general endorsement of MDN's discourse no doubt but it did not dampen the general enthusiasm for new crops and new techniques. In the agricultural fields both the discourse of modern agribusiness and MDN's ideology coexisted. Confrontations occurred only when MDN launched his direct democratic action campaigns against government policies and multinational agribusiness corporations. This situation kindled my interest to probe deeper into the role that the KRRS under MDN's leadership played in opposing trends of contemporary globalization in Karnataka.[4]

KRRS: TRAJECTORY OF ITS EVOLUTION AS AN ANTI-GLOBALIZATION MOVEMENT

The KRRS like several other peasant/farmer organizations in India is a child of the 'green revolution'. The KRRS was formed in 1980 when farmers of the Malaprabha and Ghataprabha irrigation areas agitating against the imposition of water tax and betterment levy[5] (a levy for the enhanced value of land after irrigation was provided) were fired upon by the police, leaving two farmers dead. In the beginning a Farmers' Coordination Committee consisting of independent peasant organizations from all over the state and representatives of political parties was set up to struggle against the adverse policies of the government. But as politicians had their own party agenda that prevented united action, a state-level organization—the KRRS—was formed with a specific provision to keep out political parties. Such an organization was required because the introduction of Green Revolution technology had eroded the self-reliance of peasants. Economic viability of agriculture now depended in a large measure on the decisions taken by government agencies in determining the prices of inputs and of outputs. The Green Revolution technology promoted the cultivation of high-yielding varieties (HYV) of seeds that had to be purchased from the agriculture department.[6] The farmer's dependence on external agencies for supplies of HYV seeds, chemical fertilizers and pesticides and electricity or diesel to energize pump sets to lift water converted agriculture from a gamble on the monsoons into a gamble on the decisions of the government. The government that was committed to the creation of a 'socialist pattern of society' controlled the supply and prices of critical inputs that had to be imported. Commitment to socialism also required the government to fix prices of agricultural products to ensure that food grains and other 'essential commodities'[7] are relatively cheap in the market. The farmers started complaining about agriculture having become a losing economic proposition; their cost of production kept increasing while the government deliberately kept the price of agricultural products under check to satisfy urban consumers. The KRRS under the leadership of MDN resorted to novel forms of collective protest such as *Rasta Roko* (road blockade) campaigns, mass siege and blockades of government offices, and mass protests and demonstrations to squeeze from successive governments free supply of electricity, loans at low rates of interest, loans waivers, remunerative prices for their agricultural outputs and such other benefits. MDN demonstrated his skills in organizing agitations and soon acquired a big reputation for his civil disobedience campaigns in which he called upon the farmers to refuse to pay their electricity bills or water taxes. At one stage in the 1980s, KRRS boasted a membership of more than 10 million members. He became adept at organizing mass demonstrations to ridicule government decisions that harmed the farming community. He courted arrest several times in defiance of policies and decisions that, in his view, harmed farmers' interests. His methods of public protests won him a large following among the farmers and he became the president of the KRRS. His capacity for organizing mammoth farmers' rallies created an aura around him and politicians as well as political parties tried to compete with each other to win over his favours. Although he was sceptical of electoral politics, in 1989 he got the KRRS registered as a political party and contested for the Davangere seat in the State Assembly elections. He lost the subsequent election in 1994 and the experience changed his mind about the role of KRRS in electoral politics. He said that electoral politics co-opts farmers into party politics thereby compromising with their collective interests.

In the 1980s, MDN emerged as a major peasant leader in national politics, but the era of green revolution agriculture confined him to the economism[8] of the middle and rich farmers. It was in the 1990s when liberal economic reforms were introduced in the country that he acquired a new global avatar, as it were. The state of Karnataka offered him an early opportunity to wrestle with the forces of contemporary globalization and elaborate his radically transformed vision of the world. In 1992, under his leadership the KRRS became perhaps the first farmers' organization to launch a movement against the Dunkel Proposals on the inclusion of agriculture and intellectual property rights under the WTO regime and he vehemently opposed it in the Karnataka Legislative Assembly. He was clear that the Dunkel Proposals would sacrifice the collective rights of Indian farmers to promote the interests of multinational agribusiness corporations. He organized a rally against the Dunkel Proposals in 1993 that attracted more than half a million farmers. Subsequently, the KRRS joined 200 other organizations worldwide to oppose the application of W.R. Grace and Company for a patent on a pesticidal extract from *neem* in the US Patent and Trade Mark Office.

The KRRS caught worldwide attention when MDN launched what he called seed satyagraha. MDN opposed the entry of Cargill Seeds into India. He contended that the seed corporation intended to erode the autonomy of the Indian farmer and compel him to purchase its branded seeds at the beginning of every agricultural season. He saw Cargill Seeds as a big threat to the agricultural tradition of producing one's own seeds and of exchanging seeds with other farmers. In

December 1992, as part of his seed satyagraha he led a group of about a thousand members of the *hasiru sene* (green army)—a youth wing of the KRRS—to ransack the office of Cargill Seeds India in Bangaluru. He repeated the act eight months later in a raid of the seed unit of the corporation in Bellary. The protesters used iron rods to damage property of the corporation and make a ceremonial bonfire of it, but MDN claimed that his campaign was Gandhian and 'non-violent' because it did not damage life but only inanimate objects. He argued that in fact it was the multinational corporations who were guilty of violence because they denied the poor their right to life!

MDN's next target of 'non-violent' attack was the Kentucky Fried Chicken (KFC) outlet that was inaugurated for the first time in India in Bangaluru. His reason was that the KFC was a part of Pepsico which had committed itself to the Export Promotion Council of India to bring modern livestock technology into India to increase meat exports. MDN argued that meat exports would not only deplete Indian cattle species but also undermine food security of the poor because enormous quantities of food grains would be converted into cattle feed.

MDN carried forward his struggle against globalization when the multinational agribusiness firm Monsanto decided in 1998 to introduce genetically modified cotton crop called Bt cotton in India by collaborating with some scientists of the Indian Institute of Science, Bangaluru, and with an Indian agribusiness firm called MAHYCO. MDN charged Monsanto of producing 'terminator seeds', that is, seeds that produce only sterile seeds so that farmers will become entirely dependent on the company for their seeds. He also argued that genetically modified (GM) crops were a major threat to the tradition of Indian agriculture because the new strain could diffuse to other plant varieties, thereby permanently changing the genetic biodiversity of India. In 1998 MDN launched 'Cremation of Monsanto' campaigns to mobilize the KRRS and to set fire to standing Bt cotton plants on some of the approved experimental plots in Karnataka. He also demanded that Indian scientists should terminate their collaboration with Monsanto and threatened to lay siege to the Indian Institute of Science to force them to do it. Partly in response to this campaign in June 2000 Monsanto's research and development facility in bio-informatics at the Institute was closed.

A major success of KRRS lies in casting doubts on the credibility of the government and of the scientists. MDN used modern media to challenge the claims made by the government, scientists and multinational corporations. A senior Indian scientist working in the Monsanto laboratories of the Indian Institute of Science told me that their field trials of Bt cotton had been successful both in regard to reduction of the use of pesticides and about the increase in yield, but as Herring points out, the data could be interpreted in several ways.[9]

KRRS' campaigns against globalization marked a new chapter in the history of peasant movements in India. The direct action campaigns he initiated provided agency to the farmers to embarrass the government and compel it to succumb to their demands. For instance, one effect of the Cremation of Monsanto campaign was the announcement of suspension of Bt cotton trials by the minister for agriculture in Karnataka (although I was told that suspension was later surreptitiously withdrawn). MDN trained KRRS farmers to repair their electricity transformers so that they need not approach the government electricity department that would have compelled them to clear their arrears before agreeing to undertake the repair. The KRRS therefore set a unique example in the peaceful defiance of authority. As a shrewd IPS officer battling the Naxalite movement (a Maoist guerrilla movement that has now spread to several states in India) that has recently surfaced put it, MDN was a 'Gandhian Naxalite'. He stated that the government could handle Naxalites with guns and it could handle Gandhians too by paying respect to service to Gandhi as the father of the nation, but it did not have an answer to this blend of Gandhi and Mao! While Gandhi advocated passive resistance, MDN, he said, shaped a new tool—that of active non-violent resistance.

MDN, it can be said, actually went beyond both Gandhi and Mao. He converted his local battles against globalization into struggles against the global centres of globalization by establishing networks both at the national and at the global levels. He established an alliance with the Bharatiya Kisan Union of Uttar Pradesh to form the Joint Action Forum of Indian People to campaign against India's acceptance of the WTO regime of free trade, investment policies and intellectual property rights. The worldwide visibility that his spectacular campaigns brought gave MDN access to networks of NGOs fighting against globalization. The KRRS became a prominent member of the People's Global Action Against Free Trade (PGA). A PGA meeting held under the auspices of the KRRS in Bangaluru adopted a declaration to the effect that the PGA 'rejects all forms and systems of domination and discrimination including but not limited to, patriarchy, racism and religious fundamentalism of all creeds'. The declaration was an attempt to distance the PGA from political parties and NGOs that promoted fundamentalist ideologies as well as those that were inclined towards centralization of power in the state.

In May–June 1999, the KRRS took part in the Intercontinental Caravan (ICC) organized by Via Campesina and the PGA in which about 400 farmers from India, Nepal, Bangladesh and Sri Lanka participated. The Caravan visited European sites of farmers' grievances to focus people's attention on 'the systems of exploitation that multinational corporations, Western governments and multilateral institutions were imposing on the farmers in the south' as MDN, the leader of the Caravan, put it. The Caravan held demonstrations against Cargill Seeds and Pioneer Hi Breed in Amsterdam, the Monsanto Technical European Centre in Belgium, Nuffield Foundation in London, sites of the European Union summit and that of the G8 conference in Cologne on two different dates, the European Patent Office in Munich and the Bayer Plant in Leverkusen, Belgium. MDN also took part in the first meeting of the World Social Forum (WSF) although he subsequently distanced himself from its activities. The KRRS as a member of the global AGM organized a mammoth farmers' rally in Bangaluru in a show of solidarity with the NGOs' siege of the WTO ministerial meeting scheduled for 29 November 1999 in Seattle, USA. The KRRS meeting held the next day attracted thousands of farmers. The meeting demanded that Monsanto 'Quit India'.[10] This spectacular demonstration was bigger than the demonstration at Seattle and gave KRRS the status of a global leader in the AGM.

The global network of NGOs and voluntary organizations that the AGM represents highlights a new phase in the history of social movements. To coordinate with NGOs professing diverse, if not contrary, ideologies and synergize their energies to engage and combat with powerful multinational enterprises and government organizations demands organizational and media management skills of a high order. Protests and demonstrations, in order that they create the optimum impact will have to be carefully choreographed. Demonstrators have to be taught to abjure violence, they have to be trained to deal with water cannon charges, with tear gas shells that are lobbed at them and with first-aid in the event of a breakout of violence.

The impressive success of the AGM in paralysing the 1999 WTO meeting in Seattle dramatically highlighted the weaknesses of the dominant institutions and governance structures that support multinational corporations. Subsequently, the impressive convergence of movements in the gatherings of the WSF held in 2001 in Porto Alegre in Brazil proved to be yet another significant milestone in the history of AGM. The WSF has now diversified into regional forums that meet in different parts of the world. Its annual meetings are scheduled to coincide with the meetings of the World Economic Forum (WEF) at Davos in Switzerland so that media attention is diverted to the real issues of the people rather than concentrate on the issues of the rich countries. The WSF has been so effective in mobilizing diverse groups of excluded and marginalized people from different parts of the world that even the WEF is now forced to address issues of equity and poverty eradication in its meetings in order to retain its credibility.

The KRRS evolved into a major exemplar of the AGM and the successes achieved by the latter is also because it coordinated with the KRRS under the imaginative leadership of MDN.

KRRS AND THE GLOBALIZATION PROCESS

MDN as the spokesperson of KRRS was clear that he was fundamentally opposed to globalization because it threatened to rob India of its biodiversity and deprive Indian agriculture of its seed variety, knowledge and practices. MDN had a total vision of Indian society built around the Gandhian concept of the 'village republic'. He thought that traditional Indian agriculture was designed for the predominantly rural society of India whereas Western agriculture could only support a rural population of about 20 per cent. Adoption of Western agricultural practices would therefore deprive livelihoods of vast majority of the population thereby creating an irresolvable crisis. He extended this view to the sphere of culture as well; he and his *hasiru sene* volunteers were in the forefront of protests against India's first Miss World contest held in 1996 in Bangalore. His objection to the beauty pageant stemmed from his concerns for gender equality. The KRRS encouraged simple weddings without the mediation of a Brahmin priest in which the newly wedded couple would pledge their commitment to gender equality.

MDN was not a developmentalist; he was of the opinion that organic farming was best suited to the Indian conditions because it would provide food security for all. He was sceptical of development because it displaces the poor and deprives them of their livelihoods. He thought that organic farming was also suited to the organic life of the Indian village. His campaigns against Bt cotton were about ecology, no doubt, but his primary objection was that it would lead to the genetic contamination of Indian plant and seed varieties. Following Gandhi he advocated a principle of decentralization with the village as the basic unit. He wanted local people to govern themselves and be in control of the local economy. His scheme of decentralization commended that all decisions that affect the life of the village should be taken at the village level and only decisions affecting villages at the district level should be taken at that level and so on. This model would reduce the power that units at higher levels wield thereby institutionalizing a true democratic form of governance. The organizational structure of the KRRS reflected his line of thinking.

At the ideological level, the KRRS as a movement dominated the social discourse of rural Karnataka. The farmers acknowledge that MDN salvaged their dignity by giving them the pride of place in his scheme of things. By foregrounding farmers' issues, MDN ensured that farmers were in the vanguard of 'revolution'. Kadilal Shamanna, a former close political associate, who had been thrown out of the KRRS for showing dissent by MDN, pointed out that the politicians and bureaucrats who were hitherto merely paying lip service to the theme of farmers forming the backbone of the nation were now compelled to recognize the centrality of the farmer in social development, thanks to MDN.[11] Even scientists whose advice used to be considered as authoritative during the 1960s and 1970s, found themselves in an awkward position in responding to MDN's criticisms. Their scientific training and professionalism did not allow them to issue categorical denials of the exaggerated criticisms and the consequent demonization of biotechnology. As a result, Monsanto and the Genetic Engineering Approval Committee of the Ministry of Environment of the Government of India preferred to extend the trials in response to the pressures applied on it by the AGM even when the results from the trials seemed satisfactory. This is indeed the sign of changing times, an instance of scientific methodology undermining its own legitimacy. The discourse on the merits of biotechnology in agriculture calls for a large dose of belief in science itself.

Ideological hegemony of the AGM in India did not produce expected results in practice. While an extremely vocal section of the

AGM did indeed dominate the public discourse on agricultural policies to resist globalization, some of the peasants' associations were either against the dominant discourse, as was the case with the influential and powerful leader of Maharashtra's Shetkari Sanghatana, Sharad Joshi, or were ambivalent, as was the case with Mahendra Singh Tikait of Uttar Pradesh's Bharatiya Kisan Union. Further, the discourse did not offer a viable alternative to globalization. MDN propagated organic farming and even set up a centre for sustainable agriculture called Amrita Bhoomi but he was not able to convert farmers on a large scale to his ideas on the subject.

To some extent, MDN's failure to create a mass following for organic farming was a consequence of the green revolution of the 1960s and 1970s that had extraverted India's agriculture and with it the village society as well. The Green Revolution technology had already made the farmers dependent on industries and laboratories that were then mainly under state patronage as socialism was the hegemonic discourse of that time. Traditional agriculture proved to be unviable and uneconomic. Traditional animal husbandry that relied on traditional crops with long stems but the new dwarf varieties compelled the farmer reduce his cattle stock. The consequent shortage of farmyard manure forced the farmer to buy chemical fertilizers that also promised higher yields. The new hybrid varieties with their shorter growth cycles were more attractive because they reduced the risks of unforeseen losses due to weather fluctuations. Hence traditional farming methods atrophied even though they left behind a myth about the great virtues of traditional crops.[12] The farmers believe that while traditional organic farming did indeed make for better tasting and more nutritive food grains, they feel they are condemned, under the changed circumstances, to the cultivation of inferior hybrid varieties.

Rural social life lost its organic unity partly as a consequence of the green revolution. Heavy dependence on water and erratic power supply to energize pump sets encouraged the middle and rich farmers to move away from the village and build their houses on their own farms. Flow of seasonal migrant labour loosened patron-client relations within the village.[13] As patrons lost the social prestige they had enjoyed earlier, they increasingly turned their attention to farming. A new kind of economism emerged that veered the farmers towards practices propagated by modern agribusiness firms because of the promise of higher profits they held out. Hence it is not at all surprising that in

1998 when MDN ceremonially 'cremated' Monsanto Bt cotton, a respected member of the KRRS, Shankarikoppa Mahalingappa of Adur village in Haveri taluk decided to put MDN's statement to test by trying out the cultivation of Bt cotton on his own. Mahalingappa's trials testified to the advantages of Bt cotton and allayed his fears about terminator seeds. Around the same time, in Gujarat, the farmers bypassed the controversy over Monsanto by trying out Bt cotton reportedly imported from Australia, confirming Mahadevappa's experience. Farmers' movements in India got divided between those who vehemently opposed genetically modified crops and those who wanted the government to ensure that the 'farmers' right to the fruits of modern science and technology were not denied to them'.[14] The situation has become more complex with the proliferation of companies informally developing varieties of Bt cotton for the Indian farmers. Sharad Joshi organized a mammoth campaign against the Government of India's decision to burn Bt cotton crops that had not been cleared for trials by urging that 'Development should not be locked up in the cities. The marvel of technology should reach the villages.' By choosing to focus on Monsanto as the metonymy of its struggle against multinational agribusiness, the AGM campaigns in India lost their credibility with the farmers.[15]

It is paradoxical that occasionally the AGM recoils from the contradictions of its own success. One such instance was in 2001 when the KRRS, coordinating with other NGOs, successfully lobbied to get the Protection of Plant Varieties and Farm Rights Act passed by the Parliament. The Act allowed farmers to sell loosely packed seeds in the retail market. This success indirectly contributed to the growing incidence of farmers' suicides because they purchased cheap spurious seeds that could now be sold in loose packets.

The economic consequences of globalization have become so complex that it is not possible to anticipate losers and gainers with any degree of precision. There are of course instances of small and marginal farmers being displaced by globalization but there are also counter instances that have reversed economic decline and poverty. In the villages of Ranebennur taluk in Karnataka, the success of contract seed farming for international agribusiness firms has benefited even small and marginal farmers who can profitably lease out their lands to rich and medium farmers. By leasing out land they also attain the mobility to move out to urban areas where high wage employment opportunities are available. Similarly, in some parts of Bangaluru district agricultural workers, especially women, have gained by the introduction of floriculture. They now get secure jobs in floriculture units at what they consider as attractive wages because they have acquired the reputation for tending to plants with care and sensitivity. In rural Karnataka market opportunities have multiplied because of a boom in horticulture and floriculture. Hence, even a marginal farmer who sold his small patch of land to a floriculture unit and now is engaged as a labourer in the same unit is able to rationalize his loss of land by stating that as a labourer now he earns more than he used to as a landowner![16]

KRRS AND AGM: AN ASSESSMENT

Even the brief narration of the movement and its principal architect sketched above suggests that there are contradictions between the movement and the actual process of globalization. It is indeed surprising that despite the weaknesses inherent in the KRRS and in MDN as a person the movement had a powerful presence and dominated the rural scene in Karnataka for more than two decades. One of the major constraints on the movement has been the rising trend of economism in Karnataka. This trend is a reflection of the new market orientation for rural Karnataka. The farmers, who had hitherto been dependent on the government for the economic viability of their small plots of land[17] became eager to cultivate crops that provide them assured returns in the market. Besides floriculture, they took to the cultivation of non-food crops such as cotton, gherkins and vanilla under subcontracting systems with both multinational and Indian agribusiness units to enhance their returns.

A major reason for the decline of the appeal of the KRRS and its ideology can also be attributed to the role played by MDN as its leader. According to several accounts, he ruled the KRRS like a dictator although he forcefully advocated decentralized democracy and direct action against authoritarian rule. Further, analysts point out that when MDN, intoxicated with the worldwide approbation that he richly deserved, in trying to project himself on the global scene neglected organizational issues that led to factionalism and fragmentation within the KRRS.[18]

The KRRS seemed to have failed in changing the attitudes and conservative views of its members. Reports on the planning and execution of the ICC highlight MDN's tendencies to bully the

European organizers into accepting his decisions. By taking upon himself the burden of using the internet to communicate and coordinate with the European organizers of the Caravan, MDN ensured that his position as a leader was not challenged. During the demonstrations and protests organized by MDN, the members of the Caravan articulated views that not only disappointed their hosts but also embarrassed them a good deal. One of the demonstrators was reported to have objected to the presence of scantily clad European women joining their demonstrations, and another expressed his moral outrage at the open display of sexuality in the streets of Europe. A third Indian participant is reported to have even expressed his unreserved admiration for Hitler in an impromptu interview with a German television channel![20] Several women participants and participants from Sri Lanka and Nepal reportedly complained about MDN's authoritarian and patriarchal attitudes to their hosts. The Caravan therefore was a disaster in terms of projecting the image of the AGM.

It becomes evident from a close study of the KRRS that the global network against globalization contained several contrary ideologies and attitudes and that its 'weak relations' were fragile as well. This is revealed in a widely circulated letter dated 4 December 2002 that MDN wrote to the organizers of the WSF. Justifying his decision to stay away from WSF 2001 he quotes an organizer of the WSF commenting that the reputed international NGO ATTAC had become close to President Bush![20] The letter complains about the prominence given to latecomer NGOs that had no grassroots support in India as against the tested and proven ones like the KRRS. MDN therefore declines the invitation to the KRRS to participate in the Asian Social Forum of 2003 and in the WSF 2003.[21] This letter hints at intense rivalries and conflicts that plague the AGM network. It is remarkable that the network proved to be an effective mobilizer despite such differences.

The global network against globalization is unable to prevent participant organizations from abandoning the goals of the movement when they get co-opted by powerful multilateral governance structures such as the World Bank and the Food and Agriculture Organization (FAO). A case in point is the International Federation of Agricultural Producers (IFAP) that was ideologically close to Via Campesina as it believed that international trade regulations were necessary to establish fair rules and markets for food and agriculture. IFAP, however, gradually changed its position to accept and support liberalization policies of the WTO. Some of its critics trace this changed stance to the invitations the IFAP received to participate in the meetings of the WTO. Members of Via Campesina who regard themselves as consistent in their pursuit of food security for the poor hold that it is easy for institutions such as the World Bank and the FAO to co-opt their opponents by inviting them for their meetings and by disbursing grants for their various projects. The fine print of agreements, protocols involved in the distribution of grants and the accommodative approach of the multilateral institutions in regard to the less important items of the agenda contribute to the dilution of the radical idealism of the AGM. To maintain its credibility and legitimacy the AGM has been forced to project itself as a flexible and democratic network accommodating diverse viewpoints. This has in practice weakened the AGM from offering unrelenting opposition to globalization. Considering these drawbacks it is commendable that the AGM has indeed offered trenchant criticisms of globalization and has been able to include some pro-poor items in the agenda of global institutions. Several alternatives ranging from the abolition of the WTO, removing agriculture from the WTO agenda to provision of training and other facilities to enable the poorer farmers to compete in world trade have been offered but differences within the AGM persist. Ironing out such differences may prove damaging because the fragile unity that has been built up with care may get ruptured. Hence, it appears that the AGM is condemned to work within this world even as it is critical of it. The AGM therefore has produced reformist, rather than revolutionary programmes.

The criticisms mentioned above may lead us to conclude that the value of the AGM lies merely in the rhetoric it has generated. Such a judgement hides the fact that the rhetoric in itself turns out to be valuable in this era of globalization. The rhetoric amplified by modern media compels institutions of global governance and multinational corporations to defend themselves with an appropriate response. They have the option of ignoring such criticisms but this may damage their image and erode their legitimacy. President Jacques Chirac of France in his speech at the WEF meeting in 2005 in Davos proposed a tax on international financial transactions to raise resources for combating AIDS and malaria and for improving the conditions of the poor in the southern countries. Although he immediately clarified that he was not proposing a Tobin Tax (a levy on international financial transactions proposed by an economist that had obtained the support of the AGM and become controversial) his rationale stemmed from the growing income disparities between the developed and developing countries—a point that the AGM has been making for long.[22] Another way in which the AGM has been effective is in slightly tilting the balance in favour of the South countries in the negotiations at the WTO. The Development Round of the WTO negotiations have not resulted in an agreement mainly because India, Brazil and eighteen other countries have been forcefully taking up some of the proposals that the AGM has put across. The rich nations of the North have now lost their ability to push through their agendas at the WTO meetings. They have been forced to adopt defensive postures and opt for compromise, as they desperately need new markets to ensure the buoyancy of their economies. At another level, Monsanto announced that it has abandoned the project of development of terminator seeds partly in reaction to the KRRS campaign against it.

Hence, the KRRS by forcing itself upon the global and local discourses on globalization has altered the discourse itself. While it is too early to conclude that the alteration has been radical the hegemony of the north cannot any longer be taken for granted. This should be considered as a major contribution of KRRS and its maverick leader Professor M.D. Nanjundaswamy.

In conclusion, in this era of globalization we note that the character of social movements has changed considerably. The effectiveness of the social movement is at the surface level but that is what counts. Social movements that concentrate on transforming the social consciousness of the participants as well as that of the society at large may not succeed in the changed global context.

NOTES

1. This also reflects the current state of scientific discourse, especially in biotechnology, that permits only qualified, conditional statements unlike the categorical, universal laws that dominated scientific enquiry a few decades ago.
2. See M. Hardt and A. Negri (2003), 'Foreword', in W.F. Fisher and T. Ponniah (eds.), *Another World is Possible: Popular Alternatives to Globalization at the World Social Forum,* London: Zed Books, pp. xvi–xix and Greame Chesters, 'Global Complexity and Global Civil Society', www.istr.org/conferences/toronto/workingpapers/chesters.greame.pdf

3. See Department of Agriculture, Government of Karnataka, *Agricultural Policy Resolution*, Bangalore, 1995.
4. As both MDN and KRRS have captured the imagination of the cyber world, I found the internet a treasure trove of data on MDN and his comrades and on the history of the KRRS.
5. A levy imposed by the government for the higher value of land consequent upon the construction of a canal to supply water to the field. Land that was hitherto classified as 'rain fed' would now be classified as superior 'wet land' thereby attracting higher land tax.
6. The new technology was only suitable for irrigated areas with adequate supply of water but even peasants in semi-arid regions took to the new technology because it promised high yields. They started digging bore wells to supply water required for the new crops.
7. Under the Essential Commodities Act of 1955, the state government can declare any farm product as an'essential commodity' and regulate its price and distribution.
8. By economism I refer to the preference of farmers to weigh practical economic considerations such as productivity and profitability over ideals, values and traditions of farming.
9. See Ronald Herring, ' Miracle Seeds, Suicide Seeds and the Poor: GMOs, NGOs, Farmers and the State', 2003. It is this ambiguity of interpretation that has led to the controversy on the application of biotechnology in agriculture thereby undermining the credibility of the scientists.
10. 'Quit India' was the slogan that Gandhi coined in 1942 to campaign against the perpetuation of British rule in India. MDN deliberately used the slogan to evoke the fear of a second East India Company rule in India.
11. See 'Time to Rethink: Farmers' Leader Kadidal Shamanna on the Future of Farmers' Movement in Karnataka', *Deccan Herald*, http://www.deccanhearald/feb102004/spt1.asp
12. See Vasavi (1994), 'Hybrid Times, Hybrid People', *Man: Journal of Royal Anthropological Society*, 29(2).
13. See Polly Hill (1982), *Dry Grain Farming Families*, Cambridge: Cambridge University Press.
14. See Ronald Herring, 'Miracle Seeds, Suicide Seeds and the Poor'.
15. The fact that even in Andhra Pradesh where AGM campaigns have seemingly won over the small and marginal farmers, complaints from NGOs that the multinational agribusiness firms are 'tempting' farmers with exaggerated promises of high returns indirectly admits the economism of farmers there and their inclination towards agribusiness practices.
16. The situation of expanding employment opportunities is not incongruent with reports of farmers' suicides in the context of Karnataka. Farmers' suicides are more a reflection of their market orientation, erosion of

village solidarity with the rise of individuation and continued drought conditions that prevailed in the state during 2002–4.

17. See R.S. Deshpande and K.V. Raju (2001), 'Agricultural Development and Policy in Karnataka', in Arun Bali (ed.), *Refashioning the New Economic Order: Karnataka in Transition,* New Delhi: Indian Council of Social Science Research, pp. 129–30.
18. On MDN's dictatorial attitudes Kadidal Shamanna's interview reported in the *Deccan Herald* of 10 February 2004. Vandana Shiva's criticisms of MDN's style of leadership and reports of the Inter Continental Caravan available on the internet also support the view.
19. See Ronald Herring (op. cit.) and 'The Intercontinental Caravan: A Critical Analysis', *Do or Die,* isssue no. 8, pp. 28–9.
20. In the AGM circle there can no worse abuse than being connected to the arch enemy Bush.
21. See http://www.nadir.org/nadir/initiativ/agp///free/wsf/asia2003/krrs.htm
22. See http://www.gavialliance org/Media_Center/Press_Releases/pr_WEF_26Jan2005_JChiracSpeech.php

IV. GLOBALIZATION, STATE AND NEW IDENTITY

CHAPTER 15

Dynamic of Contention: Post-electoral Movement in Mexico

SERGIO TAMAYO

INTRODUCTION

The mobilization against electoral fraud and in support of democracy that Mexico saw in 2006 was a dynamic and innovating process. As a movement it opened a period of transition; it arose transgressing institutions and it created a ample space for protest and for political and social change. The institutional transgression can be understood as the beginning of an episode of contention (cf. McAdam, Tarrow and Tilly 2003 [2001]; and Tarrow 1998) and the starting point of a space for citizen conflict (cf. Tamayo 2006). However, that *space* or *episode* was constituted later by processes and trajectories of action that limited the movement or that were limited by the movement itself.

It is in this perspective that the present paper exposes the dynamics of the post-electoral movement against fraud and for substantive democracy in Mexico that was formed and revalued in the course of the social struggle (Touraine 1988; Thompson 1963; Przeworski 1985).

McAdam, Tarrow and Tilly (2003 [2001]) have developed a perspective that they call 'contention politics or dynamics' (Contention: as a dispute, rivalry, competition, conflict, response, of responding, the one that responds, and the one that rejects). This approach is close to what I have called 'spaces of citizenship as spaces of conflict', 'contention space' or better 'confrontation space', as in terms of episodes of confrontation like in the process and dynamic character of the conflict (Tamayo 2006). The intention of explaining the movement against electoral fraud starts off by articulating both visions. The referred authors have tried a synthesis of diverse classic models on social movements, of which it would be possible to indicate the emphasis in the structural determinants, the structure of political opportunities, the mobilization of resources, the rational choice, the organizational analysis of the movements, the repertoires of mobilization, the cycles of protest, the frame alignment, and the construction of collective identities, amongst others. The objective of the model of McAdam, Tarrow and Tilly is to make the static perspective of the movements flexible, where the dynamic of the mobilization is being reconstructed. It is about putting in movement those constituent, but rigid parts, of the classical agenda, in the sense of: (a) to go from the analysis of the structure of political opportunities (EOP) to the examination of *attribution that the actors give to the challenges and opportunities that make the action possible*; (b) to leave behind the analysis of the resource mobilization theory and organizational structures of mobilization (that is to say, the study of the organizations in itself) and to emphasize what the authors call *the social appropriation* of their own social organization; (c) to transform the vision of strategic interpretative framework (ideological schemes) and frame analysis into the analysis of *the social construction and the collective efforts of interpretation* (cf. Chihu 2006); and finally (d) to go from the repertoires of the mobilization to an *innovative collective action.*

As can be inferred, the role of social and political subjects are fundamental in this review. From this perspective, there are four causal mechanisms: (a) the analysis of the opportunities and challenges of mobilization should not have to be treated as if they were objective categories. The analysis will always depend on the form in which the actors in confrontation attribute or not those possibilities of action; (b) The organizational structures can be preexisting or be created in the course of the confrontation, but in any case, they need to be *appropriated socially* by the base, to turn them into effective vehicles of struggle; (c) The frame alignments are constructed in the social interaction. This means that as much as the episodes of confrontation, as well as its actors and their actions, are interpreted by the participants, these adversaries, the mass media and an important number of directly or indirectly involved observers; (d) the already established repertoires of action selected, but action is innovating and impacts at the same time the episode of confrontation. It introduces new disturbances, opportunities and challenges that always generate uncertainty in the resolution of the conflict.

The dynamics of this mobilization occurs through *episodes of confrontation* that show the interactive relationship of the described causal mechanisms. The mobilization, thus, can be understood partly like a function of this interaction of mechanisms; articulation that explains the episodes as processes; and these, at the same time, expose the trajectory of action.

In consequence, what I do is analyse the sequence of the movement against fraud and for democracy. I highlight the ways in which the actors had opportunities and risks that determined the type of mobilization and the possibilities of success of social control. I define the pre-existing organizations and the new forms of organization of the participants. I point out the discursive spaces in confrontation that reflect the interpretation and meaning of the situations, actions and adversaries. And I go over the forms of collective action, classical as well as innovative, as symbolic forms of confrontation.

With the movement for democracy seen as an episode of confrontation or as a space of conflict, the empirical closeness that takes place includes systematic observation through various methods of political ethnography and situational analysis (cf. Tamayo y Cruz 2006). In this manner a seminary of observation and follow-up was conformed. The objective was to carry out a systematic follow-up of the movement against electoral fraud and after the constitution of the Democratic National Convention (DNC).

The procedure for the gathering of information was based on four strategies: (a) to carry out a situational analysis parting from three theoretical methodological elements: the limitation of ethnographical space, the definition and interaction of the 'political actors, and the description of the socio-political context parting from the attribution of opportunities and political challenges, (b) to create a database of the movement that includes aspects like chronology and periodization of the actions (Granados 2007), the analysis of the controversy of the sentence of validation of the presidential elections (Claudio 2007), as well as a biographical picture of Andrés Manuel López Obrador (García Bartolo 2007). The ethnographical essays point out the mega marches and the mega sit-in on Reforma Ave. (Minor y Gómez 2007); to a diary of events of the fraud from the offices of Sedesol located at Av. Paseo de la Reforma (Villagrana 2007); and the work of the Democratic National Convention (Darán 2007).

What follows is an account of the dynamics of the movement.

THE BEGINNING OF AN EPISODE

A movement has a beginning and an end (Stewart et al. 1989) and can be analysed in a linear trajectory, from its origin, its development and conclusion. Also, from an organizational perspective, the formation of primary groups would arise, from which, and through distinctive strategies of persuasion, the movement is developed and it reaches its peak, only to initiate its descent until its disappearance. The movement, nevertheless, cannot be compared with linear or organizational trajectories, at least not exclusively. A movement is a conflict field. It is an uninterrupted public challenge. And the post-electoral movement shows evidence of all this. It had its beginning as a result of a conjuncture determined by the harms of the presidential election. They were primary groups, political parties, coalitions and pre-existing organizations that impelled it. But the type of answer shows historical extensions that go back further in time, articulating themselves with struggles against fraud and the taking away of AMLOs political rights in previous years, in which the same actors and organizations also participated.

In an interview, the outgoing neoconservative president Vicente Fox told Jose Woldenberg, ex-president of the Federal Electoral Institute (IFE in Spanish, that organizes federal elections in Mexico), that when he was a candidate for the presidency in 2000, he always feared a possible fraud in the elections, by virtue that it had been a very 'unequal' day. The institutions and the mechanisms could have been very well designed and the boundaries set, he said, but the 'mapachería', the robbing of the ballot boxes, could have been next on the daily schedule. Paradoxically, in the elections of 2006, the majority of those who had promoted electoral democratization after 2000 election—many of them national electoral advisors, President Fox himself, and the whole conservative National Action Party (PAN)—vindicated the electoral results and electoral institutions as infallible. In fact, they were justifying the designation of the new *panista* candidate Felipe Calderón, in spite of the very doubtful obtained electoral results.

Many analysts (Palma 2004; Becerra, Salazar y Woldenberg 2000;

Salazar 2001, between others) had focused on the presidential shift of the year 2000, to the existence of divided governments, a plurality of houses and the autonomy of the IFE as guarantees that Mexico had entered a new democratic period. Nevertheless, the celebration lasted a very short while.

The reason for the directly affected, López Obrador and the 'por el Bien de Todos' Coalition (for the good of all, poor first), to denounce the fraud were numerous, amongst them the climate of terror that promoted the vote of fear through television and radio spots, the use of public resources by the PAN to generate an enormous neo-corporate relationship with the poor, the buying of votes, the purges of the electoral register, the use of information of the state to benefit the *panist* campaign, the manipulation of the primary results to induce a favourable public opinion towards Felipe Calderón, etc. These actions helped to disqualify López Obrador. Since 2005 President Fox wanted to AMLO's leadership accusing of corruption. Later on IFE upper functionaries handled the electoral council by including members linked to their own group and official party interest. The uncertain results of the election showed an ideologically divided and politically polarized country.

It should not surprise us then that the issues of these elections, the struggle between the left and right, between rich and poor, between progressives and conservatives, between north and south, would re-emerge. The right had its blow ready. Its gaining of power using methods similar to those used by the PRI—the method it had criticized beforehand—are the evidence of the farce of democratic speech.

But even the left, political and social, was divided. On the one side, although with frictions, was the Alliance between the PRD, the *Partido del Trabajo* (PT in Spanish, the Labor Party) and *Convergencia* (*ex-priista*, Convergence). This alliance was the starting point of the *Convención Nacional Democrática* (CND in Spanish, the National Democratic Convention) and the *Frente Amplio Progresista* (FAP in Spanish, the Progressive Ample Front). This social democratic thought was reinforced in action, and it could remain, because of the enormous mobilizations that preceded the electoral day. It could gather important intellectuals, numerous workers and members of unions, communities, teachers, peasants, indigenous people, popular organizations that saw in López Obrador the symbolic representation of genuine democratic change.

On the other hand, the leftist forces and the trade unions—the organizations of the *Diálogo Nacional* (National Dialogue), la Coordinadora Nacional de Trabajadores de la Educación (Teachers' National Organization), y la Promotora Nacional de Unidad Contra el Neoliberalismo (National United Organization Against Neoliberalism)—suggested the struggle against electoral fraud, the respect for popular will and for a coordinated mobilization of all the popular sectors of the democratic movement. Moreover, some socialist political organizations were confronted with hegemonic abstentionist positions inside *La Otra Campaña* ('The Other Campaign' spearheaded in 2006 by the EZLN, Zapatista National Liberation Army, coordinating political actions in opposition to the institutional electoral campaign).

Indeed, a third leftist position was that assumed by sub-commander Marcos, the EZLN, and the majority of *La Otra Campaña*. They expressed their lack of confidence in the leadership of movement: 'They are going to fix it at the top', they said. 'To keep the confidence on institutions like the IFE is useless.' Thus, their position was consistent with the attitude assumed on election-day, since 'The other Campaign' was organized parallel to the institutional campaigns. Marco's speech was belligerent, aimed against the political class, mainly against López Obrador.

The intellectuals were divided. Some discarded the evidence of electoral fraud and were prepared to defend the IFE and what they believed was the symbol of Mexican democracy. Others placed themselves next to the movement of López Obrador and against electoral fraud. There is no doubt, however, that the fundamental criticism of the movement was centred on the characterization of the leader, and from there to the whole movement. For the dissident group, the candidate was a populist leader who was also elevated as a candidate of a left that was likewise populist.

Consequently, society began to feel uncomfortable at the institutional response, with enormous doubts of validity. Society was already polarized and the voting process testified this. In such a scenario, the political and social forces positioned themselves and decided to start a movement against electoral fraud.

HOW DID THE MOVEMENT GROW?

In an atmosphere of confrontation, an initial stage was opened in the movement against fraud. This stage considered the attributions that the political actors gave to the structure of opportunities and political restrictions. I emphasize three strategies in this period of accumulation of forces and preparation of evidence that justified the purpose of the mobilization: (a) direct actions that served to pressure, (b) the legal actions, and (c) mediatic actions that divulged and persuaded on the merit of the movement. Strategies were designed within the framework of these attributions on the opportunity to mobilize themselves, to advance in their demands and, in consequence, open new spaces of opportunity. In the same manner, the adversaries valued the strategic possibilities and tried to restrict them to the maximum.

Let us look at the legal strategy. Before the closing of the counting for the presidential election and the affirmation by the IFE of the triumph of Calderon, López Obrador announced that he would oppose the results. He demanded a vote by vote and voting booth by voting booth review because he believed that the election had been manipulated. The refutation generated heated discussions between the political forces about the validity and inappropriateness of the measure. It tightened the divisions in society even more. There were sporadic incidents of violence against the candidate of the PAN, Felipe Calderon. The space of confrontation was extended to the media and other national and international actors. The pressure of the actions of Lopez Obrador was violent due to the incidents that could not wait. The problem was that Felipe Calderon had not yet received evidence of the majority vote and there was a political *impasse* that took away legitimacy from him. Deep down, there was the uncertainty of who had really won the election. On the other hand, the IFE was mobilized. It denied that it had manipulated the primary results and it received the endorsement of the United Nations (UN). Then the governments of the United States, Canada and Spain quickly went on to congratulate Calderon, although they backed off shortly thereafter, asserting that they would wait for the results of the court.

The direct actions occurred in parallel with this legal strategy. While the legal resources were mobilized, Lopez Obrador summoned the first informative assembly. More than half a million supporters attended. There Lopez Obrador called for the construction of a pacific national mobilization. A mega march would be organized that would depart from the 300 electoral districts in all the country and would culminate in the Zocalo of Mexico City.

The links between the organizations created an immense network which would sustain the movement against fraud. In the Second Informative Assembly a million citizens attended. There, Lopez Obrador called to make actions of resistance. The movement was being transformed and self-defining itself as 'the movement of peaceful civil resistance' and their demand 'vote by vote, voting booth by voting booth' was sustained in the mobilization.

THE SYMBOLIC APPROPRIATION OF THE SPACE: STRATEGIES OF MOBILIZATION

This period shows the climax of the movement. It emphasizes the symbolic forms of appropriation of public space by mobilizing action. It is part of the repertoire of mobilizations and at the same time it expresses the innovation of collective action. It permits us to see the ample calling power that Lopez Obrador and the Political Party Coalition have, as well as the articulation and construction of citizenship networks, the construction of a political identity around a charismatic leader, a greater mobilization of resources and the linkage between party and movement.

The central mobilization was the demonstration of 30 July and the installation of the sit-in that remained during a month and a half, but the repertoire included the planning of various actions and parallel protests. The objective of the mobilization was to pressure the decision of the court on the recount, but the highest electoral authority rejected the demand of a total recount. The sit-in remained in protest for the outcome.

The Third Informative Assembly took place with the attendance of close to 2 million citizens, the biggest demonstration in the political and social history of the country (Granados 2007). Lopez Obrador was euphoric and called to install a mega camp-out until the court gave its last word. The speech of AMLO made reference to the symbolic and social appropriation of the public space. It assumed that the space represented the history of justice and liberty. For example, Madero Street was named after the apostle of democracy in the Revolution of 1910, when the aristocrats saw as subversive and rebellious. Also, Juarez Avenue was named after the founding father who constructed the Republic in nineteenth century. It meant a charismatic liberal leader who resisted the conservatives and the French intervention. And, finally, Reforma: it meant an broad avenue that was constructed by the French Empire in the nineteenth century. It turned, later on, into the strolling place of the nineteenth century liberals, where the local bourgeoisie *flaneured* daily. In this metaphoric space were constructed part of the values of the movement, parting from their own attributes that the actors reinvented to bond their own struggle and memory with history.

Canvases and tents were extended all through the trajectory. You could observe the precision of limits and boundaries between the organizations. There were dining halls, chess tables and places for meetings. The Zocalo was full. They placed cots, they put altars against President Fox, and they took the electricity from the posts and from the local government office, and set up televisions. Rivers of people walking, passing, looking, stopping for the artistic spectacle, before the debates. Thousands of tents and discussion forums every 100 metres made up movie theatres with plastic chairs inside a space limited by duct tape on the floor, dozens of people in front of televisions that showed documentaries about Lopez Obrador, historic revolutionary movies like *The Battle of Argelia* and *Animal Farm*. There were dozens of cultural forms, folk dances and groups of young 'rockers'. The people would gather around and shout: 'AMLO, you are not alone.' It was a space where the supporters could go. The atmosphere was of camaraderie, identification, and solidarity. They took advantage to divulge the materials of the civil networks, social, civic and socialist organization.

The sit-in is the best way of projecting the organization of a movement, the articulation of organizations, associations and citizens. The mobilization of financial and material resources of the local government that was supporting Lopez Obrador made the movement known. The creativity and innovation of actions were directly proportional to the magnitude of the movement and the participation of the social organizations.

The reactions did not wait. Representatives of the bourgeoisie, conservative *panist* legislators, the media and the church demanded the evacuation of the sit-in: 'The city had been kidnapped by the lopezobradorism—as they said it—and turned into its general military headquarters.' Various groups came out polarizing their positions. The PRD challenged the outgoing president Fox to evacuate the sit-in with the Federal Police Corps (PFP in Spanish). The preventive police of the federal district was mobilized by the local government to act as a shield of the demonstrators in the case in which the PFP decided to evacuate, which finally did not happen.

The sit-in lasted 48 days. Entrepreneurs' organizations estimated a negative impact of 8 thousand million pesos. Some 3,900 people had lost their jobs and the PRD would owe 14 million for spending on maintenance. According to an estimate the spending for the camps ascended to about 24 million 500 thousand pesos for the concept of 176 mobile restrooms, 195 carps, 350 canvases and 2 cranes of 5 tons each.

THE STRAIGHT CONFRONTATION

The stage showed strong frictions between the political adversaries. The movement was confronted at the highest level of the political system. Its actions transgressed the institutional space that bothered the political class and the media. Lopez Obrador in his diatribe sent 'the institutions to the devil'. Actions were planned that literally crossed the civic calendar: 1 September, the day of the Presidential report: 15 September, commemoration of anniversary of the Mexico's independence, 16 September, day on which the Mexican army and the air force carried out the traditional military parade.

The first of these strategies of mobilization was the design of actions and symbolic forms of disqualification and de-legitimization of the presidential figure. The tensions in the Legislative Palace became more profound. Fences and police surrounded and heavily protected the perimeters of the building against the threat of the demonstrators.

On 1 September an unexpected and dramatic episode was generated in the political life of Mexico. President Fox could not render his governmental report. If it is true that Fox could get to the Legislative Palace, it was impossible for him to enter the room where the sessions took place. The episode, indignant for some, exciting for others, was recorded by a private television and relayed on the air by the Congress channel. For some analysts what occurred in the tribunes was a challenge to the presidential investiture. The international media did not wait for answers. *Los Angeles Times* wrote: 'The Presidential Crisis Grows': *Washington Post:* 'The Political Crisis in Mexico Deepens'; *Granma*: 'An Unedited Event in Mexican Politics'; *El Pais*: 'Fox had to Limit Himself to Read the Report in a Televised Message.'

THE DEMOCRATIC NATIONAL CONVENTION

Under the un-revocability of the sentence, López Obrador abandoned the electoral topic and centred on the strategy that would give the movement legitimization, organization and perspective: the Democratic National Convention.

The CND (in Spanish) justified itself on the basis of historical memory and on norms taken from the constitution. Article 39 of the constitution says to the word: 'National Sovereignty resides essentially and originally on the people. All public power comes from the people and is instituted in favor of it. The people have, at all times, the unalienable right to alter or modify their form of government.'

Now, the proposal of the CND by Lopez Obrador generated ample discussions and tensed the interior forces. For some it meant, above all, the consolidation of a political alliance of the parties that had begun as an electoral coalition but that no longer had any major expectation of development. This alliance transformed into the *Frente Amplio Progresista* (Progressive Ample Front) between the PRD, PT (Labor Party) and *Convergencia*.

For the radical groups of the movement, the convention meant a qualitative leap in the struggle against imposition. It should work as an inducement for an independent organization of the citizens and a possibility of implanting the workers' organization. For it, they had to ensure that the Convention did not become just a forum acclaiming López Obrador as the legitimate president. Rather, it had to be a front of deeper organization and social struggle.

Thousands of people started their way from very early on. A dense network of yellow colours and nametags of the CND emerged from all points of the great metropolis. More than 10,000 popular assemblies were carried out and 150 debate forums were held in the entire Republic. Thousands of individual and collective speeches were received. 10,25,724 delegates registered before the organizing committee. Of all the proposals, three were common: (1) to disown the declaration of validity of the presidential election announced by the Electoral Court; (2) to support the call of the CND; and (3) to convene a Constituting Congress to re-found the Republic (Darin 2007).

Ten resolutions of the CND were voted, among them: the overtaking is rejected and Felipe Calderon is not recognized as the president of México. Instead, the triumph of López Obrador is recognized and he is declared as the legitimate president. Besides everything, the act of foundation looked like a symbolic act of ovation to López Obrador as the 'legitimate president'. It was a day of synthesis of previous work, but not structured, which, in spite of everything, generated confusion in many groups. It let down the most enthusiastic promoters who wanted to turn the Convention into an instrument of debate and action.

Nevertheless, the act was solemn and emotional for thousands of citizens who were just beginning their collective experience and who relied on the charisma of their leader. A charisma that, nonetheless, was not based on the personal attributes in a psychological sense, as the opposition wanted to picture him, but on one that was being constructed on the basis of the symbolic interaction, in the radicalization of a speech that was always pressured and evaluated from the base, and in the own political experience of the movement.

COROLLARY

The post-electoral movement, against fraud and for democracy has not ended. It is present in hundreds of activities, declarations and political work of the commissions. Yet, be it for the lack of a greater articulation between the movement, the organizations and the political challenge, the truth is that the formation of the CND on 16 September meant at the same time the culmination of a cycle in the history of the movement. After all, Felipe Calderón took office as the constitutional president. The majority of the citizens who saw the consummation of the act on a television controlled totally by the federal executive, felt a mix of helplessness and frustration. The impotent mobilization of 2 million citizens had stayed behind.

The social movements that emerged parallel to the movement against fraud and for democracy, like the struggle in San Salvador Atenco and the Popular Assembly of the Peoples of Oaxaca were violently repressed and are now in a stage of reflux. The Convention lost the chance of articulating itself with these movements, to fortify them and to fortify itself with this alliance.

What followed was a meeting of the CND in March 2007. But the political impact of the movement on the existing institutions has dwindled. The mobilization of diverse resources has fallen noticeably: legal and electoral resources (through FAP), political resources (through the declaration of the legitimate president and the poor advances in the organization of the new constituency), organizing resources (generated through weak networks and alliances with trade unions and popular organizations), and resources of resistance (through minimum collective actions of a different kind).

Has the movement ended? Is it entering a new cycle of protests? Losses? Could we see now the marks left on the democratic process? Somethings, may be, seen through the interconnection of various causal mechanisms of the mobilization. Factors that were interwoven with each of the facets are described below. We could value (a) the attribution that the actors gave to the challenges like the opportunities that made the type of action possible, (b) the appropriation of the social organization by the supporters and activists of the movement, (c) the social construction of the speeches that interpreted the opposition as well as the same episode of conflict, systematically evaluating it, and (d) new forms of innovative action that were paired off with old strategies of action.

I will concentrate on two aspects. The first is the qualitative effect that the size of the movement had, in this case extraordinary, on the perception and reaction of the episode of contention, by the supporters as well as by the political adversaries. This decisively impacted the structure of political opportunity. The second aspect is the importance of the symbolic space as a political strategy. The appropriation, re-appropriation, interpretation and re-interpretation of the public space, by actors as well as adversaries, constituted one of the most important mechanisms that permitted us to explain the distinctive symbolic forms of politics and the dynamics of confrontation.

This episode clearly demonstrates the social construction of a citizenship space.

REFERENCES

Alberoni, F. (1984), *Movement and Institution*, New York: Columbia University Press.

——— (1993), *Enamoramiento y amor*, España: Gedisa.

Chihu Amparán Aquiles (2006) (coord.), *El análisis de los marcos en la sociología de los movimientos sociales*, México: Miguel Ángel Porrúa y Universidad Autónoma Metropolitana.

Becerra, Ricardo, Pedro Salazar y José Woldenberg (2000), *La mecánica del cambio político en México: elecciones, partidos y reformas*, México: Cal y Arena.

Claudio Piedras, Guillermo (2007), 'Debate y controversia frente al dictamen de validez de la elección presidencial 2006 en los principales diarios del Distrito Federal', En Dossier 'Procesos y etnografías de un movimiento. Dossier', Revista *El Cotidiano*, no. 141, enero-febrero 2007.

Darán Martínez, Óscar (2007), 'La Convención Nacional Democrática 'Por el bien de todos', En Dossier 'Procesos y etnografías de un movimiento. Dossier', Revista *El Cotidiano*, no. 141, enero-febrero 2007.

García Bartolo, Moisés Sinhué (2007), 'La construcción de un liderazgo: esbozo Biográfico de Andrés Manuel López Obrador', En Dossier 'Procesos y etnografías de un movimiento. Dossier', Revista *El Cotidiano,* no. 141, enero-febrero 2007.

Giddens, Anthony (2001), *La tercera vía y sus críticos*, México: Taurus.

Gilly, Adolfo (1998), *La revolución interrumpida*, México: Editorial Era.

Granados, Moctezuma, Azucena S. (2007), 'Movimiento voto por voto: una cronología'. En Dossier 'Procesos y etnografías de un movimiento. Dossier', Revista *El Cotidiano*, no. 141, enero-febrero 2007.

Salazar, Luis (2001) (coord), *México 2000, alternancia y transición a la democracia*, México: Ediciones Cal y Arena.

McAdam, Doug, Tarrow, Sidney y Tilly, Charles (2001 [2003]), *Dynamics of Contention*, Cambridge: Cambridge University Press.

Minor, Fredy y Gómez, Juan Carlos (2007), 'La apropiación del espacio público: las Mega Marchas y el Mega Plantón del Movimiento postelectoral 2006', En Dossier 'Procesos y etnografías de un movimiento. Dossier', Revista *El Cotidiano*, no. 141, enero-febrero 2007.

Mouffe, Chantal (2000), *La Paradoja Democrática*, Barcelona: gedisa editorial.

Palma, Esperanza (2004), *Las bases políticas de la alternancia en México. Un estudio del PAN y el PRD durante la democratización*, México: Universidad Autónoma Metropolitana, Azcapotzalco.

Przeworski, A. (1985), 'Proletariat into a Class: The Process of Class Formation', in A.P. Przeworski, *Capitalisms and Social Democracy*, Cambridge: Cambridge University Press.

Reveles, José (2006), *Las manos sucias del PAN. Historia de un atraco multimillonario a los más pobres*, México: Editorial Planeta Mexicana.

Smelser, N.J. (1995), *Teoría del comportamiento colectivo*, México: Fondo de Cultura Económica.

Stewart, Ch., C. Smith y R. Denton (1989), *Persuasion and Social Movements*, Prospect Heights, Illinois: Waveland Press.

Tamayo, S. (1999), *Los Veinte Octubres Mexicanos: ciudadanías e identidades colectivas*, México: Universidad Autónoma Metropolitana, Azcapotzalco, colección de estudios urbanos.

——— (2005), 'Los límites de la desobediencia civil y la resistencia pacífica: experiencias distintas, discursos distintos'. En revista *El Cotidiano*, *no. 132*, julio-agosto de 2005, año 20. Universidad Autónoma Metropolitana, Azcapotzalco, pp. 55–63.

——— (2006), 'Espacios de ciudadanía, espacios de conflicto', En *Sociológica*, año 21, número 61, mayo-agosto de 2006, pp. 11–40

——— (2007) (coord.), 'Procesos y etnografías de un movimiento. Dossier', En Revista *El Cotidiano*, no. 141, enero-febrero 2007.

Tamayo, Sergio y Xóchitl Cruz (2006), 'Espacio etnográfico, hermenéutica y contexto socio-político: una análisis situacional'. En Patricia Ramírez

Kuri y Miguel Ángel Aguilar (coords.), *Pensar y Habitar la Ciudad*, Barcelona: Anthropos y UAM Iztapalapa.

Tarrow, Sydney (1998), *Power in Movement: Social Movements and Contentious Politics*, Cambridge: Cambridge University Press.

Thompson, E.P. (1963), *The Making of the English Working Class*, New York: Vintage Books.

Tilly, Charles (1995), 'Los movimientos sociales como agrupaciones históricamente específicas de actuaciones políticas', En *Sociológica*, año 10, no. 28, UAM/Azcapotzalco.

Touraine, A. (1988), *Return of the Actor: Social Theory in Postindustrial Society*, Minneapolis: University of Minnesota Press.

——— (1994), *Crítica de la Modernidad*, México: Fondo de Cultura Económica.

Villagrana Velásquez, Erika (2007), 'Postelecciones 2006. Crónica de un fraude anunciado desde una perspectiva gubernamental' En Dossier 'Procesos y etnografías de un movimiento. Dossier', Revista *El Cotidiano*, no. 141, enero-febrero 2007.

CHAPTER 16

Combating Historical Ethnic Stigmatization: BRASPOL in Brazil

ELŻBIETA BUDAKOWSKA

This paper will briefly examine the characteristics of the new generation of social movements and the main elements of Polish immigration to Brazil. It will then present some of the research findings on the dynamic role of the new social movement BRASPOL in stimulating the Polish post-immigrant generations' actions to challenge negative historical stigmatization of their ancestors in the pluralist society of Brazil. The full result of the research is extensively presented in the recently published book, *Wposzukiwaniu etniczności. Ruch BRASPOL w Brazylii—współczesna interpretacja*, WUW 2007, (*In Search of Ethnicity. The BRASPOL Movement in Brazil—A Contemporary Interpretation*).

NEW SOCIAL MOVEMENTS AS SOCIAL MOVEMENTS OF A NEW GENERATION

The *new social movements* (NSM) are currently recognized by many social theorists as a crucial factor determining contemporary mechanisms of social life. As new generation movements vigorously challenging the social reality in recent times, they are regarded as possible and relevant agents of social transformation. Societies are increasingly organized around global capitalism and resistance to it shapes new movements. However, NSMs do not advocate the radical, revolutionary restructuring of the state through violent revolution. Rather, their approach is to increase activism and large-scale participation in grassroots collective mobilization within the civil society to achieve the necessary change.

Contrary to the old social movements, the NSMs do not appeal to any classical ideological systems. Their aim is the mobilization of civil society, not seizure of power. They mostly exist outside the political sphere. Consequently, advocates of such movements, in general, do not come from one social class. They often represent various social and professional groups. So one can say that the structure of the NSMs is defined by the plurality of pursuits and purposes, as well as goals and orientations.

These types of social activism deal with new problems and social matters resulting from the present state of civilization in particular societies. The passage from industrial to post-industrial societies makes NSMs authentic representatives of post-industrial social forces connected with the change and the emergent new needs. The current transformation of societies from modernism to post-modernism offers a new representation of society, which defines itself by *new* types of collectivities based on open and not hierarchic collective social actions. Key concepts characterizing these movements are: activity, direct participation, engagement as well as responsible and conscious action. The major new feature is that focus is laid on transformation of values, identities and symbols, in other words, the creation of alternative lifestyles—what can be achieved in the discursive interaction of the social actors.

There is a variety of sociological perspectives on the NSMs since the new type of collective social action embraces a complex and broad range of organizations and struggles. Some of them emerged in the wake of the students' movements of the 1960s. They also include the women's liberation movement, the peace movement, the anti-nuclear movements, regionalist movements, the environmentalist and green organizations, alternative movements and many others. However, different theoretical concepts of current grassroot mobilizations are beyond the limit of this article.

The NSMs, being anchored in their collective form in culture, are usually decentralized, and to a certain extent function as networks. They pave the way not only for specific actions, but they continue to function during the actions and remain in operation after the event. Thus, undertakings brought about by new actions are not only visible quantitative facts, but many a time they become a qualitative process.

Due to increased complexity, pluralization and individualism, the social movements of the new generation rejected the contempt for the *Otherness*. They support minorities' rights. This is why they support the collectivity based on individuals' rights to protect their identity and to build proud individuals out of it. In contrast to the previous vertical relationships, NSMs emerging in the new era of horizontal activities provide an important intersection between internal subject and external manifestation of identity.

The social theorists indicate that one of the NSMs' manifestations is ethnicity. Growing on the basis of the bond shared by successors of immigrants with inherited culture, ethnicity may be treated as a manifestation of the changes in the awareness of individual processes as well as of new tendencies in the perception of the role of renewed collective identities. Being concerned with the cultural sphere and innovation, NSMs can challenge the present traditional values and change attitudes towards ethnicity in multicultural neighbourhoods.

NSMs can also develop a praxis that will challenge traditionally exercised marginalization, especially in overcoming the marginalization connected with negative ethnic stigmatization, and gaining recognition for the contributions of different immigrant groups into a pluralistic society. The main change would then let the post-immigrant generations of the previously marginalized groups celebrate their ethnicity without feelings of inferiority and low self-esteem. Simultaneously, a new sense of solidarity could be viewed as the source of NSMs' significance. Therefore, to comprehend the nature of the assertion at the cultural level it is important to trace shortly the trajectory of inter-linkage between history (in a sense of development of the plural society) and recent heterogeneous mobilization.

DEMOCRATIC CHANGES IN BRAZIL AS A STIMULI OF ETHNIC NSMs

The condition *sine qua non* of the emergence of NSMs is a democratic system. The actions may differ from region to region and even country to country, depending on the historical heritage, nature of the political system and the level of economic development. Democratic traditions themselves can be limited by the form of power.

In many countries, especially post-colonial ones, interplaying elements of modernity and post-modernity produce a social scene crisscrossed by classical social movements as well as NSMs. So we can say that the present forms of collective actions, both in their content and direction oscillate between the past and the future.

Another important feature of multi-ethnic and multi-racial post-colonial societies is that their policy of cultural pluralism may simultaneously enforce the processes of cultural differentiation of their civil societies. Sometimes that process leads to reconstruction of historical ethnic identities; and sometimes it leads to more complex individual cultural identity created by the individuals in the conditions of their increased free choice. Within the multiculturalism, social actors can join the elements of different cultures, including that ones which they rediscover being engaged in the NSM.

Distinction partly corresponds with Wieviorka's two approaches towards cultural differences: reproduction and production. As he puts it: '*Reproduction* ensures the survival, unchanged, of differences; while an approach in terms of *production* considers differences as subject to change, invention, including differences that appear to be traditional.'

In Brazil, the mobilization to create a new social and ethnic dynamic intensified in the 1990s. It resulted from the earlier transition to democracy and the return of civilians to power. The civil society became a new political space where citizens could mobilize and express their dissatisfaction with the state of the matters. The democratization process caused new forms of organization to develop, not always having well-articulated aims. However, they motivated the wider grassroots mobilization of the social actors.

The new attitude shaped by socialization promoted individual reflecion, criticism, responsibility and evolution of democracy. The new democratic reality became an important stimuli for undertaking social actions connected with the rights of every individual to create her/his individual identity. Their value was based on the growing awareness of the ability to create new meanings and forms of social life and action.

However, ethnically diversified and deeply blended population of Brazil, cannot use the colour of one's skin as decisive factor to indicate an ancestor. It is despite the changes in social mentality that reenforces the need of ethnic basis of recognition and belonging and building a positive image of their own group.

POLISH IMMIGRANTS IN BRAZIL AND THEIR STIGMATIZATION

Brazil has one of the largest immigrant populations in the world. During the nineteenth and twentieth centuries about five million immigrants of different nationalities came to Brazil. Most of them settled in the large cities and along the coastal strip, creating the ethnically diversified population of the country. However, the peasant settlement followed D. João VI's decree of 1808 permitting the selling of land to foreigners. It was also the reason Polish immigration became a historical component of the European immigration to Brazil, leading to structural differentiation of the new nation.

Beginning with the nineteenth century, emigration from Poland to Brazil coincided with the process of development of the wild tropics. The Brazilian state introduced the geopolitical strategy of widening the expansion of settlements towards the south. For that reason vigorous propaganda was directed toward strengthening the attractiveness of settlement in that area. As a result of it 1,29,515 Poles moved to Brazil in the years 1820–1955. This early influx though numerically large, did not contain members of the intelligentsia. Later, between 1955 and 1970, about 15,000 more immigrants arrived, but this group was more socially differentiated. There were no successive waves of immigration, so Brazilians of Polish descent were mostly identified with their ancestors of the early Polish peasant immigrants.

The historic evolution of the status of the Polish group and its identity over almost 150 years shows that the process was not a systematic continuity of reproduction. Achieving higher social-economic status from one post-immigrant generation to another progressively constituted the milieu for the future social change. So one can say that the community of Polish immigrants in Brazil experienced a three-stage evolution: from the status of the pioneer *comunidade polaca* through the intermediary status of *polono-brasileira* to the contemporary *brasileiro-polonesa*. The sequence of adjectives is reflected in the name of the new ethnic movement—the Central Representation of the Brazilian–Polish Community in Brazil, BRASPOL.

In its historical development, the early Polish communities were passing from the dominant stage of the national canon, brought from the old country and practised in the closed system of the immigrant group, through biculturalism to the individualized status of a Brazilian citizen of Polish descent, who to a higher or lower degree retained knowledge of his/her Polish heritage. As the traditional cultural landscape slowly began to change, its impact on the individual's cultural world became more visible. It underwent transformation from the empirical stage to a symbolic one influencing bonds and social relations in the private and public spheres of life. In many cases the hyphenated world was replaced by multiple identities.

The process did not lack drastic interventional factors, such as Getúlio Vargasa's integrative policy. His decrees of nationalization issued in 1938–9 were to speed up assimilation of the younger generation and deprive the descendants of immigrants of their material cultural heritage. This policy caused the disruption of activity of numerous Polish societies and the nationalization of a considerable part of the communities' material resources. The integrative policy announced by President Vargas also resulted in language assimilation of masses of newcomers, who were forbidden to use their national languages in public places.

The Polish immigrants in Brazil, unavoidably like other national groups, were subject to stereotyping which they had to get rid off in the process of social advancement. Lacking the objective opportunities their pioneers enjoyed, they remained on the periphery of the modernizing society.

There are multiple sources of stigmatization. Stigmatized groups are usually perceived through the prism of a few characteristics interpreted in a negative way like physical looks, traditional way of dressing, or others. Stigma is historically changeable and culturally conditioned. People can be stigmatized because of the context of a given culture, historical event, economic or social situation. Stigmatization is closely connected with human interaction and its consequences for the individual are psychological in nature. As Goffman puts it, a stigmatized person has a 'spoiled identity'. Such an individual, while feeling 'different', doesn't know-how he/she is seen by others in the course of social interaction and whether to avoid contact with the others. So, it is often raised in specialist literature that negative stigma results, in addition, in a feeling of isolationism, which does not necessarily have to be of psychological nature but of the spatial distance as well.

Belonging to a certain national group can also be the source of stigmatization. Pejoratively labelled groups suffer all sort of disadvantages. It is especially the case if the new immigrants' behaviour is 'strange' because of not knowing the language, specific costumes and traditions, and different mentality of the new country. Nationalisms and ethnic biases have strengthened divisions and social distances among the colonizers. What is important is that national stigmatization can disqualify and be transferred to the next generations. Negative generalizations play an important role in creating social relationships and inter-group communication. Even when new information about a given group is spreading out, it is still difficult to combat its negative stereotype. Maintaining asymmetrical relationships in the society potentially can become a reason for tension and contradictions in different domains. A sort of inter-group conflict can appear especially at the local level.

In the case of the Polish pioneers, their ethno-social classification persisted for several decades and had several consequences for the group. The occupational structure of the pioneers was interrelated with their later asymmetric social position, since they didn't take active part in the urbanization process and the urban labour market. This excluded them from the modernizing mainstream of the society, especially at that historical period when participation in a free urban labour market was recognized as a crucial input for development. Many a time the very name of the group—*polacos*—was linked to information about its place in the social hierarchy and society.

Various factors influenced the categorization of the Poles and their descendants in the early pioneering phase. Stereotypes of Polish immigrants to Brazil was the result not only of their differences but also the wave they came to Brazil with. Their world was part of the nationally fragmented settlement despite the efforts of the authorities to overcome and not to support specific ethnic homogenization.

Stereotypes very often led to marginalization and to inferiority complex. While the social relations created by the discrimination of the dominated enforced her/his closeness in relations with the *Others*.

Another reason was that the negative classification of the Poles was to diminish their contribution to the economic growth and the creation of a regional social space, while the social composition of the Polish settlers was principally determined by selective immigration policy subjected to Brazil's colonization plans. Peasant families were included in the process of construction of small, self-supporting agricultural properties which were to balance the latyfundium (great landed estates specializing in export-oriented commercial agriculture in coffee, olive oil, wine, suger, etc.) form of economy.

There is no question that they participated in the move of the civilization southward. The pioneers changed from emigrant 'after bread' to colonizer of *frontier society*, and to a large extent actively took part in modernization and the development of the new country.

As a colonizer, the Polish newcomer contributed several elements which civilized the environment. He was an active subject contributing to the effective colonization and the development of European agriculture in the south of Brazil. Despite the crucial role played by the agricultural newcomers their activities remained stigmatized and considered demeaning for upward social and cultural mobility. This is why it became necessary to revise the view of the Polish peasant immigrants. So the main dilemma of stigmatized identities was to transform historical *negative* into *present* positive, in other words, shame based on stigma into proud based on real contribution.

That became more obvious when the post-immigrant generations began to witness the competing ethnic actions on evaluating the contribution of different ethnic and racial groups to the formation of Brazil. Then the rise of the NSMs started and differences became a central relation between collective mobilization and diversities. All participating sides wanted to be socially recognized in the public space.

THE BRASPOL MOVEMENT IN COMBATING HISTORICAL STIGMATIZATION

Since stigma is a social construct, it can be remodelled. Similarly the process of marginalization is also culturally constructed. The post-immigrant generations' access to social mobility caused some sort of conflict between achieved status and historically prescribed position. The new consciousness emerged mostly as a function of changing self-definition and perception. Upward mobility, increasing occupational diversification and higher social status implied that a series of collective actions would have to be undertaken to bring about the required change. The democratic state supplied an instrument to make such a change—the NSM. If this emerges in heterogeneous society, the grassroot mobilization would have to interact or compete with other ethnic groups in society.

Since the majority of Poles—like other European nationalities—were directed to colonize undeveloped areas and not to work on *fazendas*, the settlement process of the pioneers from Poland could be analysed from the perspective of *integrated history*, and not only from the position of expulsive factors in the country of departure. An analysis of the origin of the Polish element from the point of *integrated history* of the state meant that for contemporaries the history of migratory movements constitutes an element of modernization of the country and the construction of a modern history of Brazilian society.

Therefore a great many of the common stereotypes could be easily refuted by referring to the *paradigm of integrated history* and by demonstrating more decisively the positive contribution of Polish settlers to the development of the South of Brazil.

Such an approach appeared of great importance in interpreting the ancestors' history by the post-immigrant generations and enabled viewing them in the context of social-economic relations in the contemporary state. So collective history of a stigmatized group was a starting point in seeking the abolition of the stigma and regaining recognition of the ethnic identity.

A formal mobilizing structure of the NSM of Polish post-immigrant generations in the pluralistic society of Brazil was the *Central Representation of the Brazilian-Polish Community in Brazil* or BRASPOL (A Representação Central da Comunidade Brasileiro-Polonesa no Brasil—BRASPOL). It was founded on 27 January 1990 in Curitiba, which has the largest density of people of Polish origin in the state of Parana and in the whole of Brazil.

BRASPOL focused its attention on redefining the cultural identity of partly assimilated descendents of Polish origin and based its existence on the idea of collective activity in a civic society.

Simultaneously, as a new phenomenon it was a manifestation of the re-evaluation of the organizational formula of social activity typical of early, closed Polish immigrant communities to an open social movement of a nowadays non-territorial ethnic group. Inspired by the ethnic leaders' discourse, it enforced individual and collective identity processes, along with an alteration in the treatment of the cultural heritage in the pluralistic society.

The BRASPOL movement spread out very fast and began to play an important role in creating the contemporary ethnicity of the Brazilian post-immigrant generations of Polish descent. They are estimated around 2 million Polish descendants in Brazil now.

I began my research when the movement was active among people of Polish origin in the sixteen states of Brazil. Material collected during empirical research conducted in 85 local branches (*nucleos*) in 13 states of Brazil allowed me to make contemporary interpretation of the Polish model of ethnicity in Brazil. It had been created by the communities of post-immigrant generations, not strengthened by new waves of immigrants, after the historical isolation from the remote country of origin and feeble contact with its cultural canon.

They started with the usage of the now common name *Polônicos* instead of *polacos* which had negative social connotation. So the process of revalourization of origin can shortly be called from *polacos* to *Polônicos*. Participants from broad range of social background have engaged in building the new image of the group.

The new repertoire of actions was raised in the name of re-evaluation of the negative categorization of the *polacos* coming from the early period of Polish settlement in Brazil. Simultaneously, the creation of a positive collective identity of the *Polônicos* in contemporary *comunidade brasileiro-polonesa* served as a good example of how NSMs based on cultural heritage can challenge the historical ethnic stigmatization of a group.

As it appeared, the model of new ethnicity embraces four main ingredients: *knowledge* (cognition) about the central core value of the culture of ethnic origin; *collective social activity* (based on common belonging and tradition); building the modern *Brazilian–Polish international relations*; and focusing on the *Brazilian context* (in a sense of re-evaluation of the significance of Polish pioneers' contributions and strengthening the Polish-background cultural component in the pluralistic society).

The findings proved that the model of *integrated history* appeared most suitable for an understanding of contemporary identity processes, and can be contrasted with M.L. Hansen's three-generation concept applied to North America and frequently used to explain the ethnic phenomena outside of that continent.

An important initiative in this respect was returning to historical memory. People of further generations, even fourth, fifth and sixth ones, engaged in the movement started to research on the historical facts, famous persons, and places connected with the pioneering times to show their significance in the formation of Brazil.

The movement, evolving in accordance with the local social and ethnic resources—at the same time accumulated preserved historical memory, symbols of local material, immigrant heritage, the specificity and regional tradition to build through inter-ethnic cultural contacts, new knowledge about the Polish ethnic group in the pluralistic society and to effect a revalourization of its contribution to local development.

A new project entitled Projeto Memórial (The Project to Remember) for renewing the historical traces of first pioneers had been announced by the movement leaders. The project was to motivate post-immigrant generations to rediscover and preserve the material culture connected with the presence of the Polish ancestors and commemorate in local communities their contribution to the development of Brazil.

The findings showed the association between space, memory and ethnicity. Memories were rediscovered by the symbolic perception of space. The respondents showed a new approach towards historical heritage and recognized that material heritage was an important internal asset. A series of collective actions conducted to bring about change in the local environment had been guided by the vision of the undertaken goals. The post-immigrant generations confronted the previous pioneers' space with the current developments of the state. Although the efforts undertaken ranged widely in terms of historical recourses connected with the particular locality, nevertheless it resulted in the preservation, reconstruction or reservation of group historical cultural property. The post-immigrant generations took the effort of reconstructing many historical objects like houses of the first settlers serving now as local museums, the crosses built to show the road to the settlements in the tropical forest, small chapels in historical style with old ethnic decorations, which I could visit during my fieldwork.

The model of ethnicity declared by the post-immigrants showed that despite the intensive assimilation, the language of the country of origin is still perceived as a strong attribute of Polish ethnicity in Brazil. It is also a fact that the aspirations connected with the post-materialistic value system led to satisfying the new needs of creating a positive, harmonic cultural identity overthrowing the negative stigmatization of origin and the inferiority complex that it led to. It was based on equal evaluation of contribution and the pride of one's roots in a competitive, pluralistic society.

The NSM broke the historical stigmatization in Brazil's pluralist society. Everyday activity of the movement were mostly based on direct contacts, so people began openly to manifest their pride at being of Polish descent. That had a big influence on overthrowing some still existing prejudices and stereotypes of the group. Another observation made was the increase of participants of non-Polish Brazilians in the BRASPOL cultural events as a result of high evaluations of them by the *Others*. Due to this perception, the movement did not have a clear-cut boundary, but apart from leading activists and participants, it also had sympathizers from different ethnic backgrounds. Besides in some localities, other groups, not being so much organized, started to follow BRASPOLS's patterns of grassroots activity to raise their own ethnic pride.

Another sign of combating the negative historical stigmatization could be seen in initiating contacts with Poland as the modern country of their ancestors. In an open multicultural world, virtual contacts play an important role. The Internet has given some impetus to growth of knowledge about contemporary Poland and its position in the international arena, including the European Union membership. Contacts with relatives have begun to go significantly beyond old national boundaries. It has created a new sense of solidarity. Attempts at direct contact and communication have also been reported, mutual visits and tourist trips being the most popular of them.

The attempts at learning Polish as the means to communicate with Poland's people has also been acknowledged by the research. Raising Polish to the group of other foreign languages in the personal feelings, can be interpreted as a significant change in overcoming the inferiority complex. Language assimilation, partly forced by the state integrative policy, diminished effectively the interest in learning the national languages, even after liberalization.

CONCLUSION

Social mobilization to redress issues of historical stigmatization is closely linked to individual and collective identity processes. On one hand, identity-oriented mobilization is correlated with the socially and culturally fragmented context that could lead to a fragmented identity. On the other, the processes of individual and collective identity intertwine with the global and local context of social development.

Multiculturalism, based on the recognition and acceptance of differences, lets new forms of differenc continually present themselves. Since the national culture is plural and not a cultural vision of one group, coherent macro-culture is seen as something in a constant state of becoming. The interaction and intercultural exchange led to deepening citizenship, especially in an isolated Brazilian interior. Multicultural context thus served as a background for the revalourization of origin.

The general conclusion is that NSM in its creation of a positive collective identity is based on the cultural heritage of the active social actors. It can help in overcoming marginalization when it is mostly based on the historical stigmatization in a pluralist society.

REFERENCES

BRASPOL (1993), *Representação Central da Comunidade Brasileiro–Polonesa no Brasil–'Projeto Memórial'*, Curitiba.

Budakowska, E. (2007), *W poszukiwaniu etniczności. Ruch BRASPOL w Brazylii–współczesna interpretacja*. WUW, Warszawa.

——— (2005), *Tożsamość bez granic. Współczesne wyzwania*, WUW, Warszawa.

——— (2004), Ruch BRASPOL w społeczeństwie pluralistycznym. *Wspólnota Polska, pismo poświęone Polonii i Polakom za granicą*, nr 1, s.11–14.

Carneiro, F. (1950), *Imigração e Colonização no Brasil*, Rio de Janeiro: Editora Brasiliences.

Czykwin, E. (2007), *Stygmat społeczny*, PWN, Warszawa.

Goffman, E. (2000), *Człowiek w teatrze życia codziennego*, PWN.

Hausen, M.L. (1948), *The Immigrant in American History*, Cambridge: Cambridge University Press.

Ianni, O. (1992), *A Ideia de Brasil Moderno, São Paulo.*

McAdam, D., J.D. McCarthy and M.N. Zald (eds.) (1996), *Comparative Perspectives on Social Movements: Political Opportunities, Mobilizing Structures, and Cultural Framing*, Cambridge: Cambridge University Press.

Scott, A. (1990), *Ideology and the New Social Movements*, London: Unwin Hyman.

Sokół, W. (2000), 'Nowe ruchy społeczne', *Encyklopedia Politologii*, vol. 4. *Myśl społeczna i ruchy polityczne współczesnego świata*, pp. 260–2, Zakamycze.

Wieviorka, M. (2004), 'The Making of Differences', *International Sociology*, vol. 19, no. 3, September.

CHAPTER 17

Students' Protest and Activism in Sub-Sahara Africa

LEO ZEILIG

INTRODUCTION

University students in the period following the independence of African countries were a transitory social group, who held well-founded expectations of rewards and high status employment after graduation. The 1970s began to erode many of these assurances as countries that had attempted to implement state-led development faced international recession and internal corruption and decay. State funding of higher education by the late 1970s was being targeted for restructuring. Student activism was affected: while students clung onto a self-conscious elitism, the reality of student poverty and the financial crises of African universities transformed their activism (Bathily et al. 1995). These processes, however, were inherently contradictory. Seeing their status as a privileged group collapse, there was an unprecedented 'convergence of forces' (Kagoro, interview 23 June 2003) between students and the popular classes (Seddon 2002). The ivory tower had been turned inside out by the austerity imposed by structural adjustment and national governments. This convergence was expressed in the waves of resistance from the mid-1970s and later the 'democratic transitions' that swept the continent from the late 1980s and 1990s.

This paper surveys the role of students, the nature of their protest and their relationship with civil society in the processes that brought about a wave of multi-party elections and democratic struggles in sub-Saharan Africa. The paper focuses specifically on the literature that relates to student activism and protest, although it is acknowledged that this activism brings into play many other factors. The context in which students become political actors in contemporary Africa is tied to the transformation of higher education in sub-Saharan Africa, often under the auspices of the IMF and World Bank (WB) led reforms. The paper asks a number of related questions: Have university students become a marginalized social group? If their status as a pampered post-colonial elite has collapsed, has there been a convergence of the student and the urban population? And how has this impacted on their activism?

The early sections of the paper explore the changing nature of higher education in the political economy of sub-Saharan Africa, focusing on the changed circumstances that student activists have been forced to negotiate in the last twenty-five years. The final sections of the paper discuss both the evolution of student activism, the way it has been characterized in the recent literature and the involvement of students in the 'convergence of forces' and the popular protests that was typical of the democratic transitions. The paper intentionally presents the broad political and economic changes in higher education in sub-Saharan Africa, and details the role of students in the actual transitions that took place in the 1990s. The history of these transitions must be, in Thompson's word, 'embodied . . . in a real context' (Thompson 1991: 8).

UNIVERSITIES IN CRISIS

Universities have been analysed as sites of contestation where the democratization process took place, incorporating a range of political forces and agencies (Akam and Ducasse 2002). The literature, however, finds unanimity in the description of the university as a neglected institution, a crumbling edifice housing impoverished students and lecturers. The physical decay of higher education is a feature common in many sub-Saharan African universities (see Box 17.1).

It is important not to generalize uncritically from Aborisade's observations, although much of the literature tends to corroborate his observations (Lebeau, 1997; Caffentzis 2000). In Malawi, Kerr and Mapanje (2002: 90) note that the physical collapse of the University of Malawi, the non-payment of staff and declining facilities for students have helped to create an 'atmosphere of marginalization' that has often led 'students to anti-social behaviour.' They describe the increase in sexual assaults on female students and lecturers from 1994 as a 'cowardly attempt among male students to find an easy

BOX 17.1

Femi Aborisade (2002)—a Nigerian academic and trade unionist—describes the situation at institutions of higher educations in Nigeria, typical in much of the literature:

1. INADEQUATE INFRASTRUCTURAL FACILITIES

Classrooms are inadequate, both in terms of number and size considering the increase in the number of students offered admission on a yearly basis. There is the trend of phenomenal growth in the number of students without corresponding preparation for the growth. The management and government are concerned about the size of income to be generated from the students in terms of . . . fees and other types of levies. Physical clashes occasionally occur between students of different classes as lecture timetables are often not observed—students scramble to outpace fellow students in being the first to occupy classrooms.

2. STAFFING SITUATION

Higher education is grossly understaffed in many states. In the Department of Business and Public Administration where I was teaching, for example, there were just eleven academic staff teaching 1,109 students as of December 1999.

3. LIBRARIES

Libraries are inadequate, in terms of size, number of books and the age of the books. Current literatures are hardly available. Yet, many students are too poor to buy books of their own. Thus the lack of reading materials tends to further strengthen the development of cultism among students and lecturers.

4. PAYMENT OF SALARIES

Salaries are never paid as and when due. Unfortunately, this situation encourages lecturers to unlawfully seek to pass the burden of their domestic problems on students through imposition of all sorts of levies, inducements and threats of failure. A common example is the practice whereby lecturers make it compulsory for students to buy photocopied lecture notes, etc.

5. WATER, ELECTRICITY AND OTHER CONVENIENCES

Supply of electricity is erratic. Evening lectures stop whenever electricity supply is arbitrarily cut-off. There is no regular supply of water. This affects conveniences such as toilets,—which are usually locked up. Lecturers and students have to make use of nearby bushes.

6. UNDER-FUNDING

A major cause of the hostile environment in which the academic staff works is traceable largely to under-funding of education. The problem of under-funding is not because Nigeria is poor but because higher education has been de-prioritized. As the student population increases, funding (for both recurrent and capital expenditure) declines! (Interview, 24 September 2002).

scapegoat for a much broader set of frustrations'. Nkongolo (2000) describes a similar 'set of frustrations' among students at the University of Lubumbashi in the early 1990s. Describing how the students were humiliated, he writes:

> Us, students and tomorrow's elite of Zaire, the youth of the *Mouvement Populaire de la Révolution* (JMPR) were compelled to go to the toilet in the bush, like animals. We went there every day, in the hot and rainy season. The night like the day . . . even the 'largest library in central Africa' was not saved, and was used as a WC. . . . The outside world must know the extent that Mobutu had humiliated us. (Nkongolo, 2000: 96–8)

It is clear that there is a remarkable symmetry in the decay of sub-Saharan African universities over the last twenty years: countries thousands of miles apart experienced the same 'erosion' of higher education. Piet Konings (2002: 181) writes about the crisis of the University of Yaounde in Cameroon in the 1990s: 'First and foremost, there was growing dissatisfaction with deepening crisis within the university and the lack of employment prospects for university graduates. Mockingly, students referred to their university as 'the bachelors' cemetery'.

Konings goes on to describe how student numbers have swelled from 10,000 in 1982 to more than 42,000 ten years later, even though the university infrastructure is only built to cope with a maximum of 7,000 students. Consequently:

> Lecture rooms, libraries, laboratories, and office space for lecturers were inadequate and lacked necessary equipment. The university hostel could offer accommodation to a limited number of students, often on the basis of patronage or ethnic criteria, and the vast majority of students were compelled to look for accommodation themselves. (Konings 2002: 181)

Even in Makerere University, regarded as a model for the rest of Africa, half the students questioned in a survey failed to attend lectures because there were not enough seats (Musisi and Muwanga 2003: 43). Alternative, private accommodation was invariably in overpriced 'mini-cities' surrounding the university.

The same pattern of decay affected Kenya's university system. Although Maurice Amutabi (2002) tends to romanticize student activism,[1] his descriptions of conditions in Kenya's universities is convincing:

> The lecture theatres and libraries are not only congested but also run down. The hostels have become overcrowded, sanitary conditions have worsened, and food quality has deteriorated. University buildings are dilapidated, making the university conditions not different from any slum or poor neighbourhood in Kenya. (Amutabi 2002: 163)

Amutabi argues that the resulting impoverishment of student life has radically altered their position in Kenyan society. They are now, he maintains, 'bedfellows' with the population as a whole. They share the same economic crisis and live the same poverty. Students, though, still have a role as 'societal watchdogs' and only their vigilance will ensure that the gains of multi-partyism and democratization are maintained.

The conditions of higher education in Africa seen from the perspective of the university's physical infrastructure and the pauperization of staff and students has declined steeply since the 1980s (Zeilig and Seddon 2002). A number of writers point to the effects of structural adjustment programmes (SAPs) that have greatly exacerbated the withdrawal of state funding for universities, teaching staff and students (Konings 2002; Frederici 2000). They argue that these policies have deprioritized higher education in Africa, compelling national governments to slash State support to university budgets and insisting on the introduction of tuition fee and 'levies' on students.

REFORM OF HIGHER EDUCATION IN SUB-SAHARAN AFRICA

From the early 1980s to the early 1990s the World Bank produced a number of important studies stressing the importance of higher education reform. These studies advocated the dramatic reduction of higher education expenditure in Africa. The most important of these reports, *Accelerated Development in Sub-Saharan Africa*, which became known as the Berg Report, was produced in 1981. It focused on the general priorities for African development and prescribed policy reforms to unregulate national states. These reforms included the wholesale reconfiguration of university education in Africa. The report has become the subject of considerable and mostly hostile discussion (Sandbrook 1993; Diouf and Mamdani 1994). The report (1981) determined the approach of donor agencies to education in Africa. The problem was simple: too much money was being spent on education:

> Expenditure on schooling already claims a large part of GDP—around 4% in two-thirds of the countries for which data are available. And, more important, they claim a sizeable share of public expenditure—about 16% of the total, on average, more than any other government function except general administration. In a significant number of African countries, recurrent expenditure on education is between 25 and 35% of total recurrent spending. In the 1970s, when government revenues rose rapidly in most of the continent, the average African country's incremental share going to education was 13%—again larger than any other single item except general administration. (WB 1981: 81–2)

The report recommended fundamental reforms that centred on 'cost-analysis', which pitted the economic returns of primary education against those of the tertiary sector. The report explained the calculation:

> Given Africa's extreme shortage of fiscal resources and the many claims on revenue, all educational strategies must have a key objective of greater efficiency in resource use. African education is expensive not only in the sense that it absorbs a significant share of public sector resources; it is expensive also in terms of average cost per pupil, especially at the higher level. By contrast primary education is cheap in comparison with industrialised countries. Primary education cost per student year as a per cent of per capita GNP in Africa are about as much as in other developing areas; secondary education costs are 4 to 5 times as much and higher education costs 5 to 10 times as much. (WB 1981: 82)

While the report provided the blueprint for higher education reform in the 1980s, it was criticized by another WB report released in 1989. The report recognized that tight budgets in the 1980s had led to a decline in primary to post-secondary education. Indeed education had been the focus of an important report the previous year, *Education in Sub-Saharan Africa* (WB 1988). By the end of the decade it was obvious to the WB—if also contradictory—that there was a need to improve 'human resources'. The 1989 report even stated that donors should fund capital expenditure in tertiary education (Sandbrook 1993: 83–4). The effect of years of reform was clear: the rapid decline in salaries and the deterioration of higher education had led to shortfalls in doctors, managers, accountants and economists. The crisis even forced Babangida, the military ruler in Nigeria, to set up the *Presidential Task Force on the Brain Drain* in 1988. As Sandbrook (1993: 43) argued:

> A widespread decline in the quality of secondary and university education in the 1980s aggravated the problem of finding qualified staff. Economic crisis and budget cutbacks have deprived educational institutions of the resources they require.

Even so the reforms did not go far enough for some. At the 1986 Conference of African Vice-Chancellors in Harare, the WB questioned the very existence of universities in Africa (Iman and Mama 1994: 73). Another conference two years later described the bleak state of higher education, ravaged by structural adjustment. The conference—Human Dimensions of Africa's Economic Recovery and Development—noted that far from structural adjustment increasing the rate of primary school enrolment, the opposite was the case as all sectors of education had suffered:

> Primary school enrolment declined by 65% between 1980–5. Secondary school enrolment during the same period dropped from 13.7% to 10.9%. And in higher education, the annual enrolment declined by 66% between 1980–5. The drastic growth in brain drain involving middle and high-level manpower is another disturbing trend. A joint ECA/ILO report estimated that, in six months to 1987, 70,000 Africans left the continent, up from 40,000 in 1985. This represents approximately 30% of Africa's skilled human resources. While the lucky ones flee to Europe, those less fortunate take up jobs as teachers and doctors in some of South Africa's homelands. (quoted in Bako 1994: 152)

The argument that runs through the reports is that the 'repriori-tization' of education will ensure that African countries see a more equal distribution of resources across the education sector. Critics of the reforms who followed these reports cite the fact that after five years of SAPs, social spending in sub-Saharan African countries had declined by 26 per cent (between the years 1980 and 1986).

Governments already facing financial crisis were pressurized to cut subsides to secondary and tertiary level students. The WB responded by claiming that they intended to reorganize funding on education because for too long governments had regarded universities as 'sacred cows', when in reality they were bloated, overfunded and inefficient (Caffentzis 2000).

A report carried out by the academic M. Kelly (1991) for the WB sought to describe the nature of post-colonial education typical of Africa. Zambia had suffered a severe economic crisis in 1977 with the collapsing price of copper, the country's leading export. The fall in copper prices meant that by 1977 Zambia, which depended on copper for half of its GDP, received no income from its most important resource (Marfleet 1998: 104). Despite the crisis the government continued to increase funding in higher education to the detriment of primary and secondary schools (Akam and Ducasse 2002). This led Kelly (1991: 61) to argue that 'too much was devoted to the refined needs of too few at the higher level, and too little to the general needs of too many at the lower level'. In addition the report concluded that higher education was inefficient, citing the 'tradition' of not charging fees.

The WB argued that, unlike higher education, the primary sector had a higher return on investment, 28 per cent against 13 per cent for tertiary education. As Caffentzis (2000: 5) explains, 'In other words university graduates received about two and half times more income over outlay than the government; and they received from the government thirty times more than what primary students received.' Reports pointed out that while the 'white collar sector' comprised 6 per cent of the population, they received in State revenue more than 27 per cent of the education budget (Caffentzis 2000: 5). The WB maintained that the thrust of their policies was to ensure a more egalitarian allocation of funding: by reallocating funds from 'urban elites' an educational egalitarianism could be achieved.

In Senegal despite almost two decades of structural adjustment, and a concerted effort in the 1990s from the WB and IMF to force the government to reduce the enrolment of students into higher education, enrolment had increased (some estimate that there are now more than 30,000 students at Cheikh Anta Diop Université in Dakar, UCAD). The higher education sector by 2001 was still absorbing roughly 27 per cent of the national education budget, whereas primary education received 38.4 per cent of the budget

(Niang 2004: 67). The point of highlighting these figures is not to argue in favour of WB and IMF reform but to explain how unsuccessful their policies have been.

There is considerable controversy over the number of university students in sub-Saharan Africa. According to one important study (Caffentzis 2000: 9) there are fewer than 500,000 students in higher education in the whole of Africa. Considering that there is a continental population of about 500 million, that makes roughly one student per 1,000 people. This figure is unreliable. Mama (2005: 98) states that, 'Gross enrolment in African universities increased dramatically . . . to over 1.75 million in 1995 and are still growing fast in most places.' Caffentzis states that in 1986 the enrolment rates for higher education were about 2 per cent of the pertinent age group; this had reached 3 per cent by 1995 ('Higher Education in Developing Countries', WB 2000: 107). This means that Africa has among the lowest enrolment rates in the world, much less than Latin America's 12 per cent, and 7 per cent for the developing world as a whole. However, there are no reliable figures for sub-Saharan Africa, and Mama's enrolment numbers are contested by Altbach and Teferra (2003). This is largely due to the fact that under the impact of World Bank and IMF reforms in the 1980s cash-strapped universities stopped producing their own statistics. But at the same time these organizations demanded figures on student enrolment in order to assess the progress of reforms. Often institutions were left to 'create' numbers that had previously been collated by the university administration (Lebeau, 1997). Enrolment rates can be seen in Tables 17.1 and 17.2.

However, various reports disguise the huge discrepancies within the Third World so that the enrolment rates for Africa are lost in the figure for the Third World as a whole (see Table 17.1). This has the effect of disguising the stagnant and in some cases falling enrolment figures for Africa. Table 17.2 clarifies the situation on the continent.

However, there are wide differences within sub-Saharan Africa. The university system varies widely across the region as the following examples illustrate. The two public universities in Zaire had a combined enrolment of approximately 2,000 students in 1960 at the time of the country's independence (WB 2000). Five years after independence the gross enrolment rate in the country was still bouncing around zero, while the figure for Latin America was about 4 per cent at the same time (see Table 17.2). By 1995 enrolment for

TABLE 17.1: THE EVOLUTION OF ENROLMENT RATES 1980–95

(*in per cent*)

Count	Least Dev.	Less Dev.	World Total	Dev.
1980	2	4	11	36
1985	2	4	12	38
1990	2	6	13	48
1995	3	.6	15	62

Source: World Bank, 2000.

TABLE 17.2: GROSS ENROLMENT RATES

	Secondary		Tertiary			
	1965	1995	1965	1975	1985	1995
Low/middle income	21	55	4	7	7	10
Sub-Saharan Africa	5	25	1	1	2	3
East Asia/Pacific	23	64	5	5	4	7
South Asia	24	44	4	7	8	6
Europe/Central Asia	39	83	9	14	13	32
Latin America and Caribbean	19	55	4	13	16	18
Middle East and N. Africa	20	62	3	7	11	15

Source: World Bank, 2000.

single courses offered at the university could exceed the entire number of students at the university thirty years previously. The WB reports that in the academic year 1995–6 'nearly 2,500 freshmen packed a single class in biomedical sciences' (WB 2000: 18).

Makerere University is an example of higher education in Africa celebrated by the WB. According to research (Musisi and Nansozi 2003), the university managed to extricate itself from a crisis in the early 1990s, returning to its former pre-eminence as one of the foremost universities in East Africa. The Bank highlights how the university managed to increase enrolment rates and the number of students paying fees: almost 70 per cent of the student population was contributing towards its fees by the end of the 1990s. Where previously the university was funded completely by the national government, today 30 per cent of the revenue is raised 'internally' (WB 2000: 54–5). The WB (2000: 55) emphasizes the case of Makerere to stress the importance of 'releasing' universities from state funding and control in Africa,

The Makerere accomplishment has lessons for other universities in Africa that face similar resource constraints. It shows that expansion—and the maintenance of quality—can be achieved simultaneously in a context of reduced state funding. It puts to rest the notion that the state must be the sole provider of higher education in Africa.

A series of academic studies conducted since mid-1990s emphasize these points. They stress that higher education in Africa has a future only if the liberalization of several key African universities is emulated.[2] As the preface to the series describes:

> Much of sub-Saharan Africa has suffered deep stagnation over the last two decades and is staggering under the weight of domestic and international conflict, disease, poverty, corruption and natural disaster. Its universities—once the shining lights of intellectual excitement and promise—suffered from enormous decline in the government resources for education. In the last half of the last decade however this began to change in a number of countries. . . . Our interest was captured by the renewal and resurgence that we saw in several African nations and at their universities bought about by stabilisation, democratization, decentralisation and economic liberalization. (Musisi and Muwanga 2003)

What is remarkable about this quotation is the absence of concern for the role of external factors in the subcontinent's decline. Indeed, the case studies that make up the series are highly contradictory.[3]

The WB envisaged the total transformation of the university system in Africa, for the reforms aimed at creating 'centres of excellence' for a smaller number of students of 'high quality'. For many students who would have previously gravitated towards higher education, a system of 'on-the-job' training was envisaged that would be provided by the private sector and subsidised by the government, where 'worker-students' would receive training for lower wages. In primary and secondary education, schools would be run by local communities, religious institutions and private companies who would pay for the cost of teaching staff and the upkeep of buildings (Caffentzis 2000). In Senegal, Dakar has returned to being the educational focal point for the sub-region, with students making pilgrimages to a pedagogical world almost entirely privatized. The city has been turned into a training centre; according to a recent pamphlet advertising *Enseignement supérieur* there are now eighty public and private establishments almost all based in the capital Dakar and offering an array of internationally recognized degrees, certificates and diplomas. Most of these schools, colleges and universities are private (sixty-five of these are private, and fifteen public), and the majority of their students come from elsewhere in West Africa. The massive expansion in private colleges is connected to the liberalization of higher education in Senegal since 1994 (*Etudier au Sénégal* 2003: 4).

Many of the premises that form the backbone of these proposals appear to make sense. Certainly it cannot be objected that 'primary education' in the context of small national budgets should be a national educational priority or that higher education should also aim for 'high quality'. Shrinking resources affect most sub-Saharan African countries and require a realistic approach to the policy of educational provision. Some commentators have argued that the WB reforms and the re-shifting of provision to primary education are the only serious and viable options for African economies (e.g. Verspoor 2001).

One of the central questions in considering these arguments is the effect of Structural Adjustment Plans (SAP) on social policy and economic development in Africa. Many write how SAPs have deepened the crisis that has afflicted sub-Saharan society (Bond 2002; Seddon and Dwyer 2002). The reality of life for students and lecturers in much of the continent could not contrast more to the image of higher education as 'spoilt' and 'over bloated' that the WB presents. Higher education in Africa does not thrive, but in many places faces a battle for survival. If the objective is to 'streamline' higher education then the question that demands answering is: where from? Africa has the lowest enrolment rates in higher education in the world; further restrictions would limit access to higher education to an almost imperceptible minority of privileged and 'elite' students.[4]

This has led one writer to comment: 'any policy that lowers enrolment rates—hovering now near zero—can be seen as a policy of academic exterminism' (Caffentzis 2002: 9). There is a further dimension to this debate. The WB is correct to maintain that there is 'excessive demand' for higher education in Africa. The university system is seen by the youth as a crucial entry point to a world of greater opportunities, and a way to escape poverty. The effect of the crisis that has gripped many African economies is to leave the 'youth' without the prospect of work. Politicized youth, or the 'youth factor' (Richards 1996; 2002), has fuelled conflict in Africa; youth have been recruited for movements of social breakdown in Sierra Leone, Ivory Coast, Senegal and Zimbabwe. 'Youth' in this context has not, as Richards argued, supplanted 'ethnicity', but has often turned secessionist and political conflicts in Africa into 'ethnic-youth' movements. The tendency to deprioritize higher education in the Third World has been an important contributing factor in these conflicts (Krueger and Maleckova 2002).

If the WB advocates a system of loans and fees—introduced almost without exception across Africa—then there needs to be a pool of students who are able to take up and pay the loans. This is contingent on two factors, real wages that can sustain a system of loans and fees, and employment for students after graduation to ensure the repayment of these loans (White House 2002). There is an additional problem connected to the relationship between primary and tertiary education. If the WB is motivated by a desire to expand primary education then by necessity it requires a complementary expansion of teaching graduates from universities. Caffentzis (2002: 11) has argued that if the yearly influx from tertiary education must increase by 10 per cent a year then an enrolment growth rate of 1 per cent can not keep up with the stated demands of expanding primary education and the WB is 'subverting its own alleged objective: the expansion and improvement of primary education'.

The centrepiece of WB reform for higher education in Africa (and the Third World) is the 'economic' return on education provision. In resource-strapped economies limited funds must not be diverted to the low returns of higher education but must re-emphasize the primary and secondary sectors where there are higher real returns on the money invested from state budgets. Bloom (2001) has criticized this pattern of reforms:

> Take someone who has no education, someone who has been to primary school, someone who has completed secondary school, and someone with a degree. How much more does each earn than the previous? This differential is then compared to the amount invested in their education to find the return. The results suggest that higher education yields a lower return than primary or secondary education—and has been used to justify the skewing of government budgets (and development funds) away from higher education institutions.

This approach has the effect of reducing education to a zero-sum game that places primary education in a competitive struggle with higher and university education. Rather, as Bloom argues, education is a 'positive sum game'.[5] The report of the 'Higher Education and Developing Countries: Peril and Promise' (2000), funded by the WB includes an important criticism of the approach previously taken by the Bank:

> Since the 1980s, many national governments and international donors have assigned higher education a relatively low priority. Narrow—and, in our view, misleading—economic analysis has contributed to the view that public investment in universities and colleges brings meagre returns compared to investment in primary and secondary schools, and that higher education magnifies income inequality. (WB 2000: 10)

The report notes that although 85 per cent of the world's population lives in the Third World, less than half of the world's 80 million students in higher education are from these parts of the world. The report stresses the problems for students in the Third World:

> They are taught by poorly-qualified, poorly-motivated and (no surprise) poorly-compensated faculty, struggling with inadequate facilities and outmoded curricula. The secondary education system has often failed to prepare these students adequately for advanced study—and, once on campus, political activism, violence, cheating, corruption and discrimination can undermine their progress. (Bloom 2001)

These are not reasons to undermine higher education but, on the contrary, 'We have educated more and more young people to primary and secondary level—but, like Oliver Twist, they want more! They realize something that even the richest governments are only beginning to wake up to: in today's world, higher education is basic education. Education that is needed by the masses—and can no longer be confined to a tiny elite' (Bloom 2001). In the report the university sector is regarded as a system to both generate national elites to respond to the 'challenges' of globalization and 'to promote prosperity among people with talent and motivation, irrespective of their social origins' (Bloom 2001). However, there are few signs that the WB or IMF have accepted these criticisms, or that after twenty years they can see the importance of higher education in Africa.

NEW STUDENT MOVEMENTS OR DESCENT INTO CORPORATISM?

There is the danger of exceptionalizing the experience of higher education in Africa, that the university system is uniquely affected by catastrophe and crisis. This is an important consideration when examining the state of student activism in higher education in Africa.

The literature tends to emphasize the same 'tragedy', with students and youth seen as the quintessential 'lost generation' (Cruise O'Brien 1996). Can we speak as Barkan (1975: 128–30) did 30 years ago of an 'African pattern' dividing the behaviour of African university students and European and American ones? The implication in this example was that students in the West were driven by higher political ideals. Frederici (2000: 103) is unequivocal about the question: 'we can speak today of an international student movement, and that African students are paying by far the heaviest cost for the effort this movement is making to reverse the corporate agenda by which education is being reshaped worldwide'.[6] The argument finds a parallel in Boren (2001) whose global survey of 'student resistance' makes a case for the same pan-student approach.

There is an important divide in the literature on student activism that has ramifications for the understanding of student politics not just in the current period but historically. One strand of opinion is propagated by the editorial board of the important American newsletter Committee for Academic Freedom in Africa (CAFA) and summarized in *A Thousand Flowers: Social Struggles against Structural Adjustment in African Universities*, a collection of essays by the authors of the newsletter. Their arguments are very persuasive: They state their objectives in the introduction to the collection:

> Although the state is the immediate perpetrator, the ultimate responsibility for many violations of academic rights on the African campuses is borne by international financial institutions and more specifically, by the policy of 'adjustment' adopted by Washington and the European Union in the 1980s, that calls for the virtual recolonisation of Africa's educational systems.
>
> The attack on the universities is part of a broader attack on the place of Africa in the International Division of Labor, on the value of African workers, and on the capacity of Africans to achieve self-determination, the still unrealised goal of the anti-colonial struggle.
>
> Defending the struggles of students and teachers in Africa is to defend the right of the African youth to study. This means the right to have equal access, with European and North American youth, and the youth of other countries across the world, to the knowledge and the wealth produced internationally, rather than being condemned to poverty and migration, the lot reserved for them in the plans of international financial institutions now ruling Africa's political economy. (Alidou et al. 2000: xiii)

They have provided a running critique of the policies of the WB and IMF in Africa from the point of view of popular protest and student resistance (CAFA 1991, 1996). They maintain that in the escalation of student protest since the introduction of SAPs in Africa from the early 1980s there has emerged a new 'pan-African student movement, continuous in its political aspirations with the student activism that developed in the context of the anti-colonial struggle, and yet more radical in its challenges to the established political power' (Frederici 2000: 88). The effects of SAPs have massively proletarianized the African student body, breaking them from their recent post-colonial past as members of the elite (Frederici 2000: 93).

The partial withdrawal of the state from higher education in Africa has altered the nature of elite formation at the university. Much of the literature confirms these arguments. Piet Koning (2002: 180–1) makes a similar point to CAFA in reference to the student rebellions in the late 1980s and early 1990s:

> As a result of such state withdrawal, African universities no longer appeared to be serving as centres of elite formation. . . . Little wonder that they have been inclined to see corrupt and authoritarian regimes as responsible for their predicament and to perceive a 'democratic transition' as a necessary condition for change in society in general and in universities in particular.

Equally, Mamdani (1994) has seen a similar development as part of a process transforming the African class system, where the limited expansion of the African 'middle classes' after independence has been reversed as state directed initiatives receded from the 1970s onwards. The impact on higher education was clear:

> the growth in a state-financed higher and secondary education sector, whose enrolment came less and less from affluent families, went alongside shrinking opportunities for middle class advancement in a crisis-prone economy.
>
> (Mamdani 1994: 258)

There has been a process of 'institutional liberalization' that has caused explosions in student activism in recent years. The new *proletarianized* student population that has resisted the polices of SAPs and their application to higher education have created a qualitatively different form of student activism. This allows us to view the 'present phase of student activism not as a set of separate struggles but as one pan-African student movement' (Frederici 2000: 96).

Some writers and activists argue that there was a 'convergence of forces' between previously privileged—now proletarianized students and the urban poor. The case is put most forcefully by the former student leader at the University of Zimbabwe, Brian Kagoro (2003). Referring to a period of activism in the mid-1990s he said:

> so you now had students supporting their parents on their student stipends which were not enough, because their parents had been laid off work. So in a sense as poverty increases you have a *reconvergence of these forces.* And the critique started . . . around issues of social economic justice, [the] right to a living wage . . . students started couching their demands around a right to livelihood (interview 23 June 2003).

Seddon (2002) raises many similar themes, defining these 'new' popular forces as including the urban and rural working classes broadly defined as well as other categories, including the so-called 'lumpen proletariat', day-labourers and the unemployed, workers in the informal sector, small (and sometimes medium) peasants, small retailers, craftsmen and artisans, petty commodity producers (see also Zeilig and Seddon 2005). If we extend Kagoro's argument we can say that the social expectations (and pauperization) of students 'converged' with these 'forces' during the period of structural adjustment. As Harrison (2002: 114) has noted, 'One can see the decline of corporatism and the increasing informalisation of the urban economy '[as] . . . the reformulation of . . . political identities into a realm of fiscal austerity and speculation.' The 'hybridization' of these social forces bringing together exceedingly motley groups has altered the mobilisation and activism of students.'

These arguments contrast with much of the commentary: for example, Bathily et al. reverse the categorization made by *CAFA* and *A Thousand Flowers.* It is necessary, they argue, to separate student activism from its perceived heyday in the 1960s and 1970s to the disintegration of the movement during the last twenty years. Today students are written off, 'left with their daily corporatism and the inefficiency of their fights' (Bathily et al. 1995: 401). Yesterday they were harbingers of a brighter future: 'If prior to World War II students tacitly accepted being petty bourgeois with colonial linkages, up to the mid-1970s they claimed a left vanguard status' (Bathily et al. 1995: 401). They make their argument by charting the evolution of student activism:

> But at the end of the day, they only managed some vigils with hardly any support. They appeared at most as the enlightened conscience of their people on the path to complete emancipation and modernisation. They managed

to shift from their role as supporters of the Western system . . . to that of rejecting it totally. . . . By the late 1970s . . . students saw themselves [as] . . . political and economic failures. (Bathily et al. 1995: 401)

The argument asserts that with the collapse of the post-colonial 'social pact' student engagement has become 'corporatist', concerned only with issues of 'bread and butter'. In the case of Senegal, 'By the late 1970s Senegalese students saw themselves more modestly as symbols of the independent stalemate, of the political and economic failure of a regime which was unable to provide them with clear survival prospects.' Students, following this argument, have lost their status 'from providers of modernity they became aid applicants' (Bathily et al. 1995: 405). The respected scholar Cruise O'Brien makes a similar point about student protests in defence of their 'elite status': 'And students will riot for their privileges too . . . defending their "right" to better scholarship' (Cruise O'Brien 1996: 65).

While these arguments tend to avoid the heroic discourse with students 'counter-posing and confronting the abuses of state power' (Boyer 2002: 210), they miss the 'novelty' in the wave of popular protest that has swept Africa in the last fifteen years. Far from understanding the 'role of students in the "democratic transition" ' (Konings 2002: 180) as part of a generalized revolt, these arguments dismiss the significance of student revolt. Frederici (2000: 101) sees 'students' struggle to defend education as "an inalienable right"; they are fighting not in defense of a privilege or a corporatist interest, but against it.' Students are, on the contrary, attempting to 'reverse the corporate agenda by which education is being reshaped world-wide' (Frederici 2000: 103).

However, there is a tendency in *CAFA* and *A Thousand Flowers* to downplay the ambiguity of student protest. While they describe the significance and celebrate the resistance of the student population in Africa, they miss the way student movements have become, in certain respects, subject to manipulation and co-option. They capture the 'novelty' of the new resistance among students but neglect the new directions that this activism can take. Students today are 'situated in a complex field of societal power, class interest . . . and moral positions' (Boyer 2002: 211) that create, in conditions of social breakdown, unique and challenging forms of activism. Historically the argument remains that university students—a small minority—attending higher education in the 1960 and 1970s were regarded as either destined to become members of the ruling elite or important state functionaries. Although the case for describing students of the period as elites is well made, there is a tendency to overstate the argument (Federici 2000; Hanna 1975).

STUDENTS AND THE DEMOCRATIC TRANSITION

In his celebrated popular history of student resistance, Boren (2001: 240) notes that the last decade of the millennium saw students in Africa play a leading role in the democratic transition: 'In the wake of Eastern European revolutions against Communism, and the rampant local economic difficulties, many African students increased pro-democracy efforts and campaigned for the establishment of multiple-party political systems.' Commentators celebrated the student revolts across Africa: 'political liberalization, starting at the end of the 1980s unleashed an unprecedented wave of student rebellion on university campuses in West and Central Africa' (Konings 2002: 180). News reports of the day were replete with analysis of the democratic struggles in Africa, often questioning the role of students.[8] Still, there is a recognized lack of serious research on the role of students in democratic transition (Buijtenhuijs and Thiriot 1995; Mills 2004: 671). Students were part of the broad and popular alliances that developed between opposition groups during, and immediately after, the processes of democratic change.

Perhaps it is advisable to express a certain caution about the connection that is often (and lazily) made between events in Africa and eastern Europe. Boren (2001) makes the common assumption that the events in Africa in the early 1990s were a direct corollary of the revolutions that swept aside the Stalinist regimes in eastern Europe. This idea received some support from incumbent regimes conscious of the events in Europe. Mazrui (1994) has questioned these assumptions: 'we cannot trace all democratic forces in Africa to the . . . impact of Eastern Europe' (1994: 172). He states that the origins of these movements can be properly traced back to earlier acts of democratic struggle—long predating the upheavals in Eastern Europe (see Table 17.3). Indeed some commentators state that the origins of these movements are found in the first wave of 'bread riots' in Egypt in 1977 and early anti-SAP revolts (Marfleet 2000; Alexander and Renton 2002; Seddon and Walton 1994).[9]

Mazrui (1994: 172) continues to press his point, 'What should be borne in mind is that the role model for Africa has not been

TABLE 17.3: INCIDENTS OF STUDENT ACTIVISM DURING THE DEMOCRATIC TRANSITION 1985–95

Year	No. of incidents
1985	6
1986	5
1987	10
1988	6
1989	11
1990	11
1991	15
1992	15
1993	16
1994	22
1995	5

Source: Federici (2000: 112).

necessarily the impact of demonstrations across the Berlin Wall. It has been youthful riots against armed apartheid.' Although the influence of pan-African struggles has an important impact on the mobilization of student and trade union militants, it was the shared nature of the economic crisis gripping Africa that brought these movements together (Saul 2001). Still it is important not to completely discount the effect of the changes in the USSR and eastern Europe. These countries had functioned as the ideological glue for generations of left-wing activists, students and intellectuals, as well as providing scholarships for students to the Soviet bloc (Zeilig and Seddon 2002). The dismantling of these regimes undermined the states in Africa politically connected to and funded by the USSR, and the political confidence of militants and intellectuals whose ideological moorings had been tied to Stalinism. Marzui (1994: 173) summarized the main points at the time:

> The speedy abandonment of one-partyism by Eastern European countries has made it harder for its African champions to carry adequate conviction on its behalf. It is in that sense that glasnost and perestroika in Eastern Europe and the Soviet Union have helped the cause of the liberal revival in Africa—though that liberal revival was already underway regardless of events in Europe.

While these events might have broken the confidence of an older generation of activists, they gave new life to student politics that many argued had collapsed irredeemably into 'corporatism' and 'factionalism'. In 1989, the movement started in the West African state of Bénin when students demonstrated against the government in January, demanding overdue grants and a guarantee of public sector employment after graduation. The government, crippled by financial scandals, capital flight and falling tax revenue, thought it could respond as it had always done, by suppressing the protest. But the movement grew during the year to incorporate trade unions and the urban poor. Half way through the year in the hope of placating the demonstrators President Mathieu Kérékou invited a human rights campaigner into his government. In a pattern followed by other countries he set up a commission that eventually created a 'national reconciliation conference' that included the opposition movement, trade unions, students and religious associations (*Jeune Afrique,* 1991).

Students at the University of Kinshasa in Zaire were the first to initiate the protests that almost unseated Mobutu, and led to a largely urban protest movement and transition that lasted into the middle of the 1990s (Martins 2002; Renton et al. 2006). They demonstrated on 5 May 1990 asserting that the reforms announced by the dictator ten days early were 'irrevocable'. The demonstration ended violently after security forces attacked it. The students immediately issued an appeal to other universities and colleges across the country to rise up in solidarity. '[D]o not cross your arms. Follow our example. The dictatorship is finished. We cannot go back. Take on the state. Demonstrate! March!' (Nkongolo 2000: 182).

The call to arms was answered. Students at the University of Lubumbashi responded to the call, demonstrating daily in the city and at the university from 9 May. On 11 May the student uprising in Katanga (the southern most region of Zaire) was bought to a swift and violent end: a 'squadron of death' was sent to the university by the president. Dozens of students who had led the strikes and demonstrations were killed, and their bodies disappeared. Their parents were unable to complain. Without wider protests the students could be picked up, killed and isolated. For thousands the massacre in Lubumbashi exposed the reality of Mobutu's 'reforms'. There was strong condemnation of the massacre from humanitarian organizations, and the Belgian government announced immediate suspension of official bilateral assistance to Zaire. After some procrastination and strenuous denial of the reports, Mobutu authorized an official parliamentary enquiry, as a result of which a provincial governor and other senior local officials were arrested and charged with having organized the killing of one student and the injury of 13 others. Despite a news blackout, it emerged that the massacre had sparked serious clashes between students and government forces in other towns, including Kisangani, Bukavu and Mbanza-Ngungu. The massacre was in many ways pivotal to the early stages of the transition in Zaire, and it is still the subject of controversy and debate (Nzongola-Ntalaja 2002: 155–6; Munikengi and Sangol 2004: 99).

Students were crucial to spearheading the resistance in Zimbabwe. In 1989 a student leaflet denounced the Investment Code that further facilitated foreign investment in Zimbabwe. It argued that the code would lead to further entrenchment of capitalism in Zimbabwe, . . . an acquiescence to the IMF and World Bank sponsored programmes . . . and incompatible with the doctrine of socialism' (quoted in Tengenende 1996: 389–92). Many students attended the May Day rallies in Harare, whilst the Students Union condemned the suppression of a strike by doctors: 'The use of force which was exercised on Doctors while they were airing their clear, legitimate grievances is really an authoritarian and neo-fascist tendency and hence it has to be condemned.' When the university was closed on 4 October 1989 following the arrest of students union leaders for organizing a celebration of the previous year's Anti-Corruption Demonstration, the Zimbabwe Congress of Trade Unions (ZCTU) general secretary, Morgan Tsvangirai, denounced the arrest in strong terms and was detained for over four weeks (Gwisai 2002b). At the 1991 May Day celebrations, the ZCTU organized an event under the theme 'Liberalization or Liberation'. Workers paraded with banners denouncing SAP: 'Employers liberated, workers sacrificed'; 'Are we going to make 1991 the Year of the World Bank Storm?'; 'The Year of the People's Misery'. Meanwhile the Ministry of Labour distributed its own leaflets telling workers to 'Suffer Now and Benefit later' (quoted in Tengenende 1996: 427). The criticism of the ZCTU mirrored that of the University of Zimbabwe Students Union (Gwisai 2002b).

In Mali, according to one important account, it was not university students but young unemployed college graduates who initiated the first protests on 15 October 1990 against the one-party state. The mobilization was small, roughly 15 young men marched through the centre of the capital with banners that declared 'Down with the UDPM [*Union Démocratique du Peuple Malien*]'. The demonstrators were attacked and arrested by the police. As Brenner (2001: 242) contends, 'their initiative immediately preceded, and may well have helped to precipitate the emergence into public of the clandestine opposition movement which had been actively organising and plotting for some years against the regime of Moussa Traoré' (see also Buijtenhuijs and Thirot 1995).

The collapse into sectarian factionalism affected the student body when the transition was frustrated or after it had been achieved. The examples of Mali and Cameroon are illustrative of these processes. Mali experienced a period of 'democratic transition' at the same time as other countries in the region. There had been major demonstrations against the regime of Moussa Traoré in January 1990, when thousands took part in street protests demanding political reform and an end to Traoré's 22-year rule. The government was finally bought down in April 1991. The central role of students inside the *Association des Elèves et Etudiants du Mali* (AEEM) in the democratic transition is widely recognized (Brenner 2001; Smith 1997).[10] A 'memorandum' was issued listing student demands in return for an immediate end to strikes. It included a 50 per cent rise in the scholarship, followed by a further 25 per cent in six months; the expansion of the scholarship to include secondary school students; and physical improvements to the university and schools. While there was a widely recognized appreciation of the justness of these demands there was a similar understanding by the government that they could not hope to meet them (Smith 1997). Within a short space of time the new government of Alpha Oumar Konaré confronted the wrath of his erstwhile political allies.[11]

By 1993 students in AEEM were calling for action against the government for failing to honour the promises made in the memorandum. Class-boycotts, strikes and demonstrations punctuated the following years. In 1993 the leadership of AEEM was divided between those supporting the government and those arguing for more militant action. The government were keen to exploit these divisions: 'In response to this unrest, the government attempted to manipulate divisions within the AEEM leadership by funding a "palace coup" in which a faction of the student leaders . . . tried to replace the elected leader' (Smith 1997: 249). One student expressed the dilemmas for many AEEM leaders with the recent experience of the 'revolution' (democratic transition):

> I was young, I still am and I love Alpha and marched with ADEMA [*Alliance pour la Démocratie au Mali*] during the revolution to bring down Moussa.

> Imagine, I am a student leader and I am called by the president of my country, he invites me to his office and flatters me telling me how much potential I have. He then tells me that our activities are threatening democracy and asks for my help to save the country. I thought then what I did was in the best interest of democracy. (Smith, 1997: 251)

The government manipulated the student movement thoroughly, providing scholarships to foreign universities for several leading members of AEEM. By 1995 the students union was so divided that it had lost the support of the population and could only rely on the fractured and intermittent loyalty of its own members. AEEM even split at one point with the new organization calling itself 'Friends of the Schools' which, amid accusations that it was funded by the government, argued for the opening of schools and the resumption of classes. The rupture with the ruling party was complete by the time of the next elections, and the damage to the AEEM seemingly irreparable. Student protests were broken up by tear gas and students who had previously declared their love of Alpha 'burned campaign posters of Konaré and banners of the ADEMA party' (Smith 1997: 263).

The experience of 'democratic transition' in Cameroon contrasts with many of the examples already given. The process of political liberalization was protracted and violent, yet it provided students with a space to express themselves (Konings 2002). This expression took both a party and ethnic line. The government exploited these differences, which resulted in the emergence of two groups at the University of Yaoundé. The student body was divided between 'strangers', students organized in the Student's Parliament aligned to the opposition, and the 'indigenous' Beti students, loyal to the ruling regime and organized in the Committee for Self-Defence and the Beti Militia. The nature of the 'democratic transition' led to violence and disruption at the university that continued practically unabated from 1990 to 1996.

Students at the University of Yaoundé were deemed to be relatively privileged: the low level of political activism prior to 1991 testifies to this fact (Konings 2002). Even in the late 1970s when the openings for university graduates began to shrink, President Ahidjo and then his successor Paul Biya forced vacancies for them in the state administration. Student numbers at the university exceeded 40,000 in 1992 although the conditions for students and staff were diabolical (Konings 2002: 182). However, part of the reason for this was a high degree of political repression that out-lawed student organizations, and police spies repeatedly disguised themselves as students to infiltrate the campus. The processes of political liberalization in the 1990s combined with deep dissatisfaction at the deterioration of conditions under the impact of SAP. The introduction of multi-partyism did not cleanse the regime of undemocratic habits but led them to use the 'liberalization' to divide the student body. As early as March 1991, *Jeune Afrique* had noted the contradiction in the progress of the 'democratic transition' in Cameroon; one article was titled *Le pluralisme en marche au Cameroun, mais l'Etat est en panne.*[12]

The regional and ethnic cleavages became more prominent after the formation of the opposition SDF, which was founded in Anglophone Cameroon (Mbembe 1991). The reaction of the regime and Beti supporters formed support groups, including the Commando Delta, Direct Action and the National Front for Beti Liberation. The support that Fru Ndi and the SDF received in the southern capital Yaoundé was frequently from the 'Anglo-Bami' communities living in the city. National political cleavages found a similar expression in the political activism of students on the campus. The president exploited ethnic divisions, emphasizing his Beti origin and allying Beti students on the campus to the ruling CPDM, explicitly opposed to Anglophone Bamileke 'strangers' who often regarded the anglophone John Fru Ndi in the SDF as their champion. Although there were historical roots to the crisis that now afflicted Cameroon and the university, they had not expressed themselves so virulently in the period prior to political liberalization. 'Parliament' members seeing themselves as revolutionaries were allied to militant elements in the opposition, that saw the overthrow of the regime as the only answer to the political stalemate in the country and at the university. The Committee for Self-Defense attempted to respond to the perceived threat from opposition members on the campus, regarding the objectives of the Parliament as tantamount to the destruction of 'their' university and country. The committee members—a small minority of students—were permitted to carry knives, clubs and guns to intimidate Parliament members and they worked in tandem with other vigilante groups. The Parliament formed its own 'self-defence' groups (Konings 2002).

The first political crisis at the university occurred in 1990, when students marched in favour of the SDF and multi-partyism. This led to the permanent presence of gendarmes—or ninjas as they were called by students—on the campus. Students used the political opening allowed in the country at the time to set up their first autonomous organizations that, as we have seen, quickly became polarized. By 1991, along with the opposition, students called for a sovereign national conference, a political formation that was a popular demand during the 'democratic transitions' in Africa. The year ended with a prolonged student strike against the late payment of scholarships. As the chaos on the campus escalated over the next few years the university authorities resorted to further desperate measures. In 1993 the university chancellor Peter Aghor Tabi ordered the Beti militias on the campus to step up their attacks on students (Zeilig and Seddon 2002).

By 1996 another group directly affiliated to Biya's party, PRESBY ('President Biya's Youth'), had replaced the self-defense groups. Like earlier formations, this group was a constellation 'composed mainly of university students and other sections of the educated youth either engaged in informal-sector activities or unemployed, including a number of university graduates and dropouts' (Konings 2002: 201). The process of political liberalization in Cameroon demonstrates diverse patterns of political behaviours and activism in the period of 'democratic transition'. Students do not appear here as heroes or as a permanent political avant-garde, but rather as contradictory social actors, prone to political manipulation and division. The defining elements in student protests in these examples are the wider configurations of political forces involved in the 'democratic transition'.

CONCLUSION

Students were not isolated political actors behaving simply as democratic vanguards; they were neither 'demons nor democrats' as some commentary has expressed the distinction (Smith 1997). Their role in the 'democratic transitions' was complex because it was inextricably tied to the liberalization of political space and the manipulations of these processes by incumbent governments and political parties. The 'success' of student activism was linked to the wider social forces that they could help animate and identify with. It was tied to their ability to 'converge' their struggles with broader popular forces. Mamdani (1994) is correct to recognize that when students were effective they succeeded in 'forcing an opening up' even if they lacked an alternative strategy: 'Its possibilities depended far more on the character of forces that student action succeeded in mobilizing than its own internal energies' (Mamdani 1994: 259).

Popular mobilizations were a response to widespread disaffection with the policies of austerity and structural adjustment, yet these movements were responding in new ways. Class structures in sub-Saharan Africa had been transformed, and resistance did not simply take old forms (Alavi and Shanin 1982; Cohen 1982). The processes of class alignment and resistance brought in new and heterogeneous forces (Harrison 2002; Seddon 2002; see also Seddon and Zeiling 2005). Seddon (2002) defines the role of the 'popular classes' in Africa, describing a shifting constellation of political forces that included the unemployed, informal sector traders and trade unionists. This paper argues that students and unemployed graduates also form an important part of the popular classes. As Harrison (2002: 119–20) correctly formulates the issues:

> The salience of youth identities derives from a broader set of changes. Economic crisis has had a direct and negative impact on the postcolonial social political project of modernisation. The ensuing ruptures of social life have impacted on . . . urban society—notably they are part of the context in which the working class has become fractured and 'informalised'. . . . But the particular situation of youth, either leaving school to find employment, dignity and independence, or leaving university to join the middle classes, predominately through linkages with the state, gives a peculiarly sharpened twist to the experience of Africa's recent economic decline.

This 'informalization' or 'hybridization' of the social structure is not the effect of 'indeterminacy of political identity' but the product of the political economy in much of Africa (Harrison 2002: 113). These circumstances form the inherited structures that contemporary students have been forced to negotiate. Students are not 'free-floating' above the political and economic crisis. The resulting hybrity of social groups in Africa has transformed their activism and identity and affected their ability to exercise political agency. We can say that students expressed their status as politically privileged actors in diverse forms during the political transitions, yet repeatedly they have sparked wider protests in a period that has seen the 'convergence of social forces'.

Higher education reforms, as we have seen, have transported student identity into the maelstrom of the structural crisis. Mamdani (1994: 258–9), in an important study on class and the intelligentsia, has seen these processes at work: 'previously a more or less guaranteed route to position and privilege, higher education seemed to lead more and more students to the heart of the economic and social crisis' Students are no longer the 'transitory' social group waiting to be allotted government employment; on the contrary they have become pauperized, converging more and more with the wider urban poor: social groups that they had historically regarded as their 'responsibility' to liberate. Are they a marginal social group? They are only marginal in so far as the whole of urban society has become marginalized from the formal economy, forced increasingly into a precarious world of causal and informal employment. In one important extent they have become less marginal to the social world that they sought to change in the 1960s and 1970s.

There is an international dimension to these developments that should not be ignored. It can be argued that the neo-liberal processes that have led to the privatisation and commodification of university education in sub-Saharan Africa have had a global reach. Across the world student movements have grappled with the changing nature of university education. Nowhere is this clearer than in France, where globally the student movement is perhaps at its strongest. Here there is a direct symmetry in the lives and experiences of students and the working class. This is explained brilliantly by the Marxist writer Daniel Bensaid, when he describes the differences between the current period and the so-called high-point of student unrest in 1968:

> The present movement is directly based on a social question—the destruction of workplace regulations and the generalized casualisation of employment, which is common both in education and to workers. The question of the link, and not just solidarity, between the two is therefore immediate.
>
> Finally, the fundamental difference is with the general context and in particular with the way unemployment weighs on things. In 1968, the unemployed were counted in tens of thousands in a period of great expansion, so students had no worries about the future.

This is a central issue. Unemployment in the 1960s counted in tens of thousands, was practically full employment, meaning that unemployment one week would be followed by employment the next. Students were a privileged part of this stable economic milieu. However, in France today Bensaid continues, 'six million people are either without work or causally employed'. This has impacted enormously on the identity of students today, who require no ideological leap to connect their activism to the labour movement.

The link, as Bensaid argues, is immediate. Students do not simply dabble in the social world outside the university campus—committed as they might have been in 1968 to building the bonds of solidarity with the labour movement—they are a central component of it. Often this connection is explicit in terms of student involvement in the labour force, but there is also a political dimension to these changes:

> The link is natural, and the labour movement is less closed, or even hostile, than it was towards students in 1968.
>
> At the time this hostility, or wariness, was fostered in particular by the workerist demagoguery of the Communist Party. . . .
>
> Today relations are not so closed. On the one hand the ability of the bureaucratic machines to control things has been considerably weakened.
>
> On the other the overall expansion of secondary and higher education means it is no longer possible to portray students as an exclusively middle class layer. (Socialist Worker, 4 April 2006)

These comments could as easily be made about the experience in much of Africa, buffeted by the same blows of globalization. However student activism internationally is still instilled with an important element of elitism, though now tempered by the realities of campus poverty. They have a considerable ability to mobilize in relatively autonomous urban spaces, achieving an organizational coherence that is rarely matched by other social groups. The power of students to set-off wider social protests was again vividly demonstrated by French students earlier in 1996.

This paper has concentrated on the neo-liberal reform of education across the continent in the 1980s and 1990s and the patterns of student resistance and activism. One of the central factors influencing student politics was the ability to contest the ideological foundations of structural adjustment. The capacity of student organizations to confront the 'world-view' presented by their governments (before and after the transitions) and the IFIs, helped shape their political agency. But their ability to do this was influenced by wider political forces in society, and they were disabled by the lack of a coherent ideological alternative to neo-liberal reforms. Students found themselves buffeted together with the popular classes, by the resumption of a more or less unopposed politics of adjustment and austerity.

Student activism has been affected by the vacillations in the popular movements that they have helped to mobilize. Once new governments had been installed (Senegal, Mali) or old regimes revived (Cameroon, Zimbabwe), the tempo of resistance and student activism receded, often returning to the 'corporatist' and piecemeal demands that many commentators have wrongly interpreted as representing a new phase in student activism. The 'corporatism'—or economism[13]—of student politics is not symptomatic of a new and qualitatively different student movement, nor, as Bathily et al. (1995: 401) imply, of a slide into irrelevance:

> [S]tudents . . . are only in a transition, over which they have no control because they have no impact on the socio-economic stakes. So instead of being actors/initiators of this change, they have turned into mere artefacts of this evolution.

According to this account, the only barrier preventing students from assuming their full role as 'actors/initiators' is their temporality. However, the status of 'student'—at university, as graduate, as a 'cartouchard'[14] or part of the mass of unemployed—is not impermanent. The crisis for students in sub-Saharan Africa is precisely because they are not in 'transition'; on the contrary they are increasingly permanent 'artefacts' in the post-colonial impasse. Their activism—always complex and contradictory—retreats into a routine of 'economic' and factional contestation when wider popular and democratic movements in society decline or are frustrated.

In Malawi students at the university together with academic staff were important in the mobilizations that eventually toppled the Banda regime in the multiparty elections in 1994. As Kerr and Mapanje (2002: 86) have stated, 'students and staff marched in protest against the regime during the demonstrations sparked by the Catholic Bishops' Pastoral Letter of March 1992 and during the riots of May in the same year'. Although they note a wave of activism during the transition from 1991 to 1993, they also lament the decline of student politics into 'corporatist' concerns after this period. By 1994 there were even cases of male students at the university attacking and ridiculing female students and lecturers.

After the victory of Bakilli Muluzi and his United Democratic Front, the Malawian government participated uncritically in the project of structural adjustment and economic liberalization that had given the resistance to the previous regime such impetus. The University of Malawi continued to deteriorate: 'Research funding was available only for programs financed by donor communities with specific agendas. Government subventions for salaries and such essential resources as books, journals, computers, photocopiers, paper . . . remained pitifully small' (Kerr and Mapanji 2002: 87). The 'lassitude' that Kerr and Mapanji claim affected students after the elections in 1994 was tied to the resumption of economic structural adjustment programmes after a period of democratic transition. The same disillusionment and 'lassitude' gripped student politics in dozens of campuses across sub-Saharan Africa as governments that had emerged from the 'transition' committed themselves to implementing the IMF and WB reforms. The predominance of neo-liberalism across the continent after the democratic transition ensured a quick death for the African renaissance and the movements that had heralded it.

NOTES

1. Amutabi argues that the student movement managed, almost uniquely, to hold aloft the banner of democratization.
2. Five countries were nominated as case studies, all apparently showing positive signs of such liberalization. These countries were Uganda, Ghana, South Africa, Tanzania and Mozambique.
3. How the experience of Makerere University in Uganda demonstrates the benefits of 'democratization' in higher education in a country that has specifically outlawed 'democratization' is never explained.
4. However, the great majority of privileged students are not sent, and will not be sent, to improved and more selective national universities. On the contrary the trend is to educate the children of a wealthy elite in the United States (the country of preference for everyone), France (particularly for students from Senegal) and the UK. In Zimbabwe, South Africa is a closer and far cheaper option, with a large number of relatively well-funded universities. This suggests that South Africa is at variance with some of the arguments made in the paper.
5. This implies that there cannot be a simple economic trade off between primary and tertiary education, as they fulfil distinct roles in society. However, for years this was exactly how the WB viewed education reform in Africa.
6. There are, of course, additional dangers of conflating the behaviour of African students with their European and American counterparts. It is hard to see any point in investigating African student movements if they are simply elements of an already existing international student movement as Frederici et al. (2000) contend. To what extent do students—in Africa and Europe—regard themselves as part of such an 'international movement'? Or are these categories imposed on essentially national 'movements'? While it is possible to argue that they are linked to an international wave

of resistance to structural adjustment (Walton and Seddon 1994) and neo-liberalism, for this resistance to be part of a 'movement'—let alone an international one—surely these links have to be conscious and explicit among the students themselves?

7. However, it is important to caution against generalizing about the proletarianized status of students. The picture varies across the continent. A survey of students at the national university in Maputo in Mozambique revealed the over-representation of Maputo students at universities and a correlation between prestigious degree courses and family status (Mario and Fry 2003: 31). Mills (2004) suggests that the elite status of students in higher education in Mozambique is demonstrated at Eduardo Mondlane University in Maputo where 80 per cent of students speak Portuguese as a first language.
8. 'La démocratie envers et contre tout', *Jeune Afrique*, 27 March–2 April 1991; 'Que veulent les étudiants?', *Jeune Afrique*, 11–16 July 1991.
9. Some even extend these hypotheses by arguing that the current anti-capitalist movement originates in the Third World and comes out of the 'bread riots' that greeted the impact of structural adjustment policies (Caffentzis 2002).
10. The slogan of the AEEM conjures up the atmosphere of the period *Oser lutter, c'est oser vaincre, la lutte continue* (To dare to fight is to dare to overcome, the struggle continues).
11. It is worth noting that Zeric Kay Smith (1997: 264) interviewed members of the donor community who unanimously maintained that AEEM had a negative impact on the country's democratic governance: 'This negative view was also amply evident in interviews I conducted with members of the World Bank mission in Mali.'
12. 'Multi-partyism makes progress in Cameroon but the state has broken down'
13. Interestingly the same criticism of 'economism' is made of the trade union movement, forgetting that an umbilical cord connects political and economic struggles. This was a point made powerfully by Rosa Luxemburg (1906) in her book *The Mass Strike*.
14. Term used in Senegal to describe students who have exhausted almost all of their chances (literately their 'cartridges') giving them just one more chance in the annual exams (Bianchini 2002: 368).

REFERENCES

Abrahamsen, R. (2000), *Disciplining Democracy: Development Discourse and Good Governance in Africa*, London: Zed Books.

Federici, S., G. Caffentzis and O. Alidou (2000), *A Thousand Flowers: Social Struggles Against Structural Adjustment in African Universities*, Trenton, Asmara: Africa World Press.

Bako, S. (1994), 'Education and Adjustment in Nigeria', in M. Diouf and M. Mamdani (eds.), *Academic Freedom in Africa*, Dakar: CODESRIA.

Barkan, J.D. (1975), *An African Dilemma: University Students, Development and Politics in Ghana, Tanzania and Uganda*, Nairobi: Oxford University Press.

Bathily, A., M. Diouf and M. Mbodj (1995), 'The Senegalese Student Movement from its Inception to 1989', in M. Mamdani and E. Wamba-Dia-Wamba (eds.), *African Studies in Social Movements and Democracy*, Dakar: CODESRIA.

Bathily, A. (1992), *Mai 68 à Dakar ou la Révolte Universitaire et la Démocratie*, Paris: Chaka.

Bianchini, P. (2002), 'Le mouvement étudiant Sénégalais. Un essai d'interprétation', in M.C. Diop, *La Société Sénéglaise entre le local et le global*, Paris: Karthala.

Bloom, D. (2001), 'Opening Address' at the conference *Globalization and Higher Education: Views from the South*, Education Policy Unit at the University of the Western Cape, http://www.tfhe.net/resources/Cape_town.htm.

Bond, P. (2002), *Against Global Apartheid: South Africa Meets the World Bank, IMF and International Finance*, Cape Town: University of Cape Town Press.

Boyer, D. (2002), 'The African Crisis in Context: Comparative Encounters with Educational Rationalization', *African Studies Review*, 45(2), pp. 205–18.

Boren, M.E. (2001), *Student Resistance: A History of the Unruly Subject*, New York: Routledge.

Brenner, L. (2001), *Controlling Knowledge: Religion, Power and Schooling in a West African Muslim Society*, Bloomington: Indiana University Press.

Caffentzis, G. (2000), 'The World Bank and Education in Africa', in O. Alidou, G. Caffentzis and S. Federici (eds.), *A Thousand Flowers: Social Struggles Against Structural Adjustment in African Universities*, New Jersey: Africa World Press, Inc.

Diouf, M. and M. Mamdani (1994), *Academic Freedom in Africa*, Dakar: CODESRIA.

Dwyer, P. and D. Seddon (2002), 'The New Wave? A Global Perspective on Popular Protest', Paper presented at the Eight International Conference on Alternative Futures and Popular Protest, 2–4 April 2002, Manchester Metropolitan University.

Étudier au Senegal: Guide de l'Enseignement Supérieur et Professionnel (Pamphlet, 2003), Dakar: Senco 5.

Frederici, S. (2000), 'The New Student Movement', in O. Alidou, G. Caffentzis and S. Frederici (eds.), *A Thousand Flowers: Social Struggles*

Against Structural Adjustment in African Universities, New York: Africa World Press.

Gwisai, M. (2002), *Revolutionaries, Resistance and Crisis in Zimbabwe: Anti-Neo-liberal Struggles in Periphery Capitalism*, Harare: I.S.O. Pamphlet.

Hanna, W.J. and J.L. Hanna (eds.) (1975), *University Students and African Politics*, New York-London: Africana Publishing Company.

Hanna, W.J. (1975), 'Students, Universities and Political Outcomes', in W.J. Hanna and J. Hanna (eds.), *University Students and African Politics*, London: Africana Publishing Company.

Hanna, W.J. and J.L. Hanna (1975), 'Students as Elites', in Hanna and Hanna (eds.), *University Students and African Politics*, London: Africana Publishing Company.

Harrison, G. (2002), *Issues in the Contemporary Politics of Sub-Saharan Africa: The Dynamics of Struggle and Resistance*, New York: Palgrave.

Hosni, D. (2000), *Higher Education in Developing Countries: Peril and Promise: The Task Force on Higher Education and Society*, Washington, D.C: The World Bank.

Hutchful, E. (1991), 'Eastern Europe: Consequences for Africa', *Review of African Political Economy*, 18(50), pp. 51–9.

Imam, A. and A. Mama (1994), 'The Role of Academics in Limiting and Expanding Academic Freedom', in Diouf and Mamdani (eds.), *Academic Freedom in Africa*, Dakar: CODESRIA

Jeune Afrique (1991), 'Le Bon Mauvais Example', 29 March–2 April.

Kelly, M. (1991), *Education in a Declining Economy: The Case of Zambia, 1975-1985*, Washington, D.C.: World Bank

Kerr, D. and J. Mapanje (2002), 'Academic Freedom and the University of Malawi', *African Studies Review*, 45(2), pp. 73–92.

Klein, N. (2000), *No Logo: No Space, No Choice, No Jobs: Taking Aim at the Brand Bullies*, London: Flamingo.

Konings, P. (2002), 'University Students' Revolt, Ethnic Militia, and Violence During Political Liberalization in Cameroon', *African Studies Review*, 45(2), pp. 179–204.

Lebeau, Y. (1997), *Étudiants et campus du Nigéria: recomposition du champ universitaire et sociabilités étudiantes*, Paris: Karthala.

Maier, K. (2000), *This House has Fallen*, London: Penguin.

Mamdani, M. (1994), 'The Intelligentsia, the State and Social Movements in Africa', in M. Diouf and M. Mamdani (eds.), *Academic Freedom in Africa*, Dakar: CODESRIA.

Mamdani, M. and E. Wamba-dia-Wamba (1995) (eds.), *African Studies in Social Movements and Democracy*, Dakar: CODESRIA.

Marfleet, P. (1998), 'Globalization and the Third World', *International Socialism Journal*, 2(81), pp. 91–130.

Mario, M. and P. Fry (2003), *Higher Education in Mozambique: A Case Study*, Oxford: James Currey.

Martins, L. (2002), *Kabila et la révolution congolaise, panafricanisme ou neocolonialisme? Tome 1*, Anvers: Editions EPO.

Mazrui, A. (1994), 'The Impact of Global Changes on Academic Freedom in Africa: A Preliminary Assessment', in M. Diouf, and M. Mamdani, (eds.), *Academic Freedom in Africa*, Dakar: CODESRIA.

Mills, D. (2004), 'The "New" African Higher Education?', *African Affairs*, 103(413), pp. 667–75.

Mkude, D., B. Cooksey and L. Levey (2003), *Higher Education in Tanzania: A Case Study*, Oxford: James Currey.

Munikengi, T.T. and W. Sangol (2004), 'The Diploma Paradox: University of Kinshasa between Crisis and Salvation', in Trefon (ed.), *Reinventing Order in the Congo*, London: Zed Books.

Musisi, N.B. and K.M. Nansozi (2003), *Makerere University in Transition: 1993-2000*, Oxford: James Currey.

Ngugi, wa Thiong'o (1987), *Decolonising the Mind*, Harare: Zimbabwe Publishing House.

Nkomo, M.O. (1984), *Student Culture and Activism in Black South African Universities: The Roots of Resistance*, Westport, Connecticut-London: Greenwood Press.

Nkongolo, M.N. (2000), *Le Campus Martyr*, Paris: L'Harmattan.

Nyamnjoh, F.B. and N.B. Jua (2002), 'African Universities in Crisis and the Promotion of a Democratic Culture: The Political Economy of Violence in African Educational Systems', *African Studies Review*, 45(2), pp. 1–26.

Nzongola-Ntalaja (2002), *A People's History of the Congo*, London: Zed Books.

O'Brien, D.C. (1996), 'A Lost Generation? Youth Identity and State Decay in West Africa', in R.P. Werbner and T.O. Ranger (eds.), *Post-colonial Identities in Africa*, London: Zed Books.

Renton, D., D. Seddon and L. Zeiling, *The Congo: Plunder and Resistance 1880-2005*, London: Zed Books.

Richards, P. (1996), *Fighting for the Rain Forest: War, Youth And Resources in Sierra Leone*, London: International African Institute in association with James Currey.

Richards, P. (2002), 'Youth, Food and Peace: A Reflection on Some African Security Issues at the Millennium', in T. Zack-Williams et al. (eds.), *Africa in Crisis*, London: Pluto Press.

Riley, S. and T. Parfitt (1994), 'Economic Adjustment and Democratization in Africa', in J. Walton and D. Seddon (eds.), *Free Markets and Food Riots: The Politics of Global Adjustment*, Oxford: Blackwell.

Sandbrook, R. (1993), *The Politics of Africa's Economic Recovery*, Cambridge: Cambridge University Press.

———. (2000), *Closing the Circle: Democratization and Development in Africa*, London: Zed Books.

Saul, J. (2001), *Millennial Africa: Capitalism, Socialism, Democracy*, New Jersey: Africa World Press.

——— (2003), 'Africa: The Next Liberation Struggle', *Review of African Political Economy*, 30(96), pp. 187–202.

Seddon, D. (2002), 'Popular Protest and Class Struggle in Africa: An Historical Overview', in L. Zeiling (ed.), *Class Struggle and Resistance in Africa*, Cheltenham: New Clarion Press.

Seddon, D. and L. Zeiling (2005), 'Class and Protest in Africa: New Waves', *Review of African Political Economy*, 31(103), pp. 9–27.

Smith, Z.K. (1997), 'From Demons to Democrats: Mali's Student Movement 1991–1996', *Review of African Political Economy*, 24(72), pp. 249–63.

Socialist Worker (2006), 'Daniel Bensaid: This movement is directly based on the social question', 4 April.

Teferra, D. and P. Altbach (eds.), (2003), *African Higher Education: An International Reference Handbook*, Bloomington: Indiana University Press.

Tengende, N. (1994), 'Workers, Students and the Struggles for Democracy: State-Civil Society Relations in Zimbabwe', Ph.D dissertation, Roskilde University, Denmark.

Thompson, E.P. (1991), *The Making of the English Working Class*, London: Penguin.

Verspoor, A. (2001), *A Chance to Learn: Knowledge and Finance for Education in Sub-Saharan Africa*, Washington, D.C.: World Bank.

Walton, J. and D. Seddon (1994), *Free Markets and Food Riots: The Politics of Global Adjustment*, Oxford: Blackwell.

World Bank (1981), *Accelerated Development in Sub-Saharan Africa*, Washington, D.C.: World Bank.

——— (1988), *Education in Sub-Saharan Africa: Policies for Adjustment, Revitalization, and Expansion*, Washington, D.C.: World Bank.

——— (1992), *Revitalisation de l'Enseignement Supérieur: les Enjeux de la Réforme*, Dakar: Départment du Sahel, Bureau régional de la Banque mondiale.

——— (2000), *Higher Education in Developing Countries: Peril and Promise*, Washington, D.C.

Zack-Williams, T., D. Frost and A. Thomson (2002) (eds.), *Africa in Crisis: New Challenges and Possibilities*, London: Pluto Press.

Zeilig, L. (ed.) (2002a), *Class Struggle and Resistance in Africa*, Cheltenham: New Clarion Press.

Zeilig, L. and D. Seddon (2002), 'Marxism, Class and Resistance in Africa', in L. Zeiling (ed.), *Class Struggle and Resistance in Africa*, Cheltenham: New Clarion Press.

CHAPTER 18

Kshatriyahood to Statehood: Voices of the Rajbansis of North Bengal

SWARAJ BASU

INTRODUCTION

The Rajbansis are indigenous inhabitants of North Bengal having a distinct socio-cultural identity. Among various ethnic groups living in North Bengal, numerically the Rajbansis are the most dominant. As per the *Census of India*, 2001, in the six districts of North Bengal, besides the Rajbansis, there are other Scheduled Castes and Tribes like the Namasudras, Paliyas, Santals, Oraons, Mundas, Rabhas, Bhutias, and Lepchas. Socially and economically the Rajbansis along with other lower castes are in the margins compared to the upper castes of the region. During the colonial rule in Bengal, the Rajbansis organized a caste movement for upward social mobility and under the banner of the Kshatriya Samiti asserted their demand for social equity and justice. The Kshatriya Samiti took part in the electoral politics in pre-Partition India and in the legislative assembly elections their representatives won in the constituencies of North Bengal. In post-independent India the Rajbansi Kshatriya movement lost its momentum, but over a period of time from a perceived sense of marginalization the Rajbansis raised their voices for a separate state—either in the name of 'Uttarakhand' or 'Kamtapur' or 'Greater Cooch Behar'. The Rajbansi community strongly feels dominated by 'others'. The 'others' are primarily the migrated Bengalis who have settled in different districts of North Bengal for various reasons over a long period of time. There is a created feeling among the indigenous people of North Bengal that the migrated Bengalis are primarily responsible for their misery. A section within the community has tried to capitalize the grievances of the Rajbansis by mobilizing them on ethnic lines against the migrant Bengalis.

In the recent past, India has witnessed a number of movements for a separate state and many such movements have succeeded in creating independent states. The Rajbansis' demand for a separate state may be partly influenced by such movements. The members living in Assam are also demanding a separate state. The entire movement of the Rajbansis for a separate state needs to be looked at in a broader perspective. This paper makes an attempt to analyse the reasons for the Rajbansi movement, first for Kshatriya identity and then for a separate state. The response of different political parties towards the demands of the Rajbansis would also be analysed. At the end the point I would like to make is that the mere creation of a state will not lead to the end of the existing problems of the Rajbansis or other indigenous groups unless the state machinery gears up to undertake corrective measures to remove socio-economic disparities.

MOVEMENT FOR KSHATRIYAHOOD

The Rajbansis constitute the largest Scheduled Caste (SC) group in the districts of North Bengal and particularly in Cooch Behar and Jalpaiguri districts, where the percentage of SC population to the total population is 50.11 per cent and 36.71 per cent respectively.[1] Despite their numerical dominance in North Bengal there is a strong sense of deprivation among the Rajbansis against the upper caste Bengalis settled in the region. The sense of marginalization and also cultural subordination by the upper caste Hindus influenced the Rajbansis time and again to assert for respectable social identity and also for a separate state. It is essential to understand the Rajbansi Kshatriya movement of the early twentieth century in order to analyse the recent movements by the Rajbansis for a separate state.

The origin of the name Rajbansi is debatable and there are contradictory interpretations given by the colonial ethnographers, administrators and the Rajbansi scholars. In the official records of the colonial ethnographers the dominant view is that the Koches, after undergoing Kshatriyaization, assumed the name Rajbansi, a Hinduized synonym of the Koch. The Rajbansi scholars like Hara Kishor Adhikari, Panchanan Barman and Upendranath Barman tried to prove the royal lineage of the Rajbansis and their Kshatriyahood.[2]

The Rajbansis's assertion for Kshatriya status is very much linked to the socio-economic and political development of the early twentieth-century Bengal. The Rajbansis, being the indigenous dominant social group in North Bengal, did not face the problem of social inferiority till a large number of caste-Hindu immigrants started settling in this region, which was very much linked with the colonization of the region. A sense of caste hierarchy and social superiority among the migrated caste Hindus in North Bengal created a line of difference between the Rajbansis and other caste Hindus and in the process the Rajbansis faced humiliation and social suppression. Writings of Panchanan Barman, Upendranath Barman, and others, the leaders of the community, provide references to such humiliation faced by the Rajbansis.

Besides the issue of socio-cultural domination, the settlement of caste-Hindus led to transfer of lands to the non-Rajbansis and that made the Rajbansis economically dependent on the upper caste Hindus. Educationally being more advanced, whatever jobs were available in the government service at the local level were mostly cornered by the upper castes. In the given socio-economic setting the Rajbansis further felt the need for social assertion because of the colonial government's policy of census enumeration based on caste rank and governmental assistance based on caste status. This was also the period when the colonial government initiated the process of decentralization of powers through representation of various groups in the local bodies as well as the state legislatures. Therefore the changing socio-economic and political situation had a major influence behind the mobilization of the Rajbansis for Kshatriya status.

It was not the Rajbansis alone who felt the need to create a glorified past in order to claim higher social status; throughout India different caste groups tried to legitimize their position as one of the three twice-born castes, namely the Brahman, Kshatriya and Vaishya. The point I would like to make here is that the Kshatriya movement launched by the Rajbansis was not only influenced by the grievances that the community was having, but that the policies of the colonial government had a direct bearing on the movement. The Rajbansi Kshatriya movement instead of attacking the caste system—which was primarily responsible for their ascribed lower social status—tried to legitimize their Kshatriya identity by emphasizing their distinctiveness from the Koch and by practising Brahmanical cultural values.

The efforts of the Rajbansi leaders towards upward social mobility did not bring the desired change in social interaction between the Rajbansis and other upper caste Hindus and neither did it help them to elevate their social status. However, in the process of Kshatriyaization the Rajbansi caste leaders distanced themselves from other local indigenous social groups like the Koch, Rabha, and Mech. Even within the Rajbansi community there are several strands and the Kshatriya movement did not evoke the same response from the entire community.[3] The differentiation within the community in terms of economic position resulted in differential response to the Kshatriyaization movement. This became more evident during the Tebhaga movement in 1946.

During the end of 1939 and the beginning of 1940 peasants and *adhiars* in the districts of North Bengal raised their voices against the collection of tolls in *haats* (local markets) and other exactions realized from the *adhiars*. The *jotedars* collected not only half of the produce but on various pretexts compelled the *adhiars* to pay additional levies. The Communists and the Krishak Samiti leaders mobilized the peasants and the *adhiars* to check the exploitation by the *jotedars*. Studies on the *adhiar* movement in North Bengal show how, in spite of pressures put up by the Rajbansi *jotedars* and Kshatriya Samiti leaders describing the *adhiar* movement as a ploy of the migrant upper caste Bengalis, the *adhiars* did not respond to the call given by their caste elders.[4] In 1946 the *adhiar* movement got new impetus when the Bengal Provincial Kishan Sabha gave the call for Tebhaga (two-thirds share of the harvest in favour of the *adhiars*). Studies on the Tebhaga movement show that a large number of Rajbansi peasants and *adhiars*, both men and women, took active part in the movement in which caste and community appeal failed to evoke any response. Without going into the detail of either the Kshatriya movement or the Tebhaga movement, the point I would like to stress is that the mobilization around the Kshatriya identity could not influence the different strands of the Rajbansi community because of its focus merely on upward social mobility without taking into account the economic hardships of the Rajbansi peasants and *adhiars*. The Tebhaga movement is a classic example of mass mobilization cutting across caste and community affiliations for the common cause of the poor peasants.

Another important development that needs our attention in this context is the mobilization of the Rajbansis and other indigenous people living in and around Cooch Behar for making the region an independent state during the time of the Partition of India in 1947. This was the time when within Cooch Behar a section of the local indigenous people formed an association by the name of Hitasadhani Sabha. The Sabha was very vocal against the migrated Bengalis in the region and wanted Cooch Behar to remain independent of the Union of India. It is even alleged that members of this association were in favour of the merger of Cooch Behar with Pakistan. The Rajbansis residing in the Western Duars of Jalpaiguri district tried to mobilize the indigenous people for including them within the Cooch Behar kingdom. Let me cite here an appeal made by the Rajbansis of Western Duars:

> To the Rajbansis and Indigenous Muslim Inhabitants
> Brothers,
>
> For the Rajbansis and indigenous Muslim inhabitants present time is not the time for remaining asleep. You know that before the British period the Western Duars area of Jalpaiguri district was under our Rajbansi kingdom of Koch Bihar rajya. During the British period we have become separated from the [Rajbansi] national empire of Koch Bihar. The British rulers are leaving and the Maharaj (Koch Bihar ruler) has demanded the restoration of our ancestral land—the Duars area [to Koch Bihar]. To make this demand a success and the national movement victorious each and every Rajbaṇsi and Muslim of the area will have to unite. So we make a sincere request to our indigenous brothers to devote themselves in the sacred task of strengthening a united Rajasthan and . . . build up the national glory through the inclusion of the duars area into the Koch Bihar kingdom.[5]

The point to be noted is that because of ethnic and cultural distinctiveness there was always a line of separation between the Rajbansis and the migrated Bengalis. The Rajbansis being marginalized by the Bengalis tried to assert for social equality and justice and made efforts to get back their lost glory and power.

DEMAND FOR STATEHOOD

In post-independent India there was large-scale migration of people from the eastern part of Bengal into North Bengal. As we have already discussed, with the immigration of upper caste Hindu gentry into this region since the late nineteenth century, transfer of land from Rajbansis to the migrated gentry became a predominant phenomenon. The reasons for migration were primarily the abundance of land, prospects of good business and better job opportunities in government offices and tea gardens as the local people were not much educated and therefore not competitive for jobs. Following the economic depression of the 1920s and the Second World War there was rise in prices of food grains. The famine in Bengal further resulted in hardships for the common people. Merchants, moneylenders and speculators, taking advantage of the economic condition, invested money in land and middle and poor peasants became victims of this economic crisis. In effect, the lands which were owned by the Rajbansis and other indigenous people began to change hands and a new class of landed gentry, mostly belonging to upper caste Hindus, became dominant in the region. Economic and social dominance of the migrated gentry along with their sense of cultural superiority fostered a sense of solidarity among the Rajbansis.[6] The fight for Kshatriya identity was one way of asserting their rightful place in the social hierarchy but this was not enough to gain economic and political rights. Failure of the movement for Kshatriyahood made the Rajbansis realize that without economic and political power the community would not be able to protect itself from marginalization.

Alienated from their ancestral land, the Rajbansis now constitute a major section of rickshaw pullers, construction workers and domestic servants. The caste leaders have tried to capitalize this condition of the Rajbansis in order to widen the rift between them and the non-Rajbansis. The Rajbansi leaders stress that the hardships of the community are caused by the migrated Bengalis and the end of their miseries lies in the creation of an independent state. In spite of having natural resources, most people of the region feel that the state government has not done much for the overall development of the region. Poverty, unemployment, economic disparities and political marginalization are the issues agitating the minds of the Rajbansis.

In the Lok Sabha in a call attention motion, P.R. Das Munsi raised the matter on regional imbalance in the development of North Bengal region under the Seventh, Eighth, Ninth and Tenth Plan periods. He drew the attention of the House to 'the lack of infrastructure development like road network, health, rural electrification, industry, education and construction of overbridges on railway crossings, etc., in the North Bengal area as also relating to the socio-economic and cultural development of backward communities like Rajbanshis of the North Bengal'. A study by the Institute of Applied Manpower Research, an autonomous institution under the Planning Commission in September 2001 also points to the sharp disparity between the

North Bengal districts and the rest of the state. Although the best quality of timber, dolomite, tea and jute are available in North Bengal, there is no tangible infrastructure development in the region beyond the Fifth Five Year Plan. Das Munsi argues that the underdevelopment of the region has led to the Gorkhaland and Kamtapur movements.[7]

North Bengal in the 1980s witnessed the mobilization of the Gorkhas in the district of Darjeeling for a separate state in the name of 'Gorkhaland'. After prolonged agitation and violence the government acceded to create an autonomous Gorkha Council which the leaders accepted after negotiation. This was also the period when the Rajbansis started agitating for the creation of a separate state of Uttarakhand comprising the six districts of North Bengal. After the failure of the Uttarakhand movement the Rajbansis formed the Kamtapur People's Party (KPP) in 1995.[8] Besides the formation of the Kamtapuri state with Cooch Behar, Jalpaiguri, Darjeeling, South and North Dinajpur and Malda districts on the basis of a common linguistic identity, the Rajbansis are also asking for inclusion of the Kamtapuri language in the Eighth Schedule of the Constitution. The KPP has threatened economic blockade and has declared that it would stop transportation of tea, oranges, timber and jute products from North Bengal districts to South Bengal. The Kamtapuris have also resorted to violence to uphold their cause. Like the terrorists outfits in Assam, there is also the Kamtapur Liberation Organisation (KLO), a terrorist front of Rajbansi youth, whose leader, 'Tumar Das alias Jiban Singha, hailing from Cooch Behar district, has an army of more than a hundred men trained in Bhutan camps'.[9] The KPP has a student wing, the All Kamtapur Students Union and also a women's wing called Kamtapur Women's Rights Forum. 'Ahead of the 2001 West Bengal assembly elections KPP joined the All India Trinamool Congress-led Bangla Bachao Front. In spring 2003 KPP suffered an internal division. Atul Roy, considered as a moderate, was dethroned and replaced by a more hardline leader, Nikhil Roy. Ahead of the 2004 Lok Sabha elections KPP formed a front together with the Jharkhand Mukti Morcha.'[10]

Parallel to the movement for Kamtapur we find that a section of indigenous people in Cooch Behar formed the Greater Cooch Behar People's Association (GCPA) and announced a 21-member executive committee with Asutosh Barman as its president. The party decided to take part in electoral politics and it considers the Left as the stumbling block in its way to fulfilling its demand for a greater Cooch Behar state.[11] The GCPA reportedly has links with the United Liberation Front of Assam and the Kamtapuri Liberal Organization. Suhrid Sankar Chattopadhyay reported the violent movement by the activists of GCPA in September 2005 in Cooch Behar. In his report he suggested that seeing the participation of a small section of population in the movement for a separate state it seems that there was no mass support. 'Although it is unlikely that the movement for a 'Greater Cooch Behar' will gather enough momentum to be a cause for concern for the state government, it has the potential to be a tool in the hands of extremist and separatist groups—something the state government has reason to worry about.'[12] 'Five persons, including an additional superintendent of police, were killed and 25 injured as violence erupted near the North Bengal town of Cooch Behar on Monday after which authorities clamped curfew. The violence erupted when a 22,000-strong mob attacked the police contingent led by Additional SP.'[13]

So we find that over a period of time the Rajbansis of North Bengal have been trying to assert themselves for the creation of a separate state and the recognition of their language. What is important to look into in this context is the response of various political parties towards the demand of the Rajbansis.

RESPONSE OF POLITICAL PARTIES

Commenting on the Kamtapuri movement, *Ganashakti*, the newspaper of the CPI(M), reported that with the coming of the Left in power in West Bengal the *jotedars* and *mahajans* in North Bengal have lost control over local administrative set up and the *adhiars*' exploitation by the landed gentry has eased. With the political support of the anti-left forces the *jotedars* and *mahajans* are organizing the movement for an independent state so that they get back their old authority. Leaders of the Kamtapuri movement are trying to make the Rajbansis realize that it is because of the migrated population in North Bengal that the indigenous people are not getting jobs and are being marginalized.[14] The CPI(M) state leadership believes that lack of developmental activities, dispossession of land and unemployment are major reasons for the grievances of the Rajbansis. However, they are of the opinion that dispossessed local landlords, at the instigation of the political opponents of the left, are trying to destabilize the local government. There are a number of attacks by the KLO on the members of the CPI(M) or its allies.

The CPI(ML) Liberation State Committee argues that the continued neglect and deprivation of North Bengal gave birth to discontent and separatist movements of the Kamtapuri people. Agriculture in North Bengal is in a bad shape and lack of irrigation facilities has reduced it to a single crop a year. Impact of land reforms is not felt by the poor peasants. The mushrooming of unauthorized tea-gardens, mostly through the acquisition of land from the Rajbansi people, has made many of the Rajbansis dispossessed peasants. Although the CPI(ML) shares the agony of the poor Rajbansis, yet the leadership states,

> We do not support the demand of a separate state of Kamtapur. The Rajvanshi community does not also constitute the majority in North Bengal, and most of the people here are also not in favour of a separate state. But the question remains: how could such separatist aspirations raise their head even after so many years of the LF rule? The LF has utterly failed in developing North Bengal and the problems of the people remain unsolved.[15]

The Congress party in West Bengal decided to launch a prolonged agitation in North Bengal to mobilize public opinion on the issue of state government's negligence towards the development of North Bengal. The Congress leadership feels that the lack of development has led to divisive movements like those of the Uttarakhand, Gorkhaland and Kamtapur.[16] The Congress party is not supportive of the demand for a separate state but appeals to the government to listen to the Rajbansi's demand for development of North Bengal and recognition of their language. The Congress leader P.R. Das Munsi said, 'When Santhali language got recognized on the other day, Rajbongshis cried as to why their language should not be recognized. When Maithili dialect, which is from Hindi, could be recognized as a language by the Constitution, why can Rajbongshi dialect not be considered by the Constitution?'[17]

From the responses of the major political parties discussed above it appears that so far as the under-development of the region and economic hardship of the Rajbansis are concerned there is no difference of opinion among the political parties. If the Left is ruling the state of West Bengal for the last 30 years, the Congress also ruled the state since independence for about two decades. However, the economic hardships of the Rajbansis and other poor people of the region remain unaddressed. It is not only the issue of development but the growing awareness of real or perceived discrimination that influences marginalized population to assert for autonomy. In a country like India, having multicultural/pluralist identities, there is always the possibility of manipulation of these identities by groups aiming to capture power. Even to meet their rising aspirations they may take recourse to violence. Analysing the causes of rising ethno-cultural assertions in India A.K. Behuria has observed that 'the shrinking capacity of the state, underdevelopment, and the politicization of plural peripheral identities, together with the search for power by neo-elites at the margins, have snapped the interethnic and intercultural bonds that have so far drawn them together. This has created new identities and led to an overwhelming craze for autonomy or self-legislation.'[18] The electoral alliance of the Kamtapur People's Party with the Trinamool Congress and the Jharkhand Mukti Morcha for the West Bengal Assembly and the Lok Sabha elections—definitely shows the rising aspirations of the Kamtapuri leaders to get into the power structure. The leaders tactfully use the cultural and ethnic distinctiveness of the Rajbansis in their efforts to sharpen the divide between them and the migrated Bengalis and this divisive politics helps the leadership to consolidate its political base. The charter of demands of the KPP fails to reflect the basic issues of the common Rajbansis. It is not the Rajbansis alone who are the victims of under-development but they have been forced to believe that the 'Bhatias', migrated Bengalis, are responsible for the cause of their poverty. It also needs to be clarified that there are a good number of Rajbansis who are ideologically inclined to other political parties and do not share the views of Kamtapuri leaders.

CONCLUSION

Daniel Bell argued that 'The breakup of the traditional authority structures and the previous effective social units—historically nation and class . . . make the ethnic attachment more salient.'[19] In India the state initiative of providing socio-economic protection through the policy of reservation has already created a situation where different groups are fighting for inclusion in the lists of SC, ST and OBC. The recent demand of the Gujars in Rajasthan to be included in the list of ST was vehemently opposed by groups already enjoying the benefits of ST status. The same story is being repeated in Assam. The All

Koch Rajbongshi Students' Union launched a movement not only for a separate state but also for inclusion in the ST list. Biswajit Rai, president of AKRSU, alleged that despite Koch Rajbongshis fulfilling the criteria needed for inclusion in the ST category, political parties have ditched their legitimate demand. AKRSU also flayed tribal organizations, especially the leaders, who reportedly opposed granting of ST status to six new communities, including Koch Rajbongshis.[20] Assam is witnessing strong movements by various ethnic groups for protection of their rights and privileges. The mobilization of various ethnic groups in the region clearly shows that they do not believe much in the leadership of various political parties.

Arguing against identity politics Hobsbawm suggests that

> Today both the right and the left are saddled with identity politics. . . . Government is not just about getting elected and then re-elected. This is a process which, in democratic politics, implies enormous quantities of lying in all its forms. Elections become contests in fiscal perjury. Unfortunately, politicians, who have as short a time-horizon as journalists, find it hard to see politics as other than a permanent campaigning season. Yet there is something beyond. There lies what government does and must do. There is the future of the country. There are the hopes and fears of the people as a whole—not just 'the community', which is an ideological cop-out, or the sum-total of earners and spenders. . . .[21]

These observations of Hobsbawm in the specific context of Europe are equally true in the context of Indian polity. The relative and perceived sense of subordination and economic deprivation is a very common cause of ethnic conflict. Using of ethnic contradictions by various political groups for narrow political gains has further contributed to ethnic tensions. It is believed that growing mobilization around caste and ethnic identity is because of the erosion of ideology and lack of socio-economic programmes among political parties. The under-development of the region, lack of job opportunities, proper education facilities and particularly the indifferent attitude of the state machinery have forced the marginalized to raise voices for equal rights and justice. But the genuine grievances of the people are manipulated by some vested interests for their personal benefit. Economic issues do not get reflected in the agenda of such mobilizations, rather mobilizations around ethnic identities are sometimes pitting the oppressed against the oppressed. Social discrimination and economic exploitation of marginalized groups deserve to be condemned and need to be stopped. But the tendency of some sections to make use of the marginalized for their own agenda has to be checked or we may have to face serious consequences in future. Identity politics hardly mobilizes more than a minority but if can even isolate the minorities. Not the creation of state but the proactive measures of the government to address the issues of development may provide the answer to the problems of people living in North Bengal.

NOTES

1. *Census of India*, 2001.
2. For, detailed discussion on the Rajbansi identity see S. Basu (2003), *Dynamics of a Caste Movement: The Rajbansis of North Bengal, 1910-1947,* Delhi: Manohar; R. Mukhopadhyay (2006), 'Conversion vs Construction: A Discourse on Hindu Identity of the Rajbansis', in A.K. Haldar and P.K. Bhowmick (eds.), *Societies and Culture in India*, (vol. 2), Kolkata: R.N. Bhattacharya Publisher.
3. For a detailed discussion on the differential responses to the Kshatriya movement, see S. Basu (2003), *Dynamics of a Caste Movement: The Rajbansis of North Bengal, 1910-1947.*
4. R. Dasgupta (1992), *Economy, Society and Politics in Bengal: Jalpaiguri 1869-1947*, Delhi: Oxford University Press; S. Basu (2003), *Dynamics of a Caste Movement: The Rajbansis of North Bengal, 1910-1947.*
5. Cited in R. Dasgupta (1992), *Economy, Society and Politics in Bengal: Jalpaiguri 1869-1947*, p. 254.
6. P. Chatterjee (1984), *Bengal 1920-1947: The Land Question,* vol. I, Calcutta: K.P. Bagchi; S. Bose (1986), *Agrarian Bengal: Economy, Social Structure and Politics, 1919-1947,* Cambridge: Cambridge University Press; R. Dasgupta (1992), *Economy, Society and Politics in Bengal: Jalpaiguri 1869-1947*, Delhi; S. Basu (2003), *Dynamics of a Caste Movement: The Rajbansis of North Bengal, 1910–1947.*
7. Lok Sabha Debates, Part II Proceedings Other than Questions and Answers (XIII Lok Sabha), http//164.100.24.208/debate/debetxt).
8. I. Sarkar (2006), 'The Kamtapur Movement: Towards a Separate State in North Bengal', in G.C. Rath (ed.), *Tribal Development in India: The Contemporary Debate,* New Delhi: Sage, p. 157.
9. Report by Sumit Mitra, www.indiatoday.com/webexclusive/dispatch/20020915/mitra.html.
10. wikipedia.org/wiki/kamtapur_peoples party.
11. *The Telegraph*, 21 August 2006.
12. S.S. Chattopadhyaya, 'Separatist Trouble', *Frontline*, vol. 22, issue 21, 8–21 October 2005.
13. http://in.rediff.com/news/2005/sep/21cooch.htm.
14. Kamtapuri—What and Why, www.ganashakti.com/old/1999.

15. J. Mitra, www.cpiml.org/liberation/year_2001/february.
16. Report by S. Sen, *Times of India*, 20 February 2002, www.timesofindia.indiatimes.com.
17. Lok Sabha Debates, Part-II Proceedings Other than Questions and Answers (XIII Lok Sabha), http//164.100.24.208/debate/debetxt.
18. A.K. Behuria, 'Demands for Autonomy: Internal Weaknesses of a Multiethnic, Multicultural and Multinational State', www.manipuronline.com/features/September2006.
19. D. Bell, 'Ethnicity and Social Change', in N. Glazer and D.P. Moynihan (eds.) (1975), *Ethnicity: Theory and Experience*, Cambridge: Harvard University Press, p. 171, cited in E. Hobsbawm, *Identity Politics and the Left*, Harvard University Press. www.amielandmelburn.org.uk/articles/1996.
20. *Times of India*, Guwahati edition, 10 December 07.
21. E. Hobsbawm, *Identity Politics and the Left*, www.amielandmelburn.org.uk/articles/1996.

V. GRASSROOT INITIATIVE IN A GLOBALIZED WORLD

CHAPTER 19

Adivasi Social Movement in Orissa: Development, Marginalization and Dispossession

DIP KAPOOR AND TEJWANT CHANA

INTRODUCTION

According to the International Work Group for Indigenous Affairs (IWGIA) and the UN's Working Group on Indigenous Populations, 'problems faced by indigenous peoples of Asia include plundering of resources; forced relocation; cultural genocide; militarization; forced integration of indigenous peoples into market economies; and bigotry and discrimination' (Eversole, McNeish, and Cimadamore 2005: 32). This observation resonates with the Indian context, home to some 80 million plus Adivasis (2001 census), as Adivasis account for 40 per cent of development-displaced persons while constituting 8 per cent of the Indian population (Fernandes 2006). Behura and Panigrahi (2006: 209) state that the Adivasis continue to be subjected to a 'systematic process of exploitation, which has marginalized and impoverished them. . . . State policies on land and land-based resources instead of encouraging the tribals have depressed them and opened up the tribal economy for others to exploit'.

Prompted by such critical observations on the contemporary situation of the Adivasis, this paper elaborates on the preliminary findings of a qualitative research study (which commenced in 2006 and is being undertaken by the Centre for Research and Development Solidarity or CRDS, Orissa) which partially aims to construct Adivasi social movement perspectives on development and its implications for Adivasis and Adivasi social movements in Orissa. Specifically, this paper will: (a) provide a brief overview of the contemporary Adivasi land-forest context in Orissa, (b) address the methodological orientation of the research, (c) present some emergent themes (analysis of data pertaining to Adivasi movement leader conceptions/ understandings in particular) from the research, and (d) provide a brief concluding summary pertaining to emergent findings and observations.

ADIVASI LAND-FOREST CONTEXT IN ORISSA

Adivasis belong to 62 different Scheduled Tribes and number over 8 million people, constituting almost a quarter of Orissa's population, 80 per cent of which lives in the state's 57,000 villages. The tribes rely primarily on shifting cultivation, horticulture, animal husbandry, the collection and sale of minor forest products and seasonal work on government construction sites (or as migratory labour) for their living. The land and forests are not just economic assets with material significance but are of great cultural and spiritual significance, a point that is often disregarded by State/outside interests (Behura and Panigrahi 2006).

The systematic process of penetration and colonization of Adivasi space was initiated by the British who first restricted customary rights of the tribals over land and forests in 1855. The Indian Forest Act of 1878, of 1927 and the Government of India Act of 1935 successively consolidated the power of the imperial government over forests and emphasized the revenue yield aspects and the resource requirements of British military, commercial and industrial sectors. During 200 years of colonial rule, the British brought changes to land use patterns (e.g. opening up of tribal areas to outsiders through improved communications); exploited forest resources and mineral ores, and introduced cash crops, thus distorting the land structure, ecology, forest resources, and flora and fauna, with grave implications for the Adivasis (Behura and Panigrahi 2006: 35). British colonial rule began the process of detribalization of tribal land and forests, whereby the various Forest and Land Acts reduced the tribals to the status of encroachers on their own territories. This process was met with determined tribal resistance and rebellion (including Chhota Nagpur, Munda, Kol, Santhal and Rampha rebellions), which did result in acts of amelioration and legislative measures to recognize some tribal rights.

The post-Independence Forest Policy of 1952 was a reiteration of the bureaucratic management of forests and the promotion of State

Capitalism in the forest sector, a major reason for continued unrest in Adivasi areas in Orissa and elsewhere (Rath 2006). According to the Asia Centre for Human Rights (ACHR 2005: 4–5), despite constitutional provisions in the Fifth and Sixth Schedules that recognize tribal ownership rights over land and forests in Scheduled/Protected Areas, 'contradictory legal provisions and failure to implement or translate Constitutional Provisions into reality' undermine these rights of Adivasis. For example, forest laws that confer 'usufruct rights' to use minor forest products without right to ownership are subject to 'whimsical no damage to the forest' determination by forest officials which contradict the ownership rights provisions of the Fifth Schedule.

Under the Forest Conservation Act (1980), the Wild Life Protection Act (1972), and the Land Acquisition Act (1894/pre-Independence), 'The government has the sovereign right to evict people for undefined public interest or "larger interest" but the affected people do not have the right to question the decision of the government on forceable evictions' (ACHR 2005: 9). In fact, until just recently, the Land Acquisition Act, which has been instrumental in evicting tribal peoples for more than a century, has had no provisions for resettlement and rehabilitation, not to mention right to free, prior, and informed consent (the Right to Information is a recent legal innovation in India).

The New Economic Policy (NEP) of 1991 (neoliberal policy prescriptions to marketize, privatize and open up the Indian economy to foreign direct ownership/investment) has exacerbated the process of Adivasi land alienation, as Pimple and Sethi (2005: 239) conclude from their study that 'under the application of neoliberal land policies . . . traditional occupiers of land under customary law confront the prospect and reality of becoming illegal encroachers on land they have cultivated and sustained for generations—they are vulnerable and subject to summary eviction'.

In the case of Orissa, where they make up 22 per cent of the population, Adivasis account for 42 per cent of 'displaced persons' (Fernandes 2006), as Orissa's rich mineral deposits are now open (post-1991 liberalization) for economic exploitation by national and multinational corporate interests. About 95 per cent of the mining activity (e.g. for Bauxite/Alumina) takes place on Adivasi lands while a third of Adivasis have been rendered landless through such avenues for capitalist-developmentalist-exploitation in Orissa (Behura and

Panigrahi 2006: 192). According to conservative estimates, 24,124 hectares of land (until 1999) have been deforested as a result of development projects in tribal areas including dams, mines, roads, railways and new industry (Behura and Panigrahi 2006: 192).

The NEP continues to encourage such exploitation as the abundance of steel, coal, iron ore, bauxite, aluminum, and other minerals in the mountainous regions of Orissa has attracted both local and foreign investment by large national and multinational companies, the most recent case being that of POSCO-India (Pohang Steel Company) which is the largest single foreign direct investment in India. POSCO signed a memorandum of understanding (MOU) with the Government of Orissa in June 2005 in which it committed $18 billion to various steel projects in the central-east area. Presently, Orissa has approximately 50 billion tonnes of iron ore of which POSCO has secured 600 million tonnes over the next thirty years. According to Conway Data Inc., POSCO presently produces approximately 28 million tonnes of steel annually; the steel mills in Orissa will add another 12 million tonnes to the annual pool for worldwide consumption by 2016 (Rosenquist 2005). In order to facilitate this process the Government of Orissa has initially allocated 1,132 acres of land and forests for such large-scale mining.

Although the NEP has provided POSCO and other corporations with a favourable business investment environment, such developments rooted in resource extraction and capitalist accumulation raise contradictory prospects for Adivasis and agri-based communities whose people predominantly rely on agriculture and forest culture. Increased trans/national corporatization in India, on the lands, lives, and culture of the Adivasis has predictably exacerbated relations between them and the government and catalyzed social movement processes in contemporary India (Ray and Katzenstein 2005).

QUALITATIVE RESEARCH METHODOLOGY: A CASE STUDY OF ADIVASI MOVEMENT PERSPECTIVES ON DEVELOPMENT IN ORISSA

Scholarship concerning the Adivasis seldom, if ever, moves from the assumption that Adivasis are agents and architects of their own social processes. It continues to 'anthropologize the native as an inert object of study and analysis in a colonial project of assessment, taxonomy, and assimilation' (Kapoor 2007: 3), with little regard for their own analysis, understanding and agency concerning their relations with modern developmentalism and its vanguards including the state, the corporations and consumer-caste groups (rural and urban) that benefit from this process. The primary purpose for undertaking this qualitative participatory case study with the Kondh and Saora Adivasis and Panos (Scheduled Caste group) of South Orissa, was to understand and construct their movement articulations, as asserted by the Adivasi Dalit Ekta Abhijan (ADEA), which advocates for 120 villages or some 16,000 plus Kondhs, Saoras and Panos in South Orissa. The key questions of inquiry pertinent to this paper include:

- What are Adivasi movement perspectives on development? How do the Adivasis explain their relations with the developmentalist-state and other dominant social groups/outsiders (e.g. dominant caste groups, agents of the state, and commercially-motivated social groups)?
- What are the main purposes of the ADEA movement in relation to development-instigated issues being faced by Adivasis? What are some related and culturally-specific expressions of movement articulations?

The research methodology is a combination of participatory 'indigenous approaches' (Smith 1999) and an 'exploratory intrinsic case study' approach that seeks 'first time knowledge' about Adivasi movement constructions of developmentalism, defined by its 'particularity' and the interest in 'telling the stories of those living the case' (Stake 2000: 437). The research employs a combination of what Linda Tuhiwai-Smith in *Decolonizing Methodologies* refers to as a 'strategy of consultation where efforts are made to seek support and consent' from the Adivasis and a 'strategy of making space' where the research process consciously brings more Adivasi 'researchers and voices' into the research process (Smith 1999: 177). CRDS's long and close association with the ADEA since the early 1990s was instrumental in adopting this approach to the research.

Research participants were primarily Kondh Adivasis, located within a regional wing of a 120 village movement organization. A total of 12 villages in one panchayat/local administrative unit were part of a purposive sample. Research was carried out with a gender-balanced team of six community-based research assistants (RA), all of whom belonged to the communities of the ADEA and were familiar with 'doing research', given previous research initiatives with CRDS. Data sets were and are being developed around 'mini research projects' defined by the team, often in conjunction with representatives of the ADEA leadership or specific village communities facing pressing issues being addressed by the movement. Some examples include: (i) tapes/notes on ADEA leadership gatherings on four occasions (day-long sessions); (ii) a five-village case study pertaining to land and forest struggle as a microcosm of the broader struggle of the ADEA [employing interviews with key informants (e.g. elders); village gatherings as 'focus groups'; participant observation in ceremonies celebrating Adivasi assertions and historic struggles; observation of critical incidents, later shared and discussed/analysed with concerned communities; documents, such as community or state land records]; and (iii) collection and discussion of poetry, laments, narrations and oral renditions with implications for movement issues/concerns. Research methods (including the ethics and politics of 'doing research') were discussed before, during and after the 'mini research projects'. The enthusiasm was infectious and as one RA relatively new to the research relationship put it,

> I thought research means doing surveys and getting people to share personal information about themselves that the government will use on them—statistical stuff that they bother our people about all the time but nothing changes for our communities. But this, what you are sharing with us, is about us and about the people—it is our way. If this is research, then I am with you!

Typically, the research team would meet with people from a particular village or the ADEA regional representatives of participating villages in the early morning hours from anywhere between 2–4 hours a session, depending on the course of these conversations. Such gatherings usually took place in the village square (on the *mandap* or raised platform built for such occasions) and the intent of each meeting was to discuss problematic issues (especially in relation to land and forests) for Adivasis and their implications for defining the purposes of the ADEA movement in the region and related positions on development. More often than not, all residents of a village (children, women and men) would gather for these discussions, with the elders and leaders/ADEA representatives (women and men) seated on the *mandap* while the others lined the periphery of the *mandap*.

Data consisted of observation and interview notes, diagrammatic and pictorial representations and taped songs/poetry and narrations, copies of which were given to the communities when on request. The data was either in Kui (Kondh Adivasi language) or Oriya (dominant state language) and translated by the team into English. Three members of the team were proficient in Kui, Oriya and English and played a significant role around discussions concerning translations. English versions were subjected to discussion and 'corrected' by the team when necessary, run by the community/groups concerned for advice and accuracy of interpretations. Similarly, data analysed by the team for patterns and emergent themes (Miles and Huberman 1994) were subject to member checks when necessary and analysed on a regular rotation to ensure that when saturation points are reached, 'when new data is redundant with previously collected data' (Mayrkut and Morehouse 1994: 62), data collection on that front is brought to a close. Whenever necessary, as in instances where the team was 'uncomfortable with analytical interpretations' being made by the group, the data and participants were revisited and re-engaged. Whenever possible, data was jointly analysed with the village communities or participants (like the ADEA leadership), as in the case of analysis of laments or narratives or of observations around rituals and ceremonies.

Issues of trustworthiness of data and emergent reflections are important to the extent that representations are not a distortion/ misrepresentation of participant's constructions and have catalytic validity (Lather 1993) or some utility for the movement. To this end, triangulation approach has been used here as the emphasis has been on the use of multiple investigator, multiple sources of data and methods of data collection which taken together to confirm emergent finding. Member checks and joint analysis of data enhanced the plausibility of interpretations.

Methodological positioning is also informed by select theoretical propositions from subaltern studies (Guha 1983) in terms of its Gramscian–Marxist strains and relatively more recent post-colonial-culturalist preoccupations with representation, voice, agency and language. The fundamental assumption and overarching theme in subaltern studies is that subalterns are subjects of history and the makers of their own destinies. Subaltern studies demonstrate 'the extent to which peasant politics possessed autonomy within . . . encompassing structures of subordination' (Arnold 1984: 169) and that despite British colonialism and post-Independence modernization and development, subaltern collectivities like the Adivasis and the ADEA 'have continued to exist vigorously and even develop new forms and content' (Ludden 2005: 100). Subaltern studies have always emphasized the politics of the lower orders (subaltern groups) and their political consciousness and the central focus of this scholarship has been on these groups, their struggles and movements and activities, while dominant Euro–American traditions (from the left and the right) and Indian party politics shaped by the same, have either chosen to assimilate, ignore, or obscure the politics of the subaltern by failing to acknowledge there is a 'subaltern consciousness separate from hegemonic cultural forms . . . realized in the practice of rural resistance' (Sivaramakrishnan 2005: 217). Specific critiques of subaltern studies, such as the tendency to obscure questions of unity among subalterns and related fissures of domination/oppression, have also proved useful in relation to aiding this research process in the manner of providing possible probes/avenues for exploration, not to mention pointing to possible dimensions that may not have emerged through grounded discussion in a participatory case study with the Adivasis. Finally, this study takes up Spivak's invocation to intellectuals to make the importance of subalterns to history known (Loomba 2005: 203).

DATA ANALYSIS: EMERGENT THEMES AND ADIVASI CONSTRUCTIONS

Emergent themes and Adivasi constructions pertaining to development and related movement purposes are presented here with the view to capture the variety and similarity across participant perspectives shared at various venues and at different points in time during the data gathering process. Collaborative analysis (CRDS team and ADEA movement leader participants) of data aided by additional member checks and peer assessments of emergent themes are based on both 'typical constructions' and 'additional/differing insights' that elaborate/extend a constellation of related and/or cumulative meanings. Contradictions are investigated further to determine convergences and divergences with the view to portray movement positions and understandings in a manner that is consistent with the dominant expressions of movement aspirations/analysis of development/actors.

A. Adivasi Movement Perspectives on Development and Developers

Injustice and suffocation of mulo nivasi (*root peoples*). A Kondh Adivasi leader expresses his frustration with state-led development, likening it to a process of suffocation of indigenous peoples:

We are the *mulo nivasi* (root people) and the people who dominated us, as history has taught us, came here 5,000 years ago. They fought with our ancestors with superior weapons and war tactics and defeated our peoples. They divided us into many divisions and sub-divisions and created *bhed-bhav* (or differences), took away our land and forests and created livelihood pressures so that we, the *Adivasis*, would continue to fight each other for survival.

The *sarkar* (government) is doing a great injustice (*anyayo durniti*) and is involved in corrupt practices. . . . With regard to land, they have given over 90 per cent of the land to upper classes and castes (*goshtis*) and we, the 80 per cent who are poor, have just 5 per cent of the cultivable land to meet our purposes. And the way they have framed laws around land-holding and distribution, we the poor are being squashed and are stampeding into each other's spaces and getting suffocated (*dalachatta hoi santholito ho chonti*). This creation of inequality (*taro tomyo*) is so widespread and so true—we see it in our lives. This is the root of all problems and we hold the government responsible for this.

He goes on to elaborate on life in towns and how urban living is predicated on the encroachment of Adivasi lands, as the Adivasis themselves are *reduced to silent spectators and to dust* by urban development as a process of usurption.

Life in the town is not created for our type of life. The people of *shahar* (city) will never think about us. They would rather enjoy life from the benefits that come from the forest and mountains, like water and forest products. They tell us they want to modernize, make machines and industries for themselves. To do this, they are encroaching on our land—they are all over our hills and stones. They are coming quietly to our forests and hills and in secrecy they are making plans to dig them up and destroy them (mining). Not only this, they are diverting our water to the towns (dams) for their use. They are making dams and water reservoirs, where our villages are to be submerged and we have to leave the place, leave the land and become landless and homeless. We have become silent spectators (*niravre dekhuchu*) to a repeated snatching away of our resources.

Whenever we have tried to assert our land rights, we have been warned by the upper castes, their politician friends and the wealthy and have faced innumerable threats and retaliations. The *ucho-barga* (dominant castes and classes) will work to divide and have us fight each other till we are reduced to dust (*talitalanth*).

He elaborates on the exercise of legal manipulations in the interests of dominant caste-class groups as the state develops some at the expense of others (selective application of laws and rules in the interests of profit/corporates and the dominant development process/related social segments).

People come from nearby towns and stay in our forests overnight. They cut our *pia sal* (costly timber for furniture) and take them away. The government and the companies come and take away truckloads of bamboo. The forests which our ancestors nurtured (*banchaye chanti*) are getting destroyed by these *bahari ko lok* (outsiders). When these things happen, the forest guards give them protection and when we have needs, they ask us if we have paid our royalty or the tax on the tamarind trees—we are taxed for each of these trees. When they take truckloads of sal timbers and bamboos and the paper mills exploit this place for their business, how can the *Adivasis* be held responsible for destroying the forests? When the *Adivasis* depend on the forest for their life, the *vyavasahi* (business people) and the government are destroying them for their own profit (*labho*).

Or as similarly expressed by another Adivasi leader,

When we clear up wasted forest land to do cultivation, the officers trouble us, but they are the same people who are quietly taking away bamboo and timber in truckloads. The government and the companies do this (*sarkar o company bhethore achanti*). And when we get a small piece of wood for repairing our house, they put their seal on it and file a case against us for illegal felling.

Racism and cultural chauvinism of developers. Several participants allude to the racist and chauvinistic attitudes of the agents of development and their related conceptions of the Adivasis. A woman leader expresses her sentiments as follows:

The *sarkar* (government) and their workers think that we Adivasis do not know anything and we are good for nothing, that we are weak and powerless and will not question them if they treat us unjustly. That is why they think that they do not need to ask us anything before going ahead. That's why they think they can put their pressure and power on us (*shakti a bong prayogo karanti*). To the government, we are of no significance (*sarkar amar prathi heyogyano karuchi*). They are selling our forests, they are selling our water and they are selling our land and may be they will sell us also.

Not only are the Adivasis perceived as being insignificant, as another leader suggests, they are likened (by the developmentalist state, its agents and outsiders—often referred to as 'they') to the stained, the sinful and the despised; characterizations that are reinforced by various forms of power:

> They have the power of *dhana* (wealth) and *astro-shastro* (armaments). They have the power of *kruthrima ain* (of artificial laws and rules)—they created these laws just to maintain their own interests . . . and where we live, they call this area *adhusith* (or *Adivasi* infested, pejoratively understood as 'pest-infestation') . . . we are condemned to the life of *ananta paapi* (eternal sinners), as *colonkitha* (dirty/black/stained), as *ghruniya* (despised and hated).

Protecting the forests from the developers: Protecting development from itself. In her analysis of the government's actions, the same Kondh Adivasi woman leader argued that it is the Adivasis that need to protect the forests from the self-serving agenda of a developmentalist State.

> The Forest Department comes and asks us to create a Forest Protection Committee (*jungle surakshya manch*). Protection from whom, I ask? They are the ones who lie and take bribes from outsiders who destroy the forest, people from the cities who come and destroy our timbers, cut them and take them away while the Forest Department Officials protect them and these activities! They could have enforced the law that they talk to us about all the time. But if we cut a small piece of wood here and there to make a cot/bed, chair or door panel, these people come into our houses as if we have decimated the forests! They are not serving the public as public servants but rather, they are serving themselves (*shae mane chakiriya hisab re amo paey sbha koru na hanthi*)—so we do not cooperate because they really do not care about the forest! We need to protect the forest from them!

B. Adivasi (ADEA) Movement Purposes

The struggle to save the wealth of the Gods',

> We are the real protectors of the forest (*ame jangalo surokhya kariba lokho*) because we are the ones that have always depended on the forests for our well-being. For us all plants and animals are equally valuable whether it is *pia sal, kalami* and *mahul.* Our forests are our history and our culture (*amor jangalo, amaro itihas ote avom a thi amoro sanskriti*). . . .
>
> The Gods have given us all this wealth and surrounding. But the government says the land on which you have *patta* (title) is yours and the

rest is the government's! This is not our way and the government does not understand. The water, for instance, does not belong to anyone like the government seems to think—it is given by God for the forests, the animals and humans alike. But the government would not understand this. This soil does not belong to the government or the government's parents (*sarkar kimba aur tanko bapar ko mati nahi tho*). They have been given to us by the Gods through the ages. Who is this government (*e sarkar kee?*) that lets the paper mills take the longest bamboo and best wood and then asks us for royalty and taxes for small cuts for poles? . . .

Protecting our way of life and the struggle for food, land, water, forest and unity.

The ADEA is there to fight collectively (*sangram*) to save (*raksha*) the forests and to protect our way of life. The ADEA is a means of collective struggle for the forest (*ame samastha mishi sangram o kariba*). We are all members of the ADEA and our struggle is around *khadyo, jamin, jalo, jangalo o ektha* (food, land, water, forest and unity).

The above definition of the ADEA movement's purposes as expressed by a Saora male Adivasi leader and a Panos woman leader, makes explicit the key platforms and *raison d'être* of the movement. Other leaders extend these definitions of the movement's purpose to include specific movement claims on the state and to highlight the importance of the movement as a unifier of subaltern groups (Adivasis and Dalits/Panos).

ADEA movement and our claims on the state. A Panos woman leader addresses the government/state voicing ADEA claims:

. . . we are laying a claim on the government which is supposed to serve all the people in this land. We are demanding a place for ourselves—we are questioning the government and asking them to help us develop our land using our ways. ADEA's idea is that our livelihood should be protected and our traditional occupations and relationships to the land and forest be protected in the form of community control over land and forests in our areas. This is our understanding of our constitutional rights too. There is no contradiction. Once this is understood, we can cooperate and when necessary, work with the government to take care of the land and forests. If they can help the *shaharis* (modern/urban people) destroy the forests, then they can and should help us to protect it and listen to our story too.

The government should not evict people from the land they have occupied and need. People have the right to cultivable land which they have been using in accordance with their knowledge and traditions. The government should rather help us to develop our agriculture by finding ways to support us. And instead of big dams, it should erect check dams (small-scale irrigation) to help our agriculture.

ADEA and the unity-knot of subalterns

Ekta Abhijan (ADEA) stands on a root called unity (*ekta*) and the promotion of unity will always be the primary requirement—a unity of minds, hearts and feeling of togetherness. The artificially created sense of difference, divisions and *jati-goshti* (caste-class feelings) need to be destroyed. Our *dhwoja* (flag) is unity (*ekta*) and we have to fly it high (*oraiba*). The flag that ADEA flies is of the people who have lost their land and their forests and who are losing their very roots.

We have a hope in our movement (ADEA). We need to take strong action so that *shahari* (city) people and outside exploiters will not capture our land, forests, hills and water. ADEA will work to ensure that they have no clue as to how to continue this process of control. When the time is right, we will need to tie our knot (*samoyo thao thao ganthi bandhiba darkar*). The people will be activated by the ADEA so that the dominant groups cannot continue to shock us. We need to face the Oriya caste who look down on us as *neech* (lowly). It is a significant development to see that poor people who were lying low for years are actively tightening their belts (*onta bhirunchanti*) and in our region, this has already happened and will continue to happen.

C. Forms of Cultural Expression and the Articulation of Movement Purposes

The ADEA movement's purposes are articulated at various forums employing different culturally-specific mediums of movement expression including, though not restricted to: (a) lamentation and (b) narratives of elders, brief examples of which are shared below.

At one of the proceedings, the following *song/lamentation* was sung by three women (while playing a one-stringed instrument):

> This forest, this mountain and this land is ours
> Given by our Gods to our ancestors
> But people are destroying the forests,
> They are cutting the trees,
> They are plucking leaves and making them barren
> Is this now left as ours for name sake?
> How can we depend on it if everything is gone?
>
> Oh God of sun (surjo devta), oh moon God (chandra devta), why are you giving us sorrows? . . . [and they call for the Gods to help them in their struggle, including *Gungi* (forest goddess), *Pahar devta* (mountain

god), *ghaso devta* (God of green grass), *Dhuli devta* (God of dust), *Durga pena* (rain god), etc.].

In olden times oh brothers and oh sisters
In the time of the British rule,
the Britishers used our grandparents like servants
and beat them severely to make them work
During that period oh brothers and sisters,
the revenue collectors came and took
the measurement of our lands and paddy fields
They said, 'you will be given land, paddy fields and dry land'
We went to work even when we did not have anything to eat
But when the work was done
Our land, our paddy fields and dry land
were transferred to the rich people and the big people, the outsiders
From then we lost our way, from then we are hopeless

One of the women singers explains:

Through this song we remember our past, how, from the time of the British until today, we have been exploited by the outsiders and the rich. How in hunger and in sickness we have not stopped working. Even when we have been wounded we have not stopped working. Our bad days continue till today. We remember this through this song and our souls weep (*atma kanduchi*). We weep together, young and old as you can see (pointing to the gathering).

An elderly man illustrates the use of *elder-narratives* as he discusses the alienation and loss (fertile valley bottoms) of Adivasi lands, supplanted by grazing land or military land by the *sarkar* (government) for itself. As the elder explained:

The flat land is no longer accessible to us. We, the Adivasis, have access to only hilly land for cultivation to sustain us (stony land, sloping and often degraded/waste land). The British prospered while we boiled as cultivators and today the government still exploits us like the British did by taking away our land. We are people of the land and forest and without them, there is nothing. We sing this song because this is an expression of our *sangharsh* (struggle).

He goes on to say:

In the past, in the time of our grandparents, we (these two villages) had one common graveyard. We had a system of sharing (or *bheda* in the Saora language, in relation to sharing of fruits, forest products, meat and land/forest usage). We had a collective contribution system to support one another. Land was not assigned to any particular person or family—it was a common claim that went back to our ancestors. We were together in joys and sorrows.

But since the government's revenue demarcation of land and forests, what belonged to all of us suddenly got divided into two *moujas*/areas of claim and people have started saying, 'this is mine and this is mine'. . . . This is not our way.

He went on to discuss the divide and rule tactics of the state and upper caste groups to ensure their commercial interests.

There is communal conflict around land and forests because the political powers, in order to keep their control over and access to these vital resources, are promoting division and hatred among the communities (Domb, Kondh and Saora). Our communities once had equal access to land and forests, which today has been controlled using outside methods of the *sarkar* (government) and the *vyaparis* (business classes) and upper castes (Brahmins). They want to perpetuate their ways and ideas among us and keep us divided. We are all *garib sreni* (poor class) and land and forest are vital for our survival. If they succeed in controlling our resources, they end up controlling our lives. As has been the case over the ages, they want us to live in disharmony and difference so that they can be the *shashaks* (rulers) all the time. So they have done this.

Elders narratives like these caution the young and the community against this 'historic strategy', calling for unity among the Adivasi peoples.

CONCLUSION

Phase one of this research has sought to understand and construct Adivasi movement conceptions of development, 'outsiders', state-corporate and caste-class interests and their implications for the Adivasi struggle as exemplified in the ADEA movement purposes and related cultural expressions pertaining to desired movement directions. It is increasingly evident from the preceding exposition of emergent themes that this movement seeks to affirm Adivasi ways and secure Adivasi land and forest spaces through a concerted attempt to build unity and collective action, given the increasing incursions (e.g. divide and scatter/isolate tactics) by state-capitalist and caste/outsider developmentalist and political-economic interests. The ADEA lays its own claims on the state as citizens of the country, outlining alternatives in relation to state-Adivasi engagements around protection and promotion of their ways of land and forest use, respect for them and their cultural and material spaces and the acceptance of a process of change that is predicated on the recognition of Adivasi agency.

In the absence of such proposed state collaborations, movements like the ADEA will continue to assert themselves. For instance, the movement has encouraged and developed an organized approach towards taking control over (*akthiar*) land and some 6,000 hectares of are currently in dispute, while claims are being made on the basis of the Directives of State Policy and the Fifth Schedule, rights which make it possible for Adivasis and people living below the poverty line (BPL) to use unclaimed land and unused state land for the purposes of subsistence. ADEA villages have moved *en masse* to begin such land takeovers. Plantation (fruit orchards in the forested areas) and agricultural (growing millet, lentils and grains) activities are being undertaken on 're-possessed' lands, with an eye on land that gives them such legal and constitutional grounds for takeover (as opposed to previous occupations that placed disorganized individuals on more vulnerable terms with the state). Through collective pressure the ADEA has secured hutment pattas for over 60 per cent of the region whose people are now not susceptible to summary evictions as encroachers. As one research participant put it, 'We are giving importance to land occupation (*padar bari akthiar*) and land use (*chatriya chatri*). We are now beginning to see the fruits of occupation.'

The adoption of the UN Declaration on the Rights of Indigenous Peoples by 144 nations (including India) of the General Assembly on 13 September 2007 (with Canada, USA, New Zealand and Australia as the only countries to vote against the Declaration), has now catapulted indigenous people's economic, political and socio-cultural rights onto the international stage, some 25 years since the Draft Declaration was first proposed. Such international and national legitimation of indigenous peoples has created new opportunities for Adivasis to stand in solidarity with one another, both, locally and globally. India's overt recognition of indigenous and Adivasi peoples in such global forums will compel a re-evaluation of the prevailing ideologies of the 1960s which asserted that 'these "backward" people would eventually become extinct' (Colchester 2005; cited in Gupta 2006) at the turn of the twenty-first century. This case study of the ADEA exemplifies the resolve as is expressed by an elder/leader of the ADEA:

> Who wants to go to the city to join the Oriyas and do business and open shops and be *shahari* (city/modern) if they give you a chance or to do labour like donkeys to get one meal? Even if they teach us, we do not want to go

to the cities—these are not the ways of the Adivasi. We cannot leave our forests (*ame jangale chari paribo nahi*). The forest is our second home (after the huts). We have a deep relationship with our forests (*jangale sahitho gobhiro sampark*). There is no distance between our homes and the forest. You just come out and you have everything you would need. You have stream water. You have *jhuna* (type of incense). If you want to hunt for deer, wild goats and boars, you need not run any where. You will get them easily. In our forests, tell me what you can not find? We have roots and tubers which we can eat. We have herbs to treat our sickness. We have tamarind and for our clothes we grow cotton. We grow millet and we have ropes, thatch and bamboo for making our homes. It is difficult even to leave our own forest and go to another to live because in our forest we know what is where. My friends and brothers, we are from the forest. That is why we use the small sticks of the *karanja* tree to brush our teeth—not tooth brushes. Our relationship with the forest is like a finger nail is to flesh (*nakho koo mangsho*)—we cannot be separated. The past is the present and the present is the past and they are the future, past and present. We are as we are, we are as we have been and we will be as we are and have been. That is why we are *Adivasi*.

REFERENCES

Arnold, D. (1984), 'Gramsci and the Peasant Subalternity in India', *Journal of Peasant Studies*, vol. 11, no. 4, pp. 155–77.

Asian Centre for Human Rights (2005), 'Promising Picture or Broken Future? Commentary and Recommendations on the Draft National Policy on Tribals of the Government of India', http:// www.achrweb.org.

Behura, N. and N. Panigrahi (2006), *Tribals and the Indian Constitution: Functioning of the Fifth Schedule in Orissa*, New Delhi: Rawat Publications.

Eversole, R., J. McNeish and D. Cimadamore (2005), *Indigenous Peoples and Poverty: An International Perspective*, London: Zed Books.

Fernandes, W. (2006), 'Development Related Displacement and Tribal Women', in G. Rath (ed.), *Tribal Development in India: The Contemporary Debate*, New Delhi: Sage.

Guha, R. (1983), *Elementary Aspects of Peasant Insurgency in Colonial India*, New Delhi: Oxford.

Gupta, R. (2006), 'The Dynamics Between States, Resources, and Indigenous Peoples in South Asia: Implications for Common Property Resource Governance', http://www.indiana.edu/~iascp/bali/papers/Gupta_Radhika.pdf.

Kapoor, D. (2007), 'Subaltern Social Movement Learning and the Decolonization of Space in India', *International Education*, vol. 37, no. 1, pp. 10–41.

Lather, P. (1993), 'Fertile Obsession: Validity after Poststructuralism', *The Sociological Quarterly*, vol. 34, no. 4, pp. 673–93.

Loomba, A. (2005), *Colonialism/Postcolonialism*, NY: Routledge.

Ludden, D. (ed.) (2005), *Reading Subaltern Studies: Critical History, Contested Meaning and the Globalization of South Asia*, New Delhi: Paul's Press.

Mayrkut, P. and R. Moorehouse (1994), *Beginning Qualitative Research: A Philosophic and Practical Guide*, London: Falmer Press.

Miles, M., and A. Huberman (1994), *Qualitative Data Analysis: An Expanded Source Book*, London: Sage.

Pimple, M., and M. Sethi (2005), 'Occupation of Land in India: Experiences and Challenges', in S. Moyo and P. Yeras (eds.), *Reclaiming the Land: The Resurgence of Rural Movements in Africa, Asia and Latin America*, London: Zed Books.

Rath, G. (ed.) (2006), *Tribal Development in India: The Contemporary Debate*, New Delhi: Sage.

Ray, R. and M. Katzenstein (eds.) (2005), *Social Movements in India: Poverty, Power, and Politics*, Lanham, MD: Rowman and Littlefield.

Rosenquist, G. (2005), 'Posco, Tata Boost India's Steel Industry', http://md1.csa.com/partners/viewrecord.php?requester=gs&collection=TRD&recid=200605S206513MB&q=POSCO+Orissa&uid=791526001&setcookie=yes

Sivaramakrishnan, K. (2005), 'Situating the Subaltern: History and Anthropology in the Subaltern Studies Project', in D. Ludden (ed.), *Reading Subaltern Studies: Critical History, Contested Meaning and the Globalization of South Asia*, New Delhi: Paul's Press.

Smith, G. (1992), *Research Issues Related to Maori Education*, Auckland: University of Auckland.

Smith, L. (1999), *Decolonizing Methodologies: Research and Indigenous Peoples*, London: Zed Books.

Stake, R. (2000), 'Case Study', in N. Denzin and Y. Lincoln (eds.), *Handbook of Qalitative Research*, London: Sage.

CHAPTER 20

Mahila Panchayat: An Alternative Mode of Collective Action

ARCHANA PRASAD

BACKDROP

Violence against women (VAW) is 'a manifestation of historically unequal power relations between men and women, and is at the root cause of inequality and subordination'. The Declaration on the Elimination of Violence Against Women, adopted by the UN General Assembly in 1993, defines violence against women as 'any act of gender-based violence that results in, or is likely to result in, physical, sexual or psychological harm, or suffering to women including threats of such acts, coercion or arbitrary deprivation of liberty; whether occurring in public or private life'. According to Indira Jaising, senior advocate and activist:

> Violence is a fact of every woman's life. Her condition seems to be defined by the violence she faces, be it in the home, at the workplace or anywhere else. Be it from strangers, intimate partners or armed forces of the state. Be it in the public or in the so-called 'private' domain. Be it by exclusion or by inclusion. This makes violence against women systematic, pervasive and of epidemic proportion in our societies. It must therefore, serve a function, as any other system does. Considering it happens to women and not to men, one obvious function of violence is to keep women in a position of subordination that is inequality. (Jaisingh 2007)

For a long time domestic violence was being perceived as a private matter within the four walls of the home. From this perspective, VAW was seen to be a matter of individual responsibilility of either adjusting more adequately to the situation as dictated by cultural norms or of developing an acceptable method of suffering silently. This understanding of VAW and especially domestic violence as a private affair has been strongly challenged by women's activists and civil society. As a result of feminist advocacy, the shift has been in perceiving domestic violence within the human rights framework. Women's human rights advocates stress that unless women are free from the threat of violence, they are unable to realize their other rights, and thus unable to participate in the process of development. It has become increasingly evident that VAW thus needs to be viewed not only as a serious human rights issue, but as one impacting development because violence contradicts every goal of development, be it social, economic or political.

Since 1990s, VAW and domestic violence have been specifically highlighted as endemic and pervasive realities of women's lives as well as fundamental violations of human rights. Globally, the Vienna Congress Rights (1994) and the Fourth World Conference of Women at Beijing (1995) included these issues as critical areas of concern. As a result, several initiatives have been taken by both national governments and international bodies to ensure the fulfilment of women's right as human rights and the goals of development more broadly. These initiatives have been somewhat instrumental in creating a shift in perspective from viewing the issue of violence as a private domain to one that merits 'public' concern (Mathur 2004).

The most crucial and recent initiative in the Indian context has been the passing of the new legislation on domestic violence, Protection of Women against Domestic Violence Act, 2005 (PWDVA). The PWDVA, which was notified on 25 October 2006, is path-breaking in more ways than one. Most significant perhaps is its definition of 'domestic violence' as spelt out in Chapter II of the Act. All forms of physical, sexual, verbal, emotional or economic abuse are defined as 'domestic violence' by this law. It offers women victims of such violence civil remedies of a kind not available to them earlier. Till now, women could use Section 498A of the Indian Penal Code to file a complaint against an abusive spouse. But this did not give the woman the right, for instance, to stay on in her matrimonial home or to demand a maintenance if thrown out or seek protection orders from the abusive partner. The law now provides her these civil remedies that are as important as the punishment provided under the law for committing the offence. The Act is significant because for the first time the term 'domestic violence' has been widened in meaning and scope from the culture-specific restriction of 'dowry deaths' and penal provisions to positive civil rights of protection and injunction.

The law came into effect after more than a decade of struggle by women's groups, lawyers and activists. The salient feature of the new legislation is that it is a civil law whereby an aggrieved woman can directly approach the magistrate for an emergency order to protect her from further violence. However, like the previous legislations the new law suffers from several shortcomings due to lack of political will in effectively implementing the law to make justice available to marginalized poor women.

> Though violence against women continues to increase in India, the law and the criminal justice system in many ways have failed to respond to or deal effectively with it. Indeed in crime against women the rate of conviction is reported to be less than 4 per cent. Very little efforts in terms of making the law more sensitive to women and in terms of enforcing the existing law has been made by the State to actually curb or deal with violence against women.
> (Singh 2004)

VAW is rapidly on the increase in spite of existing legislations. Every hour that ticks by in India inflicts more brutality on women, with two rapes, two kidnappings, four molestations and seven incidents of cruelty from husbands and relatives, reveal the latest national crime statistics. According to the National Crime Records Bureau (NCRB), on an average every hour at least 18 women in the country were victimized in 2006 and more disturbingly, the numbers are swiftly increasing. Therefore the challenge is to return to roots, and draw strength and sustenance from those who believe in the values behind the law.

When the administration, the police and the courts refuse to implement the law, where does a victim of violence go to seek justice? Do they turn towards their community for collective support? Does grassroots democracy offer fresh opportunities for enforcing collective values? How much moral authority can any collective exercise? How does one ensure safeguards for justice and ethics over the brute force of democratic majorities? These are the questions addressed in this paper in an attempt to understand strategies to combat VAW.

Gender-based violence is a manifestation of inequality within the home and therefore, it is not enough to advocate for the implementation of laws criminalizing domestic violence. There is a need to create an enabling environment in which a woman is able to assert her rights and seek legal recourse. It is essential to address the inequality within the home and recognize rights that counter such inequality to enable women to seek legal action. Given the lack of support for women, it is unlikely that a woman will ever resort to legal remedies unless she is assured, at a minimum, of a right to reside in her home.

In recent years, as a result of activism by women's group and NGOs, community-level initiatives have emerged as alternative forums for countering violence. These are strategies employed at the grassroot level by women from marginalized communities.

The term community is not necessarily used here to describe an idealized homogeneous setting. The reference here is to women from resettlement colonies occupied in large number by the economically poor class. It is basically in these communities that the Mahila Panchayat is functional. These colonies were set up to relocate the large slum colonies that had appeared in Delhi due to large-scale migration of rural labour seeking opportunity in the city.

Grassroots movement refers to 'community-based initiatives, action and/or organization that address issues of practical concern to their constituents and are generally committed to making better the lives of local people' (Bystydzienski and Sekhon 1999). To call these as alternate systems of justice would not be a misnomer because they are functioning outside the formal legal system and derive their legitimacy from the community of men and women. These alternative modes of collective action are challenging at once, norms entrenched in one of the most patriarchal institutions namely the justice system and simultaneously have established an identity that is being reckoned by the community and the law enforcement machinery (Rajan and Bhatla 2002).

This paper is an attempt to understand the structure and function of one such initiative, called as 'Mahila Panchayat' operating in the urban slums of Delhi. Through this forum, women are attempting to bring an end to the violence in their lives. The aim of the paper is to critically assess the structure, function and legitimacy of the Mahila Panchayat as a forum for women's access to justice. The idea is to understand the success of the forum in terms of resolution, in comparison to the formal structure of judiciary, thereby leading to women's empowerment.

Mahila Panchayat is combination of two terms 'Mahila' meaning women and 'Panchayat' meaning a forum of five elders. The usage of these two terms jointly is to question two widely-held notions. Firstly the assumption that power is traditionally a masculine concept and women are not associated with it. Kate Millet define power as: 'the essence of politics, views patriarchal governments as the institutions whereby half the population, which is female is controlled by the half which is male' (Millet 1970).

It has often been noted that politics is a man's game and government a men's club. For women participating in politics it is not a simple matter of taking up a new activity. Rather, it is participating in activities and institutions designed and populated primarily by men (Shapria 1984). This notion prevented women from participating in politics for a very long time. The second assumption is the traditional concept of women's real place being within the four walls of the house and thus historically women's mobility in public space was restricted. The formation of Mahila Panchayat is thus an attempt to question the two assumptions in order to create an environment for women's empowerment.

The Mahila Panchayat is a redressal forum for disputes in the community and serves as a vigil group on violence against women and children, especially girl children. Its functioning is similar to that of Panchayats in rural areas. A group of women, who are the leaders of the community and are respected by the community, constitute the Mahila Panchayat, which acts as a fact-finding team, a pressure group and offers solutions to the problems, which are in turn honoured by the community. The Mahila Panchayat is also a powerful women's forum putting pressure on the family and the community to resolve marital and other disputes.

The emergence of the Mahila Panchayat as a justice redressal forum can be traced backed the following three factors:

- Dominance of male members in traditional forms of village panchayat,
- Patriarchal attitude and functioning of the State, and
- Significance of collective strength of community.

Dominance of Male Members in Panchayats

The earliest form of panchayat consisted of five men of the village who acted as a forum to resolve conflicts. The panchayat was considered as an important public space of power as it was a legitimate forum for conflict resolution. In this traditional form of a panchayat, women and lowers castes were not allowed membership. As a result the cases that were resolved suffered from gender bias. Resolutions tried to preserve the patriarchal order of the society. This traditional concept of panchayat underwent changes with the introduction of Panchayati Raj Institutions in 1953. Here the term was retained for use for local self-government. However, its meaning and usage has become more political, referring to a formal body of elected representative for decentralized governance. Further the 73rd (Panchayati Raj) and 74th (urban local self-administration) Constitutional Amendments made beginning of questioning the above two assumptions. The constitutional amendments were made to create space for the entry of women into politics with 33 per cent reservation of seats in all panchayats for women.

The reservation of seats opened a new pandora's box. Some studies have indicated that entry of women in politics has led to their empowerment while other studies have documented the limitation whereby women have not been able to totally utilize the space provided to them due to several problems. It has been observed that by and large where men had not been able to contest due to reservation for women, their female counterparts had contested (MARG 1996; Leiten 1997). These studies have further reported that women do not go for panchayat meetings, take no interest in matters/issues being discussed in the panchayat, and act as proxies and namesake members. The patriarchal and feudal values have constrained the political participation of women. The country report prepared by the Government of India has mentioned that the climate of criminalization, corruption, muscle power and violence inhibits full participation in the political process (GOI 1995: 75). Therefore what is needed is a change in the power structure and gender relations for transformative politics that would allow not only participation of women in politics but also the full utilization of politics by women themselves for their empowerment.

Patriarchal Attitude and the Functioning of State

Catherine McKinnon once said that the state is male in feminist sense and the law sees and treats women the way men see and treat women. The Indian state has from its very inception been portraying gender sensitivity by formulating several provisions towards gender equality. Article 14 of the Constitution of India mandates that the state shall not deny to any person equality before law or the equal protection of the laws within the territory of India. Article 15 of the Constitution of India mandates that the state shall not discriminate against any citizen on grounds of religion, race, caste, sex, place of birth or any of them be subjected to any disability. Further the Directive Principles State Policy provide specific instances in Articles 39 and 42 of what the state should do to ensure equity and promote equality. But unfortunately such constitutional guarantees have not been able to achieve substantive equality for women. It has been said that the patriarchal attitudes and values held by the Indian states have prevented them from implementing the constitutional mandate of equality in its true spirit (Nigam 2005).

Besides the existing constitutional provisions, the central and state governments have taken several steps to protect women through enactment of legislations and to prosecute those who perpetrate violence against them. The Indian Penal Code (IPC) has been amended several times in relation to crimes against women largely as a result of campaigns against violence led by the women's movement in the country.

> Almost every campaign against gender-based violence on women in the 1980s resulted in a new legislation providing protection to them. Each enactment resulted in making the punishment provisions more stringent, setting time limits for pending cases and extending compensation to the victims. Violence in its different dimensions has been sought to be tackled by legislative reforms, innovations in the structure and working of the police force, measures to sensitise the bureaucracy, media campaigns and new institutional structures. (Extract from the Government of India's report to CEDAW, UN doc: CEDAW/C/IND/1, 10 March 1999, para 93)

In 1983 and 1986, amendments were made to the existing criminal law to take on board the category of 'cruelty to wives' in terms that were diffuse or incomplete in definition, difficult to implement within the procedures of criminal law and easy to circumvent. For instance, 'cruelty' was defined as the causing of 'grave injury or danger to life, limb or death', thus leaving outside its ambit the mundane or non-physical forms of violence of everyday life (Agnes 1995: 121–6). As mentioned earlier the most recent step taken by the government is the enactment of the new law, Protection of Women from Domestic Violence Act, 2005. But as a means to prevent and (or punish) acts of domestic violence and find restitution for its victims, the legislation has so far been of limited efficacy and of dubious benefits to women.

So, while there are laws to protect women, the system in which they function results in many of these laws reinforcing gendered ideas of society and preserving family along patriarchal lines (Kapur 1998; ICRW 2002). The paternalistic approaches adopted by the state institutions and society often synthesizes together to produce a system that acts against the interest of women (Nigam 2005). Gender biases, which exist within institutions of redress, are often exacerbated by ingrained caste and other biases against members of disadvantaged communities.

> Not many of these cases reach the courts for trial, partly in view of the shame and honour involved and partly due to the existing difficult and complicated procedural laws. It was also noticed that the police are generally apathetic to the registration of complaints involving rape. Even in those cases which come up to courts for trial after going through all the investigations and medical examinations, our courts had not been sensitive to the trauma undergone by the rape victims, both during the actual commission of the offence and during trial in the courts. The courts are also oblivious of the social stigma and ostracism a victim of rape has to face throughout her life and all rapists to be acquitted on wholly irrelevant and flimsy grounds of age, religion, caste, status and other considerations. [National Commission for Women Annual Report for 1995–6]

Perhaps it is only once women entered within the realm of law and justice do they recognize that the platform provided by the state is no different as an arbiter than their family and kinship ties. The state therefore is hard seen as a practical and political choice by women (Nigam 2005). Attempts by women to seek justice through the criminal justice system are regularly forestalled. Although legislation exists, measures to ensure its full implementation—including communicating provisions to the public, training officials responsible for administering the legislation, providing legal support services to enable beneficiaries to invoke legislation, monitoring implementation and ensuring further development of legislation in response to the reality on the ground—have not been sufficient. Unless supported by male relatives or a strong social group, women victims of crime are at a severe disadvantage within the criminal justice system. Threats and harassment by perpetrators and their communities and social pressures, which exist within families and communities, force them towards compromise or withdrawal rather than pursuing justice.

Significance of Collective Strength of Community

The formal legal system in India has failed to deliver justice for many women. While there are laws to protect women from violence, the patriarchal attitudes of society, the government and its institutions prevent these laws being used to protect women's right effectively. The lack of an adequate formal justice system and the recognition of the detrimental effects of its absence has resulted in the establishment of informal community-level initiatives that attempt to gain justice for women. The civil society and women's groups have played an important role in organizing community response to handle violence against women.

The roots of community-based initiative led by women's group and NGOs can to a large extent be traced to the government's Women Development Programme (WDP) launched in 1984. The WDP addressed a wide range of women's issues and involved women in the analysis of their situation and in seeking solutions to their position of subordination. The collective becomes a forum for sharing passion emotions and experiences and creates environment-establishing women to 'voice' their experiences.

Throughout India there are a number of community-level initiatives, mostly run by women's groups that attempt to gain justice for women in a variety of cases from dowry disputes to domestic violence. These initiatives use various strategies such as public shaming, mock funerals and community-level dispute resolution forums (ICRW 2002). Many of the more formalized initiatives run variation models that involve all-women councils or committees that hear, investigate and rule on cases that come before them. These community-based approaches have often proved more effective then the formal system dealing with gender-based violence and other crimes against women. Initiatives such as these currently function in many areas of India including the Nari Adalat (women's court) in Gujarat and Uttar Pradesh, the Mahila Panch (women's council) in Gujarat, the Sahara Sanghs (support groups) in the hill district of Tehri Garhwal, the Shalishi in West Bengal and the Mahila Panchayats in Delhi. Many of these grew out of community-level women's groups established to deal with varying issues such as women's education, women's rights, or developmental issues around resource use, and savings and loans schemes. For many of these groups, cases concerning violence against women became impossible to ignore and more formalized units were established to deal specifically with such cases (ICRW 2002: 1) note that 'the fact that women-initiated dispute resolution mechanisms have emerged independently from any wider national strategy or government directive is worthy of close attention'.

GENESIS OF MAHILA PANCHAYAT

At the height of the women's autonomous movements in the 1980s, Action India, a grassroot-based NGO, initiated forums that enabled women from the community to articulate discontent and recognize underlying patterns of discrimination in their lives. The forums introduced a safe space to share the reality of domestic violence, dowry burning, rape and sexual harassment. As these collectives developed, they evolved into Mahila Panchayat in 1994, which formalized the role that women had begun to play in resolving disputes and conflict situations within their family and community.

Action India is a community-based organization working in the resettlement colonies of Delhi since 1976. Its experience of working with women from the resettlement colonies made it realize that laws of marriage, custody and maintenance, inheritance and property rights do not serve the needs of a whole variety of conjugal arrangements that have come into being (Action India 1996:1).

> It was through the experience of 'women helping women' that we learned of the need for crises counselling, support groups, shelters and alternative forums for dispute resolution. The birth of Mahila Panchahayat in the resettlement colonies of Delhi in 1994 was an innovative yet traditional concept developed by Action India. (Action India 1996)

The model of Mahila Panchayat attracted the attention of the government. In 2001, women's NGOs in Delhi were asked by the Delhi Commission for Women (DCW) to come up with a model to help deal with the gulf between women and the knowledge and uptake of their legal rights. Action India's model of Mahila Panchayat was recognized by the government and given support for spearheading the process of replicating the model with other NGOs across Delhi.

The Panchayats are funded partially by the DCW and partially by the users who pay a fee for each case (a minimum amount of Rs 50 is taken as fee charge from the users). While being funded by DCW they function autonomously as separate units responsible to their community. Each Panchayat is supported by an NGO which provides funds and trained paralegal workers who work full time for each Panchayat. Paralegal workers meet regularly with the NGOs and with one another for training, to discuss issues that arise and new initiatives.

The establishment of the Mahila Panchayat was done on a number of founding principles. *Firstly* they are to provide a 'women's space' where women feel safe to speak freely and openly about their situation without fear of castigation. *Secondly* they are to provide justice for women by women. The Panchayats were set up by all women members on the ground that women can more easily establish the concerns of other women and therefore provide women-friendly outcomes. *Thirdly* they are to give balanced and fair judgements. It was essential for the Mahila Panchayats' success that they be perceived by the community, both men and women, as being fair and not simply taking the women's side. *Fourthly*, it is essential that community women position the Panchayat in the community and run it.

With these guiding principles the objectives of the Mahila Panchayat are:

- To create community-based support systems for women in crisis and victims of domestic violence.
- To provide a forum to solve family disputes and enable women to assert themselves and live with dignity.
- To build capacity of the grassroot women to become legally aware, gender sensitive and non-judgemental and to listen with empathy to victims of domestic violence.
- To train paralegal workers to handle case work and counsel women to know their human rights to take decisions and to act to get out of violent situations when conflict is not resolved.
- To prepare women for legal action and seek legal aid whenever necessary.

The Mahila Panchayat is thus a female version of the *biradri* or the caste panchayat. The caste panchayat is a body of elders of a particular caste who hear and resolve conflicts among members of the caste. The caste panchayat traditionally delivered governance and justice in India and in some areas still does. However, they are few in Delhi and do not play a role in impeding love marriages. Caste-based panchayats that are known for meting out social boycotts, fines and punishments have lost their credibility in Delhi as the courts, Mahila Panchayats and human rights organizations offer alternative routes to justice and marital arbitration. They serve as an informal judicial system designed by women, run by women, for women, all at the grassroot level. They hear and counsel cases specifically of importance to women such as violence in the homes, marital discord, maintenance and dowry demand (Magar 2003).

Structure and Functioning

The structure of the Mahila Panchayat consists of several NGOs as partner organizations throughout Delhi. At present there is a Mahila Panchayat network consisting of 16 NGOs. The NGOs that are part of the Mahila Panchayat network are Action India, ADHAAR, MAMTA, Child Survival India, MRYDO, Bal Vikas Dhara, Navshristi, Yuva Chetna Mandal, Vikashini, DBS, Lady Help, Guild of Service, BAADR, Surnirman, INDCARE, and Navjyoti Development Society. Each NGO has two or three panchayats, though Action India has eight. In each panchayat there are around 25 women, thereby the strength of the entire network consists of around 1,500 women. By 2012 with the support of Delhi Commission of Women, the network intends to expand by multiplying the existing panchayats. And with the addition of six new NGOs, the Mahila Panchayat Network would get more than doubled. At present the number of panchayat is 38, which would increase to 84, with each NGO having to add two more panchayats to the network.

The Mahila Panchayat Network therefore foresees the creation of 'Women's Task Force' for combating all forms of violence against women. It would effectively provide arbitration forums at the community level to resolve family disputes and would be accessible to the economically weaker sections of the capital's population.

Membership

The members of Mahila Panchayat consists of the following:

(*i*) *Coordinators* from NGOs that are part of the Mahila Panchayat Network.

(*ii*) *Paralegals* are women from the same or similar communities, generally with some formal education. Some have been through the process themselves and have gone on to establish their own panchayat (Magar 2003). Their role is to listen to women when they come to the office and to investigate the case should the woman choose to file a formal complaint.

(*iii*) *Women from the communities*, or neighbourhood groups of women who volunteer their time and support to victims of violence enabling a process for dispute resolution.

The members of the panchayats are women from the communities, often older respected women but also young women passionate about women's rights. They are not educated upper-class women but women like the users themselves who live as they do and understand the issues and constraints which they face. They are also made up of women from different castes.

All the members of the panchayat are women and they function with the understanding of women's particular vulnerabilities due to her gender. The paralegals as well as the other members of the panchayat have received training in law, conflict resolution and gender sensitization by women activists and lawyers.

Panchayat Office

The panchayat offices are located in the communities that they serve, in the resettlement and low-income communities that they were established to help. One or two paralegals staff the panchayat office six days a week and are available at any time in case of emergency. The panchayat meets once a week for discussing and resolving conflicts.

Process of Dispute Resolution

The process of dispute resolution consists of the following procedures:

- *Case Registration:* A case can be registered in two ways. In the first case the aggrieved woman herself approaches the panchayat office and shares her problem with panchayat members. When the woman approaches the panchayat for the first time the attempt is to try and make her talk about her problem openly and without any hesitation. She is encouraged to narrate the entire problem in detail and what she wants as a resolution to her problem. In the second method, a member of the panchayat brings a woman who has been suffering but lacked the courage to speak out, to the panchayats. In either case, the woman may choose to simply talk about her situation or she may decide to register a complaint. In case the woman decides to lodge a complain against the accused, a case is registered.
- *Investigation and Notice Delivery:* Once a case is registered the paralegals will visit neighbours of the complainant or other relevant individuals, to investigate the case. Following this they will send a notice stating the details of the case to the other party, indicating a date when they should attend a hearing or consultation.

- *Hearing:* The hearing, held once a week, will be attended by usually 18 to 25 of the panchayat members as well as paralegals. There, the woman who has brought the case will have the opportunity to speak about it in her own words. During this time she is not to be interrupted. Then the other party has the same opportunity. The paṇchayat asks further questions and deliberates on the issue. In cases of violence and ill-treatment by a spouse, the panchayat members will ask the man why he acts this way and also encourage him to list any issues he has with his wife. There is discussion around what has been done about it and what should be the future course of action.
  The offending party is called to the next session of the proceedings through a letter. If the offending party does not come to the next hearing the case is discussed in detail trying to figure out the reason for the absence of the offender. In case the opposite party does not turn up despite repeated letters (usually twice) then members of the Mahila Panchayat personally visit the offender's residence as to find out why he is not showing up. The panchayat's visit builds pressure on the man to attend the hearing. In the course of repeated hearings a mutually acceptable and feasible solution is arrived at through meetings, arbitration and counselling of both parties.
- *Arbitration and Passing the Judgement:* It is important for the panchayat to be impartial and not simply favour women. So each side lists the minimum requirements it has of the other. Then both sign the agreement and are each given a copy of it. Often there will be discussion and a compromise found. The man and the woman may be encouraged to interact face to face because in many cases the problem arises due to non-communication between spouses. If the two parties cannot come to an agreement they may reconvene another meeting in 15 days, giving both sides an opportunity to further consider their options. Where issues cannot be resolved legal intervention is sought and the panchayats support the women to separate from and divorce their husbands.
- *Follow up:* After the case is resolved, the paralegals are responsible for follow-up of the case to ensure adherence to the agreed outcome and the safety of the women involved, especially when they are returning to abusive partners and extended family.

Women who come to the meeting for the first time gain an idea of the proceedings and the nature of interaction in the MP. The women feel reassured and supported. Hearing other women speak about their experience boosts their confidence and reduces their apprehension and sense of isolation. It also validates their decision to approach the forum for help and go public with their problem.

The Mahila Panchayat serves to function as a:

1. Dispute resolution forum
2. Platform for empowerment of women
3. Grassroots democratization of women from marginalized communities.

MAHILA PANCHAYAT AS A DISPUTE RESOLUTION FORUM

The Mahila Panchayat over the years has evolved successfully as a dispute resolution forum, especially for women from the poor and marginalized communities for whom access to the formal justice redressal forum is not easily available. The various types of cases coming to the panchayat are wife beating, alcohol abuse/gambling husbands, doubts on wife, maintenance, dowry, extra-marital affairs, bigamy, sexual harassment, teasing, rape, forceful intercourse, kidnapping, right to residence for woman, divorce, cheating in marriage, custody of children, quarrel with neighbours, property, run-away girls, harassment by in-laws and other gender-related issues.

Over the years the Mahila Panchayat has witnessed tremendous success in resolving disputes as is evident from Table 20.1.

From Table 20.1 it is evident that the number of cases coming to the Mahila Panchayat has increased from 1169 to 1859 in a period of three years, i.e. an increase in 690 cases. However, the rate of solving the cases has come down from 83.83 per cent to 64.60 per

TABLE 20.1: MAHILA PANCHAYAT NETWORK ANNUAL CASE DATA 2004–7

Dates	Total Case	Solved Case	Rate of Success (%)
14 September 2004 to 15 September 2005	1,169	980	83.83
14 September 2005 to 15 September 2006	1,471	1,293	87.89
14 September 2006 to 15 September 2007	1,859	1,201	64.60
Total	4,499	3,474	77.21

cent, indicating the need to make a legitimate and formal structure. The total number of cases coming to the Mahila Panchayat annually is more than 1,000. This is much higher compared to the number of cases registered in formal courts; that is out of a total of 604 cases coming to the Mahila Panchayat in Delhi only 5 per cent of the cases are referred to the government courts. It illustrates that women prefer to go to informal resources such as the Mahila Panchayat rather than going to the formal institutions like police or courts.

Besides being involved in the resolution of cases being registered with them, the members of the Mahila Panchayat, also being part of the women's groups, are actively involved in conducting legal literacy workshops for educating grassroots women on legal rights, in capacity building of community women and in providing legal aid and counselling to women in crises situations.

FACTORS FOR SUCCESS OF MP

The main factor for the success of the MP is the capacity to give fair justice to women after listening to their problems and decisions arrived at after understanding what she wants. Also, the decision is taken through a process of mediation in which both parties are involved. The advantages of taking a care to the MP are:

- It does not require any proof to file a complaint.
- It is not time bound—people are given time to think and rethink before they take a final decision.
- The decision is not final and binding—the possibility of renegotiation open.
- It is not based on punishment for the perpetrators of violence.
- The MPs are neutral and objective—they find out the facts about the case give equal opportunity for both sides to talk and tell their side of the story.
- It involves discussion with the larger community.
- Money and vested interest do not influence the process.
- It is an all-empowering process with local participation.
- MPs provide transparency in the process of face-to-face interaction.

MAHILA PANCHAYAT *VIS-Á-VIS* LEGAL SYSTEM

There is no denying that the Mahila Panchayat is being legitimately used by community women for dispute resolution and the members of the panchayat are seen as those who can take decisions to end violence in women's lives. The process of what happens in these panchayats is to be seen along the continuum of the existing legal system and the formation of the panchayat as being different from that of the mainstream legal system.

LEGITIMACY OF MAHILA PANCHAYAT

Seeing the success of the Mahila Panchayat in resolving cases in relation to the formal legal system, it is important to understand the reason for it existence and the factors for it being accepted as a legitimate forum for dispute resolution. The several factors for wide-spread acceptance within the community are:

(i) *Quasi-judicial forum at pre-litigation stage:* The Mahila Panchayat has been delegated power by the Delhi Commission of Women to listen to the problems of couples (both men and women) and work towards compromise/settlement of the problem. The forum is recognized as an alternate forum to reduce the burden of the judiciary. Only those cases are taken to the court that fail to get resolved at the Mahila Panchayat forum.

(ii) *Institutionalized form of functioning:* The panchayat functions in ways similar to the functioning of formal courts. The letter sent out to the abuser/person against whom complaint is filed is on an official letterhead and with stamps. The institutionalized form of functioning gives the panchayat legitimacy. Another strategy that the panchayats may employ is the calling of a guarantor. In cases of domestic violence or mistreatment, the panchayat may ask the man to bring in a responsible person to act as a guarantor that he will refrain from beating and mistreating his wife. This means that another member of the household takes the responsibility for ensuring the well-being of the woman involved.

(iii) *Community pressure:* Social pressure and fear of the so-called 'private' matter becoming public compel men to adhere to the decisions taken by the MP. While there is a level of social acceptance of violence within home, it is not openly discussed and most men would wish to avoid such issues being openly discussed in the community. The fear of community ostracism and sanctions play an important role in enforcing the decisions of such informal initiatives (Burton et al. 2002). Community

APPROACH OF THE MAHILA PANCHAYAT TOWARDS SOCIAL ISSUES

Issues	Legal System	Mahila Panchayat
I. Access to system		
(i) By whom	Mainly women from upper class and caste access the legal system. Difficult for women from poor and marginalized communities to access the system	The panchayat consists of women from the community and its office is located in the community itself. It is very convenient for the women to access the panchayat.
(ii) Obstacles	Lack of information on judicial procedure to be followed.	There is easy dissemination of information about the functioning of the panchayat by its members
(iii) Financial cost	High financial cost in terms of fees to be paid to lawyers, filing of case, transportation for going to the court on hearing, etc.	Minimal cost is charged as registration fee from the complainant. Since the hearing takes place in the community itself no transportation cost is involved.
(iv) Fear & stigma	Women suffer from fear and stigma in approaching courts and police stations.	The aim of the Mahila Panchayat is to make the aggrieved women feel comfortable and provide a space where she can share her problems without any fear and stigma.
(v) Patriarchal attitudes	The patriarchal attitude of the state machinery prevents women from accessing the system.	The panchayat works with a gender neutral ideology with the intention of creating gender equality.
II. Lacunae in procedures		
(i) Identity Proof	Registration of case in the courts requires identity proof like proof of residence, etc. Many women	Registration of case does not require any identity proof. Most of the complainants are women from the areas in which

	from the marginalized communities often do not have the proof and hence unable to register their case.	the panchayats function and hence are known to each other.
(ii) Time limit	Once the case is disposed off in the courts the decision is time bound and the decision is binding.	In the procedures followed in the Mahila Panchayat there is no time boundness. Women are given time to think and rethink before they take the final decision. There is also the possibility of renegotiation.
(iii) Final decision	The final decision in court cases end with punishment for the perpetrators. Often many women do not approach the legal system with the fear that their partners would be punished.	There is no punishment for the perpetrator. The aim of the panchayat is to bring change in attitude and behaviour. This is often done through counselling and community pressure.

sanctions make it hard for an individual to earn a living or buy goods, which may be devastating.

(iv) *Knowledge about legal procedures*: The panchayat members use their legal knowledge to pressure the offending party into complying. They may threaten further court action if the man or his family members do not change their ways.

(v) *Using collective strength*: The panchayats also utilize the strength of their size. Defendants attending a hearing where twenty-five vocal women surround him and emphasize that his behaviour is unacceptable is bound to be affected by it. Community-based strategies also allow men to see the collective strength of women directly where they live (DCW 2000). The fact that the judgement is arrived in consultation with so many women has value.

(vi) *Support of NGO network*: Another factor at work is the burgeoning strength of women through their association with the panchayats and NGOs. Sen found that one important contributor to ending violence was establishment of networks within families and communities and with women's organization and legal aid centres. Networks are important both as support and advice in the long run, and for immediate interventions during bouts of violence.

(vii) *Acts as a facilitating agency*: The panchayat work in a number of ways as facilitating agencies. They help women to define their goals by giving them space and opportunity to think and speak about them. The panchayat provides a space where women can come and discuss their problem and where they are not told to be silent, Mosedale (2005) believes it is when women can gather to discuss their mutual circumstances and look at ways to deal with problems that empowerment can begin. Women may find strength in meeting other women who are facing similar situations or have done so in the past and have found a resolution to their problems. They also have the opportunity to learn about their rights and entitlements.

(viii) *Challenges the patriarchal norms and values*: The panchayat fiercely challenges the ingrained norm that violence against women is acceptable, especially within the confines of the home. The members and paralegal workers emphasize during their hearings and consultation that violence is not only unacceptable but also illegal. For many men, this would be the first time they have openly been berated over their actions. It has been observed that simply making men aware of the fact that domestic violence is a crime and that by perpetrating it they are becoming criminals works to deter men from violence (Ahmed-Ghosh 2004).

(ix) *Functions as an inexpensive and easily available forum of redressal*: It is an inexpensive and an accessible forum. What adds to the acceptability of the forum is the fact that the decision-making involves giving time to think of the best solution, rather than focusing on absolute positions of wrong and right.

(x) *Wide coverage of other social and legal issues*: The reason the MP commands community respect is because the MP's area of work extends beyond dealing with violence. They are well informed about government schemes meant for upliftment of poor and also work on education and health. Along with sensitivity to women's issues and an understanding of violence, they also draw upon an intuitive cultural sense of the beliefs, values and normative codes of the area. This contributes to the effectiveness of their judgement, which is based on an understanding of the cultural value system and the information gathered from the immediate community about the family and circumstances.

The panchayat uses an array of interacting and cumulative strategies in an attempt to gain compliance to the outcomes of the cases. They use both legal proceedings and social embarrassment to compel abusers to modify their behaviour. They emphasize a clear message of accountability and responsibility of individuals to their family. The panchayat members do not allow offenders to minimize their actions. Comments like 'I only drink sometimes', 'I may have slapped but I am not violent' are challenged.

EMPOWERMENT THROUGH COLLECTIVITY

The effectiveness of the panchayat stems from the fact that there is collective analysis and decision making. The Mahila Panchayat represents a constituency of membership—of women who are its members. They support this process and promote it. That it has the possibility of going beyond is unquestionable. For it represents the effort to reinvent the local conflict management/resolution heritage without perpetuating the exclusion of women, dalits, minorities and other weaker sections of the society, and the domination and exploitation of landlords (Hayden 1999).

The existence of MP as a collective forum also provides a platform for empowerment of women from the marginalized communities. Oakley and Rowland (1998) argue that empowerment is not only about opening up access to decision making, but also includes processes that lead people to perceive themselves as being able and entitled to occupy that decision-making space. Participation is at the heart of the empowerment process as individuals come together with equally valid but different perspectives, sharing problems and exploring answers.

The Mahila Panchayat involves women in perceiving themselves as being entitled to make decisions. Seeing women like themselves as panchayat members, having legal knowledge and the confidence to speak and stand up against the abusive partners helps to facilitate this perception of poor, low-caste women as decision makers. The

Mahila Panchayat works in a large number of ways in facilitating empowerment of women:

- Provides a platform to challenge the ingrained norm that violence against women is acceptable, especially within the confines of the home. Panchayat members are dogged in their denunciation of violence, openly challenging the perception that a little bit of hitting is acceptable, and in some cases necessary to discipline a misbehaving wife or daughter. The panchayat members emphasize during hearings and consultations the consistent message that violence is not only unacceptable but also illegal. Further the panchayat openly challenges the norm that dispensing justice is the privilege of men.
- They help women to define their goals by giving them the space and opportunity to think and speak about their life.
- Provide an open space where women from different classes, castes and religions can come and discuss their problems. Many of them are persuaded to break their silence. Women may find strength in meeting other women who are facing similar situation or have done so in past and have found a resolution to their problems. They also have the opportunity to learn about their rights and entitlements.
- Provide an avenue to take decisions in life and act upon them to bring end to the violence in their life.

With the support of women's groups and the civil society, members of the Mahila Panchayat build advocacy campaigns for promotion and implementation of various legislations. This is done through participation, networking and dissemination of information on legal rights to create public opinion in the community and in the family to press for change at the policy level.

While operating as a viable alternative to the formal system, the Mahila Panchayats also leverage on linkages with the administration and the police because of the legal authority vested in them. In many cases they take recourse to the police and courts for enabling women to access justice. The relationship between the Mahila Panchayat as an informal system and the formal legal setup needs to be strengthened so as to provide responsive support to women and make violence-free homes a reality. This is seen most effectively in implementing the new legislation on domestic violence whereby members of the Mahila Panchayat and paralegal workers are working as support systems so as to make justice easily accessible to women.

GRASSROOTS DEMOCRATIZATION PROCESS

The above description of the structure and functioning of the Mahila Panchayat illustrates the nature of empowerment of women through collective action. The struggle for social justice and equality at the grassroots is characterized by the democratic process of the Mahila Panchayat. The analysis draws our attention away from macro-level studies that focus only on state-oriented activities and electoral politics. At the micro-level there is the same democratic process functioning to bring about social change. Such action plays important role in pressuring the state to make it more accountable.

The Mahila Panchayat illustrates that an informal response based within the immediate community can provide a valuable space for dialogue and within which women can gain confidence in devising their own strategies, speaking their minds and gaining recognition of their own rights. These responses incorporate a strong element of preventive justice. They differ from traditional justice forums by incorporating a perspective that is feminist and a process that is truly democratic. In order to resolve a domestic dispute effectively, they create a forum where a large number of stakeholders gather to air their private grievances and engage in spirited arguments. The process relies on the community's right to enter the sphere of private family matters in order to restore collective peace and accepts its responsibility in a public shaming of the guilty party. The forum operates under the assumption that community pressure can indeed act as an effective deterrent to further violence.

FUTURE DIRECTIONS

In spite of the wide success of the Mahila Panchayat, it has not been recognized as a formal and institutionalized forum due to certain limitations due to which their decisions are devalued by the caste panchayat and the formal legal setup. These limitations are:

- *Patriarchal environment*: Most restricting is the environment of patriarchy in which they have to operate.
- *Representative of women's issues*: The forums are becoming representative of women's issues and not community arbitration forums. In that sense their influence can be limiting. They perhaps need to debate on how the role of the forum can be broad-based to include other issues of discrimination and exploitation.
- *Dominance of matrimonial dispute cases*: They are in their present

form able to influence mainly matrimonial relationships and the norms related to the same. Issues related to other forms of gender-based violence, caste, and so on remain outside their purview.

What is needed is greater recognition and formalization of the informal forum so that it is considered as a legitimate alternative for the state machinery. For example, courts could recognize the testimony gathered and decisions made by the Mahila Panchahyat as valid evidences to be used in the formal legal system.

Such plural conflict management/resolution mechanisms and processes would add to the socio-economic-political health of India. They would also become quite vital in India where justice is often delayed (and hence denied) by the slow, overburdened and increasingly expensive courts. (Hayden 1999)

There is also need for macro-micro linkages. At a time when the courts are overburdened and speedy trial difficult there is the urgency for a linkage between exiting state machinery and Mahila Panchayat for effective resolution of conflicts. There is need for such initiatives to expand, and seek wider legitimacy in the social as well as the judicial domains. The effort in this direction is being already taken up by women's groups and the civil society whereby the model of Mahila Panchayat is being extended to form a network of NGOs, police, civil society and state departments that would work effectively allow women irrespective of their economic class and caste to access justice. The development of the Delhi model for the implementation of the law on domestic violence indicates the acceptance of informal structures by the state and vice versa. The growth of the Mahila Panchayat from a small groups of 25 women to a network of more than 1,000 women tells the success story of women's groups in organizing collectively at the grassroots to address social problems.

REFERENCES

Action India (1996), Annual Report, unpublished, Delhi.

Agnes, F. (1995), 'State, Gender and Rhetoric of Law Reform', Mumbai: SNDT University Research Center for Women's Studies.

Ahmed-Ghosh (2004), 'Chattels of Society', *Violence Against Women*, vol. 10, no. 1, pp. 94–118.

Burton, B. Rajan and Nandita Bhatla (2002), 'Introduction', in *Domestic Violence in India: Exploring Strategies, Promoting Dialogue Women-initiated Community Level Responses to Domestic Violence*, Washington: ICRW.

Bystydzienski, J. and M. Sekhon (eds.) (1999), *Democratisation and Women's Grassroot Movements*, Bloomington: Indiana University Press.

Coomaraswamy R. (1999), 'Reinventing International Law: Women's Right as Human Right in the International Community', in P. Van Nissled, *Debating Human Rights:* London: Routlegde.

DCW, Mahila Panchayat, http://dcw.delhigovt.nic.in/MPs.htm

Gill, A. and G. Rehman (2004), 'Empowerment through Activism: Responding to Domestic Violence in the South Asian Community in London', *Gender and Development*, 12(1), pp. 75–82.

GOI (1995), Delhi: Country Report for Beijing Conference.

Hayden, Robert M. (1999), *Disputes and Arguments Amongst Nomads: A Caste Council in India*, New Delhi: Oxford University Press.

ICRW (2002), *Domestic Violence in India: Exploring Strategies, Promoting Dialogue: A Summary of Three Studies*, Delhi: ICRW.

Jaising, Indira (2007), 'One Step Closer to Equality', *The Little Magazine*, Delhi: Lawyer's Collective.

Kabeer, N. (1999), 'Response, Agency, and Achievements: Reflections on the Measurement of Women's Empowerment', *Development and Change*, 30, pp. 435–64.

Kapur, R. (1995), 'Who Draws the Line', *The Times of India*, 25 September 1995, p. 6.

NCRB (2006), 'Crime in India, 2006', http://ncrb.nic.in/cii2006/cii-2006/CHAP5.pdf

Nigam, Shalu (2005), 'Understanding Justice Delivery Mechanism from the Perspective of Women Litigants as Victims of Domestic Violence in India', Occasional paper no. 39, Delhi: CWDS.

Leiten, G.K. (1997), 'Panchayat in Western Uttar Pradesh, Namesake Members', *Economic Political Weekly,* XXX, no. 39, pp. 2700–5.

Magar, V. (2003), 'Empowerment Approaches to Gender-based Violence: Women's Courts in Delhi Slums', *Women's Studies International Forum,* vol. 26, no. 6, November, pp. 509–23(15).

Marg (1997), 'They Call Me Member Saab—A Study of Panchayat in Karnal District of Haryana', Delhi: Marg.

Mathur, Kanchan (2004), *Countering Gender Violence: Initiatives Towards Collective Action in Rajasthan*, Jaipur: Institute of Development Studies.

Mosedale, S. (2005), 'Policy Arena, Assessing Women's Empowerment: Towards a Conceptual Framework', *Journal of International Development*, 17(2), pp. 243–57.

Pateman, C. (1998), *The Sexual Contract Standard*, Chicago: Standford University Press.

Sen, P. (1998a), 'Development Practice and Violence against Women', *Gender and Development,* vol. 6, no. 3, November, pp. 7–16.

——— (1998b), 'Violence in Intimate Relationships: A Research Project in

India', in H. Afshar and Maynard, *Women and Empowerment: Illustrations from the Third World*, London: MacMillan Press Ltd.

Shapario, M. (ed.) (1984), *Language and Politics*, New York: University Press.

Sharma, B.R. and M. Gupta (2004), 'Gender-based Violence in India—A Never-ending Phenomenon', *Journal of International Women Studies*, 6(1), p. 114.

Singh, Kirti (2004), 'Violence Against Women and the India Law', in Savitri Goonesekere (ed.), *Violence, Law and Women's Right in South Asia*, New Delhi: Sage.

Srivastava, Alka (2006), A Long Journey Ahead—Women in Panchayati Raj: A Study in Rajasthan', New Delhi: Indian Social Institute.

Umbreit (1994), Victims Meet Offender—The Impact of Restorative Justice and Mediation, NY: Criminal Justices Press: Monsey.

Virginia S. (1984), *The Political Integration of Women, Roles, Socialization and Politics*, Urbana and Chicago: University of Illinois Press.

Contributors

SWARAJ BASU is a Professor of History at the School of Social Sciences, Indira Gandhi National Open University.

TOVA BENSKI is currently a senior lecturer and chair of the department of Behavioral Sciences at the College of Management—Academic Studies, Rishon Leziyon, Israel.

SHARIT BHOWMIK is presently the Dean, School of Management and Labour Studies in the Tata Institute of Social Sciences, Mumbai.

ELŻBIETA BUDAKOWSKA is Professor of Sociology at University of Warsaw, Poland.

TEJWANT K. CHANA is currently a Ph.D. candidate and Sessional Lecturer at the University of Alberta, in the Department of Educational Policy Studies.

JAMES GOODMAN works at the Faculty of Arts and Social Sciences, University of Technology, Sydney, Australia.

MARK HERKENRATH, D.Phil., is Lecturer in Sociology at the University of Zurich.

DIP KAPOOR is an Associate Professor in International Education, University of Alberta, Canada and a voluntary Research Associate in the Centre for Research and Development Solidarity, Orissa, India.

DANIEL KÜNZLER, Ph.D. is Doctoral Assistant at the Department of Social Sciences at the University of Fribourg in Switzerland.

LAUREN LANGMAN is Professor of Sociology at Loyola University.

PARTHA NATH MUKHERJI was the holding the A.K. Dey Chair, in the Institute of Social Sciences, New Delhi until recently.

GAIL OMVEDT is sociologist and writer.

M.N. PANINI has recently retired from the Centre for the Study of Social Systems, Jawaharlal Nehru University.

ARÇAHNA PRASAD is researcher in sociology.

HELEN SCHWENKEN is Assistant Professor in the Department for Social Sciences at the University of Kassel (Germany).

DEBAL K. SINGHAROY is Professor of Sociology, in the Faculty of Sociology, School of Social Sciences, Indira Gandhi National Open University.

SERGIO TAMAYO is a sociologist and Chair of the Research Group on Political Analysis, Department of Sociology, Universidad Autonoma Metropolitana at Mexico City.

BENJAMÍN TEJERINA is Professor of Sociology at the University of the Basque Country and Director of the Collective Identity Research Centre.

HÅKAN THÖRN is Professor of Sociology at the Department of Sociology, and at the Centre for Globalization and Development Gothenburg University, Sweden.

SHASHI BHUSHAN UPADHYAY is an Assistant Professor of History, Indira Gandhi National Open University, New Delhi.

LEO ZEILIG is currently a Research Fellow in the Centre for Sociological Research, University of Johannesburg, South Africa.